# Why Do You Need This New Edition?

**If you're wondering why you should buy this new edition of *The Blair Reader,* here are a few great reasons!**

1. More than fifty new reading selections will stimulate interest and introduce you to the enduring issues you will confront as a citizen in the twenty-first century. These new selections include articles, book excerpts, speeches, fiction, and poetry, helping you discover your own voice and express your own ideas.

2. More than thirty new images for analysis are reproduced in the chapter openers, in the Focus units, and in the new photo essay on tattoos and cultural identity in Chapter 6, "Culture and Identity." These images will help you approach, understand, and read visuals critically.

3. A new Chapter 6, "Culture and Identity," explores this important contemporary topic, including readings on cultural groups who define themselves based on race, religion, ethnicity, geography, economics, and sexual orientation.

4. A new Chapter 10, "Facing the Future," offers a glimpse into various visions of the future, including readings on the future of our country, of our environment, and of our creative potential.

5. New Focus units appear in revised Chapters 1, 2, 7, 8, and 9, exploring such questions as whether college is worth the money, whether undocumented immigrants should have a path to citizenship, whether internships are work experience or exploitation, and what has happened to academic integrity.

6. New Focus units appear in new Chapters 6 and 10, exploring the questions "Are We Moving toward a Post-Racial Society?" and "What Comes Next?"

7. A new set of prompts, "Beyond the Classroom," appears in the chapters' "Widening the Focus" sections. These prompts encourage you to write about your own observations and experiences.

**PEARSON**

# THE BLAIR READER

## EXPLORING ISSUES AND IDEAS

### EIGHTH EDITION

EDITED BY

# LAURIE G. KIRSZNER

*University of the Sciences, Emeritus*

# STEPHEN R. MANDELL

*Drexel University*

**PEARSON**

Boston Columbus Indianapolis New York San Francisco Upper Saddle River
Amsterdam Cape Town Dubai London Madrid Milan Munich Paris Montreal Toronto
Delhi Mexico City Sao Paulo Sydney Hong Kong Seoul Singapore Taipei Tokyo

**Senior Acquisitions Editor:** Brad Potthoff
**Senior Marketing Manager:** Sandra McGuire
**Executive Digital Producer:** Stefanie A. Snajder
**Digital Project Manager:** Janell Lantana
**Digital Editor:** Sara Gordus
**Production Manager:** S.S. Kulig
**Project Coordination, Text Design, and Electronic Page Makeup:** Cenveo Publisher Services
**Cover Designer/Manager:** John Callahan
**Cover Art:** (clockwise from upper left) Zhu Difeng/Shutterstock.com, Kostenko Maxim/Shutterstock.com, Juli Hansen/Shutterstock.com, Chris Alcock/Shutterstock.com, Lisa S./Shutterstock.com, Bloomua/Shutterstock.com, Katharina M./Shutterstock.com, Patryk Kosmider/Shutterstock.com
**Senior Manufacturing Buyer:** Dennis Para
**Printer/Binder:** R.R. Donnelley
**Cover Printer:** Lehigh Phoenix

This title is restricted to sales and distribution in North America only.

Credits and acknowledgments for material borrowed from other sources and reproduced, with permission, in this textbook appear on-page or at the back of the book on pages 565–570.

**Library of Congress Control Number: 2012954092**

10 9 8 7 6 5 4 3 2 1—DOC—18 17 16 15 14 13

Student edition
ISBN 10: 0-205-90184-0
ISBN 13: 978-0-205-90184-5

www.pearsonhighered.com

# CONTENTS

# TOPICAL CLUSTERS

## *Conformity and Rebellion*

## Self-Image

## Social and Economic Class

## Stereotyping

## Speeches

*Note:* Speeches are listed in alphabetical order.

# RHETORICAL TABLE OF CONTENTS

*Note:* Selections are listed alphabetically within categories.

*Exemplification*

*Argument & Persuasion*

# PREFACE

After many years of teaching composition, we have come to see reading and writing as interrelated activities: if students are going to write effectively, they must first be able to read actively and critically. In addition, we see writing as both a private and a public act. As a private act, it enables students to explore their feelings and reactions and to discover their ideas about subjects that are important to them. As a public act, writing enables students to see how their own ideas fit into larger discourse communities, where ideas gain meaning and value. We believe that students are enriched and engaged when they view the reading and writing they do as a way of participating in ongoing public discussions about ideas that matter to them. From the beginning, our goal in *The Blair Reader* has always been to encourage students to contribute to these discussions in the wider world by responding to the ideas of others.

The core of *The Blair Reader* is, of course, its reading selections. As we selected the readings for this book, our goal was to introduce students to the enduring issues they confront as citizens in the twenty-first century. Many of these readings are contemporary; many are also quite provocative. Whenever possible, however, we also include classic readings that give students the historical context they need. For example, Chapter 2, "Issues in Education," includes "School Is Bad for Children" by John Holt; Chapter 3, "The Politics of Language," includes "Learning to Read and Write" by Frederick Douglass; and Chapter 7, "The American Dream," includes "I Have a Dream" by Martin Luther King, Jr. It was also important to us that the selections in *The Blair Reader* represent a wide variety of rhetorical patterns and types of discourse as well as a range of themes, issues, and positions. In addition to essays and articles from print and electronic sources, *The Blair Reader* includes speeches, short stories, and poems. It is our hope that exposure to this wide variety of formats, topics, and viewpoints can help students discover their own voices and express their own ideas.

As teachers, we—like you—expect a thematic reader to include compelling reading selections that involve instructors and students in spirited exchanges. We also expect readings that reflect the diversity of ideas that characterizes our society and questions that challenge students to respond critically to what they have read. In short, we expect a book that stimulates discussion and that encourages students to discover new ideas and see familiar ideas in new ways. These expectations guided us as we initially created *The Blair Reader*, and they continued to guide us as we worked on this new eighth edition.

## What's New in the Eighth Edition?

In response to the thoughtful comments of the many instructors who generously shared with us their reactions (and their students' reactions) to *The Blair Reader*, we have made many changes in this new edition, adding two new thematic units, new readings, new study questions and writing and research prompts, and new visuals.

- **Two new thematic units,** "Culture and Identity" and "Facing the Future," provide background on important contemporary issues, including essays by writers such as Clara E. Rodríguez, Neal Gabler, and Neal Stephenson and Focus sections on the questions "Are We Moving toward a Post-Racial Society?" and "What Comes Next?"

- **New Focus sections** showcase related essays that examine contemporary concerns, zeroing in on questions such as "Are Internships Work Experience or Exploitation?" and "What Has Happened to Academic Integrity?"

- **New "Beyond the Classroom" prompts** in each chapter's "Widening the Focus" sections encourage students to write about first-hand observation and experience.

- **Updated treatment of visual literacy** draws attention to this important skill. In the Introduction to the text, "Reacting to Visual Texts" offers a series of questions to help students approach and understand visuals and includes a sample visual with student annotations. In addition, we include a new full-color photo essay in Chapter 6, "Culture and Identity," as well as new visuals in chapter openers and Focus sections.

- **New readings** have been added to stimulate student interest and to introduce them to some of the challenging issues that they confront as students and as citizens. Among the many essays that are new to this edition are Amy Chua's "Why Chinese Mothers Are Superior," Scott Adams's "How to Get a Real Education," Jasmin Darznik's "Persian, English," Nicholas Carr's "Does the Internet Make You Dumber?," Sherry Turkle's "Connectivity and Its Discontents," Jose Antonio Vargas's "Outlaw: My Life in America as an Undocumented Immigrant," and Richard A. Posner's "The Truth about Plagiarism." New poetry, such as Rhina Espaillat's

"Bilingual/Bilingue" and Pat Mora's "La Migra," and new speeches, such as commencement addresses by Hilda Solis and Colin Powell, have also been added.

## Resources for Students

We designed the apparatus in The *Blair Reader* to involve students and to encourage them to respond critically to what they read. These responses can lay the groundwork for the more focused thinking that they will do when they write. In order to help students improve their critical reading and writing skills, we have included the following features:

- **Introduction: Becoming a Critical Reader** explains and illustrates the process of reading and reacting critically to texts (including visual texts) and formulating original responses.

- **Paired visuals** introduce each thematic chapter. These visuals engage students by encouraging them to identify parallels and contrasts. In addition, they introduce students to the themes that they will be considering as they read the essays in the chapter.

- A brief **chapter introduction** places each chapter's broad theme in its social, historical, or political context, helping students to understand the complexities of the issues being discussed. This chapter introduction is followed by **Preparing to Read and Write**, a list of questions designed to help students focus their responses to individual readings and relate these responses to the chapter's larger issues.

- **Headnotes** that introduce each selection provide biographical and other background information as well as insight into the writer's purpose.

- **Responding to Reading** questions that follow each selection address thematic and rhetorical considerations. By encouraging students to think critically, these questions help them to see reading as an interactive and intellectually stimulating process.

- A **Responding in Writing** prompt after each reading selection gives students the opportunity to write an informal response.

- A **Focus** section at the end of each chapter is introduced by a provocative question related to the chapter's theme, followed by a visual that is accompanied by **Responding to the Image** questions. The heart of the Focus section is a group of readings that take a variety of positions on the issue, encouraging students to add their voices to the debate and demonstrating that complex issues elicit different points of view. Each reading is followed by "Responding to Reading" questions and a "Responding in Writing" prompt.

- At the end of each Focus section, a **Widening the Focus** feature includes a writing prompt ("For Critical Reading and Writing") that asks students to tie the readings together; a list of essays in other chapters of the book that also address the issues raised by the Focus question; an Internet research assignment; and a field research assignment ("Beyond the Classroom").

- **Writing** suggestions at the end of each chapter ask students to respond to one or more of the chapter's readings.

- A **Rhetorical Table of Contents,** located at the front of the book on pages xxi–xxx, groups the text's readings according to the way they arrange material: narration, description, process, comparison and contrast, and so on.

- **Topical Clusters,** narrowly focused thematic units (pp. x–xx), offer students and teachers additional options for grouping readings.

## Additional Resources for Instructors and Students

### Instructor's Manual (0321838564)

Because we wanted *The Blair Reader* to be a rich and comprehensive resource for instructors, a thoroughly revised and updated *Instructor's Resource Manual* has been developed to accompany the text. Designed to be a useful and all-inclusive tool, the manual contains teaching strategies, collaborative activities, and suggested answers for "Responding to Reading" questions. The manual includes Web and/or multimedia teaching resources for almost every reading. It also contains new questions for stimulating classroom discussions of the new chapter-opening images. Contact your local Pearson representative for details.

### Pearson MyLabs

The Pearson English MyLabs empower students to improve their skills in writing, grammar, research, and documentation with market-leading instruction, multimedia tutorials, exercises, and assessment tools. Students can use the MyLab on their own, benefiting from self-paced diagnostics and extra practice in content knowledge and writing skills. Instructors can use MyLabs in ways that best complement their courses and teaching styles. They can work more efficiently and more closely with students by creating their own assignments and using time-saving administrative and assessment tools. Enhanced online resources and assessments are available to students through the Pearson e-text, which is also available in an iPad version. To learn more, visit www.pearsonhighered .com/englishmylabs <http://www.pearsonhighered.com/englishmylabs> or ask your Pearson representative.

## Acknowledgments

*The Blair Reader* is the result of a fruitful collaboration between the two of us, between us and our students, between us and Pearson, and between us and you—our colleagues who told us what you want in a reader.

At Pearson, we want to thank Brad Potthoff, Senior Acquisitions Editor, and Joe Opiela, Senior Vice President and Editorial Director. We also appreciate the efforts of Lauren Cunningham, Editorial Assistant, as well as our copyeditor, David Abel.

Karen R. Mauk, our wonderful developmental editor, spent a great deal of time and effort making this book as good as it is. As always, her patience, professionalism, and hard work are greatly appreciated. At Cenveo Publisher Services, we want to thank Susan McIntyre, Senior Project Manager, for seeing this book through to completion.

In preparing *The Blair Reader*, Eighth Edition, we benefited at every stage from the assistance and suggestions of colleagues from across the country: Marlene Allen, Fayetteville State University; Katie Thomas, Community College of Beaver County; Gail Charrier, Delaware Technical and Community College; Kimberly Greenfield, Lorain County Community College; Aura Imbarus, El Camino College; Nicole S. Wilson, Bowie State University; Dr. Ryan D. Stryffeler, Western Nevada College; Robyn Lyons-Robinson, Columbus State Community College; and Robert Lunday, Houston Community College.

We would also like to thank the following reviewers of previous editions for their valuable insight: Jacob Agatucci, Central Oregon Community College; Jesse T. Airaudi, Baylor University; Linda A. Archer, Green River Community College; Anthony Armstrong, Richland College; Stephen R. Armstrong, Eastern Carolina University; Patricia Baldwin, Pitt Community College; Lisa Beckelhimer, University of Cincinnati; Chere Berman, College of the Canyons; Charlene Bunnell, University of Delaware; Jason Chaffin, Cape Fear Community College; Peggy Cole, Arapahoe Community College; Carla L. Dando, Idaho State University; Rosemary Day, Albuquerque Community College; Emily Dial-Driver, Rogers State University; Janet Eldred, University of Kentucky; Anne Fernald, Fordham University; Robert G. Ford, Houston Community College; Web Freeman, Ozarks Technical Community College; Ruth Gerik, University of Texas at Arlington; Janet Gerstner, San Juan College; Lisa Gordon, Columbus State Community College; Judy A. Hayden, University of Tampa; David Holper, College of the Redwoods; Pamela Howell, Midland College; Tara Hubschmitt, Lakeland College; Lu Ellen Huntley, University of North Carolina at Wilmington; Jessica Hyatt, Ozarks Technical Community College; Robert S. Imbur, University of Toledo; JoAnne James, Pitt Community College; James Jenkins, Mt. San Antonio College; Amanda Jerome, Saddleback College; Terry Jolliffe, Midland College; Alan Kaufman,

Bergen Community College; Dimitri Keriotis, Modesto Junior College; Robert Leston, University of Texas at Arlington; John Lucarelli, Community College of Allegheny County; Dani McLean, Saddleback College; Camilla Mortensen, University of Oregon; Kathryn Neal, York Technical College; Paul Northam, Johnson County Community College; Marguerite Parker, Eastern Carolina University; Andrea Penner, San Juan College; Angie Pratt, Montgomery College; Jeannette E. Riley, UMass Dartmouth; CC Ryder, West L.A. College; Debra Shein, Idaho State University; Margaret Simonton, East Arizona College; Katie Singer, Fairleigh Dickinson University; Darlene Smith-Worthington, Pitt Community College; Derek Soles, Drexel University; Lori Ann Stephens, Richland College; Sharon Strand, Black Hills State University; Diane Sweet, Wentworth Institute of Technology; Cara Unger, Portland Community College; Jennifer Vanags, Johnson County Community College; Stephen H. Wells, Community College of Allegheny County; Mary Williams, Midland College; Mary Ellen Williams, UC Davis; and K. Siobhan Wright, Carroll Community College.

On the home front, we once again "round up the usual suspects" to thank. And, of course, we thank each other: it really has been a "beautiful friendship."

# INTRODUCTION: BECOMING
# A CRITICAL READER

In his autobiographical essay "The Library Card" (p. 346), Richard Wright describes his early exposure to the world of books:

> The plots and stories in the novels did not interest me so much as the point of view revealed. I gave myself over to each novel without reserve, without trying to criticize it; it was enough for me to see and feel something different. Reading was like a drug.

It is a rare person today for whom reading can hold this magic or inspire this awe. Most of us take the access to books for granted. As a student, you've probably learned to be pragmatic about your reading. In fact, "reading a book" may have come to mean just reading assigned pages in a textbook. Whether the book's subject is modern American history, principles of corporate management, or quantum mechanics, you probably tend to read largely for information, expecting a book's ideas to be accessible and free of ambiguity and the book to be clearly written and logically organized.

In addition to reading textbooks, however, you also read essays and journal articles, fiction and poetry, Web sites and blogs. These texts present special challenges because you read them not just for information but also to discover your own ideas about what the writer is saying—what the piece of writing means to you, how you react to it, why you react as you do, and how your reactions differ from the responses of other readers. And, because the writers express opinions and communicate impressions as well as facts, your role as a reader must be more active than it is when you read a textbook. In these cases, reading becomes not only a search for information, but also a search for meaning.

## Reading and Meaning

Many of the texts you read during your years as a student will be challenging. In college, you read to expand your horizons, so it makes sense

1

that some ideas and concepts that you encounter in your assigned reading may be difficult or unfamiliar. When you approach an academic text for the first time, you may feel intimidated, or even overwhelmed, and you may find yourself wondering where to start and what to look for. This is natural. Fortunately, reading strategies that can make it easier for you to understand unfamiliar texts are explained and illustrated later in this Introduction.

Like many readers, you may assume that the meaning of a text is hidden somewhere between the lines and that you only have to ask the right questions or unearth the appropriate clues to discover exactly what the writer is getting at. But reading is not a game of hide-and-seek in which you search for ideas that have been hidden by the writer. As current reading theory demonstrates, meaning is created by the interaction between a reader and a text.

One way to explain this interactive process is to draw an analogy between a text—a work being read—and a word. A word is not the natural equivalent of the thing it signifies. The word *dog*, for example, does not evoke the image of a furry, four-legged animal in all parts of the world. To speakers of Spanish, the word *perro* elicits the same mental picture *dog* does in English-speaking countries. Not only does the word *dog* have meaning only in a specific cultural context, but even within that context it also evokes different images in different people. Some people may picture a collie, others a poodle, and still others a particular pet.

Like a word, a text can have different meanings in different cultures—or even in different historical time periods. Each reader brings to the text associations that come from his or her own cultural community. These associations are determined by readers' experience and education as well as by their ethnic group, social class, religion, gender, and many other factors that contribute to how they view the world. Each reader also brings to the text beliefs, expectations, desires, and biases that influence how he or she reacts to and interprets it. Thus, it is entirely possible for two readers to have very different, but equally valid, interpretations of the same text. (This does not mean, of course, that a text can mean whatever any individual reader wishes it to mean. To be valid, an interpretation must be supported by the text itself.)

To get an idea of the range of possible interpretations that can be suggested by a single text, consider some of the responses different readers might have to E. B. White's classic essay "Once More to the Lake" (p. 18).

In "Once More to the Lake," White tells a story about his visit with his son to a lake in Maine in the 1940s, comparing this visit with those he made as a boy with his own father in 1904. Throughout the essay, White describes the changes that have occurred since his first visit. Memories from the past flood his consciousness, causing him to remember things that he did when he was a boy. At one point, after he and his son have been feeding worms to fish, he remembers doing the same thing with his father and has trouble separating the past from the present.

Eventually, White realizes that he will soon be just a memory in his son's mind—just as his father is only a memory in his.

White had specific goals in mind when he wrote this essay. His title, "Once More to the Lake," indicates that he intended to compare his childhood and adult visits to the lake. The organization of ideas in the essay, the use of flashbacks, and the choice of particular transitional words and phrases reinforce this purpose. In addition, descriptive details—such as the image of the tarred road that replaced the dirt road—remind readers, as well as White himself, that the years have made the lake site different from what it once was. The essay ends with White suddenly feeling the "chill of death."

Despite White's specific intentions, each person reading "Once More to the Lake" will respond to it somewhat differently. Young male readers might identify with the boy. If they have ever spent a vacation at a lake, they might have experienced the "peace and goodness and jollity" of the whole summer scene. Female readers might also want to share these experiences, but they might feel excluded because only males are described in the essay. Readers who have never been on a fishing trip might not feel the same nostalgia for the woods that White feels. To them, living in the woods away from the comforts of home might seem an unthinkably uncomfortable ordeal. Older readers might identify with White, sympathizing with his efforts as an adult to recapture the past and seeing his son as naively innocent of the challenges of life.

Thus, although each person who reads White's essay will read the same words, each will be likely to interpret it differently and to see different things as important. This is because much is left open to interpretation. All essays leave blanks or gaps—missing ideas or images—that readers have to fill in. In "Once More to the Lake," for example, readers must imagine what happened in the years that separated White's last visit to the lake with his father and the trip he took with his son.

These gaps in the text create ambiguities—words, phrases, descriptions, or ideas that need to be interpreted by the reader. For instance, when you read the words "One summer, along about 1904, my father rented a camp on a lake," how do you picture the camp? White's description of the setting contains a great deal of detail, but no matter how much information he supplies, he cannot paint a complete verbal picture of the lakeside camp. He must rely on his readers' ability to visualize the setting and to supply details from their own experience.

Readers also bring their emotional associations to a text. For example, how readers react to White's statement above depends, in part, on their feelings about their own fathers. If White's words bring to mind a parent who is loving, strong, and protective, they will most likely respond favorably; if the essay calls up memories of a parent who is distant, bad-tempered, or even abusive, they may respond negatively.

Because each reader views the text from a slightly different angle, each may also see a different focus as central to "Once More to the

Lake." Some might see nature as the primary element in the essay and believe that White's purpose is to condemn the encroachment of human beings on the environment. Others might see the passage of time as the central focus. Still others might see the initiation theme as being the most important element of the essay: each boy is brought to the lake by his father, and each eventually passes from childhood innocence to adulthood and to the awareness of his own mortality.

Finally, each reader may evaluate the essay differently. Some readers might find "Once More to the Lake" boring because it has little action and deals with a subject in which they have no interest. Others might believe the essay is a brilliant meditation that makes an impact through its vivid description and imaginative figurative language. Still others might see the essay as falling between these two extremes—for example, they might grant that White is an accomplished stylist but also see him as self-centered and self-indulgent. After all, they might argue, the experiences he describes are available only to relatively privileged members of society and are irrelevant to others.

## Reading Critically

**Reading critically** means interacting with a text, questioning the text's assumptions, and formulating and reformulating judgments about its ideas. Think of reading as a dialogue between you and the text: sometimes the writer will assert himself or herself; at other times, you will dominate the conversation. Remember, though, that a critical voice is a thoughtful and responsible one, not one that shouts down the opposition. Linguist Deborah Tannen makes this distinction clear in an essay called "The Triumph of the Yell":

> In many university classrooms, "critical thinking" means reading someone's life work, then ripping it to shreds. Though critique is surely one form of critical thinking, so are integrating ideas from disparate fields and examining the context out of which they grew. Opposition does not lead to truth when we ask only "What's wrong with this argument?" and never "What can we use from this in building a new theory, a new understanding?"

In other words, being a critical reader does not necessarily mean arguing and contradicting; more often, it means asking questions and exploring your reactions—while remaining open to new ideas.

Asking the following questions as you read will help you to become aware of the relationships between the writer's perspective and your own:

- **Who is the writer addressing?** Who is the writer's intended audience? For example, the title of John Holt's essay on early childhood education, "School Is Bad for Children" (p. 72), suggests that Holt expects his readers to have preconceived notions about the value of a traditional education—notions his essay will challenge.

- **What is the writer's purpose?** Exactly what is the writer trying to accomplish in the essay? For example, is the writer attempting to explain, persuade, justify, evaluate, describe, debunk, entertain, preach, browbeat, threaten, or frighten? Or, does the writer have some other purpose (or combination of purposes)? For example, is the writer trying to explain causes and effects, as Sherry Turkle is in "Connectivity and Its Discontents" (p. 235)? To reflect on his or her life experiences, as Oscar Hijuelos is in "Lost in Time and Words, a Child Begins Anew" (p. 131)? Or to move readers to action, as Arlie Hochschild is in "The Second Shift" (p. 412)? What strategies does the writer use to achieve his or her purpose? For example, does the writer rely primarily on logic or on emotion? Does the writer appeal to the prejudices or fears of his or her readers or in any other way attempt to influence readers unfairly?

- **What voice does the writer use?** Does the writer seem to talk directly to readers? If so, does the writer's subjectivity get in the way, or does it help to involve readers? Does the writer's voice seem distant or formal? Different voices have different effects on readers. For example, an emotional tone, like the one Martin Luther King, Jr., uses in "I Have a Dream" (p. 370), can inspire; an intimate tone, like the one Lynda Barry uses in "The Sanctuary of School" (p. 69), can create reader identification and empathy; a straightforward, forthright voice, like that of Karen S. Sibert in "Don't Quit This Day Job" (p. 260), can make ideas seem reasonable and credible. An ironic tone can either amuse readers or alienate them; a distant, reserved tone can evoke either respect or discomfort.

- **What emotional response is the writer trying to create?** In his Inaugural Address (p. 510), John F. Kennedy uses stirring language and an emotional tone to inspire pride in the United States and give his listeners a sense of their collective responsibility to contribute something to their nation. In "Letter from Birmingham Jail" (p. 464), Martin Luther King, Jr., maintains a calm, unemotional tone even though he is writing about injustices that have wounded him deeply. By maintaining a dignified tone and avoiding bitterness and resentment, he succeeds in inspiring sympathy and respect. Other writers may attempt to elicit other emotional responses: amusement, nostalgia, curiosity, wonder over the grandeur or mystery of the world that surrounds us, or even anger or fear.

- **What position does the writer take on the issue?** Sometimes a work's title reveals a writer's position—for example, "Amy Chua

Is a Wimp" (p. 57) or "Plan B: Skip College" (p. 116). The choice of the word *war* in Christina Hoff Sommers's title "The War against Boys" (p. 283) clearly reveals her position on society's attitude toward boys; in the same way, the title of John Humphrys's essay "I h8 txt msgs" (p. 174) conveys his attitude toward texting. Keep in mind, though, that a writer's position may not always be as obvious as it is in these examples. As you read, look carefully for specific language that suggests the writer's position on a particular subject or issue—or for explicit statements that make that position clear. Also, be sure you understand how you feel about the writer's position, particularly if it is an unusual or controversial one. Do you agree or disagree? Can you explain your reasoning? Of course, a writer's advocacy of a position that is at odds with your own does not automatically render the work suspect or its ideas invalid. Remember, ideas that you might consider shocking or absurd may be readily accepted by many other readers. Unexpected, puzzling, or even repellent positions should encourage you to read carefully and thoughtfully, trying to understand the larger historical and cultural context of a writer's ideas.

- **How does the writer support his or her position?** What kind of supporting evidence is provided? Is it convincing? Does the writer use a series of individual examples, as Alleen Pace Nilsen does in "Sexism in English: Embodiment and Language" (p. 148), or a single extended example, as Claire McCarthy does in "Dog Lab" (p. 479)? Does the writer use statistics, as Christina Hoff Sommers does in "The War against Boys" (p. 283), or does he or she rely primarily on personal experiences, as Brent Staples does in "Just Walk On By" (p. 356)? Does the writer quote experts, as Deborah Tannen does in "Marked Women" (p. 268), or present anecdotal information, as Jonathan Kozol does in "The Human Cost of an Illiterate Society" (p. 159)? Why does the writer choose a particular kind of support? Does the writer supply enough information to support the essay's points? Are all the examples actually relevant to the issues being discussed? Is the writer's reasoning valid, or do the arguments seem forced or unrealistic? Are any references in the work unfamiliar to you? If so, do they arouse your curiosity, or do they discourage you from reading further?

- **What beliefs, assumptions, or preconceived ideas do you have that color your responses to a work?** Does the writer challenge any ideas that you accept as "natural" or "obvious"? For example, does the parent–child relationship described in Amy Chua's "Why Chinese Mothers Are Superior" (p. 52) shock you? Does the fact that you are opposed to the concept of a path to citizenship for undocumented immigrants make it hard for you to sympathize with the struggles described by Jose Antonio Vargas in "Outlaw: My Life in America as an Undocumented Immigrant" (p. 377)?

- **Does your own background or experience give you any special insights that enable you to understand or interpret the writer's ideas?** Are the writer's experiences similar to your own? Is the writer like you in terms of age, ethnic background, gender, and social class? How do the similarities between you and the writer affect your reaction to the work? For example, you may be able to understand Amy Tan's "Mother Tongue" (p. 134) better than other students because you, like Tan, speak one language at home and another in public. Or, you may have a unique perspective on the problems Lynda Barry describes in "The Sanctuary of School" (p. 69) because you also had a difficult childhood. Any experiences you may have had can help you to understand a writer's ideas and shape your response to them.

## Recording Your Reactions

It is a good idea to read any text at least twice: first to get a general sense of the writer's ideas and then to react critically to these ideas. As you read critically, you interact with the text and respond in ways that will help you to interpret it. This process of coming to understand the text will prepare you to discuss the work with others and, perhaps, to write about it.

As you read and reread, record your responses; if you don't, you may forget some of your best ideas. Two activities can help you keep a record of the ideas that come to you as you read: **highlighting** (using a system of symbols and underlining to identify key ideas) and **annotating** (writing down your responses and interpretations in the margins of the text).

When you react to what you read, don't be afraid to question the writer's ideas. As you read and make annotations, you may disagree with or even challenge some of these ideas; when you have time, you can think more about what you have written. These informal responses may be the beginning of a thought process that will lead you to original insights.

Highlighting and annotating helped a student to understand the passage on page 8, which is excerpted from Brent Staples's essay "Just Walk On By" (p. 356). As she prepared to write about the essay, the student identified and summarized the writer's key points and made a connection with another essay, Judith Ortiz Cofer's "The Myth of the Latin Woman" (p. 308). As she read, she underlined some of the passage's important words and ideas, using arrows to indicate relationships between them. She also circled a few words to remind her to look up their meanings later on, and she wrote down questions and comments as they occurred to her.

<u>The fearsomeness mistakenly attributed to me in public places often has a perilous flavor.</u> The most frightening of these confusions occurred in the <u>late 1970s and early 1980s</u> when I worked as a journalist in Chicago. One day, rushing into the office of a magazine I was writing for with a deadline story in hand, I was mistaken for a burglar. The office manager called security and, with an ad hoc posse, pursued me through the labyrinthine halls, nearly to my editor's door. I had no way of proving who I was. I could only move briskly toward the company of someone who knew me.

*(Fear creates danger)*

Still applies today?

*(?)*

*First experience*

*(?)*

Another time I was on assignment for a local paper and killing time before an interview. I entered a jewelry store on the city's affluent Near North Side. The proprietor excused herself and returned with an enormous red Doberman pinscher straining at the end of a leash. She stood, the dog extended toward me, silent to my questions, her eyes bulging nearly out of her head. I took a cursory look around, nodded, and bade her good night. Relatively speaking, however, I never fared as badly as another black male journalist. He went to nearby Waukegan, Illinois, a couple of summers ago to work on a story about a murderer who was born there. Mistaking the reporter for the killer, police hauled him from his car at gunpoint and but for his press credentials would probably have tried to book him. <u>Such episodes are not uncommon. Black men trade tales like this all the time.</u>

*Second experience*

*(?)*

*Compare with Cofer's experience w/ stereotypes*

*

## Reacting to Visual Texts

Many of the written texts you read—from newspapers and magazines to Web sites to textbooks such as this one—include visuals. Some of these visuals (charts, tables, maps, graphs, scientific diagrams, and the like) primarily present information; others (fine art, photographs, cartoons, and advertisements, for example) may be designed to have an emotional impact on readers or to persuade them to change their minds or to take some kind of action.

Visuals can be analyzed, interpreted, and evaluated just as written texts are. You begin this process by looking critically at the visual, identifying its most important elements, and considering the relationships of various elements to one another and to the image as a whole. Then, you try to identify the purpose for which the image was created, and you consider your own personal response to the image.

As you examine a visual text, finding answers to the following questions will help you to understand it better:

- **What audience is the visual aimed at?** Does the visual seem to address a wide general audience or some kind of specialized audience, such as new parents, runners, or medical professionals? Is it aimed at adults or at children? Does it seem likely to appeal mainly to people from a particular region or ethnic group, or is it likely to resonate with a broad range of people? Often, knowing where a visual appeared—in a popular magazine, on a political blog, in a professional journal, or in a trade publication, for example—will help you to identify the audience the visual is trying to reach.

- **For what purpose was the visual created?** Is the visual designed to evoke an emotional response—fear or guilt, for example? Is it designed to be humorous? Or is its purpose simply to present information? To understand a visual's purpose, you need to consider not only its source but also what images it contains and how it arranges them. (Some visuals contain written text, and if this is the case, you will have to consider this written text as well.)

- **What elements does the visual use to achieve its purpose?** What is the most important image? Where is it placed? What other images are present? Does the visual depict people? What are they doing? How much space is left blank? How does the visual use color and shadow? Does it include written text? How are words and images juxtaposed? For example, a visual designed to be primarily informative may use written text and straightforward graphics (such as graphs or scientific diagrams), while one that aims to persuade may use a single eye-catching image surrounded by blank space.

- **Does the visual make a point?** If so, how does it use images to get its message across? What other elements help to convey that message? If the visual is designed to convince its audience of something—for example, to change unhealthy behavior, donate to a charity, vote for a candidate, or buy a product—exactly how does it communicate this message? For example, a photograph of starving children on a charity's Web site might convey the idea that a donation will bring them food, but statistics about infant mortality might make the image even more persuasive. Moreover, a close-up of one hungry child might be more convincing than a distant photo of a crowd. Similarly, an ad might appeal to consumers either by showing satisfied customers using a product or by setting a memorable slogan against a contrasting background.

- **Do you have any beliefs or assumptions that help to determine your response to the visual?** Is there anything in your background or experience that influences your reaction? Just as with written texts, different people react differently to different visual texts. For example, if you have expertise in economics, you may approach a chart depicting economic trends with greater interest—or greater skepticism—than a general audience would. If you know very little about fine art, your reaction to a painting is more likely to be emotional than analytical. And, as a loyal Democrat or Republican, you may react negatively to a political cartoon that is critical of your party. Finally, if you or a family member has struggled with illness or addiction, you might not respond favorably to a visual that took a superficial, lighthearted, or satirical approach to such a problem.

The following visual is a parody of an ad for Marlboro cigarettes. The visual, which appeared on the Web site www.adbusters.org, was annotated by a student who was assigned to analyze it. As he examined the ad, he identified its key elements and recorded his reactions in handwritten notes.

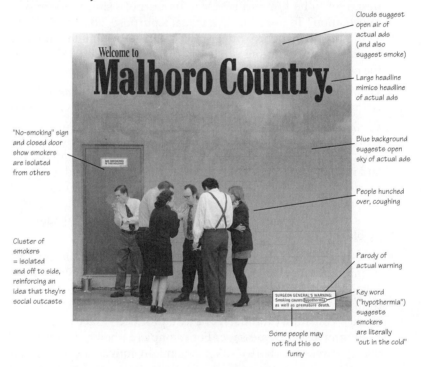

### Reading to Write

Much of the reading you will do as a student will be done to prepare you for writing. Writing helps you focus your ideas about various issues; in addition, the process of writing can lead you in unexpected directions, thereby enabling you to discover new ideas. With this in mind, we have included in *The Blair Reader* a number of features that will help you as you read its selections and prepare to write about them.

The readings in *The Blair Reader* (classic and contemporary essays as well as speeches, fiction, and poetry) are arranged in ten thematic chapters, each offering a variety of different vantage points from which to view the chapter's central theme. Each chapter opens with a brief introduction, which provides a context for the chapter's theme and includes a list of **Preparing to Read and Write** questions to guide your thinking as you read. These questions are designed to help you to sharpen your critical skills and begin to apply those skills effectively. Each chapter introduction also includes a pair of contrasting visual images—photographs, advertisements, Web pages, and so on—designed to introduce you to the chapter's theme and to help you begin thinking about the issues it suggests.

Following each reading are three questions that encourage you to think about and respond to what you have read. These **Responding to Reading** questions ask you to think critically about the writer's ideas, perhaps focusing on a particular strategy the writer has used to achieve his or her purpose. In some cases, these questions may ask you to examine your own ideas or beliefs. Following the **Responding to Reading** questions is a **Responding in Writing** prompt that asks you to write a brief informal response. These prompts may ask you to link the writer's experiences or ideas to your own; to do some kind of writing exercise, such as making a list, writing a summary, or drafting an email; or to respond more critically to the writer's ideas.

Following the essays on each chapter's general theme is a **Focus** section that zeroes in on a specific issue. The Focus section's central question—for example, "Does Social Networking Connect Us or Keep Us Apart?" (Chapter 4) or "Who Has It Harder, Girls or Boys?" (Chapter 5)—introduces a cluster of thought-provoking essays that take different positions on a single complex issue; a related visual image is also included here. Each Focus essay is accompanied by three **Responding to Reading** questions and a **Responding in Writing** prompt; **Responding to the Image** questions follow each visual. The Focus section ends with **Widening the Focus**, which includes "For Critical Reading and Writing" (a comprehensive essay prompt), "For Further Reading" (a list of related readings in other chapters of the book), "For Focused Research" (a guided research assignment that relies on Web sources), and "Beyond the Classroom" (a prompt designed to encourage you to write about your first-hand observations and experiences).

At the end of each chapter are suggestions for writing assignments that are longer and more formally structured than those suggested by the **Responding in Writing** prompts. These writing assignments ask you to examine some aspect of the chapter's theme by analyzing, interpreting, or evaluating ideas explored in various essays, sometimes considering parallels and contrasts with other essays in the book—or with your own life experiences.

As you read and write about the selections in this book, remember that you are learning how to think about yourself and about the world. By considering and reconsidering the ideas of others, by rejecting easy answers, by considering a problem from many different angles, and by appreciating the many factors that can influence your responses, you will develop critical thinking skills that you will use throughout your life. In addition, by writing about the themes discussed in this book, you will participate in an ongoing conversation within the community of scholars and writers who care deeply about the issues that shape our world.

# 1

## FAMILY AND MEMORY

The ties that bind us to family, and to our family history, are like no other human connections. In this chapter, writers search their memories, trying to understand, recapture, or re-create the past, to see across the barriers imposed by time. In some cases, memories appear in sharp focus; in others, they are blurred, confused, or even partially invented. Many writers focus on themselves; others focus on their parents or other family members, struggling to close generational gaps, to replay events, to see through the eyes of others—and, in this way, to understand their families and themselves more fully.

Alice Walker with her mother

In this chapter's Focus section, "Are 'Chinese Mothers' Superior?" (p. 52), three writers discuss the pros and cons of a strict, somewhat "old-fashioned" parenting style in the twenty-first century.

## PREPARING TO READ AND WRITE

As you read and prepare to write about the selections in this chapter, you may consider the following questions:

- How does the writer define *family?*

- Does the writer focus on a single person, on a relationship between two people, or on wider family dynamics?

- Does the writer focus on one generation or on more than one?

- How important is the setting in which the events the writer describes take place?

- Do you think the writer's perspective is *subjective* (shaped by his or her emotional responses or personal opinions) or *objective* (based mainly on observation and fact rather than on personal impressions)?

David Jacobsen with his mother

- What insights does the writer have that he or she did not have when the events occurred? What has the writer learned—and how?

- Are the memories generally happy or unhappy ones?

- Are family members presented in a favorable, unfavorable, neutral, or ambivalent way?

- Does the writer feel close to or distant from family members? Does the writer identify with a particular family member?

- Does one family member seem to have had a great influence over the writer? If so, is this influence positive or negative?

- What social, political, economic, or cultural forces influenced the family dynamics?

- What is the writer's primary purpose? For example, is the writer's purpose to observe? re-examine? explore? discover? explain? persuade?

- Do you identify with the writer or with another person the writer describes? What makes you identify with that person?

- Which selections seem most similar in their views of family? How are they similar?

- Which selections seem most different in their views of family? How are they different?

- Which family seems most like your own? Why?

# Heritage

## Linda Hogan

### 1947–

*A Chickasaw Native American, Linda Hogan writes poetry, novels, plays, and essays. She has published numerous works, including, most recently,* Indios: A Poem to Be Spoken *(2011). In the following poem, Hogan explores the complexity of her heritage.*

From my mother, the antique mirror
where I watch my face take on her lines.
She left me the smell of baking bread
to warm fine hairs in my nostrils,
she left the large white breasts that weigh down          5
my body.

From my father I take his brown eyes,
the plague of locusts that leveled our crops,
they flew in formation like buzzards.
From my uncle the whittled wood          10
that rattles like bones
and is white
and smells like all our old houses
that are no longer there. He was the man
who sang old chants to me, the words          15
my father was told not to remember.

From my grandfather who never spoke
I learned to fear silence.
I learned to kill a snake
when you're begging for rain.          20

And grandmother, blue-eyed woman
whose skin was brown,
she used snuff.
When her coffee can full of black saliva
spilled on me          25
it was like the brown cloud of grasshoppers
that leveled her fields.
It was the brown stain

that covered my white shirt,
30   my whiteness a shame.
That sweet black liquid like the food
she chewed up and spit into my father's mouth
when he was an infant.
It was the brown earth of Oklahoma
35   stained with oil.
She said tobacco would purge your body of poisons.
It has more medicine than stones and knives
against your enemies.

That tobacco is the dark night that covers me.
40   She said it is wise to eat the flesh of deer
so you will be swift and travel over many miles.
She told me how our tribe has always followed a stick
that pointed west
that pointed east.

45   From my family I have learned the secrets
of never having a home.

## Responding to Reading

1. What has the speaker inherited from her parents? from her grandparents? from her tribe? Which inheritance does she seem to value most? Why?
2. What do you think the speaker means in the poem's last lines when she says, "From my family I have learned the secrets / of never having a home"?
3. What feelings does the speaker have about her family's past? Do you see these as mixed feelings?

## Responding in Writing

In lines 21–38, the speaker describes her grandmother in terms of the colors she associates with her. Write a paragraph in which you describe a family member in this way.

# THOSE WINTER SUNDAYS
## Robert Hayden
### 1913–1980

*Robert Hayden's work includes poems about slave rebellions and the historical roots of racism as well as about more personal subjects. Hayden's first book of poetry,* Heart-Shaped in the Dust, *was published in 1940. Other works include* Angle of Ascent: New and Selected Poems *(1975), in which "Those Winter Sundays" appeared, and* Complete Poems *(1985). In the following poem, the speaker expresses his ambivalence about his father's sacrifices.*

Sundays too my father got up early
and put his clothes on in the blueblack cold,
then with cracked hands that ached
from labor in the weekday weather made
banked fires blaze. No one ever thanked him.                    5

I'd wake and hear the cold splintering, breaking.
When the rooms were warm, he'd call,
and slowly I would rise and dress,
fearing the chronic angers of that house,

Speaking indifferently to him,                                 10
who had driven out the cold
and polished my good shoes as well.
What did I know, what did I know
of love's austere and lonely offices?

## Responding to Reading

1. Other than having "driven out the cold," what has the father done for his son? To what might "chronic angers" (line 9) refer?
2. What important lessons has the speaker learned? When do you think he learned them? Do you see these lessons as primarily theoretical or practical?
3. In what respects does this poem sound like conversational speech? In what respects is it "poetic"?

## Responding in Writing

What do you now know about your parents' responsibilities and sacrifices that you did not know when you were a child? How has this knowledge changed your feelings about your parents?

# ONCE MORE TO THE LAKE

## E. B. White

### 1899–1985

*Well known for his children's stories, Elwyn Brooks White was also a talented essayist and a witty observer of contemporary society. His expansion of Will Strunk's* The Elements of Style *remains one of the most popular and concise grammar and style texts in use today. White wrote for the* New Yorker *and* Harper's Magazine, *and his essays are collected in* Essays of E. B. White *(1977). In 1939, he moved to a farm in North Brooklin, Maine, where he wrote the children's classics* Stuart Little *(1945) and* Charlotte's Web *(1952). As a youth, White vacationed with his family on a lake in Maine. It is to this lake that he returned with his son, and he describes his experience in the following essay.*

One summer, along about 1904, my father rented a camp on a lake in Maine and took us all there for the month of August. We all got ring-worm from some kittens and had to rub Pond's Extract on our arms and legs night and morning, and my father rolled over in a canoe with all his clothes on; but outside of that the vacation was a success and from then on none of us ever thought there was any place in the world like that lake in Maine. We returned summer after summer—always on August 1st for one month. I have since become a salt-water man, but sometimes in summer there are days when the restlessness of the tides and the fearful cold of the sea water and the incessant wind which blows across the afternoon and into the evening make me wish for the placid-ity of a lake in the woods. A few weeks ago this feeling got so strong I bought myself a couple of bass hooks and a spinner and returned to the lake where we used to go, for a week's fishing and to revisit old haunts.

I took along my son, who had never had any fresh water up his nose and who had seen lily pads only from train windows. On the journey over to the lake I began to wonder what it would be like. I wondered how time would have marred this unique, this holy spot—the coves and streams, the hills that the sun set behind, the camps and the paths behind the camps. I was sure the tarred road would have found it out and I wondered in what other ways it would be desolated. It is strange how much you can remember about places like that once you allow your mind to return into the grooves which lead back. You remember one thing, and that suddenly reminds you of another thing. I guess I remembered clearest of all the early mornings, when the lake was cool and motionless, remembered how the bedroom smelled of the lumber it was made of and of the wet woods whose scent entered through the screen. The partitions in the camp were thin and did not extend clear to the top of the rooms, and as I was always the first up I would dress softly so as not to wake the others, and sneak out into the sweet outdoors and start out in the canoe, keeping close along the shore in the long shadows of the pines. I remembered being very careful never to rub my paddle against the gunwale for fear of disturbing the stillness of the cathedral.

The lake had never been what you would call a wild lake. There were cottages sprinkled around the shores, and it was in farming country although the shores of the lake were quite heavily wooded. Some of the cottages were owned by nearby farmers, and you would live at the shore and eat your meals at the farmhouse. That's what our family did. But although it wasn't wild, it was a fairly large and undisturbed lake and there were places in it which, to a child at least, seemed infinitely remote and primeval.

I was right about the tar: it led to within half a mile of the shore. But when I got back there, with my boy, and we settled into a camp near a farmhouse and into the kind of summertime I had known, I could tell that it was going to be pretty much the same as it had been before—I knew it, lying in bed the first morning, smelling the bedroom, and hearing the boy sneak quietly out and go off along the shore in a boat. I began to sustain the illusion that he was I, and therefore, by simple transposition, that I was my father. This sensation persisted, kept cropping up all the time we were there. It was not an entirely new feeling, but in this setting it grew much stronger. I seemed to be living a dual existence. I would be in the middle of some simple act, I would be picking up a bait box or laying down a table fork, or I would be saying something, and suddenly it would be not I but my father who was saying the words or making the gesture. It gave me a creepy sensation.

We went fishing the first morning. I felt the same damp moss covering the worms in the bait can, and saw the dragonfly alight on the tip of my rod as it hovered a few inches from the surface of the water. It was the arrival of this fly that convinced me beyond any doubt that everything was as it always had been, that the years were a mirage and there had been no years. The small waves were the same, chucking the rowboat under the chin as we fished at anchor, and the boat was the same boat, the same color green and the ribs broken in the same places, and under the floor-boards the same freshwater leavings and débris— the dead helgramite,[1] the wisps of moss, the rusty discarded fishhook, the dried blood from yesterday's catch. We stared silently at the tips of our rods, at the dragonflies that came and went. I lowered the tip of mine into the water, tentatively, pensively dislodging the fly, which darted two feet away, poised, darted two feet back, and came to rest again a little farther up the rod. There had been no years between the ducking of this dragonfly and the other one—the one that was part of memory. I looked at the boy, who was silently watching his fly, and it

5

---
[1] The nymph of the May-fly, used as bait. [Eds.]

was my hands that held his rod, my eyes watching. I felt dizzy and didn't know which rod I was at the end of.

We caught two bass, hauling them in briskly as though they were mackerel, pulling them over the side of the boat in a businesslike manner without any landing net, and stunning them with a blow on the back of the head. When we got back for a swim before lunch, the lake was exactly where we had left it, the same number of inches from the dock, and there was only the merest suggestion of a breeze. This seemed an utterly enchanted sea, this lake you could leave to its own devices for a few hours and come back to, and find that it had not stirred, this constant and trustworthy body of water. In the shallows, the dark, water-soaked sticks and twigs, smooth and old, were undulating in clusters on the bottom against the clean ribbed sand, and the track of the mussel was plain. A school of minnows swam by, each minnow with its small individual shadow, doubling the attendance, so clear and sharp in the sunlight. Some of the other campers were in swimming, along the shore, one of them with a cake of soap, and the water felt thin and clear and unsubstantial. Over the years there had been this person with the cake of soap, this cultist, and here he was. There had been no years.

Up to the farmhouse to dinner through the teeming, dusty field, the road under our sneakers was only a two-track road. The middle track was missing, the one with the marks of the hooves and the splotches of dried, flaky manure. There had always been three tracks to choose from in choosing which track to walk in; now the choice was narrowed down to two. For a moment I missed terribly the middle alternative. But the way led past the tennis court, and something about the way it lay there in the sun reassured me; the tape had loosened along the backline, the alleys were green with plantains and other weeds, and the net (installed in June and removed in September) sagged in the dry noon, and the whole place steamed with midday heat and hunger and emptiness. There was a choice of pie for dessert, and one was blueberry and one was apple, and the waitresses were the same country girls, there having been no passage of time, only the illusion of it as in a dropped curtain—the waitresses were still fifteen; their hair had been washed, that was the only difference—they had been to the movies and seen the pretty girls with the clean hair.

Summertime, oh summertime, pattern of life indelible, the fade-proof lake, the woods unshatterable, the pasture with the sweetfern and the juniper forever and ever, summer without end; this was the background, and the life along the shore was the design, the cottagers with their innocent and tranquil design, their tiny docks with the flagpole and the American flag floating against the white clouds in the blue sky, the little paths over the roots of the trees leading from camp to camp and the paths leading back to the outhouses and the can of lime for sprinkling, and at the souvenir counters at the store the miniature birch-bark canoes and the post cards that showed things looking a little better than they looked. This was the American family at play, escaping the city heat, wondering whether the newcomers in the camp at the head of the cove were "common" or "nice," wondering whether it was true that the people who drove up for Sunday dinner at the farmhouse were turned away because there wasn't enough chicken.

It seemed to me, as I kept remembering all this, that those times and those summers had been infinitely precious and worth saving. There had been jollity and peace and goodness. The arriving (at the beginning of August) had been so big a business in itself, at the railway station the farm wagon drawn up, the first smell of the pine-laden air, the first glimpse of the smiling farmer, and the great importance of the trunks and your father's enormous authority in such matters, and the feel of the wagon under you for the long ten-mile haul, and at the top of the last long hill catching the first view of the lake after eleven months of not seeing this cherished body of water. The shouts and cries of the other campers when they saw you, and the trunks to be unpacked, to give up their rich burden. (Arriving was less exciting nowadays, when you sneaked up in your car and parked it under a tree near the camp and took out the bags and in five minutes it was all over, no fuss, no loud wonderful fuss about trunks.)

Peace and goodness and jollity. The only thing that was wrong now, really, was the sound of the place, an unfamiliar nervous sound of the outboard motors. This was the note that jarred, the one thing that would sometimes break the illusion and set the years moving. In those other summertimes all motors were inboard; and when they were at a little distance, the noise they made was a sedative, an ingredient of summer sleep. They were one-cylinder and two-cylinder engines, and some were make-and-break and some were jump-spark,[2] but they all made a sleepy sound across the lake. The one-lungers throbbed and fluttered, and the twin-cylinder ones purred and purred, and that was a quiet sound too. But now the campers all had outboards. In the day-time, in the hot mornings, these motors made a petulant, irritable sound; at night, in the still evening when the afterglow lit the water, they whined about one's ears like mosquitoes. My boy loved our rented outboard, and his great desire was to achieve singlehanded mastery over it, and authority, and he soon learned the trick of choking it a little (but not too much), and the adjustment of the needle valve. Watching him I would remember the things you could do with the old one-cylinder engine with the heavy flywheel, how you could have it eating out of your hand if you got really close to it spiritually. Motor boats in those days didn't have clutches, and you would make a landing by shutting off the motor at the proper time and coasting in with a dead rudder. But there was a way of reversing them, if you learned the trick, by cutting the

10

---

[2]Methods of ignition timing. [Eds.]

switch and putting it on again exactly on the final dying revolution of the flywheel, so that it would kick back against compression and begin reversing. Approaching a dock in a strong following breeze, it was difficult to slow up sufficiently by the ordinary coasting method, and if a boy felt he had complete mastery over his motor, he was tempted to keep it running beyond its time and then reverse it a few feet from the dock. It took a cool nerve, because if you threw the switch a twentieth of a second too soon you would catch the flywheel when it still had speed enough to go up past center, and the boat would leap ahead, charging bull-fashion at the dock.

We had a good week at the camp. The bass were biting well and the sun shone endlessly, day after day. We would be tired at night and lie down in the accumulated heat of the little bedrooms after the long hot day and the breeze would stir almost imperceptibly outside and the smell of the swamp drift in through the rusty screens. Sleep would come easily and in the morning the red squirrel would be on the roof, tapping out his gay routine. I kept remembering everything, lying in bed in the mornings—the small steamboat that had a long rounded stern like the lip of a Ubangi, and how quietly she ran on the moonlight sails, when the older boys played their mandolins and the girls sang and we ate doughnuts dipped in sugar, and how sweet the music was on the water in the shining night, and what it had felt like to think about girls then. After breakfast we would go up to the store and the things were in the same place—the minnows in a bottle, the plugs and spinners disarranged and pawed over by the youngsters from the boys' camp, the fig newtons and the Beeman's gum. Outside, the road was tarred and cars stood in front of the store. Inside, all was just as it had always been, except there was more Coca-Cola and not so much Moxie and root beer and birch beer and sarsaparilla. We would walk out with a bottle of pop apiece and sometimes the pop would backfire up our noses and hurt. We explored the streams, quietly, where the turtles slid off the sunny logs and dug their way into the soft bottom; and we lay on the town wharf and fed worms to the tame bass. Everywhere we went I had trouble making out which was I, the one walking at my side, the one walking in my pants.

One afternoon while we were there at that lake a thunderstorm came up. It was like the revival of an old melodrama that I had seen long ago with childish awe. The second-act climax of the drama of the electrical disturbance over a lake in America had not changed in any important respect. This was the big scene, still the big scene. The whole thing was so familiar, the first feeling of oppression and heat and a general air around camp of not wanting to go very far away. In midafternoon (it was all the same) a curious darkening of the sky, and a lull in everything that had made life tick; and then the way the boats suddenly swung the other way at their moorings with the coming of a breeze out of the new quarter, and the premonitory rumble. Then the kettle drum, then the snare, then the bass drum and cymbals, then crackling light against the dark, and the gods grinning and licking their chops in the hills. Afterward the calm, the rain steadily rustling in the calm lake, the return of light and hope and spirits, and the campers running out in joy and relief to go swimming in the rain, their bright cries perpetuating the deathless joke about how they were getting simply drenched, and the children screaming with delight at the new sensation of bathing in the rain, and the joke about getting drenched linking the generations in a strong indestructible chain. And the comedian who waded in carrying an umbrella.

When the others went swimming my son said he was going in too. He pulled his dripping trunks from the line where they had hung all through the shower, and wrung them out. Languidly, and with no thought of going in, I watched him, his hard little body, skinny and bare, saw him wince slightly as he pulled up around his vitals the small, soggy, icy garment. As he buckled the swollen belt suddenly my groin felt the chill of death.

## Responding to Reading

1. How is White's "holy spot" different when he visits it with his son from how it was when he visited it with his father?
2. Is this essay primarily about a time, a place, or a relationship? Explain.
3. Why does White feel "the chill of death" as he watches his son? Do you identify more with White the father or White the son?

## Responding in Writing

Write two short paragraphs about a place that was important to you as a child: one from the point of view of your adult self, and one from the point of view of your childhood self. How are the two paragraphs different?

# NO NAME WOMAN

## Maxine Hong Kingston

### 1940–

*Maxine Hong Kingston was born in Stockton, California, the daughter of Chinese immigrants who ran a gambling house and, later, a laundry where she and her five siblings worked. Since her first book,* The Woman Warrior: Memoirs of a Girlhood among Ghosts *(1976), was published, Kingston has been acclaimed as a writer of fiction and nonfiction. Her most recent book is* I Love a Broad Margin to My Life *(2011), a memoir in free verse. In the following autobiographical essay from* The Woman Warrior, *Kingston speculates about the life and death of a family member she has never met.*

"You must not tell anyone," my mother said, "what I am about to tell you. In China your father had a sister who killed herself. She jumped into the family well. We say that your father has all brothers because it is as if she had never been born.

"In 1924 just a few days after our village celebrated seventeen hurry-up weddings—to make sure that every young man who went 'out on the road' would responsibly come home—your father and his brothers and your grandfather and his brothers and your aunt's new husband sailed for America, the Gold Mountain. It was your grand-father's last trip. Those lucky enough to get contracts waved good-bye from the decks. They fed and guarded the stowaways and helped them off in Cuba, New York, Bali, Hawaii. 'We'll meet in California next year,' they said. All of them sent money home.

"I remember looking at your aunt one day when she and I were dressing; I had not noticed before that she had such a protruding melon of a stomach. But I did not think, 'She's pregnant,' until she began to look like other pregnant women, her shirt pulling and the white tops of her black pants showing. She could not have been pregnant, you see, because her husband had been gone for years. No one said anything. We did not discuss it. In early summer she was ready to have the child, long after the time when it could have been possible.

"The village had also been counting. On the night the baby was to be born the villagers raided our house. Some were crying. Like a great saw, teeth strung with lights, files of people walked zigzag across our land, tearing the rice. Their lanterns doubled in the dis-turbed black water, which drained away through the broken bunds. As the villagers closed in, we could see that some of them, probably men and women we knew well, wore white masks. The people with long hair hung it over their faces. Women with short hair made it stand up on end. Some had tied white bands around their foreheads, arms, and legs.

5      "At first they threw mud and rocks at the house. Then they threw eggs and began slaughtering our stock. We could hear the animals scream their deaths—the roosters, the pigs, a last great roar from the ox. Familiar wild heads flared in our night windows; the villagers encir-cled us. Some of the faces stopped to peer at us, their eyes rushing like searchlights. The hands flattened against the panes, framed heads, and left red prints.

"The villagers broke in the front and the back doors at the same time, even though we had not locked the doors against them. Their knives dripped with the blood of our animals. They smeared blood on the doors and walls. One woman swung a chicken, whose throat she had slit, splattering blood in red arcs about her. We stood together in the middle of our house, in the family hall with the pictures and tables of the ancestors around us, and looked straight ahead.

"At the time the house had only two wings. When the men came back, we would build two more to enclose our courtyard and a third one to begin a second courtyard. The villagers pushed through both wings, even your grandparents' rooms, to find your aunt's, which was also mine until the men returned. From this room a new wing for one of the younger families would grow. They ripped up her clothes and shoes and broke her combs, grinding them underfoot. They tore her work from the loom. They scattered the cooking fire and rolled the new weaving in it. We could hear them in the kitchen breaking our bowls and banging the pots. They overturned the great waist-high earthenware jugs; duck eggs, pickled fruits, vegetables burst out and mixed in acrid torrents. The old woman from the next field swept a broom through the air and loosed the spirits-of-the-broom over our heads. 'Pig.' 'Ghost.' 'Pig,' they sobbed and scolded while they ruined our house.

"When they left, they took sugar and oranges to bless themselves. They cut pieces from the dead animals. Some of them took bowls that were not broken and clothes that were not torn. Afterward we swept up the rice and sewed it back up into sacks. But the smells from the spilled preserves lasted. Your aunt gave birth in the pigsty that night. The next morning when I went for the water, I found her and the baby plugging up the family well.

"Don't let your father know that I told you. He denies her. Now that you have started to menstruate, what happened to her could happen to you. Don't humiliate us. You wouldn't like to be forgotten as if you had never been born. The villagers are watchful."

Whenever she had to warn us about life, my mother told stories 10 that ran like this one, a story to grow up on. She tested our strength to establish realities. Those in the emigrant generations who could not reassert brute survival died young and far from home. Those of us in the first American generations have had to figure out how the invisible world the emigrants built around our childhoods fit in solid America.

The emigrants confused the gods by diverting their curses, misleading them with crooked streets and false names. They must try to confuse their offspring as well, who, I suppose, threaten them in similar ways—always trying to get things straight, always trying to name the unspeakable. The Chinese I know hide their names; sojourners take new names when their lives change and guard their real names with silence.

Chinese-Americans, when you try to understand what things in you are Chinese, how do you separate what is peculiar to childhood, to poverty, insanities, one family, your mother who marked your growing with stories, from what is Chinese? What is Chinese tradition and what is the movies?

If I want to learn what clothes my aunt wore, whether flashy or ordinary, I would have to begin, "Remember Father's drowned-in-the-well sister?" I cannot ask that. My mother has told me once and for all the useful parts. She will add nothing unless powered by Necessity, a riverbank that guides her life. She plants vegetable gardens rather than lawns; she carries the odd-shaped tomatoes home from the fields and eats food left for the gods.

Whenever we did frivolous things, we used up energy; we flew high kites. We children came up off the ground over the melting cones our parents brought home from work and the American movie on New Year's Day—*Oh, You Beautiful Doll* with Betty Grable one year, and *She Wore a Yellow Ribbon* with John Wayne another year. After the one carnival ride each, we paid in guilt; our tired father counted his change on the dark walk home.

15      Adultery is extravagance. Could people who hatch their own chicks and eat the embryos and the heads for delicacies and boil the feet in vinegar for party food, leaving only the gravel, eating even the gizzard lining—could such people engender a prodigal aunt? To be a woman, to have a daughter in starvation time was a waste enough. My aunt could not have been the lone romantic who gave up everything for sex. Women in the old China did not choose. Some man had commanded her to lie with him and be his secret evil. I wonder whether he masked himself when he joined the raid on her family.

Perhaps she encountered him in the fields or on the mountain where the daughters-in-law collected fuel. Or perhaps he first noticed her in the marketplace. He was not a stranger because the village housed no strangers. She had to have dealings with him other than sex. Perhaps he worked an adjoining field, or he sold her the cloth for the dress she sewed and wore. His demand must have surprised, then terrified her. She obeyed him; she always did as she was told.

When the family found a young man in the next village to be her husband, she stood tractably beside the best rooster, his proxy, and promised before they met that she would be his forever. She was lucky that he was her age and she would be the first wife, an advantage secure now. The night she first saw him, he had sex with her. Then he left for America. She had almost forgotten what he looked like. When she tried to envision him, she only saw the black and white face in the group photograph the men had had taken before leaving.

The other man was not, after all, much different from her husband. They both gave orders: she followed. "If you tell your family, I'll beat you. I'll kill you. Be here again next week." No one talked sex, ever. And she might have separated the rapes from the rest of living if only she did not have to buy her oil from him or gather wood in the same forest. I want her fear to have lasted just as long as rape lasted so that the fear could have been contained. No drawn-out fear. But women at sex hazarded birth and hence lifetimes. The fear did not stop but permeated everywhere. She told the man, "I think I'm pregnant." He organized the raid against her.

On nights when my mother and father talked about their life back home, sometimes they mentioned an "outcast table" whose business they still seemed to be settling, their voices tight. In a commensal[1] tradition, where food is precious, the powerful older people made wrongdoers eat alone. Instead of letting them start separate new lives like the Japanese, who could become samurais and geishas, the Chinese family, faces averted but eyes glowering sideways, hung on to the offenders and fed them leftovers. My aunt must have lived in the same house as my parents and eaten at an outcast table. My mother spoke about the raid as if she had seen it, when she and my aunt, a daughter-in-law to a different household, should not have been living together at all. Daughters-in-law lived with their husbands' parents, not their own; a synonym for marriage in Chinese is "taking a daughter-in-law." Her husband's parents could have sold her, mortgaged her, stoned her. But they had sent her back to her own mother and father, a mysterious act hinting at disgraces not told me. Perhaps they had thrown her out to deflect the avengers.

She was the only daughter; her four brothers went with her father, husband, and uncles "out on the road" and for some years became western men. When the goods were divided among the family, three of the brothers took land, and the youngest, my father, chose an education. After my grandparents gave their daughter away to her husband's family, they had dispensed all the adventure and all the property. They expected her alone to keep the traditional ways, which her brothers, now among the barbarians, could fumble without detection. The heavy, deep-rooted women were to maintain the past against the flood, safe for returning. But the rare urge west had fixed upon our family, and so my aunt crossed boundaries not delineated in space.

The work of preservation demands that the feelings playing about in one's guts not be turned into action. Just watch their passing like cherry blossoms. But perhaps my aunt, my forerunner, caught in a slow life, let dreams grow and fade and after some months or years went toward what persisted. Fear at the enormities of the forbidden kept her desires delicate, wire and bone. She looked at a man because she liked the way the hair was tucked behind his ears, or she liked the question-mark line of a long torso curving at the shoulder and straight at the hip. For warm eyes or a soft voice or a slow walk—that's all—a few hairs, a line, a brightness, a sound, a pace, she gave up family. She offered us up for a charm that vanished with tiredness, a pigtail that didn't toss when the wind died. Why, the wrong lighting could erase the dearest thing about him.

It could very well have been, however, that my aunt did not take subtle enjoyment of her friend, but, a wild woman, kept rollicking company. Imagining her free with sex doesn't fit, though. I don't know any

---

[1]Eating at the same table; sharing meals as table companions. [Eds.]

women like that, or men either. Unless I see her life branching into mine, she gives me no ancestral help.

To sustain her being in love, she often worked at herself in the mirror, guessing at the colors and shapes that would interest him, changing them frequently in order to hit on the right combination. She wanted him to look back.

On a farm near the sea, a woman who tended her appearance reaped a reputation for eccentricity. All the married women blunt-cut their hair in flaps about their ears or pulled it back in tight buns. No nonsense. Neither style blew easily into heart-catching tangles. And at their weddings they displayed themselves in their long hair for the last time. "It brushed the backs of my knees," my mother tells me. "It was braided, and even so, it brushed the backs of my knees."

25    At the mirror my aunt combed individuality into her bob. A bun could have been contrived to escape into black streamers blowing in the wind or in quiet wisps about her face, but only the older women in our picture album wear buns. She brushed her hair back from her forehead, tucking the flaps behind her ears. She looped a piece of thread, knotted into a circle between her index fingers and thumbs, and ran the double strand across her forehead. When she closed her fingers as if she were making a pair of shadow geese bite, the string twisted together catching the little hairs. Then she pulled the thread away from her skin, ripping the hairs out neatly, her eyes watering from the needles of pain. Opening her fingers, she cleaned the thread, then rolled it along her hairline and the tops of her eyebrows. My mother did the same to me and my sisters and herself. I used to believe that the expression "caught by the short hairs" meant a captive held with a depilatory string. It especially hurt at the temples, but my mother said we were lucky we didn't have to have our feet bound when we were seven. Sisters used to sit on their beds and cry together, she said, as their mothers or their slave removed the bandages for a few minutes each night and let the blood gush back into their veins. I hope that the man my aunt loved appreciated a smooth brow, that he wasn't just a tits-and-ass man.

Once my aunt found a freckle on her chin, at a spot that the almanac said predestined her for unhappiness. She dug it out with a hot needle and washed the wound with peroxide.

More attention to her looks than these pullings of hairs and pickings at spots would have caused gossip among the villagers. They owned work clothes and good clothes, and they wore good clothes for feasting the new seasons. But since a woman combing her hair hexes beginnings, my aunt rarely found an occasion to look her best. Women looked like great sea snails—the corded wood, babies, and laundry they carried were the whorls on their backs. The Chinese did not admire a bent back; goddesses and warriors stood straight. Still there must have been a marvelous freeing of beauty when a worker laid down her burden and stretched and arched.

Such commonplace loveliness, however, was not enough for my aunt. She dreamed of a lover for the fifteen days of New Year's, the time for families to exchange visits, money, and food. She plied her secret comb. And sure enough she cursed the year, the family, the village, and herself.

Even as her hair lured her imminent lover, many other men looked at her. Uncles, cousins, nephews, brothers would have looked, too, had they been home between journeys. Perhaps they had already been restraining their curiosity, and they left, fearful that their glances, like a field of nesting birds, might be startled and caught. Poverty hurt, and that was their first reason for leaving. But another, final reason for leaving the crowded house was the never-said.

She may have been unusually beloved, the precious only daughter, 30 spoiled and mirror gazing because of the affection the family lavished on her. When her husband left, they welcomed the chance to take her back from the in-laws; she could live like the little daughter for just a while longer. There are stories that my grandfather was different from other people, "crazy ever since the little Jap bayoneted him in the head." He used to put his naked penis on the dinner table, laughing. And one day he brought home a baby girl, wrapped up inside his brown western-style greatcoat. He had traded one of his sons, probably my father, the youngest, for her. My grandmother made him trade back. When he finally got a daughter of his own, he doted on her. They must have all loved her, except perhaps my father, the only brother who never went back to China, having once been traded for a girl.

Brothers and sisters, newly men and women, had to efface their sexual color and present plain miens.[2] Disturbing hair and eyes, a smile like no other, threatened the ideal of five generations living under one roof. To focus blurs, people shouted face to face and yelled from room to room. The immigrants I know have loud voices, unmodulated to American tones even after years away from the village where they called their friendships out across the fields. I have not been able to stop my mother's screams in public libraries or over telephones. Walking erect (knees straight, toes pointed forward, not pigeon-toed, which is Chinese-feminine) and speaking in an inaudible voice, I have tried to turn myself American-feminine. Chinese communication was loud, public. Only sick people had to whisper. But at the dinner table, where the family members came nearest one another, no one could talk, not the outcasts nor any eaters. Every word that falls from the mouth is a coin lost. Silently they gave and accepted food with both hands. A preoccupied child who took his bowl with one hand got a sideways glare. A complete moment of total

---

[2]Appearances. [Eds.]

attention is due everyone alike. Children and lovers have no singularity here, but my aunt used a secret voice, a separate attentiveness.

She kept the man's name to herself throughout her labor and dying; she did not accuse him that he be punished with her. To save her inseminator's name she gave silent birth.

He may have been somebody in her own household, but intercourse with a man outside the family would have been no less abhorrent. All the village were kinsmen, and the titles shouted in loud country voices never let kinship be forgotten. Any man within visiting distance would have been neutralized as a lover—"brother," "younger brother," "older brother"—one hundred and fifteen relationship titles. Parents researched birth charts probably not so much to assure good fortune as to circumvent incest in a population that has but one hundred surnames. Everybody has eight million relatives. How useless then sexual mannerisms, how dangerous.

As if it came from an atavism[3] deeper than fear, I used to add "brother" silently to boys' names. It hexed the boys, who would or would not ask me to dance, and made them less scary and as familiar and deserving of benevolence as girls.

35    But, of course, I hexed myself also—no dates. I should have stood up, both arms waving, and shouted out across libraries, "Hey, you! Love me back." I had no idea, though, how to make attraction selective, how to control its direction and magnitude. If I made myself American-pretty so that the five or six Chinese boys in the class fell in love with me, everyone else—the Caucasian, Negro, and Japanese boys—would too. Sisterliness, dignified and honorable, made much more sense.

Attraction eludes control so stubbornly that whole societies designed to organize relationships among people cannot keep order, not even when they bind people to one another from childhood and raise them together. Among the very poor and the wealthy, brothers married their adopted sisters, like doves. Our family allowed some romance, paying adult brides' prices and providing dowries so that their sons and daughters could marry strangers. Marriage promises to turn strangers into friendly relatives—a nation of siblings.

In the village structure, spirits shimmered among the live creatures, balanced and held in equilibrium by time and land. But one human being flaring up into violence could open up a black hole, a maelstrom that pulled in the sky. The frightened villagers, who depended on one another to maintain the real, went to my aunt to show her a personal, physical representation of the break she had made in the "roundness." Misallying couples snapped off the future, which was to be embodied in true offspring. The villagers punished her for acting as if she could have a private life, secret and apart from them.

---

[3]The reappearance of a characteristic after a long absence. [Eds.]

If my aunt had betrayed the family at a time of large grain yields and peace, when many boys were born, and wings were being built on many houses, perhaps she might have escaped such severe punishment. But the men—hungry, greedy, tired of planting in dry soil, cuckolded—had had to leave the village in order to send food-money home. There were ghost plagues, bandit plagues, wars with the Japanese, floods. My Chinese brother and sister had died of an unknown sickness. Adultery, perhaps only a mistake during good times, became a crime when the village needed food.

The round moon cakes and round doorways, the round tables of graduated size that fit one roundness inside another, round windows and rice bowls—these talismans had lost their power to warn this family of the law: a family must be whole, faithfully keeping the descent line by having sons to feed the old and the dead, who in turn look after the family. The villagers came to show my aunt and her lover-in-hiding a broken house. The villagers were speeding up the circling of events because she was too shortsighted to see that her infidelity had already harmed the village, that waves of consequences would return unpredictably, sometimes in disguise, as now, to hurt her. This roundness had to be made coin-sized so that she would see its circumference: punish her at the birth of her baby. Awaken her to the inexorable. People who refused fatalism because they could invent small resources insisted on culpability. Deny accidents and wrest fault from the stars.

After the villagers left, their lanterns now scattering in various directions toward home, the family broke their silence and cursed her. "Aiaa, we're going to die. Death is coming. Death is coming. Look what you've done. You've killed us. Ghost! Dead ghost! Ghost! You've never been born." She ran out into the fields, far enough from the house so that she could no longer hear their voices, and pressed herself against the earth, her own land no more. When she felt the birth coming, she thought that she had been hurt. Her body seized together. "They've hurt me too much," she thought. "This is gall, and it will kill me." With forehead and knees against the earth, her body convulsed and then relaxed. She turned on her back, lay on the ground. The black well of sky and stars went out and out and out forever; her body and her complexity seemed to disappear. She was one of the stars, a bright dot in blackness, without home, without a companion, in eternal cold and silence. And agoraphobia[4] rose in her, speeding higher and higher, bigger and bigger; she would not be able to contain it; there would be no end to fear.

Flayed, unprotected against space, she felt pain return, focusing her body. This pain chilled her—a cold, steady kind of surface pain. Inside,

[4]Pathological fear of being helpless or embarrassed in a public situation, characterized by avoidance of public places. [Eds.]

spasmodically, the other pain, the pain of the child, heated her. For hours she lay on the ground, alternately body and space. Sometimes a vision of normal comfort obliterated reality: she saw the family in the evening gambling at the dinner table, the young people massaging their elders' backs. She saw them congratulating one another, high joy on the mornings the rice shoots came up. When these pictures burst, the stars drew yet further apart. Black space opened.

She got to her feet to fight better and remembered that old-fashioned women gave birth in their pigsties to fool the jealous, pain-dealing gods, who do not snatch piglets. Before the next spasms could stop her, she ran to the pigsty, each step a rushing out into emptiness. She climbed over the fence and knelt in the dirt. It was good to have a fence enclosing her, a tribal person alone.

Laboring, this woman who had carried her child as a foreign growth that sickened her every day, expelled it at last. She reached down to touch the hot, wet, moving mass, surely smaller than anything human, and could feel that it was human after all—fingers, toes, nails, nose. She pulled it up on to her belly, and it lay curled there, butt in the air, feet precisely tucked one under the other. She opened her loose shirt and buttoned the child inside. After resting, it squirmed and thrashed and she pushed it up to her breast. It turned its head this way and that until it found her nipple. There, it made little snuffling noises. She clenched her teeth at its preciousness, lovely as a young calf, a piglet, a little dog.

She may have gone to the pigsty as a last act of responsibility: she would protect this child as she had protected its father. It would look after her soul, leaving supplies on her grave. But how would this tiny child without family find her grave when there would be no marker for her anywhere, neither in the earth nor the family hall? No one would give her a family hall name. She had taken the child with her into the wastes. At its birth the two of them had felt the same raw pain of separation, a wound that only the family pressing tight could close. A child with no descent line would not soften her life but only trail after her, ghost-like, begging her to give it purpose. At dawn the villagers on their way to the fields would stand around the fence and look.

45   Full of milk, the little ghost slept. When it awoke, she hardened her breasts against the milk that crying loosens. Toward morning she picked up the baby and walked to the well.

Carrying the baby to the well shows loving. Otherwise abandon it. Turn its face into the mud. Mothers who love their children take them along. It was probably a girl; there is some hope of forgiveness for boys.

"Don't tell anyone you had an aunt. Your father does not want to hear her name. She has never been born." I have believed that sex was unspeakable and words so strong and fathers so frail that "aunt" would do my father mysterious harm. I have thought that my family, having settled among immigrants who had also been their neighbors in the ancestral land, needed to clean their name, and a wrong word would incite the kinspeople even here. But there is more to this silence: they want me to participate in her punishment. And I have.

In the twenty years since I heard this story I have not asked for details nor said my aunt's name; I do not know it. People who can comfort the dead can also chase after them to hurt them further—a reverse ancestor worship. The real punishment was not the raid swiftly inflicted by the villagers, but the family's deliberately forgetting her. Her betrayal so maddened them, they saw to it that she would suffer forever, even after death. Always hungry, always needing, she would have to beg food from other ghosts, snatch and steal it from those whose living descendants give them gifts. She would have to fight the ghosts massed at crossroads for the buns a few thoughtful citizens leave to decoy her away from village and home so that the ancestral spirits could feast unharassed. At peace, they could act like gods, not ghosts, their descent lines providing them with paper suits and dresses, spirit money, paper houses, paper automobiles, chicken, meat, and rice into eternity—essences delivered up in smoke and flames, steam and incense rising from each rice bowl. In an attempt to make the Chinese care for people outside the family, Chairman Mao[5] encourages us now to give our paper replicas to the spirits of outstanding soldiers and workers, no matter whose ancestors they may be. My aunt remains forever hungry. Goods are not distributed evenly among the dead.

My aunt haunts me—her ghost drawn to me because now, after fifty years of neglect, I alone devote pages of paper to her, though not origamied into houses and clothes. I do not think she always means me well. I am telling on her, and she was a spite suicide, drowning herself in the drinking water. The Chinese are always very frightened of the drowned one, whose weeping ghost, wet hair hanging and skin bloated, waits silently by the water to pull down a substitute.

## Responding to Reading

1. How accurate do you think Kingston's "facts" are? Do you think strict accuracy is important in this essay? Why or why not?
2. Kingston never met her aunt; in fact, she doesn't even know her name. Even so, in what sense is this essay about her relationship with her aunt (and with other family members, both known and unknown)?
3. In paragraph 49, Kingston says, "My aunt haunts me—." Why do you think Kingston is "haunted" by her aunt's story?

---

[5]Mao Zedong (1893–1976), founder and leader of the communist People's Republic of China from 1949 until his death. [Eds.]

## Responding in Writing

Write a one-paragraph biographical sketch of a family member whose memory "haunts" you. Or, write a short obituary of a deceased relative.

# BEAUTY: WHEN THE OTHER DANCER IS THE SELF

## Alice Walker

### 1944–

*Alice Walker, best known for her award-winning novel* The Color Purple *(1982), is recognized as an important voice among African-American women writers. Born in Georgia, the daughter of sharecroppers, Walker received scholarships to Spelman College in Atlanta and Sarah Lawrence College in Bronxville, New York. Her work, which often focuses on racism and sexism, includes poetry, novels, short stories, essays, criticism, a biography of Langston Hughes, and an edition of Zora Neale Hurston's collection* I Love Myself When I Am Laughing *(1979). Walker's most recent work is* The Chicken Chronicles *(2011), a memoir. Like much of her writing, the following essay moves from pain and despair to self-celebration.*

It is a bright summer day in 1947. My father, a fat, funny man with beautiful eyes and a subversive wit, is trying to decide which of his eight children he will take with him to the county fair. My mother, of course, will not go. She is knocked out from getting most of us ready: I hold my neck stiff against the pressure of her knuckles as she hastily completes the braiding and then beribboning of my hair.

My father is the driver for the rich old white lady up the road. Her name is Miss Mey. She owns all the land for miles around, as well as the house in which we live. All I remember about her is that she once offered to pay my mother thirty-five cents for cleaning her house, raking up piles of her magnolia leaves, and washing her family's clothes, and that my mother—she of no money, eight children, and a chronic earache—refused it. But I do not think of this in 1947. I am two and a half years old. I want to go everywhere my daddy goes. I am excited at the prospect of riding in a car. Someone has told me fairs are fun. That there is room in the car for only three of us doesn't faze me at all. Whirling happily in my starchy frock, showing off my biscuit-polished patent-leather shoes and lavender socks, tossing my head in a way that makes my ribbons bounce, I stand, hands on hips, before my father. "Take me, Daddy," I say with assurance; "I'm the prettiest!"

Later, it does not surprise me to find myself in Miss Mey's shiny black car, sharing the back seat with the other lucky ones. Does not surprise me that I thoroughly enjoy the fair. At home that night I tell the unlucky ones all I can remember about the merry-go-round, the man who eats live chickens, and the teddy bears, until they say: "That's enough, baby Alice. Shut up now, and go to sleep."

It is Easter Sunday, 1950. I am dressed in a green, flocked, scalloped-hem dress (handmade by my adoring sister, Ruth) that has its own smooth satin petticoat and tiny hot-pink roses tucked into each scallop. My shoes, new T-strap patent leather, again highly biscuit-polished. I am six years old and have learned one of the longest Easter speeches to be heard that day, totally unlike the speech I said when I was two: "Easter lilies/pure and white/blossom in/the morning light." When I rise to give my speech I do so on a great wave of love and pride and expectation. People in the church stop rustling their new crinolines. They seem to hold their breath. I can tell they admire my dress, but it is my spirit, bordering on sassiness (womanishness), they secretly applaud.

"That girl's a little *mess*," they whisper to each other, pleased.    5

Naturally I say my speech without stammer or pause, unlike those who stutter, stammer, or, worst of all, forget. This is before the word "beautiful" exists in people's vocabulary, but "Oh, isn't she the *cutest* thing!" frequently floats my way. "And got so much sense!" they gratefully add . . . for which thoughtful addition I thank them to this day.

*It was great fun being cute. But then, one day, it ended.*

I am eight years old and a tomboy. I have a cowboy hat, cowboy boots, checkered shirt and pants, all red. My playmates are my brothers, two and four years older than I. Their colors are black and green, the only difference in the way we are dressed. On Saturday nights we all go to the picture show, even my mother; Westerns are her favorite kind of movie. Back home, "on the ranch," we pretend we are Tom Mix, Hopalong Cassidy, Lash LaRue (we've even named one of our dogs Lash LaRue); we chase each other for hours rustling cattle, being outlaws, delivering damsels from distress. Then my parents decide to buy my brothers guns. These are not "real" guns. They shoot "BBs," copper pellets my brothers say will kill birds. Because I am a girl, I do not get a gun. Instantly I am relegated to the position of Indian. Now there appears a great distance between us. They shoot and shoot at everything with their new guns. I try to keep up with my bow and arrows.

One day while I am standing on top of our makeshift "garage"— pieces of tin nailed across some poles—holding my bow and arrow and looking out toward the fields, I feel an incredible blow in my right eye. I look down just in time to see my brother lower his gun.

Both brothers rush to my side. My eye stings, and I cover it with    10 my hand. "If you tell," they say, "we will get a whipping. You don't want that to happen, do you?" I do not. "Here is a piece of wire," says the older brother, picking it up from the roof; "say you stepped on one end of it and the other flew up and hit you." The pain is beginning to start. "Yes," I say, "Yes, I will say that is what happened." If I do not say this is what happened, I know my brothers will find ways to make me wish I had. But now I will say anything that gets me to my mother.

Confronted by our parents we stick to the lie agreed upon. They place me on a bench on the porch and I close my left eye while they examine the right. There is a tree growing from underneath the porch that climbs past the railing to the roof. It is the last thing my right eye sees. I watch as its trunk, its branches, and then its leaves are blotted out by the rising blood.

I am in shock. First there is intense fever, which my father tries to break using lily leaves bound around my head. Then there are chills: my mother tries to get me to eat soup. Eventually, I do not know how, my parents learn what has happened. A week after the "accident" they take me to see a doctor. "Why did you wait so long to come?" he asks, looking into my eye and shaking his head. "Eyes are sympathetic," he says. "If one is blind, the other will likely become blind too."

This comment of the doctor's terrifies me. But it is really how I look that bothers me most. Where the BB pellet struck there is a glob of whitish scar tissue, a hideous cataract, on my eye. Now when I stare at people—a favorite pastime, up to now—they will stare back. Not at the "cute" little girl, but at her scar. For six years I do not stare at anyone, because I do not raise my head.

Years later, in the throes of a mid-life crisis, I ask my mother and sister whether I changed after the "accident." "No," they say, puzzled. "What do you mean?"

15      *What do I mean?*

I am eight, and, for the first time, doing poorly in school, where I have been something of a whiz since I was four. We have just moved to the place where the "accident" occurred. We do not know any of the people around us because this is a different county. The only time I see the friends I knew is when we go back to our old church. The new school is the former state penitentiary. It is a large stone building, cold and drafty, crammed to overflowing with boisterous, ill-disciplined children. On the third floor there is a huge circular imprint of some partition that has been torn out.

"What used to be here?" I ask a sullen girl next to me on our way past it to lunch.

"The electric chair," says she.

At night I have nightmares about the electric chair, and about all the people reputedly "fried" in it. I am afraid of the school, where all the students seem to be budding criminals.

20      "What's the matter with your eye?" they ask, critically.

When I don't answer (I cannot decide whether it was an "accident" or not), they shove me, insist on a fight.

My brother, the one who created the story about the wire, comes to my rescue. But then brags so much about "protecting" me, I become sick.

After months of torture at the school, my parents decide to send me back to our old community, to my old school. I live with my grandparents and the teacher they board. But there is no room for Phoebe, my cat. By the time my grandparents decide there *is* room, and I ask for my cat, she cannot be found. Miss Yarborough, the boarding teacher, takes me under her wing, and begins to teach me to play the piano. But soon she marries an African—a "prince," she says—and is whisked away to his continent.

At my old school there is at least one teacher who loves me. She is the teacher who "knew me before I was born" and bought my first baby clothes. It is she who makes life bearable. It is her presence that finally helps me turn on the one child at the school who continually calls me "one-eyed bitch." One day I simply grab him by his coat and beat him until I am satisfied. It is my teacher who tells me my mother is ill.

My mother is lying in bed in the middle of the day, something I 25 have never seen. She is in too much pain to speak. She has an abscess in her ear. I stand looking down on her, knowing that if she dies, I cannot live. She is being treated with warm oils and hot bricks held against her cheek. Finally a doctor comes. But I must go back to my grandparents' house. The weeks pass but I am hardly aware of it. All I know is that my mother might die, my father is not so jolly, my brothers still have their guns, and I am the one sent away from home.

"You did not change," they say.

*Did I imagine the anguish of never looking up?*

I am twelve. When relatives come to visit I hide in my room. My cousin Brenda, just my age, whose father works in the post office and whose mother is a nurse, comes to find me. "Hello," she says. And then she asks, looking at my recent school picture, which I did not want taken, and on which the "glob," as I think of it, is clearly visible, "You still can't see out of that eye?"

"No," I say, and flop back on the bed over my book.

That night, as I do almost every night, I abuse my eye. I rant and 30 rave at it, in front of the mirror. I plead with it to clear up before morning. I tell it I hate and despise it. I do not pray for sight. I pray for beauty.

"You did not change," they say.

I am fourteen and baby-sitting for my brother Bill, who lives in Boston. He is my favorite brother and there is a strong bond between us.

Understanding my feelings of shame and ugliness he and his wife take me to a local hospital, where the "glob" is removed by a doctor named O. Henry. There is still a small bluish crater where the scar tissue was, but the ugly white stuff is gone. Almost immediately I become a different person from the girl who does not raise her head. Or so I think. Now that I've raised my head I win the boyfriend of my dreams. Now that I've raised my head I have plenty of friends. Now that I've raised my head classwork comes from my lips as faultlessly as Easter speeches did, and I leave high school as valedictorian, most popular student, and *queen,* hardly believing my luck. Ironically, the girl who was voted most beautiful in our class (and was) was later shot twice through the chest by a male companion, using a "real" gun, while she was pregnant. But that's another story in itself. Or is it?

"You did not change," they say.

It is now thirty years since the "accident." A beautiful journalist comes to visit and to interview me. She is going to write a cover story for her magazine that focuses on my latest book. "Decide how you want to look on the cover," she says. "Glamorous, or whatever."

35 Never mind "glamorous," it is the "whatever" that I hear. Suddenly all I can think of is whether I will get enough sleep the night before the photography session: if I don't, my eye will be tired and wander, as blind eyes will.

At night in bed with my lover I think up reasons why I should not appear on the cover of a magazine. "My meanest critics will say I've sold out," I say. "My family will now realize I write scandalous books."

"But what's the real reason you don't want to do this?" he asks.

"Because in all probability," I say in a rush, "my eye won't be straight."

"It will be straight enough," he says. Then, "Besides, I thought you'd made your peace with that."

40 And I suddenly remember that I have.

*I remember:*

I am talking to my brother Jimmy, asking if he remembers anything unusual about the day I was shot. He does not know I consider that day the last time my father, with his sweet home remedy of cool lily leaves, chose me, and that I suffered and raged inside because of this. "Well," he says, "all I remember is standing by the side of the highway with Daddy, trying to flag down a car. A white man stopped, but when Daddy said he needed somebody to take his little girl to the doctor, he drove off."

*I remember:*

I am in the desert for the first time. I fall totally in love with it. I am so overwhelmed by its beauty, I confront for the first time, consciously, the meaning of the doctor's words years ago: "Eyes are sympathetic.

If one is blind, the other will likely become blind too." I realize I have dashed about the world madly, looking at this, looking at that, storing up images against the fading of the light. *But I might have missed seeing the desert!* The shock of that possibility—and gratitude for over twenty-five years of sight—sends me literally to my knees. Poem after poem comes—which is perhaps how poets pray.

### On Sight

I am so thankful I have seen
The Desert
And the creatures in the desert
And the desert Itself.

The desert has its own moon
Which I have seen
With my own eye.
There is no flag on it.

Trees of the desert have arms
All of which are always up
That is because the moon is up
The sun is up
Also the sky
The stars
Clouds
None with flags.

If there were flags, I doubt
the trees would point.
Would you?

*But mostly, I remember this:*    45

I am twenty-seven, and my baby daughter is almost three. Since her birth I have worried about her discovery that her mother's eyes are different from other people's. Will she be embarrassed? I think. What will she say? Every day she watches a television program called "Big Blue Marble." It begins with a picture of the earth as it appears from the moon. It is bluish, a little battered-looking, but full of light, with whitish clouds swirling around it. Every time I see it I weep with love, as if it is a picture of Grandma's house. One day when I am putting Rebecca down for her nap, she suddenly focuses on my eye. Something inside me cringes, gets ready to try to protect myself. All children are cruel about physical differences, I know from experience, and that they don't always mean to be is another matter. I assume Rebecca will be the same.

But no-o-o-o. She studies my face intently as we stand, her inside and me outside her crib. She even holds my face maternally between her dimpled little hands. Then, looking every bit as serious and lawyerlike as her father, she says, as if it may just possibly have slipped my attention: "Mommy, there's a *world* in your eye." (As in, "Don't be alarmed, or do anything crazy.") And then, gently, but with great interest: "Mommy, where did you get that world in your eye?"

For the most part, the pain left then. (So what, if my brothers grew up to buy even more powerful pellet guns for their sons and to carry real guns themselves. So what, if a young "Morehouse man"[1] once nearly fell off the steps of Trevor Arnett Library because he thought my eyes were blue.) Crying and laughing I ran to the bathroom, while Rebecca mumbled and sang herself off to sleep. Yes indeed, I realized, looking into the mirror. There was a world in my eye. And I saw that it was possible to love it: that in fact, for all it had taught me of shame and anger and inner vision, I *did* love it. Even to see it drifting out of orbit in boredom, or rolling up out of fatigue, not to mention floating back at attention in excitement (bearing witness, a friend has called it), deeply suitable to my personality, and even characteristic of me.

That night I dream I am dancing to Stevie Wonder's song "Always" (the name of the song is really "As," but I hear it as "Always"). As I dance, whirling and joyous, happier than I've ever been in my life, another bright-faced dancer joins me. We dance and kiss each other and hold each other through the night. The other dancer has obviously come through all right, as I have done. She is beautiful, whole and free. And she is also me.

## Responding to Reading

1. Although she is remembering past events, Walker uses present tense ("It is a bright summer day in 1947") to tell her story. Why do you think she does this? Is the present tense more effective than the past tense ("It was a bright summer day in 1947") would be? Explain.
2. At several points in the essay, Walker repeats the words her relatives used to reassure her: "You did not change." Why does she repeat this phrase? Were her relatives correct?
3. What circumstances or individuals does Walker blame for the childhood problems she describes? Who do you think is responsible for her misery? Would you be as forgiving as Walker seems to be?

## Responding in Writing

Using present tense, write a paragraph or two about a painful incident from your childhood. Begin with a sentence that tells how old you are ("I am _____.").

---

[1]A student at Morehouse College, a historically black college in Atlanta, Georgia. [Eds.]

# SIXTY-NINE CENTS
## Gary Shteyngart
### 1972–

*Born in Leningrad (now called Saint Petersburg), Russia, Gary Shteyngart immigrated to the United States when he was seven years old. The author of three highly acclaimed novels*—The Russian Debutante's Handbook *(2002),* Absurdistan *(2006), and* Super Sad True Love Story *(2010)*— *Shteyngart has also published numerous essays and short stories in publications such as the* New York Times Magazine, *the* New Yorker, Esquire, *and* GQ. *In the following essay, Shteyngart recalls the mixed feelings he had about his family on a childhood trip to Disney World.*

When I was fourteen years old, I lost my Russian accent. I could, in theory, walk up to a girl and the words "Oh, hi there" would not sound like Okht Hyzer, possibly the name of a Turkish politician. There were three things I wanted to do in my new incarnation: go to Florida, where I understood that our nation's best and brightest had built themselves a sandy, vice-filled paradise; have a girl, preferably native-born, tell me that she liked me in some way; and eat all my meals at McDonald's. I did not have the pleasure of eating at McDonald's often. My parents believed that going to restaurants and buying clothes not sold by weight on Orchard Street[1] were things done only by the very wealthy or the very profligate, maybe those extravagant "welfare queens" we kept hearing about on television. Even my parents, however, as uncritically in love with America as only immigrants can be, could not resist the iconic pull of Florida, the call of the beach and the Mouse.

And so, in the midst of my Hebrew-school winter vacation, two Russian families crammed into a large used sedan and took I-95 down to the Sunshine State. The other family—three members in all—mirrored our own, except that their single offspring was a girl and they were, on the whole, more ample; by contrast, my entire family weighed three hundred pounds. There's a picture of us beneath the monorail at EPCOT Center, each of us trying out a different smile to express the déjà-vu feeling of standing squarely in our new country's greatest attraction, my own megawatt grin that of a turn-of-the-century Jewish peddler scampering after a potential sidewalk sale. The Disney tickets were a freebie, for which we had had to sit through a sales pitch for an Orlando time-share. "You're from Moscow?" the time-share salesman asked, appraising the polyester cut of my father's jib.

---

[1] A shopping street on New York City's Lower East Side, a destination for generations of immigrants. [Eds.]

"Leningrad."

"Let me guess: mechanical engineer?"

5    "Yes, mechanical engineer. . . . Eh, please Disney tickets now."

The ride over the MacArthur Causeway to Miami Beach was my real naturalization ceremony. I wanted all of it—the palm trees, the yachts bobbing beside the hard-currency mansions, the concrete-and-glass condominiums preening at their own reflections in the azure pool water below, the implicit availability of relations with amoral women. I could see myself on a balcony eating a Big Mac, casually throwing fries over my shoulder into the sea-salted air. But I would have to wait. The hotel reserved by my parents' friends featured army cots instead of beds and a half-foot-long cockroach evolved enough to wave what looked like a fist at us. Scared out of Miami Beach, we decamped for Fort Lauderdale, where a Yugoslav woman sheltered us in a faded motel, beach-adjacent and featuring free UHF reception. We always seemed to be at the margins of places: the driveway of the Fontainebleau Hilton, or the glassed-in elevator leading to a rooftop restaurant where we could momentarily peek over the "Please Wait to Be Seated" sign at the endless ocean below, the Old World we had left behind so far and yet deceptively near.

To my parents and their friends, the Yugoslav motel was an unquestioned paradise, a lucky coda to a set of difficult lives. My father lay magnificently beneath the sun in his red-and-black striped imitation Speedo while I stalked down the beach, past baking Midwestern girls. "Oh, hi there." The words, perfectly American, not a birthright but an acquisition, perched between my lips, but to walk up to one of those girls and say something so casual required a deep rootedness to the hot sand beneath me, a historical presence thicker than the green card embossed with my thumbprint and freckled face. Back at the motel, the *Star Trek* reruns looped endlessly on Channel 73 or 31 or some other prime number, the washed-out Technicolor planets more familiar to me than our own.

On the drive back to New York, I plugged myself firmly into my Walkman, hoping to forget our vacation. Sometime after the palm trees ran out, somewhere in southern Georgia, we stopped at a McDonald's. I could already taste it: The sixty-nine-cent hamburger. The ketchup, red and decadent, embedded with little flecks of grated onion. The uplift of the pickle slices; the obliterating rush of fresh Coca-Cola; the soda tingle at the back of the throat signifying that the act was complete. I ran into the meat-fumigated coldness of the magical place, the larger Russians following behind me, lugging something big and red. It was a cooler, packed, before we left the motel, by the other mother, the kindly, round-faced equivalent of my own mother. She had prepared a full Russian lunch for us. Soft-boiled eggs wrapped in tinfoil; *vinigret,* the Russian beet salad, overflowing a reused container of sour cream; cold chicken served between crisp white furrows of a *bulka*.[2] "But it's not allowed," I pleaded. "We have to buy the food here."

I felt coldness, not the air-conditioned chill of southern Georgia but the coldness of a body understanding the ramifications of its own demise, the pointlessness of it all. I sat down at a table as far away from my parents and their friends as possible. I watched the spectacle of the newly tanned resident aliens eating their ethnic meal—jowls working, jowls working—the soft-boiled eggs that quivered lightly as they were brought to the mouth; the girl, my coeval, sullen like me but with a hint of pliant equanimity; her parents, dishing out the chunks of beet with plastic spoons; my parents, getting up to use free McDonald's napkins and straws while American motorists with their noisy towheaded children bought themselves the happiest of meals.

My parents laughed at my haughtiness. Sitting there hungry and all alone—what a strange man I was becoming! So unlike them. My pockets were filled with several quarters and dimes, enough for a hamburger and a small Coke. I considered the possibility of redeeming my own dignity, of leaving behind our beet-salad heritage. My parents didn't spend money, because they lived with the idea that disaster was close at hand, that a liver-function test would come back marked with a doctor's urgent scrawl, that they would be fired from their jobs because their English did not suffice. We were all representatives of a shadow society, cowering under a cloud of bad tidings that would never come. The silver coins stayed in my pocket, the anger burrowed and expanded into some future ulcer. I was my parents' son.

## Responding to Reading

1. In paragraph 8, Shteyngart describes in detail the "full Russian lunch" his mother served the family. Why does he include this information?
2. This essay contrasts the familiar world of Shteyngart's home and family with the unfamiliar world of Miami. List some of the contrasts he identifies. What other differences would you imagine exist between these two worlds?
3. How do you suppose Shteyngart's memories of this trip differ from his parents' memories?

## Responding in Writing

Shteyngart's longing for a McDonald's hamburger and a Coke parallels his longing to be "American." What other products and brand names do you see as typically American? Why?

---

[2]Russian bread roll. [Eds.]

# REFLECTIONS: GROWING-UP GROWN

## David Jacobsen

*An assistant editor for and contributor to* DailyGrito.com, *where the following essay first appeared, David Jacobsen writes about culture, politics, and LGBT (lesbian, gay, bisexual, and transgender) issues. His work has also appeared in the student newspaper the* New Hampshire, *the magazine* American Record Guide, *and the online publication* Politic365. *In "Reflections: Growing-Up Grown," Jacobsen considers his past as the son of a struggling Latina.*

I graduated college, an increasing rarity for Latino males. Now, I reside in the so-called "real" world.

It is not uncommon for the children of Latina/os to be a family's translator. As far back as I can remember—at the age of ten—I was arguing with the electric company, ordering cable, fighting parking tickets in court, doing income-tax returns, cooking and cleaning the house. Many of us have been in the real world all our lives.

As a non-English speaking Latina, my mother began to work as a bartender in the early '90s. Soon after, because of economic need, she began working as an exotic dancer in the highway crack-dens of Northern New Jersey. One of the most spectacular memories of my childhood took place at a court in Paterson, N.J. I was sixteen or so. I had known for years now that my mother was a dancer. She asked me to go with her to court as she had had a "problem" a couple years ago that needed resolution. She explained to me that as she was dancing, an undercover cop (enjoying the show nevertheless) had slipped a dollar into her belt (this is illegal). She was arrested, and needed to clear her record before applying for citizenship. I thought it was going to be another quick ten-minute argument with the credit card company. Come to find out, she was charged with a felony for prostitution and clearly had no idea what had gone on.

By sixteen, I was working in Newark as a piano instructor, taking the 39 bus in the late and lonely nights of Penn Station. By seventeen, I was applying to college, (by myself) filing FAFSA,[1] while the only instruction I had from my mother was, "good men go to college."

5      Despite her hard work and dedication, my mother was always at odds with this country—both culturally and financially. In search of providing me with a middle-class lifestyle, she sacrificed much of her selfhood. We originally lived in West New York, N.J. and lived a very modest lifestyle. Because of our search for Americanism, she decided to move us out of W.N.Y. because there were "too many Hispanics." Internalized racism is a hugely damaging element in immigrant culture.

---

[1]Free Application for Federal Standard Aid [Eds.]

The obsession with arriving at Americanism whatever that means—often makes us work against our interests and turn on our communities.

With the job situation worsening for my mother, and the excessive demands of a young son, trying to invent himself in our world of fast-pace demand and consumerism, everyday life became unbearable. We fell into debt, and lost everything, months before I left to attend the University of New Hampshire.

I agonize over the fact that my mother's financial situation was in such despair at the time of my entering college. My mother was left in the street, her car repossessed, her apartment lost, her furniture on the curb, her life destroyed. But, her son was attending an American university. My education would not have happened if I did not have my grandmother's financial support. Making the reality this: many Latinos who do not have the privilege I had, could never aspire to go to a place like the University of New Hampshire, especially now, when they are nearly private because of the "live free or die" nonsense that runs that crazy state. The people of New Hampshire are wonderful, and I enjoyed my time in the state, but their idea of funding public education is profoundly misguided.

I struggle with the fact that after twenty five years of my mother living in this country she still does not know English. She understands here and there, but I never made an effort to teach her. Now, I write about her experience in a language that she cannot read. It is difficult to see where the line is between my using my mother's experience as yet another way to exploit the experience of Latina women, and as an honest gesture of my love for her and respect for her life.

I might now be a "proper" member of American society, yet my mother is left with nothing.

The day before graduating college, I sat on my porch in Dover, New 10 Hampshire, and watched the sunrise as the bitter cold of New England pulled at my skin. Looking outward, I felt fear—fear of graduating without a job, of bringing the romantics of my adolescence to an end, panic of not knowing, of moving in with my mother, of having no direction.

I am slowly realizing my foolishness, and assessing the reality now, that I can live a comfortable life because of her sacrifice. What is even more difficult is that her sacrifice comes with purely authentic love, and that she did all she did happily. And that is truly something worth noting as an "American Dream," [that] millions of Latino parents want the dream for their children and [accept] a nightmare for themselves. We can surely do better.

All became relevant—painfully relevant—to see the face of unimaginable joy and euphoria on my mother's face the day I graduated. She will forever be a warrior, and I am proud to be a product of her greatness. The opportunity to obtain an education needs to be widely available, as it will help us work collectively for a more just future. That is our duty and responsibility above all others.

## Responding to Reading

1.  What images of his mother does Jacobsen remember most vividly? Why?
2.  In paragraph 5, Jacobsen says his mother was "always at odds with this country—both culturally and financially." What does he mean? What (or whom) does he seem to blame for this state of affairs? Why?
3.  Do you think Jacobsen feels guilty about succeeding while his mother "is left with nothing" (9)? Do you think he *should* feel guilty? Do you think his use of his mother's life as subject matter for his essay is "yet another way to exploit the experience of Latina women" (8)? Explain.

## Responding in Writing

Reread paragraph 7. What is your reaction to Jacobsen's comments about New Hampshire's "idea of funding public education"? Do you see these comments as a digression or as an integral part of his essay?

## THE STORYTELLER

## Sandra Cisneros

### 1954–

*A highly acclaimed novelist, poet, and essayist, Sandra Cisneros frequently writes about her Mexican-American roots. Her works include* The House on Mango Street *(1983),* My Wicked Wicked Ways *(1987),* Woman Hollering Creek and Other Stories *(1991),* Loose Woman: Poems *(1994),* Caramelo, or, Puro Cuento: A Novel *(2002), and the forthcoming book* Have You Seen Marie? *In the following essay, which was adapted from the introduction to the twenty-fifth anniversary edition of* The House on Mango Street, *Cisneros explores the role of family and memory in shaping a writer.*

The young woman in [a photograph I remember is] me when I was writing *The House on Mango Street*. She's in her office, a room that had probably been a child's bedroom when families lived in this apartment. It has no door and is only slightly wider than the walk-in pantry. But it has great light and sits above the hallway door downstairs, so she can hear her neighbors come and go. She's posed as if she's just looked up from her work for a moment, but in real life she never writes in this office. She writes in the kitchen, the only room with a heater.

It's Chicago, 1980, in the down-at-the-heels Bucktown neighborhood before it's discovered by folks with money. The young woman lives at 1814 N. Paulina, second floor front. Nelson Algren[1] once wandered these streets. Saul Bellow's[2] turf was over on Division Street,

---

[1]American writer (1909–1981). [Eds.]
[2]American writer (1915–2005). [Eds.]

walking distance away. It's a neighborhood that reeks of beer and urine, of sausage and beans.

The young woman fills her "office" with things she drags home from the flea market at Maxwell Street. Antique typewriters, alphabet blocks, asparagus ferns, bookshelves, ceramic figurines from Occupied Japan, wicker baskets, birdcages, hand-painted photos. Things she likes to look at. It's important to have this space to look and think. When she lived at home, the things she looked at scolded her and made her feel sad and depressed. They said, "Wash me." They said, "Lazy." They said, "You ought." But the things in her office are magical and invite her to play. They fill her with light. It's the room where she can be quiet and still and listen to the voices inside herself. She likes being alone in the daytime.

As a girl, she dreamed about having a silent home, just to herself, the way other women dreamed of their weddings. Instead of collecting lace and linen for her trousseau,[3] the young woman buys old things from the thrift stores on grimy Milwaukee Avenue for her future house-of-her-own—faded quilts, cracked vases, chipped saucers, lamps in need of love.

The young woman returned to Chicago after graduate school and  5 moved back into her father's house, 1754 N. Keeler, back into her girl's room with its twin bed and floral wallpaper. She was 23 and a half. Now she summoned her courage and told her father she wanted to live alone again, like she did when she was away at school. He looked at her with that eye of the rooster before it attacks, but she wasn't alarmed. She'd seen that look before and knew he was harmless. She was his favorite, and it was only a matter of waiting.

The daughter claimed she'd been taught that a writer needs quiet, privacy, and long stretches of solitude to think. The father decided too much college and too many gringo friends had ruined her. In a way he was right. In a way she was right. When she thinks to herself in her father's language, she knows sons and daughters don't leave their parents' house until they marry. When she thinks in English, she knows she should've been on her own since 18.

For a time father and daughter reached a truce. She agreed to move into the basement of a building where the oldest of her six brothers and his wife lived, 4832 W. Homer. But after a few months, when the big brother upstairs turned out to be Big Brother, she got on her bicycle and rode through the neighborhood of her high school days until she spotted an apartment with fresh-painted walls and masking tape on the windows. Then she knocked on the storefront downstairs. That's how she convinced the landlord she was his new tenant.

Her father can't understand why she wants to live in a hundred-year-old building with big windows that let in the cold. She knows her

---

[3]Collection of a bride's belongings. [Eds.]

apartment is clean, but the hallway is scuffed and scary, though she and the woman upstairs take turns mopping it regularly. The hall needs paint, and there's nothing they can do about that. When the father visits, he climbs up the stairs muttering with disgust. Inside, he looks at her books arranged in milk crates, at the futon on the floor in a bedroom with no door, and whispers, "Hippie," in the same way he looks at boys hanging out in his neighborhood and says, "Drogas."[4] When he sees the space heater in the kitchen, the father shakes his head and sighs, "Why did I work so hard to buy a house with a furnace so she could go backward and live like this?"

When she's alone, she savors her apartment of high ceilings and windows that let in the sky, the new carpeting and walls white as typing paper, the walk-in pantry with empty shelves, her bedroom without a door, her office with its typewriter, and the big front-room windows with their view of a street, rooftops, trees, and the dizzy traffic of the Kennedy Expressway.

10    Her father calls every week to say, "*Mija*,[5] when are you coming home?" What does her mother say about all this? She puts her hands on her hips and boasts, "She gets it from me." When the father is in the room, the mother just shrugs and says, "What can I do?" The mother doesn't object. She knows what it is to live a life filled with regrets, and she doesn't want her daughter to live that life, too. She always supported the daughter's projects, so long as she went to school. The mother who painted the walls of their Chicago homes the color of flowers; who planted tomatoes and roses in her garden; sang arias; practiced solos on her son's drum set; boogied along with the *Soul Train* dancers; glued travel posters on her kitchen wall with Karo syrup; herded her kids weekly to the library, to public concerts, to museums; wore a button on her lapel that said FEED THE PEOPLE NOT THE PENTAGON; who never went beyond the ninth grade. *That* mother. She nudges her daughter and says, "Good lucky you studied."

The father wants his daughter to be a weather girl on television, or to marry and have babies. She doesn't want to be a TV weather girl. Nor does she want to marry and have babies. Not yet. Maybe later, but there are so many other things she must do in her lifetime first. Travel. Learn how to dance the tango. Publish a book. Live in other cities. Win a National Endowment for the Arts Award. See the northern lights. Jump out of a cake.

She stares at the ceilings and walls of her apartment the way she once stared at the ceilings and walls of the apartments she grew up in, inventing pictures in the cracks in the plaster, inventing stories to go with these pictures. At night, under the circle of light from a cheap metal lamp clamped to the kitchen table, she sits with paper and a pen and pretends she's not afraid. She's trying to live like a writer.

---

[4]Spanish for *drugs*. [Eds.]
[5]Spanish term of endearment for *daughter*. [Eds.]

The woman I am in the photo was working on a series of vignettes, little by little, along with her poetry. I already had a title—*The House on Mango Street*. Fifty pages had been written, but I still didn't think of it as a novel. It was just a jar of buttons, like the mismatched embroidered pillowcases and monogrammed napkins I tugged from the bins at the Goodwill. I wrote these things and thought of them as "little stories," though I sensed they were connected to each other. I hadn't heard of story cycles yet. I hadn't read Ermilo Abreu Gómez's *Canek*, Elena Poniatowska's *Lilus Kikus*, Gwendolyn Brooks's *Maud Martha*, Nellie Campobello's *My Mother's Hands*. That would come later, when I had more time and solitude to read.

The young woman is modeling her book-in-progress after *Dreamtigers*, by Jorge Luis Borges—a writer she'd read since high school, story fragments that ring like Hans Christian Andersen, or Ovid, or entries from the encyclopedia. She wants to write stories that ignore borders between genres, between written and spoken, between highbrow literature and children's nursery rhymes, between New York and the imaginary village of Macondo, between the United States and Mexico. It's true, she wants the writers she admires to respect her work, but she also wants people who don't usually read books to enjoy these stories, too. She doesn't want to write a book that a reader won't understand and would feel ashamed for not understanding.

She thinks stories are about beauty. Beauty that is there to be 15 admired by anyone, like a herd of clouds grazing overhead. She thinks people who are busy working for a living deserve beautiful little stories, because they don't have much time and are often tired. She has in mind a book that can be opened at any page and will still make sense to the reader who doesn't know what came before or comes after.

She experiments, creating a text that is as succinct and flexible as poetry, snapping sentences into fragments so that the reader pauses, making each sentence serve her and not the other way round, abandoning quotation marks to streamline the typography and make the page as simple and readable as possible. So that the sentences are pliant as branches and can be read in more ways than one.

Sometimes the woman I once was goes out on weekends to meet with other writers. Sometimes I invite these friends to come to my apartment to workshop each other's writing. We come from black, white, Latino communities. What we have in common is our sense that art should serve our communities. Together we publish an anthology—*Emergency Tacos*, because we finish our collaborations in the early hours before dawn and gather at the same 24-hour taqueria on Belmont Avenue, like a multicultural version of Hopper's *Nighthawks* painting. The *Emergency Tacos* writers organize monthly arts events at my brother Keek's apartment—Galeria Quique. We do this with no capital except our valuable time. We do this because the world we live in is a house on fire and the people we love are burning.

The young woman in the photograph gets up in the morning to go to the job that pays the rent on her Paulina Street apartment. She teaches at a school in Pilsen, her mother's old neighborhood on Chicago's South Side, a Mexican neighborhood where the rent is cheap and too many families live crowded together. Landlords and the city take no responsibility for the rats, trash that isn't collected often enough, porches that collapse, apartments without fire escapes, until a tragedy happens and several people die. Then they hold investigations for a little while, but the problems go on until the next death, the next investigation, the next bout of forgetting.

The young woman works with students who have dropped out of high school but have decided to try again for their diplomas. She learns from her students that they have more difficult lives than her storyteller's imagination can invent. Her life has been comfortable and privileged compared with theirs. She never had to worry about feeding her babies before she went to class. She never had a father or boyfriend who beat her at night and left her bruised in the morning. She didn't have to plan an alternative route to avoid gangs in the school hallway. Her parents didn't plead with her to drop out of school so she could help them earn money.

20　　The young woman's teaching job leads to the next, and now she finds herself a counselor/recruiter at her alma mater, Loyola University, on the north side, in Rogers Park. I have health benefits. I don't bring work home anymore. My workday ends at 5 P.M. Now I have evenings free to do my own work. I feel like a real writer.

On the weekends, if I can sidestep guilt and avoid my father's demands to come home for Sunday dinner, I'm free to stay home and write. I feel like a bad daughter ignoring my father, but I feel worse when I don't write. Either way, I never feel completely happy.

Often all I have is a title with no story—"The Family of Little Feet"—and I have to make the title kick me in the behind to get me going. Or sometimes all I've got is a first sentence—"You can never have too much sky." One of my Pilsen students said I had said this, and she never forgot it. Good thing she remembered and quoted it back to me. "They came with the wind that blows in August. . . ." This line came to me in a dream. Sometimes the best ideas come in dreams. Sometimes the worst ideas come from there, too!

Whether the idea came from a sentence I heard buzzing around somewhere and saved in a jar, or from a title I picked up and pocketed, the stories always insist on telling me where they want to end. They often surprise me by stopping when I had every intention of galloping along a little further. They're stubborn. They know best when there's no more to be said. The last sentence must ring like the final notes at the end of a mariachi song—*tan-tán*—to tell you when the song is done.

I meet Norma Alarcón. She is to become one of my earliest publishers and my lifetime friend. The first time she walks through the rooms of the apartment on N. Paulina, she notices the quiet rooms, the collection of typewriters, the books and Japanese figurines, the windows with the view of freeway and sky. She walks as if on tiptoe, peering into every room, even the pantry and closet as if looking for something. "You live here . . ." she asks, "alone?"

"Yes."                                                                                    25

"So . . ." She pauses. "How did you do it?"

Eventually I took a job in San Antonio. Left. Came back. And left again. I kept coming back lured by cheap rent. Affordable housing is essential to an artist. I could, in time, even buy my own first house, a hundred-year-old home once periwinkle, but now painted a Mexican pink.

Two years ago my office went up in my backyard, a building created from my Mexican memories. I am writing this today from this very office, Mexican marigold on the outside, morning-glory violet on the inside. Wind chimes ring from the terrace. Trains moan in the distance all the time, ours is a neighborhood of trains. The same San Antonio River tourists know from the Riverwalk wends its way behind my house to the Missions and beyond until it empties into the Gulf of Mexico. From my terrace you can see the river where it bends into an S.

White cranes float across the sky like a scene painted on a lacquered screen. The river shares the land with ducks, raccoons, possums, skunks, buzzards, butterflies, hawks, turtles, snakes, owls, even though we're walking distance to downtown. And within the confines of my own garden there are plenty of other creatures too—yappy dogs, kamikaze cats, one lovesick parrot with a crush on me.

This is my house.                                                                          30

Bliss.

## Responding to Reading

1. Although she is writing largely about past events in her own life, Cisneros often uses third person and present tense: "The young woman fills her 'office' . . ." (3); "It's Chicago, 1980 . . ." (2). Why? Where does she use first person? Where does she use past tense? Can you explain these shifts? Are they justified?
2. What is the source of Cisneros's conflict with her father? What does he want for her? What does she want for herself? Is this conflict ever resolved?
3. Do you think the primary focus of this essay is on Cisneros's life as a writer, her life as a daughter, or her life as a woman? Explain.

## Responding in Writing

Cisneros focuses on a variety of places that were important to her—for example, her first "office" (3), her "apartment of high ceilings and windows that let in the sky" (9), and her house in San Antonio. Write a few paragraphs about places that have been important to you. Introduce each place with a "snapshot" sentence that identifies and describes it.

---
## FOCUS
---

### Are "Chinese Mothers" Superior?

Amy Chua and her daughters at home in New Haven, CT

### Responding to the Image

1. The photo above shows writer Amy Chua at home with her daughters, Louisa and Sophia. What message does this photo convey about the family? For example, what can you infer about the family's economic status or educational level?
2. This photograph accompanied Chua's essay when it was published in the *Wall Street Journal*. Note that Chua's husband, who lives with the family, is not pictured here. Is his absence in any way significant?

## WHY CHINESE MOTHERS ARE SUPERIOR

### Amy Chua

#### 1962–

*The John M. Duff, Jr. Professor of Law at Yale Law School, Amy Chua specializes in such topics as ethnic conflict and globalization. She is the author of* World on Fire: How Exporting Free Market Democracy Breeds Ethnic Hatred and Global Instability *(2003),* Day of Empire: How Hyperpowers Rise to Global Dominance—and Why They Fall *(2007), and* Battle Hymn of the Tiger Mother *(2011), from which the following essay is excerpted. In this essay, Chua contrasts two distinct parenting styles.*

A lot of people wonder how Chinese parents raise such stereotypically successful kids. They wonder what these parents do to produce so many math whizzes and music prodigies, what it's like inside the family, and whether they could do it too. Well, I can tell them, because I've done it. Here are some things my daughters, Sophia and Louisa, were never allowed to do:

- attend a sleepover
- have a playdate
- be in a school play
- complain about not being in a school play
- watch TV or play computer games
- choose their own extracurricular activities
- get any grade less than an A
- not be the No. 1 student in every subject except gym and drama
- play any instrument other than the piano or violin
- not play the piano or violin.

I'm using the term "Chinese mother" loosely. I know some Korean, Indian, Jamaican, Irish and Ghanaian parents who qualify too. Conversely, I know some mothers of Chinese heritage, almost always born in the West, who are not Chinese mothers, by choice or otherwise. I'm also using the term "Western parents" loosely. Western parents come in all varieties.

All the same, even when Western parents think they're being strict, they usually don't come close to being Chinese mothers. For example, my Western friends who consider themselves strict make their children practice their instruments 30 minutes every day. An hour at most. For a Chinese mother, the first hour is the easy part. It's hours two and three that get tough.

Despite our squeamishness about cultural stereotypes, there are tons of studies out there showing marked and quantifiable differences between Chinese and Westerners when it comes to parenting. In one study of 50 Western American mothers and 48 Chinese immigrant mothers, almost 70% of the Western mothers said either that "stressing academic success is not good for children" or that "parents need to foster the idea that learning is fun." By contrast, roughly 0% of the Chinese mothers felt the same way. Instead, the vast majority of the Chinese mothers said that they believe their children can be "the best" students, that "academic achievement reflects successful parenting," and that if children did not excel at school then there was "a problem" and

CHAPTER 1   FOCUS

parents "were not doing their job." Other studies indicate that compared to Western parents, Chinese parents spend approximately 10 times as long every day drilling academic activities with their children. By contrast, Western kids are more likely to participate in sports teams.

5      What Chinese parents understand is that nothing is fun until you're good at it. To get good at anything you have to work, and children on their own never want to work, which is why it is crucial to override their preferences. This often requires fortitude on the part of the parents because the child will resist; things are always hardest at the beginning, which is where Western parents tend to give up. But if done properly, the Chinese strategy produces a virtuous circle. Tenacious practice, practice, practice is crucial for excellence; rote repetition is underrated in America. Once a child starts to excel at something—whether it's math, piano, pitching or ballet—he or she gets praise, admiration and satisfaction. This builds confidence and makes the once not-fun activity fun. This in turn makes it easier for the parent to get the child to work even more.

Chinese parents can get away with things that Western parents can't. Once when I was young—maybe more than once—when I was extremely disrespectful to my mother, my father angrily called me "garbage" in our native Hokkien dialect.[1] It worked really well. I felt terrible and deeply ashamed of what I had done. But it didn't damage my self-esteem or anything like that. I knew exactly how highly he thought of me. I didn't actually think I was worthless or feel like a piece of garbage.

As an adult, I once did the same thing to Sophia, calling her garbage in English when she acted extremely disrespectfully toward me. When I mentioned that I had done this at a dinner party, I was immediately ostracized. One guest named Marcy got so upset she broke down in tears and had to leave early. My friend Susan, the host, tried to rehabilitate me with the remaining guests.

The fact is that Chinese parents can do things that would seem unimaginable—even legally actionable—to Westerners. Chinese mothers can say to their daughters, "Hey fatty—lose some weight." By contrast, Western parents have to tiptoe around the issue, talking in terms of "health" and never ever mentioning the f-word, and their kids still end up in therapy for eating disorders and negative self-image. (I also once heard a Western father toast his adult daughter by calling her "beautiful and incredibly competent." She later told me that made her feel like garbage.)

Chinese parents can order their kids to get straight As. Western parents can only ask their kids to try their best. Chinese parents can say, "You're lazy. All your classmates are getting ahead of you." By contrast, Western parents have to struggle with their own conflicted feelings

---

[1] A Chinese dialect spoken in Southeast Asia. [Eds.]

about achievement, and try to persuade themselves that they're not disappointed about how their kids turned out.

I've thought long and hard about how Chinese parents can get away with what they do. I think there are three big differences between the Chinese and Western parental mind-sets.

First, I've noticed that Western parents are extremely anxious about their children's self-esteem. They worry about how their children will feel if they fail at something, and they constantly try to reassure their children about how good they are notwithstanding a mediocre performance on a test or at a recital. In other words, Western parents are concerned about their children's psyches. Chinese parents aren't. They assume strength, not fragility, and as a result they behave very differently.

For example, if a child comes home with an A-minus on a test, a Western parent will most likely praise the child. The Chinese mother will gasp in horror and ask what went wrong. If the child comes home with a B on the test, some Western parents will still praise the child. Other Western parents will sit their child down and express disapproval, but they will be careful not to make their child feel inadequate or insecure, and they will not call their child "stupid," "worthless" or "a disgrace." Privately, the Western parents may worry that their child does not test well or have aptitude in the subject or that there is something wrong with the curriculum and possibly the whole school. If the child's grades do not improve, they may eventually schedule a meeting with the school principal to challenge the way the subject is being taught or to call into question the teacher's credentials.

If a Chinese child gets a B—which would never happen—there would first be a screaming, hair-tearing explosion. The devastated Chinese mother would then get dozens, maybe hundreds of practice tests and work through them with her child for as long as it takes to get the grade up to an A.

Chinese parents demand perfect grades because they believe that their child can get them. If their child doesn't get them, the Chinese parent assumes it's because the child didn't work hard enough. That's why the solution to substandard performance is always to excoriate, punish and shame the child. The Chinese parent believes that their child will be strong enough to take the shaming and to improve from it. (And when Chinese kids do excel, there is plenty of ego-inflating parental praise lavished in the privacy of the home.)

Second, Chinese parents believe that their kids owe them everything. The reason for this is a little unclear, but it's probably a combination of Confucian filial piety[2] and the fact that the parents have sacrificed and done so much for their children. (And it's true that Chinese mothers get in the trenches, putting in long grueling hours personally tutoring, training,

_____
[2]Respect for elders. [Eds.]

interrogating and spying on their kids.) Anyway, the understanding is that Chinese children must spend their lives repaying their parents by obeying them and making them proud.

By contrast, I don't think most Westerners have the same view of children being permanently indebted to their parents. My husband, Jed, actually has the opposite view. "Children don't choose their parents," he once said to me. "They don't even choose to be born. It's parents who foist life on their kids, so it's the parents' responsibility to provide for them. Kids don't owe their parents anything. Their duty will be to their own kids." This strikes me as a terrible deal for the Western parent.

Third, Chinese parents believe that they know what is best for their children and therefore override all of their children's own desires and preferences. That's why Chinese daughters can't have boyfriends in high school and why Chinese kids can't go to sleepaway camp. It's also why no Chinese kid would ever dare say to their mother, "I got a part in the school play! I'm Villager Number Six. I'll have to stay after school for rehearsal every day from 3:00 to 7:00, and I'll also need a ride on weekends." God help any Chinese kid who tried that one.

Don't get me wrong: It's not that Chinese parents don't care about their children. Just the opposite. They would give up anything for their children. It's just an entirely different parenting model. . . .

Western parents worry a lot about their children's self-esteem. But as a parent, one of the worst things you can do for your child's self-esteem is to let them give up. On the flip side, there's nothing better for building confidence than learning you can do something you thought you couldn't.

20    There are all these new books out there portraying Asian mothers as scheming, callous, overdriven people indifferent to their kids' true interests. For their part, many Chinese secretly believe that they care more about their children and are willing to sacrifice much more for them than Westerners, who seem perfectly content to let their children turn out badly. I think it's a misunderstanding on both sides. All decent parents want to do what's best for their children. The Chinese just have a totally different idea of how to do that.

Western parents try to respect their children's individuality, encouraging them to pursue their true passions, supporting their choices, and providing positive reinforcement and a nurturing environment. By contrast, the Chinese believe that the best way to protect their children is by preparing them for the future, letting them see what they're capable of, and arming them with skills, work habits and inner confidence that no one can ever take away.

## Responding to Reading

1. In paragraph 2, Chua clarifies what she means by the term "Chinese mother." Why do you suppose she feels a need to do this? Do you find her explanation convincing?

2. How are Chinese parents different from Western parents? Why, according to Chua, are Chinese mothers superior? Does she present sufficient evidence to support her position? If not, what should she add?

3. Explain your reaction to each of the following statements:

   • "What Chinese parents understand is that nothing is fun until you're good at it." (5)

   • "Chinese parents can get away with things that Western parents can't." (6)

   • "Western parents worry a lot about their children's self-esteem. But as a parent, one of the worst things you can do for your child's self-esteem is to let them give up." (19)

How do you think David Brooks (below) and Sophia Chua-Rubenfeld (p. 60) would react to each of these statements?

## Responding in Writing

How are Chua's rules for her children like and unlike the rules your parents set for you? Which set of rules makes more sense to you? Why?

# AMY CHUA IS A WIMP

## David Brooks

### 1961–

*A* New York Times *columnist and a radio and television political commentator, David Brooks has been an* Atlantic *correspondent, a* Weekly Standard *senior editor, and a* Newsweek *contributing editor. Brooks has published widely on American political and social issues. His latest book is* The Social Animal: The Hidden Sources of Love, Character, and Achievement *(2011). In the following essay, Brooks takes a hard look at Amy Chua's parenting techniques and at her claims about what it takes for a child to succeed.*

Sometime early last week, a large slice of educated America decided that Amy Chua is a menace to society. Chua, as you probably know, is the Yale professor who has written a bracing critique of what she considers the weak, cuddling American parenting style.

Chua didn't let her own girls go out on play dates or sleepovers. She didn't let them watch TV or play video games or take part in garbage activities like crafts. Once, one of her daughters came in second to a Korean kid in a math competition, so Chua made the girl do 2,000 math problems a night until she regained her supremacy. Once, her daughters gave her birthday cards of insufficient quality. Chua rejected them and demanded new cards. Once, she threatened to burn all of one of her daughter's stuffed animals unless she played a piece of music perfectly.

As a result, Chua's daughters get straight As and have won a series of musical competitions.

In her book, *Battle Hymn of the Tiger Mother*, Chua delivers a broadside against American parenting even as she mocks herself for her own extreme "Chinese" style. She says American parents lack authority and produce entitled children who aren't forced to live up to their abilities.

5    The furious denunciations began flooding my in-box a week ago. Chua plays into America's fear of national decline. Here's a Chinese parent working really hard (and, by the way, there are a billion more of her) and her kids are going to crush ours. Furthermore (and this Chua doesn't appreciate), she is not really rebelling against American-style parenting; she is the logical extension of the prevailing elite practices. She does everything over-pressuring upper-middle-class parents are doing. She's just hard core.

Her critics echoed the familiar themes. Her kids can't possibly be happy or truly creative. They'll grow up skilled and compliant but without the audacity to be great. She's destroying their love for music. There's a reason Asian-American women between the ages of 15 and 24 have such high suicide rates.

I have the opposite problem with Chua. I believe she's coddling her children. She's protecting them from the most intellectually demanding activities because she doesn't understand what's cognitively difficult and what isn't.

Practicing a piece of music for four hours requires focused attention, but it is nowhere near as cognitively demanding as a sleepover with 14-year-old girls. Managing status rivalries, negotiating group dynamics, understanding social norms, navigating the distinction between self and group—these and other social tests impose cognitive demands that blow away any intense tutoring session or a class at Yale.

Yet mastering these arduous skills is at the very essence of achievement. Most people work in groups. We do this because groups are much more efficient at solving problems than individuals (swimmers are often motivated to have their best times as part of relay teams, not in individual events). Moreover, the performance of a group does not correlate well with the average I.Q. of the group or even with the I.Q.'s of the smartest members.

10    Researchers at the Massachusetts Institute of Technology and Carnegie Mellon have found that groups have a high collective intelligence when members of a group are good at reading each others' emotions—when they take turns speaking, when the inputs from each member are managed fluidly, when they detect each others' inclinations and strengths.

Participating in a well-functioning group is really hard. It requires the ability to trust people outside your kinship circle, read intonations and moods, understand how the psychological pieces each person brings to the room can and cannot fit together.

This skill set is not taught formally, but it is imparted through arduous experiences. These are exactly the kinds of difficult experiences Chua shelters her children from by making them rush home to hit the homework table.

Chua would do better to see the classroom as a cognitive break from the truly arduous tests of childhood. Where do they learn how to manage people? Where do they learn to construct and manipulate metaphors? Where do they learn to perceive details of a scene the way a hunter reads a landscape? Where do they learn how to detect their own shortcomings? Where do they learn how to put themselves in others' minds and anticipate others' reactions?

These and a million other skills are imparted by the informal maturity process and are not developed if formal learning monopolizes a child's time.

So I'm not against the way Chua pushes her daughters. And I loved 15 her book as a courageous and thought-provoking read. It's also more supple than her critics let on. I just wish she wasn't so soft and indulgent. I wish she recognized that in some important ways the school cafeteria is more intellectually demanding than the library. And I hope her daughters grow up to write their own books, and maybe learn the skills to better anticipate how theirs will be received.

## Responding to Reading

1. In what sense, according to Brooks, is Amy Chua a "wimp"? Do you think Brooks's title is effective, or do you see it as inappropriate—or possibly even offensive? Explain.
2. In paragraphs 2 through 4, Brooks summarizes some of Chua's key points. Is his summary accurate? Is it sufficiently detailed, or does he leave out any important pieces of information?
3. According to Brooks, what do some critics say is wrong with Chua's child-rearing philosophy? What objections to her practices does Brooks himself have? How do you suppose Chua would defend her family against these criticisms?

## Responding in Writing

Which do you see as more important, the academic success Chua wants for her daughters or the social skills Brooks discusses? Do you think it is possible to excel both academically and socially?

# WHY I LOVE MY STRICT CHINESE MOM

## Sophia Chua-Rubenfeld

### 1993–

*Sophia Chua-Rubenfeld is the daughter of Amy Chua. In the following letter, which appeared in the* New York Post, *Chua-Rubenfeld defends her mother's intense parenting style. According to Chua-Rubenfeld, her mother's strict way of raising her and her sister helped her to learn "that even creativity takes effort."*

Dear Tiger Mom,

You've been criticized a lot since you published your memoir, *Battle Hymn of the Tiger Mother*. One problem is that some people don't get your humor. They think you're serious about all this, and they assume Lulu and I are oppressed by our evil mother. That is so not true. Every other Thursday, you take off our chains and let us play math games in the basement.

But for real, it's not their fault. No outsider can know what our family is really like. They don't hear us cracking up over each other's jokes. They don't see us eating our hamburgers with fried rice. They don't know how much fun we have when the six of us—dogs included—squeeze into one bed and argue about what movies to download from Netflix.

I admit it: Having you as a mother was no tea party. There were some play dates I wish I'd gone to and some piano camps I wish I'd skipped. But now that I'm 18 and about to leave the tiger den, I'm glad you and Daddy raised me the way you did. Here's why.

A lot of people have accused you of producing robot kids who can't think for themselves. Well, that's funny, because I think those people are . . . oh well, it doesn't matter. At any rate, I was thinking about this, and I came to the opposite conclusion: I think your strict parenting forced me to be more independent. Early on, I decided to be an easy child to raise. Maybe I got it from Daddy—he taught me not to care what people think and to make my own choices—but I also decided to be who I want to be. I didn't rebel, but I didn't suffer all the slings and arrows of a Tiger Mom, either. I pretty much do my own thing these days—like building greenhouses downtown, blasting Daft Punk in the car with Lulu and forcing my boyfriend to watch *Lord of the Rings* with me over and over—as long as I get my piano done first.

5      Everybody's talking about the birthday cards we once made for you, which you rejected because they weren't good enough. Funny how

some people are convinced that Lulu and I are scarred for life. Maybe if I had poured my heart into it, I would have been upset. But let's face it: The card was feeble, and I was busted. It took me 30 seconds; I didn't even sharpen the pencil. That's why, when you rejected it, I didn't feel you were rejecting me. If I actually tried my best at something, you'd never throw it back in my face.

I remember walking on stage for a piano competition. I was so nervous, and you whispered, "Soso, you worked as hard as you could. It doesn't matter how you do."

Everybody seems to think art is spontaneous. But Tiger Mom, you taught me that even creativity takes effort. I guess I was a little different from other kids in grade school, but who says that's a bad thing? Maybe I was just lucky to have nice friends. They used to put notes in my backpack that said "Good luck at the competition tomorrow! You'll be great!" They came to my piano recitals—mostly for the dumplings you made afterward—and I started crying when I heard them yelling "bravo!" at Carnegie Hall.

When I got to high school, you realized it was time to let me grow up a little. All the girls started wearing makeup in ninth grade. I walked to CVS to buy some and taught myself how to use it. It wasn't a big deal. You were surprised when I came down to dinner wearing eyeliner, but you didn't mind. You let me have that rite of passage.

Another criticism I keep hearing is that you're somehow promoting tunnel vision, but you and Daddy taught me to pursue knowledge for its own sake. In junior year, I signed myself up for a military-history elective (yes, you let me take lots of classes besides math and physics). One of our assignments was to interview someone who had experienced war. I knew I could get a good grade interviewing my grandparents, whose childhood stories about World War II I'd heard a thousand times. I mentioned it to you, and you said, "Sophia, this is an opportunity to learn something new. You're taking the easy way out." You were right, Tiger Mom. In the end, I interviewed a terrifying Israeli paratrooper whose story changed my outlook on life. I owe that experience to you.

There's one more thing: I think the desire to live a meaningful life 10 is universal. To some people, it's working toward a goal. To others, it's enjoying every minute of every day. So what does it really mean to live life to the fullest? Maybe striving to win a Nobel Prize and going skydiving are just two sides of the same coin. To me, it's not about achievement or self-gratification. It's about knowing that you've pushed yourself, body and mind, to the limits of your own potential. You feel it when you're sprinting, and when the piano piece you've practiced for hours finally comes to life beneath your fingertips. You feel it when you encounter a life-changing idea, and when you do something on your own that you never thought you

CHAPTER 1  FOCUS

could. If I died tomorrow, I would die feeling I've lived my whole life at 110 percent.

And for that, Tiger Mom, thank you.

## Responding to Reading

1. In paragraph 3, Chua-Rubenfeld says she is glad she was raised the way she was. How does she support this statement in her letter? Do you find this support convincing? Why or why not?
2. Given how closely Amy Chua has supervised her children, do you think her daughter's letter in her defense is completely sincere—and completely uncensored? Explain.
3. In paragraph 10, Chua-Rubenfeld asks, "So what does it really mean to live life to the fullest?" How would you answer this question? What is the relationship between this question and Chua-Rubenfeld's defense of her mother's parenting style?

## Responding in Writing

Write a letter to one or both of your parents, explaining why you are (or are not) satisfied with the way you were raised. Be very specific in your explanation of the rules and guidelines that were set for you.

# WIDENING THE FOCUS

## For Critical Reading and Writing

Referring specifically to the three readings in this chapter's Focus section, write an essay in which you answer the question, "Are 'Chinese Mothers' Superior?"

## For Further Reading

The following readings can suggest additional perspectives for thinking and writing about different kinds of parent–child relationships.

- Lynda Barry, "The Sanctuary of School" (p. 69)
- Amy Tan, "Mother Tongue" (p. 134)
- Kirin Desai, "Fatherland" (p. 360)
- Gary Soto, "One Last Time" (p. 404)

## For Focused Research

Recent years have seen an increase in the number of afterschool programs designed to improve children's academic performance. One such program is offered by Kumon Learning Centers <http://www.kumon.com>. Do a *Google* search for afterschool enrichment programs, and select two program Web sites. Then, write an essay that analyzes these programs. What is their purpose? Why were they developed? Why is their popularity increasing? Are they a good thing for children, or do they create too much pressure for them to excel? Use information from the Web sites you have chosen to support your conclusions.

## Beyond the Classroom

Conduct an email survey of the friends and classmates in your address book. After explaining Chua's distinction between "Chinese mothers" and "Western mothers," ask each recipient the following questions:

- Which type of mother did you have?
- Did this kind of parenting encourage you to succeed or hold you back?
- Which of these two types of parents do you plan to be, and why?

When you have gathered all your responses, write an essay that summarizes your findings and draws a conclusion about the relative value of each of the two parenting styles.

CHAPTER 1  FOCUS

--- **WRITING** ---

## FAMILY AND MEMORY

1. What exactly is a family? Is it a group of people bound together by love? by marriage? by blood? by history? by shared memories? by economic dependency? by habit? What unites family members, and what divides them? Does *family* denote only a traditional nuclear family or also a family broken by divorce and blended by remarriage? Define *family* as it is portrayed in several of the readings in this chapter.

2. Leo Tolstoy's classic Russian novel *Anna Karenina* opens with this sentence: "Happy families are all alike; every unhappy family is unhappy in its own way." Write an essay in which you agree with or challenge this statement, supporting your position with references to several of the readings in this chapter.

3. In a sense, memories are like snapshots: a series of disconnected candid pictures, sometimes unflattering, often out of focus, gradually fading. Writers of autobiographical memoirs often explore this similarity. For example, Alice Walker (p. 34) sees her painful childhood as a series of snapshots, and Sandra Cisneros (p. 46) also refers to photographs as she remembers her past. Using information from your own family life as well as from your reading, discuss the relationship between memories and photographs. If you like, you may describe and discuss some of your own family photographs. (You might begin by examining the photographs that open this chapter.)

4. In "No Name Woman" (p. 23), Maxine Hong Kingston presents a detailed biographical sketch of a family member she never knew. Using her essay as a guide, write a detailed biographical essay about a member of your own family (living or deceased). Prepare for this assignment by interviewing several family members.

5. When you think about your childhood and your young adulthood, what music do you imagine playing in the background? Write a musical autobiography that gives readers a sense of who you were at different times of your life. Try to help readers understand the times you grew up in and the person you were (and became). Or, remember the smells and tastes of the food you grew up with, and write a culinary autobiography instead.

6. How do your parents' notions of success and failure affect you? Do you think your parents tend to expect too much of you? too little? Explore these ideas in an essay, referring to readings in this chapter and in Chapter 7, "The American Dream."

7. What traits, habits, and values (positive or negative) have you inherited from your parents? What qualities do you think you will pass

on to your children? Read the poem "Heritage" (p. 15) and the essay "Why I Love My Strict Chinese Mom" (p. 60), and then write a letter to your parents in which you answer these two questions. Be sure to illustrate the characteristics you discuss with examples of specific incidents.

8. "Those Winter Sundays" (p. 17), told from the point of view of an adult looking back on his childhood, views the parent–child relationship with a mixture of regret and resignation. Write an essay exploring the similarly ambivalent feelings this work—and others in this chapter—convey about the relationship between child and parent.

9. In "Why Chinese Mothers Are Superior" (p. 52), Amy Chua draws a distinction between Chinese "tiger mothers" and Western parents. Which of the parents described in this chapter's readings do you see as "Chinese," and which do you see as "Western"? Choose two readings in each category, and use them to illustrate the differences between the two parenting styles.

10. In many of the essays in this chapter, writers see their parents through two different lenses: as they were in the past and as they are in the present. Write an essay in which you discuss the two different views of their parents described by David Jacobsen, Alice Walker, and Sandra Cisneros. How did each writer view his or her parents when they were young? What is their impression of their parents now? How do you explain the differences?

# 2

# ISSUES IN EDUCATION

In the nineteenth century, people had little difficulty defining the purpose of education: they assumed it was the school's job to prepare students for the roles they would play as adults. To accomplish this end, public school administrators made sure that the elementary school curriculum gave students a good dose of the basics: arithmetic, grammar, spelling, reading, composition, and penmanship. High school students studied literature, history, geography, and civics. At the elite private schools, students studied subjects that would prepare them for the leadership positions that they would eventually occupy as adults. They learned physics, rhetoric, and elocution—as well as Latin and Greek so that they could read the classics in the original.

Today, educators seem to have a great deal of difficulty agreeing on what purpose schools are supposed to serve. No longer can a group of

Nineteenth-century college classroom

school administrators simply proscribe a curriculum. Parents, students, politicians, academics, special interest groups, and religious leaders all attempt to influence what is taught. The result, according to some educators, is an environment in which it is almost impossible for any real education to take place. In fact, in many of today's schools, more emphasis seems to be placed on increasing self-esteem, avoiding controversy, and passing standardized tests than on challenging students to discover new ways of thinking about themselves and about the world. In this milieu, classic books are censored or rewritten to eliminate passages that might offend, ideas are presented as if they all have equal value, and the curriculum is revised so that teachers can "teach to the test." The result is an educational environment that has all the intellectual appeal of elevator music. Many people—educators included—seem to have forgotten that ideas must be unsettling if they are to make us think. After all, what is education but a process that encourages us to think critically about our world and to develop a healthy skepticism—to question, evaluate, and reach conclusions about ideas and events?

The Focus section of this chapter (p. 113) addresses the question, "Is a College Education Worth the Money?" The essays in the section present a variety of opinions on the value of a college education. For example, should the value of higher education be judged solely in financial terms? Given the high cost of college, should the economic benefits of a college degree be taken into consideration? And is there a case to be made for credible vocational alternatives for students who are not suited for college?

Contemporary college classroom

──────────── **PREPARING TO READ AND WRITE** ────────────

As you read and prepare to write about the selections in this chapter, you may consider the following questions:

- How does the writer define *education*? Is this definition consistent with yours?

- What does the writer think the main goals of education should be? Do you agree?

- Which does the writer believe is more important, formal or informal education?

- On what aspect or aspects of education does the writer focus?

- Who does the writer believe bears primary responsibility for a student's education? The student? The family? The school? The community? The government?

- Does the writer use personal experience to support his or her points? Does he or she use facts and statistics or expert opinion as support? Do you find the writer's ideas convincing?

- What changes in the educational system does the writer recommend? Do you agree with these recommendations?

- Are the writer's educational experiences similar to or different from yours? How do these similarities or differences affect your response to the essay?

- In what way is the essay similar to or different from other essays in this chapter?

# THE SANCTUARY OF SCHOOL
## Lynda Barry
### 1956–

*Lynda Barry grew up as part of an extended Filipino family (her mother was Filipino, her father an alcoholic Norwegian-Irishman). The first member of her family to pursue higher education, she majored in art and began her career as a cartoonist shortly after graduation. Barry is known as a chronicler of adolescent angst both in her syndicated comic strip* Ernie Pook's Comeek *and in the semi-autobiographical* One Hundred Demons *(2002). Her latest collections are* Nearsighted Monkey *(2009) and* Blabber Blabber Blabber: Volume 1 of Everything *(2011). Barry has also written a novel,* The Good Times Are Killing Me *(1988), which was turned into a successful musical. In the following essay, Barry remembers her Seattle grade school in a racially mixed neighborhood as a nurturing safe haven from her difficult family life.*

I was 7 years old the first time I snuck out of the house in the dark. It was winter and my parents had been fighting all night. They were short on money and long on relatives who kept "temporarily" moving into our house because they had nowhere else to go.

My brother and I were used to giving up our bedroom. We slept on the couch, something we actually liked because it put us that much closer to the light of our lives, our television.

At night when everyone was asleep, we lay on our pillows watching it with the sound off. We watched Steve Allen's mouth moving. We watched Johnny Carson's mouth moving. We watched movies filled with gangsters shooting machine guns into packed rooms, dying soldiers hurling a last grenade and beautiful women crying at windows. Then the sign-off finally came and we tried to sleep.

The morning I snuck out, I woke up filled with a panic about needing to get to school. The sun wasn't quite up yet but my anxiety was so fierce that I just got dressed, walked quietly across the kitchen and let myself out the back door.

It was quiet outside. Stars were still out. Nothing moved and no one    5
was in the street. It was as if someone had turned the sound off on the world.

I walked the alley, breaking thin ice over the puddles with my shoes. I didn't know why I was walking to school in the dark. I didn't think about it. All I knew was a feeling of panic, like the panic that strikes kids when they realize they are lost.

That feeling eased the moment I turned the corner and saw the dark outline of my school at the top of the hill. My school was made up of about 15 nondescript portable classrooms set down on a fenced concrete lot in a rundown Seattle neighborhood, but it had the most beautiful view of the Cascade Mountains. You could see them from anywhere on the playfield and you could see them from the windows of my classroom—Room 2.

I walked over to the monkey bars and hooked my arms around the cold metal. I stood for a long time just looking across Rainier Valley. The sky was beginning to whiten and I could hear a few birds.

In a perfect world my absence at home would not have gone unnoticed. I would have had two parents in a panic to locate me, instead of two parents in a panic to locate an answer to the hard question of survival during a deep financial and emotional crisis.

10      But in an overcrowded and unhappy home, it's incredibly easy for any child to slip away. The high levels of frustration, depression and anger in my house made my brother and me invisible. We were children with the sound turned off. And for us, as for the steadily increasing number of neglected children in this country, the only place where we could count on being noticed was at school.

"Hey there, young lady. Did you forget to go home last night?" It was Mr. Gunderson, our janitor, whom we all loved. He was nice and he was funny and he was old with white hair, thick glasses and an unbelievable number of keys. I could hear them jingling as he walked across the playfield. I felt incredibly happy to see him.

He let me push his wheeled garbage can between the different portables as he unlocked each room. He let me turn on the lights and raise the window shades and I saw my school slowly come to life. I saw Mrs. Holman, our school secretary, walk into the office without her orange lipstick on yet. She waved.

I saw the fifth-grade teacher Mr. Cunningham, walking under the breezeway eating a hard roll. He waved.

And I saw my teacher, Mrs. Claire LeSane, walking toward us in a red coat and calling my name in a very happy and surprised way, and suddenly my throat got tight and my eyes stung and I ran toward her crying. It was something that surprised us both.

15      It's only thinking about it now, 28 years later, that I realize I was crying from relief. I was with my teacher, and in a while I was going to sit at my desk, with my crayons and pencils and books and classmates all around me, and for the next six hours I was going to enjoy a thoroughly secure, warm and stable world. It was a world I absolutely relied on. Without it, I don't know where I would have gone that morning.

Mrs. LeSane asked me what was wrong and when I said "Nothing," she seemingly left it at that. But she asked me if I would carry her purse for her, an honor above all honors, and she asked if I wanted to come into Room 2 early and paint.

She believed in the natural healing power of painting and drawing for troubled children. In the back of her room there was always a drawing table and an easel with plenty of supplies, and sometimes during the day she would come up to you for what seemed like no good reason and quietly ask if you wanted to go to the back table and "make some pictures for Mrs. LeSane." We all had a chance at it—to sit apart from the class for a while to paint, draw and silently work out impossible problems on 11 × 17 sheets of newsprint.

Drawing came to mean everything to me. At the back table in Room 2, I learned to build myself a life preserver that I could carry into my home.

We all know that a good education system saves lives, but the people of this country are still told that cutting the budget for public schools is necessary, that poor salaries for teachers are all we can manage and that art, music and all creative activities must be the first to go when times are lean.

Before- and after-school programs are cut and we are told that public schools are not made for baby-sitting children. If parents are neglectful temporarily or permanently, for whatever reason, it's certainly sad, but their unlucky children must fend for themselves. Or slip through the cracks. Or wander in a dark night alone. 20

We are told in a thousand ways that not only are public schools not important, but that the children who attend them, the children who need them most, are not important either. We leave them to learn from the blind eye of a television, or to the mercy of "a thousand points of light"[1] that can be as far away as stars.

I was lucky. I had Mrs. LeSane. I had Mr. Gunderson. I had an abundance of art supplies. And I had a particular brand of neglect in my home that allowed me to slip away and get to them. But what about the rest of the kids who weren't as lucky? What happened to them?

By the time the bell rang that morning I had finished my drawing and Mrs. LeSane pinned it up on the special bulletin board she reserved for drawings from the back table. It was the same picture I always drew—a sun in the corner of a blue sky over a nice house with flowers all around it.

Mrs. LeSane asked us to please stand, face the flag, place our right hands over our hearts and say the Pledge of Allegiance. Children across the country do it faithfully. I wonder now when the country will face its children and say a pledge right back.

## Responding to Reading

1. What information about her school does Barry provide? What information does she not provide? How can you explain these omissions?
2. In paragraph 22, Barry asks two questions. Why doesn't she answer them? What do you think the answers to these questions might be?
3. Barry's essay ends on a cynical note. How effective is this conclusion? What does Barry gain or lose with this concluding strategy?

## Responding in Writing

Has school been a sanctuary for you as it was for Barry? Write a paragraph or two in which you answer this question.

---

[1]Catchphrase for President George H. W. Bush's plan to substitute volunteerism for government programs. [Eds.]

# SCHOOL IS BAD FOR CHILDREN

## John Holt

### 1923–1985

*John Holt, a teacher and education theorist, believed that traditional schooling suppresses children's natural curiosity about life. In his writings about educa-tion, Holt suggests that students be allowed to pursue whatever interests them. Holt worked for an international peace group, traveled in Europe, and then worked at the private Colorado Rocky Mountain School in Carbondale, Colorado, where he taught high school English, French, and mathematics and coached soccer and baseball. His many books include* How Children Fail *(1964),* How Children Learn *(1967),* Education *(1976), and* Learning All the Time *(1989). In the following essay, first published in 1969, Holt makes a plea to free children from the classroom, a "dull and ugly place, where nobody ever says anything very truthful," and to "give them a chance to learn about the world at first hand." Holt was also a major supporter of the Home Schooling movement.*

Almost every child, on the first day he sets foot in a school building, is smarter, more curious, less afraid of what he doesn't know, better at finding and figuring things out, more confident, resourceful, persistent and independent than he will ever be again in his schooling—or, unless he is very unusual and very lucky, for the rest of his life. Already, by paying close attention to and interacting with the world and people around him, and without any school-type formal instruction, he has done a task far more difficult, complicated and abstract than anything he will be asked to do in school, or than any of his teachers has done for years. He has solved the mystery of language. He has discovered it—babies don't even know that language exists—and he has found out how it works and learned to use it. He has done it by exploring, by experimenting, by developing his own model of the grammar of lan-guage, by trying it out and seeing whether it works, by gradually changing it and refining it until it does work. And while he has been doing this, he has been learning other things as well, including many of the "concepts" that the schools think only they can teach him, and many that are more complicated than the ones they do try to teach him.

In he comes, this curious, patient, determined, energetic, skillful learner. We sit him down at a desk, and what do we teach him? Many things. First, that learning is separate from living. "You come to school to learn," we tell him, as if the child hadn't been learning before, as if living were out there and learning were in here, and there were no con-nection between the two. Secondly, that he cannot be trusted to learn and is no good at it. Everything we teach about reading, a task far sim-pler than many that the child has already mastered, says to him, "If we don't make you read, you won't, and if you don't do it exactly the way we tell you, you can't." In short, he comes to feel that learning is a passive process, something that someone else does *to* you, instead of something you do for yourself.

In a great many other ways he learns that he is worthless, untrustworthy, fit only to take other people's orders, a blank sheet for other people to write on. Oh, we make a lot of nice noises in school about respect for the child and individual differences, and the like. But our acts, as opposed to our talk, say to the child, "Your experience, your concerns, your curiosities, your needs, what you know, what you want, what you wonder about, what you hope for, what you fear, what you like and dislike, what you are good at or not so good at—all this is of not the slightest importance, it counts for nothing. What counts here, and the only thing that counts, is what we know, what we think is important, what we want you to do, think and be." The child soon learns not to ask questions—the teacher isn't there to satisfy his curiosity. Having learned to hide his curiosity, he later learns to be ashamed of it. Given no chance to find out who he is—and to develop that person, whoever it is—he soon comes to accept the adults' evaluation of him.

He learns many other things. He learns that to be wrong, uncertain, confused, is a crime. Right Answers are what the school wants, and he learns countless strategies for prying these answers out of the teacher, for conning her into thinking he knows what he doesn't know. He learns to dodge, bluff, fake, cheat. He learns to be lazy. Before he came to school, he would work for hours on end, on his own, with no thought of reward, at the business of making sense of the world and gaining competence in it. In school he learns, like every buck private, how to goldbrick, how not to work when the sergeant isn't looking, how to know when he is looking, how to make him think you are working even when he is looking. He learns that in real life you don't do anything unless you are bribed, bullied or conned into doing it, that nothing is worth doing for its own sake, or that if it is, you can't do it in school. He learns to be bored, to work with a small part of his mind, to escape from the reality around him into daydreams and fantasies—but not like the fantasies of his preschool years, in which he played a very active part.

The child comes to school curious about other people, particularly 5 other children, and the school teaches him to be indifferent. The most interesting thing in the classroom—often the only interesting thing in it—is the other children, but he has to act as if these other children, all about him, only a few feet away, are not really there. He cannot interact with them, talk with them, smile at them. In many schools he can't talk to other children in the halls between classes; in more than a few, and some of these in stylish suburbs, he can't even talk to them at lunch. Splendid training for a world in which, when you're not studying the other person to figure out how to do him in, you pay no attention to him.

In fact, he learns how to live without paying attention to anything going on around him. You might say that school is a long lesson in how to turn yourself off, which may be one reason why so many young people, seeking the awareness of the world and responsiveness to it they had when they were little, think they can only find it in drugs. Aside from being boring, the school is almost always ugly, cold, inhuman— even the most stylish, glass-windowed, $20-a-square-foot schools.

And so, in this dull and ugly place, where nobody ever says anything very truthful, where everybody is playing a kind of role, as in a charade, where the teachers are no more free to respond honestly to the students than the students are free to respond to the teachers or each other, where the air practically vibrates with suspicion and anxiety, the child learns to live in a daze, saving his energies for those small parts of his life that are too trivial for the adults to bother with, and thus remain his. It is a rare child who can come through his schooling with much left of his curiosity, his independence or his sense of his own dignity, competence and worth.

So much for criticism. What do we need to do? Many things. Some are easy—we can do them right away. Some are hard, and may take some time. Take a hard one first. We should abolish compulsory school attendance. At the very least we should modify it, perhaps by giving children every year a large number of authorized absences. Our compulsory school-attendance laws once served a humane and useful purpose. They protected children's right to some schooling, against those adults who would otherwise have denied it to them in order to exploit their labor, in farm, store, mine or factory. Today the laws help nobody, not the schools, not the teachers, not the children. To keep kids in school who would rather not be there costs the schools an enormous amount of time and trouble—to say nothing of what it costs to repair the damage that these angry and resentful prisoners do every time they get a chance. Every teacher knows that any kid in class who, for whatever reason, would rather not be there not only doesn't learn anything himself but makes it a great deal tougher for anyone else. As for protecting the children from exploitation, the chief and indeed only exploiters of children these days *are* the schools. Kids caught in the college rush more often than not work 70 hours or more a week, most of it on paper busy-work. For kids who aren't going to college, school is just a useless time waster, preventing them from earning some money or doing some useful work, or even doing some true learning.

Objections. "If kids didn't have to go to school, they'd all be out in the streets." No, they wouldn't. In the first place, even if schools stayed just the way they are, children would spend at least some time there because that's where they'd be likely to find friends; it's a natural meeting place for children. In the second place, schools wouldn't stay the way they are, they'd get better, because we would have to start making them what they ought to be right now—places where children would *want* to be. In the third place, those children who did not want to go to school could find, particularly if we stirred up our brains and gave them a little help, other things to do—the things many children now do during their summers and holidays.

There's something easier we could do. We need to get kids out of the 10 school buildings, give them a chance to learn about the world at first hand. It is a very recent idea, and a crazy one, that the way to teach our young people about the world they live in is to take them out of it and shut them up in brick boxes. Fortunately, educators are beginning to realize this. In Philadelphia and Portland, Oreg., to pick only two places I happen to have heard about, plans are being drawn up for public schools that won't have any school buildings at all, that will take the students out into the city and help them to use it and its people as a learning resource. In other words, students, perhaps in groups, perhaps independently, will go to libraries, museums, exhibits, court rooms, legislatures, radio and TV stations, meetings, businesses and laboratories to learn about their world and society at first hand. A small private school in Washington is already doing this. It makes sense. We need more of it.

As we help children get out into the world, to do their learning there, we get more of the world into the schools. Aside from their parents, most children never have any close contact with any adults except people whose sole business is children. No wonder they have no idea what adult life or work is like. We need to bring a lot more people who are *not* full-time teachers into the schools and into contact with the children. In New York City, under the Teachers and Writers Collaborative, real writers, working writers—novelists, poets, playwrights— come into the schools, read their work, and talk to the children about the problems of their craft. The children eat it up. In another school I know of, a practicing attorney from a nearby city comes in every month or so and talks to several classes about the law. Not the law as it is in books but as he sees it and encounters it in his cases, his problems, his work. And the children love it. It is real, grown-up, true, not *My Weekly Reader,* not "social studies," not lies and baloney.

Something easier yet. Let children work together, help each other, learn from each other and each other's mistakes. We now know, from the experience of many schools, both rich-suburban and poor-city, that children are often the best teachers of other children. What is more important, we know that when a fifth- or sixth-grader who has been having trouble with reading starts helping a first-grader, his own reading sharply improves. A number of schools are beginning to use what some call Paired Learning. This means that you let children form partnerships with other children, do their work, even including their tests, together, and share whatever marks or results this work gets—just like grownups in the real world. It seems to work.

Let the children learn to judge their own work. A child learning to talk does not learn by being corrected all the time—if corrected too much, he will stop talking. *He* compares, a thousand times a day, the difference between language as he uses it and as those around him use it. Bit by bit, he makes the necessary changes to make his language like other people's. In the same way, kids learning to do all the other things they learn without adult teachers—to walk, run, climb, whistle, ride a bike, skate, play games, jump rope—compare their own performance with what more skilled people do, and slowly make the needed changes. But in school we never give a child a chance to detect his mistakes, let alone correct them. We do it all for him. We act as if we thought he would never notice a mistake unless it was pointed out to him, or correct it unless he was made to. Soon he becomes dependent on the expert. We should let him do it himself. Let him figure out, with the help of other children if he wants it, what this word says, what is the answer to that problem, whether this is a good way of saying or doing this or that. If right answers are involved, as in some math or science, give him the answer book, let him correct his own papers. Why should we teachers waste time on such donkey work? Our job should be to help the kid when he tells us that he can't find a way to get the right answer. Let's get rid of all this nonsense of grades, exams, marks. We don't know now, and we never will know, how to measure what another person knows or understands. We certainly can't find out by asking him questions. All we find out is what he doesn't know—which is what most tests are for, anyway. Throw it all out, and let the child learn what *every* educated person must someday learn, how to measure his own understanding, how to know what he knows or does not know.

We could also abolish the fixed, required curriculum. People remember only what is interesting and useful to them, what helps them make sense of the world, or helps them get along in it. All else they quickly forget, if they ever learn it at all. The idea of a "body of knowledge," to be picked up in school and used for the rest of one's life, is nonsense in a world as complicated and rapidly changing as ours. Anyway, the most important questions and problems of our time are not *in* the curriculum, not even in the hotshot universities, let alone the schools.

15    Children want, more than they want anything else, and even after years of miseducation, to make sense of the world, themselves, and other human beings. Let them get at this job, with our help if they ask for it, in the way that makes most sense to them.

## Responding to Reading

1. In what specific ways does Holt believe schools fail children?
2. According to Holt, what should schools do to correct their shortcomings? Do you think his suggestions are practical? realistic? Why or why not?

3.  In paragraph 13, Holt says, "Let's get rid of all this nonsense of grades, exams, marks." Do you agree? What would be the advantages and disadvantages of this course of action?

### Responding in Writing

What would your ideal elementary school be like? How would it be like the schools you attended? How would it be different?

# GRADUATION

## Maya Angelou

### 1928–

*Maya Angelou was raised in Arkansas by her grandmother, who ran a general store. She began a theatrical career when she toured with* Porgy and Bess *in 1954–1955. Angelou is now a poet, writer, lecturer, and teacher. She read her poem "On the Pulse of Morning" at the 1993 presidential inauguration of Bill Clinton. Angelou's most recent books are* Letter to My Daughter *(2008) and* Great Food All Day Long: Cook Splendidly, Eat Smart *(2010). In "Graduation," excerpted from her autobiography* I Know Why the Caged Bird Sings *(1969), Angelou remembers the anger and pride of graduation day at her segregated school in Stamps, Arkansas.*

The children in Stamps trembled visibly with anticipation. Some adults were excited too, but to be certain the whole young population had come down with graduation epidemic. Large classes were graduating from both the grammar school and the high school. Even those who were years removed from their own day of glorious release were anxious to help with preparations as a kind of dry run. The junior students who were moving into the vacating classes' chairs were tradition-bound to show their talents for leadership and management. They strutted through the school and around the campus exerting pressure on the lower grades. Their authority was so new that occasionally if they pressed a little too hard it had to be overlooked. After all, next term was coming, and it never hurt a sixth grader to have a play sister in the eighth grade, or a tenth-year student to be able to call a twelfth grader Bubba. So all was endured in a spirit of shared understanding. But the graduating classes themselves were the nobility. Like travelers with exotic destinations on their minds, the graduates were remarkably forgetful. They came to school without their books, or tablets or even pencils. Volunteers fell over themselves to secure replacements for the missing equipment. When accepted, the willing workers might or might not be thanked, and it was of no importance to the pregraduation rites. Even teachers were respectful of the now quiet and aging seniors, and tended to speak to them, if not as equals, as beings only slightly lower than themselves. After tests were returned and grades given, the student body, which acted like an extended family, knew who did well, who excelled, and what piteous ones had failed.

Unlike the white high school, Lafayette County Training School distinguished itself by having neither lawn, nor hedges, nor tennis court, nor climbing ivy. Its two buildings (main classrooms, the grade school and home economics) were set on a dirt hill with no fence to limit either its boundaries or those of bordering farms. There was a large expanse to the left of the school which was used alternately as a baseball diamond or basketball court. Rusty hoops on swaying poles represented the permanent recreational equipment, although bats and balls could be borrowed from the P.E. teacher if the borrower was qualified and if the diamond wasn't occupied.

Over this rocky area relieved by a few shady tall persimmon trees the graduating class walked. The girls often held hands and no longer bothered to speak to the lower students. There was a sadness about them, as if this old world was not their home and they were bound for higher ground. The boys, on the other hand, had become more friendly, more outgoing. A decided change from the closed attitude they projected while studying for finals. Now they seemed not ready to give up the old school, the familiar paths and classrooms. Only a small percentage would be continuing on to college—one of the South's A & M (agricultural and mechanical) schools, which trained Negro youths to be carpenters, farmers, handymen, masons, maids, cooks and baby nurses. Their future rode heavily on their shoulders, and blinded them to the collective joy that had pervaded the lives of the boys and girls in the grammar school graduating class.

Parents who could afford it had ordered new shoes and ready-made clothes for themselves from Sears and Roebuck or Montgomery Ward. They also engaged the best seamstresses to make the floating graduating dresses and to cut down secondhand pants which would be pressed to a military slickness for the important event.

5    Oh, it was important, all right. Whitefolks would attend the ceremony, and two or three would speak of God and home, and the Southern way of life, and Mrs. Parsons, the principal's wife, would play the graduation march while the lower-grade graduates paraded down the aisles and took their seats below the platform. The high school seniors would wait in empty classrooms to make their dramatic entrance.

In the Store I was the person of the moment. The birthday girl. The center. Bailey[1] had graduated the year before, although to do so he had had to forfeit all pleasures to make up for his time lost in Baton Rouge.

---

[1]Angelou's brother. The store was run by Angelou's grandmother, whom she called Momma, and Momma's son, Uncle Willie. [Eds.]

My class was wearing butter-yellow piqué dresses, and Momma launched out on mine. She smocked the yoke into tiny crisscrossing puckers, then shirred the rest of the bodice. Her dark fingers ducked in and out of the lemony cloth as she embroidered raised daisies around the hem. Before she considered herself finished she had added a crocheted cuff on the puff sleeves, and a pointy crocheted collar.

I was going to be lovely. A walking model of all the various styles of fine hand sewing and it didn't worry me that I was only twelve years old and merely graduating from the eighth grade. Besides, many teachers in Arkansas Negro schools had only that diploma and were licensed to impart wisdom.

The days had become longer and more noticeable. The faded beige of former times had been replaced with strong and sure colors. I began to see my classmates' clothes, their skin tones, and the dust that waved off pussy willows. Clouds that lazed across the sky were objects of great concern to me. Their shiftier shapes might have held a message that in my new happiness and with a little bit of time I'd soon decipher. During that period I looked at the arch of heaven so religiously my neck kept a steady ache. I had taken to smiling more often, and my jaws hurt from the unaccustomed activity. Between the two physical sore spots, I suppose I could have been uncomfortable, but that was not the case. As a member of the winning team (the graduating class of 1940) I had outdistanced unpleasant sensations by miles. I was headed for the freedom of open fields.

Youth and social approval allied themselves with me and we trammeled memories of slights and insults. The wind of our swift passage remodeled my features. Lost tears were pounded to mud and then to dust. Years of withdrawal were brushed aside and left behind, as hanging ropes of parasitic moss.    10

My work alone had awarded me a top place and I was going to be one of the first called in the graduating ceremonies. On the classroom blackboard, as well as on the bulletin board in the auditorium, there were blue stars and white stars and red stars. No absences, no tardinesses, and my academic work was among the best of the year. I could say the preamble to the Constitution even faster than Bailey. We timed ourselves often: "WethepeopleoftheUnitedStatesinordertoformamoreperfectunion . . ." I had memorized the Presidents of the United States from Washington to Roosevelt in chronological as well as alphabetical order.

My hair pleased me too. Gradually the black mass had lengthened and thickened, so that it kept at last to its braided pattern, and I didn't have to yank my scalp off when I tried to comb it.

Louise and I had rehearsed the exercises until we tired out ourselves. Henry Reed was class valedictorian. He was a small, very black boy with hooded eyes, a long, broad nose and an oddly shaped head.

I had admired him for years because each term he and I vied for the best grades in our class. Most often he bested me, but instead of being disappointed I was pleased that we shared top places between us. Like many Southern Black children, he lived with his grandmother, who was as strict as Momma and as kind as she knew how to be. He was courteous, respectful and soft-spoken to elders, but on the playground he chose to play the roughest games. I admired him. Anyone, I reckoned, sufficiently afraid or sufficiently dull could be polite. But to be able to operate at a top level with both adults and children was admirable.

His valedictory speech was entitled "To Be or Not to Be." The rigid tenth-grade teacher had helped him write it. He'd been working on the dramatic stresses for months.

15      The weeks until graduation were filled with heady activities. A group of small children were to be presented in a play about buttercups and daisies and bunny rabbits. They could be heard throughout the building practicing their hops and their little songs that sounded like silver bells. The older girls (nongraduates, of course) were assigned the task of making refreshments for the night's festivities. A tangy scent of ginger, cinnamon, nutmeg and chocolate wafted around the home economics building as the budding cooks made samples for themselves and their teachers.

In every corner of the workshop, axes and saws split fresh timber as the woodshop boys made sets and stage scenery. Only the graduates were left out of the general bustle. We were free to sit in the library at the back of the building or look in quite detachedly, naturally, on the measures being taken for our event.

Even the minister preached on graduation the Sunday before. His subject was, "Let your light so shine that men will see your good works and praise your Father, Who is in Heaven." Although the sermon was purported to be addressed to us, he used the occasion to speak to backsliders, gamblers and general ne'er-do-wells. But since he had called our names at the beginning of the service we were mollified.

Among Negroes the tradition was to give presents to children going only from one grade to another. How much more important this was when the person was graduating at the top of the class. Uncle Willie and Momma had sent away for a Mickey Mouse watch like Bailey's. Louise gave me four embroidered handkerchiefs. (I gave her crocheted doilies.) Mrs. Sneed, the minister's wife, made me an undershirt to wear for graduation, and nearly every customer gave me a nickel or maybe even a dime with the instruction "Keep on moving to higher ground," or some such encouragement.

Amazingly the great day finally dawned and I was out of bed before I knew it. I threw open the back door to see it more clearly, but Momma said, "Sister, come away from that door and put your robe on."

I hoped the memory of that morning would never leave me. Sun- 20 light was itself young, and the day had none of the insistence maturity would bring it in a few hours. In my robe and barefoot in the backyard, under cover of going to see about my new beans, I gave myself up to the gentle warmth and thanked God that no matter what evil I had done in my life He had allowed me to live to see this day. Somewhere in my fatalism I had expected to die, accidentally, and never have the chance to walk up the stairs in the auditorium and gracefully receive my hard-earned diploma. Out of God's merciful bosom I had won reprieve.

Bailey came out in his robe and gave me a box wrapped in Christmas paper. He said he had saved his money for months to pay for it. It felt like a box of chocolates, but I knew Bailey wouldn't save money to buy candy when we had all we could want under our noses.

He was as proud of the gift as I. It was a soft-leather-bound copy of a collection of poems by Edgar Allan Poe, or, as Bailey and I called him, "Eap." I turned to "Annabel Lee" and we walked up and down the garden rows, the cool dirt between our toes, reciting the beautifully sad lines.

Momma made a Sunday breakfast although it was only Friday. After we finished the blessing, I opened my eyes to find the watch on my plate. It was a dream of a day. Everything went smoothly and to my credit I didn't have to be reminded or scolded for anything. Near evening I was too jittery to attend to chores, so Bailey volunteered to do all before his bath.

Days before, we had made a sign for the Store, and as we turned out the lights Momma hung the cardboard over the doorknob. It read clearly: CLOSED. GRADUATION.

My dress fitted perfectly and everyone said that I looked like a 25 sunbeam in it. On the hill, going toward the school, Bailey walked behind with Uncle Willie, who muttered, "Go on, Ju." He wanted him to walk ahead with us because it embarrassed him to have to walk so slowly. Bailey said he'd let the ladies walk together, and the men would bring up the rear. We all laughed, nicely.

Little children dashed by out of the dark like fireflies. Their crepe-paper dresses and butterfly wings were not made for running and we heard more than one rip, dryly, and the regretful "uh uh" that followed.

The school blazed without gaiety. The windows seemed cold and unfriendly from the lower hill. A sense of ill-fated timing crept over me, and if Momma hadn't reached for my hand I would have drifted back to Bailey and Uncle Willie, and possibly beyond. She made a few slow jokes about my feet getting cold, and tugged me along to the now-strange building.

Around the front steps, assurance came back. There were my fellow "greats," the graduating class. Hair brushed back, legs oiled, new dresses and pressed pleats, fresh pocket handkerchiefs and little handbags, all homesewn. Oh, we were up to snuff, all right. I joined my comrades and didn't even see my family go in to find seats in the crowded auditorium.

The school band struck up a march and all classes filed in as had been rehearsed. We stood in front of our seats, as assigned, and on a signal from the choir director, we sat. No sooner had this been accomplished than the band started to play the national anthem. We rose again and sang the song, after which we recited the pledge of allegiance. We remained standing for a brief minute before the choir director and the principal signaled to us, rather desperately I thought, to take our seats. The command was so unusual that our carefully rehearsed and smooth-running machine was thrown off. For a full minute we fumbled for our chairs and bumped into each other awkwardly. Habits change or solidify under pressure, so in our state of nervous tension we had been ready to follow our usual assembly pattern: the American national anthem, then the pledge of allegiance, then the song every Black person I knew called the Negro National Anthem. All done in the same key, with the same passion and most often standing on the same foot.

30     Finding my seat at last, I was overcome with a presentiment of worse things to come. Something unrehearsed, unplanned, was going to happen, and we were going to be made to look bad. I distinctly remember being explicit in the choice of pronoun. It was "we," the graduating class, the unit, that concerned me then.

The principal welcomed "parents and friends" and asked the Baptist minister to lead us in prayer. His invocation was brief and punchy, and for a second I thought we were getting on the high road to right action. When the principal came back to the dais, however, his voice had changed. Sounds always affected me profoundly and the principal's voice was one of my favorites. During assembly it melted and lowed weakly into the audience. It had not been in my plan to listen to him, but my curiosity was piqued and I straightened up to give him my attention.

He was talking about Booker T. Washington, our "late great leader," who said we can be as close as the fingers on the hand, etc. . . . Then he said a few vague things about friendship and the friendship of kindly people to those less fortunate than themselves. With that his voice nearly faded, thin, away. Like a river diminishing to a stream and then to a trickle. But he cleared his throat and said, "Our speaker tonight, who is also our friend, came from Texarkana to deliver the commencement address, but due to the irregularity of the train schedule, he's going to, as they say, 'speak and run.'" He said that we understood and wanted the man to know that we were most grateful for the time he was able to give us and then something about how we were willing always to adjust to another's program, and without more ado—"I give you Mr. Edward Donleavy."

Not one but two white men came through the door off-stage. The shorter one walked to the speaker's platform, and the tall one moved to the center seat and sat down. But that was our principal's seat, and already occupied. The dislodged gentleman bounced around for a long breath or two before the Baptist minister gave him his chair, then with more dignity than the situation deserved, the minister walked off the stage.

Donleavy looked at the audience once (on reflection, I'm sure that he wanted only to reassure himself that we were really there), adjusted his glasses and began to read from a sheaf of papers.

He was glad "to be here and to see the work going on just as it was 35 in the other schools."

At the first "Amen" from the audience I willed the offender to immediate death by choking on the word. But Amens and Yes, sir's began to fall around the room like rain through a ragged umbrella.

He told us of the wonderful changes we children in Stamps had in store. The Central School (naturally, the white school was Central) had already been granted improvements that would be in use in the fall. A well-known artist was coming from Little Rock to teach art to them. They were going to have the newest microscopes and chemistry equipment for their laboratory. Mr. Donleavy didn't leave us long in the dark over who made these improvements available to Central High. Nor were we to be ignored in the general betterment scheme he had in mind.

He said that he had pointed out to people at a very high level that one of the first-line football tacklers at Arkansas Agricultural and Mechanical College had graduated from good old Lafayette County Training School. Here fewer Amen's were heard. Those few that did break through lay dully in the air with the heaviness of habit.

He went on to praise us. He went on to say how he had bragged that "one of the best basketball players at Fisk[2] sank his first ball right here at Lafayette County Training School."

The white kids were going to have a chance to become Galileos and 40 Madame Curies and Edisons and Gauguins,[3] and our boys (the girls weren't even in on it) would try to be Jesse Owenses and Joe Louises.[4]

Owens and the Brown Bomber were great heroes in our world, but what school official in the white-goddom of Little Rock had the right to

---

[2]Highly regarded, historically black university in Nashville. [Eds.]

[3]Inventors, scientists, and artists. [Eds.]

[4]The black track star and Olympic gold medalist, and the longtime world heavyweight boxing champion known as the "Brown Bomber." [Eds.]

decide that those two men must be our only heroes? Who decided that for Henry Reed to become a scientist he had to work like George Washington Carver, as a bootblack, to buy a lousy microscope? Bailey was obviously always going to be too small to be an athlete, so which concrete angel glued to what country seat had decided that if my brother wanted to become a lawyer he had to first pay penance for his skin by picking cotton and hoeing corn and studying correspondence books at night for twenty years?

The man's dead words fell like bricks around the auditorium and too many settled in my belly. Constrained by hard-learned manners I couldn't look behind me, but to my left and right the proud graduating class of 1940 had dropped their heads. Every girl in my row had found something new to do with her handkerchief. Some folded the tiny squares into love knots, some into triangles, but most were wadding them, then pressing them flat on their yellow laps.

On the dais, the ancient tragedy was being replayed. Professor Parsons sat, a sculptor's reject, rigid. His large, heavy body seemed devoid of will or willingness, and his eyes said he was no longer with us. The other teachers examined the flag (which was draped stage right) or their notes, or the windows which opened on our now-famous playing diamond.

Graduation, the hush-hush magic time of frills and gifts and congratulations and diplomas, was finished for me before my name was called. The accomplishment was nothing. The meticulous maps, drawn in three colors of ink, learning and spelling decasyllabic words, memorizing the whole of *The Rape of Lucrece*[5]—it was for nothing. Donleavy had exposed us.

45      We were maids and farmers, handymen and washerwomen, and anything higher that we aspired to was farcical and presumptuous.

Then I wished that Gabriel Prosser and Nat Turner[6] had killed all whitefolks in their beds and that Abraham Lincoln had been assassinated before the signing of the Emancipation Proclamation, and that Harriet Tubman[7] had been killed by that blow on her head and Christopher Columbus had drowned in the *Santa Maria.*

It was awful to be a Negro and have no control over my life. It was brutal to be young and already trained to sit quietly and listen to charges brought against my color with no chance of defense. We should all be dead. I thought I should like to see us all dead, one on top of the other. A pyramid of flesh with the whitefolks on the bottom, as the broad base, then the Indians with their silly tomahawks and teepees and wigwams and treaties, the Negroes with their mops and recipes and cotton sacks and spirituals sticking out of their mouths. The Dutch

---

[5]*The Rape of Lucrece* is a long narrative poem by Shakespeare. [Eds.]

[6]Prosser and Turner both led slave rebellions. [Eds.]

[7]Harriet Tubman (1820–1913) was an African-American abolitionist who became one of the most successful guides on the Underground Railroad. [Eds.]

children should all stumble in their wooden shoes and break their necks. The French should choke to death on the Louisiana Purchase (1803) while silkworms ate all the Chinese with their stupid pigtails. As a species, we were an abomination. All of us.

Donleavy was running for election, and assured our parents that if he won we could count on having the only colored paved playing field in that part of Arkansas. Also—he never looked up to acknowledge the grunts of acceptance—also, we were bound to get some new equipment for the home economics building and the workshop.

He finished, and since there was no need to give any more than the most perfunctory thank-you's, he nodded to the men on the stage, and the tall white man who was never introduced joined him at the door. They left with the attitude that now they were off to something really important. (The graduation ceremonies at Lafayette County Training School had been a mere preliminary.)

The ugliness they left was palpable. An uninvited guest who wouldn't leave. The choir was summoned and sang a modern arrangement of "Onward, Christian Soldiers," with new words pertaining to graduates seeking their place in the world. But it didn't work. Elouise, the daughter of the Baptist minister, recited "Invictus,"[8] and I could have cried at the impertinence of "I am the master of my fate, I am the captain of my soul."

My name had lost its ring of familiarity and I had to be nudged to go and receive my diploma. All my preparations had fled. I neither marched up to the stage like a conquering Amazon, nor did I look in the audience for Bailey's nod of approval. Marguerite Johnson,[9] I heard the name again, my honors were read, there were noises in the audience of appreciation, and I took my place on the stage as rehearsed.

I thought about colors I hated: ecru, puce, lavender, beige and black.

There was shuffling and rustling around me, then Henry Reed was giving his valedictory address, "To Be or Not to Be." Hadn't he heard the whitefolks? We couldn't be, so the question was a waste of time. Henry's voice came out clear and strong. I feared to look at him. Hadn't he got the message? There was no "nobler in the mind" for Negroes because the world didn't think we had minds, and they let us know it. "Outrageous fortune"? Now, that was a joke. When the ceremony was over I had to tell Henry Reed some things. That is, if I still cared. Not "rub," Henry, "erase." "Ah, there's the erase." Us.

Henry had been a good student in elocution. His voice rose on tides of promise and fell on waves of warnings. The English teacher had

---

[8]An inspirational poem written in 1875 by William Ernest Henley (1849–1903). Its defiant and stoic sentiments made it extremely popular with nineteenth-century readers. [Eds.]

[9]Angelou's given name. [Eds.]

helped him to create a sermon winging through Hamlet's soliloquy. To be a man, a doer, a builder, a leader, or to be a tool, an unfunny joke, a crusher of funky toadstools. I marveled that Henry could go through with the speech as if we had a choice.

55  I had been listening and silently rebutting each sentence with my eyes closed; then there was a hush, which in an audience warns that something unplanned is happening. I looked up and saw Henry Reed, the conservative, the proper, the A student, turn his back to the audience and turn to us (the proud graduating class of 1940) and sing, nearly speaking,

> "Lift ev'ry voice and sing
> Till earth and heaven ring
> Ring with the harmonies of Liberty . . ."

It was the poem written by James Weldon Johnson. It was the music composed by J. Rosamond Johnson. It was the Negro national anthem. Out of habit we were singing it.

Our mothers and fathers stood in the dark hall and joined the hymn of encouragement. A kindergarten teacher led the small children onto the stage and the buttercups and daisies and bunny rabbits marked time and tried to follow:

> "Stony the road we trod
> Bitter the chastening rod
> Felt in the days when hope, unborn, had died.
> Yet with a steady beat
> Have not our weary feet
> Come to the place for which our fathers sighed?"

Each child I knew had learned that song with his ABC's and along with "Jesus Loves Me This I Know." But I personally had never heard it before. Never heard the words, despite the thousands of times I had sung them. Never thought they had anything to do with me.

On the other hand, the words of Patrick Henry had made such an impression on me that I had been able to stretch myself tall and trembling and say, "I know not what course others may take, but as for me, give me liberty or give me death."

60  And now I heard, really for the first time:

> "We have come over a way that with tears
> has been watered,
> We have come, treading our path through
> the blood of the slaughtered."

While echoes of the song shivered in the air, Henry Reed bowed his head, said "Thank you," and returned to his place in the line. The tears that slipped down many faces were not wiped away in shame.

We were on top again. As always, again. We survived. The depths had been icy and dark, but now a bright sun spoke to our souls. I was no longer simply a member of the proud graduating class of 1940; I was a proud member of the wonderful, beautiful Negro race.

Oh, Black known and unknown poets, how often have your auctioned pains sustained us? Who will compute the lonely nights made less lonely by your songs, or the empty pots made less tragic by your tales?

If we were a people much given to revealing secrets, we might raise monuments and sacrifice to the memories of our poets, but slavery cured us of that weakness. It may be enough, however, to have it said that we survive in exact relationship to the dedication of our poets (include preachers, musicians and blues singers).

## Responding to Reading

1. Angelou's graduation took place in 1940. What expectations did educators have for Angelou and her classmates? How were these expectations different from the expectations Angelou and her fellow students had?
2. In what sense did Mr. Donleavy's speech "educate" the graduates? How did Angelou's thinking change as she listened to him?
3. In paragraph 62, Angelou says, "We were on top again." In what sense were she and the graduates "on top"? Do you think Angelou is being overly optimistic in light of what she had just experienced?

## Responding in Writing

In the 1954 *Brown v. Board of Education* decision, the Supreme Court of the United States ruled that the "separate but equal" education that Angelou experienced was unconstitutional. How do you suppose her education would have been different had she attended high school in 1960 instead of in 1940?

# THE GOOD IMMIGRANT STUDENT

## Bich Minh Nguyen

### 1974–

*Bich Minh Nguyen is an associate professor of English and the director of Asian-American Studies at Purdue University and winner of the PEN American Center's 2005 PEN/Jerard Award in nonfiction for her memoir,* Stealing Buddha's Dinner *(2007). She has also coedited three anthologies and written for* Gourmet *magazine, the* Chicago Tribune, *and other publications. Her latest work is a novel,* Short Girls *(2009). In the following essay, Nguyen explores the implications of bilingual education for immigrants in America.*

My stepmother, Rosa, who began dating my father when I was three years old, says that my sister and I used to watch *Police Woman* and rapturously repeat everything Angie Dickinson said. But when the show was over Anh and I would resume our Vietnamese, whispering together, giggling in accents. Rosa worried about this. She had the idea that she could teach us English and we could teach her Vietnamese. She would make us lunch or give us baths, speaking slowly and asking us how to say *water*, or *rice*, or *house*.

After she and my father married, Rosa swept us out of our falling-down house and into middle-class suburban Grand Rapids, Michigan. Our neighborhood surrounded Ken-O-Sha Elementary School and Plaster Creek, and was only a short drive away from the original Meijer's Thrifty Acres. In the early 1980s, this neighborhood of mis-matching street names—Poinsettia, Van Auken, Senora, Ravanna—was home to families of Dutch heritage, and everyone was Christian Reformed, and conservative Republican. Except us. Even if my father hadn't left his rusted-through silver Mustang, the first car he ever owned, to languish in the driveway for months we would have stuck out simply because we weren't white. There was my Latina stepmother and her daughter, Cristina; my father, sister, grandmother, and I, refu-gees from Saigon; and my half-brother born a year after we moved to the house on Ravanna Street.

Although my family lived two blocks from Ken-O-Sha, my step-mother enrolled me and Anh at Sherwood Elementary, a bus ride away, because Sherwood had a bilingual education program. Rosa, who had a master's in education and taught ESL and community ed in the pub-lic school system, was a big supporter of bilingual education. School mornings, Anh and I would be at the bus stop at the corner of our street quite early, hustled out of the house by our grandmother who con-stantly feared we would miss our chance. I went off to first grade, Anh to second. At ten o'clock, we crept out of our classes, drawing glances and whispers from the other students, and convened with a group of Vietnamese kids from other grades to learn English. The teachers were Mr. Ho, who wore a lot of short-sleeved button-down shirts in neutral hues, and Miss Huong, who favored a maroon blouse with puffy shoul-ders and slight ruffles at the high neck and wrists, paired with a tweed skirt that hung heavily to her ankles. They passed out photocopied booklets of Vietnamese phrases and their English translations, with themes such as "In the Grocery Store." They asked us to repeat slowly after them and took turns coming around to each of us, bending close to hear our pronunciations.

Anh and I exchanged a lot of worried glances, for we had a secret that we were quite embarrassed about: we already knew English. It was the Vietnamese part that gave us trouble. When Mr. Ho and Miss Huong gave instructions, or passed out homework assignments, they did so in Vietnamese. Anh and I received praise for our English, but were reprimanded for failing to complete our assignments and failing to pay attention. After a couple of weeks of this Anh announced to Rosa that we didn't need bilingual education. Nonsense, she said. Our father just shrugged his shoulders. After that, Anh began skipping bilingual classes, urging me to do the same, and then we never went back. What was amazing was that no one, not Mrs. Eunice, my first grade teacher, or Mrs. Hankins, Anh's teacher, or even Mr. Ho or Miss Huong said anything directly to us about it. Or if they did, I have forgotten it entirely. Then one day my parents got a call from Miss Huong. When Rosa came to talk to me and Anh about it we were watching television the way kids do, sitting alarmingly close to the screen. Rosa confronted us with "Do you girls know English?" Then she suddenly said, "Do you know Vietnamese?" I can't remember what we replied to either question.

For many years, a towering old billboard over the expressway 5 downtown proudly declared Grand Rapids "An All-American City." For me, that all-American designation meant all-white. I couldn't believe (and still don't) that they meant to include the growing Mexican-American population, or the sudden influx of Vietnamese refugees in 1975. I often thought it a rather mean-spirited prank of some administrator at the INS, deciding with a flourish of a signature to send a thousand refugees to Grand Rapids, a city that boasted having more churches per square mile than any other city in the United States. Did that administrator know what Grand Rapids was like? That in school, everywhere I turned, and often when I closed my eyes, I saw blond blond blond? The point of bilingual education was assimilation. To my stepmother, the point was preservation: she didn't want English to take over wholly, pushing the Vietnamese out of our heads. She was too ambitious. Anh and I were Americanized as soon as we turned on the television. Today, bilingual education is supposed to have become both a method of assimilation and a method of preservation, an effort to prove that kids can have it both ways. They can supposedly keep English for school and their friends and keep another language for home and family.

In Grand Rapids, Michigan, in the 1980s, I found that an impossible task.

I transferred to Ken-O-Sha Elementary in time for third grade, after Rosa finally admitted that taking the bus all the way to Sherwood was pointless. I was glad to transfer, eager to be part of a class that wasn't, in my mind, tainted with the knowledge of my bilingual stigma. Third grade was led by Mrs. Alexander, an imperious, middle-aged woman of many plaid skirts held safe by giant gold safety pins. She had a habit of turning her wedding ring around and around her finger while she stood at the chalkboard. Mrs. Alexander had an intricate system of rewards for good grades and good behavior, denoted by colored star stickers on a piece of poster board that loomed over us all. One glance and you could see who was behind, who was striding ahead.

I was an insufferably good student, with perfect Palmer cursive and the highest possible scores in every subject. I had learned this trick at Sherwood. That the quieter you are, the shyer and sweeter and better-at-school you are, the more the teacher will let you alone. Mrs. Alexander should have let me alone. For, in addition to my excellent marks, I was nearly silent, deadly shy, and wholly obedient. My greatest fear was being called on, or in any way standing out more than I already did in the class that was, except for me and one black student, dough-white. I got good grades because I feared the authority of the teacher; I felt that getting in good with Mrs. Alexander would protect me, that she would protect me from the frightful rest of the world. But Mrs. Alexander was not agreeable to this notion. If it was my turn to read aloud during reading circle, she'd interrupt me to snap, "You're reading too fast" or demand, "What does that word mean?" Things she did not do to the other students. Anh, when I told her about this, suggested that perhaps Mrs. Alexander liked me and wanted to help me get smarter. But neither of us believed it. You know when a teacher likes you and when she doesn't.

Secretly, I admired and envied the rebellious kids, like Robbie Andrews who came to school looking bleary-eyed and pinched, like a hungover adult; Robbie and his ilk snapped back at teachers, were routinely sent to the principal's office, were even spanked a few times with the principal's infamous red paddle (apparently no one in Grand Rapids objected to corporal punishment). Those kids made noise, possessed something I thought was confidence, self-knowledge, allowing them to marvelously question everything ordered of them. They had the ability to challenge the given world.

10    Toward the middle of third grade Mrs. Alexander introduced a stuffed lion to the pool of rewards: the best student of the week would earn the privilege of having the lion sit on his or her desk for the entire week. My quantity of gold stars was neck and neck with that of my two competitors, Brenda and Jennifer, both sweet-eyed blond girls with pastel-colored monogrammed sweaters and neatly tied Dock-Sides. My family did not have a lot of money and my stepmother had terrible taste. Thus I attended school in such ensembles as dark red parachute pants and a nubby pink sweater stitched with a picture of a unicorn rearing up. This only propelled me to try harder to be good, to make up for everything I felt was against me: my odd family, my race, my very face. And I craved that stuffed lion. Week after week, the lion perched on Brenda's desk or Jennifer's desk. Meanwhile, the class spelling bee approached. I didn't know I was such a good speller until I won it, earning a scalloped-edged certificate and a candy bar.

That afternoon I started toward home, then remembered I'd forgotten my rain boots in my locker. I doubled back to school and overheard Mrs. Alexander in the classroom talking to another teacher. "Can you believe it?" Mrs. Alexander was saying. "A foreigner winning our spelling bee!"

I waited for the stuffed lion the rest of that year, with a kind of patience I have no patience for today. To no avail. In June, on the last day of school, Mrs. Alexander gave the stuffed lion to Brenda to keep forever.

The first time I had to read aloud something I had written—perhaps it was in fourth grade—I felt such terror, such a need not to have any attention upon me, that I convinced myself that I had become invisible, that the teacher could never call on me because she couldn't see me.

More than once, I was given the assignment of writing a report about my family history. I loathed this task, for I was dreadfully aware that my history could not be faked; it already showed on my face. When my turn came to read out loud the teacher had to ask me several times to speak louder. Some kids, a few of them older, in different classes, took to pressing back the corners of their eyes with the heels of their palms while they chanted, "Ching-chong, ching-chong!" during recess. (This continued until Anh, who was far tougher than me, threatened to beat them up.)

I have no way of telling what tortured me more: the actual snickers and remarks and watchfulness of my classmates, or my own imagination, conjuring disdain. My own sense of shame. At times I felt sickened by my obedience, my accumulation of gold stickers, my every effort to be invisible.

Yet Robbie Andrews must have felt the same kind of claustrophobia, trapped in his own reputation, in his inability to be otherwise. I learned in school that changing oneself is not easy, that the world makes up its mind quickly.  15

I've heard that Robbie dropped out of high school, got a girl pregnant, found himself in and out of first juvenile detention, then jail.

What comes out of difference? What constitutes difference? Such questions, academic and unanswered, popped up in every other course description in college. But the idea of difference is easy to come by, especially in school; it is shame, the permutations and inversions of difference and self-loathing, that we should be worrying about.

Imagined torment, imagined scorn. When what is imagined and what is desired turn on each other.

Some kids want to rebel; other kids want to disappear. I wanted to disappear. I was not brave enough to shrug my shoulders and flaunt my difference; because I could not disappear into the crowd, I wished to disappear entirely. Anyone might have mistaken this for passivity.

20      Once, at the end of my career at Sherwood Elementary, I disappeared on the bus home. Mine was usually the third stop, but that day the bus driver thought I wasn't there, and she sailed right by the corner of Ravanna and Senora. I said nothing. The bus wove its way downtown, and for the first time I got to see where other children lived, some of them in clean orderly neighborhoods, some near houses with sagging porches and boarded-up windows. All the while, the kid sitting across the aisle from me played the same cheerful song over and over on his portable boom box. *Pass the doochee from the left hand side, pass the doochee from the left hand side.* He and his brother turned out to be the last kids off the bus. Then the bus driver saw me through the rearview mirror. She walked back to where I was sitting and said, "How come you didn't get off at your stop?" I shook my head, don't know. She sighed and drove me home.

I was often doing that, shaking my head silently or staring up wordlessly. I realize that while I remember so much of what other people said when I was a child, I remember little of what I said. Probably because I didn't say much at all.

I recently came across in the stacks of the University of Michigan library *A Manual for Indochinese Refugee Education 1976–1977.* Some of it is silly, but much of it is a painstaking, fairly thoughtful effort to let school administrators and teachers know how to go about sensitively handling the influx of Vietnamese children in the public schools. Here is one of the most wonderful items of advice: "The Vietnamese child, even the older child, is also reported to be afraid of the dark, and more often than not, believes in ghosts. A teacher may have to be a little more solicitous of the child on gloomy, wintery days." Perhaps if Mrs. Alexander had read this, she would not have upbraided me so often for tracking mud into the classroom on rainy days. In third grade I was horrified and ashamed of my muddy shoes. I hung back, trying to duck behind this or that dark-haired boy. In spite of this, in spite of bilingual education, and shyness, and all that wordless shaking of my head, I was sent off every Monday to the Spectrum School for the Gifted and Talented. I still have no idea who selected me, who singled me out. Spectrum was (and still is) a public school program that invited students from every public elementary school to meet once a week and take specialized classes on topics such as the Middle Ages, Ellis Island, and fairy tales. Each student chose two classes, a major and minor, and for the rest of the semester worked toward final projects in both. I loved going to Spectrum. Not only did the range of students from other schools prove to be diverse, I found myself feeling more comfortable, mainly because Spectrum encouraged individual work. And the teachers seemed happy to be there. The best teacher at Spectrum was Mrs. King, whom every student adored. I still remember the soft gray sweaters she wore, her big wavy hair, her art-class handwriting, the way she'd often tell us to close our eyes when she read us a particular story or passage.

I believe that I figured out how to stop disappearing, how to talk and answer, even speak up, after several years in Spectrum. I was still deeply self-conscious, but I became able, sometimes, to maneuver around it.

Spectrum may have spoiled me a little, because it made me think about college and freedom, and thus made all the years in between disappointing and annoying.

In seventh grade I joined Anh and Cristina at the City School, a  25 seventh through twelfth grade public school in the Grand Rapids system that served as an early charter school; admission was by interview, and each grade had about fifty students. The City School had the advantage of being downtown, perched over old cobblestone roads, and close to the main public library. Art and music history were required. There were no sports teams. And volunteering was mandatory. But kids didn't tend to stay at City School; as they got older they transferred to one of the big high schools nearby, perhaps wishing to play sports, perhaps wishing to get away from City's rather brutal academic system. Each half semester, after grades were doled out, giant dot-matrix printouts of everyone's GPAs were posted in the hallways.

I didn't stay at City, either. When my family moved to a different suburb, my stepmother promptly transferred me to Forest Hills Northern High School. Most of the students there came from upper-middle-class or very well-to-do families; the ones who didn't stood out sharply. The rich kids were the same as they were anywhere in America: they wore a lot of Esprit and Guess, drove nice cars, and ran student council, prom, and sports. These kids strutted down the hallways; the boys sat in a row on the long windowsill near a group of lockers, whistling or calling out to girls who walked by. Girls gathered in bathrooms with their Clinique lipsticks.

High school was the least interesting part of my education, but I did accomplish something: I learned to forget myself a little. I learned the sweetness of apathy. And through apathy, how to forget my skin and body for a minute or two, almost not caring what would happen if I walked into a room late and all heads swiveled toward me. I learned the pleasure that reveals itself in the loss, no matter how slight, of self-consciousness. These things occurred because I remained the good immigrant student, without raising my hand often or showing off what I knew. Doing work was rote, and I went along to get along. I've never gotten over the terror of being called on in class, or the dread in knowing that I'm expected to contribute to class discussion. But there is a slippage between being good and being unnoticed, and in that sliver of freedom I learned what it could feel like to walk in the world in plain, unself-conscious view.

I would like to make a broad, accurate statement about immigrant children in schools. I would like to speak for them (us). I hesitate; I cannot. My own sister, for instance, was never as shy as I was. Anh disliked school from the start, choosing rebellion rather than silence. It was a good arrangement: I wrote papers for her and she paid me in money or candy; she gave me rides to school if I promised not to tell anyone about her cigarettes. Still, I think of an Indian friend of mine who told of an elementary school experience in which a blond schoolchild told the teacher, "I can't sit by her. My mom said I can't sit by anyone who's brown." And another friend, whose family immigrated around the same time mine did, whose second grade teacher used her as a vocabulary example: "Children, this is what a *foreigner* is." And sometimes I fall into thinking that kids today have the advantage of so much more wisdom, that they are so much more socially and politically aware than anyone was when I was in school. But I am wrong, of course. I know not every kid is fortunate enough to have a teacher like Mrs. King, or a program like Spectrum, or even the benefit of a manual written by a group of concerned educators; I know that some kids want to disappear and disappear until they actually do. Sometimes I think I see them, in the blurry background of a magazine photo, or in a gaggle of kids following a teacher's aide across the street. The kids with heads bent down, holding themselves in such a way that they seem to be self-conscious even of how they breathe. Small, shy, quiet kids, such good, good kids, *immigrant, foreigner,* their eyes watchful and waiting for whatever judgment will occur. I reassure myself that they will grow up fine, they will be okay. Maybe I cross the same street, then another, glancing back once in a while to see where they are going.

## Responding to Reading

1. What does Nguyen mean when she says that today bilingual education is supposed to be "both a method of assimilation and a method of preservation" (5)? Does she believe this assessment is accurate?
2. In paragraph 17, Nguyen asks, "What comes out of difference? What constitutes difference?" How does she answer these questions? In what way does her own sense of difference affect her education?
3. What is "the good immigrant student"? How did Nguyen's education reinforce this stereotype? How did it help her move beyond it?

## Responding in Writing

In paragraph 28, Nguyen says, "I would like to make a broad, accurate statement about immigrant children in schools. I would like to speak for them (us). I hesitate; I cannot." What do you think she means? Why can't she make "a broad, accurate statement"?

# SHOULD THE OBAMA GENERATION DROP OUT?

## Charles Murray

### 1943–

*A scholar at the American Enterprise Institute for Public Policy Research, Charles Murray has written extensively on social issues ranging from the history of liberal education to welfare reform. His latest books are* Real Education: Four Simple Truths for Bringing America's Schools Back to Reality *(2008) and* Coming Apart: The State of White America, 1960–2010 *(2012). In the following provocative essay, Murray questions the value of a college degree.*

Barack Obama has two attractive ideas for improving post-secondary education—expanding the use of community colleges and tuition tax credits—but he needs to hitch them to a broader platform. As president, Mr. Obama should use his bully pulpit to undermine the bachelor's degree as a job qualification. Here's a suggested battle cry, to be repeated in every speech on the subject: "It's what you can do that should count when you apply for a job, not where you learned to do it."

The residential college leading to a bachelor's degree at the end of four years works fine for the children of parents who have plenty of money. It works fine for top students from all backgrounds who are drawn toward academics. But most 18-year-olds are not from families with plenty of money, not top students, and not drawn toward academics. They want to learn how to get a satisfying job that also pays well. That almost always means education beyond high school, but it need not mean four years on a campus, nor cost a small fortune. It need not mean getting a bachelor's degree.

I am not discounting the merits of a liberal education. Students at every level should be encouraged to explore subjects that will not be part of their vocation. It would be even better if more colleges required a rigorous core curriculum for students who seek a traditional bachelor's degree. My beef is not with liberal education, but with the use of the degree as a job qualification.

For most of the nation's youths, making the bachelor's degree a job qualification means demanding a credential that is beyond their reach. It is a truth that politicians and educators cannot bring themselves to say out loud: A large majority of young people do not have the intellectual ability to do genuine college-level work.

If you doubt it, go back and look through your old college text- 5 books, and then do a little homework on the reading ability of high school seniors. About 10 percent to 20 percent of all 18-year-olds can absorb the material in your old liberal arts textbooks. For engineering and the hard sciences, the percentage is probably not as high as 10.

No improvements in primary and secondary education will do more than tweak those percentages. The core disciplines taught at a true college level are tough, requiring high levels of linguistic and logical-mathematical ability. Those abilities are no more malleable than athletic or musical talent.

You think I'm too pessimistic? Too elitist? Readers who graduated with honors in English literature or Renaissance history should ask themselves if they could have gotten a B.S. in physics, no matter how hard they tried. (I wouldn't have survived freshman year.) Except for the freakishly gifted, all of us are too dumb to get through college in many majors.

But I'm not thinking just about students who are not smart enough to deal with college-level material. Many young people who have the intellectual ability to succeed in rigorous liberal arts courses don't want to. For these students, the distribution requirements of the college degree do not open up new horizons. They are bothersome time-wasters.

A century ago, these students would happily have gone to work after high school. Now they know they need to acquire additional skills, but they want to treat college as vocational training, not as a leisurely journey to well-roundedness.

10    As more and more students who cannot get or don't want a liberal education have appeared on campuses, colleges have adapted by expanding the range of courses and adding vocationally oriented majors. That's appropriate. What's not appropriate is keeping the bachelor's degree as the measure of job preparedness, as the minimal requirement to get your foot in the door for vast numbers of jobs that don't really require a B.A. or B.S.

Discarding the bachelor's degree as a job qualification would not be difficult. The solution is to substitute certification tests, which would provide evidence that the applicant has acquired the skills the employer needs.

Certification tests can take many forms. For some jobs, a multiple-choice test might be appropriate. But there's no reason to limit certifications to academic tests. For centuries, the crafts have used work samples to certify journeymen and master craftsmen. Today, many computer programmers without college degrees get jobs by presenting examples of their work. With a little imagination, almost any corporation can come up with analogous work samples.

The benefits of discarding the bachelor's degree as a job qualification would be huge for both employers and job applicants. Certifications would tell employers far more about their applicants' qualifications than a B.A. does, and hundreds of thousands of young people would be able to get what they want from post-secondary education without having to twist themselves into knots to comply with the rituals of getting a bachelor's degree.

Certification tests would not eliminate the role of innate ability—the most gifted applicants would still have an edge—but they would strip away much of the unwarranted halo effect that goes with a degree from a prestigious university. They would put everyone under the same spotlight.

Discrediting the bachelor's degree is within reach because so many 15 employers already sense that it has become education's Wizard of Oz. All we need is someone willing to yank the curtain aside. Barack Obama is ideally positioned to do it. He just needs to say it over and over: "It's what you can do that should count when you apply for a job, not where you learned to do it."

## Responding to Reading

1. Why does Murray think it is a mistake to make a college degree a job qualification? Why does he think this goal is not realistic for most high school students?
2. What objections to his ideas does Murray mention? Do you think he successfully addresses these objections?
3. What job qualification does Murray think should replace a college degree? What are the benefits of "discarding the bachelor's degree as a job qualification" (11)?

## Responding in Writing

After reading Murray's op-ed, several people wrote letters to the editor in which they voiced the following objections to his ideas:

- Murray's "reforms" would institute a class system in the United States.

- Liberal arts courses teach skills our country desperately needs.

- A liberal arts degree shows an employer that an applicant has the ability to accomplish something.

- A liberal arts degree teaches students how to learn.

Which of these objections to Murray's ideas do you think is the most convincing? Which is the least convincing? Write two paragraphs in which you express your views.

# HOW TO GET A REAL EDUCATION

## Scott Adams

### 1957–

*Scott Adams is the creator of* Dilbert, *the long-running comic strip about office mediocrity. He is also the author of more than eighty comic books featuring the antics of Dilbert and his coworkers, including, most recently,* I'm Tempted to Stop Acting Randomly: Dilbert *(2010). In the following essay, Adams outlines the ideal education for entrepreneurs.*

I understand why the top students in America study physics, chemistry, calculus and classic literature. The kids in this brainy group are the future professors, scientists, thinkers and engineers who will propel civilization forward. But why do we make B students sit through these same classes? That's like trying to train your cat to do your taxes—a waste of time and money. Wouldn't it make more sense to teach B students something useful, like entrepreneurship?

I speak from experience because I majored in entrepreneurship at Hartwick College in Oneonta, N.Y. Technically, my major was economics. But the unsung advantage of attending a small college is that you can mold your experience any way you want.

There was a small business on our campus called The Coffee House. It served beer and snacks, and featured live entertainment. It was managed by students, and it was a money-losing mess, subsidized by the college. I thought I could make a difference, so I applied for an opening as the so-called Minister of Finance. I landed the job, thanks to my impressive interviewing skills, my can-do attitude and the fact that everyone else in the solar system had more interesting plans.

The drinking age in those days was 18, and the entire compensation package for the managers of The Coffee House was free beer. That goes a long way toward explaining why the accounting system consisted of seven students trying to remember where all the money went. I thought we could do better. So I proposed to my accounting professor that for three course credits I would build and operate a proper accounting system for the business. And so I did. It was a great experience. Meanwhile, some of my peers were taking courses in art history so they'd be prepared to remember what art looked like just in case anyone asked.

5      One day the managers of The Coffee House had a meeting to discuss two topics. First, our Minister of Employment was recommending that we fire a bartender, who happened to be one of my best friends. Second, we needed to choose a leader for our group. On the first question, there was a general consensus that my friend lacked both the will and the potential to master the bartending arts. I reluctantly voted with the majority to fire him.

But when it came to discussing who should be our new leader, I pointed out that my friend—the soon-to-be-fired bartender—was tall, good-looking and so gifted at b.s. that he'd be the perfect leader. By the end of the meeting I had persuaded the group to fire the worst bartender that any of us had ever seen . . . and ask him if he would consider being our leader. My friend nailed the interview and became our Commissioner. He went on to do a terrific job. That was the year I learned everything I know about management.

At about the same time, this same friend, along with my roommate and me, hatched a plan to become the student managers of our dormitory and to get paid to do it. The idea involved replacing all of the professional staff, including the resident assistant, security guard and even the cleaning crew, with students who would be paid to do the work. We imagined forming a dorm government to manage elections for various jobs, set out penalties for misbehavior and generally take care of business. And we imagined that the three of us, being the visionaries for this scheme, would run the show.

We pitched our entrepreneurial idea to the dean and his staff. To our surprise, the dean said that if we could get a majority of next year's dorm residents to agree to our scheme, the college would back it.

It was a high hurdle, but a loophole made it easier to clear. We only needed a majority of students who said they *planned* to live in the dorm next year. And we had plenty of friends who were happy to plan just about anything so long as they could later change their minds. That's the year I learned that if there's a loophole, someone's going to drive a truck through it, and the people in the truck will get paid better than the people under it.

The dean required that our first order of business in the fall would  10 be creating a dorm constitution and getting it ratified. That sounded like a nightmare to organize. To save time, I wrote the constitution over the summer and didn't mention it when classes resumed. We held a constitutional convention to collect everyone's input, and I listened to two hours of diverse opinions. At the end of the meeting I volunteered to take on the daunting task of crafting a document that reflected all of the varied and sometimes conflicting opinions that had been aired. I waited a week, made copies of the document that I had written over the summer, presented it to the dorm as their own ideas and watched it get approved in a landslide vote. That was the year I learned everything I know about getting buy-in.

For the next two years my friends and I each had a private room at no cost, a base salary and the experience of managing the dorm. On some nights I also got paid to do overnight security, while also getting paid to clean the laundry room. At the end of my security shift I would go to The Coffee House and balance the books.

My college days were full of entrepreneurial stories of this sort. When my friends and I couldn't get the gym to give us space for our informal games of indoor soccer, we considered our options. The gym's rule was that only organized groups could reserve time. A few days later we took another run at it, but this time we were an organized soccer club, and I was the president. My executive duties included filling out a form to register the club and remembering to bring the ball.

By the time I graduated, I had mastered the strange art of transforming nothing into something. Every good thing that has happened to me as an adult can be traced back to that training. Several years later, I finished my MBA at Berkeley's Haas School of Business. That was the fine-tuning I needed to see the world through an entrepreneur's eyes.

If you're having a hard time imagining what an education in entrepreneurship should include, allow me to prime the pump with some lessons I've learned along the way.

## Combine Skills

15    The first thing you should learn in a course on entrepreneurship is how to make yourself valuable. It's unlikely that any average student can develop a world-class skill in one particular area. But it's easy to learn how to do several different things fairly well. I succeeded as a cartoonist with negligible art talent, some basic writing skills, an ordinary sense of humor and a bit of experience in the business world. The "Dilbert" comic is a combination of all four skills. The world has plenty of better artists, smarter writers, funnier humorists and more experienced business people. The rare part is that each of those modest skills is collected in one person. That's how value is created.

## Fail Forward

If you're taking risks, and you probably should, you can find yourself failing 90% of the time. The trick is to get paid while you're doing the failing and to use the experience to gain skills that will be useful later. I failed at my first career in banking. I failed at my second career with the phone company. But you'd be surprised at how many of the skills I learned in those careers can be applied to almost any field, including cartooning. Students should be taught that failure is a process, not an obstacle.

## Find the Action

In my senior year of college I asked my adviser how I should pursue my goal of being a banker. He told me to figure out where the most innovation in banking was happening and to move there. And so I did.

Banking didn't work out for me, but the advice still holds: Move to where the action is. Distance is your enemy.

## Attract Luck

You can't manage luck directly, but you can manage your career in a way that makes it easier for luck to find you. To succeed, first you must *do* something. And if that doesn't work, which can be 90% of the time, do something else. Luck finds the doers. Readers of the *Journal*[1] will find this point obvious. It's not obvious to a teenager.

## Conquer Fear

I took classes in public speaking in college and a few more during my corporate days. That training was marginally useful for learning how to mask nervousness in public. Then I took the Dale Carnegie course. It was life-changing. The Dale Carnegie method ignores speaking technique entirely and trains you instead to enjoy the experience of speaking to a crowd. Once you become relaxed in front of people, technique comes automatically. Over the years, I've given speeches to hundreds of audiences and enjoyed every minute on stage. But this isn't a plug for Dale Carnegie. The point is that people can be trained to replace fear and shyness with enthusiasm. Every entrepreneur can use that skill.

## Write Simply

I took a two-day class in business writing that taught me how to write 20 direct sentences and to avoid extra words. Simplicity makes ideas powerful. Want examples? Read anything by Steve Jobs or Warren Buffett.

## Learn Persuasion

Students of entrepreneurship should learn the art of persuasion in all its forms, including psychology, sales, marketing, negotiating, statistics and even design. Usually those skills are sprinkled across several disciplines. For entrepreneurs, it makes sense to teach them as a package.

That's my starter list for the sort of classes that would serve B students well. The list is not meant to be complete. Obviously an entrepreneur would benefit from classes in finance, management and more.

Remember, children are our future, and the majority of them are B students. If that doesn't scare you, it probably should.

---

[1] The *Wall Street Journal*. [Eds.]

## Responding to Reading

1. Adams says that making B students take physics and classic literature is "like trying to train your cat to do your taxes—a waste of time and money" (1). Do you think this analogy makes sense? Do you agree with the point Adams is making here?
2. Adams says that during the year he worked at The Coffee Shop and as a student manager of his dorm, he learned everything he knows today about management and buy-ins. What did he learn?
3. Adams lists classes that he thinks would benefit B students. Do you agree with his suggestions? What other classes should he have included?

## Responding in Writing

In paragraph 16, Adams says, "failure is a process, not an obstacle." What do you think he means? Explain why you agree or disagree with his statement.

# ONLINE HIGHER EDUCATION'S
# INDIVIDUALIST FALLACY
## Johann N. Neem

*An associate professor of history at Western Washington University, Johann N. Neem specializes in the history of the early American republic. He is the author of* Creating a Nation of Joiners: Democracy and Civil Society in Early National Massachusetts *(2008). In the following essay, Neem argues for the value of "institutional culture" in higher education.*

There has been much talk of the "online revolution" in higher education. While there is a place for online education, some of its boosters anticipate displacing the traditional campus altogether. A close reading of their arguments, however, makes clear that many share what might be called the "individualist fallacy," both in their understanding of how students learn and how professors teach.

Of course, individualism has a long, noble heritage in American history. From the "age of the self-made man" onward, we have valued those who pull themselves up by their own bootstraps. But, as Warren Buffett[1] has made clear, even the most successful individuals depend heavily on the cultural, economic, legal, political, and social contexts in which they act. This is as true for Buffett as it is for other so-called self-made men, such as Bill Gates. And it is certainly true for students.

But many advocates of online learning ignore this simple point. The economist Richard Vedder, for example, believes that being on

---

[1]Investor and philanthropist (1930–). [Eds.]

campus is only useful for "making friends, partying, drinking, and having sex." Anya Kamenetz, in her book *DIY U*, celebrates the day when individuals are liberated from the constraints of physical campuses, while Gates anticipates that "five years from now on the Web for free you'll be able to find the best lectures in the world. It will be better than any single university."

These advocates of online higher education forget the importance of *institutional culture* in shaping how people learn. College is about more than accessing information; it's about developing an attitude toward knowledge.

There is a difference between being on a campus with other stu- 5 dents and teachers committed to learning and sitting at home. Learning, like religion, is a social experience. Context matters. No matter how much we might learn about God and our obligations from the Web, it is by going to church and being surrounded by other congregants engaged in similar questions, under the guidance of a thoughtful, caring pastor, that we really change. Conversion is social, and so is learning.

Like all adults, students will pursue many activities during their time on campus, but what distinguishes a college is that it embodies ideals distinct from the rest of students' lives. If we take college seriously, we need people to spend time in such places so that they will leave different than when they entered.

Some argue that large lecture courses make a mockery of the above claims. Admittedly, in a better world, there would be no large lecture courses. Still, this argument misleads for several reasons. First, it generalizes from one kind of course, ignoring the smaller class sizes at community colleges and the upper-division courses in which students interact closely with each other and their professors. Second, it dismisses the energy of being in a classroom, even a large one, with real people when compared to being on our own. Even in large classes, good teachers push their students to think by asking probing questions, modeling curiosity, and adapting to the class's needs. Finally, it disregards the importance of the broader campus context in which all classes, large and small, take place.

The goal of bringing students to campus for several years is to immerse them in an environment in which learning is the highest value, something online environments, no matter how interactive, cannot simulate. Real learning is hard; it requires students to trust each other and their teachers. In other words, it depends on relationships. This is particularly important for the liberal arts.

Of course, as Richard Arum and Josipa Roksa's recent study *Academically Adrift* makes clear, there are great variations in what college students are learning. All too often, higher education does not fulfill our aspirations. But none of the problems Arum and Roksa identify are ones that online higher education would solve. As Arum and Roksa make clear, students learn more on campuses where learning is valued and expectations are high. If anything, we need to pay more attention to institutional culture because it matters so much.

10 This does not mean that we should reject technology when it can further learning, as in new computer programs that help diagnose students' specific stumbling blocks. But computers will never replace the inspiring, often unexpected, conversations that happen among students and between students and teachers on campuses. Because computers are not interpretive moral beings, they cannot evaluate assignments in which students are asked to reflect on complicated ideas or come up with new ones, especially concerning moral questions. Fundamentally, computers cannot cultivate curiosity because machines are not curious.

Technology is a tool, not an end in itself. As the computer scientist Jaron Lanier has written in his book *You Are Not A Gadget*, computers exist to support human endeavors, not the other way around. Many techno-utopists proclaim that computers are becoming smarter, more human, but Lanier wonders whether that is because we tend to reduce our human horizons to interact with our machines. This certainly is one of the dangers of online higher education.

The individualist fallacy applies not just to online advocates' understandings of students, but also their conception of what makes great teachers and scholars. Vedder, for example, echoes Gates in his hope that someday there will be a Wikipedia University, or that the Gates Foundation will start a university in which a few "star professors" are paid to teach thousands of students across the nation and world. Of course, this has been happening since the invention of cassette tapes that offer "the great courses." This is hardly innovative, nor does it a college education make.

Vedder ignores how star professors become great. How do they know what to teach and to write? Their success, like Buffett's, is social: they converse with and read and rely on the work of hundreds, even thousands, of other scholars. Read their articles and books, listen to their lectures, and you can discern how deeply influenced and how dependent they are on the work of their peers. In short, there would be no star professors absent an academy of scholars committed to research.

Schools like the online, Gates Foundation–funded Western Governors University free-ride off the expensive, quality research completed by traditional professors when they rely on open course ware and curricula. Take away the professors, and many online schools will teach material that is out of date or inaccurate or, worse, hand control over to other entities who are not interested in promoting the truth—from textbook companies seeking to maximize sales to coal and pharmaceutical companies offering their own curriculums for "free."

The Web and new technologies are great tools; they have made   15
more information more accessible to more people. This is to be celebrated. Citizens in a democracy should be able to access as much information as freely as possible. A democratic society cannot allow scholars,
or anyone else, to be the gatekeepers to knowledge.

Certainly, we will expand online higher education, if for no other
reason than because wealthy foundations like Gates and ambitious for-
profit entities are putting their money and power behind it. For certain
students, especially working adults pursuing clearly defined vocational
programs rather than a liberal arts education, online programs may
allow opportunities that they would have otherwise foregone. But
online higher education will never replace, much less replicate, what
happens on college campuses.

Even as we expand online, therefore, we must deepen our commitment to those institutions that cultivate a love of learning in their students, focus on the liberal arts, and produce the knowledge that online
and offline teaching requires.

## Responding to Reading

1. What is the "individualist fallacy" (1)? How does Neem use this concept to
   refute the arguments presented by supporters of online education?
2. What is the importance of "institutional culture" in shaping the way students
   learn (4)? According to Neem, how does distance learning undercut institutional culture in higher education?
3. What does Neem mean when he says, "Technology is a tool, not an end in
   itself" (11)? In what sense does he believe that online schools "free-ride off
   the expensive, quality research completed by traditional professors" (14)?

## Responding in Writing

Do you think students need to be in a traditional classroom to get an education?
Why or why not?

# FOR MORE BALANCE ON CAMPUSES

## Christina Hoff Sommers

### 1950–

*Christina Hoff Sommers, who calls herself an "equity feminist," is currently
a resident scholar at the American Enterprise Institute. Sommers is the
author of essays in a wide variety of periodicals and has published several
books but is best known for* Who Stole Feminism? How Women Have
Betrayed Women *(1994) and* The War against Boys: How Misguided
Feminism Is Harming Our Young Men *(2000). Her latest book is the
compilation* The Science on Women and Science *(2009). In the following*

*essay, the introduction to a longer essay that appeared in the* Atlantic Monthly, *Sommers makes a plea for more political diversity on America's college campuses.*

Washington—In a recent talk at Haverford College, I questioned the standard women's studies teaching that the United States is a patriarchal society that oppresses women.

For many in the audience, this was their first encounter with a dissident scholar. One student was horrified when I said that the free market had advanced the cause of women by affording them unprecedented economic opportunities. "How can anyone say that capitalism has helped women?" she asked.

Nor did I win converts when I said that the male heroism of special forces soldiers and the firefighters at ground zero should persuade gender scholars to acknowledge that "stereotypical masculinity" had some merit. Later an embarrassed and apologetic student said to me, "Haverford is just not ready for you."

After my talk, the young woman who invited me told me there was little intellectual diversity at Haverford and that she had hoped I would spark debate. In fact, many in the audience were quietly delighted by the exchanges. But two angry students accused her of providing "a forum for hate speech."

5    As the 2000 election made plain, the United States is pretty evenly divided between conservatives and liberals. Yet conservative scholars have effectively been marginalized, silenced, and rendered invisible on most campuses. This problem began in the late '80s and has become much worse in recent years. Most students can now go through four years of college without encountering a scholar of pronounced conservative views.

Few conservatives make it past the gantlet of faculty hiring in political-science, history, or English departments. In 1998, when a reporter from Denver's *Rocky Mountain News* surveyed the humanities and social sciences at the University of Colorado, Boulder, he found that of 190 professors with party affiliations, 184 were Democrats.

There wasn't a single Republican in the English, psychology, journalism, or philosophy departments. A 1999 survey of history departments found 22 Democrats and 2 Republicans at Stanford. At Cornell and Dartmouth there were 29 and 10 Democrats, respectively, and no Republicans.

The dearth of conservatives in psychology departments is so striking, that one (politically liberal) professor has proposed affirmative-action outreach. Richard Redding, a professor of psychology at Villanova University, writing in a recent issue of *American Psychologist*, notes that of the 31 social-policy articles that appeared in the journal between 1990 and 1999, 30 could be classified as liberal, one as conservative.

The key issue, Professor Redding says, is not the preponderance of Democrats, but the liberal practice of systematically excluding conservatives. Redding cites an experiment in which several graduate departments received mock applications from two candidates nearly identical, except that one "applicant" said he was a conservative Christian. The professors judged the nonconservative to be the significantly better candidate.

Redding asks, rhetorically: "Do we want a professional world 10 where our liberal world view prevents us from considering valuable strengths of conservative approaches to social problems . . . where conservatives are reluctant to enter the profession and we tacitly discriminate against them if they do? That, in fact, is the academic world we now have . . . ."

Campus talks by "politically incorrect" speakers happen rarely; visits are resisted and almost never internally funded. When Dinesh D'Souza, Andrew Sullivan, David Horowitz, or Linda Chavez do appear at a college, they are routinely heckled and sometimes threatened. The academy is now so inhospitable to free expression that conservatives buy advertisements in student newspapers. But most school newspapers won't print them. And papers that do are sometimes vandalized and the editors threatened.

The classical liberalism articulated by John Stuart Mill in his book *On Liberty* is no longer alive on campuses, having died of the very disease Mr. Mill warned of when he pointed out that ideas not freely and openly debated become *dead dogmas.* Mill insisted that the intellectually free person must put himself in the *mental position of those who think differently* adding that dissident ideas are best understood *by hear[ing] them from persons who actually believe them.*

Several groups are working to bring some balance to campus. The Intercollegiate Studies Institute, Young America's Foundation, Clare Boothe Luce Policy Institute, and Accuracy in Academia sponsor lectures by leading conservatives and libertarians. Students can ask these groups for funds to sponsor speakers.

More good news is that David Horowitz's Center for the Study of Popular Culture has launched a "Campaign for Fairness and Inclusion in Higher Education." It calls for university officials to:

1. Establish a zero-tolerance policy for vandalizing newspapers or heckling speakers.
2. Conduct an inquiry into political bias in the allocation of student program funds, including speakers' fees, and seek ways to promote underrepresented perspectives.
3. Conduct an inquiry into political bias in the hiring process of faculty and administrators and seek ways to promote fairness toward—and inclusion of—underrepresented perspectives.

15    Were even one high-profile institution like the University of Colorado to adopt a firm policy of intellectual inclusiveness, that practice
would quickly spread, and benighted students everywhere would soon
see daylight.

## Responding to Reading

1. Why does Sommers say she is a "dissident scholar" (2)? What generally
   accepted beliefs does she question? During her talk at Haverford College,
   why do her remarks cause uneasiness?
2. According to Sommers, conservatives have been marginalized on most
   American college campuses. What does she mean? How has this occurred?
   What evidence does Sommers present to support her claim? Is her evidence
   persuasive?
3. In Sommers's view, what is the effect of excluding conservatives from the
   intellectual life of a college or university? What does Sommers say is being
   done "to bring some balance to campus" (13)?

## Responding in Writing

Sommers says that students almost never hear campus talks by "'politically
incorrect' speakers" (11). Do you agree with Sommers, or do you believe that at
your college or university you are exposed to a cross-section of ideas?

# THE FIRST DAY
## Edward P. Jones
### 1950–

*Edward P. Jones studied writing at the University of Virginia. His book* Lost
in the City *(1992) is a collection of stories set in the hometown of his childhood, Washington, D.C., a city of working-class black men and women who
struggle heroically in their daily lives. The book was nominated for the
National Book Award and lauded by critics both for addressing racial issues
and for transcending them. His first novel,* The Known World, *published
in 2003, was chosen as one of the year's nine best books (and four best novels) by the editors of the* New York Times Book Review. The Known
World *also won the fiction prize of the National Book Critics Circle and the
2004 Pulitzer Prize for fiction. His latest book,* All Aunt Hagar's Children
*(2006), is a collection of stories. The short story that follows, from* Lost in
the City, *is the poignant story of a mother who takes her daughter to her
first day of school.*

In an otherwise unremarkable September morning, long before I learned to be ashamed of my mother, she takes my hand and we set off down New Jersey Avenue to begin my very first day of school. I am wearing a checkeredlike blue-and-green cotton dress, and scattered about these colors are bits of yellow and white and brown. My mother has uncharacteristically spent nearly an hour on my hair that morning, plaiting and replaiting so that now my scalp tingles. Whenever I turn my head quickly, my nose fills with the faint smell of Dixie Peach hair grease. The smell is somehow a soothing one now and I will reach for it time and time again before the morning ends. All the plaits, each with a blue barrette near the tip and each twisted into an uncommon sturdiness, will last until I go to bed that night, something that has never happened before. My stomach is full of milk and oatmeal sweetened with brown sugar. Like everything else I have on, my pale green slip and underwear are new, the underwear having come three to a plastic package with a little girl on the front who appears to be dancing. Behind my ears, my mother, to stop my whining, has dabbed the stingiest bit of her gardenia perfume, the last present my father gave her before he disappeared into memory. Because I cannot smell it, I have only her word that the perfume is there. I am also wearing yellow socks trimmed with thin lines of black and white around the tops. My shoes are my greatest joy, black patent-leather miracles, and when one is nicked at the toe later that morning in class, my heart will break.

I am carrying a pencil, a pencil sharpener, and a small ten-cent tablet with a black-and-white speckled cover. My mother does not believe that a girl in kindergarten needs such things, so I am taking them only because of my insistent whining and because they are presents from our neighbors, Mary Keith and Blondelle Harris. Miss Mary and Miss Blondelle are watching my two younger sisters until my mother returns. The women are as precious to me as my mother and sisters. Out playing one day, I have overheard an older child, speaking to another child, call Miss Mary and Miss Blondelle a word that is brand new to me. This is my mother: When I say the word in fun to one of my sisters, my mother slaps me across the mouth and the word is lost for years and years.

All the way down New Jersey Avenue, the sidewalks are teeming with children. In my neighborhood, I have many friends, but I see none of them as my mother and I walk. We cross New York Avenue, we cross Pierce Street, and we cross L and K, and still I see no one who knows my name. At I Street, between New Jersey Avenue and Third Street, we enter Seaton Elementary School, a timeworn, sad-faced building across the street from my mother's church, Mt. Carmel Baptist.

Just inside the front door, women out of the advertisements in *Ebony* are greeting other parents and children. The woman who greets us has pearls thick as jumbo marbles that come down almost to her navel, and she acts as if she had known me all my life, touching my shoulder, cupping her hand under my chin. She is enveloped in a perfume that I only know is not gardenia. When, in answer to her question, my mother tells her that we live at 1227 New Jersey Avenue, the woman first seems to be picturing in her head where we live. Then she shakes her head and says that we are at the wrong school, that we should be at Walker-Jones.

5    My mother shakes her head vigorously. "I want her to go here," my mother says. "If I'da wanted her someplace else, I'da took her there." The woman continues to act as if she has known me all my life, but she tells my mother that we live beyond the area that Seaton serves. My mother is not convinced and for several more minutes she questions the woman about why I cannot attend Seaton. For as many Sundays as I can remember, perhaps even Sundays when I was in her womb, my mother has pointed across I Street to Seaton as we come and go to Mt. Carmel. "You gonna go there and learn about the whole world." But one of the guardians of that place is saying no, and no again. I am learning this about my mother: The higher up on the scale of respectability a person is—and teachers are rather high up in her eyes—the less she is liable to let them push her around. But finally, I see in her eyes the closing gate, and she takes my hand and we leave the building. On the steps, she stops as people move past us on either side.

"Mama, I can't go to school?"

She says nothing at first, then takes my hand again and we are down the steps quickly and nearing New Jersey Avenue before I can blink. This is my mother: She says, "One monkey don't stop no show."

Walker-Jones is a larger, newer school and I immediately like it because of that. But it is not across the street from my mother's church, her rock, one of her connections to God, and I sense her doubts as she absently rubs her thumb over the back of her hand. We find our way to the crowded auditorium where gray metal chairs are set up in the middle of the room. Along the wall to the left are tables and other chairs. Every chair seems occupied by a child or adult. Somewhere in the room a child is crying, a cry that rises above the buzz-talk of so many people. Strewn about the floor are dozens and dozens of pieces of white paper, and people are walking over them without any thought of picking them up. And seeing this lack of concern, I am all of a sudden afraid.

"Is this where they register for school?" my mother asks a woman at one of the tables.

10    The woman looks up slowly as if she has heard this question once too often. She nods. She is tiny, almost as small as the girl standing beside her. The woman's hair is set in a mass of curlers and all of those curlers are made of paper money, here a dollar bill, there a five-dollar

bill. The girl's hair is arrayed in curls, but some of them are beginning to droop and this makes me happy. On the table beside the woman's pocketbook is a large notebook, worthy of someone in high school, and looking at me looking at the notebook, the girl places her hand possessively on it. In her other hand she holds several pencils with thick crowns of additional erasers.

"These the forms you gotta use?" my mother asks the woman, picking up a few pieces of the paper from the table. "Is this what you have to fill out?"

The woman tells her yes, but that she need fill out only one.

"I see," my mother says, looking about the room. Then: "Would you help me with this form? That is, if you don't mind."

The woman asks my mother what she means.

"This form. Would you mind helpin me fill it out?"                          15

The woman still seems not to understand.

"I can't read it. I don't know how to read or write, and I'm askin you to help me." My mother looks at me, then looks away. I know almost all of her looks, but this one is brand new to me. "Would you help me, then?"

The woman says Why sure, and suddenly she appears happier, so much more satisfied with everything. She finishes the form for her daughter and my mother and I step aside to wait for her. We find two chairs nearby and sit. My mother is now diseased, according to the girl's eyes, and until the moment her mother takes her and the form to the front of the auditorium, the girl never stops looking at my mother. I stare back at her. "Don't stare," my mother says to me. "You know better than that."

Another woman out of the *Ebony* ads takes the woman's child away. Now, the woman says upon returning, let's see what we can do for you two.

My mother answers the questions the woman reads off the form.  20 They start with my last name, and then on to the first and middle names. This is school, I think. This is going to school. My mother slowly enunciates each word of my name. This is my mother: As the questions go on, she takes from her pocketbook document after document, as if they will support my right to attend school, as if she has been saving them up for just this moment. Indeed, she takes out more papers than I have ever seen her do in other places: my birth certificate, my baptismal record, a doctor's letter concerning my bout with chicken pox, rent receipts, records of immunization, a letter about our public assistance payments, even her marriage license—every single paper that has anything even remotely to do with my five-year-old life. Few of the papers are needed here, but it does not matter and my mother continues to pull out the documents with the purposefulness of a magician pulling out a long string of scarves. She has learned that money is the beginning and end of everything in this world, and when the woman finishes, my mother offers her fifty cents, and the woman accepts it without hesitation. My mother and I are just about the last parent and child in the room.

My mother presents the form to a woman sitting in front of the stage, and the woman looks at it and writes something on a white card, which she gives to my mother. Before long, the woman who has taken the girl with the drooping curls appears from behind us, speaks to the sitting woman, and introduces herself to my mother and me. She's to be my teacher, she tells my mother. My mother stares.

We go into the hall, where my mother kneels down to me. Her lips are quivering. "I'll be back to pick you up at twelve o'clock. I don't want you to go nowhere. You just wait right here. And listen to every word she say." I touch her lips and press them together. It is an old, old game between us. She puts my hand down at my side, which is not part of the game. She stands and looks a second at the teacher, then she turns and walks away. I see where she has darned one of her socks the night before. Her shoes make loud sounds in the hall. She passes through the doors and I can still hear the loud sounds of her shoes. And even when the teacher turns me toward the classrooms and I hear what must be the singing and talking of all the children in the world, I can still hear my mother's footsteps above it all.

## Responding to Reading

1. Why does the narrator's mother want to enroll her in Seaton Elementary School? Why is she unable to? What does the mother's reaction to this situation tell you about her?
2. What are the mother's limitations? What are her strengths?
3. Do you think that this story is primarily about the mother or her daughter? How do you explain the mother's reaction as she leaves her daughter? Why does the daughter still remember this reaction years later as she is telling this story? Why do you think the story ends with the sound of the mother's footsteps?

## Responding in Writing

Write a paragraph describing your earliest memory of school.

--- FOCUS ---

## Is a College Education Worth the Money?

"Graduating with a total college loan debt of
$120,000, Marissa Kulver... Graduating with a
total debt of $107,000, James Lehman..."

### Responding to the Image

1. The cartoon above addresses the issues of high college tuition and student debt. Who is the cartoon's audience? How can you tell?
2. In what sense is this cartoon ironic? What point do you think the cartoonist wants to make with his use of irony? Do you think he gets his point across? Why or why not?

# IS COLLEGE WORTH THE MONEY?

## Daniel S. Cheever, Jr.

### 1942–

*Former president of Boston's Simmons College, Daniel S. Cheever, Jr., is cred-
ited with numerous improvements to the school during his tenure, including
efforts to modernize college facilities and to diversify the faculty, staff, and*

*student population. At the college's centennial celebration, Cheever noted, "The unique character of Simmons lies in its people. . . . " In the following essay, Cheever urges people to look at factors other than cost when judging the value of a college education.*

The annual trials and tribulations of college acceptance are over for most students and parents. The vast majority of college-bound high school seniors now know where they'll be going to school in the fall.

What never seems to end for students and parents, however, is understandable anxiety over paying for college. The relentless rise in the costs of higher education alarms payers and the public. According to the College Board, over the last 10 years average tuition and fees rose 51 percent at public four-year colleges and 36 percent at private institutions, outpacing the consumer price index. Undergraduate tuition and fees at elite private schools such as Harvard grew even faster. For example, Harvard undergraduate tuition and fees are $27,448 this year, up from $17,851 in 1995 and $9,500 in 1985. With room and board added, next year's bill at Harvard will be an attention-getting $42,000. That's as much as the average family income in the United States.

College officials must take this issue more seriously. There's no question political leaders feel the heat. In response to a growing public outcry over escalating college costs in the late '90s, Congress established the National Commission on the Cost of Higher Education. The commission's report, while politically safe, offered some useful recommendations. As is often the case, however, the commission's work produced few results. College costs continued to rise far faster than inflation or family income.

Now the drumbeat to reform ever-rising college costs is once again echoing throughout Washington. Can a new round of congressional hearings be far away?

5 But the focus on the cost of higher education misses a fundamental point. The real question is whether students are getting their money's worth. In most other consumer markets, cost is a function of quality, real or perceived. This is a fact of life when purchasing a luxury car or high-caliber professional services. There is a "value paradox" in higher education, however, since families rarely consider cost in the context of the quality delivered. That's partly because most colleges don't know how to measure their quality. But if education is truly an investment in a young person, shouldn't we be able to understand the return on that investment? By focusing on cost alone, we're avoiding more serious conversations about value.

Most parents are willing to invest or borrow $100,000 to help produce highly employable graduates with proven critical thinking and communication skills and strong professional preparation. Because a college graduate earns nearly $1 million more in pay over a working career than a high school graduate, while the same college tuition investment in the stock market would yield more than $2 million over that same period, we had better insist the value of higher education be measured in more than cost terms.

Focusing on educational value, and not solely on cost, means that students, parents, faculty, and administrators must ask tough questions. For example, who's doing the teaching? What are students really learning? Perhaps a student is willing to pay a high price for education when professors, not graduate student teaching assistants, are guaranteed to teach the course and grade the papers. Maybe a parent is willing to pay market rates for a course whose small class size lets professors establish personal working relationships with students. Right now, many professors prefer their research "opportunities" over their teaching "load." Yet isn't it obvious the quality of education erodes when professors are absent, classes are unmanageably large, or most students get honor grades?

Parents and school leaders might also ask how well colleges prepare students to become economically productive, community-minded citizens. Will the graduate get a good job at a fine salary, making the investment worthwhile?

Colleges also need to work harder at serving students long after graduation. For their considerable investment, alumni should receive a lifetime of services to help with their professional and personal growth. While some colleges offer engaging, high-quality alumni services, many do not. And students certainly lose out when they fail to think of their college investment in terms of its lifetime value.

As the cost discussion heats up again, it's imperative that we define   10 it in terms of quality as well as cost. Only then can we achieve a true measure of the value we receive from investments in higher education. When higher education is assessed in value terms, it seems inevitable that students and parents will demand proven, verifiable outcomes that measure the return on their considerable investment.

## Responding to Reading

1. According to Cheever, what "fundamental point" does "the focus on the cost of higher education" (5) miss?
2. In paragraph 6, Cheever compares the value of a college education with the value of tuition if it were invested in the stock market. Do you think this comparison is valid? Do you think it is fair? What point does Cheever make with this comparison?
3. How does Cheever define "educational value"? Do you agree with his definition? What factors (if any) do you think he fails to consider?

## Responding in Writing

Consider your own college education. Do you think you are receiving your money's worth? What return on your investment do you think you are getting?

# PLAN B: SKIP COLLEGE

## Jacques Steinberg

*A* New York Times *staff reporter and a national education correspondent, Jacques Steinberg writes about issues in American education. He is the author of* The Gatekeepers: Inside the Admissions Process of a Premier College *(2002) and* You Are an Ironman: How Six Weekend Warriors Chased Their Dream of Finishing the World's Toughest Triathlon *(2011). In the following essay, Steinberg explores "credible alternatives" to a college degree.*

What's the key to success in the United States?

Short of becoming a reality TV star, the answer is rote and, some would argue, rather knee-jerk: Earn a college degree.

The idea that four years of higher education will translate into a better job, higher earnings and a happier life—a refrain sure to be repeated this month at graduation ceremonies across the country—has been pounded into the heads of schoolchildren, parents and educators. But there's an underside to that conventional wisdom. Perhaps no more than half of those who began a four-year bachelor's degree program in the fall of 2006 will get that degree within six years, according to the latest projections from the Department of Education. (The figures don't include transfer students, who aren't tracked.)

For college students who ranked among the bottom quarter of their high school classes, the numbers are even more stark: 80 percent will probably never get a bachelor's degree or even a two-year associate's degree.

5      That can be a lot of tuition to pay, without a degree to show for it.

A small but influential group of economists and educators is pushing another pathway: for some students, no college at all. It's time, they say, to develop credible alternatives for students unlikely to be successful pursuing a higher degree, or who may not be ready to do so.

Whether everyone in college needs to be there is not a new question; the subject has been hashed out in books and dissertations for years. But the economic crisis has sharpened that focus, as financially struggling states cut aid to higher education.

Among those calling for such alternatives are the economists Richard K. Vedder of Ohio University and Robert I. Lerman of American University, the political scientist Charles Murray, and James E. Rosenbaum, an education professor at Northwestern. They would steer some students toward intensive, short-term vocational and career training, through expanded high school programs and corporate apprenticeships.

"It is true that we need more nanosurgeons than we did 10 to 15 years ago," said Professor Vedder, founder of the Center for College Affordability and Productivity, a research nonprofit in Washington. "But the numbers are still relatively small compared to the numbers of nurses' aides we're going to need. We will need hundreds of thousands of them over the next decade."

And much of their training, he added, might be feasible outside the college setting. 10

College degrees are simply not necessary for many jobs. Of the 30 jobs projected to grow at the fastest rate over the next decade in the United States, only seven typically require a bachelor's degree, according to the Bureau of Labor Statistics.

Among the top 10 growing job categories, two require college degrees: accounting (a bachelor's) and postsecondary teachers (a doctorate). But this growth is expected to be dwarfed by the need for registered nurses, home health aides, customer service representatives and store clerks. None of those jobs require a bachelor's degree.

Professor Vedder likes to ask why 15 percent of mail carriers have bachelor's degrees, according to a 1999 federal study.

"Some of them could have bought a house for what they spent on their education," he said.

Professor Lerman, the American University economist, said some 15 high school graduates would be better served by being taught how to behave and communicate in the workplace.

Such skills are ranked among the most desired—even ahead of educational attainment—in many surveys of employers. In one 2008 survey of more than 2,000 businesses in Washington State, employers said entry-level workers appeared to be most deficient in being able to "solve problems and make decisions," "resolve conflict and negotiate," "cooperate with others" and "listen actively."

Yet despite the need, vocational programs, which might teach such skills, have been one casualty in the push for national education standards, which has been focused on preparing students for college.

While some educators propose a radical renovation of the community college system to teach work readiness, Professor Lerman advocates a significant national investment by government and employers in on-the-job apprenticeship training. He spoke with admiration, for example, about a program in the CVS pharmacy chain in which aspiring pharmacists' assistants work as apprentices in hundreds of stores, with many going on to study to become full-fledged pharmacists themselves.

"The health field is an obvious case where the manpower situation is less than ideal," he said. "I would try to work with some of the major employers to develop these kinds of programs to yield mastery in jobs that do demand high expertise."

While no country has a perfect model for such programs, Professor 20 Lerman pointed to a modest study of a German effort done last summer by an intern from that country. She found that of those who passed the Abitur, the exam that allows some Germans to attend college for almost no tuition, 40 percent chose to go into apprenticeships in trades, accounting, sales management, and computers.

"Some of the people coming out of those apprenticeships are in more demand than college graduates," he said, "because they've actually managed things in the workplace."

Still, by urging that some students be directed away from four-year colleges, academics like Professor Lerman are touching a third rail of the education system. At the very least, they could be accused of lowering expectations for some students. Some critics go further, suggesting that the approach amounts to educational redlining, since many of the students who drop out of college are black or non-white Hispanics.

Peggy Williams, a counselor at a high school in suburban New York City with a student body that is mostly black or Hispanic, understands the argument for erring on the side of pushing more students toward college.

"If we're telling kids, 'You can't cut the mustard, you shouldn't go to college or university,' then we're shortchanging them from experiencing an environment in which they might grow," she said.

25    But Ms. Williams said she would be more willing to counsel some students away from the precollege track if her school, Mount Vernon High School, had a better vocational education alternative. Over the last decade, she said, courses in culinary arts, nursing, dentistry and heating and ventilation system repair were eliminated. Perhaps 1 percent of this year's graduates will complete a concentration in vocational courses, she said, compared with 40 percent a decade ago.

There is another rejoinder to the case against college: People with college and graduate degrees generally earn more than those without them, and face lower risks of unemployment, according to figures from the Bureau of Labor Statistics.

Even those who experience a few years of college earn more money, on average, with less risk of unemployment, than those who merely graduate from high school, said Morton Schapiro, an economist who is the president of Northwestern University.

"You get some return even if you don't get the sheepskin," Mr. Schapiro said.

He warned against overlooking the intangible benefits of a college experience—even an incomplete experience—for those who might not apply what they learned directly to their chosen work.

30    "It's not just about the economic return," he said. "Some college, whether you complete it or not, contributes to aesthetic appreciation, better health and better voting behavior."

Nonetheless, Professor Rosenbaum said, high school counselors and teachers are not doing enough to alert students unlikely to earn a college degree to the perilous road ahead.

"I'm not saying don't get the B.A," he said. "I'm saying, let's get them some intervening credentials, some intervening milestones. Then, if they want to go further in their education, they can."

## Responding to Reading

1. Why do some economists and educators believe that there should be alternatives for students who are not likely to succeed in (or are not ready for) college? Do you agree? Does Steinberg?
2. Where does Steinberg discuss the disadvantages of counseling students not to go to college? What specific disadvantages do his sources identify?
3. Do you think Steinberg's article makes a more convincing case *for* or *against* encouraging some students to "skip college"? Do you agree with Professors Vedder and Lerman (discussed in paragraphs 7–21) or with the educators quoted in paragraphs 22–31?

## Responding in Writing

Do you think all students should be encouraged to go to college? Why or why not?

# Is College Worth the Money?

## Stephen G. Emerson

*A graduate of Haverford College, Stephen G. Emerson went on to become the college's thirteenth president. In 2011, he stepped down to become a professor of biology. A clinical hematologist/oncologist, Emerson specializes in bone marrow stem cell disorders. In the following essay, he argues for the value of a college degree.*

If you have paid, or are about to pay, an astronomical amount of money to a college or university, I'm pleased to report that you're making a good investment.

But that isn't news: With a single Google search you can turn up countless articles, essays and analyses proving that nearly all degrees more than pay for themselves. (An M.A. in a few fields is the sole soft spot.) Some degrees, such as those you get for studying law or medicine, generally pay enormous dividends.

But I propose that those of us in higher education—administrators, teachers, students and parents—take another look at this question by changing the very question itself. Instead of asking, "Is college worth the money?" what if we ask, "How valuable is a college degree?"

Sure, financial factors figure into such an equation. But how can your degree—and the experience of earning it—enrich your life and the world in which you live it? After all, if you're going to spend six figures in cash and four, eight or 10 years' time obtaining your degree, shouldn't it keep paying dividends, beyond the financial, forever?

College should literally change your life. It should shape your values and your ambitions, as well as provide you with analytical skill sets

5

you will need to achieve and sustain those ambitions. If college achieves these goals, it is absolutely worth the money.

A Class of '74 graduate of Haverford College, I recently returned to be its president after a career as a hematologist-oncologist and stem cell biologist. And what I now realize after two decades of clinical practice and scientific study is that a school like Haverford, which is informed by the Quaker tradition of community both socially and academically, isn't just minting graduates. We're creating stem cells.

You heard me right. The 300 or so young men and women who will receive diplomas in May are remarkably similar to the stem cells that I have worked with in the lab, and I believe that such similarity reveals the true, enduring value of a college education.

Stem cells are rare cells, maybe one in a million in any organ or tissue, but they are precious and potent. Each stem cell has the ability to give rise to daughter cells that can build and repair surrounding tissues, while also growing, developing and renewing itself.

These educated stem cells can travel, and they can learn to do different tasks, in different sites, depending on the needs of their world. Stem cells need to be nurtured in particular microenvironments, in which they educate and are educated by their surrounding cells.

10    So without much of a metaphorical stretch, I believe that a college is, indeed, a source of the most important stem cells for our world: the students who we have the privilege of learning from and training.

Through their lives in a community with deeply engaged faculty and staff, Haverford students are steeped in the most radical learning, take continuing joy in the adventures of discovery in which they engage, and prepare for lives of renewal. They become leaders in business, medicine, law, education and the arts and, in Haverford's case—given our need-blind admission policy—have been enabled to do so regardless of socioeconomic background.

The investment is clearly worthwhile, given the result: students who will go on to change the world. So where's the value in a college degree? Only this: the value you place in being able to teach, to learn, to heal, to bridge difference—to change the world, and yourselves.

## Responding to Reading

1. Emerson says that people who ask whether college is worth the money are asking the wrong question. What question does he believe they *should* be asking? Why?

2. According to Emerson, the college students who are graduating from Haverford College are "remarkably similar to stem cells" (7). How? Do you think this analogy is effective? Explain.

3. Haverford is a prestigious and expensive private college. Do the points Emerson makes about the value of a college degree apply just to Haverford

students, or do they also apply to students at state universities and community colleges?

## Responding in Writing

How do you think each of the six students interviewed for Liz Dwyer's article (below) would respond to Emerson's essay?

# IS COLLEGE WORTH THE MONEY?
# ANSWERS FROM SIX NEW GRADUATES
## Liz Dwyer

*In the following article from* GOOD *magazine, education editor Liz Dwyer compiles the responses of six 2011 college graduates to the question examined in this Focus section: Is a college education worth the money? An experienced teacher and an avid blogger, Dwyer writes about educational issues, parenting, and race. Her work has appeared in* Good Housekeeping *magazine, the online publication* DivineCaroline, *and numerous blogs, including her own,* Los Angelista.

Students are racking up astronomical amounts of debt and moving home with mom and dad after graduation because there are no jobs to be found. PayPal founder Peter Thiel is even encouraging students to drop out and try entrepreneurship instead because, he says, college isn't worth it. So we decided to ask some graduates from the class of 2011 what they think. Almost all of them are worried about paying back their student loan debt, and of those not going on to grad school, none will have traditional full-time jobs. But their answers about the value of college might surprise you.

**1) The Journalist**
**Name:** Sara Fletcher
**Age:** 22
**College:** Northwestern University
**Major:** Journalism
**Post-college plans:** Fletcher's headed to Portland, Oregon, for a public relations internship.
**Is college worth the money?**

"I chose Northwestern's Medill School of Journalism because it is top in the country. The connections here are undeniable and the opportunities for internships and post-grad jobs are better than I could have hoped for had I attended school in-state. I was challenged from the moment I arrived at Medill to basically act as a full-time reporter. Those skills, which I was challenged to develop very independently in and outside of the classroom will be incredibly useful for my work in PR and marketing. That said, I think college, particularly at a top school, is somewhat of a luxury and privilege. It's a chance for a lot of people, myself included, to take four years to really focus ourselves, figure out our passions in life, and gather the skills, critical thinking and connections to live out those passions. Because of the high price, for many that I've met, the luxury of four years at an elite school to 'find yourself' sometimes isn't as immediately justifiable, particularly when a high school grad has the life skills and confidence to enter the working world."

### 2) The Dentist
**Name:** Leah Munson
**Age:** 21
**College:** Binghamton University
**Major:** Biological Sciences
**Post-college plans:** Munson's hoping to get into dental school and be an orthodontist.
**Is college worth the money?**

"I hated college while I was there because I felt like everyone was wasting my time. I have known what I wanted to do since I was 12 and sitting in yet another classroom learning material that only grazed my interest was frustrating. I rushed through my undergraduate work, graduating in 3 years so that I could finally get to where I wanted to be. Although I have learned a lot in college and looking back I believe that it was very important in shaping who I am today, I hate the fact that I just spent years of my life forcing myself to learn information that I likely won't use again. College is not shaping students for their careers but rather for society. I'm not the person I was when I went to college but not because of anything I learned in a classroom. I'm different because it was a social bootcamp of sorts. Seeing as I already know what I want to do, I took the knowledge with a grain of salt. I was glad to be learning it and found it interesting but I was forced to acknowledge that I would likely never use it again."

### 3) The Startup Guru
**Name:** Ashwin Anandani
**Age:** 22
**College:** Northwestern University
**Major:** Economics
**Post-college plans:** Anandani graduated early, managed to raise some money for a social change startup idea and moved to the Bay Area to pursue it. In the meantime, to keep a roof over his head, he also found a paid part-time job with another startup.
**Is college worth the money?**

"I don't think the value of a college is equal to the sum of its graduates' wages. I paid a couple hundred thousand dollars in total for my (almost) 4 years at university, and while I came out being able to think well, which is what I believe university is really meant to 'teach' you, I can only say that the university contributed a very small share of that ability. Now that I've been out, I'm thinking, 'I really just paid money to be assigned papers and math so I could have a piece of paper that serves as a filtering mechanism for corporations' HR departments?'

I would say my assignments and college requirements were more of a very arduous process of creating a 'fallback plan' so I don't end up on the streets if my startup fails. It's almost a monopoly in terms of options, too—'If you don't go to college, where will you go?'—so we pay the high price to be locked into a degree and we learn how to make standardized documents and take standardized tests. Too bad the world isn't standardized like my degree was."

### 4) The Teacher
**Name:** Alexis Valdez
**Age:** 22
**College:** Holy Cross College
**Major:** Elementary Education, K-6 and ENL (English as a New Language)
**Post-college plans:** Valdez, who is the first in her family to go to college, doesn't yet have a permanent teaching position. She says she plans to keep submitting applications to all the school districts in her area, and hopes to substitute teach to pay the bills.
**Is college worth the money?**

"I think that even though right now I'm in a tight spot as far as a job and finances go, college was definitely worth the money. In my specific field the job market is particularly sparse, though I wouldn't be as marketable in the teaching world if I hadn't had the opportunity to get real classroom experiences through my college program. I will admit that I'm not pleased to be deep in college debt, but in the long run, I believe that getting a college education was the best choice I could have made for myself to ensure a better future."

### 5) The Entrepreneur
**Name:** Arnela Sulovic
**Age:** 21
**School:** University of Southern California
**Major:** Communication
**Post-college plans:** Sulovic, who immigrated from war-torn Bosnia, is the first in her family to go to college and graduated in three years to save money. She wants to start her own business, but right now she's working as a summer resident adviser for off-campus housing and a sales/partnership intern at Thrillist Rewards. She's still looking for a full-time job.
**Is college worth the money?**

CHAPTER 2 FOCUS

"I strongly believe that college is worth the money. Although everything I learned in the classroom may not be applicable to my career, USC gave me access to unparalleled experiences, introduced me to incredible people and ideas, and broadened my perspective. Furthermore, the extracurricular activities that I participated in helped me build real-world skills and leadership experiences. There are many benefits that one can gain only by experiencing a higher education. If I had known exactly what I wanted to do post-graduation, I could have taken advantage of more opportunities in college. I wish all college classes were hands-on, skill building, and exploratory."

**6) The Lawyer**
**Name:** Beverly Ozowara
**Age:** 21
**College:** University of Notre Dame
**Major:** Psychology & Film, Television, Theatre
**Post-college plans:** Ozowara will be attending Valparaiso Law School and wants to be a family lawyer.
**Is college worth the money?**

"I think that college is definitely worth it, but not because I learned specific things that would be helpful with my career. It was worth it for the valuable resources and connections I formed. It was also worth it because of the priceless undergraduate experience that I couldn't have gotten easily anywhere else. For example, I had the opportunity to travel (for a third of the normal cost) to Brazil with the Notre Dame Concert Band. During the trip, I was able to do things like perform at the oldest concert hall in the Americas and to swim in the Amazon River. I will admit though that I did not learn very many things that are specific to my career. It would have been helpful if there had been a pre-law program or more advising since freshmen year of college geared toward getting internships and familiarizing myself with corporations and the business world."

## Responding to Reading

1. Several of these six new graduates believe that a college education will guarantee them a better future. Why? Do you agree?
2. What would the six students change about their undergraduate experiences? What would they keep the same?
3. On which points do these six new graduates seem to agree? On which points do they disagree?

## Responding in Writing

Do you think that college should prepare you for life or for a career?

# WIDENING THE FOCUS

## For Critical Reading and Writing

Referring specifically to the four readings in this chapter's Focus section, write an essay in which you answer the question, "Is a College Education Worth the Money?"

## For Further Reading

The following readings can suggest additional perspectives for thinking about the value of a college education.

- Frederick Douglass, "Learning to Read and Write" (p. 143)
- Nicholas Carr, "Does the Internet Make You Dumber?" (p. 216)
- Ross Perlin, "Unpaid Interns, Complicit Colleges" (p. 439)

## For Focused Research

As tuition costs continue to rise, students, educators, politicians, and the general public are increasingly asking if a college education is worth the money. In preparation for writing an essay that answers this question, search the Internet for up-to-date statistics on lifetime earnings of college graduates versus nongraduates. Then, write an essay in which you consider how having (or not having) a college degree affects lifetime employment, male versus female earnings, and initial access to the job market. Be sure to support your points with the statistics and examples you find.

## Beyond the Classroom

Interview six adults, three with four-year college degrees and three without. One person in each category should be in his or her 60s, one in his or her 40s, and one a recent college graduate in his or her 20s.

- Ask those without college degrees if they believe they have suffered financially because of their lack of higher education.
- Ask those with college degrees whether they believe the money they spent on college was worth the expense.
- Ask those in both groups to evaluate their professional and economic success.

Then, write an essay that draws some conclusions about the perceived value of a college education for people in different age groups.

CHAPTER 2  FOCUS

---
## WRITING
---

### Issues in Education

1. Both Lynda Barry (p. 69) and Maya Angelou (p. 77) describe personal experiences related to their education. Write an essay in which you describe a positive or negative experience you have had with your own education. Be specific, and make sure you include plenty of vivid descriptive details.

2. Many of the readings in this chapter try to define exactly what constitutes a "good" education. Write an essay in which you define a good education. Explain your view with specific references to readings in this chapter by John Holt (p. 72), Scott Adams (p. 98), and Liz Dwyer (p. 121).

3. According to Christina Hoff Sommers (p. 105), instructors with conservative political views are being systematically excluded from many American colleges and universities. Write a letter to Sommers in which you agree or disagree with her contentions. Make sure that you address Sommers's specific points and that you use examples from both the essay and your own experience to support your position.

4. In his short story "The First Day" (p. 108), Edward P. Jones tells the story of a child attending school for the first time. Write an essay in which you discuss your own first impressions of school. In what way have your impressions changed? How have they stayed the same? Do you agree with John Holt (p. 72) that traditional methods of education do more to hurt students than to help them?

5. In his essay "Should the Obama Generation Drop Out?" (p. 95), Charles Murray questions the idea that every student should be encouraged to go to college. In "Is College Worth the Money?" (p. 113), Daniel S. Cheever, Jr., asks if students are getting their money's worth in college. Write an essay in which you address one (or both) of these issues. Be specific, and use examples from your own experience as well as the essays to support your points.

6. In her essay "The Good Immigrant Student" (p. 87), Bich Minh Nguyen discusses the difficulties immigrant students face in American schools. At one point in her essay she says that she has never "gotten over the terror of being called on in class, or the dread in knowing that I'm expected to contribute to class discussion" (27). Assume that you are a tutor in your school's writing center and that you have been asked to write an essay to be included in an orientation booklet. In this essay, your goal is to address the concerns that Nguyen expresses. Be supportive, and give specific advice for overcoming these problems.

7. Define your educational philosophy. Then, choose one grade level and design a curriculum that reflects your philosophy. Finally, write a proposal in which you present your ideal curriculum, referring to the ideas of at least one of the writers in this chapter.

8. All the writers in this chapter believe in the power of education to change a person. For many people, this process begins with a teacher who has a profound influence on them. Write an essay in which you discuss such a teacher. What, in your opinion, made this teacher so effective? In what ways did contact with this teacher change you?

9. Write an essay in which you develop a definition of good teaching, considering the relationship of the teacher to the class, the standards teachers should use to evaluate students, and what students should gain from their educational experience. Refer to the ideas of John Holt (p. 72) and Stephen G. Emerson (p. 119) in your essay.

10. Write an essay in which you outline a career path for yourself that does not involve college. In your essay, refer to the ideas presented by Scott Adams (p. 98) and Jacques Steinberg (p. 116).

# 3

# THE POLITICS OF LANGUAGE

During the years he spent in prison, political activist Malcolm X became increasingly frustrated by his inability to express himself in writing, so he began the tedious and often frustrating task of copying words from the dictionary—page by page. The eventual result was that, for the first time, he could pick up a book and read it with understanding: "Anyone who has read a great deal," he says, "can imagine the new world that opened." In addition, by becoming a serious reader, Malcolm X was able to develop the ideas about race, politics, and economics that he presented so forcefully after he was released from prison.

Malcolm X giving a speech in Washington, D.C., 1961

In our society, language is constantly being manipulated for political ends. This fact should come as no surprise if we consider the potential power of words. Often, the power of a word comes not from its dictionary definition, or *denotation*, but from its *connotations*, the associations that surround it. These connotations can be subtle, giving language the power to confuse and even to harm. For example, whether a doctor who performs an abortion is "terminating a pregnancy" or "murdering a preborn child" is not just a matter of semantics. It is also a political issue, one that has provoked both debate and violence. This potential for misunderstanding, disagreement, deception, and possibly danger makes careful word choice very important.

The Focus section of this chapter (p. 174) addresses the question, "Is Texting Destroying the English Language?" As the essays in this section illustrate, the answer to this question is neither straightforward nor simple. Is texting ruining the English language as we know it or enriching the language by encouraging people to experiment and be linguistically creative? Or, is texting simply an interim technology that will have little effect on our language and will soon be obsolete?

John F. Kennedy giving a speech in Berlin, Germany, 1963

————————— **PREPARING TO READ AND WRITE** —————————

As you read and prepare to write about the essays in this chapter, you may consider the following questions:

- Does the selection deal primarily with written or spoken language?

- Does the writer place more emphasis on the denotations or the connotations of words?

- Does the writer make any distinctions between language applied to males and language applied to females? Do you consider such distinctions valid?

- Does the writer discuss language in the context of a particular culture? Does he or she see language as a unifying or a divisive factor?

- In what ways would the writer like to change or reshape language? What do you see as the possible advantages or disadvantages of such change?

- Does the writer believe that people are shaped by language or that language is shaped by people?

- Does the writer see language as having a particular social or political function? In what sense?

- Does the writer see language as empowering?

- Does the writer make assumptions about people's status on the basis of their use of language? Do these assumptions seem justified?

- Does the writer make a convincing case for the importance of language?

- Is the writer's focus primarily on language's ability to help or its power to harm?

- In what ways are your ideas about the power of words similar to or different from the writer's?

- How is the essay like and unlike other essays in this chapter?

# LOST IN TIME AND WORDS, A CHILD BEGINS ANEW

## Oscar Hijuelos

### 1951–

*Oscar Hijuelos is the first Hispanic novelist to win the Pulitzer Prize, which he received for his book* The Mambo Kings Play Songs of Love *(1989). This highly acclaimed novel was later adapted for film and as a Broadway musical. The author of numerous books, Hijuelos most recently published a memoir,* Thoughts without Cigarettes *(2011). In the following essay, Hijuelos explores the connections between language and home.*

To this day it is hard for me to speak about possessing any real sense of a home, at least during my childhood and adolescence. Or, to put this idea more precisely: whatever sense of a secure home life, of belonging, that I once felt as a boy was whisked out from under my feet at a tender age.

I was born in the summer of 1951 in Manhattan, at Woman's Hospital in Harlem, the first four years of my life passing serenely in our ground-floor walk-through on West 118th Street, where my parents, fresh up from Cuba, had settled in the mid-1940s. What few and primitive memories I have from those years are of a busy and boisterous household, with relatives and newly arrived boarders constantly filling the spare beds and cots we kept in a back room; and of crawling along the floors during the many weekend parties that my papi, a spendthrift Cubano to the core, often gave. On such occasions, our living room, facing the street, became a cozy, if smoke-filled, dance hall, replete with dim lights, music, food and booze—fetes that attracted Cubans and other Latinos to our home from every part of the city.

These were family affairs, with folks of every age, from old abuelitas, or grandmothers, to mothers with newborns. As songs like "The Peanut Vendor" by the Cugat orchestra gushed out of the record player, and people ate plates of arroz con pollo with tostones or some crispy lechón, others—mostly young couples in love, like Frankie the exterminator and his fiancée—took to the dance floor and mamboed away.

On one of those nights, I recall, people rushed to look out the window, pointing with excitement: some kind of crazy and haunted sound had drawn them there. My father lifted me up to see the most amusing thing in the world. There, a local man, celebrating his roots, had dressed up in kilt and tam-o'-shanter and had gone marching along the street, playing old Celtic airs on his bagpipes. So this was America!

5      Our festive apartment was a Cuban oasis in a largely non-Latino block of working-class folks and Columbia University students. My family surely stood apart from our fellow tenants. Neighbors like Mrs. Blair, the elderly and genteel woman living directly across the hall, and Mr. Hess, our German superintendent, did not know any Spanish and were surely bemused by having a little slice of Cuba in their midst.

While my father went off to his job as a morning-to-lunch shift cook at the Biltmore Hotel, it was my mother who cared for me: occasionally she'd wheel my stroller over to the nearby Columbia University campus, by whose fountains we would sit, or down the hill to Morningside Drive with its ivied walls looking eastward over the rooftops of Harlem. Just as often we stayed in the apartment, surrounded by our relatives and guests, our kitchen, with sizzling pans of food, always the busiest place.

But wherever we happened to be, Spanish, rather than English, is what I heard day in and day out. It was, after all, my mother and father's tongue—for years my mother resisted learning more than a handful of English phrases—and it was the language that I identified with the comforts and security of home.

That is, until something inside me changed.

In the summer of 1955, my mother took me to Cuba for three months, to visit with her family in Holguìn, on the rural eastern part of the island. At the end of my Cuban sojourn, I fell deathly ill from a disease of los riñones—the kidneys—a bout of nephritis so severe that, back in the States, I spent a year or so recovering in a hospital in Greenwich, Conn., the black hole of my childhood.

10      It was during that long separation from my family that I became estranged from the Spanish language and, therefore, my roots. I recall returning home from the hospital to the apartment and being only vaguely aware of just who my father, mother and older brother were; and Spanish, the language I had so glibly spoken not so long before, suddenly seemed like a foreign tongue. To my mother's chagrin, I had seemingly lost interest in Spanish, or perhaps forgotten how to speak the language. It was English, which I had absorbed during my hospital stay, that I came to prefer.

The apartment itself, with its sizzling radiators and leaky pipes, and with my souvenir conga drum from Cuba still in my room, seemed vaguely familiar and therefore somewhat comforting. Visitors like Mr. Martinez, a superintendent from up the street, or the deaf and mute Mrs. Walker, with whom my mother somehow had fluent conversations in grunts and gesticulations, were always nice to me. "This is my son, who almost died," my mother would tell them.

But because of my disengagement from Spanish and my frail health, the apartment became something of a prison. I was still considered quite susceptible to infections; as a result, for several years I rarely left home, except when I had an appointment for a checkup. My most frequent companion was my mother, who had begun to regard me, her muy americano[1] son, with increasing exasperation—"Por favor, por que no hablas español?" "Why don't you speak in Spanish?" I had more than a few problems communicating with her, and I began to experience a stranger's solitude.

I, a kid, had become an outsider within my own home.

At this point I should mention another thing: unlike my mother and father, who were dark-featured, I was fair-skinned, blond, hazel-eyed, my looks a throwback to a distant Irish ancestor. That I was so different in appearance from my own parents was something I could see in my mother's eyes, as if, indeed, the son who refused to speak Spanish truly belonged in another household. (Or at least that's my fantasy of how she sometimes saw me.)

Surely then you can imagine how cooped up and lonely I felt. In those 15 years, poised by our living room windows, and unable to play with any friends, I spent many an hour watching the street, where life, in a quite New York way, merrily unfolded. Mainly I envied those kids who were free to do as they pleased, whether it was cussing their brains out while playing cards for cigarettes on our stoop, singing doo-wop or gleefully stomping on the hoods of cars in the midst of a catch during a three-sewer stickball game. The sight of beautiful snow falling, youngsters with their sleds trailing behind them, making their way to Morningside Park, where they would zip down the steepest ice-covered stairways with abandon—it all left me faint-headed with hopes of my own.

In the meantime, before I attended school, my mother became my teacher—not in Spanish, but in English, which she could barely read herself. Spending part of nearly every day by our kitchen table with comic books open before us, we took turns reciting each word aloud: after a while, it was I who corrected her pronunciation. In a tender way, as I think about it now, those afternoons were our most peaceful and unhurried moments—and well worth it, even if my Spanish remained unchanged.

Of course, I got better, grew up and eventually left the strict confinement of my household for the outside world. Not that I easily fit in—I always had a solitary air about me—but I made my friends, among them many Latinos.

Then, as the years passed, while learning the hard way that I did not completely fit in with either group, a funny thing happened to me. Despite the strange baggage that I carried about my upbringing, and despite the relative loss of my first language, I eventually came to the point that, when I heard Spanish, I found my heart warming. And that was the moment when I began to look through another window, not out onto 118th Street, but into myself—through my writing, the process by which, for all my earlier alienation, I had finally returned home.

---

[1]Spanish for *very American*. [Eds.]

## Responding to Reading

1. In paragraph 7, Hijuelos says that Spanish was the language that he "identi-fied with the comforts and security of home." What does he mean? Did the meaning of *home* change for him?
2. What causes Hijuelos to change his opinion of Spanish? How does his year-long stay at a hospital in Connecticut make him "an outsider in his own home" (13)?
3. Does Hijuelos ever resolve the conflict between Spanish and English? What does he mean when he says, "And that was the moment when I began to look through another window, not out onto 118th Street, but into myself—through my writing, the process by which, for all my earlier alienation, I had finally arrived home" (18)?

## Responding in Writing

What do you think Hijuelos gains by primarily speaking English? What do you think he loses?

# MOTHER TONGUE

## Amy Tan

### 1952–

*Amy Tan was born to parents who had emigrated from China only a few years earlier. (Her given name is actually An-mei, which means "blessing from America.") A workaholic, Tan began writing stories as a means of personal therapy, and these stories eventually became the highly successful* The Joy Luck Club *(1987), a novel about Chinese-born mothers and their American-born daughters that was later made into a widely praised film. Tan's other books include four more novels—*The Kitchen God's Wife *(1991),* The Hundred Secret Senses *(1995),* The Bonesetter's Daughter *(2001), and* Saving Fish from Drowning *(2005)—and a work of nonfic-tion,* The Opposite of Fate: A Book of Musings *(2003) as well as two illustrated children's books. In the following essay, which was originally delivered as a speech, Tan considers her relationship with her own mother, concentrating on the different "Englishes" they use to communicate with each other and with the world.*

I am not a scholar of English or literature. I cannot give you much more than personal opinions on the English language and its variations in this country or others.

I am a writer. And by that definition, I am someone who has always loved language. I am fascinated by language in daily life. I spend a great deal of my time thinking about the power of language—the way it can evoke an emotion, a visual image, a complex idea, or a simple truth. Language is the tool of my trade. And I use them all—all the Englishes I grew up with.

Recently, I was made keenly aware of the different Englishes I do use. I was giving a talk to a large group of people, the same talk I had already given to half a dozen other groups. The nature of the talk was about my writing, my life, and my book, *The Joy Luck Club*. The talk was going along well enough, until I remembered one major difference that made the whole talk sound wrong. My mother was in the room. And it was perhaps the first time she had heard me give a lengthy speech, using the kind of English I have never used with her. I was saying things like, "The intersection of memory upon imagination" and "There is an aspect of my fiction that relates to thus-and-thus"—a speech filled with carefully wrought grammatical phrases, burdened, it suddenly seemed to me, with nominalized forms, past perfect tenses, conditional phrases, all the forms of standard English that I had learned in school and through books, the forms of English I did not use at home with my mother.

Just last week, I was walking down the street with my mother, and I again found myself conscious of the English I was using, and the English I do use with her. We were talking about the price of new and used furniture and I heard myself saying this: "Not waste money that way." My husband was with us as well, and he didn't notice any switch in my English. And then I realized why. It's because over the twenty years we've been together I've often used that same kind of English with him, and sometimes he even uses it with me. It has become our language of intimacy, a different sort of English that relates to family talk, the language I grew up with.

So you'll have some idea of what this family talk I heard sounds like, I'll quote what my mother said during a recent conversation which I videotaped and then transcribed. During this conversation, my mother was talking about a political gangster in Shanghai who had the same last name as her family's, Du, and how the gangster in his early years wanted to be adopted by her family, which was rich by comparison. Later, the gangster became more powerful, far richer than my mother's family, and one day showed up at my mother's wedding to pay his respects. Here's what she said in part:

"Du Yusong having business like fruit stand. Like off the street kind. He is Du like Du Zong—but not Tsung-ming Island people. The local people call putong, the river east side, he belong to that side local people. The man want to ask Du Zong father take him in like become own family. Du Zong father wasn't look down on him, but didn't take seriously, until that man big like become a mafia. Now important person, very hard to inviting him. Chinese way, came only to show respect, don't stay for dinner. Respect for making big celebration, he shows up. Mean gives lots of respect. Chinese custom. Chinese social life that way. If too important won't have to stay too long. He come to my wedding. I didn't see, I heard it. I gone to boy's side, they have YMCA dinner. Chinese age I was nineteen."

You should know that my mother's expressive command of English belies how much she actually understands. She reads the Forbes report, listens to *Wall Street Week,* converses daily with her stockbroker, reads all of Shirley MacLaine's[1] books with ease—all kinds of things I can't begin to understand. Yet some of my friends tell me they understand 50 percent of what my mother says. Some say they understand 80 to 90 percent. Some say they understand none of it, as if she were speaking pure Chinese. But to me, my mother's English is perfectly clear, perfectly natural. It's my mother tongue. Her language, as I hear it, is vivid, direct, full of observation and imagery. That was the language that helped shape the way I saw things, expressed things, made sense of the world.

Lately, I've been giving more thought to the kind of English my mother speaks. Like others, I have described it to people as "broken" or "fractured" English. But I wince when I say that. It has always bothered me that I can think of no way to describe it other than "broken," as if it were damaged and needed to be fixed, as if it lacked a certain wholeness and soundness. I've heard other terms used, "limited English," for example. But they seem just as bad, as if everything is limited, including people's perceptions of the limited English speaker.

I know this for a fact, because when I was growing up, my mother's "limited" English limited *my* perception of her. I was ashamed of her English. I believed that her English reflected the quality of what she had to say. That is, because she expressed them imperfectly her thoughts were imperfect. And I had plenty of empirical evidence to support me: the fact that people in department stores, at banks, and at restaurants did not take her seriously, did not give her good service, pretended not to understand her, or even acted as if they did not hear her.

10    My mother has long realized the limitations of her English as well. When I was fifteen, she used to have me call people on the phone to pretend I was she. In this guise, I was forced to ask for information or even to complain and yell at people who had been rude to her. One time it was a call to her stockbroker in New York. She had cashed out her small portfolio and it just so happened we were going to go to New York the next week, our very first trip outside California. I had to get on the phone and say in an adolescent voice that was not very convincing, "This is Mrs. Tan."

And my mother was standing in the back whispering loudly, "Why he don't send me check, already two weeks late. So mad he lie to me, losing me money."

And then I said in perfect English, "Yes, I'm getting rather concerned. You had agreed to send the check two weeks ago, but it hasn't arrived."

---

[1]Actress known for her autobiographical books, in which she traces her many past lives. [Eds.]

Then she began to talk more loudly. "What he want, I come to New York tell him front of his boss, you cheating me?" And I was trying to calm her down, make her be quiet, while telling the stockbroker, "I can't tolerate any more excuses. If I don't receive the check immediately, I am going to have to speak to your manager when I'm in New York next week." And sure enough, the following week there we were in front of this astonished stockbroker, and I was sitting there red-faced and quiet, and my mother, the real Mrs. Tan, was shouting at his boss in her impeccable broken English.

We used a similar routine just five days ago, for a situation that was far less humorous. My mother had gone to the hospital for an appointment, to find out about a benign brain tumor a CAT scan had revealed a month ago. She said she had spoken very good English, her best English, no mistakes. Still, she said, the hospital did not apologize when they said they had lost the CAT scan and she had come for nothing. She said they did not seem to have any sympathy when she told them she was anxious to know the exact diagnosis, since her husband and son had both died of brain tumors. She said they would not give her any more information until the next time and she would have to make another appointment for that. So she said she would not leave until the doctor called her daughter. She wouldn't budge. And when the doctor finally called her daughter, me, who spoke in perfect English—lo and behold—we had assurances the CAT scan would be found, promises that a conference call on Monday would be held, and apologies for any suffering my mother had gone through for a most regrettable mistake.

I think my mother's English almost had an effect on limiting my 15 possibilities in life as well. Sociologists and linguists probably will tell you that a person's developing language skills are more influenced by peers. But I do think that the language spoken in the family, especially in immigrant families which are more insular, plays a large role in shaping the language of the child. And I believe that it affected my results on achievement tests, IQ tests, and the SAT. While my English skills were never judged as poor, compared to math, English could not be considered my strong suit. In grade school I did moderately well, getting perhaps B's, sometimes B-pluses, in English and scoring perhaps in the sixtieth or seventieth percentile on achievement tests. But those scores were not good enough to override the opinion that my true abilities lay in math and science, because in those areas I achieved A's and scored in the ninetieth percentile or higher.

This was understandable. Math is precise; there is only one correct answer. Whereas, for me at least, the answers on English tests were always a judgment call, a matter of opinion and personal experience. Those tests were constructed around items like fill-in-the-blank sentence completion, such as, "Even though Tom was _____ , Mary thought he was _____." And the correct answer always seemed to be the most bland combinations of thoughts, for example, "Even though Tom was shy, Mary thought he was charming," with the grammatical structure "even though" limiting the correct answer to some sort of semantic opposites, so you wouldn't get answers like, "Even though Tom was foolish, Mary thought he was ridiculous." Well, according to my mother, there were very few limitations as to what Tom could have been and what Mary might have thought of him. So I never did well on tests like that.

The same was true with word analogies, pairs of words in which you were supposed to find some sort of logical, semantic relationship—for example, "*Sunset* is to *nightfall* as _____ is to _____." And here you would be presented with a list of four possible pairs, one of which showed the same kind of relationship: *red* is to *stoplight, bus* is to *arrival, chills* is to *fever, yawn* is to *boring*. Well, I could never think that way. I knew what the tests were asking, but I could not block out of my mind the images already created by the first pair, "*sunset* is to *nightfall*"—and I would see a burst of colors against a darkening sky, the moon rising, the lowering of a curtain of stars. And all the other pairs of words—red, bus, stoplight, boring—just threw up a mass of confusing images, making it impossible for me to sort out something as logical as saying: "A sunset precedes nightfall" is the same as "a chill precedes a fever." The only way I would have gotten that answer right would have been to imagine an associative situation, for example, my being disobedient and staying out past sunset, catching a chill at night, which turns into feverish pneumonia as punishment, which indeed did happen to me.

I have been thinking about all this lately, about my mother's English, about achievement tests. Because lately I've been asked, as a writer, why there are not more Asian Americans represented in American literature. Why are there few Asian Americans enrolled in creative writing programs? Why do so many Chinese students go into engineering? Well, these are broad sociological questions I can't begin to answer. But I have noticed in surveys—in fact, just last week—that Asian students, as a whole, always do significantly better on math achievement tests than in English. And this makes me think that there are other Asian-American students whose English spoken in the home might also be described as "broken" or "limited." And perhaps they also have teachers who are steering them away from writing and into math and science, which is what happened to me.

Fortunately, I happen to be rebellious in nature and enjoy the challenge of disproving assumptions made about me. I became an English major my first year in college, after being enrolled as pre-med. I started writing nonfiction as a freelancer the week after I was told by my former boss that writing was my worst skill and I should hone my talents toward account management.

But it wasn't until 1985 that I finally began to write fiction. And at 20 first I wrote using what I thought to be wittily crafted sentences, sentences that would finally prove I had mastery over the English language. Here's an example from the first draft of a story that later made its way into *The Joy Luck Club*, but without this line: "That was my mental quandary in its nascent state." A terrible line, which I can barely pronounce.

Fortunately, for reasons I won't get into today, I later decided I should envision a reader for the stories I would write. And the reader I decided upon was my mother, because these were stories about mothers. So with this reader in mind—and in fact she did read my early drafts—I began to write stories using all the Englishes I grew up with: the English I spoke to my mother, which for lack of a better term might be described as "simple"; the English she used with me, which for lack of a better term might be described as "broken"; my translation of her Chinese, which could certainly be described as "watered down"; and what I imagined to be her translation of her Chinese if she could speak in perfect English, her internal language, and for that I sought to preserve the essence, but neither an English nor a Chinese structure. I wanted to capture what language ability tests can never reveal: her intent, her passion, her imagery, the rhythms of her speech and the nature of her thoughts.

Apart from what any critic had to say about my writing, I knew I had succeeded where it counted when my mother finished reading my book and gave me her verdict: "So easy to read."

## Responding to Reading

1. Why does Tan begin her essay with the disclaimer, "I am not a scholar of English or literature. I cannot give you much more than personal opinions" (1)? Do these statements add to her credibility or detract from it? Explain.
2. Tan implies that some languages are more expressive than others. Do you agree? Are there some ideas you can express in one language that are difficult or impossible to express in another? Give examples if you can.
3. Do you agree with Tan's statement in paragraph 15 that the kind of English spoken at home can have an effect on a student's performance on IQ tests and the SAT?

## Responding in Writing

Do you think the English you speak at home has had a positive or a negative effect on your performance in school?

# PERSIAN, ENGLISH

## Jasmin Darznik

### 1973–

*An assistant professor of English at Washington and Lee University, Jasmin Darznik writes essays and stories that explore her Iranian cultural heritage. Her work has appeared in such publications as the* Los Angeles review, *the* Los Angeles Times *magazine, the* New York Times, San Francisco Chronicle *magazine, and the* Washington Post *magazine. She is the author of* The Good Daughter: A Memoir of My Mother's Hidden Life *(2011). In the following essay, Darznik examines her complex relationship with the Persian language.*

It's the new language that leads me astray, cuts off my mother tongue and carries me off in a jumble of strange words. "Whisper." "Marshmallow." Did I ever have the language for these? Slowly I learn to look at the world backwards, train my eye to move left to right instead of the Persian way around the page. The lines of my first penmanship—lines that flowed down and across every boundary—fall to waste. In their place I trace stocky letters easily contained between dotted lines.

When we first came to America in 1979, my mother always dragged me along on her trips to the grocery store and I'd stand by mutely as she struggled to communicate with Americans. Very soon I could tell that hers was not a fashionable or exotic accent, but rough and ugly to these strangers' ears. One word out of her mouth and Americans would stare her down, hard and long. My mother seemed not to notice or care; if anything she pitied Americans their apparent stupidity. But not me. Whenever my mother spoke English, even a word or a sentence of it, I cringed. I'd inch away from her and quietly disappear behind a rack of clothes or scramble down the next grocery aisle.

Pride, I happen to believe, is not a child's native instinct. It needs to be taught and learned—and often for good reason. Shame, though, comes very easily to a child and is only very rarely undone by later experience. It can, however, inspire certain abiding talents and affections. Shame took my Persian and gave me English.

In America I might have cleaved myself to Persian, but survival—even the most basic social survival—depended on learning English and learning it fast. But once I mastered the rudiments of reading and writing, English became less a matter of survival than something beginning to resemble love. I began to make my way through stacks and stacks of library books. I polished off essays and began to walk away with all the school literary prizes. And it was here that my problems with Persian really began.

My parents prided themselves on the seeming ease with which I picked up English. In public with Americans, my mother would nudge me and whisper, "Show them how well you can speak! Even better than those Americans!" In time my parents learned to speak English well enough to make their own way in America, but for many, they had me assume the role of the family's official translator and all-purpose intermediary between "us" and "them." At home, though, I could expect nothing but reprimands for speaking "that" language instead of "ours." "Don't use your big English words on me!" my mother would often warn me as a child.

But while I grew up speaking Persian at home, mine is a diminished and misshapen native tongue, a remnant of all the imposed boundaries of my childhood. The Iranian world that my family and their friends reconstructed here in California was in fact made up of two very different worlds, each with its distinct vocabulary and distinct topics of conversation. Whenever my parents' Iranian friends used to gather for dinner parties, birthday fetes, and Norooz[1] celebrations, invariably the men and women would part ways just as soon as they stepped out of their cars and over the threshold of their host's home.

As a girl, my place was with the women. For many years I was content to sit among them, silently listening to their talk. Their fancy attire, animated gestures and gossipy conversations fascinated me as a child, and my presence was tolerated so long as I sat quietly and fulfilled my duty of replenishing their plates of food and cups of tea.

Yet with each year that went by in America, I'd cast more of a longing look at the other camp. Emboldened by my little bits of learning, I yearned to join the men in their earnest talk of Iranian politics and Persian literature. But very few women crossed that invisible boundary in those days and in those circles of ours, and it was unthinkable that I, a young girl, should pull up a chair next to grown men. It would have been indecent.

So over the years, my Persian grew up around these women's lives and the particular language they spoke to each other. And my tongue wrapped itself around the role I played at these functions, the forever deferential and soft-spoken daughter.

Now when other Iranians hear how long I have lived abroad, they will tell me how good my Persian still is. But I know the truth: my Persian is oddly and unmistakably stunted. Sure, by force of habit I've learned all the compliments and pleasantries. I speak a colloquial Persian that gets me by remarkably well in most circumstances, but it's far from a high or literary Persian. And in the Persian language that boundary makes a world of difference.

---

[1]Iranian New Year. [Eds.]

It's a discomfiting tongue on me, this Persian of mine. When I speak it now, even when I take care I hear an infantile version of myself speaking. In Persian I am more bashful, sweet, and polite. Even the tone of my voice is different—it is a far, far softer voice than my voice in English.

In America Persian has been my language of infancy, intimacy, manners, and—perhaps most of all—of boundaries. You can hear it as soon as I open my mouth, which is why as an adult I have so very often preferred silence. For me it's been English for school, work, and Americans, and Persian for home, family, and Iranians. Endearments still sound sweetest to me in Persian, and it's in expressing emotion that I'll most readily surrender to it. Ideas, though, come to my mind and out of my mouth in English.

I remember there once was a distant relative my parents loved to ridicule. One day in America, this relative up and decided he would forget he had ever spoken Persian. Other relatives would taunt him, turning the situation into a sort of contest over who would finally make him break out and speak his native language. But this man held fast. He has never, so far as anyone knows, spoken Persian again.

The truth is that I have also been eager to unburden myself of my native tongue and the world to which it bound me. For me, leaving home and my girlish self has meant long absences from this, my mother tongue. The road away is easy, too easy really—except that curious detours begin to appear far along the way. When recently I started to read Persian poetry in translation my interest was neither benign nor benevolent. I wanted to see what all the fuss was about. What was this great legacy of poetry of which every Iranian spoke but only a few seemed to know intimately and well?

15    The first surprise would be that translation itself was less than transparent and much less than innocent. When I began to read Persian poetry in translation I could hear the muffled voice of that other language, the real language that lay beneath the English translation. That voice kept slowing me down and tripping me up. I thought I could hear some of the original verses quite clearly, and I'd quarrel with the translator over his choice of words. It didn't matter if I was right. Probably I often wasn't. The point is that I still had enough Persian left in me for a fight.

I'll always speak many languages, but I have grown tired of forked tongues and split selves and mistaken identities. I want to access Iranian worlds that correspond to worlds I know in English. But first I need to suit myself up with a new Persian language. And so, embarrassed, wary, curious, and afraid, I've begun the long process of willing this old language of mine into a new form. I've begun my life in this new old language by dragging out the tattered old language primers from my childhood, the ones with the silly stories and cartoon drawings of school children. I left them behind years ago to reach instead for Keats, Bronte, Woolf and, much later, for volumes of translated Persian poetry. I just might never make it from here to meet Hāfez or Farrokhzād[2] in our common language, but at long last I'm working my way in their direction.

## Responding to Reading

1. What does Darznik mean when she says, "Shame took my Persian and gave me English" (3)?
2. What "two very different worlds" did Darznik's Iranian family and friends establish in California? How are these two worlds different? With which one does Darznik identify?
3. Why was Darznik eager to "unburden" herself of Persian (14)? Why did she consider it a burden? What is her attitude toward the Persian language now?

## Responding in Writing

To become United States citizens, immigrants must demonstrate proficiency in English. Do you think this requirement is fair, or do you think it places an unfair burden on applicants for citizenship?

# LEARNING TO READ AND WRITE
## Frederick Douglass
### 1817–1895

*Frederick Douglass was born a slave in rural Talbot County, Maryland, and later served a family in Baltimore. After escaping to the North in 1838, he settled in Bedford, Massachusetts, where he became active in the abolitionist movement. He recounts these experiences in his most famous work,* Narrative of the Life of Frederick Douglass *(1845). After spending almost two years in England and Europe on a lecture tour, Douglass returned to the United States and purchased his freedom. In 1847, he launched the antislavery newspaper* The North Star *and became a vocal supporter of both Abraham Lincoln and the Civil War. Throughout his life, Douglass believed that the United States Constitution, if interpreted correctly, would enable African Americans to become full participants in the economic, social, and intellectual life of America. In the following excerpt from his* Narrative, *Douglass writes of outwitting his owners to become literate, thereby finding "the pathway from slavery to freedom."*

I lived in Master Hugh's family about seven years. During this time, I succeeded in learning to read and write. In accomplishing this, I was compelled to resort to various stratagems. I had no regular teacher. My

---

[2]Hāfez (1325/26–1389/90) and Forugh Farrokhzād (1935–1967), Persian poets. [Eds.]

mistress, who had kindly commenced to instruct me, had, in compliance with the advice and direction of her husband, not only ceased to instruct, but had set her face against my being instructed by any one else. It is due, however, to my mistress to say of her, that she did not adopt this course of treatment immediately. She at first lacked the depravity indispensable to shutting me up in mental darkness. It was at least necessary for her to have some training in the exercise of irresponsible power, to make her equal to the task of treating me as though I were a brute.

My mistress was, as I have said, a kind and tender-hearted woman; and in the simplicity of her soul she commenced, when I first went to live with her, to treat me as she supposed one human being ought to treat another. In entering upon the duties of a slaveholder, she did not seem to perceive that I sustained to her the relation of a mere chattel,[1] and that for her to treat me as a human being was not only wrong, but dangerously so. Slavery proved as injurious to her as it did to me. When I went there, she was a pious, warm, and tender-hearted woman. There was no sorrow or suffering for which she had not a tear. She had bread for the hungry, clothes for the naked, and comfort for every mourner that came within her reach. Slavery soon proved its ability to divest her of these heavenly qualities. Under its influence, the tender heart became stone, and the lamblike disposition gave way to one of tigerlike fierceness. The first step in her downward course was in her ceasing to instruct me. She now commenced to practice her husband's precepts. She finally became even more violent in her opposition than her husband himself. She was not satisfied with simply doing as well as he had commanded; she seemed anxious to do better. Nothing seemed to make her more angry than to see me with a newspaper. She seemed to think that here lay the danger. I have had her rush at me with a face made all up of fury, and snatch from me a newspaper, in a manner that fully revealed her apprehension. She was an apt woman; and a little experience soon demonstrated, to her satisfaction, that education and slavery were incompatible with each other.

From this time I was most narrowly watched. If I was in a separate room any considerable length of time, I was sure to be suspected of having a book, and was at once called to give an account of myself. All this, however, was too late. The first step had been taken. Mistress, in teaching me the alphabet, had given me the *inch*, and no precaution could prevent me from taking the *ell*.

The plan which I adopted, and the one by which I was most successful, was that of making friends of all the little white boys whom I met in the street. As many of these as I could, I converted into teachers. With their kindly aid, obtained at different times and in different places,

---

[1]Property. [Eds.]

I finally succeeded in learning to read. When I was sent on errands, I always took my book with me, and by going one part of my errand quickly, I found time to get a lesson before my return. I used also to carry bread with me, enough of which was always in the house, and to which I was always welcome; for I was much better off in this regard than many of the poor white children in our neighborhood. This bread I used to bestow upon the hungry little urchins, who, in return, would give me that more valuable bread of knowledge. I am strongly tempted to give the names of two or three of those little boys, as a testimonial of the gratitude and affection I bear them; but prudence forbids;—not that it would injure me, but it might embarrass them; for it is almost an unpardonable offense to teach slaves to read in this Christian country. It is enough to say of the dear little fellows, that they lived on Philpot Street, very near Durgin and Bailey's ship-yard. I used to talk this matter of slavery over with them. I would sometimes say to them, I wished I could be as free as they would be when they got to be men. "You will be free as soon as you are twenty-one, *but I am a slave for life!* Have not I as good a right to be free as you have?" These words used to trouble them; they would express for me the liveliest sympathy, and console me with the hope that something would occur by which I might be free.

I was now about twelve years old, and the thought of being *a slave for life* began to bear heavily upon my heart. Just about this time, I got hold of a book entitled "The Columbian Orator."[2] Every opportunity I got, I used to read this book. Among much of other interesting matter, I found in it a dialogue between a master and his slave. The slave was represented as having run away from his master three times. The dialogue represented the conversation which took place between them, when the slave was retaken the third time. In this dialogue, the whole argument in behalf of slavery was brought forward by the master, all of which was disposed of by the slave. The slave was made to say some very smart as well as impressive things in reply to his master—things which had the desired though unexpected effect; for the conversation resulted in the voluntary emancipation of the slave on the part of the master.

In the same book, I met with one of Sheridan's mighty speeches on and in behalf of Catholic emancipation.[3] These were choice documents to me. I read them over and over again with unabated interest. They gave tongue to interesting thoughts of my own soul, which had frequently flashed through my mind, and died away for want of utterance. The moral which I gained from the dialogue was the power of truth over the conscience of even a slaveholder. What I got from Sheridan was a

---

[2]A popular textbook that taught the principles of effective public speaking. [Eds.]

[3]Richard Brinsley Sheridan (1751–1816), British playwright and statesman who made speeches supporting the right of English Catholics to vote. Full emancipation was not granted to Catholics until 1829. [Eds.]

bold denunciation of slavery, and a powerful vindication of human rights. The reading of these documents enabled me to utter my thoughts, and to meet the arguments brought forward to sustain slavery; but while they relieved me of one difficulty, they brought on another even more painful than the one of which I was relieved. The more I read, the more I was led to abhor and detest my enslavers. I could regard them in no other light than a band of successful robbers, who had left their homes, and gone to Africa, and stolen us from our homes, and in a strange land reduced us to slavery. I loathed them as being the meanest as well as the most wicked of men. As I read and contemplated the subject, behold! that very discontentment which Master Hugh had predicted would follow my learning to read had already come, to torment and sting my soul to unutterable anguish. As I writhed under it, I would at times feel that learning to read had been a curse rather than a blessing. It had given me a view of my wretched condition, without the remedy. It opened my eyes to the horrible pit, but to no ladder upon which to get out. In moments of agony, I envied my fellow-slaves for their stupidity. I have often wished myself a beast. I preferred the condition of the meanest reptile to my own. Any thing, no matter what, to get rid of thinking! It was the everlasting thinking of my condition that tormented me. There was no getting rid of it. It was pressed upon me by every object within sight or hearing, animate or inanimate. The silver trump of freedom had roused my soul to eternal wakefulness. Freedom now appeared, to disappear no more forever. It was heard in every sound, and seen in every thing. It was ever present to torment me with a sense of my wretched condition. I saw nothing without seeing it, I heard nothing without hearing it, and felt nothing without feeling it. It looked from every star, it smiled in every calm, breathed in every wind, and moved in every storm.

I often found myself regretting my own existence, and wishing myself dead; and but for the hope of being free, I have no doubt but that I should have killed myself, or done something for which I should have been killed. While in this state of mind, I was eager to hear any one speak of slavery. I was a ready listener. Every little while, I could hear something about the abolitionists. It was some time before I found what the word meant. It was always used in such connections as to make it an interesting word to me. If a slave ran away and succeeded in getting clear, or if a slave killed his master, set fire to a barn, or did any thing very wrong in the mind of a slaveholder, it was spoken of as the fruit of *abolition*. Hearing the word in this connection very often, I set about learning what it meant. The dictionary afforded me little or no help. I found it was "the act of abolishing"; but then I did not know what was to be abolished. Here I was perplexed. I did not dare to ask any one about its meaning, for I was satisfied that it was something they wanted me to know very little about. After a patient waiting, I got one of our city papers, containing an account of the number of petitions from the north, praying for the abolition of slavery in the District of Columbia, and of the slave trade between the States. From this time I understood the words *abolition* and *abolitionist*, and always drew near when that word was spoken, expecting to hear something of importance to myself and fellow-slaves. The light broke in upon me by degrees. I went one day down on the wharf of Mr. Waters; and seeing two Irishmen unloading a scow of stone, I went, unasked, and helped them. When we had finished, one of them came to me and asked me if I were a slave. I told him I was. He asked, "Are ye a slave for life?" I told him that I was. The good Irishman seemed to be deeply affected by the statement. He said to the other that it was a pity so fine a little fellow as myself should be a slave for life. He said it was a shame to hold me. They both advised me to run away to the north; that I should find friends there, and that I should be free. I pretended not to be interested in what they said, and treated them as if I did not understand them; for I feared they might be treacherous. White men have been known to encourage slaves to escape, and then, to get the reward, catch them and return them to their masters. I was afraid that these seemingly good men might use me so; but I nevertheless remembered their advice, and from that time I resolved to run away. I looked forward to a time at which it would be safe for me to escape. I was too young to think of doing so immediately; besides, I wished to learn how to write, as I might have occasion to write my own pass. I consoled myself with the hope that I should one day find a good chance. Meanwhile, I would learn to write.

The idea as to how I might learn to write was suggested to me by being in Durgin and Bailey's ship-yard, and frequently seeing the ship carpenters, after hewing, and getting a piece of timber ready for use, write on the timber the name of that part of the ship for which it was intended. When a piece of timber was intended for the larboard side, it would be marked thus—"L." When a piece was for the starboard side, it would be marked thus—"S." A piece for the larboard side forward, would be marked thus—"L. F." When a piece was for starboard side forward, it would be marked thus—"S. F." For larboard aft, it would be marked thus—"L. A." For starboard aft, it would be marked thus—"S. A." I soon learned the names of these letters, and for what they were intended when placed upon a piece of timber in the shipyard. I immediately commenced copying them, and in a short time was able to make the four letters named. After that, when I met with any boy who I knew could write, I would tell him I could write as well as he. The next word would be, "I don't believe you. Let me see you try it." I would then make the letters which I had been so fortunate as to learn, and ask him to beat that. In this way I got a good many lessons in writing, which it is quite possible I should never have gotten in any other way. During this time, my copy-book was the board fence, brick wall, and pavement; my pen and ink was a lump of chalk. With these, I learned mainly how to write. I then commenced and continued copying the Italics in Webster's Spelling Book, until I could make them all without looking on the book. By this time, my little Master Thomas had gone to school, and learned how to write, and had written over a number of copy-books. These had been brought home, and shown to some of our near neighbors, and then laid aside. My mistress used to go to class meeting at the Wilk Street meetinghouse every Monday afternoon, and leave me to take care of the house. When left thus, I used to spend the time in writing in the spaces left in Master Thomas's copy-book, copying what he had written. I continued to do this until I could write a hand very similar to that of Master Thomas. Thus, after a long, tedious effort for years, I finally succeeded in learning how to write.

## Responding to Reading

1.  What does Douglass mean in paragraph 2 when he says that slavery proved as harmful to his mistress as it did to him? In spite of his owners' actions, what strategies did Douglass use to learn to read?
2.  Douglass escaped from slavery in 1838 and became a leading figure in the antislavery movement. How did reading and writing help him develop his ideas about slavery? In what way did language empower him?
3.  What comment do you think Douglass's essay makes on the condition of African Americans in the mid-nineteenth century?

## Responding in Writing

Does this essay, written over 150 years ago, have relevance today? Explain.

# SEXISM IN ENGLISH: EMBODIMENT AND LANGUAGE

## Alleen Pace Nilsen

### 1936–

*Alleen Pace Nilsen is an educator and essayist. Her most recent book, coauthored with her husband, is* Names and Naming in Young Adult Literature *(2007). When Nilsen lived in Afghanistan in the 1960s, she observed the subordinate position of women in that society. When she returned to the United States, she studied American English for its cultural biases toward men and women. Nilsen says of that project, "As I worked my way through the dictionary, I concentrated on the way particular usages, metaphors, slang terms, and definitions reveal society's attitude toward males and females." The following essay is an updated version of Nilsen's findings from her dictionary study.*

During the late 1960s, I lived with my husband and three young children in Kabul, Afghanistan. This was before the Russian invasion, the Afghan civil war, and the eventual taking over of the country by the Taleban Islamic movement and its resolve to return the country to a strict Islamic dynasty, in which females are not allowed to attend school or work outside their homes.

But even when we were there and the country was considered moderate rather than extremist, I was shocked to observe how different were the roles assigned to males and females. The Afghan version of the *chaderi*[1] prescribed by Moslem women was particularly confining. Women in religious families were required to wear it whenever they were outside their family home, with the result being that most of them didn't venture outside.

The household help we hired were made up of men, because women could not be employed by foreigners. Afghan folk stories and jokes were blatantly sexist, as in this proverb: "If you see an old man, sit down and take a lesson; if you see an old woman, throw a stone."

But it wasn't only the native culture that made me question women's roles, it was also the American community within Afghanistan.

Most of the American women were like myself—wives and mothers whose husbands were either career diplomats, employees of USAID, or college professors who had been recruited to work on various contract teams. We were suddenly bereft of our traditional roles: The local economy provided few jobs for women and certainly none for foreigners; we were isolated from former friends and the social goals we had grown up with. Some of us became alcoholics, others got very good at bridge, while still others searched desperately for ways to contribute either to our families or to the Afghans.

When we returned in the fall of 1969 to the University of Michigan in Ann Arbor, I was surprised to find that many other women were also questioning the expectations they had grown up with. Since I had been an English major when I was in college, I decided that for my part in the feminist movement I would study the English language and see what it could tell me about sexism. I started reading a desk dictionary and making note cards on every entry that seemed to tell something different about male and female. I soon had a dog-eared dictionary, along with a collection of note cards filling two shoe boxes.

The first thing I learned was that I couldn't study the language without getting involved in social issues. Language and society are as intertwined as a chicken and an egg. The language a culture uses is telltale evidence of the values and beliefs of that culture. And because there is a lag in how fast a language changes—new words can easily be

5

---

[1]A *chaderi* is a heavily draped cloth covering the entire head and body. [Eds.]

introduced, but it takes a long time for old words and usages to disappear—a careful look at English will reveal the attitudes that our ancestors held and that we as a culture are therefore predisposed to hold. My note cards revealed three main points. While friends have offered the opinion that I didn't need to read a dictionary to learn such obvious facts, the linguistic evidence lends credibility to the sociological observations.

## Women Are Sexy; Men Are Successful

First, in American culture a woman is valued for the attractiveness and sexiness of her body, while a man is valued for his physical strength and accomplishments. A woman is sexy. A man is successful.

A persuasive piece of evidence supporting this view are the eponyms—words that have come from someone's name—found in English. I had a two-and-a-half-inch stack of cards taken from men's names but less than a half-inch stack from women's names, and most of those came from Greek mythology. In the words that came into American English since we separated from Britain, there are many eponyms based on the names of famous American men: Bartlett pear, boysenberry, Franklin stove, Ferris wheel, Gatling gun, mason jar, sideburns, sousaphone, Schick test, and Winchester rifle. The only common eponyms that I found taken from American women's names are Alice blue (after Alice Roosevelt Longworth), bloomers (after Amelia Jenks Bloomer), and Mae West jacket (after the buxom actress). Two out of the three feminine eponyms relate closely to a woman's physical anatomy, while the masculine eponyms (except for "sideburns" after General Burnsides) have nothing to do with the namesake's body, but, instead, honor the man for an accomplishment of some kind.

10    In Greek mythology women played a bigger role than they did in the biblical stories of the Judeo-Christian cultures, and so the names of goddesses are accepted parts of the language in such place names as Pomona, from the goddess of fruit, and Athens, from Athena, and in such common words as *cereal* from Ceres, *psychology* from Psyche, and *arachnoid* from Arachne. However, there is the same tendency to think of women in relation to sexuality as shown through the eponyms *aphrodisiac* from Aphrodite, the Greek name for the goddess of love and beauty, and *venereal disease* from Venus, the Roman name for Aphrodite.

Another interesting word from Greek mythology is *Amazon*. According to Greek folk etymology, the *a-* means "without," as in *atypical* or *amoral*, while *-mazon* comes from *mazos*, meaning "breast," as still seen in *mastectomy*. In the Greek legend, Amazon women cut off their right breasts so they could better shoot their bows. Apparently, the storytellers had a feeling that for women to play the active, "masculine" role the Amazons adopted for themselves, they had to trade in part of their femininity.

This preoccupation with women's breasts is not limited to the Greeks; it's what inspired the definition and the name for "mammals" (from Indo-European *mammae* for "breasts"). As a volunteer for the University of Wisconsin's *Dictionary of American Regional English (DARE),* I read a western trapper's diary from the 1830s. I was to make notes of any unusual usages or language patterns. My most interesting finding was that the trapper referred to a range of mountains as "The Teats," a metaphor based on the similarity between the shapes of the mountains and women's breasts. Because today we use the French wording "The Grand Tetons," the metaphor isn't as obvious, but I wrote to mapmakers and found the following listings: Nipple Top and Little Nipple Top near Mount Marcy in the Adirondacks; Nipple Mountain in Archuleta County, Colorado; Nipple Peak in Coke County, Texas; Nipple Butte in Pennington, South Dakota; Squaw Peak in Placer County, California (and many other locations); Maiden's Peak and Squaw Tit (they're the same mountain) in the Cascade Range in Oregon; Mary's Nipple near Salt Lake City, Utah; and Jane Russell Peaks near Stark, New Hampshire.

Except for the movie star Jane Russell, the women being referred to are anonymous—it's only a sexual part of their body that is mentioned. When topographical features are named after men, it's probably not going to be to draw attention to a sexual part of their bodies but instead to honor individuals for an accomplishment.

Going back to what I learned from my dictionary cards, I was surprised to realize how many pairs of words we have in which the feminine word has acquired sexual connotations while the masculine word retains a serious businesslike aura. For example, a callboy is the person who calls actors when it is time for them to go on stage, but a callgirl is a prostitute. Compare sir and madam. *Sir* is a term of respect, while *madam* has acquired the specialized meaning of a brothel manager. Something similar has happened to master and mistress. Would you rather have a painting "by an old master" or "by an old mistress"?

It's because the word *woman* had sexual connotations, as in "She's his woman," that people began avoiding its use, hence such terminology as ladies' room, lady of the house, and girl's school or school for young ladies. Those of us who in the 1970s began asking that speakers use the term *woman* rather than *girl* or *lady* were rejecting the idea that *woman* is primarily a sexual term.

I found two-hundred pairs of words with masculine and feminine forms; for example, *heir/heiress, hero/heroine, steward/stewardess, usher/usherette.* In nearly all such pairs, the masculine word is considered the base, with some kind of a feminine suffix being added. The masculine form is the one from which compounds are made; for example, from *king/queen* comes *kingdom* but not *queendom*, from *sportsman/sports-lady* comes *sportsmanship* but not *sportsladyship*. There is one—and only one—semantic area in which the masculine word is not the base or more powerful word. This is in the area dealing with sex, marriage, and motherhood. When someone refers to a virgin, a listener will probably think of a female unless the speaker specifies male or uses a masculine pronoun. The same is true for *prostitute*.

In relation to marriage, linguistic evidence shows that weddings are more important to women than to men. A woman cherishes the wedding and is considered a bride for a whole year, but a man is referred to as a groom only on the day of the wedding. The word *bride* appears in *bridal attendant, bridal gown, bridesmaid, bridal shower,* and even *bridegroom. Groom* comes from the Middle English *grom,* meaning "man," and in that sense is seldom used outside of the wedding. With most pairs of male/female words, people habitually put the masculine word first: *Mr. and Mrs., his and hers, boys and girls, men and women, kings and queens, brothers and sisters, guys and dolls,* and *host and hostess.* But it is the bride and groom who are talked about, not the groom and bride.

The importance of marriage to a woman is also shown by the fact that when a marriage ends in death, the woman gets the title of widow. A man gets the derived title of widower. This term is not used in other phrases or contexts, but widow is seen in widowhood, widow's peak, and widow's walk. A widow in a card game is an extra hand of cards, while in typesetting it is a leftover line of type.

Changing cultural ideas bring changes to language, and since I did my dictionary study three decades ago the word *singles* has largely replaced such gender-specific and value-laden terms as *bachelor, old maid, spinster, divorcee, widow,* and *widower.* In 1970 I wrote that when people hear a man called "a professional," they usually think of him as a doctor or a lawyer, but when people hear a woman referred to as "a professional," they are likely to think of her as a prostitute. That's not as true today because so many women have become doctors and lawyers, it's no longer incongruous to think of women in those professional roles.

20    Another change that has taken place is in wedding announcements. They used to be sent out from the bride's parents and did not even give the name of the groom's parents. Today, most couples choose to list either all or none of the parents' names. Also it is now much more likely that both the bride and groom's picture will be in the newspaper, while twenty years ago only the bride's picture was published on the "Women's" or the "Society" page. In the weddings I have recently attended, the official has pronounced the couple "husband and wife" instead of the traditional "man and wife," and the bride has been asked if she promises to "love, honor, and cherish," instead of to "love, honor, and obey."

## Women Are Passive; Men Are Active

However, other wording in the wedding ceremony relates to a second point that my cards showed, which is that women are expected to play a passive or weak role while men play an active or strong role. In the traditional ceremony, the official asks, "Who gives the bride away?" and the father answers, "I do." Some fathers answer, "Her mother and I do," but that doesn't solve the problem inherent in the question. The idea that a bride is something to be handed over from one man to another bothers people because it goes back to the days when a man's servants, his children, and his wife were all considered to be his property. They were known by his name because they belonged to him, and he was responsible for their actions and their debts.

The grammar used in talking or writing about weddings as well as other sexual relationships shows the expectation of men playing the active role. Men *wed* women while women *become* brides of men. A man *possesses* a woman; he *deflowers* her; he *performs*; he *scores*; he *takes away* her virginity. Although a woman can *seduce* a man, she cannot offer him her virginity. When talking about virginity, the only way to make the woman the actor in the sentence is to say that "she lost her virginity," but people lose things by accident rather than by purposeful actions, and so she's only the grammatical, not the real-life, actor.

The reason that women brought the term Ms. into the language to replace Miss and Mrs. relates to this point. Many married women resent being identified in the "Mrs. Husband" form. The dictionary cards showed what appeared to be an attitude on the part of the editors that it was almost indecent to let a respectable woman's name march unaccompanied across the pages of a dictionary. Women were listed with male names whether or not the male contributed to the woman's reason for being in the dictionary or whether or not in his own right he was as famous as the woman. For example:

Charlotte Brontë = Mrs. Arthur B. Nicholls
Amelia Earhart = Mrs. George Palmer Putnam
Helen Hayes = Mrs. Charles MacArthur
Jenny Lind = Mme. Otto Goldschmit
Cornelia Otis Skinner = daughter of Otis
Harriet Beecher Stowe = sister of Henry Ward Beecher
Dame Edith Sitwell = sister of Osbert and Sacheverell[2]

Only a small number of rebels and crusaders got into the dictionary without the benefit of a masculine escort: temperance leaders Frances

---

[2]Charlotte Brontë (1816–1855), author of *Jane Eyre*; Amelia Earhart (1898–1937), first woman to fly over the Atlantic; Helen Hayes (1900–1993), actress; Jenny Lind (1820–1887), Swedish soprano; Cornelia Otis Skinner (1901–1979), actress and writer; Harriet Beecher Stowe (1811–1896), author of *Uncle Tom's Cabin*; Edith Sitwell (1877–1964), English poet and critic. [Eds.]

Elizabeth Caroline Willard and Carry Nation, women's rights leaders Carrie Chapman Catt and Elizabeth Cady Stanton, birth control educator Margaret Sanger, religious leader Mary Baker Eddy, and slaves Harriet Tubman and Phillis Wheatley.

Etiquette books used to teach that if a woman had Mrs. in front of her name, then the husband's name should follow because Mrs. is an abbreviated form of Mistress and a woman couldn't be a mistress of herself. As with many arguments about "correct" language usage, this isn't very logical because Miss is also an abbreviation of Mistress. Feminists hoped to simplify matters by introducing Ms. as an alternative to both Mrs. and Miss, but what happened is that Ms. largely replaced Miss to become a catch-all business title for women. Many married women still prefer the title Mrs., and some even resent being addressed with the term Ms. As one frustrated newspaper reporter complained, "Before I can write about a woman I have to know not only her marital status but also her political philosophy." The result of such complications may contribute to the demise of titles, which are already being ignored by many writers who find it more efficient to simply use names; for example, in a business letter: "Dear Joan Garcia," instead of "Dear Mrs. Joan Garcia," "Dear Ms. Garcia," or "Dear Mrs. Louis Garcia."

25      Titles given to royalty show how males can be disadvantaged by the assumption that they always play the more powerful role. In British royalty, when a male holds a title, his wife is automatically given the feminine equivalent. But the reverse is not true. For example, a count is a high political officer with a countess being his wife. The same pattern holds true for a duke and a duchess and a king and a queen. But when a female holds the royal title, the man she marries does not automatically acquire the matching title. For example, Queen Elizabeth's husband has the title of prince rather than king, but when Prince Charles married Diana, she became Princess Diana. If they had stayed married and he had ascended to the throne, then she would have become Queen Diana. The reasoning appears to be that since masculine words are stronger, they are reserved for true heirs and withheld from males coming into the royal family by marriage. If Prince Phillip were called "King Phillip," British subjects might forget who had inherited the right to rule.

The names that people give their children show the hopes and dreams they have for them, and when we look at the differences between male and female names in a culture, we can see the cumulative expectations of that culture. In our culture girls often have names taken from small, aesthetically pleasing items; for example, Ruby, Jewel, and Pearl. Esther and Stella mean "star," and Ada means "ornament." One of the few women's names that refers to strength is Mildred, and it means "mild strength." Boys often have names with meanings of power and strength; for example, Neil means "champion"; Martin is from Mars, the God of war; Raymond means "wise protection"; Harold means "chief of the army"; Ira means "vigilant"; Rex means "king"; and Richard means "strong king."

We see similar differences in food metaphors. Food is a passive substance just sitting there waiting to be eaten. Many people have recognized this and so no longer feel comfortable describing women as "delectable morsels." However, when I was a teenager, it was considered a compliment to refer to a girl (we didn't call anyone a "woman" until she was middle-aged) as a cute tomato, a peach, a dish, a cookie, honey, sugar, or sweetie-pie. When being affectionate, women will occasionally call a man honey or sweetie, but in general, food metaphors are used much less often with men than with women. If a man is called "a fruit," his masculinity is being questioned. But it's perfectly acceptable to use a food metaphor if the food is heavier and more substantive than that used for women. For example, pin-up pictures of women have long been known as "cheesecake," but when Burt Reynolds posed for a nude centerfold the picture was immediately dubbed "beefcake," that is, a hunk of meat. That such sexual references to men have come into the language is another reflection of how society is beginning to lessen the differences between their attitudes toward men and women.

Something similar to the fruit metaphor happens with references to plants. We insult a man by calling him a "pansy," but it wasn't considered particularly insulting to talk about a girl being a wallflower, a clinging vine, or a shrinking violet, or to give girls such names as Ivy, Rose, Lily, Iris, Daisy, Camelia, Heather, and Flora. A positive plant metaphor can be used with a man only if the plant is big and strong; for example, Andrew Jackson's nickname of Old Hickory. Also, the phrases *blooming idiots* and *budding geniuses* can be used with either sex, but notice how they are based on the most active thing a plant can do, which is to bloom or bud.

Animal metaphors also illustrate the different expectations for males and females. Men are referred to as studs, bucks, and wolves, while women are referred to with such metaphors as kitten, bunny, beaver, bird, chick, and lamb. In the 1950s, we said that boys went "tom catting," but today it's just "catting around," and both boys and girls do it. When the term foxy, meaning that someone was sexy, first became popular it was used only for females, but now someone of either sex can be described as a fox. Some animal metaphors that are used predominantly with men have negative connotations based on the size and/or strength of the animals; for example, beast, bull-headed, jackass, rat, loanshark, and vulture. Negative metaphors used with women are based on smaller animals; for example, social butterfly, mousey, catty, and vixen. The feminine terms connote action, but not the same kind of large scale action as with the masculine terms.

## Women Are Connected with Negative Connotations; Men with Positive Connotations

30  The final point that my note cards illustrated was how many positive connotations are associated with the concept of masculinity, while there are either trivial or negative connotations connected with the corresponding feminine concept. An example from the animal metaphors makes a good illustration. The word *shrew* taken from the name of a small but especially vicious animal was defined in my dictionary as "an ill-tempered scolding woman," but the word *shrewd* taken from the same root was defined as "marked by clever, discerning awareness" and was illustrated with the phrase "a shrewd businessman."

Early in life, children are conditioned to the superiority of the masculine role. As child psychologists point out, little girls have much more freedom to experiment with sex roles than do little boys. If a little girl acts like a tomboy, most parents have mixed feelings, being at least partially proud. But if their little boy acts like a sissy (derived from *sister*), they call a psychologist. It's perfectly acceptable for a little girl to sleep in the crib that was purchased for her brother, to wear his hand-me-down jeans and shirts, and to ride the bicycle that he has outgrown. But few parents would put a boy baby in a white-and-gold crib decorated with frills and lace, and virtually no parents would have their little boy wear his sister's hand-me-down dresses, nor would they have their son ride a girl's pink bicycle with a flower-bedecked basket. The proper names given to girls and boys show this same attitude. Girls can have "boy" names—Cris, Craig, Jo, Kelly, Shawn, Teri, Toni, and Sam—but it doesn't work the other way around. A couple of generations ago, Beverly, Frances, Hazel, Marion, and Shirley were common boys' names. As parents gave these names to more and more girls, they fell into disuse for males, and some older men who have these names prefer to go by their initials or by such abbreviated forms as Haze or Shirl.

When a little girl is told to be a lady, she is being told to sit with her knees together and to be quiet and dainty. But when a little boy is told to be a man, he is being told to be noble, strong, and virtuous—to have all the qualities that the speaker looks on as desirable. The concept of manliness has such positive connotations that it used to be a compliment to call someone a he-man, to say that he was doubly a man. Today many people are more ambivalent about this term and respond to it much as they do to the word *macho*. But calling someone a manly man or a virile man is nearly always meant as a compliment. Virile comes from the Indo-European *vir*, meaning "man," which is also the basis of *virtuous*. Consider the positive connotations of both virile and virtuous with the negative connotations of *hysterical*. The Greeks took this latter word from their name for uterus (as still seen in *hysterectomy*). They thought that women were the only ones who experienced uncontrolled emotional outbursts, and so the condition must have something to do with a part of the body that only women have. But how word meanings change is regularly shown at athletic events where thousands of *virtuous* women sit quietly beside their *hysterical* husbands.

Differences in the connotations between positive male and negative female connotations can be seen in several pairs of words that differ denotatively only in the matter of sex. Bachelor as compared to spinster or old maid has such positive connotations that women try to adopt it by using the term *bachelor-girl* or *bachelorette.* Old maid is so negative that it's the basis for metaphors: pretentious and fussy old men are called "old maids," as are the leftover kernels of unpopped popcorn and the last card in a popular children's card game.

*Patron* and *matron* (Middle English for "father" and "mother") have such different levels of prestige that women try to borrow the more positive masculine connotations with the word *patroness,* literally "female father." Such a peculiar term came about because of the high prestige attached to patron in such phrases as a *patron of the arts* or a *patron saint.* Matron is more apt to be used in talking about a woman in charge of a jail or a public restroom.

When men are doing jobs that women often do, we apparently try 35 to pay the men extra by giving them fancy titles. For example, a male cook is more likely to be called a "chef" while a male seamstress will get the title of "tailor." The armed forces have a special problem in that they recruit under such slogans as "The Marine Corps builds men!" and "Join the Army! Become a Man." Once the recruits are enlisted, they find themselves doing much of the work that has been traditionally thought of as "women's work." The solution to getting the work done and not insulting anyone's masculinity was to change the titles as shown below:

waitress = orderly
nurse = medic or corpsman
secretary = clerk-typist
assistant = adjutant
dishwasher = KP (kitchen police) or kitchen helper

Compare *brave* and *squaw.* Early settlers in America truly admired Indian men and hence named them with a word that carried connotations of youth, vigor, and courage. But for Indian women they used an Algonquin slang term with negative sexual connotations that are almost opposite to those of brave. Wizard and witch contrast almost as much. The masculine *wizard* implies skill and wisdom combined with magic, while the feminine *witch* implies evil intentions combined with magic. When witch is used for men, as in witch-doctor, many main-stream speakers feel some carry-over of the negative connotations.

Part of the unattractiveness of both witch and squaw is that they have been used so often to refer to old women, something with which our culture is particularly uncomfortable, just as the Afghans were. Imagine my surprise when I ran across the phrases *grandfatherly advice* and *old wives' tales* and realized that the underlying implication is the same as the Afghan proverb about old men being worth listening to while old women talk only foolishness.

Other terms that show how negatively we view old women as compared to young women are *old nag* as compared to *filly, old crow* or *old bat* as compared to *bird,* and being *catty* as compared to being *kittenish.* There is no matching set of metaphors for men. The chicken metaphor tells the whole story of a woman's life. In her youth she is a chick. Then she marries and begins feathering her nest. Soon she begins feeling cooped up, so she goes to hen parties where she cackles with her friends. Then she has her brood, begins to henpeck her husband, and finally turns into an old biddy.

I embarked on my study of the dictionary not with the intention of prescribing language change but simply to see what the language would tell me about sexism. Nevertheless, I have been both surprised and pleased as I've watched the changes that have occurred over the past three decades. I'm one of those linguists who believes that new language customs will cause a new generation of speakers to grow up with different expectations. This is why I'm happy about people's efforts to use inclusive languages, to say "he or she" or "they" when speaking about individuals whose names they do not know. I'm glad that leading publishers have developed guidelines to help writers use language that is fair to both sexes. I'm glad that most newspapers and magazines list women by their own names instead of only by their husbands' names. And I'm so glad that educated and thoughtful people no longer begin their business letters with "Dear Sir" or "Gentlemen," but instead use a memo form or begin with such salutations as "Dear Colleagues," "Dear Reader," or "Dear Committee Members." I'm also glad that such words as *poetess, authoress, conductress,* and *aviatrix* now sound quaint and old-fashioned and that *chairman* is giving way to *chair* or *head, mailman* to *mail carrier, clergyman* to *clergy,* and *stewardess* to *flight attendant.* I was also pleased when the National Oceanic and Atmospheric Administration bowed to feminist complaints and in the late 1970s began to alternate men's and women's names for hurricanes. However, I wasn't so pleased to discover that the change did not immediately erase sexist thoughts from everyone's mind, as shown by a headline about Hurricane David in a 1979 New York tabloid, "David Rapes Virgin Islands." More recently a similar metaphor appeared in a headline in the *Arizona Republic* about Hurricane Charlie, "Charlie Quits Carolinas, Flirts with Virginia."

What these incidents show is that sexism is not something existing independently in American English or in the particular dictionary that I happened to read. Rather, it exists in people's minds. Language is like an X-ray in providing visible evidence of invisible thoughts. The best thing about people being interested in and discussing sexist language is that as they make conscious decisions about what pronouns they will use, what jokes they will tell or laugh at, how they will write their names, or how they will begin their letters, they are forced to think about the underlying issue of sexism. This is good because as a problem that begins in people's assumptions and expectations, it's a problem that will be solved only when a great many people have given it a great deal of thought.

## Responding to Reading

1.  What point is Nilsen making about American culture? Does your experience support her conclusions?
2.  Does Nilsen use enough examples to support her claims? What other examples can you think of? In what way do her examples—and your own—illustrate the power of language to define the way people think?
3.  Many of the connotations of the words Nilsen discusses are hundreds of years old and are also found in languages other than English. Given these widespread and long-standing connotations, do you think attempts by Nilsen and others to change this linguistic situation can succeed?

## Responding in Writing

List some words and phrases in your own speaking vocabulary that reinforce the stereotypes Nilsen discusses. What alternatives could you employ? What would be gained and lost if you used these alternatives?

# THE HUMAN COST OF AN ILLITERATE SOCIETY

## Jonathan Kozol

### 1936–

*In 1964, Jonathan Kozol took a teaching job in the Boston Public Schools System. In 1967, he published his first book,* Death at an Early Age: The Destruction of the Hearts and Minds of Negro Children in the Boston Public Schools. *Based on his experiences as a fourth-grade teacher in an inner-city school, a position from which he was fired for "curriculum deviation," this book won the National Book Award in 1968 and led to a number of specific reforms. Since then, Kozol has divided his time between teaching and social activism. His books include* Illiterate America *(1985),* Savage Inequalities *(1991),* The Shame of a Nation: The Restoration of Apartheid Schooling in America *(2005), and* On Being a Teacher *(2009). In the following essay, a chapter from* Illiterate America, *Kozol exposes the problems facing the sixty million Americans who are unable to read and argues that their plight has important implications for the nation as a whole.*

PRECAUTIONS. READ BEFORE USING.
Poison: Contains sodium hydroxide (caustic soda-lye).
Corrosive: Causes severe eye and skin damage, may cause blindness.
Harmful or fatal if swallowed.
If swallowed, give large quantities of milk or water.
Do not induce vomiting.
Important: Keep water out of can at all times to prevent contents from violently erupting . . .

—warning on a can of Drano

Questions of literacy, in Socrates' belief, must at length be judged as matters of morality. Socrates could not have had in mind the moral compromise peculiar to a nation like our own. Some of our Founding Fathers did, however, have this question in their minds. One of the wisest of those Founding Fathers (one who may not have been most compassionate but surely was more prescient than some of his peers) recognized the special dangers that illiteracy would pose to basic equity in the political construction that he helped to shape.

"A people who mean to be their own governors," James Madison wrote, "must arm themselves with the power knowledge gives. A popular government without popular information or the means of acquiring it, is but a prologue to a farce or a tragedy, or perhaps both."

Tragedy looms larger than farce in the United States today. Illiterate citizens seldom vote. Those who do are forced to cast a vote of questionable worth. They cannot make informed decisions based on serious print information. Sometimes they can be alerted to their interests by aggressive voter education. More frequently, they vote for a face, a smile, or a style, not for a mind or character or body of beliefs.

The number of illiterate adults exceeds by 16 million the entire vote cast for the winner in the 1980 presidential contest. If even one third of all illiterates could vote, and read enough and do sufficient math to vote in their self-interest, Ronald Reagan would not likely have been chosen president. There is, of course, no way to know for sure. We do know this: Democracy is a mendacious[1] term when used by those who are prepared to countenance the forced exclusion of one third of our electorate. So long as 60 million people are denied significant participation, the government is neither of, nor for, nor by, the people. It is a government, at best, of those two thirds whose wealth, skin color, or parental privilege allows them opportunity to profit from the provocation and instruction of the written word.

---

[1]Basely dishonest. [Eds.]

The undermining of democracy in the United States is one ₅ "expense" that sensitive Americans can easily deplore because it represents a contradiction that endangers citizens of all political positions. The human price is not so obvious at first.

Since I first immersed myself within this work I have often had the following dream: I find that I am in a railroad station or a large department store within a city that is utterly unknown to me and where I cannot understand the printed words. None of the signs or symbols is familiar. Everything looks strange: like mirror writing of some kind. Gradually I understand that I am in the Soviet Union. All the letters on the walls around me are Cyrillic. I look for my pocket dictionary but I find that it has been mislaid. Where have I left it? Then I recall that I forgot to bring it with me when I packed my bags in Boston. I struggle to remember the name of my hotel. I try to ask somebody for directions. One person stops and looks at me in a peculiar way. I lose the nerve to ask. At last I reach into my wallet for an ID card. The card is missing. Have I lost it? Then I remember that my card was confiscated for some reason, many years before. Around this point, I wake up in a panic.

This panic is not so different from the misery that millions of adult illiterates experience each day within the course of their routine existence in the U.S.A.

Illiterates cannot read the menu in a restaurant.

They cannot read the cost of items on the menu in the *window* of the restaurant before they enter.

Illiterates cannot read the letters that their children bring home ₁₀ from their teachers. They cannot study school department circulars that tell them of the courses that their children must be taking if they hope to pass the SAT exams. They cannot help with homework. They cannot write a letter to the teacher. They are afraid to visit in the classroom. They do not want to humiliate their child or themselves.

Illiterates cannot read instructions on a bottle of prescription medicine. They cannot find out when a medicine is past the year of safe consumption; nor can they read of allergenic risks, warnings to diabetics, or the potential sedative effect of certain kinds of nonprescription pills. They cannot observe preventive health care admonitions. They cannot read about "the seven warning signs of cancer" or the indications of blood-sugar fluctuations or the risks of eating certain foods that aggravate the likelihood of cardiac arrest.

Illiterates live, in more than literal ways, an uninsured existence. They cannot understand the written details on a health insurance form. They cannot read the waivers that they sign preceding surgical procedures. Several women I have known in Boston have entered a slum hospital with the intention of obtaining a tubal ligation and have emerged a few days later after having been subjected to a hysterectomy.[2] Unaware of their rights, incognizant of jargon, intimidated by the unfamiliar air of fear and atmosphere of ether that so many of us find oppressive in the confines even of the most attractive and expensive medical facilities, they have signed their names to documents they could not read and which nobody, in the hectic situation that prevails so often in those overcrowded hospitals that serve the urban poor, had even bothered to explain.

Childbirth might seem to be the last inalienable right of any female citizen within a civilized society. Illiterate mothers, as we shall see, already have been cheated of the power to protect their progeny against the likelihood of demolition in deficient public schools and, as a result, against the verbal servitude within which they themselves exist. Surgical denial of the right to bear that child in the first place represents an ultimate denial, an unspeakable metaphor, a final darkness that denies even the twilight gleamings of our own humanity. What greater violation of our biological, our biblical, our spiritual humanity could possibly exist than that which takes place nightly, perhaps hourly these days, within such over-burdened and benighted institutions as the Boston City Hospital? Illiteracy has many costs; few are so irreversible as this.

Even the roof above one's head, the gas or other fuel for heating that protects the residents of northern city slums against the threat of illness in the winter months become uncertain guarantees. Illiterates cannot read the lease that they must sign to live in an apartment which, too often, they cannot afford. They cannot manage check accounts and therefore seldom pay for anything by mail. Hours and entire days of difficult travel (and the cost of bus or other public transit) must be added to the real cost of whatever they consume. Loss of interest on the check accounts they do not have, and could not manage if they did, must be regarded as another of the excess costs paid by the citizen who is excluded from the common instruments of commerce in a numerate society.

15    "I couldn't understand the bills," a woman in Washington, D.C., reports, "and then I couldn't write the checks to pay them. We signed things we didn't know what they were."

Illiterates cannot read the notices that they receive from welfare offices or from the IRS. They must depend on word-of-mouth instruction from the welfare worker—or from other persons whom they have good reason to mistrust. They do not know what rights they have, what deadlines and requirements they face, what options they might choose to exercise. They are half-citizens. Their rights exist in print but not in fact.

---

[2]A hysterectomy, the removal of the uterus, is a much more radical procedure than a tubal ligation, a method of sterilization that is a common form of birth control. [Eds.]

Illiterates cannot look up numbers in a telephone directory. Even if they can find the names of friends, few possess the sorting skills to make use of the yellow pages; categories are bewildering and trade names are beyond decoding capabilities for millions of nonreaders. Even the emergency numbers listed on the first page of the phone book—"Ambulance," "Police," and "Fire"—are too frequently beyond the recognition of nonreaders.

Many illiterates cannot read the admonition on a pack of cigarettes. Neither the Surgeon General's warning nor its reproduction on the package can alert them to the risks. Although most people learn by word of mouth that smoking is related to a number of grave physical disorders, they do not get the chance to read the detailed stories which can document this danger with the vividness that turns concern into determination to resist. They can see the handsome cowboy or the slim Virginia lady lighting up a filter cigarette; they cannot heed the words that tell them that this product is (not "may be") dangerous to their health. Sixty million men and women are condemned to be the unalerted, high-risk candidates for cancer.

Illiterates do not buy "no-name" products in the supermarkets. They must depend on photographs or the familiar logos that are printed on the packages of brand-name groceries. The poorest people, therefore, are denied the benefits of the least costly products.

Illiterates depend almost entirely upon label recognition. Many 20 labels, however, are not easy to distinguish. Dozens of different kinds of Campbell's soup appear identical to the nonreader. The purchaser who cannot read and does not dare to ask for help, out of the fear of being stigmatized (a fear which is unfortunately realistic), frequently comes home with something which she never wanted and her family never tasted.

Illiterates cannot read instructions on a pack of frozen food. Packages sometimes provide an illustration to explain the cooking preparations; but illustrations are of little help to someone who must "boil water, drop the food—*within* its plastic wrapper—in the boiling water, wait for it to simmer, instantly remove."

Even when labels are seemingly clear, they may be easily mistaken. A woman in Detroit brought home a gallon of Crisco for her children's dinner. She thought that she had bought the chicken that was pictured on the label. She had enough Crisco now to last a year—but no more money to go back and buy the food for dinner.

Recipes provided on the packages of certain staples sometimes tempt a semiliterate person to prepare a meal her children have not tasted. The longing to vary the uniform and often starchy content of low-budget meals provided to the family that relies on food stamps commonly leads to ruinous results. Scarce funds have been wasted and the food must be thrown out. The same applies to distribution of food-surplus produce in emergency conditions. Government inducements to poor people to "explore the ways" in which to make a tasty meal from tasteless noodles, surplus cheese, and powdered milk are useless to nonreaders. Intended as benevolent advice, such recommendations mock reality and foster deeper feelings of resentment and of inability to cope. (Those, on the other hand, who cautiously refrain from "innovative" recipes in preparation of their children's meals must suffer the opprobrium of "laziness," "lack of imagination. . . .")

Illiterates cannot travel freely. When they attempt to do so, they encounter risks that few of us can dream of. They cannot read traffic signs and, while they often learn to recognize and to decipher symbols, they cannot manage street names which they haven't seen before. The same is true for bus and subway stops. While ingenuity can sometimes help a man or woman to discern directions from familiar landmarks, buildings, cemeteries, churches, and the like, most illiterates are virtually immobilized. They seldom wander past the streets and neighborhoods they know. Geographical paralysis becomes a bitter metaphor for their entire existence. They are immobilized in almost every sense we can imagine. They can't move up. They can't move out. They cannot see beyond. Illiterates may take an oral test for drivers' permits in most sections of America. It is a questionable concession. Where will they go? How will they get there? How will they get home? Could it be that some of us might like it better if they stayed where they belong?

25 Travel is only one of many instances of circumscribed existence. Choice, in almost all its facets, is diminished in the life of an illiterate adult. Even the printed TV schedule, which provides most people with the luxury of preselection, does not belong within the arsenal of options in illiterate existence. One consequence is that the viewer watches only what appears at moments when he happens to have time to turn the switch. Another consequence, a lot more common, is that the TV set remains in operation night and day. Whatever the program offered at the hour when he walks into the room will be the nutriment that he accepts and swallows. Thus, to passivity, is added frequency—indeed, almost uninterrupted continuity. Freedom to select is no more possible here than in the choice of home or surgery or food.

"You don't choose," said one illiterate woman. "You take your wishes from somebody else." Whether in perusal of a menu, selection of highways, purchase of groceries, or determination of affordable enjoyment, illiterate Americans must trust somebody else: a friend, a relative, a stranger on the street, a grocery clerk, a TV copywriter.

"All of our mail we get, it's hard for her to read. Settin' down and writing a letter, she can't do it. Like if we get a bill . . . we take it over to my sister-in-law . . . My sister-in-law reads it."

Billing agencies harass poor people for the payment of the bills for purchases that might have taken place six months before. Utility companies offer an agreement for a staggered payment schedule on a bill past due. "You have to trust them," one man said. Precisely for this reason, you end up by trusting no one and suspecting everyone of possible deceit. A submerged sense of distrust becomes the corollary to a constant need to trust. "They are cheating me . . . I have been tricked . . . I do not know . . ."

*Not knowing:* This is a familiar theme. Not knowing the right word for the right thing at the right time is one form of subjugation. Not knowing the world that lies concealed behind those words is a more terrifying feeling. The longitude and latitude of one's existence are beyond all easy apprehension. Even the hard, cold stars within the firmament above one's head begin to mock the possibilities for self-location. Where am I? Where did I come from? Where will I go?

"I've lost a lot of jobs," one man explains. "Today, even if you're a janitor, there's still reading and writing . . . They leave a note saying, 'Go to room so-and-so . . .' You can't do it. You can't read it. You don't know." 30

"The hardest thing about it is that I've been places where I didn't know where I was. You don't know where you are . . . You're lost."

"Like I said: I have two kids. What do I do if one of my kids starts choking? I go running to the phone . . . I can't look up the hospital phone number. That's if we're at home. Out on the street, I can't read the sign. I get to a pay phone. 'Okay, tell us where you are. We'll send an ambulance.' I look at the street sign. Right there, I can't tell you what it says. I'd have to spell it out, letter for letter. By that time, one of my kids would be dead . . . These are the kinds of fears you go with, every single day . . ."

"Reading directions, I suffer with. I work with chemicals . . . That's scary to begin with . . ."

"You sit down. They throw the menu in front of you. Where do you go from there? Nine times out of ten you say, 'Go ahead. Pick out something for the both of us.' I've eaten some weird things, let me tell you!"

Menus. Chemicals. A child choking while his mother searches for a word she does not know to find assistance that will come too late. 35 Another mother speaks about the inability to help her kids to read: "I can't read to them. Of course that's leaving them out of something they should have. Oh, it matters. You *believe* it matters! I ordered all these books. The kids belong to a book club. Donny wanted me to read a book to him. I told Donny: 'I can't read,' He said: 'Mommy, you sit down. I'll read it to you.' I tried it one day, reading from the pictures. Donny looked at me. He said, 'Mommy, that's not right.' He's only five. He knew I couldn't read . . ."

A landlord tells a woman that her lease allows him to evict her if her baby cries and causes inconvenience to her neighbors. The consequence of challenging his words conveys a danger which appears, unlikely as it seems, even more alarming than the danger of eviction.

Once she admits that she can't read, in the desire to maneuver for the time in which to call a friend, she will have defined herself in terms of an explicit impotence that she cannot endure. Capitulation in this case is preferable to self-humiliation. Resisting the definition of oneself in terms of what one cannot do, what others take for granted, represents a need so great that other imperatives (even one so urgent as the need to keep one's home in winter's cold) evaporate and fall away in face of fear. Even the loss of home and shelter, in this case, is not so terrifying as the loss of self.

"I come out of school. I was sixteen. They had their meetings. The directors meet. They said that I was wasting their school paper. I was wasting pencils . . ."

Another illiterate, looking back, believes she was not worthy of her teacher's time. She believes that it was wrong of her to take up space within her school. She believes that it was right to leave in order that somebody more deserving could receive her place.

Children choke. Their mother chokes another way: on more than chicken bones.

40      People eat what others order, know what others tell them, struggle not to see themselves as they believe the world perceives them. A man in California speaks about his own loss of identity, of self-location, definition:

"I stood at the bottom of the ramp. My car had broke down on the freeway. There was a phone. I asked for the police. They was nice. They said to tell them where I was. I looked up at the signs. There was one that I had seen before. I read it to them: ONE WAY STREET. They thought it was a joke. I told them I couldn't read. There was other signs above the ramp. They told me to try. I looked around for somebody to help. All the cars was going by real fast. I couldn't make them understand that I was lost. The cop was nice. He told me: 'Try once more.' I did my best. I couldn't read. I only knew the sign above my head. The cop was trying to be nice. He knew that I was trapped. 'I can't send out a car to you if you can't tell me where you are.' I felt afraid. I nearly cried. I'm forty-eight years old. I only said: 'I'm on a one-way street . . .'"

The legal problems and the courtroom complications that confront illiterate adults have been discussed above. The anguish that may underlie such matters was brought home to me this year while I was working on this book. I have spoken, in the introduction, of a sudden phone call from one of my former students, now in prison for a criminal offense. Stephen is not a boy today. He is twenty-eight years old. He called to ask me to assist him in his trial, which comes up next fall. He will be on trial for murder. He has just knifed and killed a man who first enticed him to his home, then cheated him, and then insulted him—as "an illiterate subhuman."

Stephen now faces twenty years to life. Stephen's mother was illiterate. His grandparents were illiterate as well. What parental curse did not destroy was killed off finally by the schools. Silent violence is repaid with interest. It will cost us $25,000 yearly to maintain this broken soul in prison. But what is the price that has been paid by Stephen's victim? What is the price that will be paid by Stephen?

Perhaps we might slow down a moment here and look at the realities described above. This is the nation that we live in. This is a society that most of us did not create but which our President and other leaders have been willing to sustain by virtue of malign neglect. Do we possess the character and courage to address a problem which so many nations, poorer than our own, have found it natural to correct?

The answers to these questions represent a reasonable test of our belief in the democracy to which we have been asked in public school to swear allegiance. 45

## Responding to Reading

1. According to Kozol, how does illiteracy undermine democracy in the United States? Do you agree with him?
2. Do you think Kozol accurately describes the difficulties illiterates face in their daily lives, or does he seem to be exaggerating? If you think he is exaggerating, what motive might he have?
3. Kozol concludes his essay by asking whether we as a nation have "the character and courage to address" illiteracy (44). He does not, however, offer any concrete suggestions for doing so. Can you offer any suggestions?

## Responding in Writing

Keep a log of your activities for a day. Then, discuss which of these activities you could and could not perform if you were illiterate.

# Saying It Is Hurtful, Banning It Is Worse

## Christopher M. Fairman

*The author of a book on "word taboo" published in 2009, Christopher M. Fairman is the Alumni Society Designated Professor of Law at the Moritz College of Law at the Ohio State University. His work has appeared in numerous law journals, such as the* Arizona Law Review, *the* Cardozo Law Review, *the* Texas Law Review, *and the* University of California at Davis Law Review. *In the following essay, Fairman considers the case for not banning offensive language.*

Does the word "retard" have less than three weeks to live?

Long before Rahm Emanuel, Sarah Palin and Rush Limbaugh made the word fodder for political controversy and late-night punch lines, a movement was underway to eliminate it from everyday conversation. Saying, irrefutably, that the word and its variations are hurtful to many, the Special Olympics is leading a campaign to end its use and is promoting a national awareness day on March 3. Nearly 60,000 people have signed on to the following promise on www.r-word.org: "I pledge and support the elimination of the derogatory use of the r-word from everyday speech and promote the acceptance and inclusion of people with intellectual disabilities."

I sympathize with the effort, but I won't be making that pledge. It's not that I've come to praise the word "retard"; I just don't think we should bury it. If the history of offensive terms in America shows anything, it is that words themselves are not the culprit; the meaning we attach to them is, and such meanings change dramatically over time and across communities. The term "mentally retarded" was itself introduced by the medical establishment in the 20th century to supplant other terms that had been deemed offensive. Similarly, the words "gay" and "queer" and even the N-word can be insulting, friendly, identifying or academic in different contexts.

The varied and evolving uses of such words ultimately render self-censorship campaigns unnecessary. And restricting speech of any kind comes with a potential price—needlessly institutionalized taboos, government censorship or abridged freedom of expression—that we should be wary of paying.

5      The latest battle over the R-word kicked into high gear with a Jan. 26 *Wall Street Journal* report that last summer White House Chief of Staff Rahm Emanuel blasted liberal activists unhappy with the pace of health-care reform, deriding their strategies as "[expletive] retarded." Palin, the mother of a special-needs child, quickly took to Facebook to demand Emanuel's firing, likening the offensiveness of the R-word to that of the N-word. Limbaugh seized the low ground, saying he found nothing wrong with "calling a bunch of people who are retards, retards," and Palin rushed to his defense, saying Limbaugh had used the word satirically. Comedy Central's Stephen Colbert took her up on it, calling Palin an "[expletive] retard" and adding, with a smile: "You see? It's satire!"

Emanuel apologized and promised to take the R-Word.org pledge, but as March 3 nears, the word may already be an endangered species. Forty-eight states have voted to remove the term "mental retardation" from government agencies and state codes, and legislation is pending in Congress to strike it from any federal statutes that still use it, such as the Individuals With Disabilities Education Act. The largest advocacy group for the intellectually disabled, the Association for Retarded Citizens, is now simply the Arc. Similarly, the American Association of

Mental Retardation is now the American Association on Intellectual and Developmental Disabilities. The Centers for Disease Control and Prevention now use "intellectual disability" in place of "mental retardation." The diagnostic manuals used by medical professionals also embrace "intellectual disability" as the official label. Behind the changes is the belief that "retardation" doesn't communicate dignity and respect.

The irony is that the use of "mental retardation" and its variants was originally an attempt to convey greater dignity and respect than previous labels had. While the verb "retard"—meaning to delay or hinder—has roots in the 15th century, its use in reference to mental development didn't occur until the late 19th and early 20th centuries, when medical texts began to describe children with "retarded mental development," "retarded children" and "mentally retarded patients." By the 1960s, "mental retardation" became the preferred medical term, gradually replacing previous diagnostic standards such as "idiot," "imbecile" and "moron"—terms that had come to carry pejorative connotations.

As I was growing up in the 1970s, my father worked for the Texas Department of Mental Health and Mental Retardation, one of the now-renamed state agencies. The term "retardation" was common in my home and life, but it was sterile and clinical. It is only in the past generation that the medical term turned into the slang "retard" and gained power as an insult. The shift is even apparent in popular movies. There was little public controversy when Matt Dillon tried to woo Cameron Diaz in the 1998 hit comedy "There's Something About Mary" by confessing his passion: "I work with retards." (Diaz's character, Mary, had a mentally disabled brother.) But 10 years later, in the comedy "Tropic Thunder," Robert Downey Jr.'s use of the phrase "full retard" led to picketing and calls for a boycott.

What happened to make the word a target for extinction?

All cultures have taboos. Western culture, particularly in the United  10 States, has several taboos surrounding sexuality, grounded largely in a subconscious fear of the parade of horribles—adultery, unwanted pregnancy, incest, venereal disease—that might befall us because of some sexual behaviors. Sometimes the taboo extends to even uttering the words that describe certain behaviors. You can see word taboo at work in the way Emanuel's blunder was reported: "[expletive] retarded." It's still okay to print the R-word. The F-word? Forget it.

For years, I've been researching taboo language and its interaction with the law, and I have written a law review article and recently a book, both titled with the unprintable four letter F-word. The resilience of word taboos, the multiple usages and meanings of a single word, the rise of self-censorship, and the risks of institutionalized taboo and ultimately censorship are all core issues surrounding the F-word, and they help explain what is happening—and may happen still—with the R-word.

Mental disorders also carry cultural taboos. For centuries, mental illness and disability were poorly understood; as recently as the 1800s, they were thought to be the work of devils and demons. Because the origins of mental illness were a mystery, fears that such conditions could be contagious led to isolation through institutionalization. Shame was often attached to individuals and their families, and the result was stigma.

Fortunately, we've come a long way from those days. It's precisely the new enlightenment and openness about mental disabilities that allow Palin to launch the controversy over "retard." But at a subconscious level, the underlying taboo may explain why we constantly seek new terms for this type of disability, new ways to avoid the old stigmas. Invariably, negative connotations materialize around whatever new word is used; "idiot" becomes an insult and gives way to "retardation," which in turn suffers the same fate, leading to "intellectual disability." This illustrates one of the recurring follies of speech restriction: While there may be another word to use, a negative connotation eventually is found. Offense—both given and taken—is inevitable.

Whatever future offensiveness may emerge, though, are we not better off by purging today's insulting language and making our discourse a little kinder? That is the argument of self-censorship advocates such as Palin, who draws parallels between the use of the R-word and the N-word—the most powerful and insulting of all racial epithets. In some respects, the comparison seems overblown. The N-word invokes some of the foulest chapters in our nation's history; "retard," however harsh, pales in comparison. But there still may be some guidance to be gleaned.

15    While the N-word endures as an insult, it is so stigmatized that its use is no longer tolerated in public discourse. This is a positive step for us all, of course, but its containment does not come without costs. As Harvard law professor Randall Kennedy described in his 2002 book on the subject, stigmatizing the word has elicited new problems, including an overeagerness to detect insult where none is intended and the use of excessively harsh punishment against those who use the word wrongly.

I've coined a term for overzealous or extreme responses to insulting words: "word fetish." Those under the influence of word fetish aren't content to refrain from using a certain word; they are set on eradicating any use by others. A classic example was the plight of David Howard, a white employee in the D.C. mayor's office in 1999. Howard told staff members that because of budget cuts, he would have to be "niggardly" with available funds. Wrongly believing "niggardly" was a variation of the N-word, black subordinates lobbied for his resignation. Howard ultimately resigned after public protests, though he was soon reinstated. If the campaign against "retard" is successful, an identical risk of word fetish exists. (Imagine that Emanuel had spoken of "retarding the opposition"—would that be unacceptable?)

Like virtually every word in our language, the N-word has multiple uses. While its use as an insult has decreased, there has been a resurgence of the word as a term of identification, even affection, among some African Americans. But should certain groups of people, to the exclusion of others, be allowed to reclaim certain words? If "retard" or "retarded" were similarly restricted, could intellectually disabled individuals appropriate the term for self-identification, essentially reclaiming its original use or developing a new one?

Over time, word fetish can evolve into censorship among private organizations and ultimately direct government control of language and institutionalized word taboo. During the 1980s and 1990s, for example, many colleges and universities sought to reduce discrimination by developing speech codes, often targeting racial hate speech such as the N-word. Even with the most combustible insults, however, there must be some accommodation to their continued use; freedom of expression surely embraces unpopular, even insulting, speech. Luckily, speech codes that have been challenged in court have generally lost because they violated the First Amendment.

The risk of direct government censorship of the word "retard" is real. The New Zealand chapter of the Special Olympics is already calling on the country's Broadcasting Standards Authority (equivalent to our Federal Communications Commission) to deem the word "retard" unacceptable for broadcast. This plea is based upon a single incident involving New Zealand television personality Paul Henry, who described the runner-up in the "Britain's Got Talent" competition, Susan Boyle, as retarded. It is not difficult to imagine calls for a similar broadcast ban emerging here.

The current public awareness campaign surrounding the use of the 20 word "gay" offers better lessons and parallels for the R-word debate. Advocacy groups contend that the phrase "that's so gay" fosters homophobia and that anti-gay language is directly related to violence and harassment against homosexuals. At the same time, there is recognition that much anti-gay language is uttered carelessly and isn't necessarily intended as hurtful—as is probably the case with uses of "retard." The Ad Council and the Gay, Lesbian and Straight Education Network have developed a Web site, ThinkB4YouSpeak.com, that, much like R-Word.org, encourages the public to sign a pledge to cease using the phrase. (The slogan: "Saying that's so gay is so yesterday.")

By increasing sensitivity and awareness, the campaign hopes to encourage people to think about the possible consequences of their word choices. Such reflection would presumably lead individuals to censor themselves once they understand that others can be hurt by their language.

Inherent in this idea is the realization that words have multiple meanings and that those meanings depend on the context and circumstances surrounding any particular statement. For example, "gay" is a term of identification for homosexuals, but it also can be used as an all-purpose put-down: "That's so gay." Those using it as an insult don't intend to say "that's so homosexual," nor do they necessarily make the conscious leap that homosexuality is bad. (Indeed, the success of the ThinkB4YouSpeak.com campaign depends on this distinction.)

Similarly, the R-word has multiple usages. When Emanuel calls fellow Democrats "retarded" for jeopardizing a legislative plan, the term is a stand-in for "stupid" or "misguided" or "dumb"—it obviously does not mean that they meet the IQ diagnostic standard for intellectual disability. It is quite another thing to look at a person with Down syndrome and call him or her a "retard." So, if there are readily identifiable alternate meanings, what is the reason for censorship?

Differing usages also give rise to reclaiming—when words that have an offensive meaning are deliberately given a new spin. The putative slur is captured, repurposed and owned by the target of insult. We see this when an African American uses the N-word as a term of identification for his friends, or when the word "queer" is reclaimed for TV shows such as "Queer Eye for the Straight Guy" and "Queer as Folk," and for queer studies and queer theory in university courses. Reclaiming the word "retard" is an option that should involve no risk to freedom of expression.

25    If interest groups want to pour resources into cleaning up unintentional insults, more power to them; we surely would benefit from greater kindness to one another. But we must not let "retard" go without a requiem. If the goal is to protect intellectually disabled individuals from put-downs and prejudice, it won't succeed. New words of insult will replace old ones.

Words are ideas, and we should be reluctant to surrender any of them. Freedom of expression has come at a dear price, and it is not worth abridging, even so we can get along a little better. That's one F-word we really can't do without.

## Responding to Reading

1. In paragraph 3, Fairman says that the history of offensive words shows that "words themselves are not the culprit." What does he mean? Do you agree with his rationale?

2. According to Fairman, "restricting speech of any kind comes with a potential price" (4). What is this price? Do you think he provides enough support for this statement?

3. Throughout his essay, Fairman himself avoids certain offensive words, using euphemisms—such as "F-word" and "N-word"—instead. Does his use of these abbreviations undercut his essay's main point?

## Responding in Writing

Many countries—for example Brazil, Canada, France, and Denmark—outlaw specific types of offensive speech.  Do you think some words are so hurtful that they should be outlawed, or do you agree with Fairman that we should not ban offensive language?

---

## FOCUS

### Is Texting Destroying the English Language?

### Responding to the Image

1.  The image above shows someone typing a text message. What advantages does texting have over a phone call? over email? What are the disadvantages of texting? Do you believe that the advantages of texting outweigh any disadvantages?
2.  Do you think texting threatens your communication skills, or do you believe it enhances or expands them? How is texting different from the other types of writing you do?

# I H8 TXT MSGS: HOW TEXTING IS WRECKING OUR LANGUAGE

## John Humphrys

### 1943–

*A radio presenter for the BBC and host of the BBC television game show* Mastermind, *John Humphrys is an award-winning journalist and broad-caster. His books include* Devil's Advocate *(1999),* The Great Food Gamble *(2002),* Lost for Words: The Mangling and Manipulating of the English Language *(2004),* Beyond Words: How Language Reveals the Way We

*Live Now (2006), and* Blue Skies & Black Olives *(2009). In the following essay, Humphrys describes what he perceives as the drawbacks of texting.*

A good dictionary is a fine thing—I yield to no man in my love for one. If I stretch out my right arm as I type, I can pluck from my shelves the two volumes of the Shorter Oxford English Dictionary.

They are as close to my heart as they are to my desk because they are so much more than a useful tool.

Leafing through a good dictionary in search of a single word is a small voyage of discovery—infinitely more satisfying than looking something up on the internet.

It's partly the physical sensation—the feel and smell of good paper—and partly the minor triumph of finding the word you seek, but it's rare to open a dictionary without being diverted somewhere else.

The eye falls on a word you've never seen before or one whose  5
meaning you have always wanted to check, and you close the dictionary just a little bit richer for the experience.

But my lifetime love affair with the OED is at risk. The sixth edition has just been published and—I feel a small shudder as I write these words—it has fallen victim to fashion.

It has removed the hyphen from no fewer than 16,000 words.

So in future we are required to spell pigeon-hole, for instance, as pigeonhole and leap-frog as leapfrog. In other cases we have two words instead of one. Pot-belly shall henceforth be pot belly.

You may very well say: so what? Indeed, you may well have functioned perfectly well until now spelling leapfrog without a hyphen.

The spell-check (sorry: spellcheck) on my computer is happy with  10
both. But that's not why I feel betrayed by my precious OED.

It's because of the reason for this change. It has happened because we are changing the way we communicate with each other, which means, says the OED editor Angus Stevenson, that we no longer have time to reach for the hyphen key.

Have you ever heard anything quite so daft? No time to make one tiny key-stroke (sorry: key stroke).

Has it really come to this? Are our lives really so pressured, every minute occupied in so many vital tasks, every second accounted for, that we cannot afford the millisecond (no hyphen) it takes to tap that key?

Obviously not. No, there's another reason—and it's far more sinister and deeply troubling.

It is the relentless onward march of the texters, the SMS (Short Mes-  15
sage Service) vandals who are doing to our language what Genghis Khan[1] did to his neighbours eight hundred years ago.

---

[1]Mongolian emperor and conqueror (1162–1227). [Eds.]

They are destroying it: pillaging our punctuation; savaging our sentences; raping our vocabulary. And they must be stopped.

This, I grant you, is a tall order. The texters have many more arrows in their quiver than we who defend the old way.

Ridicule is one of them. "What! You don't text? What century are you living in then, granddad? Need me to sharpen your quill pen for you?"

You know the sort of thing; those of us who have survived for years without a mobile phone have to put up with it all the time. My old friend Amanda Platell, who graces these pages on Saturdays, has an answerphone message that says the caller may leave a message but she'd *prefer* a text. One feels so inadequate.

20 (Or should that have been *ansafone?* Of course it should. There are fewer letters in that hideous word and think how much time I could have saved typing it.)

The texters also have economy on their side. It costs almost nothing to send a text message compared with a voice message. That's perfectly true. I must also concede that some voice messages can be profoundly irritating.

My own outgoing message asks callers to be very brief—ideally just name and number—but that doesn't stop some callers burbling on for ten minutes and always, always ending by saying: "Ooh—sorry I went on so long!"

But can that be any more irritating than those absurd little smiley faces with which texters litter their messages? It is 25 years since the emoticon (that's the posh word) was born.

It started with the smiley face and the gloomy face and now there are 16 pages of them in the texters' A–Z.

25 It has now reached the stage where my computer will not allow me to type the colon, dash and bracket without automatically turning it into a picture of a smiling face. Aargh!

Even worse are the grotesque abbreviations. It is interesting, in a masochistic sort of way, to look at how text language has changed over the years.

It began with some fairly obvious and relatively inoffensive abbreviations: "tks" for "thanks"; "u" for "you"; 4 for "for."

But as it has developed its users have sought out increasingly obscure ways of expressing themselves which, when you think about it, entirely defeats the purpose.

If the recipient of the message has to spend ten minutes trying to translate it, those precious minutes are being wasted. And isn't the whole point to "save" time?

30 Then there's the problem of ambiguity. With my vast knowledge of text language I had assumed LOL meant "lots of love," but now I discover it means "laugh out loud." Or at least it did the last time I asked.

But how would you know? Instead of aiding communication it can be a barrier. I can work out BTW (by the way) but I was baffled by IMHO U R GR8. It means: "In my humble opinion you are great." But, once again, how would you know?

Let me anticipate the reaction to this modest little rant against the text revolution and the OED for being influenced by it. Its defenders will say language changes.

It is constantly evolving and anyone who tries to get in the way is a fuddy-duddy who deserves to be run down.

I agree. One of the joys of the English language and one of the reasons it has been so successful in spreading across the globe is that it is infinitely adaptable.

If we see an Americanism we like, we snaffle it—and so we should. 35 But texting and "netspeak" are effectively different languages.

The danger—for young people especially—is that they will come to dominate. Our written language may end up as a series of ridiculous emoticons and everchanging abbreviations.

It is too late to save the hand-written letter. E-mailing has seen to that and I must confess that I would find it difficult to live without it. That does not mean I like it.

I resent the fact that I spend so much of my working day (and, even more regrettably, weekends) checking for e-mails—most of which are junk.

I am also cross with myself for the way I have adapted my own style. In the early days I treated e-mails as though they were letters. I tried to construct proper, grammatical sentences and used punctuation that would have brought a smile to the lips of that guardian of our language, Lynne Truss.

Now I find myself slipping into sloppy habits, abandoning capital 40 letters and using rows of dots.

But at least I have not succumbed to "text-speak" and I wish the OED had not hoisted the white flag either. I recall a piece of doggerel which sums up my fears nicely: *Mary had a mobile.*

*She texted day and night. But when it came to her exams She'd forgotten how to write.*

*To the editor of the OED I will simply say: For many years you've been GR8. Don't spoil it now. Tks.*

## Responding to Reading

1. Why is Humphrys so troubled by the fact that the *Oxford English Dictionary* has removed the hyphen from thousands of words? According to Humphrys, what is the reason for this change?
2. In what ways does Humphrys think texters have changed the English language? Are there any other changes that Humphrys has missed?
3. According to Humphrys, what is the danger of "text-speak"? Do you think he makes a valid point, or do you think he is overreacting?

## Responding in Writing

In paragraph 16, Humphrys says that texters are "pillaging our punctuation; savaging our sentences; raping our vocabulary. And they must be stopped." Write an email to Humphrys in which you agree or disagree with this statement. Make sure you use specific examples to support your points.

# 2B OR NOT 2B?

## David Crystal

### 1941–

*An honorary professor of linguistics at the University of Wales at Bangor, David Crystal has written extensively on issues related to language and the Internet. His most recent books include* Txtng: The Gr8 Db8 *(2008),* The Future of Language *(2009),* Just a Phrase I'm Going Through: My Life in Language *(2009), and* The Cambridge Encyclopedia of Language *(2010). Crystal is the founder-editor of* Linguistics Abstracts, *the* Journal of Child Language, *and* Child Language Teaching and Therapy. *In the following essay, Crystal argues for the benefits of text messaging.*

Last year, in a newspaper article headed "I h8 txt msgs: How texting is wrecking our language," John Humphrys argued that texters are "vandals who are doing to our language what Genghis Khan did to his neighbours 800 years ago. They are destroying it: pillaging our punctuation; savaging our sentences; raping our vocabulary. And they must be stopped."

As a new variety of language, texting has been condemned as "textese," "slanguage," a "digital virus." According to John Sutherland of University College London, writing in this paper in 2002, it is "bleak, bald, sad shorthand. Drab shrinktalk . . . Linguistically it's all pig's ear . . . it masks dyslexia, poor spelling and mental laziness. Texting is penmanship for illiterates."

Ever since the arrival of printing—thought to be the invention of the devil because it would put false opinions into people's minds—people have been arguing that new technology would have disastrous consequences for language. Scares accompanied the introduction of the telegraph, telephone, and broadcasting. But has there ever been a linguistic phenomenon that has aroused such curiosity, suspicion, fear, confusion, antagonism, fascination, excitement and enthusiasm all at once as texting? And in such a short space of time. Less than a decade ago, hardly anyone had heard of it.

The idea of a point-to-point short message service (or SMS) began to be discussed as part of the development of the Global System for

Mobile Communications network in the mid-1980s, but it wasn't until the early 90s that phone companies started to develop its commercial possibilities. Texts communicated by pagers were replaced by text messages, at first only 20 characters in length. It took five years or more before numbers of users started to build up. The average number of texts per GSM customer in 1995 was 0.4 per month; by the end of 2000 it was still only 35.

The slow start, it seems, was because the companies had trouble working out reliable ways of charging for the new service. But once procedures were in place, texting rocketed. In the UK, in 2001, 12.2bn text messages were sent. This had doubled by 2004, and was forecast to be 45bn in 2007. On Christmas Day alone in 2006, over 205m texts went out. World figures went from 17bn in 2000 to 250bn in 2001. They passed a trillion in 2005. Text messaging generated around $70bn in 2005. That's more than three times as much as all Hollywood box office returns that year.

People think that the written language seen on mobile phone screens is new and alien, but all the popular beliefs about texting are wrong. Its graphic distinctiveness is not a new phenomenon, nor is its use restricted to the young. There is increasing evidence that it helps rather than hinders literacy. And only a very tiny part of it uses a distinctive orthography.[1] A trillion text messages might seem a lot, but when we set these alongside the multi-trillion instances of standard orthography in everyday life, they appear as no more than a few ripples on the surface of the sea of language. Texting has added a new dimension to language use, but its long-term impact is negligible. It is not a disaster.

Although many texters enjoy breaking linguistic rules, they also know they need to be understood. There is no point in paying to send a message if it breaks so many rules that it ceases to be intelligible. When messages are longer, containing more information, the amount of standard orthography increases. Many texters alter just the grammatical words (such as "you" and "be"). As older and more conservative language users have begun to text, an even more standardised style has appeared. Some texters refuse to depart at all from traditional orthography. And conventional spelling and punctuation is the norm when institutions send out information messages, as in this university text to students: "Weather Alert! No classes today due to snow storm", or in the texts which radio listeners are invited to send in to programmes. These institutional messages now form the majority of texts in cyberspace—and several organisations forbid the use of abbreviations, knowing that many readers will not understand them. Bad textiquette.

---

[1]System of using letters to form words. [Eds.]

Research has made it clear that the early media hysteria about the novelty (and thus the dangers) of text messaging was misplaced. In one American study, less than 20% of the text messages looked at showed abbreviated forms of any kind—about three per message. And in a Norwegian study, the proportion was even lower, with just 6% using abbreviations. In my own text collection, the figure is about 10%.

People seem to have swallowed whole the stories that youngsters use nothing else but abbreviations when they text, such as the reports in 2003 that a teenager had written an essay so full of textspeak that her teacher was unable to understand it. An extract was posted online, and quoted incessantly, but as no one was ever able to track down the entire essay, it was probably a hoax.

10     There are several distinctive features of the way texts are written that combine to give the impression of novelty, but none of them is, in fact, linguistically novel. Many of them were being used in chatroom interactions that predated the arrival of mobile phones. Some can be found in pre-computer informal writing, dating back a hundred years or more.

The most noticeable feature is the use of single letters, numerals, and symbols to represent words or parts of words, as with b "be" and 2 "to." They are called rebuses, and they go back centuries. Adults who condemn a "c u" in a young person's texting have forgotten that they once did the same thing themselves (though not on a mobile phone). In countless Christmas annuals, they solved puzzles like this one:

YY U R YY U B I C U R YY 4 ME
("Too wise you are . . .")

Similarly, the use of initial letters for whole words (n for "no," gf for "girlfriend," cmb "call me back") is not at all new. People have been initialising common phrases for ages. IOU is known from 1618. There is no difference, apart from the medium of communication, between a modern kid's "lol" ("laughing out loud") and an earlier generation's "Swalk" ("sealed with a loving kiss").

In texts we find such forms as msg ("message") and xlnt ("excellent"). Almst any wrd cn be abbrvted in ths wy—though there is no consistency between texters. But this isn't new either. Eric Partridge published his Dictionary of Abbreviations in 1942. It contained dozens of SMS-looking examples, such as agn "again," mth "month," and gd "good"—50 years before texting was born.

English has had abbreviated words ever since it began to be written down. Words such as exam, vet, fridge, cox and bus are so familiar that they have effectively become new words. When some of these abbreviated forms first came into use, they also attracted criticism. In 1711, for example, Joseph Addison complained about the way words were being "miserably curtailed"—he mentioned pos (itive) and incog (nito). And Jonathan Swift thought that abbreviating words was a "barbarous custom."

What novelty there is in texting lies chiefly in the way it takes further some of the processes used in the past. Some of its juxtapositions create forms which have little precedent, apart from in puzzles. All conceivable types of feature can be juxtaposed—sequences of shortened and full words (hldmecls "hold me close"), logograms[2] and shortened words (2bctnd "to be continued"), logograms and nonstandard spellings (cu2nite) and so on. There are no less than four processes combined in iowan2bwu "I only want to be with you"—full word + an initialism + a shortened word + two logograms + an initialism + a logogram. And some messages contain unusual processes: in iohis4u "I only have eyes for you," we see the addition of a plural ending to a logogram. One characteristic runs through all these examples: the letters, symbols and words are run together, without spaces. This is certainly unusual in the history of special writing systems. But few texts string together long sequences of puzzling graphic units.

There are also individual differences in texting, as in any other linguistic domain. In 2002, Stuart Campbell was found guilty of the murder of his 15-year-old niece after his text message alibi was shown to be a forgery. He had claimed that certain texts sent by the girl showed he was innocent. But a detailed comparison of the vocabulary and other stylistic features of his own text messages and those of his niece showed that he had written the messages himself. The forensic possibilities have been further explored by a team at the University of Leicester. The fact that texting is a relatively unstandardised mode of communication, prone to idiosyncrasy, turns out to be an advantage in such a context, as authorship differences are likely to be more easily detectable than in writing using standard English.

Texters use deviant spellings—and they know they are deviant. But they are by no means the first to use such nonstandard forms as cos "because," wot "what," or gissa "give us a." Several of these are so much part of English literary tradition that they have been given entries in the Oxford English Dictionary. "Cos" is there from 1828 and "wot" from 1829. Many can be found in literary dialect representations, such as by Charles Dickens, Mark Twain, Walter Scott, DH Lawrence, or Alan Bleasdale ("Gissa job!").

Sending a message on a mobile phone is not the most natural of ways to communicate. The keypad isn't linguistically sensible. No one took letter-frequency considerations into account when designing it. For example, key 7 on my mobile contains four symbols, pqrs. It takes four key-presses to access the letter s, and yet s is one of the most frequently

15

---

[2]Letters or symbols that stand for words. [Eds.]

occurring letters in English. It is twice as easy to input q, which is one of the least frequently occurring letters. It should be the other way round. So any strategy that reduces the time and awkwardness of inputting graphic symbols is bound to be attractive.

Abbreviations were used as a natural, intuitive response to a technological problem. And they appeared in next to no time. Texters simply transferred (and then embellished) what they had encountered in other settings. We have all left notes in which we have replaced an *and* by an &, a *three* by a 3, and so on. Anglo-Saxon scribes used abbreviations of this kind.

20    But the need to save time and energy is by no means the whole story of texting. When we look at some texts, they are linguistically quite complex. There are an extraordinary number of ways in which people play with language—creating riddles, solving crosswords, playing Scrabble, inventing new words. Professional writers do the same—providing catchy copy for advertising slogans, thinking up puns in newspaper headlines, and writing poems, novels and plays. Children quickly learn that one of the most enjoyable things you can do with language is to play with its sounds, words, grammar—and spelling.

The drive to be playful is there when we text, and it is hugely powerful. Within two or three years of the arrival of texting, it developed a ludic dimension. In short, it's fun.

To celebrate World Poetry day in 2007, T-Mobile tried to find the UK's first "Txt laureate" in a competition for the best romantic poem in SMS. They had 200 entrants, and as with previous competitions the entries were a mixture of unabbreviated and abbreviated texts.

The winner, Ben Ziman-Bright, wrote conventionally:

The wet rustle of rain
can dampen today. Your text
buoys me above oil-rainbow puddles
like a paper boat, so that even
soaked to the skin
I am grinning.

The runner-up did not:

O hart tht sorz
My luv adorz
He mAks me liv
He mAks me giv
Myslf 2 him
As my luv porz

(The author of the latter was, incidentally, in her late 60s.)

The length constraint in text-poetry fosters economy of expression in much the same way as other tightly constrained forms of poetry do, such as the haiku or the Welsh englyn. To say a poem must be written within 160 characters at first seems just as pointless as to say that a poem must be written in three lines of five, seven, and five syllables. But put such a discipline into the hands of a master, and the result can be poetic magic. Of course, SMS poetry has some way to go before it can match the haiku tradition; but then, haikus have had a head-start of several hundred years.

There is something about the genre which has no parallel else- 25 where. This is nothing to do with the use of texting abbreviations. It is more to do with the way the short lines have an individual force. Reading a text poem, wrote Peter Sansom, who co-judged a Guardian competition in 2002, is "an urgent business . . . with a text poem you stay focused as it were in the now of each arriving line." The impact is evident even in one-liners, whose effect relies on the kind of succinctness we find in a maxim or proverb. UA Fanthorpe, Sansom's fellow judge, admired "Basildon: imagine a carpark." And they both liked "They phone you up, your mum and dad."

Several competitions have focussed on reworking famous lines, titles, or quotations:

txt me ishmael
zen & T @ f m2 cycl mn10nc

The brevity of the SMS genre disallows complex formal patterning—of, say, the kind we might find in a sonnet. It isn't so easy to include more than a couple of images, such as similes, simply because there isn't the space. Writers have nonetheless tried to extend the potential of the medium. The SMS novel, for example, operates on a screen-by-screen basis. Each screen is a "chapter" describing an event in the story. Here is an interactive example from 2005, from an Indian website called "Cloakroom":

Chptr 6: While Surching 4 Her Father, Rita Bumps In2 A Chaiwalla & Tea Spills On Her Blouse. She Goes Inside Da Washroom, & Da Train Halts @ A Station.

In Japan, an author known as Yoshi has had a huge success with his text-messaging novel *Deep Love*. Readers sent feedback as the story unfolded, and some of their ideas were incorporated into it. He went on to make a film of the novel.

A mobile literature channel began in China in 2004. The "m-novel," as it is called, started with a love story, "Distance," by writer and broadcaster Xuan Huang. A young couple get to know each other because of a wrongly sent SMS message. The whole story is 1008 Chinese characters, told in 15 chapters, with one chapter sent each day.

CHAPTER 3 FOCUS

30   Plainly, there are severe limits to the expressive power of the medium, when it is restricted to a screen in this way. So it is not surprising that, very early on, writers dispensed with the 160-character constraint, and engaged in SMS creative writing of any length using hard copy. Immediately there was a problem. By taking the writing away from the mobile phone screen, how could the distinctiveness of the genre be maintained? So the stylistic character of SMS writing changed, and texting abbreviations, previously optional, became obligatory.

Several SMS poets, such as Norman Silver, go well beyond text-messaging conventions, introducing variations in line-shape, type-size, font, and colour that are reminiscent of the concrete poetry creations of the 1960s. They illustrate the way the genre is being shaped by the more powerful applications available on computers.

In 2007 Finnish writer Hannu Luntiala published The Last Messages, in which the whole 332-page narrative consists of SMS messages. It tells the story of an IT-executive who resigns his job and travels the world, using text messages to keep in touch with everyone. And the growing independence of the genre from its mobile-phone origins is well illustrated by the French novelist Phil Marso, who published a book in 2004 written entirely in French SMS shorthand, Pas Sage a Taba vo SMS—a piece of word-play intended to discourage young people from smoking. The next year he produced L, an SMS retelling of French poetic classics.

An extraordinary number of doom-laden prophecies have been made about the supposed linguistic evils unleashed by texting. Sadly, its creative potential has been virtually ignored. But five years of research has at last begun to dispel the myths. The most important finding is that texting does not erode children's ability to read and write. On the contrary, literacy improves. The latest studies (from a team at Coventry University) have found strong positive links between the use of text language and the skills underlying success in standard English in pre-teenage children. The more abbreviations in their messages, the higher they scored on tests of reading and vocabulary. The children who were better at spelling and writing used the most textisms. And the younger they received their first phone, the higher their scores.

Children could not be good at texting if they had not already developed considerable literacy awareness. Before you can write and play with abbreviated forms, you need to have a sense of how the sounds of your language relate to the letters. You need to know that there are such things as alternative spellings. If you are aware that your texting behaviour is different, you must have already intuited that there is such a thing as a standard. If you are using such abbreviations as lol and brb ("be right back"), you must have developed a sensitivity to the communicative needs of your textees.

Some people dislike texting. Some are bemused by it. But it is 35 merely the latest manifestation of the human ability to be linguistically creative and to adapt language to suit the demands of diverse settings. There is no disaster pending. We will not see a new generation of adults growing up unable to write proper English. The language as a whole will not decline. In texting what we are seeing, in a small way, is language in evolution.

## Responding to Reading

1. Why does Crystal think that popular conceptions about the effect of texting on the English language are wrong? What examples does he use to support his position?
2. According to Crystal, what is truly novel about texting? How do his ideas contradict those of John Humphrys (p. 174)?
3. In his conclusion, Crystal says, "In texting what we are seeing, in a small way, is language in evolution" (35). What does he mean?

## Responding in Writing

Crystal gives examples of text-poetry and a chapter of a text-novel. Write your own text-poem or text-story. Then, write a paragraph in which you describe the advantages and limitations of using the text-message format for this assignment.

# THUMBSPEAK: IS TEXTING HERE TO STAY?

## Louis Menand

### 1952–

*A professor of English and American literature and language at Harvard University and a staff writer for the* New Yorker, *Louis Menand researches American studies with a focus on nineteenth- and twentieth-century cultural history. His books include* American Studies *(2002),* The Story of the Soup Cans *(2006), and* The Marketplace of Ideas: Reform and Resistance in the American University *(2010). His 2001 book* The Metaphysical Club *was the recipient of the 2002 Pulitzer Prize for history. In the following essay, a review of a book on texting by David Crystal (p. 178), Menand examines the rise and fall of texting.*

Is texting bringing us closer to the end of life as we currently tolerate it? Enough people have suggested that it is to have inspired David Crystal to produce "Txtng: The Gr8 Db8" (Oxford; $19.95). "I don't think I have ever come across a topic which has attracted more adult antagonism," he says. (On the other hand, Crystal has written more than a hundred books, so he does not require extraordinary encouragement to share his views.) Crystal is a professional linguist, and professional linguists, almost universally, do not believe that any naturally occurring changes in the language can be bad. So his conclusions are predictable: texting is not corrupting the language; people who send text messages that use emoticons, initialisms ("g2g," "lol"), and other shorthands generally know how to spell perfectly well; and the history of language is filled with analogous examples of nonstandard usage. It is good to know that the estimated three billion human beings who own cell phones, and who use them to send more than a trillion text messages every year, are having no effect on anything that we should care about. A trillion text messages, Crystal says, "appear as no more than a few ripples on the surface of the sea of language."

The texting function of the cell phone ought to have been the special province of the kind of people who figure out how to use the television remote to turn on the toaster: it's a huge amount of trouble relative to the results. In some respects, texting is a giant leap backward in the science of communication. It's more efficient than semaphore,[1] maybe, but how much more efficient is it than Morse code?[2] With Morse code, to make an "s" you needed only three key presses. Sending a text message with a numeric keypad feels primitive and improvisational—like the way prisoners speak to each other by tapping on the walls of their cells in "Darkness at Noon," or the way the guy in "The Diving Bell and the Butterfly" writes a book. And, as Crystal points out, although cell phones keep getting smaller, thumbs do not. Usually, if you can text a person you can much more quickly and efficiently call that person. But people sometimes text when they are close enough to talk face to face. People *like* to text. Why is that?

Crystal's answer is that texting is, partly, a game. It's like writing a sonnet (well, sort of): the requirement is to adapt the message to immutable formal constraints. A sonnet can't have more than fourteen lines, and a mobile-phone message can't have more than a hundred and forty bytes, which is usually enough for a hundred and sixty characters. This is a challenge to ingenuity, not an invitation to anarchy.

Most of the shortcuts used in texting are either self-evident (@ for "at" and "b" for "be") or new initialisms on the model of the old "A.S.A.P.," "R.S.V.P.," and "B.Y.O.B.": "imho" for "in my humble opinion," and so on. More imaginatively, there are the elaborated emoticons, such as 7:-) for baseball cap, and pictograms, such as @(—— for a rose and ~(_8^(|) for Homer Simpson. These are for thumb-happy aficionados, though, not the ordinary texter notifying her partner that the flight is late. There is a dialect that is used mainly by kids: "prw" for

---

[1]System of communicating with the use of flags. [Eds.]
[2]System of communicating with dots and dashes developed by Samuel F. B. Morse (1791–1872). [Eds.]

"parents are watching"; "F?" for "Are we friends again?" But Crystal thinks that texting is not the equivalent of a new language. "People were playing with language in this way long before mobile phones were invented," he points out. "Texting may be using a new technology, but its linguistic processes are centuries old." Acronyms, contractions, abbreviations, and shortened words ("phone" for "telephone," and so forth) are just part of the language. Even back in the days when the dinosaurs roamed the earth and men wrote with typewriters, the language of the office memo was studded with abbreviations: "re:," "cc.," "F.Y.I." "Luv" for "love" dates from 1898; "thanx" was first used in 1936. "Wassup," Crystal notes, originally appeared in a Budweiser commercial. @(—— is something that E. E. Cummings might have come up with.

Still, despite what they say, size matters. A trillion of anything has to     5
make some change in cultural weather patterns. Texting is international. It may have come late to the United States because personal computers became a routine part of life much earlier here than in other countries, and so people could e-mail and Instant Message (which shares a lot of texting lingo). Crystal provides lists of text abbreviations in eleven languages besides English. And it is clear from the lists that different cultures have had to solve the problem of squeezing commonly delivered messages onto the cell-phone screen according to their own particular national needs. In the Czech Republic, for example, "hosipa" is used for *"Hovno si pamatuju"*: "I can't remember anything." One can imagine a wide range of contexts in which Czech texters might have recourse to that sentiment. French texters have devised "ght2v1," which means *"J'ai acheté du vin."* In Germany, "nok" is an efficient solution to the problem of how to explain *"Nicht ohne Kondom"*—"not without condom." If you receive a text reading "aun" from the fine Finnish lady you met in the airport lounge, she is telling you *"Älä unta nää"*—in English, "Dream on."

But the lists also suggest that texting has accelerated a tendency toward the Englishing of world languages. Under the constraints of the numeric-keypad technology, English has some advantages. The average English word has only five letters; the average Inuit word, for example, has fourteen. English has relatively few characters; Ethiopian has three hundred and forty-five symbols, which do not fit on most keypads. English rarely uses diacritical marks, and it is not heavily inflected. Languages with diacritical marks, such as Czech, almost always drop them in text messages. Portuguese texters often substitute "m" for the tilde. Some Chinese texters use Pinyin—that is, the practice of writing Chinese words using the Roman alphabet.

But English is also the language of much of the world's popular culture. Sometimes it is more convenient to use the English term, but

CHAPTER 3   FOCUS

often it is the aesthetically preferred term—the cooler expression. Texters in all eleven languages that Crystal lists use "lol," "u," "brb," and "gr8," all English-based shorthands. The Dutch use "2m" to mean "tomorrow"; the French have been known to use "now," which is a lot easier to type than "*maintenant*." And there is what is known as "code-mixing," in which two languages—one of them invariably English—are conflated in a single expression. Germans write "mbsseg" to mean "mail back *so schnell es geht*" ("as fast as you can"). So texting has probably done some damage to the planet's cultural ecology, to lingo-diversity. People are better able to communicate across national borders, but at some cost to variation.

The obvious appeal of texting is its speed. There is, as it happens, a Ten Commandments of texting, as laid down by one Norman Silver, the author of "Laugh Out Loud :-D"). The Fourth of these commandments reads, "u shall b prepard @ all times 2 tXt & 2 recv." This is the new decorum in communication: you can be sloppy and you can be blunt, but you have to be fast. To delay is to disrespect. In fact, delay is the only disrespect. Any other misunderstanding can be cleared up by a few more exchanges.

Back when most computing was done on a desktop, people used to complain about how much pressure they felt to respond quickly to e-mail. At least, in those days, it was understood that you might have walked away from your desk. There is no socially accepted excuse for being without your cell phone. "I didn't have my phone": that just does not sound believable. Either you are lying or you are depressed or you have something to hide. If you receive a text, therefore, you are obliged instantaneously to reply to it, if only to confirm that you are not one of those people who can be without a phone. The most common text message must be "k." It means "I have nothing to say, but God forbid that you should think that I am ignoring your message." The imperative to reply is almost addictive, which is probably one reason that texting can be not just rude (people continually sneaking a look at their cell phones, while you're talking with them, in case some message awaits) but deadly. It was reported that the engineer in the fatal Los Angeles commuter-train crash this fall was texting seconds before the accident occurred. The *Times* noted recently that four of ten teen-agers claim that they can text blindfolded. As long as they don't think that they can drive blindfolded.

10      A less obvious attraction of texting is that it uses a telephone to avoid what many people dread about face-to-face exchanges, and even about telephones—having to have a real, unscripted conversation. People don't like to have to perform the amount of self-presentation that is required in a personal encounter. They don't want to deal with the facial expressions, the body language, the obligation to be witty or

interesting. They just want to say "flt is lte." Texting is so formulaic that it is nearly anonymous. There is no penalty for using catchphrases, because that is the accepted glossary of texting. C. K. Ogden's "Basic English" had a vocabulary of eight hundred and fifty words. Most texters probably make do with far fewer than that. And there is no penalty for abruptness in a text message. Shortest said, best said. The faster the other person can reply, the less you need to say. Once, a phone call was quicker than a letter, and face-to-face was quicker than a phone call. Now e-mail is quicker than face-to-face, and texting, because the respondent is almost always armed with his or her device and ready to reply, is quicker than e-mail.

"For the moment, texting seems here to stay," Crystal concludes. Aun, as the Finns say. It's true that all technology is, ultimately, interim technology, but texting, in the form that Crystal studies, is a technology that is nearing its obsolescence. Once the numeric keypad is replaced by the QWERTY keyboard on most mobile messaging devices, and once the capacity of those devices increases, we are likely to see far fewer initialisms and pictograms. Discourse will migrate back up toward the level of e-mail. But it will still be important to reach out and touch someone. Nok, though. Danke.

## Responding to Reading

1. According to Menand, why is texting "a giant leap backward in the science of communication" (2)? In what way does this statement contradict David Crystal (p. 178)?
2. Why, according to Crystal, do people like to text? In what way is texting like a game?
3. What does Menand see as the effect of texting? What does he mean when he says that texting "is a technology that is nearing its obsolescence" (11)?

## Responding in Writing

Write a paragraph in which you analyze the texts you send each day. What different audiences do you text? How are the messages to each audience similar? How are they different? Why do you text rather than call or email?

# WIDENING THE FOCUS

## For Critical Reading and Writing

Referring specifically to the three readings in this chapter's Focus section, write an essay in which you answer the question, "Is Texting Destroying the English Language?"

## For Further Reading

The following readings can suggest additional perspectives for thinking and writing about the effect of technology on language.

- David Carr, "Why Twitter Will Endure" (p. 231)

- Richard Wright, "The Library Card" (p. 346)

- Nicholas Carr, "Does the Internet Make You Dumber?" (p. 216)

 ## For Focused Research

Texting and social networking sites have forever changed the nature of political protests around the world. For example, texting—along with *Twitter* and *Facebook*—played a pivotal role in the protests after the 2009 Iranian presidential election (which some have called the "Twitter Revolution"): protestors used these technologies to organize and communicate with one another quickly and across geographical boundaries. In preparation for writing an essay about political uses of texting, do a *Google* search using the search terms *texting and political protests,* and then choose a recent political protest. In your essay, explain the role of texting for protestors. What has texting allowed protestors to do that they could not do before? Given these changes, do you see texting as a positive development in effecting global political change, or do you think it has made things worse? Be sure to support your position with examples and evidence from the Web sites you use.

## Beyond the Classroom

Conduct an email survey of your friends and classmates, asking them the following questions:

- How much time per week do you spend texting? How much time do you spend doing other kinds of writing (such as email and essay writing)?

- What effect has texting had on your other writing?

CHAPTER 3 FOCUS

Then, write an essay summarizing your findings and taking a position on whether texting seems to have a positive or a negative effect on other kinds of writing.

—————————————— WRITING ——————————————

### The Politics of Language

1. Several writers in this chapter discuss the uneasy relationship that exists between their native languages and English. In spite of this situation, they resist abandoning the languages of their original cultures. Write an essay in which you examine the essays by Oscar Hijuelos, Amy Tan, and Jasmin Darznik and consider what benefit each writer gets from his or her native language and what problems the pull between the two languages creates.

2. According to some educators, texting is negatively affecting the quality of students' writing. Other educators disagree. They see texting as a good thing because it enables students to say what they want to say just the way they want to say it. Rather than dismissing this technology, they say, educators should explore ways of integrating it into the curriculum. Write an essay in which you suggest ways in which texting could be made part of your educational experience. Be specific, referring to the essays in the Focus section (p. 174) as well as to specific classes that you are taking.

3. In "Mother Tongue" (p. 134), Amy Tan distinguishes between the English she speaks to her mother and the English she speaks to the rest of the world. Write an essay in which you describe the various types of English you speak—at home, at school, at work, to your friends, and so on. In what ways are these Englishes alike, and in what ways are they different? What ideas are you able to express best with each type of English?

4. Over fifty years ago, George Orwell wrote an essay in which he discussed how governments use language to control their citizens. Now, control seems to be exerted at times by a desire for political correctness—excessive focus on avoiding language that might offend others because of their politics, race, gender, age, disabilities, or religious beliefs. Write an essay in which you consider the extent to which political correctness is a factor in the language used at your school, in your workplace, and among your friends and family members. Refer to Alleen Pace Nilsen's "Sexism in English: Embodiment and Language" and Christopher M. Fairman's "Saying It Is Hurtful, Banning It Is Worse" (p. 167) as well as to your own experiences.

5. Both Amy Tan in "Mother Tongue" (p. 134) and Jasmin Darznik in "Persian, English" (p. 140) talk about how education can change one's use of language. Write an essay discussing the effect education has had on your own spoken and written language. What do you think you have gained and lost as your language has changed?

6. Which of your daily activities would you be unable to carry out if, like the people Jonathan Kozol describes in "The Human Cost of an Illiterate Society" (p. 159), you could neither read nor write? Write an article for your local newspaper in which you report on a typical day, being sure to identify specific tasks you could not do. In addition, explain some strategies you would use to hide the fact that you couldn't read or write.

7. A recent study suggests that the population worldwide that has grown up speaking English is shrinking. In the sciences, however, the use of English is expanding. Some researchers warn that this situation could divide the scientific world into the "haves" and "have-nots"— with the "haves" gaining the advantage of being able to publish in prestigious scientific journals and the "have-nots" unable to achieve access. Do you think this is fair? Write an essay in which you discuss how the privileging of one language over another gives some people advantages and undercuts the ability of others to accomplish their goals. As you write, consider the essays by Frederick Douglass (p. 143), Alleen Pace Nilsen (p. 148), and Jonathan Kozol (p. 159).

8. List some of the words you use to refer to women, minorities, and other groups. Then, write an email to Alleen Pace Nilsen (p. 148) in which you agree or disagree with her assertion that the words people use tell a lot about their values and beliefs. In addition to Nilsen's essay, consider Christopher H. Fairman's "Saying It Is Hurtful, Banning It Is Worse" (p. 167).

9. Recently, there has been a great deal of debate about the benefits and drawbacks of a multilingual society. Supporters say that a multilingual society allows people to preserve their own cultures and thus fosters pride. Detractors say that a multilingual society reinforces differences and ultimately tears a country apart. What do you see as the benefits and drawbacks of a multilingual society? As a country, what would we gain if we encouraged multilingualism? What would we lose? Refer to the essays in this chapter by Oscar Hijuelos (p. 131), Jasmin Darznik (p. 140), and Amy Tan (p. 134), to support your position.

10. For years, there has been a great deal of debate about whether English should be made the official language of the United States. Those in favor of this proposal point out that a federal law making English the official language would encourage immigrants to learn the language and to assimilate. Opponents say that such a policy would discriminate against non-native speakers and keep them out of the political mainstream. What do you think Oscar Hijuelos (p. 131), Amy Tan (p. 134), and Jasmin Darznik (p. 140) would think of this proposal? What advantages and disadvantages would they identify? Be specific, and use material from their essays to support your own position on these issues.

# 4

## MEDIA AND SOCIETY

Many forms of popular media—for example, books, newspapers, and magazines; radio, television, and film—have been around for a long time, and over the years, they have had a powerful impact on our lives. But the popular media have changed dramatically in our lifetimes.

Television is one medium that changed and yet managed to survive, and even thrive. Cable television brought us literally hundreds of stations, along with sitcom reruns that endlessly recycled our childhoods (and our parents' childhoods). Satellites brought immediacy, delivering news in real time around the clock. Other innovations also appeared on television: home shopping, reality TV, infomercials, music videos. And now, of course, television has become digital and interactive, with

Fifteenth-century illuminated manuscript depicting the angel Gabriel speaking to Mary

viewers no longer tied to a schedule or limited to watching programs on a television set.

Over the years, in response to emerging technology, other forms of media also reinvented themselves. Music evolved from vinyl records to cassettes to CDs to music downloaded onto MP3 players. Movies moved from silent to "talkies" and from black and white to color, later enhanced by sophisticated computer animation and special digital effects. Professional journals and popular magazines became available online, and today, portable digital readers permit us to read paperless newspapers and books. In an effort to hold on to readers, newspapers have constructed Web sites and published online editions, but, despite these innovations, the Internet continues to threaten the survival of the daily newspaper. (Even before the Internet existed, newspaper readership was on the decline; cities that once had several different daily newspapers, with a variety of editorial positions, now have only a few. In fact, over 98 percent of U.S. cities have just one major daily newspaper.)

Clearly, "new media" is a completely different entity from the media of even a decade ago, and this evolution has had negative as well as positive consequences. In recent years, the increasing power and scope of the Internet, and its ever-increasing ability to enable us to form networks, has changed everything. Today, our access to digital media has truly made the world into what Canadian cultural critic Marshall McLuhan once called a "global village": a world of nations—and, today,

Amazon Kindle

of individuals—that are more and more interconnected and inter-dependent. The Internet has made available a tremendous amount of information—and the ability to communicate this information almost instantly to millions of people all over the planet. Now, we exchange ideas and images through blogs, chat rooms, bulletin boards, and email as well as through instant messaging, texting, *YouTube*, and *Twitter*. But the development of new media also has a dark side. The same tools that can unite, inform, instruct, entertain, and inspire can also isolate, misin-form, frighten, deceive, stereotype, and even brainwash.

In this chapter's Focus section, "Does Social Networking Connect Us or Keep Us Apart?" writers debate whether digital social networking tools have created vibrant virtual communities or have actually replaced face-to-face communication—and led to a loss of true intimacy.

## PREPARING TO READ AND WRITE

As you read and prepare to write about the essays in this chapter, you may consider the following questions:

- Does the essay focus on one particular medium or on the media in general?

- Does the writer discuss traditional media, new media, or both?

- Is the writer's purpose to present information or to persuade?

- Does the writer see the media as a positive, negative, or neutral force? Why?

- If the writer sees negative effects, where does he or she place blame? Do you agree?

- Does the writer make any recommendations for change? Do these recommendations seem reasonable?

- Is the writer focusing on the media's effects on individuals or on society?

- Does the writer discuss personal observations or experiences? If so, are they similar to or different from your own?

- When was the essay written? Has the situation the writer describes changed since then?

- Which writers' positions on the impact of the media (or on the media's shortcomings) are most alike? Most different? Most like your own?

# So Much Media, So Little News

## Peter Funt

*An op-ed writer for the* Boston Globe, *the* New York Times, *and the* Wall Street Journal, *Peter Funt was an actor, host, and producer for the popular TV show* Candid Camera. *The president of the Laughter Therapy Foundation, Funt co-authored the book* Gotcha! *(1979) about the value of practical jokes. In the following essay, he considers the relationship between mass media and the news.*

A group of daily papers in New England calls its electronic edition *No Inky Fingers.* The point, of course, is that with digital news nothing rubs off on readers' hands. But what's rubbing off on their brains?

The disappearance of what could be called the mental rub-off effect is partly to blame for the fact that many Americans are overloaded with information, yet seem to know less than ever about current events. As news packaging shifts from general interest to specific interest, it becomes difficult for mass audiences to rub up against the news—even if accidentally.

Not long ago most American homes received at least one daily newspaper. Just idly turning the pages to find the sports section or comics, readers couldn't help but glance at the news headlines, and bits of information tended to rub off.

Television, before cable and satellite, was arranged so that most entertainment stopped at the dinner hour and again before bedtime for general-interest news broadcasts. Just turning the dial, or waiting for the weather forecast, viewers couldn't help but sample a bit of hard news.

And think how radio used to be. The government basically required 5 stations to run news or "public service" programming—so whether you were listening to rock, country or classical, every hour programs paused for a few minutes of news. The news was hard to avoid, and some of it rubbed off.

By contrast, today's boutique media allow many people to skip news altogether. You can set your Internet home page so that it serves up only what you're interested in. You can watch video via Hulu or YouTube and never encounter a smidgen of news. You can listen 24/7 to satellite radio or other digital music services and not be bothered by reportage from the outside world.

Even consumers who answer surveys by stating that they get "news" online or by watching cable channels often are referring to something that isn't really news at all. Some cable "news" channels devote virtually all of prime time to nonstop campaigns for liberal and conservative agendas, making little or no effort to summarize the major news of the day.

Many television producers and an increasing number of newspaper editors mistakenly believe that since the day's hard news is readily available, around-the-clock, from so many sources, it's no longer in their commercial interest, or the public interest, to serve it up themselves.

When I asked a college media class of 40 students recently if they read a daily newspaper, two hands went up. When I clarified that online newspaper sites qualified, three more hands were raised. Yet everyone in the class claimed to be at least generally aware of the news. I was told that "important stuff" gets relayed by text, tweet or other social media.

10   While that's often true, it contributes to the total inversion of the traditional process by which news is disseminated. Anyone who has ever worked in a newsroom is familiar with the most basic debate among journalists: Should we give the public what it *wants* to know, or what it *ought* to know? The best prescription has always been a combination of both.

However, the line that separates those considerations is moving—both because journalists are succumbing to competitive pressure and because consumers are taking it upon themselves to alter the equation. Thanks to modern media and devices, they have the tools with which to change it.

The standard pushback is that there's more information out there than ever before, and that interested consumers want to sort through it to find the news. Again: Want? Or, ought?

The sad truth is that while some of us are naturally curious about what we don't know, an increasing number of readers and viewers want only reinforcement of what they already know. While it's not the job of media to force-feed news to an uninterested audience, the system worked better when some news and information just happened to rub off.

Personally, I've always relied upon great editors and great broadcasters to tell me what they think is important each day. I'm determined to form my own opinions, but I'm not so audacious as to think I know what's important without professional help.

15   One of my favorite news slogans is one used for decades by the Scripps newspaper chain: "Give light and the people will find their own way." Yet in modern communications we seem to give off more heat than light, leaving too many information-loaded consumers stumbling around in the dark.

## Responding to Reading

1.  Funt says that in the past, news was "hard to avoid" (5), but today one can "skip news altogether" (6). Do you agree with him, or do you think that today, as in the past, "bits of information" still tend to "rub off" (3)? If so, how?

2.  In paragraph 10, Funt identifies what he calls "the most basic debate among journalists: Should we give the public what it *wants* to know, or what it *ought* to know?" Give some examples of what you believe most people want to know and what you think people *should* know. On which side of the debate do you stand?

3.  In his conclusion, Funt quotes a favorite news slogan: "Give light and the people will find their own way." What do you think this slogan means? How does it support the point Funt is making in this essay in general (and in paragraphs 13–15 in particular)?

## Responding in Writing

From what sources do you get your news? Do you seek updates actively, do you count on the news to "rub off," or do you tend to "skip news altogether" (6)?

# REALITY TV: A DEARTH OF TALENT AND THE DEATH OF MORALITY

## Salman Rushdie

### 1947–

*Born in Bombay, India, Salman Rushdie is perhaps best known for his novel* The Satanic Verses *(1988), which infuriated Muslims around the world. The book was banned in a dozen countries, caused riots in several, and led to a multimillion-dollar bounty being offered for Rushdie's assassination. In 1998, the fatwa (death sentence) was lifted by the Iranian government (although some fundamentalist Muslim groups increased the reward for killing him). Rushdie continues to publish articles, essays, and books, including* Shalimar the Clown *(2005),* Midnight's Children *(2006),* The Enchantress of Florence: A Novel *(2008), and* Luka and the Fire of Life: A Novel *(2010). In the following selection, which appeared in* The Guardian *in 2001, Rushdie offers his criticisms of reality TV and suggests some dangerous trends to come.*

I've managed to miss out on reality TV until now. In spite of all the talk in Britain about nasty Nick and flighty Mel, and in America about the fat, naked bastard Richard manipulating his way to desert-island victory, I have somehow preserved my purity. I wouldn't recognise Nick or Mel if I passed them in the street, or Richard if he was standing in front of me unclothed.

Ask me where the Big Brother house is, or how to reach Temptation Island, and I have no answer. I do remember the American *Survivor* contestant who managed to fry his own hand so that the skin peeled away until his fingers looked like burst sausages, but that's because he got on to the main evening news. Otherwise, search me. Who won? Who lost? Who cares?

The subject of reality TV shows, however, has been impossible to avoid. Their success is the media story of the (new) century, along with the ratings triumph of the big-money game shows such as *Who Wants to Be a Millionaire?* Success on this scale insists on being examined, because it tells us things about ourselves; or ought to.

And what tawdry narcissism is here revealed! The television set, once so idealistically thought of as our window on the world, has become a dime-store mirror instead. Who needs images of the world's rich otherness, when you can watch these half-familiar avatars of yourself—these half-attractive half-persons—enacting ordinary life under weird conditions? Who needs talent, when the unashamed self-display of the talentless is constantly on offer?

5    I've been watching *Big Brother 2*, which has achieved the improbable feat of taking over the tabloid front pages in the final stages of a general election campaign. This, according to the conventional wisdom, is because the show is more interesting than the election. The "reality" may be even stranger. It may be that *Big Brother* is so popular because it's even more boring than the election. Because it is the most boring, and therefore most "normal," way of becoming famous, and, if you're lucky or smart, of getting rich as well.

"Famous" and "rich" are now the two most important concepts in western society, and ethical questions are simply obliterated by the potency of their appeal. In order to be famous and rich, it's OK—it's actually "good"—to be devious. It's "good" to be exhibitionistic. It's "good" to be bad. And what dulls the moral edge is boredom. It's impossible to maintain a sense of outrage about people being so trivially self-serving for so long.

Oh, the dullness! Here are people becoming famous for being asleep, for keeping a fire alight, for letting a fire go out, for videotaping their cliched thoughts, for flashing their breasts, for lounging around, for quarrelling, for bitching, for being unpopular, and (this is too interesting to happen often) for kissing! Here, in short, are people becoming famous for doing nothing much at all, but doing it where everyone can see them.

Add the contestants' exhibitionism to the viewers' voyeurism and you get a picture of a society sickly in thrall to what Saul Bellow called "event glamour." Such is the glamour of these banal but brilliantly spotlit events that anything resembling a real value—modesty, decency, intelligence, humour, selflessness; you can write your own list—is rendered redundant. In this inverted ethical universe, worse is better. The show presents "reality" as a prize fight, and suggests that in life, as on TV, anything goes, and the more deliciously contemptible it is, the more we'll like it. Winning isn't everything, as Charlie Brown once said, but losing isn't anything.

The problem with this kind of engineered realism is that, like all fads, it's likely to have a short shelf-life, unless it finds ways of renewing itself. The probability is that our voyeurism will become more demanding. It won't be enough to watch somebody being catty, or weeping when evicted from the house of hell, or "revealing everything" on subsequent talk shows, as if they had anything left to reveal.

What is gradually being reinvented is the gladiatorial combat. The TV set is the Colosseum and the contestants are both gladiators and lions; their job is to eat one another until only one remains alive. But how long, in our jaded culture, before "real" lions, actual dangers, are introduced to these various forms of fantasy island, to feed our hunger for more action, more pain, more vicarious thrills? [10]

Here's a thought, prompted by the news that the redoubtable Gore Vidal[1] has agreed to witness the execution by lethal injection of the Oklahoma bomber Timothy McVeigh.[2] The witnesses at an execution watch the macabre proceedings through a glass window: a screen. This, too, is a kind of reality TV, and—to make a modest proposal—it may represent the future of such programmes. If we are willing to watch people stab one another in the back, might we not also be willing to actually watch them die?

In the world outside TV, our numbed senses already require increasing doses of titillation. One murder is barely enough; only the mass murderers make the front pages. You have to blow up a building full of people or machine-gun a whole royal family to get our attention. Soon, perhaps, you'll have to kill off a whole species of wildlife or unleash a virus that wipes out people by the thousand, or else you'll be small potatoes. You'll be on an inside page.

And as in reality, so on "reality TV." How long until the first TV death? How long until the second? By the end of Orwell's great novel *1984*, Winston Smith has been brainwashed. "He loved Big Brother." As, now, do we. We are the Winstons now.

## Responding to Reading

1. Salman Rushdie is a respected novelist with an international reputation, but he admits that he knows little about reality TV and has only recently begun to watch one reality show. Do you think he has the credibility to criticize reality TV?

2. Rushdie's fear is that "our voyeurism will become more demanding" (9), leading to shows that will "feed our hunger for more action, more pain, more vicarious thrills" (10). Has this fear been realized since this essay was published in 2001? Do you think Rushdie is correct to be alarmed, or do you think viewers will continue to be satisfied with today's level of action, pain, and thrills?

---

[1] Novelist and essayist. [Eds.]

[2] Executed in 2001 for killing 168 people in the 1995 bombing of a government building (which housed a daycare for employees) in Oklahoma City. [Eds.]

3. In paragraphs 12–13, Rushdie draws parallels between reality TV and news reporting, suggesting that the escalation of sensationalism in reality programs has a counterpart in news reporting. Do you think he is correct? Why or why not?

## Responding in Writing

What is it about reality shows that makes them so popular? Cite examples from contemporary programs to support your response.

# TV for Tots: Not What You Remember

## Jonathan V. Last

*Jonathan V. Last is a senior writer at* The Weekly Standard *and a columnist for the* Daily *and the* Philadelphia Inquirer. *His work has appeared in such publications as the* Los Angeles Times, *the* New York Post, Salon, Slate, *the* Wall Street Journal, *and the* Washington Post. *He also writes about journalism, sports, and other topics for the blog* Galley Slaves. *In the following essay, Last takes a critical look at children's television.*

These days the personal is the political, even on children's television. Not content to simply teach lessons about the alphabet or sharing, nearly every show has a worldview or a message to push.

In recent years, for instance, children's entertainment has struggled with the idea of manliness. To some extent, TV is just reflecting changes in the outside world, which over the past 40 years has been, to a large degree, feminized. This has been partly for good and partly for ill. To take just one example, it is undeniably good that bullying has become (at least officially) forbidden. Bullying is a very bad thing.

But as bullying was put away, so were ideas about physical courage and manliness. Not knowing how to handle such subjects in this new era, the creators of children's television choose to present strange visions of men.

The men on kids' shows tend to be either aged, and hence harmless, or young, and vaguely effete.[1] Bob, Gordon and Luis—the three bulwarks of the current cast of *Sesame Street*—are all well past Social Security age. Alan, who minds the departed Mr. Hooper's store, is right behind them. The other main male characters are a teenager (Miles) and a campy tramp (Mr. Noodle).

5      Hop over to cable and you'll find *Yo Gabba Gabba!*, a show whose master of ceremonies is a skinny fellow named DJ Lance Rock. Wearing a clingy orange track suit, oversize hipster glasses and a tall, furry orange hat, he creeps and slinks around the screen carrying a giant

---
[1]Effeminate. [Eds.]

boom box while the show's obnoxious theme song blares. He isn't exactly Clint Eastwood. Another popular show, *LazyTown*, features only two men—a hero, "Sportacus," and a villain, "Robbie Rotten," neither of whom would look out of place in a Village People tribute band.

It's easy to caricature this complaint, that the men of children's television are soft and neutered. And this isn't to say that the guys on kids' shows should walk and talk like Charles Bronson.[2] But it wouldn't hurt if, every once in a while, there was a character as traditionally masculine as, say, Gen. David Petraeus. Or to lower the bar even further, if there were male figures who resemble run-of-the-mill young fathers: a 32-year-old who looks butch enough to hold down a job, enjoy baseball and occasionally change the oil in his sensible family sedan.

"Bob the Builder" isn't a real man either, though I mean this in the literal, not the pejorative, sense. But that doesn't matter, because he teaches kids a different set of values. A stop-motion animated import from British television, Bob is a construction worker who teams up with various anthropomorphic vehicles—a dump truck named "Muck," a concrete mixer named "Dizzy"—to solve problems and build things.

For the most part, *Bob the Builder* is about normal kids' stuff: teamwork, conflict resolution, taking turns and the like. The show isn't overtly political—Bob's catchphrase, "Yes we can!" predates the Obama campaign. Instead, it peddles a slightly hectoring brand of environmentalism. Ever since Bob discovered his inner environmental conscience, he's been teaching kids about believing in recycling and being kind to Mother Gaia. "Reduce, Reuse, Recycle" has become another one of the show's catchphrases. That's fine so far as it goes—aside from those evil Republicans, who doesn't love the planet?

But it's a little rich having Bob indoctrinate children about "Reduce, Reuse, Recycle" while simultaneously prompting these children to beg their parents for plastic Bob the Builder trucks, and latex Bob the Builder balls, and plush Bob the Builder dolls. All of which are manufactured in far-away lands and shipped to our fair shores by the carbon-gobbling container-shipful. Bob the Builder is like one of those evangelists who lectures on the virtues of living green before hopping onto a private jet and flying back to his mansion in Nashville.

Of course, it's not all eco-liberalism in children's programming. *Thomas the Tank Engine*—which got its start in British storybooks during the 1940s before making its way to TV in 1984—is basically a loving paean to paternalistic capitalism.

Thomas began as a junior engine at the train yard but has since graduated to workplace parity with the other engines. Lording over this entire enterprise is Sir Topham Hatt. The only human of any consequence in the

---

[2]Actor (1922–2003) famous for playing tough-guy roles. [Eds.]

series, he is a chubby, pale-faced fellow, always dressed in a top hat and morning suit.

The trains toil diligently under the benign eye of Sir Topham Hatt, who never does any actual work himself and never pays any actual wages. What he does do is set his silly engines right whenever they act badly or get into scrapes: The boss knows best and we should all aspire to be loyal worker-bees when we grow up. In short, *Thomas the Tank Engine* is exactly the kind of system that drove Karl Marx mad.

There's nothing particularly pernicious about any of this. Bob and Thomas and *Sesame Street* have plenty of redeeming qualities. And in any case, if you don't like a particular show you can always find one that better fits your tastes. Even so, it's a shame that there isn't more of a place for children's entertainment that exists solely in its own universe, apart from adult debates and sociopolitical fashions.

### Responding to Reading

1.  Last criticizes children's TV shows for their tendency to portray "soft and neutered" (6) men rather than offering more traditionally masculine role models. How does he explain why this trend exists? Do you think he has a point?
2.  In paragraph 10, Last uses the term "eco-liberalism." What does he mean? What biases does he exhibit in the language he uses in his discussion of Bob the Builder—and in the essay as a whole?
3.  Do you think Last's criticisms of children's TV shows are justified? Do you think the problem he identifies is as serious as he suggests it is? Why or why not?

### Responding in Writing

Last's central point is that children's TV programs have "a worldview or a message to push" (1). Sample some popular children's programs, and then use examples from these shows to explain why you believe Last is correct (or incorrect).

# EMINEM IS RIGHT

## Mary Eberstadt

*Research fellow at the Hoover Institution, Mary Eberstadt is a consulting editor at* Policy Review *and author of numerous magazine and newspaper articles on various American cultural issues. Her most recent book is the satire* The Loser Letters *(2010). Originally published in her 2004 book* Home-Alone America: The Hidden Toll of Day Care, Behavioral Drugs, and Other Parent Substitutes, *the essay excerpted here examines the meanings and social implications of contemporary American popular music.*

If there is one subject on which the parents of America passionately agree, it is that contemporary adolescent popular music, especially the subgenres of heavy metal and hip-hop/rap, is uniquely degraded—and degrading—by the standards of previous generations. At first blush this seems slightly ironic. After all, most of today's baby-boom parents were themselves molded by rock and roll, bumping and grinding their way through adolescence and adulthood with legendary abandon. Even so, the parents are correct: Much of today's music *is* darker and coarser than yesterday's rock. Misogyny, violence, suicide, sexual exploitation, child abuse—these and other themes, formerly rare and illicit, are now as common as the surfboards, drive-ins, and sock hops of yesteryear.

In a nutshell, the ongoing adult preoccupation with current music goes something like this: *What is the overall influence of this deafening, foul, and often vicious-sounding stuff on children and teenagers?* This is a genuinely important question, and serious studies and articles, some concerned particularly with current music's possible link to violence, have lately been devoted to it. In 2000, the American Academy of Pediatrics, the American Medical Association, the American Psychological Association, and the American Academy of Child & Adolescent Psychiatry all weighed in against contemporary lyrics and other forms of violent entertainment before Congress with a first-ever "Joint Statement on the Impact of Entertainment Violence on Children."

Nonetheless, this is not my focus here. Instead, I would like to turn that logic about influence upside down and ask this question: *What is it about today's music, violent and disgusting though it may be, that resonates with so many American kids?*

As the reader can see, this is a very different way of inquiring about the relationship between today's teenagers and their music. The first question asks what the music *does* to adolescents; the second asks what it *tells* us about them. To answer that second question is necessarily to enter the roiling emotional waters in which that music is created and consumed—in other words, actually to listen to some of it and read the lyrics.

As it turns out, such an exercise yields a fascinating and little 5 understood fact about today's adolescent scene. If yesterday's rock was the music of abandon, today's is that of abandon*ment.* The odd truth about contemporary teenage music—the characteristic that most separates it from what has gone before—is its compulsive insistence on the damage wrought by broken homes, family dysfunction, checked-out parents, and (especially) absent fathers. Papa Roach, Everclear, Blink-182, Good Charlotte, Eddie Vedder and Pearl Jam, Kurt Cobain and Nirvana, Tupac Shakur, Snoop Doggy Dogg, Eminem—these and other singers and bands, all of them award-winning top-40 performers who either are or were among the most popular icons in America, have their own generational answer to what ails the modern teenager. Surprising though it may be to some, that answer is: dysfunctional childhood. Moreover, and just as interesting, many bands and singers explicitly link the most deplored themes in music today—suicide, misogyny, and drugs—with that lack of a quasi-normal, intact-home personal past.

To put this perhaps unexpected point more broadly, during the same years in which progressive-minded and politically correct adults have been excoriating Ozzie and Harriet as an artifact of 1950s-style oppression, many millions of American teenagers have enshrined a new generation of music idols whose shared generational signature in song after song is to rage about what *not* having had a nuclear family has done to them. This is quite a fascinating puzzle of the times. The self-perceived emotional damage scrawled large across contemporary music may not be statistically quantifiable, but it is nonetheless among the most striking of all the unanticipated consequences of our home-alone world. . . .

[An] Example of the rage in contemporary music against irresponsible adults—perhaps the most interesting—is that of genre-crossing bad-boy rap superstar Marshall Mathers or Eminem (sometime stage persona "Slim Shady"). Of all the names guaranteed to send a shudder down the parental spine, his is probably the most effective. In fact, Eminem has single-handedly, if inadvertently, achieved the otherwise ideologically impossible: He is the object of a vehemently disapproving public consensus shared by the National Organization for Women, the Gay & Lesbian Alliance Against Defamation, William J. Bennett, Lynne Cheney, Bill O'Reilly, and a large number of other social conservatives as well as feminists and gay activists. In sum, this rapper—"as harmful to America as any al Qaeda fanatic," in O'Reilly's opinion—unites adult polar opposites as perhaps no other single popular entertainer has done.

There is small need to wonder why. Like other rappers, Eminem mines the shock value and gutter language of rage, casual sex, and violence. Unlike the rest, however, he appears to be a particularly attractive target of opprobrium for two distinct reasons. One, he is white and therefore politically easier to attack. (It is interesting to note that black rappers have not been targeted by name anything like Eminem has.) Perhaps even more important, Eminem is one of the largest commercially visible targets for parental wrath. Wildly popular among teenagers these last several years, he is also enormously successful in commercial terms. Winner of numerous Grammys and other music awards and a perpetual nominee for many more, he has also been critically (albeit reluctantly) acclaimed for his acting performance in the autobiographical 2003 movie *8 Mile*. For all these reasons, he is probably the preeminent rock/rap star of the last several years, one whose singles, albums, and videos routinely top every chart. His 2002 album, *The Eminem Show*, for example, was easily the most successful of the year, selling more than 7.6 million copies.

This remarkable market success, combined with the intense public criticism that his songs have generated, makes the phenomenon of Eminem particularly intriguing. Perhaps more than any other current musical icon, he returns repeatedly to the same themes that fuel other success stories in contemporary music: parental loss, abandonment, abuse, and subsequent child and adolescent anger, dysfunction, and violence (including self-violence). Both in his raunchy lyrics as well as in *8 Mile*, Mathers's own personal story has been parlayed many times over: the absent father, the troubled mother living in a trailer park, the series of unwanted maternal boyfriends, the protective if impotent feelings toward a younger sibling (in the movie, a baby sister; in real life, a younger brother), and the fine line that a poor, ambitious, and unguided young man might walk between catastrophe and success. Mathers plumbs these and related themes with a verbal savagery that leaves most adults aghast.

Yet Eminem also repeatedly centers his songs on the crypto-    10 traditional notion that children need parents and that *not* having them has made all hell break loose. In the song "8 Mile" from the movie soundtrack, for example, the narrator studies his little sister as she colors one picture after another of an imagined nuclear family, failing to understand that *"mommas got a new man." "Wish I could be the daddy that neither one of us had,"* he comments. Such wistful lyrics juxtapose oddly and regularly with Eminem's violent other lines. Even in one of his most infamous songs, "Cleaning Out My Closet (Mama, I'm Sorry)," what drives the vulgar narrative is the insistence on seeing abandonment from a child's point of view. *"My faggot father must have had his panties up in a bunch / 'Cause he split. I wonder if he even kissed me good-bye."*

As with other rappers, the vicious narrative treatment of women in some of Eminem's songs is part of this self-conception as a child victim. Contrary to what critics have intimated, the misogyny in current music does not spring from nowhere; it is often linked to the larger theme of having been abandoned several times—left behind by father, not nurtured by mother, and betrayed again by faithless womankind. One of the most violent and sexually aggressive songs in the last few years is "Kill You" by the popular metal band known as Korn. Its violence is not directed toward just any woman or even toward the narrator's girlfriend; it is instead a song about an abusive stepmother whom the singer imagines going back to rape and murder.

Similarly, Eminem's most shocking lyrics about women are not randomly dispersed; they are largely reserved for his mother and ex-wife, and the narrative pose is one of despising them for not being better women—in particular, better mothers. The worst rap directed at his own mother is indeed gut-wrenching: *"But how dare you try to take what you didn't help me to get? / You selfish bitch, I hope you f— burn in hell for this shit!"* It is no defense of the gutter to observe the obvious: This is not the expression of random misogyny but, rather, of primal rage over alleged maternal abdication and abuse.

Another refrain in these songs runs like this: Today's teenagers are a mess, and the parents who made them that way refuse to get it. In one of Eminem's early hits, for example, a song called "Who Knew," the rapper pointedly takes on his many middle- and upper-middle-class critics to observe the contradiction between their reviling him and the parental inattention that feeds his commercial success. *"What about the make-up you allow your 12 year-old daughter to wear?"* he taunts.

This same theme of AWOL parenting is rapped at greater length in another award-nominated 2003 song called "Sing for the Moment," whose lyrics and video would be recognized in an instant by most teenagers in America. That song spells out Eminem's own idea of what connects him to his millions of fans—a connection that parents, in his view, just don't (or is that won't?) understand. It details the case of one more "problem child" created by *"His f— dad walkin' out."* "Sing for the Moment," like many other songs of Eminem's, is also a popular video. The "visuals" show clearly what the lyrics depict—hordes of disaffected kids, with flashbacks to bad home lives, screaming for the singer who feels their pain. It concludes by rhetorically turning away from the music itself and toward the emotionally desperate teenagers who turn out for this music by the millions. If the demand of all those empty kids wasn't out there, the narrator says pointedly, then rappers wouldn't be supplying it the way they do.

15    If some parents still don't get it—even as their teenagers elbow up for every new Eminem CD and memorize his lyrics with psalmist devotion—at least some critics observing the music scene have thought to comment on the ironies of all this. In discussing *The Marshall Mathers LP* in 2001 for *Music Box*, a daily online newsletter about music, reviewer John Metzger argued, "Instead of spewing the hate that he is so often criticized of doing, Eminem offers a cautionary tale that speaks to our civilization's growing depravity. Ironically, it's his teenage fans who understand this, and their all-knowing parents that miss the point." Metzger further specified "the utter lack of parenting due to the spendthrift necessity of the two-income family."[1]

That insight raises the overlooked fact that in one important sense Eminem . . . would agree with many of today's adults about one thing: The kids *aren't* all right out there after all. Recall, for just one example, Eddie Vedder's rueful observation about what kind of generation would make him or Kurt Cobain its leader. Where parents and entertainers disagree is over who exactly bears responsibility for this moral chaos. Many adults want to blame the people who create and market today's music and videos. Entertainers, Eminem most prominently,

---

[1]John Metzger, review of "Eminem: The Marshall Mathers LP," *Music Box* 8:6 (June 2001).

blame the absent, absentee, and generally inattentive adults whose deprived and furious children (as they see it) have catapulted today's singers to fame. (As he puts the point in one more in-your-face response to parents: *"Don't blame me when lil' Eric jumps off of the terrace / You shoulda been watchin him—apparently you ain't parents."*)

The spectacle of a foul-mouthed bad-example rock icon instructing the hardworking parents of America in the art of child-rearing is indeed a peculiar one, not to say ridiculous. The single mother who is working frantically because she must and worrying all the while about what her 14-year-old is listening to in the headphones is entitled to a certain fury over lyrics like those. In fact, to read through most rap lyrics is to wonder which adults or political constituencies *wouldn't* take offense. Even so, the music idols who point the finger away from themselves and toward the emptied-out homes of America are telling a truth that some adults would rather not hear. In this limited sense at least, Eminem is right.

To say that today's popular music is uniquely concerned with broken homes, abandoned children, and distracted or incapable parents is not to say that this is what all of it is about. Other themes remain a constant, too, although somewhat more brutally than in the alleged golden era recalled by some baby boomers.

Much of today's metal and hip-hop, like certain music of yesterday, romanticizes illicit drug use and alcohol abuse, and much of current hip-hop sounds certain radical political themes, such as racial separationism and violence against the police. And, of course, the most elementally appealing feature of all, the sexually suggestive beat itself, continues to lure teenagers and young adults in its own right—including those from happy homes. Today as yesterday, plenty of teenagers who don't know or care what the stars are raving about find enough satisfaction in swaying to the sexy music. As professor and intellectual Allan Bloom observed about rock in his bestseller, *The Closing of the American Mind* (Simon & Schuster, 1987), the music "gives children, on a silver platter, with all the public authority of the entertaining industry, everything their parents always used to tell them they had to wait for until they grew up and would understand later."

Even so, and putting aside such obvious continuities with previous 20 generations, there is no escaping the fact that today's songs are musically and lyrically unlike any before. What distinguishes them most clearly is the fixation on having been abandoned personally by the adults supposedly in charge, with consequences ranging from bitterness to rage to bad, sick, and violent behavior.

And therein lies a painful truth about an advantage that many teenagers of yesterday enjoyed but their own children often do not. Baby boomers and their music rebelled against parents *because* they were parents—nurturing, attentive, and overly present (as those teenagers often saw it) authority figures. Today's teenagers and their music rebel against parents because they are *not* parents—not nurturing, not attentive, and often not even there. This difference in generational experience may not lend itself to statistical measure, but it is as real as the platinum and gold records that continue to capture it. What those records show compared to yesteryear's rock is emotional downward mobility. Surely if some of the current generation of teenagers and young adults had been better taken care of, then the likes of Kurt Cobain, Eminem, Tupac Shakur, and certain other parental nightmares would have been mere footnotes to recent music history rather than rulers of it.

To step back from the emotional immediacy of those lyrics and to juxtapose the ascendance of such music alongside the long-standing sophisticated assaults on what is sardonically called "family values" is to meditate on a larger irony. As today's music stars and their raving fans likely do not know, many commentators and analysts have been rationalizing every aspect of the adult exodus from home—sometimes celebrating it full throttle, as in the example of working motherhood—longer than most of today's singers and bands have been alive.

Nor do they show much sign of second thoughts. Representative sociologist Stephanie Coontz greeted the year 2004 with one more op-ed piece aimed at burying poor metaphorical Ozzie and Harriet for good. She reminded America again that "changes in marriage and family life" are here to stay and aren't "necessarily a problem"; that what is euphemistically called "family diversity" is or ought to be cause for celebration. Many other scholars and observers—to say nothing of much of polite adult society—agree with Coontz. Throughout the contemporary nonfiction literature written of, by, and for educated adults, a thousand similar rationalizations about family "changes" bloom on.

Meanwhile, a small number of emotionally damaged former children, embraced and adored by millions of teenagers like them, rage on in every commercial medium available about the multiple damages of the disappearance of loving, protective, attentive adults—and they reap a fortune for it. If this spectacle alone doesn't tell us something about the ongoing emotional costs of parent–child separation on today's outsize scale, it's hard to see what could.

## Responding to Reading

1. Eberstadt acknowledges in her first paragraph that "contemporary adolescent popular music, especially the subgenres of heavy metal and hip-hop/rap," commonly includes themes of "Misogyny, violence, suicide, sexual exploitation, [and] child abuse. . . ." How does she explain the presence of these themes? In what sense is Eminem "right"?
2. Eberstadt's focus here is not on how music affects adolescents but on what it reveals about them. In paragraph 3, she asks, *"What is it about today's music, violent and disgusting though it may be, that resonates with so many American kids?"* How does she answer this question? How would you answer it?

3.  In what sense does Eberstadt see today's adolescent music as the music of "abandon*ment*" rather than as the "music of abandon" (5)? How does she believe what she calls "our home-alone world" (6) helps to explain Eminem's violent, misogynistic lyrics? Do you see this essay primarily as a defense of the music of performers like Eminem or as an attack on "irresponsible adults" (7)?

## Responding in Writing

Elsewhere in her writing, Eberstadt discusses the lyrics of other musical artists who appeal to today's adolescents, and she argues that their lyrics, like Eminem's, also reveal a preoccupation with family dysfunction and abandonment by parents. Give examples of such lyrics in music you are familiar with, and explain how they support her position.

# THE MOVIES THAT ROSE FROM THE GRAVE

## Max Brooks

### 1972–

*An author, screenwriter, and actor, Max Brooks often explores the zombie cultural icon in his work. He has published two books and two graphic novels, including, most recently,* The Zombie Survival Guide: Recorded Attacks *(2009). In the following essay, Brooks considers the phenomenon of the "undead explosion" in various kinds of media.*

Zombies have dominated mainstream horror for more than half a decade. They're everywhere: movies, books, videogames, comics, even a new Broadway musical adaptation of Sam Raimi's *The Evil Dead*. Not only have they replaced previous alpha-monsters such as vampires and werewolves, but they are continuing to generate more interest (and revenue) than almost all other creatures put together. Given that several years ago the living dead were considered an obscure and largely underground sub-genre, it would not be an exaggeration to state that they have enjoyed a spectacular rebirth unlike anything in the history of modern horror.

Where did these creatures come from? Why are they so popular now? And when, if ever, will their reign of terror cease?

Although many cultures have their own myths concerning the raising of the dead (one going as far back as the epic of Gilgamesh), the word "zombie" can trace its origins back to west Africa. The legend involves a "houngan" (wizard) using a magical elixir to transform a living human into a mobile, docile and obedient corpse. The fact that this legend is deeply rooted in reality (Haitian zombie powder was discovered to contain a powerful neuro-toxin that caused a live victim to behave like a resurrected corpse) may explain why, when African slaves were brought to the Americas, European colonists also embraced the notion of the living dead.

For several centuries the voodoo zombie remained the staple of tall tales, stage productions, and even early Hollywood movies such as *White Zombie* (1932) and *I Walked With a Zombie* (1943). It wasn't until 1968 that up-and-coming film maker George A. Romero gave us a whole new reason to be afraid. *Night of the Living Dead* replaced the image of a harmless voodoo-created zombie with a hostile, flesh-eating ghoul that swelled its numbers to pandemic proportions. This new ghoul was the result of science, not magic, specifically radiation from a returning space probe. This new ghoul could, likewise, only be dispatched by a scientific solution: destroying the brain or severing it from the rest of the body. This new ghoul obeyed no one, other than its own insatiable craving for living, human flesh. In fact, this new ghoul was only referred to throughout the movie as a ghoul. The word zombie was never mentioned.

5    Romero's revolutionary creation set the stage for an entirely new genre, the horror-apocalypse or "horocalypse" movie. Zombies would henceforth be associated with the collapse of modern society, a new form of walking plague that threatened to stamp out humanity. Gone were the days of suspense and darkness, of castles and swamps and remote, isolated violence. Zombies would now be waging all-out war across the silver screen, a tradition that has endured for almost 40 years.

Since the premiere of *Night of the Living Dead*, many have sought to capitalise on Romero's initial success. The Italian movie *Night of the Zombie* (1980) mixed a fictional storyline with real-life footage of cannibalism in New Guinea. A similar movie, *Zombi 2*, witnessed a battle between a corpse-like stuntman and an actual man-eating shark. One Japanese film, *Wild Zero*, attempted to combine the living dead with aliens, transsexuals and the Japanese garage band Guitar Wolf. Michael Jackson immortalised dancing zombies with his 1983 music video *Thriller*. And in 1984, Romero's former writing partner, John Russo, released the zombie comedy *The Return of the Living Dead*.

While all of these works enjoyed a loyal fan base, they remained largely a cult sensation until the turn of this century. The rise began slowly at first. Computer games such as *Resident Evil* and *House of the Dead* were becoming successful enough to warrant their development into movies. On the heels of those came Danny Boyle's *28 Days Later* and the remake of Romero's *Dawn of the Dead*, which knocked Mel Gibson's *The Passion of the Christ* off the top spot in the US. Most industry experts predicted this was just a fad. Conventional wisdom predicted a short life for the living dead. Only that didn't happen. More zombie movies were produced, including Romero's own *Land of the Dead*. *Resident Evil* spawned a sequel, as did *House of the Dead*, and *The Return of the Living Dead*.

The literary world was similarly inundated with zombie fiction, as was the world of comics. New videogames such as *Stubbs the Zombie* and the mega-hit *Dead Rising* took their place alongside *Resident Evil* and *House of the Dead*. Even US television could not escape the walking corpses. Last year, Showtime's *Masters of Horror* series broadcast one episode with dead Iraq War veterans rising from their body bags to vote against the politicians that put them there.

Why now? Why such a sudden and ravenous obsession with ghouls? Could it be the zombie authors themselves and the new levels of sophistication they are bringing to the genre? Perhaps. This new generation of writers, directors, illustrators and programmers are the first to have grown up studying the works of Romero and his contemporaries. For them, simply recreating the monsters of their childhood was not enough. Their zombie projects had to either be faster, wilder, and, in some cases, even smarter. In some cases, they have surpassed their predecessors in all aspects. But this rise in product quality does nothing to explain society's phenomenal demand for the living dead.

The answer to that question lies not in fiction, but current events. 10 The last six years have witnessed a bombardment of tragic events. Terrorism, war, viral outbreaks and natural disasters have created a global undercurrent of anxiety not seen since the darkest days of the cold war. It seems that just turning on the nightly news either shows some present calamity or one that might potentially befall us any day now.

Zombie movies present people with an outlet for their apocalyptic anxieties without directly confronting them. The living dead are a fictional threat, as opposed to tsunamis or avian flu. No matter how scary or realistic the particular story might be, their unquestionably fictional nature makes them "safe." Someone can watch, say *Dawn of the Dead*, and witness an orgy of graphic violence and destruction, but still know in the back of their minds that, once they switch off the TV, this particular threat will simply cease to exist, something that cannot be said for terrorist docu-drama *Dirty War*, or the classic nuclear nightmare *Threads*. Knowing that zombies can never really rise allows for a feeling of control, a rare and valuable thing these days.

No one can say how long this present undead explosion will be with us. Perhaps they will ebb with the current trend of global chaos. Perhaps, as the dust of this decade settles, and society returns to a semblance of stability, our macabre fascinations will return to more conventional monsters, forsaking flesh-eating ghouls for good old-fashioned werewolves or vampires. No one can say. What is certain is that nothing lasts forever. What else is certain is that the living dead might go away, but they won't be gone forever. They will simply retreat underground again, waiting patiently for the day when they rise again.

## Responding to Reading

1.  How has the portrayal of zombies in film evolved over the years? Is the information Brooks presents about this evolution a necessary part of his essay, or could he have made his case without it? Is all the other information he includes—for example, the origin of the word *zombie*—necessary? Explain.
2.  In paragraph 9, Brooks asks, "Why now? Why such a sudden and ravenous obsession with ghouls?" How does he answer this question? Do you agree with his explanation of the reasons for this trend? What other explanations can you suggest?
3.  Does Brooks expect the "undead explosion" (12) to continue? Do you? Why or why not?

## Responding in Writing

In paragraph 1, Brooks mentions the rise of zombies in a variety of media, including books. Browse <http://Amazon.com> to get a sampling of some recently published books with zombie themes. Then, discuss the needs these books seem to satisfy.

# WHEN THE INTERNET THINKS
# IT KNOWS YOU

## Eli Pariser

### 1980–

*An op-ed contributor to the* New York Times, *the* Wall Street Journal, *and the* Washington Post, *Eli Pariser is the board president of* MoveOn.org, *a progressive political action organization. In his work as a political activist, Pariser focuses on helping others, especially disenfranchised Americans, to take an active role in the political process. Pariser is the author of* The Filter Bubble: What the Internet Is Hiding from You *(2011), which, like the following essay, examines the danger inherent in the kinds of "filtering" that occur in online searches.*

Once upon a time, the story goes, we lived in a broadcast society. In that dusty pre-Internet age, the tools for sharing information weren't widely available. If you wanted to share your thoughts with the masses, you had to own a printing press or a chunk of the airwaves, or have access to someone who did. Controlling the flow of information was an elite class of editors, producers and media moguls who decided what people would see and hear about the world. They were the Gatekeepers.

Then came the Internet, which made it possible to communicate with millions of people at little or no cost. Suddenly anyone with an

Internet connection could share ideas with the whole world. A new era of democratized news media dawned.

You may have heard that story before—maybe from the conservative blogger Glenn Reynolds (blogging is "technology undermining the gatekeepers") or the progressive blogger Markos Moulitsas (his book is called *Crashing the Gate*). It's a beautiful story about the revolutionary power of the medium, and as an early practitioner of online politics, I told it to describe what we did at MoveOn.org. But I'm increasingly convinced that we've got the ending wrong—perhaps dangerously wrong. There is a new group of gatekeepers in town, and this time, they're not people, they're code.

Today's Internet giants—Google, Facebook, Yahoo and Microsoft—see the remarkable rise of available information as an opportunity. If they can provide services that sift through the data and supply us with the most personally relevant and appealing results, they'll get the most users and the most ad views. As a result, they're racing to offer personalized filters that show us the Internet that they think we want to see. These filters, in effect, control and limit the information that reaches our screens.

By now, we're familiar with ads that follow us around online based on our recent clicks on commercial Web sites. But increasingly, and nearly invisibly, our searches for information are being personalized too. Two people who each search on Google for "Egypt" may get significantly different results, based on their past clicks. Both Yahoo News and Google News make adjustments to their home pages for each individual visitor. And just last month, this technology began making inroads on the Web sites of newspapers like the *Washington Post* and the *New York Times*.

All of this is fairly harmless when information about consumer products is filtered into and out of your personal universe. But when personalization affects not just what you buy but how you think, different issues arise. Democracy depends on the citizen's ability to engage with multiple viewpoints; the Internet limits such engagement when it offers up only information that reflects your already established point of view. While it's sometimes convenient to see only what you want to see, it's critical at other times that you see things that you don't.

Like the old gatekeepers, the engineers who write the new gatekeeping code have enormous power to determine what we know about the world. But unlike the best of the old gatekeepers, they don't see themselves as keepers of the public trust. There is no algorithmic equivalent to journalistic ethics.

Mark Zuckerberg, Facebook's chief executive, once told colleagues that "a squirrel dying in your front yard may be more relevant to your interests right now than people dying in Africa." At Facebook, "relevance" is virtually the sole criterion that determines what users see. Focusing on the most personally relevant news—the squirrel—is a great business strategy. But it leaves us staring at our front yard instead of reading about suffering, genocide and revolution.

There's no going back to the old system of gatekeepers, nor should there be. But if algorithms are taking over the editing function and determining what we see, we need to make sure they weigh variables beyond a narrow "relevance." They need to show us Afghanistan and Libya as well as Apple and Kanye.

10   Companies that make use of these algorithms must take this curative responsibility far more seriously than they have to date. They need to give us control over what we see—making it clear when they are personalizing, and allowing us to shape and adjust our own filters. We citizens need to uphold our end, too—developing the "filter literacy" needed to use these tools well and demanding content that broadens our horizons even when it's uncomfortable.

It is in our collective interest to ensure that the Internet lives up to its potential as a revolutionary connective medium. This won't happen if we're all sealed off in our own personalized online worlds.

### Responding to Reading

1.  In the context of this essay, what does the word *gatekeeper* mean? In what sense does Pariser see the engineers who write code as the new gatekeepers? How are these new gatekeepers different from the old gatekeepers?
2.  What alarms Pariser about the Internet's ability to deliver customized content? Why does he think personalized information is a more serious problem than personalized advertising?
3.  What does Pariser think should be done to solve the problem he describes? Who does he think should take responsibility for solving the problem? Do you think the suggestions he makes in paragraphs 10 and 11 will (or should) be followed?

### Responding in Writing

Pariser focuses on the negative side of the Internet's ability to customize information. What positive effects might this trend have? Do you think the positive side balances (or even outweighs) the negative? Why or why not?

# Does the Internet Make You Dumber?

## Nicholas Carr

### 1959–

*Nicholas Carr writes about issues pertaining to media and society in such publications as the* Atlantic, *the* Financial Times, *the* Guardian, *the* New York Times, *the* Wall Street Journal, *and* Wired. *He is the author of four books on business and technology, including* The Shallows: What the Internet

Is Doing to Our Brains *(2010), which was nominated for the 2011 Pulitzer Prize in general nonfiction. In the following essay, Carr examines the Internet's effect on our ability to think critically.*

The Roman philosopher Seneca may have put it best 2,000 years ago: "To be everywhere is to be nowhere." Today, the Internet grants us easy access to unprecedented amounts of information. But a growing body of scientific evidence suggests that the Net, with its constant distractions and interruptions, is also turning us into scattered and superficial thinkers.

The picture emerging from the research is deeply troubling, at least to anyone who values the depth, rather than just the velocity, of human thought. People who read text studded with links, the studies show, comprehend less than those who read traditional linear text. People who watch busy multimedia presentations remember less than those who take in information in a more sedate and focused manner. People who are continually distracted by emails, alerts and other messages understand less than those who are able to concentrate. And people who juggle many tasks are less creative and less productive than those who do one thing at a time.

The common thread in these disabilities is the division of attention. The richness of our thoughts, our memories and even our personalities hinges on our ability to focus the mind and sustain concentration. Only when we pay deep attention to a new piece of information are we able to associate it "meaningfully and systematically with knowledge already well established in memory," writes the Nobel Prize–winning neuroscientist Eric Kandel. Such associations are essential to mastering complex concepts.

When we're constantly distracted and interrupted, as we tend to be online, our brains are unable to forge the strong and expansive neural connections that give depth and distinctiveness to our thinking. We become mere signal-processing units, quickly shepherding disjointed bits of information into and then out of short-term memory.

In an article published in *Science* last year, Patricia Greenfield, a leading developmental psychologist, reviewed dozens of studies on how different media technologies influence our cognitive abilities. Some of the studies indicated that certain computer tasks, like playing video games, can enhance "visual literacy skills," increasing the speed at which people can shift their focus among icons and other images on screens. Other studies, however, found that such rapid shifts in focus, even if performed adeptly, result in less rigorous and "more automatic" thinking.

In one experiment conducted at Cornell University, for example, half a class of students was allowed to use Internet-connected laptops during a lecture, while the other had to keep their computers shut. Those who browsed the Web performed much worse on a subsequent test of how well they retained the lecture's content. While it's hardly surprising that

Web surfing would distract students, it should be a note of caution to schools that are wiring their classrooms in hopes of improving learning.

Ms. Greenfield concluded that "every medium develops some cognitive skills at the expense of others." Our growing use of screen-based media, she said, has strengthened visual-spatial intelligence, which can improve the ability to do jobs that involve keeping track of lots of simultaneous signals, like air traffic control. But that has been accompanied by "new weaknesses in higher-order cognitive processes," including "abstract vocabulary, mindfulness, reflection, inductive problem solving, critical thinking, and imagination." We're becoming, in a word, shallower.

In another experiment, recently conducted at Stanford University's Communication Between Humans and Interactive Media Lab, a team of researchers gave various cognitive tests to 49 people who do a lot of media multitasking and 52 people who multitask much less frequently. The heavy multitaskers performed poorly on all the tests. They were more easily distracted, had less control over their attention, and were much less able to distinguish important information from trivia.

The researchers were surprised by the results. They had expected that the intensive multitaskers would have gained some unique mental advantages from all their on-screen juggling. But that wasn't the case. In fact, the heavy multitaskers weren't even good at multitasking. They were considerably less adept at switching between tasks than the more infrequent multitaskers. "Everything distracts them," observed Clifford Nass, the professor who heads the Stanford lab.

10    It would be one thing if the ill effects went away as soon as we turned off our computers and cellphones. But they don't. The cellular structure of the human brain, scientists have discovered, adapts readily to the tools we use, including those for finding, storing and sharing information. By changing our habits of mind, each new technology strengthens certain neural pathways and weakens others. The cellular alterations continue to shape the way we think even when we're not using the technology.

The pioneering neuroscientist Michael Merzenich believes our brains are being "massively remodeled" by our ever-intensifying use of the Web and related media. In the 1970s and 1980s, Mr. Merzenich, now a professor emeritus at the University of California in San Francisco, conducted a famous series of experiments on primate brains that revealed how extensively and quickly neural circuits change in response to experience. When, for example, Mr. Merzenich rearranged the nerves in a monkey's hand, the nerve cells in the animal's sensory cortex quickly reorganized themselves to create a new "mental map" of the hand. In a conversation late last year, he said that he was profoundly worried about the cognitive consequences of the constant distractions and interruptions the Internet bombards us with. The long-term effect on the quality of our intellectual lives, he said, could be "deadly."

What we seem to be sacrificing in all our surfing and searching is our capacity to engage in the quieter, attentive modes of thought that underpin contemplation, reflection and introspection. The Web never encourages us to slow down. It keeps us in a state of perpetual mental locomotion.

It is revealing, and distressing, to compare the cognitive effects of the Internet with those of an earlier information technology, the printed book. Whereas the Internet scatters our attention, the book focuses it. Unlike the screen, the page promotes contemplativeness.

Reading a long sequence of pages helps us develop a rare kind of mental discipline. The innate bias of the human brain, after all, is to be distracted. Our predisposition is to be aware of as much of what's going on around us as possible. Our fast-paced, reflexive shifts in focus were once crucial to our survival. They reduced the odds that a predator would take us by surprise or that we'd overlook a nearby source of food.

To read a book is to practice an unnatural process of thought. It 15 requires us to place ourselves at what T. S. Eliot, in his poem "Four Quartets," called "the still point of the turning world." We have to forge or strengthen the neural links needed to counter our instinctive distractedness, thereby gaining greater control over our attention and our mind.

It is this control, this mental discipline, that we are at risk of losing as we spend ever more time scanning and skimming online. If the slow progression of words across printed pages damped our craving to be inundated by mental stimulation, the Internet indulges it. It returns us to our native state of distractedness, while presenting us with far more distractions than our ancestors ever had to contend with.

## Responding to Reading

1. Why, according to Carr, does the Internet interfere with the "richness of our thoughts" (3)? What evidence does he offer to support this statement? Is this evidence convincing? Does he address any arguments that challenges his point? Should he?
2. Given the trend toward wired classrooms, what implications do Carr's conclusions have for the future of college education? What problems do you envision, and how might they be solved?
3. Toward the end of his essay, Carr compares "the cognitive effects of the Internet with those of an earlier information technology, the printed book" (13). What specific differences does he identify between these two technologies? Why does he make this comparison?

## Responding in Writing

Does your own experience support Carr's conclusion that the Internet is "turning us into scattered and superficial thinkers" (1)? Explain.

# MIND OVER MASS MEDIA

## Steven Pinker

### 1954–

*A Harvard College professor and the Johnstone Family Professor in the psychology department at Harvard University, Steven Pinker writes about the relationship between language and the brain. A contributor to such publications as the* New Republic, *the* New York Times, *and* Time, *Pinker has written numerous books, including, most recently,* The Better Angels of Our Nature: Why Violence Has Declined *(2011). In the following essay, Pinker argues that electronic media can have a positive effect on cognition.*

New forms of media have always caused moral panics: the printing press, newspapers, paperbacks and television were all once denounced as threats to their consumers' brainpower and moral fiber.

So too with electronic technologies. PowerPoint, we're told, is reducing discourse to bullet points. Search engines lower our intelligence, encouraging us to skim on the surface of knowledge rather than dive to its depths. Twitter is shrinking our attention spans.

But such panics often fail basic reality checks. When comic books were accused of turning juveniles into delinquents in the 1950s, crime was falling to record lows, just as the denunciations of video games in the 1990s coincided with the great American crime decline. The decades of television, transistor radios and rock videos were also decades in which I.Q. scores rose continuously.

For a reality check today, take the state of science, which demands high levels of brainwork and is measured by clear benchmarks of discovery. These days scientists are never far from their e-mail, rarely touch paper and cannot lecture without PowerPoint. If electronic media were hazardous to intelligence, the quality of science would be plummeting. Yet discoveries are multiplying like fruit flies, and progress is dizzying. Other activities in the life of the mind, like philosophy, history and cultural criticism, are likewise flourishing, as anyone who has lost a morning of work to the Web site *Arts & Letters Daily* can attest.

5      Critics of new media sometimes use science itself to press their case, citing research that shows how "experience can change the brain." But cognitive neuroscientists roll their eyes at such talk. Yes, every time we learn a fact or skill the wiring of the brain changes; it's not as if the information is stored in the pancreas. But the existence of neural plasticity does not mean the brain is a blob of clay pounded into shape by experience.

Experience does not revamp the basic information-processing capacities of the brain. Speed-reading programs have long claimed to do just that, but the verdict was rendered by Woody Allen after he read *War and Peace* in one sitting: "It was about Russia." Genuine multitasking, too, has been exposed as a myth, not just by laboratory studies but by the familiar sight of an S.U.V. undulating between lanes as the driver cuts deals on his cellphone.

Moreover, as the psychologists Christopher Chabris and Daniel Simons show in their new book *The Invisible Gorilla: And Other Ways Our Intuitions Deceive Us*, the effects of experience are highly specific to the experiences themselves. If you train people to do one thing (recognize shapes, solve math puzzles, find hidden words), they get better at doing that thing, but almost nothing else. Music doesn't make you better at math, conjugating Latin doesn't make you more logical, brain-training games don't make you smarter. Accomplished people don't bulk up their brains with intellectual calisthenics; they immerse themselves in their fields. Novelists read lots of novels, scientists read lots of science.

The effects of consuming electronic media are also likely to be far more limited than the panic implies. Media critics write as if the brain takes on the qualities of whatever it consumes, the informational equivalent of "you are what you eat." As with primitive peoples who believe that eating fierce animals will make them fierce, they assume that watching quick cuts in rock videos turns your mental life into quick cuts or that reading bullet points and Twitter postings turns your thoughts into bullet points and Twitter postings.

Yes, the constant arrival of information packets can be distracting or addictive, especially to people with attention deficit disorder. But distraction is not a new phenomenon. The solution is not to bemoan technology but to develop strategies of self-control, as we do with every other temptation in life. Turn off e-mail or Twitter when you work, put away your Blackberry at dinner time, ask your spouse to call you to bed at a designated hour.

And to encourage intellectual depth, don't rail at PowerPoint or 10 Google. It's not as if habits of deep reflection, thorough research and rigorous reasoning ever came naturally to people. They must be acquired in special institutions, which we call universities, and maintained with constant upkeep, which we call analysis, criticism and debate. They are not granted by propping a heavy encyclopedia on your lap, nor are they taken away by efficient access to information on the Internet.

The new media have caught on for a reason. Knowledge is increasing exponentially; human brainpower and waking hours are not. Fortunately, the Internet and information technologies are helping us manage, search and retrieve our collective intellectual output at different scales, from Twitter and previews to e-books and online encyclopedias. Far from making us stupid, these technologies are the only things that will keep us smart.

## Responding to Reading

1.  Pinker opens his essay by drawing a general analogy between contemporary electronic media and the "new media" of the past. Do you think this is an effective opening strategy? Why or why not?
2.  Pinker argues that, contrary to claims made by critics of new media, electronic media are not "hazardous to intelligence" (4). How does he support this conclusion?
3.  What solutions does Pinker propose for the problem of information overload and to "encourage intellectual depth" (10)? Are these solutions realistic? Explain.

## Responding in Writing

Nicholas Carr's essay (p. 216) about the effects of the Internet on cognitive processes takes a position that is opposed to Pinker's. Whose argument do you find more convincing? Why? (Note that Carr includes a good deal more specific expert opinion to support his conclusion than Pinker does.)

# REALITY IS BROKEN
## Jane McGonigal
### 1977–

*The director of Games Research & Development at the non-profit research organization Institute for the Future, Jane McGonigal creates games that, as she describes, "are designed to improve real lives and solve real problems." A writer for such publications as the* New Yorker, *the* New York Times, O *magazine, and* Vanity Fair, *McGonigal is the author of* Reality Is Broken: Why Games Make Us Better and How They Can Change the World *(2011), from whose introduction the following argument for the social value of video games is excerpted.*

Anyone who sees a hurricane coming should warn others. I see a hurricane coming.

Over the next generation or two, ever larger numbers of people, hundreds of millions, will become immersed in virtual worlds and online games. While we are playing, things we used to do on the outside, in "reality," won't be happening anymore, or won't be happening in the same way. You can't pull millions of person-hours out of a society without creating an atmospheric-level event.

If it happens in a generation, I think the twenty-first century will see a social cataclysm larger than that caused by cars, radios, and TV, combined.... The exodus of these people from the real world, from our normal daily life, will create a change in social climate that makes global warming look like a tempest in a teacup.

—Edward Castronova,
*Exodus to the Virtual World*

Gamers have had enough of reality.

They are abandoning it in droves—a few hours here, an entire weekend there, sometimes every spare minute of every day for stretches at a time—in favor of simulated environments and online games. Maybe you are one of these gamers. If not, then you definitey know some of them.

Who are they? They are the nine-to-fivers who come home and apply all of the smarts and talents that are underutilized at work to plan and coordinate complex raids and quests in massively multiplayer online games like *Final Fantasy XI* and the *Lineage* worlds. They're the music lovers who have invested hundreds of dollars on plastic *Rock Band* and *Guitar Hero* instruments and spent night after night rehearsing, in order to become virtuosos of video game performance.

They're the *World of Warcraft* fans who are so intent on mastering the challenges of their favorite game that, collectively, they've written a quarter of a million wiki articles on the WoWWiki—creating the single largest wiki after Wikipedia. They're the *Brain Age* and *Mario Kart* players who take handheld game consoles everywhere they go, sneaking in short puzzles, races, and minigames as often as possible, and as a result nearly eliminating mental downtime from their lives.

They're the United States troops stationed overseas who dedicate so many hours a week to burnishing their *Halo 3* in-game service record that earning virtual combat medals is widely known as the most popular activity for off-duty soldiers. They're the young adults in China who have spent so much play money, or "QQ coins," on magical swords and other powerful game objects that the People's Bank of China intervened to prevent the devaluation of the yuan, China's real-world currency.

Most of all, they're the kids and teenagers worldwide who would rather spend hours in front of just about any computer game or video game than do anything else.

These gamers aren't rejecting reality entirely. They have jobs, goals, schoolwork, families, commitments, and real lives that they care about. But as they devote more and more of their free time to game worlds, the *real* world increasingly feels like it's missing something.

Gamers want to know: Where, in the real world, is that gamer sense of being fully alive, focused, and engaged in every moment? Where is the gamer feeling of power, heroic purpose, and community? Where are the bursts of exhilarating and creative game accomplishment? Where is the heart-expanding thrill of success and team victory? While gamers may experience these pleasures occasionally in their real lives, they experience them almost constantly when they're playing their favorite games.

The real world just doesn't offer up as easily the carefully designed pleasures, the thrilling challenges, and the powerful social bonding afforded by virtual environments. Reality doesn't motivate us as effectively. Reality isn't engineered to maximize our potential. Reality wasn't designed from the bottom up to make us happy.

10   And so, there is a growing perception in the gaming community: Reality, compared to games, is broken.

In fact, it is more than a perception. It's a phenomenon. Economist Edward Castronova calls it a "mass exodus" to game spaces, and you can see it already happening in the numbers. Hundreds of millions of people worldwide are opting out of reality for larger and larger chunks of time. In the United States alone, there are 183 million *active gamers* (individuals who, in surveys, report that they play computer or video games "regularly"—on average, thirteen hours a week). Globally, the online gamer community—including console, PC, and mobile phone gaming—counts more than 4 million gamers in the Middle East, 10 million in Russia, 105 million in India, 10 million in Vietnam, 10 million in Mexico, 13 million in Central and South America, 15 million in Australia, 17 million in South Korea, 100 million in Europe, and 200 million in China.

Although a typical gamer plays for just an hour or two a day, there are now more than 6 million people in China who spend at least twenty-two hours a week gaming, the equivalent of a part-time job. More than 10 million "hard-core" gamers in the United Kingdom, France, and Germany spend at least twenty hours a week playing. And at the leading edge of this growth curve, more than 5 million "extreme" gamers in the United States play on average forty-five hours a week.

With all of this play, we have turned digital games—for our computers, for our mobile phones, and for our home entertainment systems—into what is expected to be a $68 billion industry annually by the year 2012. And we are creating a massive virtual silo of cognitive effort, emotional energy, and collective attention lavished on game worlds instead of on the real world.

15   The ever-skyrocketing amounts of time and money spent on games are being observed with alarm by some—concerned parents, teachers, and politicians—and eagerness by others—the many technology industries that expect to profit greatly from the game boom. Meanwhile, they are met with bewilderment and disdain by more than a few nongamers, who still make up nearly half of the U.S. population, although their numbers are rapidly decreasing. Many of them deem gaming a clear waste of time.

As we make these value judgments, hold moral debates over the addictive quality of games, and simultaneously rush to achieve massive industry expansion, a vital point is being missed. The fact that so many people of all ages, all over the world, are choosing to spend so much time in game worlds is a sign of something important, a truth that we urgently need to recognize.

The truth is this: in today's society, computer and video games are fulfilling *genuine human needs* that the real world is currently unable to satisfy. Games are providing rewards that reality is not. They are teaching and inspiring and engaging us in ways that reality is not. They are bringing us together in ways that reality is not.

And unless something dramatic happens to reverse the resulting exodus, we're fast on our way to becoming a society in which a substantial portion of our population devotes its greatest efforts to playing games, creates its best memories in game environments, and experiences its biggest successes in game worlds.

Maybe this sounds hard to believe. To a nongamer, this forecast might seem surreal, or like science fiction. Are huge swaths of civilization really disappearing into game worlds? Are we really rushing headlong into a future where the majority of us use games to satisfy many of our most important needs?

If so, it will not be the first time that such a mass exodus from real- 20 ity to games has occurred. Indeed, the very first written history of human gameplay, Herodotus' *Histories*, the ancient Greek account of the Persian Wars—dating back more than three thousand years—describes a nearly identical scenario. While the oldest known game is the ancient counting game Mancala—evidence shows it was played during Egypt's age of empires, or the fifteenth to the eleventh centuries BC—it was not until Herodotus that anyone thought to record the origins or cultural functions of these games. And from his ancient text, we can learn a great deal about what's happening today—and what's almost certainly coming next.

It's a bit counterintuitive to think about the future in terms of the past. But as a research director at the Institute for the Future—a nonprofit think tank in Palo Alto, California, and the world's oldest future-forecasting organization—I've learned an important trick: to develop foresight, you need to practice hindsight. Technologies, cultures, and climates may change, but our basic human needs and desires—to survive, to care for our families, and to lead happy, purposeful lives—remain the same. So at IFTF we like to say, "To understand the future, you have to look back at least twice as far as you're looking ahead." Fortunately, when it comes to games, we can look even farther back than that. Games have been a fundamental part of human civilization for thousands of years.

In the opening book of *The Histories*, Herodotus writes:

> When Atys was king of Lydia in Asia Minor some three thousand years ago, a great scarcity threatened his realm. For a while people accepted their lot without complaining, in the hope that times of plenty would return. But when things failed to get better, the Lydians devised a strange remedy for their problem. The plan adopted against the famine was to engage in games one day so entirely as not to feel any craving for food . . . and the next day to eat and abstain from games. In this way

they passed eighteen years, and along the way they invented the dice, knuckle-bones, the ball, and all the games which are common.

What do ancient dice made from sheep's knuckles have to do with the future of computer and video games? More than you might expect.

Herodotus invented history as we know it, and he has described the goal of history as uncovering moral problems and moral truths in the concrete data of experience. Whether Herodotus' story of an eighteen-year famine survived through gameplay is true or, as some modern historians believe, apocryphal, its moral truths reveal something important about the essence of games.

25    We often think of immersive gameplay as "escapist," a kind of passive retreat from reality. But through the lens of Herodotus' history, we can see how games could be a *purposeful* escape, a thoughtful and active escape, and most importantly an extremely helpful escape. For the Lydians, playing together as a nearly full-time activity would have been a behavior highly adaptive to difficult conditions. Games made life bearable. Games gave a starving population a feeling of power in a powerless situation, a sense of structure in a chaotic environment. Games gave them a better way to live when their circumstances were otherwise completely unsupportive and uninhabitable.

Make no mistake: we are no different from the ancient Lydians. Today, many of us are suffering from a vast and primal hunger. But it is not a hunger for food—it is a hunger for more and better engagement from the world around us.

Like the ancient Lydians, many gamers have already figured out how to use the immersive power of play to distract themselves from their hunger: a hunger for more satisfying work, for a stronger sense of community, and for a more engaging and meaningful life.

Collectively, the planet is now spending more than 3 billion hours a week gaming.

We are starving, and our games are feeding us.

## Responding to Reading

1.  What central problem does this essay identify? How does McGonigal explain the cause of this problem? Can you offer other explanations?
2.  In paragraphs 3 through 6, McGonigal discusses different kinds of gamers. What point is she making here? Are these paragraphs essential to her essay? Why or why not?
3.  Why does McGonigal quote Herodotus in paragraph 22? How does she answer the question she poses in paragraph 23: "What do ancient dice made from sheep's knuckles have to do with the future of computer and video games?"

## Responding in Writing

This selection is part of the introduction to McGonigal's book *Reality Is Broken*. Later in this introduction, she offers three possible scenarios for the future of gaming: encouraging more and more complex and appealing virtual worlds as alternatives to reality; limiting access to video games in order to encourage a greater focus on reality; or using our knowledge of gaming to help solve the problems of the real world. Which of these possibilities do you think McGonigal favors? Which scenario makes the most sense to you? Which do you think is most likely to occur?

---
### FOCUS
---

## Does Social Networking Connect Us or Keep Us Apart?

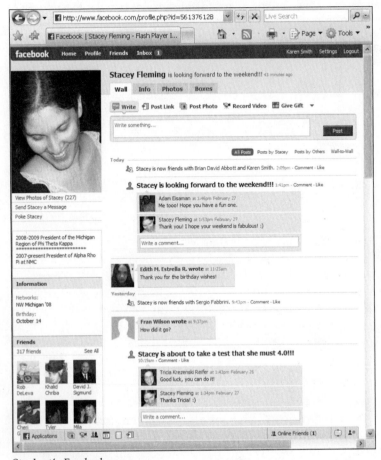

Student's *Facebook* page

## Responding to the Image

1. What information does this student supply about herself on her *Facebook* page? What additional information can you infer about her? How? What do you suppose Alice Mathias (p. 229) would say about this page?

2. This student has 317 friends, some of whom are pictured, and visitors to her page are able to see the names of Stacey's newest friends. Look carefully at the posted comments. Which sound as if they were written by friends? Which sound like the voices of acquaintances? Is there a difference?

# THE FAKEBOOK GENERATION
## Alice Mathias

*Formerly a columnist for the* Dartmouth Mirror, *Dartmouth College's weekly magazine, Alice Mathias graduated from Dartmouth in 2007 with a degree in creative writing and film and television. She has contributed to the* New York Times *blog* The Graduates, *which focuses on students' experiences and challenges as they prepare to graduate from college. In the following essay, Mathias discusses the* Facebook *phenomenon.*

The time-chugging Web site Facebook.com first appeared during my freshman year as the exclusive domain of college students. This spring, Facebook opened its pearly gates, enabling myself and other members of the class of '07 to graduate from our college networks into those of the real world.

In no time at all, the Web site has convinced its rapidly assembling adult population that it is a forum for genuine personal and professional connections. Its founder, Mark Zuckerberg, has even declared his quest to chart a "social graph" of human relationships the way that cartographers once charted the world.

Just a warning: if you're planning on following the corner of this map that's been digitally doodled by my 659 Facebook friends, you are going to end up in the middle of nowhere. All the rhetoric about human connectivity misses the real reason this popular online study buddy has so distracted college students for the past four years.

Facebook did not become popular because it was a functional tool—after all, most college students live in close quarters with the majority of their Facebook friends and have no need for social networking. Instead, we log into the Web site because it's entertaining to watch a constantly evolving narrative starring the other people in the library.

I've always thought of Facebook as online community theater. In costumes we customize in a backstage makeup room—the Edit Profile page, where we can add a few Favorite Books or touch up our About Me section—we deliver our lines on the very public stage of friends' walls or photo albums. And because every time we join a network, post a link or make another friend it's immediately made visible to others via the News Feed, every Facebook act is a soliloquy to our anonymous audience. 5

It's all comedy: making one another laugh matters more than providing useful updates about ourselves, which is why entirely phony profiles were all the rage before the grown-ups signed in. One friend announced her status as In a Relationship with Chinese Food, whose profile picture was a carry-out box and whose personal information personified the cuisine of China.

We even make a joke out of how we know one another—claiming to have met in "Intro to Super Mario Re-enactments," which I seriously doubt is a real course at Wesleyan, or to have lived together in a "spay and neuter clinic" instead of the dorm. Still, these humor bits often reveal more about our personalities and interests than any honest answers.

Facebook administrators have since exiled at least the flagrantly fake profiles, the Greta Garbos and the I Can't Believe It's Not Butters, in an effort to have the site grow up from a farce into the serious social networking tool promised to its new adult users, who earnestly type in their actual personal information and precisely label everyone they know as former co-workers or current colleagues, family members or former lovers.

But does this more reverent incarnation of Facebook actually enrich adult relationships? What do these constellations of work colleagues and long-lost friends amount to? An online office mixer? A reunion with that one other guy from your high school who has a Facebook profile? Oh! You get to see pictures of your former college sweetheart's family! (Only depressing possibilities are coming to mind for some reason.)

10   My generation has long been bizarrely comfortable with being looked at, and as performers on the Facebook stage, we upload pictures of ourselves cooking dinner for our parents or doing keg stands at last night's party; we are reckless with our personal information. But there is one area of privacy that we won't surrender: the secrecy of how and whom we search.

A friend of mine was recently in a panic over rumors of a hacker application that would allow Facebook users to see who's been visiting their profiles. She'd spent the day ogling a love interest's page and was horrified at the idea that he knew she'd been looking at him. But there's no way Facebook would allow such a program to exist: the site is popular largely because it enables us to indulge our gazes anonymously. (We might feel invulnerable in the spotlight, but we don't want to be caught sitting in someone else's audience.) If our ability to privately search is ever jeopardized, Facebook will turn into a ghost town.

Facebook purports to be a place for human connectivity, but it's made us more wary of real human confrontation. When I was in college, people always warned against the dangers of "Facebook stalking" at a library computer—the person whose profile you're perusing might be right behind you. Dwelling online is a cowardly and utterly enjoyable alternative to real interaction.

So even though Facebook offers an elaborate menu of privacy settings, many of my friends admit that the only setting they use is the one that prevents people from seeing that they are Currently Logged In. Perhaps we fear that the Currently Logged In feature advertises to everyone else that we (too!) are Currently Bored, Lustful, Socially Unfulfilled or Generally Avoiding Real Life.

For young people, Facebook is yet another form of escapism; we can turn our lives into stage dramas and relationships into comedy routines. Make believe is not part of the postgraduate Facebook user's agenda. As more and more older users try to turn Facebook into a legitimate social reference guide, younger people may follow suit and stop treating it as a circus ring. But let's hope not.

## Responding to Reading

1. Why does Mathias refer to *Facebook* as "Fakebook" in her essay's title? In what sense are she and her friends part of the "Fakebook Generation"? For example, do you think she sees herself and her friends as creative? As narcissistic?
2. What, according to Mathias, is "the real reason" *Facebook* has become so popular (3)? In what respects is *Facebook* a kind of "online community theater" (5)?
3. In paragraph 12, Mathias says, "Facebook purports to be a place for human connectivity, but it's made us more wary of real human confrontation." What does she mean? Can you think of examples besides the one she supplies to illustrate her statement?

## Responding in Writing

In paragraph 9, Mathias asks, "But does . . . Facebook actually enrich adult relationships?" Write a paragraph arguing that it does.

# WHY TWITTER WILL ENDURE

## David Carr

### 1957–

*A business columnist and a culture reporter for the* New York Times, *David Carr writes about various issues pertaining to pop culture, media, and society. His memoir,* The Night of the Gun: A Reporter Investigates the Darkest Story of His Life, His Own *(2008), chronicles the events of his troubled past. In the following essay, Carr considers the complexities of the* Twitter *cultural phenomenon.*

I can remember when I first thought seriously about Twitter. Last March, I was at the SXSW conference, a conclave in Austin, Tex., where technology, media and music are mashed up and re-imagined, and, not so coincidentally, where Twitter first rolled out in 2007. As someone who was oversubscribed on Facebook, overwhelmed by the computer-generated RSS feeds of news that came flying at me, and swamped by incoming e-mail messages, the last thing I wanted was one more Web-borne intrusion into my life.

And then there was the name. Twitter.

In the pantheon of digital nomenclature—brands within a sector of the economy that grew so fast that all the sensible names were quickly taken—it would be hard to come up with a noun more trite than Twitter. It impugns itself, promising something slight and inconsequential, yet another way to make hours disappear and have nothing to show for it. And just in case the noun is not sufficiently indicting, the verb, "to tweet" is even more embarrassing.

Beyond the dippy lingo, the idea that something intelligent, something worthy of mindshare, might occur in the space of 140 characters—Twitter's parameters were set by what would fit in a text message on a phone—seems unlikely.

5    But it was clear that at the conference, the primary news platform was Twitter, with real-time annotation of the panels on stage and critical updates about what was happening elsewhere at a very hectic convention. At 52, I succumbed, partly out of professional necessity.

And now, nearly a year later, has Twitter turned my brain to mush? No, I'm in narrative on more things in a given moment than I ever thought possible, and instead of spending a half-hour surfing in search of illumination, I get a sense of the day's news and how people are reacting to it in the time that it takes to wait for coffee at Starbucks. Yes, I worry about my ability to think long thoughts—where was I, anyway? —but the tradeoff has been worth it.

Some time soon, the company won't say when, the 100-millionth person will have signed on to Twitter to follow and be followed by friends and strangers. That may sound like a MySpace waiting to happen—remember MySpace? —but I'm convinced Twitter is here to stay.

And I'm not alone.

"The history of the Internet suggests that there have been cool Web sites that go in and out of fashion and then there have been open standards that become plumbing," said Steven Johnson, the author and technology observer who wrote a seminal piece about Twitter for *Time* last June. "Twitter is looking more and more like plumbing, and plumbing is eternal."

10    Really? What could anyone possibly find useful in this cacophony of short-burst communication?

Well, that depends on whom you ask, but more importantly whom you follow. On Twitter, anyone may follow anyone, but there is very little expectation of reciprocity. By carefully curating the people you follow, Twitter becomes an always-on data stream from really bright people in their respective fields, whose tweets are often full of links to incredibly vital, timely information.

The most frequent objection to Twitter is a predictable one: "I don't need to know someone is eating a donut right now." But if that someone is a serious user of Twitter, she or he might actually be eating the curmudgeon's lunch, racing ahead with a clear, up-to-the-second picture of an increasingly connected, busy world. The service has obvious utility for a journalist, but no matter what business you are in, imagine knowing what the thought leaders in your industry were reading and considering. And beyond following specific individuals, Twitter hash tags allow you to go deep into interests and obsession: #rollerderby, #physics, #puppets and #Avatar, to name just a few of many thousands.

The act of publishing on Twitter is so friction-free—a few keystrokes and hit send—that you can forget that others are out there listening. I was on a Virgin America cross-country flight, and used its wireless connection to tweet about the fact that the guy next to me seemed to be the leader of a cult involving Axe body spray. A half-hour later, a steward approached me and said he wondered if I would be more comfortable with a seat in the bulkhead. (He turned out to be a great guy, but I was doing a story involving another part of the company, so I had to decline the offer. @VirginAmerica, its corporate Twitter account, sent me a message afterward saying perhaps it should develop a screening process for Axe. It was creepy and comforting all at once.)

Like many newbies on Twitter, I vastly overestimated the importance of broadcasting on Twitter and after a while, I realized that I was not Moses and neither Twitter nor its users were wondering what I thought. Nearly a year in, I've come to understand that the real value of the service is listening to a wired collective voice.

Not that long ago, I was at a conference at Yale and looked at the 15 sea of open laptops in the seats in front of me. So why wasn't my laptop open? Because I follow people on Twitter who serve as my Web-crawling proxies, each of them tweeting links that I could examine and read on a Blackberry. Regardless of where I am, I surf far less than I used to.

At first, Twitter can be overwhelming, but think of it as a river of data rushing past that I dip a cup into every once in a while. Much of what I need to know is in that cup: if it looks like Apple is going to demo its new tablet, or Amazon sold more Kindles than actual books at Christmas, or the final vote in the Senate gets locked in on health care, I almost always learn about it first on Twitter.

The expressive limits of a kind of narrative developed from text messages, with less space to digress or explain than this sentence, has significant upsides. The best people on Twitter communicate with economy and precision, with each element—links, hash tags and comments—freighted with meaning. Professional acquaintances whom I find insufferable on every other platform suddenly become interesting within the confines of Twitter.

Twitter is incredibly customizable, with little of the social expectations that go with Facebook. Depending on whom you follow, Twitter can reveal a nation riveted by the last episode of "Jersey Shore" or a short-form conclave of brilliance. There is plenty of nonsense— #Tiger had quite a run—but there are rich threads on the day's news and bravura solo performances from learned autodidacts. And the ethos of Twitter, which is based on self-defining groups, is far more well-mannered than many parts of the Web—more Toastmasters than mosh pit. On Twitter, you are your avatar and your avatar is you, so best not to act like a lout and when people want to flame you for something you said, they are responding to their own followers, not yours, so trolls quickly lose interest.

"Anything that is useful to both dissidents in Iran and Martha Stewart has a lot going for it; Twitter has more raw capability for users than anything since e-mail," said Clay Shirky, who wrote *Here Comes Everybody*, a book about social media. "It will be hard to wait out Twitter because it is lightweight, endlessly useful and gets better as more people use it. Brands are using it, institutions are using it, and it is becoming a place where a lot of important conversations are being held."

20    Twitter helps define what is important by what Mr. Shirky has called "algorithmic authority," meaning that if all kinds of people are pointing at the same thing at the same instant, it must be a pretty big deal.

Beyond the throbbing networked intelligence, there is the possibility of practical magic. Twitter can tell you what kind of netbook you should buy for your wife for Christmas—thanks Twitter!—or call you out when you complain about the long lines it took to buy it, as a tweeter on behalf of the electronics store B & H did when I shared the experience on my Blackberry while in line. I have found transcendent tacos at a car wash in San Antonio, rediscovered a brand of reporter's notepad I adore, uncovered sources for stories, all just by typing a query into Twitter.

All those riches do not come at zero cost: If you think e-mail and surfing can make time disappear, wait until you get ahold of Twitter, or more likely, it gets ahold of you. There is always something more interesting on Twitter than whatever you happen to be working on.

But in the right circumstance, Twitter can flex some big muscles. Think of last weekend, a heavy travel period marked by a terrorist incident on Friday. As news outlets were scrambling to understand the implications for travelers on Saturday morning, Twitter began lighting up with reports of new security initiatives, including one from @CharleneLi, a consultant who tweeted from the Montreal airport at about 7:30 A.M.: "New security rules for int'l flights into US. 1 bag, no electronics the ENTIRE flight, no getting up last hour of flight."

It was far from the whole story and getting ahead of the news by some hours would seem like no big deal, but imagine you or someone you loved was flying later that same day: Twitter might seem very useful.

25    Twitter's growing informational hegemony is not assured. There have been serious outages in recent weeks, leading many business and

government users to wonder about the stability of the platform. And this being the Web, many smart folks are plotting ways to turn Twitter into so much pixilated mist. But I don't think so. I can go anywhere I want on the Web, but there is no guarantee that my Twitter gang will come with me. I may have quite a few followers, but that doesn't make me Moses.

## Responding to Reading

1. What were Carr's initial reservations about *Twitter*? What reservations about its widespread use does he still have?
2. Many new-media writers and critics acknowledge a divide between older and younger users of electronic media. Carr was 53 when he wrote this essay. How does your use of *Twitter* differ from his? How do the content and style of the tweets you send and receive differ from his? Do you think these differences exist solely because of the generational divide between you and Carr? Explain.
3. Why is Carr "convinced that Twitter is here to stay" (7)? What does he see as its strengths? What do you think Sherry Turkle (p. 235) might say about *Twitter?*

## Responding in Writing

Discussing his initial reservations about *Twitter,* Carr says, "And then there was the name. Twitter" (2). What associations does the word *twitter* have for you? Do you see *twitter* and *tweet* as appropriate words for what they signify? What other words might be more appropriate and evocative? Why?

# CONNECTIVITY AND ITS DISCONTENTS

## Sherry Turkle

### 1948–

*A radio and television media commentator, Sherry Turkle is the Abby Rock-efeller Mauzé Professor of the social studies of science and technology at MIT as well as the founder and director of the MIT Initiative on Technology and Self. She is the author of five books, including, most recently,* Alone Together: Why We Expect More from Technology and Less from Each Other *(2011), from which the following is excerpted. In this discussion, Turkle takes a critical look at how technology affects our interpersonal relationships.*

Online connections were first conceived as a substitute for face-to-face contact, when the latter was for some reason impractical: Don't have time to make a phone call? Shoot off a text message. But very quickly, the text message became the connection of choice. We discovered the network—the world of connectivity—to be uniquely suited to the over-worked and overscheduled life it makes possible. And now we look to the network to defend us against loneliness even as we use it to control the intensity of our connections. Technology makes it easy to communicate when we wish and to disengage at will.

A few years ago at a dinner party in Paris, I met Ellen, an ambitious, elegant young woman in her early thirties, thrilled to be working at her dream job in advertising. Once a week, she would call her grandmother in Philadelphia using Skype, an Internet service that functions as a telephone with a Web camera, Before Skype, Ellen's calls to her grandmother were costly and brief. With Skype, the calls are free and give the compelling sense that the other person is present—Skype is an almost real-time video link. Ellen could now call more frequently: "Twice a week and I stay on the call for an hour," she told me. It should have been rewarding; instead, when I met her, Ellen was unhappy. She knew that her grandmother was unaware that Skype allows surreptitious multitasking. Her grandmother could see Ellen's face on the screen but not her hands. Ellen admitted to me, "I do my e-mail during the calls. I'm not really paying attention to our conversation."

Ellen's multitasking removed her to another place. She felt her grandmother was talking to someone who was not really there. During their Skype conversations, Ellen and her grandmother were more connected than they had ever been before, but at the same time, each was alone. Ellen felt guilty and confused: she knew that her grandmother was happy, even if their intimacy was now, for Ellen, another task among multitasks.

I have often observed this distinctive confusion: these days, whether you are online or not, it is easy for people to end up unsure if they are closer together or further apart. I remember my own sense of disorientation the first time I realized that I was "alone together." I had traveled an exhausting thirty-six hours to attend a conference on advanced robotic technology held in central Japan. The packed grand ballroom was Wi-Fi enabled: the speaker was using the Web for his presentation, laptops were open throughout the audience, fingers were flying, and there was a sense of great concentration and intensity. But not many in the audience were attending to the speaker. Most people seemed to be doing their e-mail, downloading files, and surfing the Net. The man next to me was searching for a *New Yorker* cartoon to illustrate his upcoming presentation. Every once in a while, audience members gave the speaker some attention, lowering their laptop screens in a kind of curtsy, a gesture of courtesy.

5    Outside, in the hallways, the people milling around me were looking past me to virtual others. They were on their laptops and their phones, connecting to colleagues at the conference going on around them and to others around the globe. There but not there. Of course, clusters of people chatted with each other, making dinner plans, "networking" in that old sense of the word, the one that implies having a coffee or sharing a meal. But at this conference, it was clear that what people mostly want from public space is to be alone with their personal networks. It is good to come

together physically, but it is more important to stay tethered to our devices. I thought of how Sigmund Freud considered the power of communities both to shape and to subvert us, and a psychoanalytic pun came to mind: "connectivity and its discontents."

The phrase comes back to me months later as I interview management consultants who seem to have lost touch with their best instincts for what makes them competitive. They complain about the BlackBerry revolution, yet accept it as inevitable while decrying it as corrosive. They say they used to talk to each other as they waited to give presentations or took taxis to the airport; now they spend that time doing e-mail. Some tell me they are making better use of their "downtime," but they argue without conviction. The time that they once used to talk as they waited for appointments or drove to the airport was never downtime. It was the time when far-flung global teams solidified relationships and refined ideas.

In corporations, among friends, and within academic departments, people readily admit that they would rather leave a voicemail or send an e-mail than talk face-to-face. Some who say "I live my life on my BlackBerry" are forthright about avoiding the "real-time" commitment of a phone call. The new technologies allow us to "dial down" human contact, to titrate its nature and extent. I recently overheard a conversation in a restaurant between two women. "No one answers the phone in our house anymore," the first woman proclaimed with some consternation. "It used to be that the kids would race to pick up the phone. Now they are up in their rooms, knowing no one is going to call them, and texting and going on Facebook or whatever instead." Parents with teenage children will be nodding at this very familiar story in recognition and perhaps a sense of wonderment that this has happened, and so quickly. And teenagers will simply be saying, "Well, what's your point?"

A thirteen-year-old tells me she "hates the phone and never listens to voicemail." Texting offers just the right amount of access, just the right amount of control. She is a modern Goldilocks: for her, texting puts people not too close, not too far, but at just the right distance. The world is now full of modern Goldilockses, people who take comfort in being in touch with a lot of people whom they also keep at bay. A twenty-one-year-old college student reflects on the new balance: "I don't use my phone for calls any more. I don't have the time to just go on and on. I like texting, Twitter, looking at someone's Facebook wall. I learn what I need to know."

Randy, twenty-seven, has a younger sister—a Goldilocks who got her distances wrong. Randy is an American lawyer now working in California. His family lives in New York, and he flies to the East Coast to see them three or four times a year. When I meet Randy, his sister Nora, twenty-four, had just announced her engagement and wedding date via e-mail to a list of friends and family. "That," Randy says to me bitterly, "is how I got the news." He doesn't know if he is more angry or hurt, "It doesn't feel right that she didn't call," he says. "I was getting ready for a trip home. Couldn't she have told me then? She's my sister, but I didn't have a private moment when she told me in person. Or at least a call, just the two of us. When I told her I was upset, she sort of understood, but laughed and said that she and her fiancé just wanted to do things simply, as simply as possible. I feel very far away from her."

10      Nora did not mean to offend her brother. She saw e-mail as efficient and did not see beyond. We have long turned to technology to make us more efficient in work; now Nora illustrates how we want it to make us more efficient in our private lives. But when technology engineers intimacy, relationships can be reduced to mere connections. And then, easy connection becomes redefined as intimacy. Put otherwise, cyber-intimacies slide into cybersolitudes.

And with constant connection comes new anxieties of disconnection, a kind of panic. Even Randy, who longs for a phone call from Nora on such an important matter as her wedding, is never without his BlackBerry. He holds it in his hands during our entire conversation. Once, he puts it in his pocket. A few moments later, it comes out, fingered like a talisman. In interviews with young and old, I find people genuinely terrified of being cut off from the "grid." People say that the loss of a cell phone can "feel like a death." One television producer in her mid-forties tells me that without her smartphone, "I felt like I had lost my mind." Whether or not our devices are in use, without them we feel disconnected, adrift. A danger even to ourselves, we insist on our right to send text messages while driving our cars and object to rules that would limit the practice.

Only a decade ago, I would have been mystified that fifteen-year-olds in my urban neighborhood, a neighborhood of parks and shopping malls, of front stoops and coffee shops, would feel the need to send and receive close to six thousand messages a month via portable digital devices or that best friends would assume that when they visited, it would usually be on the virtual real estate of Facebook. It might have seemed intrusive, if not illegal, that my mobile phone would tell me the location of all my acquaintances within a ten-mile radius. But these days we are accustomed to all this. Life in a media bubble has come to seem natural. So has the end of a certain public etiquette: on the street, we speak into the invisible microphones on our mobile phones and appear to be talking to ourselves. We share intimacies with the air as though unconcerned about who can hear us or the details of our physical surroundings.

I once described the computer as a second self, a mirror of mind. Now the metaphor no longer goes far enough. Our new devices provide space for the emergence of a new state of the self, itself, split between the screen and the physical real, wired into existence through technology.

Teenagers tell me they sleep with their cell phone, and even when it isn't on their person, when it has been banished to the school locker, for instance, they know when their phone is vibrating. The technology has become like a phantom limb, it is so much a part of them. These young people are among the first to grow up with an expectation of continuous connection: always on, and always on them. And they are among the first to grow up not necessarily thinking of simulation as second best. All of this makes them fluent with technology but brings a set of new insecurities. They nurture friendships on social-networking sites and then wonder if they are among friends. They are connected all day but are not sure if they have communicated. They become confused about companionship. Can they find it in their lives on the screen? Could they find it with a robot? Their digitized friendships—played out with emoticon emotions, so often predicated on rapid response rather than reflection—may prepare them, at times through nothing more than their superficiality, for relationships that could bring superficiality to a higher power, that is, for relationships with the inanimate. They come to accept lower expectations for connection and, finally, the idea that robot friendships could be sufficient unto the day.

Overwhelmed by the volume and velocity of our lives, we turn to technology to help us find time. But technology makes us busier than ever and ever more in search of retreat. Gradually, we come to see our online life as life itself. We come to see what robots offer as relationship. The simplification of relationship is no longer a source of complaint. It becomes what we want. These seem the gathering clouds of a perfect storm.   15

Technology reshapes the landscape of our emotional lives, but is it offering us the lives we want to lead? Many roboticists are enthusiastic about having robots tend to our children and our aging parents, for instance. Are these psychologically, socially, and ethically acceptable propositions? What are our responsibilities here? And are we comfortable with virtual environments that propose themselves not as places for recreation but as new worlds to live in? What do we have, now that we have what we say we want—now that we have what technology makes easy? This is the time to begin these conversations, together. It is too late to leave the future to the futurists.

## Responding to Reading

1. What does Turkle mean by the terms *connectivity* (title), *cyberintimacies* and *cybersolitudes* (10), and *robot friendships* (14)? According to Turkle, what is the difference between "relationships" and "connections" (10)?

2. Relying on extended examples of Skype, texting, and email (and mentioning *Facebook* only in passing), Turkle describes a world in which people are increasingly "unsure if they are closer together or further apart" (4) and

somehow "There but not there" (5). She says, "The world is now full of modern Goldilockses, people who take comfort in being in touch with a lot of people whom they also keep at bay" (8). What does she mean? In what respects do her observations apply to *Facebook* use as well as to the examples she cites?

3. In her conclusion, Turkle says, "It is too late to leave the future to the futurists" (16). Do you think she is right to be alarmed at the trends she identifies? Or, do you think the changes she cites—for example, her statement that "Technology makes it easy to communicate when we wish and to disengage at will" (1)—are, on balance, essentially positive? Explain.

## Responding in Writing

Throughout her essay, Turkle cites examples of people she met or interviewed. Do these people's stories seem atypical, or do any of them remind you of people you know? In other words, do the concerns they cite hit home for you? Explain.

# WIDENING THE FOCUS

### For Critical Reading and Writing

Referring specifically to the three readings in this chapter's Focus section, write an essay in which you answer the question, "Does Social Networking Connect us or Keep us Apart?"

### For Further Reading

The following readings can suggest additional perspectives for reading and writing about the kinds of communities created online—and how they are different from face-to-face communities.

- Lynda Barry, "The Sanctuary of School" (p. 69)

- Gary Soto, "One Last Time" (p. 404)

- David A. Hoekema, "The Unacknowledged Ethicists on Campuses" (p. 453)

- William C. Symonds, Brian Grow, and John Cady, "Earthly Empires" (p. 525)

### For Focused Research

Web Links

The question of whether social networking helps to foster meaningful connections or whether it creates new levels of isolation is complicated. One thing, however, is certain: online social networking sites abound, and more and more Web space is being devoted to services and resources that allow users to interact online. In 2009, *Google* started its *Social Web Blog* "for anyone interested or involved in helping to make the Web more social." Its introductory post asks users to "Tell us about what you've been doing to make the web more social, what you've seen others successfully do, or simply what you think about our posts." Visit *Google's Social Web Blog* <http://googlesocialweb.blogspot.com>, and read some of the postings. Then, write an essay-length post in which you assess the value of an online space such as this one for connecting people online.

### Beyond the Classroom

Observe the people you see at a museum, restaurant, sporting event, film, concert, or performance—or on public transportation. How much time do they spend interacting with people (friends or strangers), and how much time do they spend on their smartphones? Take notes on their behavior, and then write an essay in which you draw a conclusion about the way social media are (or are not) bringing people together.

## Writing

### Media and Society

1. What do you think the impact of the various media discussed in this chapter will be in the years to come? What trends do you see emerging that you believe will change the way you think or the way you live? Write an essay in which you speculate about future trends and their impact, using the essays in this chapter by Eli Pariser (p. 214) and Jane McGonigal (p. 222) to support the points you make.

2. Write an essay in which you consider the representation of a particular ethnic or racial group (or the portrayal of women, the elderly, or people with disabilities) in the media (movies, television, magazine ads, and so on). Do you believe the group you have chosen to write about is adequately represented? Do you think its members are portrayed fairly and accurately, or do you think they are stereotyped? Support your conclusions with specific examples.

3. Do you think newspapers will survive in their present form, or do you believe that the Internet threatens their survival? Do you believe print newspapers *should* survive—that is, that they are necessary?

4. To what extent, if any, should explicitly sexual or violent media images be censored? Write an essay in which you take a stand on this issue and explain why you believe such censorship is (or is not) necessary.

5. What danger, if any, do you see for young people in the seductive messages of the music they listen to? Do you believe that parents and educators are right to be concerned about the effect the messages in rock and rap music have on teenagers and young adults, or do you think they are overreacting? Support your position with quotations from popular music lyrics. If you like, you can also interview friends and relatives and use their responses to help you develop your argument. Before you begin, read Mary Eberstadt's "Eminem Is Right" (p. 204).

6. What qualities, if any, do printed books have that their electronic counterparts lack—and vice versa? After reading "Learning to Read and Write" in Chapter 3, and "The Library Card" in Chapter 7, write an essay in which you assess the relative merits of print and electronic books.

7. Write an analysis of a Web site, considering the techniques it uses to appeal to its target audience. Who is being addressed, what message is conveyed, and how successfully is this message communicated?

8. Reread Alice Mathias's essay about *Facebook* on page 229. Then, write an essay analyzing and evaluating your own relationship with

*Facebook.* You may consider topics such as how *Facebook* connects you to your world, how you communicate with different kinds of friends, how you protect your privacy, and how you prevent information overload. All in all, is *Facebook* a positive or negative part of your life?

9. In "Does the Internet Make You Dumber?" (p. 216), Nicholas Carr expresses his concerns about the possibility that the Internet is creating distracted thinkers. In "Mind over Mass Media" (p. 220), Steven Pinker disagrees with Carr and other critics of new media. Read these two essays, summarize the writers' positions, and explain which writer you agree with, and why.

10. Write an analysis of a current popular reality TV show. Start by describing the program's basic premise, setting, and participants. Then, consider some or all of the following questions:

- What explains this program's appeal to viewers?

- What trends in society does the program reflect?

- Does the program rely on sensationalism?

- Has the program had any impact on society?

Before you begin writing, read Salman Rushdie's essay on page 199.

# 5

# GENDER AND IDENTITY

Attitudes about gender have changed dramatically over the past forty years, and they continue to change. For some, these changes have resulted in confusion as well as liberation. One reason for this confusion is that people can no longer rely on fixed gender roles to tell them how to behave in public and how to function within their families. Still, many men and women—uncomfortable with the demands of confining gender roles and unhappy with the expectations those roles create—yearn for even less rigidity, for an escape from stereotypes into a society where roles are not strictly defined by gender.

In spite of these changes, many people still see men and women in terms of outdated or unrealistic stereotypes. Men are strong, tough, and brave, and women are weak, passive, and in need of protection. Men

Two young boys playing with toy swords

understand mathematics and science and have a natural aptitude for mechanical tasks. They also have the drive, the aggressiveness, the competitive edge, and the power to succeed. They are never sentimental and never cry. Women are better at small, repetitive tasks and shy away from taking bold, decisive actions. They enjoy, and are good at, domestic activities, and they have a natural aptitude for nurturing. Although women may like their jobs, they will leave them to devote themselves to husband and children.

As you read the preceding list of stereotypes, you may react neutrally (or even favorably), or you may react with annoyance; how we react tells us something about our society and something about ourselves. As a number of writers in this chapter point out, however, stereotypes can limit the way people think, the roles they choose to assume, and, ultimately, the positions they occupy in society.

As the Focus section of this chapter, "Who Has It Harder, Girls or Boys?" (p. 274) illustrates, both men and women have problems living up to the images they believe they should conform to and filling the roles that have been set for them. Some believe that it is boys who have suffered more, because as parents and teachers have focused on the girls, they have ignored the needs of boys. Others say that before the problems boys and girls face can be addressed, society—especially educators—must stop spreading ideas about gender differences that are either misleading or incorrect. Still others assert that, in today's society, young women are presented with an impossible set of expectations that make it difficult, if

Two young girls playing with dolls

not impossible, for them to function. Only by broadening the dialogue, and by challenging conventional wisdom, will our society be able to ensure that both males and females are able to realize their full potential.

## PREPARING TO READ AND WRITE

As you read and prepare to write about the essays in this chapter, you may consider the following questions:

- Is the writer male or female? Can you determine the writer's gender without reading his or her name or the headnote? Does the writer's gender matter?

- Does the writer focus on males, on females, or on both?

- Does the essay's date of publication affect its content?

- Does the essay seem fair? Balanced?

- Does the writer discuss gender as a sexual, political, economic, or social issue?

- What does the writer suggest are the specific advantages or disadvantages of being male? Of being female? Of being gay or straight?

- Does the writer support the status quo, or does he or she suggest that change is necessary? That change is possible? That change is inevitable?

- Does the writer recommend specific societal changes? What are they?

- Does the writer think that men and women are fundamentally different? If so, does he or she suggest that these differences can (or should) be overcome, or at least lessened?

- Does the writer think gender differences are the result of environment, heredity, or both?

- Does the essay challenge any of your ideas about male or female roles?

- In what ways is the essay like other essays in this chapter?

# BARBIE DOLL

## Marge Piercy
### 1936–

*Marge Piercy's work includes the novels* Small Changes *(1972),* He, She, and It *(1991),* Three Women *(1999), and* Sex Wars: A Novel of Gilded Age New York *(2005) and the poetry collections* The Art of Blessing the Day *(1999),* The Crooked Inheritance *(2006), and* The Hunger Moon: New and Selected Poems, 1980–2010 *(2011). According to Piercy, who has been active in the women's movement since 1969, the movement "has been a great source (as well as energy sink!) and healer of the psyche for me." The following poem from* Circles in the Water *(1988) is an ironic look at the influence of the doll that has become a controversial icon.*

This girlchild was born as usual
and presented dolls that did pee-pee
and miniature GE stoves and irons
and wee lipsticks the color of cherry candy.
Then in the magic of puberty, a classmate said:                5
You have a great big nose and fat legs.

She was healthy, tested intelligent,
possessed strong arms and back,
abundant sexual drive and manual dexterity.
She went to and fro apologizing.                               10
Everyone saw a fat nose on thick legs.
She was advised to play coy,
exhorted to come on hearty,
exercise, diet, smile and wheedle.
Her good nature wore out                                       15
like a fan belt.
So she cut off her nose and her legs
and offered them up.

In the casket displayed on satin she lay
with the undertaker's cosmetics painted on,                    20
a turned-up putty nose,
dressed in a pink and white nightie.
Doesn't she look pretty? everyone said.
Consummation at last.
To every woman a happy ending.                                 25

## Responding to Reading

1. What is the significance of the poem's title? To whom (or to what) does it refer? What toys was the "girlchild" (line 1) given after she was born? What effect did these toys have on the child?
2. What happened to the "girlchild" when she reached "the magic of puberty" (line 5)? Was this change inevitable? Explain.
3. Piercy ends on a cynical note. Is this an effective conclusion? What does she gain (or lose) with this kind of ending?

## Responding in Writing

What toy (or toys) did you have as a child that defined your "femaleness" or "maleness"? Do you think Piercy accurately portrays the impact of such toys on children, or do you think she exaggerates?

# RITE OF PASSAGE
## Sharon Olds
### 1942–

*Sharon Olds was thirty-seven years old when she published her first book of poems. Her collections include* The Gold Cell *(1987),* The Wellspring *(1996),* Blood, Tin, Straw *(1999),* The Unswept Room *(2002),* Strike Sparks: Selected Poems 1980–2002 *(2004),* One Secret Thing *(2008), and* Stag's Leap: Poems *(2012). Much of her poetry focuses on family relationships. Olds is active in community outreach programs, such as the writing workshop at Goldwater Hospital in New York City. In her poetry, Olds often dwells on relationships among parents and children, using plain language that reveals surprising emotional depths. In the following poem, Olds implies that her young son and his male friends already possess the violent tendencies of adult men.*

As the guests arrive at my son's party
they gather in the living room—
short men, men in first grade
with smooth jaws and chins.
5    Hands in pockets, they stand around
jostling, jockeying for place, small fights
breaking out and calming. One says to another
*How old are you? Six. I'm seven. So?*
They eye each other, seeing themselves
10    tiny in the other's pupils. They clear their
throats a lot, a room of small bankers,
they fold their arms and frown. *I could beat you*

*up*, a seven says to a six,
the dark cake, round and heavy as a
turret, behind them on the table. My son,                    15
freckles like specks of nutmeg on his cheeks,
chest narrow as the balsa keel[1] of a
model boat, long hands
cool and thin as the day they guided him
out of me, speaks up as a host                               20
for the sake of the group.
*We could easily kill a two-year-old,*
he says in his clear voice. The other
men agree, they clear their throats
like Generals, they relax and get down to                    25
playing war, celebrating my son's life.

## Responding to Reading

1. Look up the definition of "rite of passage." Why do you think Olds gives her poem this title?
2. Why does Olds refer to the children at her son's birthday party as "men"?
3. What comment do you think Olds is making about what it means to be male in contemporary American society?

## Responding in Writing

Do you think that Olds's portrayal of boys is accurate, or do you think it is exaggerated? Why do you think that she characterizes boys as she does?

# The M/F Boxes

## E. J. Graff

### 1958–

*A senior fellow at the Schuster Institute for Investigative Journalism and a resident scholar at the Brandeis Women's Studies Research Center, E. J. Graff is a widely published author of articles on gender equality and family issues. She is a senior correspondent at the* American Prospect; *a contributor to* Out *magazine and* Slate.com; *and the author of two books—*What Is Marriage For? The Strange History of Our Most Intimate Institution *(1999) and, with Evelyn F. Murphy,* Getting Even: Why Women Don't Get Paid Like Men—and What to Do about It *(2005). The following essay questions conventional male/female distinctions and argues that either/or labels falsely prepackage identity and gender.*

---

[1]The long, narrow bottom of a wooden ship. [Eds.]

A 15-year-old girl is incarcerated in a Chicago mental hospital in 1981 and kept there for three years because she won't wear a dress. A Winn-Dixie truck driver is fired from a job he held for twenty years when his boss learns that he wears women's clothes at home. A small-time hustler in Falls City, Nebraska, is raped and then murdered when he's discovered to be physically female. A woman bleeds to death after a Washington, DC, hit-and-run accident when, after finding male genitals under her clothes, paramedics stand by laughing.

M or F? For most of us that's a simple question, decided while we were in utero. Checking off that box—at the doctor's, on the census, on a driver's license—takes scarcely a thought. But there's an emerging movement of increasingly vocal people whose bodies or behavior unsettle that clear division. They're calling themselves "transgendered": It's a spongy neologism that, at its broadest, absorbs everyone from medically reassigned transsexuals to cross-dressing men to women so masculine that security guards are called to eject them from women's restrooms. Fellow travelers include intersexuals (once called hermaphrodites), whose bodies are both/and rather than either/or. The slash between M/F cuts painfully through these lives.

And so they've started to organize. Brought together by the Internet, inspired by the successes of the gay rights movement, and with national sympathy gained from the movie *Boys Don't Cry*, intersex and transgender activists are starting to get a hearing in organizations ranging from college campuses to city councils, from lesbian and gay rights groups to pediatric conferences. And, like the feminist and gay rights movements before them, the new sex-and-gender activists may force us to rethink, in life and in law, how we define and interpret the basics of sex.

A first clue to how zealously the M/F border is guarded—to how sex is literally constructed—comes at birth. One in 2,000 infants is born with genitalia ambiguous enough to make doctors hem and haw when parents ask that first question: boy or girl? Since the late 1950s/early 1960s, standard medical procedure has been to lie and obfuscate. Rather than explain that the child is "a mixture of male and female," writes Anne Fausto-Sterling, author of *Sexing the Body*, medical manuals advise physicians to reassign the child surgically to one sex or another, telling parents only that "the gonads were incompletely developed . . . and therefore required removal." A large clitoris may be cut down; a micropenis may be removed and a vagina built; a testis or testes are sliced out—sometimes over the parents' explicit objections.

5      Now some of those children have come of age and are telling their stories: severe depression, sexual numbness and a long-time despair at having been folded, spindled and mutilated. The leader of this nascent movement is Cheryl Chase, who in 1993 organized the Intersex Society of North America. ISNA opposes reassignment surgery on intersex

infants and advocates raising intersex children as social males or
females, educating them about their bodies and letting them choose at
puberty whether they'd like surgical assistance or a shift in social sex.
ISNA's cause was helped when Johns Hopkins sex researcher and PhD
John Money, who wrote the intersex silence-and-reassignment protocol,
was profoundly discredited. After a child he called "John" was accidentally castrated soon after birth, Money advised his parents to have him
undergo surgery to construct a vagina, raise him as "Joan" and give
him female hormones at puberty. Money reported this involuntary sex
reassignment as fully successful. But in 1997, both a medical journal
report and a *Rolling Stone* article revealed that the reassignment had
been a disaster. Despite the insistence of parents, doctors, psychologists
and teachers, "Joan" had always insisted that she was "just a boy with
long hair in girl's clothes." In adolescence, John took back his manhood.

How did John "know" he was male—and by extension, how do any
of us decide we're girls or boys? One theory is that, in utero, John had
undergone the androgen bath that turns an undifferentiated fetus—
which otherwise becomes female—male, giving him a male identity
and masculine behavior. In the other rare cases where XY infants lose
penises and are raised as girls, some insist on being boys—but others
happily identify as (masculine, lesbian) women, which suggests that
things aren't quite so simple. Scientists recognize that our brains and
nervous systems are somewhat plastic, developing in response to environmental stimuli. Sexuality—all of it, from identity to presentation to
sexual orientation—is no exception; it develops as a biological interaction between inborn capacities and outside influences. As a result, most
of us have a narrow range in which we feel "natural" as we gender
ourselves daily through clothes, stance, stride, tone. For most, that gendered behavior is consonant with biological sex: Girls present as female,
if not feminine, and fall in love with boys; boys present as male or
masculine and fall in love with girls. But those in whom gendered
behavior is vice versa—feminine boys, highly masculine girls—get
treated as unnatural, even though their gendering is just as biological
as the rest of ours. What happens to these transgendered folks can be
so brutal that the pediatric surgeons who cut off infant clitorises or
penises look like merely the advance guard of the M/F border patrol.

Take, for instance, Daphne Scholinski, so masculine that at age 6,
strangers chastised her when she tried to use women's restrooms. In
her dry, pitiless memoir *The Last Time I Wore a Dress*, Scholinski tells the
story of being committed to a mental hospital at 15 for some very real
problems, including severe neglect, her father's violence and her own
delinquency. The hospital ignored her shocking childhood and instead
"treated" her masculinity. Scholinski got demerits if she didn't wear
makeup. She was put on a boys' ward, where she was twice raped, to
encourage her to be more feminine. Her confinement was so disturbing

that she still gets posttraumatic stress flashbacks, including nightmares so terrifying that she wakes up and vomits. And so Scholinski is starting an organization dedicated to reforming the diagnosis of childhood GID, or gender identity disorder, under which she was treated.

Or consider the treatment of Darlene Jespersen and Peter Oiler. After working for Harrah's Reno casino for eighteen years, in the summer of 2000, Jespersen was fired from her bar-tending job when Harrah's launched a new policy requiring all its female employees to wear foundation, powder, eye-liner, lipstick and so on. "I tried it," says Jespersen in a plaintive voice, "but I felt so naked." The obverse happened to Peter Oiler, a weathered, middle-aged man with large aviator glasses, a pleasant drawl and a bit of an overbite. After twenty years of being rotated through progressively more responsible jobs in Winn-Dixie's shipping yards, in 1999 Oiler was driving a fifty-foot truck delivering grocery supplies throughout southeastern Louisiana—until Winn-Dixie learned that he called himself "transgendered." Oiler tried to explain that he simply wore women's clothes on the weekends: He wasn't going to become a woman; he didn't want to wear makeup and heels on company time. In January 2000 Oiler was fired.

Jespersen and Oiler are stunned. Jespersen is suing Harrah's. Says Oiler, "I was raised to believe that if you do an honest day's work, you'll get an honest day's pay." The ACLU Lesbian and Gay Rights Project has taken up his case, in part because of the sheer injustice—and in part to get courts to treat discrimination against people who violate sex stereotypes as illegal sex discrimination. If a woman can wear a dress, or if a man can refuse makeup, why not vice versa? In doing so, the ACLU, like the three national lesbian and gay legal organizations, would be building on the 1989 Supreme Court decision *Price Waterhouse v. Ann Hopkins*. Price Waterhouse had told Hopkins that she wasn't going to make partner because she was too masculine—and, in actual written memos, advised her to wear jewelry and makeup, to go to charm school, to be less aggressive. The Supreme Court declared such stereotyping to be sex discrimination.

10    Will judges see Peter Oiler's dismissal as illegal sex stereotyping? There have been some recent hints that they might. In Massachusetts, for instance, the US Court of Appeals for the First Circuit said Lucas Rosa could sue a bank that instructed feminine Rosa, who had shown up to apply for a loan wearing a dress, to go home and come back in men's clothes; a female, after all, would have been considered for the loan. Another Massachusetts judge said that a male student could come to school in a dress, since female students could. A Washington transsexual prisoner raped by a prison guard, and two New York municipal employees harassed for being gay, were allowed to sue when judges ruled they'd been attacked for violating stereotyped expectations of their sex.

Our society has learned to see why women would want masculine privileges like playing soccer and serving on the Supreme Court, but there's been no matching force expanding the world for males. Boys and men still patrol each other's masculinity with a Glengarry Glen Ross level of ridicule and violence that can seem, to women, nearly surreal. Those males who violate the M-box's limits on behavior are quite literally risking their lives.

Which means that, if you're a performing drag queen, a cross-dressing straight man like Peter Oiler, or a transsexual who still has some male ID, do not under any circumstances get stopped by a cop. In New York City, says Pauline Park, a co-founder of NYAGRA (New York Association for Gender Rights Advocacy), even if the police don't actually beat you, "you could be arrested and detained for days or weeks. They don't let people out until they plead guilty to prostitution. They put them in the men's cell, where they're often assaulted and sometimes raped, as a tactic to get people to plead guilty."

And don't turn to emergency medical personnel. In August 1995 Tyra Hunter's car crashed in Washington, DC. When firefighting para-medics cut away her dress and found male genitals, they laughed and mocked her. She bled to death in the hospital. In August 2000 a jury awarded Hunter's mother $1.75 million in a wrongful-death action. Hunter's experience, unfortunately, is not unusual. Once a month, someone transgendered is murdered, and those are just the docu-mented cases. Transgender activists are beginning to mark November 28, the anniversary of another such death, as a Day of Remembrance, with candlelight vigils and a determination to slow the steady drum-beat of murder.

"We're despised. We're pariahs in this society," says Miranda Stevens-Miller, chair of the transgender rights organization It's Time, Illinois, about transsexuals and otherwise transgendered people. Many transsexuals are fired once they begin to transition. Others lose custody and visitation rights, houses, leases. Many are shut out of office and other public restrooms for years—an indignity that cuts to the very core of being human, since every living body needs to pee. And so the most urgent transgender organizing is happening locally, in organizations such as TGNet Arizona, NYAGRA and It's Time, Oregon. They're teach-ing Trans 101 to local employers, doctors, city councils, lesbian and gay organizations, judges, families, landlords, friends. They're attempting to collect statistics on firings, beatings, murders, bathroom harassment, police abuse. Often these groups are driven by the energy and determi-nation of one or two people who spend their own time and pennies writing and photocopying leaflets, giving workshops for corporate and college groups, and lobbying city councils and lesbian and gay organi-zations for inclusion in hate-crimes and antidiscrimination laws. Lately, they're having remarkable success at adding "gender identity and expression" to the protected categories in local and state employment nondiscrimination and hate-crimes laws; they've won in locales ranging from Portland, Oregon, to DeKalb, Illinois, to the state of Rhode Island.

15        Nationally, trans groups are still in the skirmishing phase faced by any new movement, with the inevitable splits over strategy and personality. The group with the most name recognition, GenderPAC, angers some transgender activists by avoiding the "T" word in its advocacy, saying that it aims at gender freedom for everyone; it acts on behalf of such people as Darlene Jespersen and Peter Oiler, or boys called "faggot" for not being noticeably masculine. Currently the most significant transgender organizations nationally are IFGE (International Foundation for Gender Education), GEA (Gender Education and Advocacy) and the Working Group on Trans Equality, a loose network of grass-roots trans activists aiming at a coordinated national presence. Perhaps the biggest success so far is that all the major lesbian and gay organizations and many smaller ones have added transgendered folks to their mission statements as folks who are equally, if differently, queer.

Or is it so different? All of us deviate from what's expected from our sex. While the relationship between transgender activists and lesbian and gay groups has at times been contentious, some lesbian and gay activists, notably Chai Feldblum, Georgetown law professor, are starting to urge that we all organize around our common deviance from sex stereotypes. The differences between homosexual, transgender and transsexual experiences are not that great: All are natural variations on the brain's gendered development that have cropped up throughout human history, from Tiresias to Radclyffe Hall, from Billy Tipton to Quentin Crisp. For the most part, the mainstream sees us on one sliding scale of queerness. And occasionally our struggles and goals intersect quite neatly. For instance, homos can't always tell whether we're harassed at work because someone figures out that we date others of the same sex, or simply because we're too butch or too fey.

And none of us can rely on having our marriages recognized by the institutions around us when we need them—because marriage is one of the last laws on the books that discriminate based on sex. Recently, Joe Gardiner asked a Kansas court to invalidate his dead father's marriage to transwoman (born male, medically and legally reassigned as female) J'Noel Gardiner, saying J'Noel was "really" a man—and therefore could not have legally married a man. The lower court agreed with the son that XY = man, which meant the son would inherit his father's fat estate. But the Kansas appeals judge remanded the case back down for a new trial. Sex, the appeals court declared, isn't decided simply by a chromosome test. Rather, sex is a complex constellation of characteristics that includes not only chromosomes but also "gonadal sex, internal morphologic sex, external morphologic sex, hormonal sex, phenotypic sex, assigned sex and gender of rearing, and sexual identity." The court approvingly quoted Johns Hopkins researcher and medical doctor William Reiner, who wrote, "The organ that appears to be critical to psychosexual development and adaptation is not the external genitalia, but the brain."

## Responding to Reading

1. How does Graff define the term *transgendered?* What does she mean when she says, "The slash between M/F cuts painfully through these lives" (2)?
2. In paragraph 4, Graff says that the border between male and female is "zealously . . . guarded." What does she mean by this statement? How effectively does her essay support it?
3. Graff says that boys and men "patrol each other's masculinity with a . . . level of ridicule and violence that can seem, to women, nearly surreal" (11). Do you agree with this contention? Do you believe that "males who violate the M-box's limits on behavior are quite literally risking their lives" (11)?

## Responding in Writing

In paragraph 3, Graff says, "like the feminist and gay rights movements before them, the new sex-and-gender activists may force us to rethink, in life and in law, how we define and interpret the basics of sex." Do you agree with this statement? How is the situation of transgendered individuals similar to and different from that of women and gays?

# IS MY MARRIAGE GAY?

## Jennifer Finney Boylan

### 1958–

*A professor of English at Colby College, Jennifer Finney Boylan is a fiction and memoir writer who specializes in gender studies. A contributor to* Condé Nast Traveler, *the* New York Times, *and* Salon, *Boylan is the author of twelve published books and one forthcoming book,* Stuck in the Middle with You *(2013), a memoir about "parenthood in two genders." In the following essay, Boylan explores the complex relationship between gender and marriage.*

As many Americans know, last week Gov. John Baldacci of Maine signed a law that made this state the fifth in the nation to legalize gay marriage. It's worth pointing out, however, that there were some legal same-sex marriages in Maine already, just as there probably are in all

50 states. These are marriages in which at least one member of the couple has changed genders since the wedding.

I'm in such a marriage myself and, quite frankly, my spouse and I forget most of the time that there is anything particularly unique about our family, even if we are—what is the phrase?—"differently married."

Deirdre Finney and I were wed in 1988 at the National Cathedral in Washington. In 2000, I started the long and complex process of changing from male to female. Deedie stood by me, deciding that her life was better with me than without me. Maybe she was crazy for doing so; lots of people have generously offered her this unsolicited opinion over the years. But what she would tell you, were you to ask, is that the things that she loved in me have mostly remained the same, and that our marriage, in the end, is about a lot more than what genders we are, or were.

Deirdre is far from the only spouse to find herself in this situation; each week we hear from wives and husbands going through similar experiences together. Reliable statistics on transgendered people always prove elusive, but just judging from my e-mail, it seems as if there are a whole lot more transsexuals—and people who love them—in New England than say, Republicans. Or Yankees fans.

5    I've been legally female since 2002, although the definition of what makes someone "legally" male or female is part of what makes this issue so unwieldy. How do we define legal gender? By chromosomes? By genitalia? By spirit? By whether one asks directions when lost?

We accept as a basic truth the idea that everyone has the right to marry somebody. Just as fundamental is the belief that no couple should be divorced against their will.

For our part, Deirdre and I remain legally married, even though we're both legally female. If we had divorced last month, before Governor Baldacci's signature, I would have been allowed on the following day to marry a man only. There are states, however, that do not recognize sex changes. If I were to attempt to remarry in Ohio, for instance, I would be allowed to wed a woman only.

Gender involves a lot of gray area. And efforts to legislate a binary truth upon the wide spectrum of gender have proven only how elusive sexual identity can be. The case of J'noel Gardiner, in Kansas, provides a telling example. Ms. Gardiner, a postoperative transsexual woman, married her husband, Marshall Gardiner, in 1998. When he died in 1999, she was denied her half of his $2.5 million estate by the Kansas Supreme Court on the ground that her marriage was invalid. Thus in Kansas, any transgendered person who is anatomically female is now allowed to marry only another woman.

Similar rulings have left couples in similar situations in Florida, Ohio and Texas. A 1999 ruling in San Antonio, in *Littleton v. Prange*, determined that marriage could be only between people with different chromosomes. The result, of course, was that lesbian couples in that jurisdiction were then allowed to wed as long as one member of the couple had a Y chromosome, which is the case with both transgendered male-to-females and people born with conditions like androgen insensitivity syndrome. This ruling made Texas, paradoxically, one of the first states in which gay marriage was legal.

A lawyer for the transgendered plaintiff in the Littleton case noted 10 the absurdity of the country's gender laws as they pertain to marriage: "Taking this situation to its logical conclusion, Mrs. Littleton, while in San Antonio, Tex., is a male and has a void marriage; as she travels to Houston, Tex., and enters federal property, she is female and a widow; upon traveling to Kentucky she is female and a widow; but, upon entering Ohio, she is once again male and prohibited from marriage; entering Connecticut, she is again female and may marry; if her travel takes her north to Vermont, she is male and may marry a female; if instead she travels south to New Jersey, she may marry a male."

Legal scholars can (and have) devoted themselves to the ultimately frustrating task of defining "male" and "female" as entities fixed and unmoving. A better use of their time, however, might be to focus on accepting the elusiveness of gender—and to celebrate it. Whether a marriage like mine is a same-sex marriage or some other kind is hardly the point. What matters is that my spouse and I love each other, and that our legal union has been a good thing—for us, for our children and for our community.

It's my hope that people who are reluctant to embrace same-sex marriage will see that it has been with us, albeit in this one unusual circumstance, for years. Can we have a future in which we are more concerned with the love a family has than with the sometimes unanswerable questions of gender and identity? As of last week, it no longer seems so unthinkable. As we say in Maine, you can get there from here.

## Responding to Reading

1. What does Boylan mean by the term "differently married" (2)? Do you agree with her that her marriage is about a lot more than gender?
2. In paragraph 4, Boylan says her emails suggest that there are a lot more transsexuals in New England than Republicans or Yankee fans. What point is she trying to make?
3. In the body of her essay, Boylan spends a great deal of time challenging traditional definitions of male and female as well as traditional definitions of marriage. Why? Is this an effective strategy?

## Responding in Writing

In paragraph 11, Boylan says whether a marriage like hers is "a same-sex marriage or some other kind" doesn't matter. What matters most is that she and her partner love each other and that the union is good for their family and their community. Do you agree?

# Who You Callin' a Lady?

## Kathleen Deveny

*The deputy editor and global business editor at* Newsweek, *Kathleen Deveny manages the magazine's coverage of issues pertaining to business, economics, and technology. She also explores family and parenting topics in the* News-week *column "Modern Family." In the following essay, Deveny takes a critical look at gender expectations in the United States.*

Everybody loves a catfight. So it was no surprise that the recent video of a University of New Mexico soccer player yanking a rival to the ground by her ponytail went viral. I, for one, watched Elizabeth Lambert, 20, throwing punches and pulling hair several times.

What was surprising was that the incident sparked a sanctimonious debate on women and sportsmanship. What Lambert did was wrong. Her team suspended her—indefinitely. Lambert quickly apologized to practically everyone in New Mexico—and last week told the *New York Times*: "I have so much regret. I can't believe I did that." But by then my media colleagues had already worked themselves into a frenzy. The *Today* show, among others, tsk-tsked at Lambert's shameful behavior. In the U.K., where they know something about red cards, Sky TV called her the "dirtiest ever" female soccer player.

If it had been two men in a Division 1 college game, I doubt we would have gotten so exercised. When Oregon running back LeGarrette Blount punched an opposing player in the face earlier this season, his video also made the rounds. But while Blount was initially suspended for the season, he has already been reinstated. Even Michael Vick is playing football again—and he killed puppies!

The difference is that we expect bad behavior from men—on the field and off. (In some ways, men justify our low opinion of them: they are 10 times more likely to murder, according to the Bureau of Justice Statistics.) But we expect better from women. We didn't fight this hard to be involved in organized sports just so we could act like a bunch of dumb jocks, right? We want women to be honest, compassionate, and nice—you know, like our moms.

5    So what's the harm in expecting the fairer sex to play fairer? It's what George W. Bush might call the soft bigotry of high expectations. If we insist on holding women and girls to higher standards than men, we set them up to disappoint us. It makes me worry about my 9-year-old daughter, and not because I hope she will someday pull hair with the best of them. I think she is sometimes held to stricter behavior standards than her boys-will-be-boys classmates. Those higher expectations follow us onto the job, where women are allegedly not only better behaved and more honest but cheaper—you only have to pay us 80 cents on the dollar! So why aren't we represented at the highest

levels of business? One problem is that women aren't supposed to be aggressive or self-promoting—that's nasty male behavior—even though it's often rewarded. And yet if professional women are too nice and cuddly, they don't seem decisive or tough enough to be leaders. "The 'women are wonderful' effect does have a terrible downside," says Alice H. Eagly, a psychology professor and coauthor of *Through the Labyrinth: The Truth About How Women Become Leaders*. "If you're too nice, you're seen as not really appropriate for high-level positions."

Our more virtuous status certainly hasn't been translated into success in politics. Women make up only 17 percent of the members of the House of Representatives and the Senate; the White House has remained out of reach. When it comes to being honest, intelligent, and hardworking—traits voters value in elected officials—the public rates women as superior to men, according to a 2008 survey by the Pew Research Center. Yet only 6 percent of those queried say women make better political leaders.

We may have only ourselves to blame for our supposed moral superiority. During the 19th century, American women were judged by themselves (and their husbands) largely by four cardinal virtues: piety, purity, submissiveness, and domesticity. Called the Cult of True Womanhood, the code held that a woman's "proper sphere" was the home. But suffragists themselves later used women's supposed piety and purity to bolster their case for voting rights, reasoning that women would make morally superior choices. Even today some advocates argue that companies should promote women because they will help make organizations more ethical, transparent, and family friendly.

I'd like to think that when women are finally sufficiently represented in the executive suite and on the field, we will stop viewing them as proxies for their entire gender—superior or not. What I hope for my daughter, and for Elizabeth Lambert, is that we will be able to see them as individuals, flaws and all.

## Responding to Reading

1. Watch a *YouTube* video of Elizabeth Lambert's fight. Does Deveny describe it accurately? Do you agree that if the fight had been between two men, people would have reacted differently? Explain.
2. In paragraph 4, Deveny says, "We want women to be honest, compassionate, and nice—you know, like our moms." Do you think this is true? Do you agree that we expect "the fairer sex to play fairer" (5) and "expect bad behavior from men'"(4)? Is this an example of "the soft bigotry of high expectations" (5)?
3. In paragraph 7, Deveny says that women may have only themselves to blame for their "supposed moral superiority." What does she mean? Do you agree?

## Responding in Writing

How does Deveny characterize men in her essay? Do you think this characterization is accurate? Fair?

# DON'T QUIT THIS DAY JOB

## Karen S. Sibert

*A New York Times op-ed contributor, Karen S. Sibert is a Los Angeles–based anesthesiologist. She also writes for the California Society of Anesthesiologists and has appeared on the NPR show On Point with Tom Ashbrook. The following essay, which examines cultural expectations for female doctors, sparked intense debate when it was published in 2011.*

I'm a doctor and a mother of four, and I've always practiced medicine full time. When I took my board exams in 1987, female doctors were still uncommon, and we were determined to work as hard as any of the men.

Today, however, increasing numbers of doctors—mostly women—decide to work part time or leave the profession. Since 2005 the part-time physician workforce has expanded by 62 percent, according to recent survey data from the American Medical Group Association, with nearly 4 in 10 female doctors between the ages of 35 and 44 reporting in 2010 that they worked part time.

This may seem like a personal decision, but it has serious consequences for patients and the public.

Medical education is supported by federal and state tax money both at the university level—student tuition doesn't come close to covering the schools' costs—and at the teaching hospitals where residents are trained. So if doctors aren't making full use of their training, taxpayers are losing their investment. With a growing shortage of doctors in America, we can no longer afford to continue training doctors who don't spend their careers in the full-time practice of medicine.

5        It isn't fashionable (and certainly isn't politically correct) to criticize "work–life balance" or part-time employment options. How can anyone deny people the right to change their minds about a career path and choose to spend more time with their families? I have great respect for stay-at-home parents, and I think it's fine if journalists or chefs or lawyers choose to work part time or quit their jobs altogether. But it's different for doctors. Someone needs to take care of the patients.

The Association of American Medical Colleges estimates that, 15 years from now, with the ranks of insured patients expanding, we will face a shortage of up to 150,000 doctors. As many doctors near retirement and aging baby boomers need more and more medical care, the shortage gets worse each year.

The decline in doctors' pay is part of the problem. As we look at Medicare and Medicaid spending cuts, we need to be careful not to drive the best of the next generation away from medicine and into, say, investment banking.

But the productivity of the doctors currently practicing is also an important factor. About 30 percent of doctors in the United States are female, and women received 48 percent of the medical degrees awarded in 2010. But their productivity doesn't match that of men. In a 2006 survey by the American Medical Association and the Association of American Medical Colleges, even full-time female doctors reported working on average 4.5 fewer hours each week and seeing fewer patients than their male colleagues. The American Academy of Pediatrics estimates that 71 percent of female pediatricians take extended leave at some point—five times higher than the percentage for male pediatricians.

This gap is especially problematic because women are more likely to go into primary care fields—where the doctor shortage is most pronounced—than men are. Today 53 percent of family practice residents, 63 percent of pediatric residents and nearly 80 percent of obstetrics and gynecology residents are female. In the low-income areas that lack primary and prenatal care, there are more emergency room visits, more preventable hospitalizations and more patients who die of treatable conditions. Foreign doctors emigrate to the United States to help fill these positions, but this drains their native countries of desperately needed medical care.

If medical training were available in infinite supply, it wouldn't 10 matter how many doctors worked part time or quit, because there would always be new graduates to fill their spots. But medical schools can only afford to accept a fraction of the students who apply.

An even tighter bottleneck exists at the level of residency training. Residents don't pay tuition; they are paid to work at teaching hospitals. Their salaries are supported by Medicare, which pays teaching hospitals about $9 billion a year for resident salaries and teaching costs as well as patient care.

In 1997, Congress imposed a cap on how many medical residencies the government could subsidize as part of the Balanced Budget Act. Last year, the Senate failed to pass an amendment to the health care bill that would have created thousands of new residency positions. Even if American medical schools could double their graduating classes, there wouldn't be additional residency positions for the new doctors. Federal and state financing to expand medical education will be hard to find in today's economic and political climate.

We often hear the argument that nurse practitioners, nurse anesthetists and physician assistants can stand in for doctors and provide cheaper care. But when critical decisions must be made, patients want a fully qualified doctor to lead the health care team.

Policy makers could encourage more doctors to stay in the profession by reforming the malpractice system to protect them from frivolous lawsuits, safeguarding their pay from further Medicare cuts and lightening the burden of bureaucratic regulations and paperwork. And in a perfect world, hospitals and clinics could keep more female doctors working full time by setting up child care centers—with long operating hours—on site.

15      In the meantime, we can only depend on doctors' own commitment to the profession.

Students who aspire to go to medical school should think about the consequences if they decide to work part time or leave clinical medicine. It's fair to ask them—women especially—to consider the conflicting demands that medicine and parenthood make before they accept (and deny to others) sought-after positions in medical school and residency. They must understand that medical education is a privilege, not an entitlement, and it confers a real moral obligation to serve.

I recently spoke with a college student who asked me if anesthesiology is a good field for women. She didn't want to hear that my days are unpredictable because serious operations can take a long time and emergency surgery often needs to be done at night. What she really wanted to know was if my working life was consistent with her rosy vision of limited work hours and raising children. I doubt that she welcomed my parting advice: If you want to be a doctor, be a doctor.

You can't have it all. I never took cupcakes to my children's homerooms or drove carpool, but I read a lot of bedtime stories and made it to soccer games and school plays. I've ridden roller coasters with my son, danced at my oldest daughter's wedding and rocked my first grandson to sleep. Along the way, I've worked full days and many nights, and brought a lot of very sick patients through long, difficult operations.

Patients need doctors to take care of them. Medicine shouldn't be a part-time interest to be set aside if it becomes inconvenient; it deserves to be a life's work.

## Responding to Reading

1.  Why does Sibert begin her essay by telling readers that she is both a doctor and a mother of four? What would she have gained or lost by omitting either—or both—of these two pieces of information?
2.  The number of female doctors is rising each year, but many work only part-time. According to Sibert, what problems does this cause? What solution does she propose?
3.  In paragraph 17, Sibert tells a female college student, "If you want to be a doctor, be a doctor." What does she mean?

## Responding in Writing

Do you think Sibert is giving good advice to aspiring female doctors, or do you think she is being unrealistic, unsympathetic, or unfair? Explain.

# WHY I WANT A WIFE

## Judy Brady

### 1937–

*Judy Brady studied art before getting married, having a family, and starting her writing career. A breast cancer survivor, Brady cofounded the Toxic Links Coalition, an environmental advocacy group based in California. She has edited two books about cancer, including* Women and Cancer *(1980) and a collection of essays and poems written by women with cancer* One in Three: Women with Cancer Confront an Epidemic *(1991). The following essay, "Why I Want a Wife," appeared in the first issue of* Ms. *magazine in 1972. In this essay, Brady takes a satirical look at what it means to be a wife and mother.*

I belong to that classification of people known as wives. I am A Wife. And, not altogether incidentally, I am a mother.

Not too long ago a male friend of mine appeared on the scene fresh from a recent divorce. He had one child, who is, of course, with his ex-wife. He is looking for another wife. As I thought about him while I was ironing one evening, it suddenly occurred to me that I, too, would like to have a wife. Why do I want a wife?

I would like to go back to school so that I can become economically independent, support myself, and, if need be, support those dependent upon me. I want a wife who will work and send me to school. And while I am going to school I want a wife to take care of my children. I want a wife to keep track of the children's doctor and dentist appointments. And to keep track of mine, too. I want a wife to make sure my children eat properly and are kept clean. I want a wife who will wash the children's clothes and keep them mended. I want a wife who is a good nurturant attendant to my children, who arranges for their schooling, makes sure that they have an adequate social life with their peers, takes them to the park, the zoo, etc. I want a wife who takes care of the children when they are sick, a wife who arranges to be around when the children need special care, because, of course, I cannot miss classes at school. My wife must arrange to lose time at work and not lose the job. It may mean a small cut in my wife's income from time to time, but I guess I can tolerate that. Needless to say, my wife will arrange and pay for the care of the children while my wife is working.

I want a wife who will take care of *my* physical needs. I want a wife who will keep my house clean. A wife who will pick up after me. I want a wife who will keep my clothes clean, ironed, mended, replaced when need be, and who will see to it that my personal things are kept in their proper place so that I can find what I need the minute I need it. I want a wife who cooks the meals, a wife who is a *good* cook. I want a wife who will plan the menus, do the necessary grocery shopping, prepare the meals, serve them pleasantly, and then do the cleaning up while I do my studying. I want a wife who will care for me when I am sick and sympathize with my pain and loss of time from school. I want a wife to go along when our family takes a vacation so that someone can continue to care for me and my children when I need a rest and change of scene.

5　　　I want a wife who will not bother me with rambling complaints about a wife's duties. But I want a wife who will listen to me when I feel the need to explain a rather difficult point I have come across in my course of studies. And I want a wife who will type my papers for me when I have written them.

I want a wife who will take care of the details of my social life. When my wife and I are invited out by friends, I want a wife who will take care of the babysitting arrangements. When I meet people at school that I like and want to entertain, I want a wife who will have the house clean, will prepare a special meal, serve it to me and my friends, and not interrupt when I talk about the things that interest me and my friends. I want a wife who will have arranged that the children are fed and ready for bed before my guests arrive so that the children do not bother us. I want a wife who takes care of the needs of my guests so that they feel comfortable, who makes sure that they have an ashtray, that they are passed the hors d'oeuvres, that they are offered a second helping of the food, that their wine glasses are replenished when necessary, that their coffee is served to them as they like it. And I want a wife who knows that sometimes I need a night out by myself.

I want a wife who is sensitive to my sexual needs, a wife who makes love passionately and eagerly when I feel like it, a wife who makes sure that I am satisfied. And, of course, I want a wife who will not demand sexual attention when I am not in the mood for it. I want a wife who assumes the complete responsibility for birth control, because I do not want more children. I want a wife who will remain sexually faithful to me so that I do not have to clutter up my intellectual life with jealousies. And I want a wife who understands that *my* sexual needs may entail more than strict adherence to monogamy. I must, after all, be able to relate to people as fully as possible.

If, by chance, I find another person more suitable as a wife than the wife I already have, I want the liberty to replace my present wife with another one. Naturally, I will expect a fresh, new life; my wife will take the children and be solely responsible for them so that I am left free.

When I am through with school and have a job, I want my wife to quit working and remain at home so that my wife can more fully and completely take care of a wife's duties.

10　　My God, who *wouldn't* want a wife?

## Responding to Reading

1. Why does Brady begin her essay by saying that she is both a wife and a mother? How does her encounter with a male friend lead her to decide that she would like to have a wife?
2. This essay, written more than thirty years ago, has been anthologized many times. To what do you attribute its continued popularity? In what ways, if any, is the essay dated? In what ways is it still relevant?
3. Brady wrote her essay to address a stereotype and a set of social conventions that she thought were harmful to women. Could you make the case that Brady's characterization of a "wife" is harmful both to women and to feminism?

## Responding in Writing

What is your definition of a wife? How is it different from (or similar to) Brady's?

# STAY-AT-HOME DADS

## Glenn Sacks

### 1964–

*The executive director of the nonprofit organization Fathers and Families, Glenn Sacks is a columnist who writes about men's and fathers' issues. His columns have appeared in the* Chicago Tribune, *the* Los Angeles Times, Newsday, *the* Philadelphia Inquirer, Insight Magazine, *and other publications. Before embarking on a career as a columnist and radio and TV personality, Sacks taught high school, elementary school, and adult education courses in Los Angeles and Miami. In the following essay, Sacks discusses the difficulties men (as well as their wives) face if they want to devote themselves to childrearing and housework.*

The subtext to the wave of concern over the recently announced epidemic of childlessness in successful career women is that women can't have it all after all—and it's men's fault. Why? Because men interfere with their wives' career aspirations by their refusal to become their children's primary caregivers, forcing women to sidetrack their careers if they want children.

Despite the criticism, men generally focus on their careers not out of selfishness but because most women still expect men to be their family's primary breadwinners. For women willing to shoulder this burden themselves, replacing the two-earner couple with a female breadwinner and a stay-at-home dad (SAHD) can be an attractive option. I became a SAHD with the birth of my daughter four years ago, and the arrangement has benefited my family immensely.

My wife and I sometimes remark that if we had met in the era before women had real career opportunities, we'd both be pretty unhappy. As a lone breadwinner I would feel deprived of time with my children. My wife, an ambitious woman who loves her career, would feel stifled as a stay-at-home mom. Since each of us would want to be doing what the other is doing, we would probably resent each other. Instead, the freedom to switch gender roles has allowed each of us to gravitate towards what we really want in life.

Men need not fear a loss of power when they become a SAHD. While SAHDs are sometimes stereotyped as being at the mercy of their stronger wives' commands, in reality, I have more power in the family now than I ever did when I was the family breadwinner. The most important issue in any marriage is deciding how to raise the children. While my wife is an equal partner in any major decision regarding the children, I supervise the children on a day to day basis and I make sure that things are done the way I want them done.

5    Women also benefit from SAHDs because, with reduced familial responsibilities, they can compete on a level playing field with career-oriented men. For men, it is an opportunity to witness the countless magical, irreplaceable moments of a young child's life, and to enjoy some of the subtle pleasures our fathers never knew, like making dinner with a three-year-old's "help," or putting the baby down for a midday nap in a hammock.

Still, there are adjustments that both men and women will need to make. Women will need to discard the popular yet misguided notion that men "have it all," and understand that being the breadwinner comes with disadvantages as well as advantages.

One disadvantage can be the loss of their primary status with their young children. Mom is #1 not because of biology or God's law but because mom is the one who does most of the child care. This can change when dad becomes the primary caregiver. When my young daughter has a nightmare and cries at 2 AM, my wife is relieved that she's not the one who has to get up and comfort her. The price that my wife has had to accept is that her child insists on being comforted not by her but by "yaddy."

Another disadvantage is that taking on the main breadwinner role reduces a woman's ability to cut back her work schedule or look for a more rewarding job if her career disappoints her. This is one of the reasons many women prefer life as a frazzled two-earner couple— keeping the man on career track as the main breadwinner helps to preserve women's options.

Men will also have to make adjustments. For one, they will have to endure the unconscious hypocrisy of a society which often wrings its hands over the lot of the housewife yet at the same time views SAHDs as freeloaders who have left their working wives holding the bag.

SAHDs also have to contend with the societal perception that being 10 a househusband is unmanly. The idea is so pervasive that even I still tend to think "wimp" when I first hear about a SAHD.

Working women sometimes complain that men in the workplace don't take them as seriously as they take men. As a SAHD I have the same complaint. For example, last year I attended a school meeting with my wife, my son's elementary school teacher, and some school officials, most of whom knew that I drove my son to and from school, met with his teachers, and did his spelling words with him every day. Yet the woman who chaired the meeting introduced herself to my wife, began the meeting, and then, only as an afterthought, looked at me and said "and who might you be?"

In addition, while many stay-at-home parents face boredom and social isolation, it can be particularly acute for SAHDs, since there are few other men at home, and connections with stay-at-home moms can be difficult to cultivate.

None of these hurdles are insurmountable, and they pale in comparison to the benefits children derive from having a parent as a primary caregiver—particularly a parent grateful for the once-in-a-lifetime opportunity that he never knew he wanted, and never thought he would have.

## Responding to Reading

1. According to Sacks, what is the "subtext to the wave of concern over the recently announced epidemic of childlessness in successful career women" (1)? Why does he think most men concentrate on their careers? What does he think is a good alternative to this situation?
2. What are the advantages of being a stay-at-home dad? What does Sacks see as the disadvantages? How practical do you think his solution is?
3. Could you make the argument that Sacks and his wife are simply switching traditional male/female roles? Are there any other models for work and childcare that Sacks and his wife could consider? Do any of these seem preferable to the one they currently follow?

## Responding in Writing

Would you want your husband to be (or would you want to be) a stay-at-home dad? Why or why not?

# MARKED WOMEN

## Deborah Tannen

### 1945–

*Deborah Tannen, a professor of linguistics at Georgetown University, has written books for both scholarly and popular audiences, with most of her work focusing on communication between men and women. Tannen is best known for her bestseller* You Just Don't Understand: Women and Men in Conversation *(1990); her most recent book is* You Were Always Mom's Favorite!: Sisters in Conversation throughout Their Lives *(2009). The following essay, written in 1993, is a departure from Tannen's usual work. Here she focuses not on different communication styles but on the contrast she finds between the neutral way men in our culture present themselves to the world and the more message-laden way women present themselves.*

Some years ago I was at a small working conference of four women and eight men. Instead of concentrating on the discussion I found myself looking at the three other women at the table, thinking how each had a different style and how each style was coherent.

One woman had dark brown hair in a classic style, a cross between Cleopatra and Plain Jane. The severity of her straight hair was softened by wavy bangs and ends that turned under. Because she was beautiful, the effect was more Cleopatra than plain.

The second woman was older, full of dignity and composure. Her hair was cut in a fashionable style that left her with only one eye, thanks to a side part that let a curtain of hair fall across half her face. As she looked down to read her prepared paper, the hair robbed her of bifocal vision and created a barrier between her and the listeners.

The third woman's hair was wild, a frosted blond avalanche falling over and beyond her shoulders. When she spoke she frequently tossed her head, calling attention to her hair and away from her lecture.

5    Then there was makeup. The first woman wore facial cover that made her skin smooth and pale, a black line under each eye and mascara that darkened already dark lashes. The second wore only a light gloss on her lips and a hint of shadow on her eyes. The third had blue bands under her eyes, dark blue shadow, mascara, bright red lipstick and rouge; her fingernails flashed red.

I considered the clothes each woman had worn during the three days of the conference: In the first case, man-tailored suits in primary colors with solid-color blouses. In the second, casual but stylish black T-shirts, a floppy collarless jacket and baggy slacks or a skirt in neutral colors. The third wore a sexy jump suit; tight sleeveless jersey and tight yellow slacks; a dress with gaping armholes and an indulged tendency to fall off one shoulder.

Shoes? No. 1 wore string sandals with medium heels; No. 2, sensible, comfortable walking shoes; No. 3, pumps with spike heels. You can fill in the jewelry, scarves, shawls, sweaters—or lack of them.

As I amused myself finding coherence in these styles, I suddenly wondered why I was scrutinizing only the women. I scanned the eight men at the table. And then I knew why I wasn't studying them. The men's styles were unmarked.

The term "marked" is a staple of linguistic theory. It refers to the way language alters the base meaning of a word by adding a linguistic particle that has no meaning on its own. The unmarked form of a word carries the meaning that goes without saying—what you think of when you're not thinking anything special.

The unmarked tense of verbs in English is the present—for example, *visit*. To indicate past, you mark the verb by adding *ed* to yield *visited*. For future, you add a word: *will visit*. Nouns are presumed to be singular until marked for plural, typically by adding *s* or *es*, so *visit* becomes *visits* and *dish* becomes *dishes*.    10

The unmarked forms of most English words also convey "male." Being male is the unmarked case. Endings like *ess* and *ette* mark words as "female." Unfortunately, they also tend to mark them for frivolousness. Would you feel safe entrusting your life to a doctorette? Alfre Woodard, who was an Oscar nominee for best supporting actress, says she identifies herself as an actor because "actresses worry about eyelashes and cellulite, and women who are actors worry about the characters we are playing." Gender markers pick up extra meanings that reflect common associations with the female gender: not quite serious, often sexual.

Each of the women at the conference had to make decisions about hair, clothing, makeup and accessories, and each decision carried meaning. Every style available to us was marked. The men in our group had made decisions, too, but the range from which they chose was incomparably narrower. Men can choose styles that are marked, but they don't have to, and in this group none did. Unlike the women, they had the option of being unmarked.

Take the men's hair styles. There was no marine crew cut or oily longish hair falling into eyes, no asymmetrical, two-tiered construction to swirl over a bald top. One man was unabashedly bald; the others had hair of standard length, parted on one side, in natural shades of brown or gray or graying. Their hair obstructed no views, left little to toss or push back or run fingers through and, consequently, needed and attracted no attention. A few men had beards. In a business setting, beards might be marked. In this academic gathering, they weren't.

There could have been a cowboy shirt with string tie or a three-piece suit or a necklaced hippie in jeans. But there wasn't. All eight men wore brown or blue slacks and nondescript shirts of light colors. No man wore sandals or boots; their shoes were dark, closed, comfortable and flat. In short, unmarked.

15    Although no man wore makeup, you couldn't say the men didn't wear makeup in the sense that you could say a woman didn't wear makeup. For men, no makeup is unmarked.

I asked myself what style we women could have adopted that would have been unmarked, like the men's. The answer was none. There is no unmarked woman.

There is no woman's hair style that can be called standard, that says nothing about her. The range of women's hair styles is staggering, but a woman whose hair has no particular style is perceived as not caring about how she looks, which can disqualify her for many positions, and will subtly diminish her as a person in the eyes of some.

Women must choose between attractive shoes and comfortable shoes. When our group made an unexpected trek, the woman who wore flat, laced shoes arrived first. Last to arrive was the woman in spike heels, shoes in hand and a handful of men around her.

If a woman's clothing is tight or revealing (in other words, sexy), it sends a message—an intended one of wanting to be attractive, but also a possibly unintended one of availability. If her clothes are not sexy, that too sends a message, lent meaning by the knowledge that they could have been. There are thousands of cosmetic products from which women can choose and myriad ways of applying them. Yet no makeup at all is anything but unmarked. Some men see it as a hostile refusal to please them.

20    Women can't even fill out a form without telling stories about themselves. Most forms give four titles to choose from. "Mr." carries no meaning other than that the respondent is male. But a woman who checks "Mrs." or "Miss" communicates not only whether she has been married but also whether she has conservative tastes in forms of address—and probably other conservative values as well. Checking "Ms." declines to let on about marriage (checking "Mr." declines nothing since nothing was asked), but it also marks her as either liberated or rebellious, depending on the observer's attitudes and assumptions.

I sometimes try to duck these variously marked choices by giving my title as "Dr."—and in so doing risk marking myself as either uppity (hence sarcastic responses like *Excuse me!*") or an overachiever (hence reactions of congratulatory surprise like "Good for you!").

All married women's surnames are marked. If a woman takes her husband's name, she announces to the world that she is married and has traditional values. To some it will indicate that she is less herself, more identified by her husband's identity. If she does not take her husband's name, this too is marked, seen as worthy of comment: she has done something; she has "kept her own name." A man is never said to have "kept his own name" because it never occurs to anyone that he might have given it up. For him using his own name is unmarked.

A married woman who wants to have her cake and eat it too may use her surname plus his, with or without a hyphen. But this too announces her marital status and often results in a tongue-tying string. In a list (Harvey O'Donovan, Jonathan Feldman, Stephanie Woodbury McGillicutty), the woman's multiple name stands out. It is marked.

I have never been inclined toward biological explanations of gender differences in language, but I was intrigued to see Ralph Fasold bring biological phenomena to bear on the question of linguistic marking in his book *The Sociolinguistics of Language.* Fasold stresses that language and culture are particularly unfair in treating women as the marked case because biologically it is the male that is marked. While two X chromosomes make a female, two Y chromosomes make nothing. Like the linguistic markers *s, es* or *ess*, the Y chromosome doesn't "mean" anything unless it is attached to a root form—an X chromosome.

Developing this idea elsewhere, Fasold points out that girls are 25 born with fully female bodies, while boys are born with modified female bodies. He invites men who doubt this to lift up their shirts and contemplate why they have nipples.

In his book, Fasold notes "a wide range of facts which demonstrates that female is the unmarked sex." For example, he observes that there are a few species that produce only females, like the whiptail lizard. Thanks to parthenogenesis, they have no trouble having as many daughters as they like. There are no species, however, that produce only males. This is no surprise, since any such species would become extinct in its first generation.

Fasold is also intrigued by species that produce individuals not involved in reproduction, like honeybees and leaf-cutter ants. Reproduction is handled by the queen and a relatively few males; the workers are sterile females. "Since they do not reproduce," Fasold says, "there is no reason for them to be one sex or the other, so they default, so to speak, to female."

Fasold ends his discussion of these matters by pointing out that if language reflected biology, grammar books would direct us to use "she" to include males and females and "he" only for specifically male referents. But they don't. They tell us that "he" means "he or she," and that "she" is used only if the referent is specifically female. This use of "he" as the sex-indefinite pronoun is an innovation introduced into English by grammarians in the 18th and 19th centuries, according to Peter Mühlhäusler and Rom Harré in *Pronouns and People.* From at least about 1500, the correct sex-indefinite pronoun was "they," as it still is in casual spoken English. In other words, the female was declared by grammarians to be the marked case.

Writing this article may mark me not as a writer, not as a linguist, not as an analyst of human behavior, but as a feminist—which will have positive or negative, but in any case powerful, connotations for readers. Yet I doubt that anyone reading Ralph Fasold's book would put that label on him.

30    I discovered the markedness inherent in the very topic of gender after writing a book on differences in conversational style based on geographical region, ethnicity, class, age and gender. When I was interviewed, the vast majority of journalists wanted to talk about the differences between women and men. While I thought I was simply describing what I observed—something I had learned to do as a researcher—merely mentioning women and men marked me as a feminist for some.

When I wrote a book devoted to gender differences, in ways of speaking, I sent the manuscript to five male colleagues, asking them to alert me to any interpretation, phrasing or wording that might seem unfairly negative toward men. Even so, when the book came out, I encountered responses like that of the television talk show host who, after interviewing me, turned to the audience and asked if they thought I was male-bashing.

Leaping upon a poor fellow who affably nodded in agreement, she made him stand and asked, "Did what she said accurately describe you?" "Oh, yes," he answered. "That's me exactly." "And what she said about women—does that sound like your wife?" "Oh yes," he responded. "That's her exactly." "Then why do you think she's male-bashing?" He answered, with disarming honesty, "Because she's a woman and she's saying things about men."

To say anything about women and men without marking oneself as either feminist or anti-feminist, male-basher or apologist for men seems as impossible for a woman as trying to get dressed in the morning without inviting interpretations of her character.

Sitting at the conference table musing on these matters, I felt sad to think that we women didn't have the freedom to be unmarked that the men sitting next to us had. Some days you just want to get dressed and go about your business. But if you're a woman, you can't, because there is no unmarked woman.

## Responding to Reading

1.  Tannen notes that men "can choose styles that are marked, but they don't have to" (12); however, she believes that women do not have "the option of being unmarked" (12). What does she mean? Can you give some examples of women's styles that you believe are unmarked? (Note that in paragraph 16, Tannen says there are no such styles.)

2.  In paragraph 33, Tannen says, "To say anything about women and men without marking oneself as either feminist or anti-feminist, male-basher or apologist for men seems as impossible for a woman as trying to get dressed in the morning without inviting interpretations of her character." Do you agree?

3.  In paragraphs 24–28, Tannen discusses Ralph Fasold's book *The Sociolinguistics of Language.* Why does she include this material? Could she have made her point just as effectively without it?

## Responding in Writing

Consider the men and women you see every day at school or in your neighborhood. Does their appearance support Tannen's thesis?

---
## FOCUS
---

### Who Has It Harder, Girls or Boys?

Researcher working in lab

### Responding to the Image

1. What is your reaction to this image? Do you think it reinforces or defies conventional gender stereotypes? Explain.
2. Suppose you were going to use this image in an ad encouraging young women to pursue careers in science. Write two or three lines of text that you could use in your ad. How do the text and the image work together to reinforce your message?

# WHAT IS THE TRIPLE BIND?

## Stephen Hinshaw

### 1952–

*Stephen Hinshaw is a professor of psychology at the University of California at Berkeley. He researches behavior disorders in children and attention-deficit/ hyperactivity disorder (ADHD), among other topics related to child psychology. His books include* The Mark of Shame: Stigma of Mental Illness and an Agenda for Change *(2007)*, Breaking the Silence: Mental Health Professionals Disclose Their Personal and Family Experiences of Mental Illness *(2008), and* Child and Adolescent Psychopathology *(2008). The following essay is excerpted from Hinshaw's most recent book,* The Triple Bind: Saving Our Teenage Girls from Today's Pressures *(2009).*

The original notion of a double bind came from social scientists in the 1950s who studied children growing up with contradictory, impossible demands. For example, a child might be told, "Tell me everything that's going on with you," and then told (either with or without words), "Don't bother me with so much information." Trying ever more frantically to do the impossible, the double-bind child was thought to be at risk of mental illness.

Of course, mental illness has more complex origins than this picture indicates, nearly always including biological and genetic underpinnings. And the types of family messages most associated with serious disorders aren't necessarily those of the double bind. But even if double-bind-style messages don't produce clinical conditions, they certainly produce distress. When we're asked to do two contradictory things, and especially when we fear being punished for not doing them, we're in a bind: confused, frustrated, and likely to blame ourselves. Our feelings might turn into anger, despair, resignation, or an ever more desperate attempt to go in two directions at once.

Today's girl faces not only a double but actually a Triple Bind: a set of impossible, contradictory expectations. Our teenage girls are baffled, distressed, and overwhelmed as they try ever harder to meet these ever more punishing demands. They've responded with a lower age of onset of depression, increases in aggression and violence, and skyrocketing rates of self-mutilation, binge eating, and suicide. They've also responded by sacrificing key portions of their identities, developing feelings of self-hatred, and becoming overwhelmed with a general sense of pressured confusion. The Triple Bind is possibly the greatest current threat to our daughters' health and well-being, an enormous obstacle to their becoming healthy, happy, and successful adults.

Each portion of the Triple Bind is challenging enough. But it's the combination of all three aspects that makes it deadly:

1. Be good at all of the traditional girl stuff.
2. Be good at most of the traditional guy stuff.
3. Conform to a narrow, unrealistic set of standards that allows for no alternative.

Let's take a closer look.

1. **Be good at all of the traditional girl stuff.** Today's girl knows she's supposed to fulfill all the traditional "girl" expectations—

5

CHAPTER 5  FOCUS

look pretty, be nice, get a boyfriend—while excelling at the "girl skills" of empathy, cooperation, and relationship building. Any girl who wants to feel normal knows the drill: bond with your girlfriends, support your boyfriend, and make your family proud. The essence of these girl skills is maintaining relationships: doing what others expect of you while putting their needs first. It's the quality that leads a girl to spend all evening talking a friend through a crisis rather than using those hours to write her own A-level paper. It's also the quality that might lead her to suppress her own abilities or desires in order to boost a boyfriend's ego or reassure an anxious parent.

2.  **Be good at most of the traditional guy stuff.** Female skills might once have been all a girl needed—but no longer. Today, a girl isn't just looking for marriage and family; she expects to succeed at what were once traditionally considered "boy" goals, such as getting straight As and being a super-athlete. Girls, especially those from the middle- or upper-income brackets, are often expected to win acceptance to a top college. A poor or working-class girl's family may also look to her for the kind of financial support or upward mobility, through school, sports, or entertainment, that was once expected only of her brother.

    So in today's competitive environment, girl skills are not enough. A successful girl must also master the ultimate boy skills of assertion, maybe even aggression: the commitment to becoming a winner at anything you undertake, regardless of your own or others' feelings. It's the quality that leads the star football player to charge through the line, suppressing any fear he might feel, ignoring both the pain he experiences and the pain he causes. It's also the quality that might lead a boy to promise himself, "Someday, I'm going to discover a cure for cancer, no matter how hard I have to work, no matter how many hours I miss with my family, no matter how many people think I can't do it."

    As you can see, there are pluses and minuses to both approaches, but what's really difficult, if not impossible, is to master both of them at the same time. How do "best friends 4ever" fight each other over a diminishing number of college slots? What if the empowered basketball star doesn't fit into the size-2 miniskirt or can't stand letting her boyfriend win at ping-pong? What about the girl who wants to get off the merry-go-round and explore an alternative identity that allows a little more breathing room?

3.  **Conform to a narrow, unrealistic set of standards that allows for no alternative.** Enter the third component of the Triple

Bind: the way that alternatives of all types—different ways of becoming a woman, relating to society, or constructing an authentic self—have been virtually erased by the culture. This is the truly insidious aspect of the Triple Bind, which seems to offer choices with one hand only to take them away with the other.

At first glance, you might think that a girl was free to become anything she chooses. Look a little closer, though, and you'll see that whatever *else* she may decide, she must also always be sexy, thin, and pretty; have either a great boyfriend or a husband and kids, and be wildly successful at her career.

Girls used to be able to escape the narrow demands of femininity through such alternative roles as beatnik, tomboy, intellectual, hippie, punk, or goth. They'd embrace the ideals of feminism to proclaim that women didn't always have to be pretty, nice, and thin; that they didn't always have to have boyfriends; and that not all women wanted to become mothers. Or girls might follow a counterculture that challenged the notion of ascending the corporate ladder or fulfilling men's notions of the ideal woman. They'd imitate pop stars who presented alternate looks and styles of femininity: Janis Joplin, Patti Smith, Tina Turner, Cyndi Lauper. They'd take up basketball or hockey; they'd turn into bookworms or dream of being president. All of these alternatives to traditional female roles gave independent girls a little breathing room, the space to insist that they didn't necessarily have to fit into skimpy clothes or learn how to flirt at age eleven. Other types of alternatives— bohemianism, the counterculture, activism, art, humanitarian ideals— helped girls challenge the achievement-oriented culture that insisted on straight As, elite colleges, and seven-figure incomes as the only prizes worth having. A free-spirited girl might even find a way of being sexy that wasn't about how she looked, a sexual style that was uniquely her own.

Now virtually all of these possibilities have been co-opted, consumerized, and forced into an increasingly narrow, unrealistic set of roles. Standards have become narrower and less realistic for both looks ("girl stuff") and achievement ("boy stuff"), even as the cultural alternatives that might have helped girls resist these standards have been erased.

First, the definitions of "sexy" and "pretty" have narrowed enormously in recent years, with an ever-escalating demand that girls turn themselves into sexual objects. For a girl to fit the acceptable look now requires an almost superhuman commitment to dieting, waxing, applying makeup, and shopping; for some girls, plastic surgery has also come to seem like a minimum requirement. These trends begin at frighteningly young ages. Even many lesbian girls, whose choice once seemed to free them from the "male gaze" of conventional beauty, are now also expected to present themselves in sexually objectified terms, sporting the same lipstick and lingerie as their heterosexual sisters.

10     At the same time, girls face increasingly unrealistic standards for achievement. Only the top grades and test scores, combined with the most impressive extracurriculars, will fit a girl for a top college, a destination that is becoming virtually a requirement for more and more middle-class girls. Poor and working-class girls now dream of becoming superstar athletes, top models, or self-made entrepreneurs—and attending the Ivies as well. I'm all for dreaming, but girls are being given the message that anything less than the absolute best counts as failure.

So both the "girl" and "boy" requirements have become harder to meet, even as the alternatives that might have freed girls from either set of demands—feminism, bohemianism, political activism, community spirit—have all but disappeared from the cultural landscape. Our girls are truly trapped, and the crisis-level statistics I have shared with you are a key consequence.

This third aspect of the Triple Bind is particularly insidious because it's so deceptive. On the surface, all jobs, all activities, indeed all possibilities are open to every teenage girl. Look a little deeper, though and you can see the constraining need for girls to objectify themselves in order to fit the feminine mold. Yes, you might be able to do something "alternative" and unique—you can become the first female Indy driver, like Danica Patrick, or the first female presidential contender, like Hillary Clinton—but you still have to pose in a sexy outfit for *Playboy* or obsess publicly about your weight. Instead of Chrissie Hynde, we have Britney Spears; instead of Annie Lennox, we have Lindsay Lohan; instead of Queen Latifah, we have Beyoncé Knowles. Political pundits toss their hair and sport short skirts; women are told to exhibit empowerment, originality, and pride even as they don swimsuits to become the next top model. Our daughters might admire a whole roster of female athletes, but they, too, are expected to look skinny and "hot." (A colleague of mine, a sports psychologist, tells me that this is a recurring worry among the top female athletes he treats each week.) The 24/7 barrage of media images contributes to the sense that the walls are closing in. Skinny, sexy, scantily dressed teens and preteens appear everywhere, an airtight world that seems to offer no way out, reinforcing the notion that the only possible way to become a woman is to turn oneself into an object. Even the pioneering Nancy Pelosi, who will go down in history as the first female Speaker of the House, seems polite and ultrafeminine compared to such forebears as the hefty, abrasive congresswoman Bella Abzug.

Despite the apparent wealth of choices, our girls are ultimately presented with a very narrow, unrealistic set of standards that allow for no alternative. A seemingly boundless and hermetic culture insists on every female looking thin, pretty, and sexually available, whether she's a political pundit, a professional athlete, or a ten-year-old girl, even as it also demands that every girl aspire to being a wife (lesbian or straight) and mother—and all while climbing to the top of her career ladder, becoming a millionaire, and triumphing over every possible competitor. No wonder our girls are increasingly becoming depressed, expressing their anguish through binge eating, self-mutilation, acts of violence, and even suicide.

As I lay out the elements of the Triple Bind, they sound neat and discrete, easy-to-separate qualities that are clearly at odds with one another. But for the teenage girl caught in the middle of that bind, the contradictions seem to blend seamlessly together. If you want to understand how this works, just watch a few episodes of *America's Next Top Model*. The show is wildly popular with teenage girls: nearly every one of the girls I spoke with told me she loved the show, including feminists, lesbians, and girls who wouldn't be caught dead wearing makeup, let alone prancing down a runway or posing for a swimsuit ad.

The show's format is simple: it gathers a group of thirteen young  15 women of various shapes, backgrounds, and sizes, and asks them to compete for a top modeling spot. Every week, one more contestant is eliminated as the women are put through the complicated demands of photo shoots, runway modeling, and extreme athleticism. They might have to don mermaids' tails and dangle in fishing nets suspended above a canal or pose, shivering in skimpy clothing, upon ice sculptures. They also have to endure twenty-four-hour surveillance from the show's cameras and find some way to get along with the other women they're competing against. And they have to learn how to make it all seem effortless, keeping a smiling, pretty face constantly on display in case some photographer snaps an unflattering "casual" shot and sells it to the tabloids. As the show's press release puts it, "Participants are asked to demonstrate both inner and outer beauty as they learn to master complicated catwalks, intense physical fitness, fashion photo shoots, and perfect publicity skills."

Looks count: a model has to have a lovely face and body, and usually she needs to be thin, though the show almost always includes a voluptuous woman or someone with unusual looks. (In fact, on the Spring 2008 cycle, a "plus-size" model won the competition for the first time.) However, a model can't be *just* a pretty face; the judges speak contemptuously of "beauty queens" and "ordinary" pretty girls. A model, especially a top model, has to have something extra—an unusual face, a signature walk. She must both fit the mold and break the mold, and of course, no one can ever quite tell her when she must do which. One contestant is told to leave the show because she refuses to cut her hair in the style that the judges have decided is best for her. Another is informed that if she doesn't let the show's dentist fix the gap in her front teeth, she won't be eligible for the Cover Girl contract that is part of the prize package.

Both girls agonize over their decisions: they see their hair, their gaptoothed smile, as aspects of who they are, their own sort of signature. No, the judges insist, those parts of their body are the wrong ground on which to take a stand. Get rid of those elements—and then find another way to be unique. "Confidence," "personality," and "being yourself" are probably the words most often spoken on *America's Next Top Model*, but unquestioning obedience is also a requirement.

The show's creator and producer is Tyra Banks, herself a groundbreaking African American model who clearly cares deeply for her young charges. But like many caring parents of today's girls, Banks has to teach the next generation how to fit into a system that she readily acknowledges is often unfair. Accordingly, she urges the girls to "be themselves" even as she demands that they conform.

In one episode. Banks explains to one young woman that her "country" accent is getting in her way. You shouldn't cut yourself off from your roots, Banks says firmly, but you can't be bound by them, either. Learn to turn your accent on and off, or you'll never be able to sell makeup on TV. Then Banks demonstrates how to play with a non-mainstream accent, teasing the model in her own childhood "street" speech and then reverting immediately to a more cultured voice.

20   No one minds where you actually came from: on one episode, the runway coach talked about himself as someone who had grown up in the projects, and fashion icon Twiggy, who was one of the judges for several seasons, referred frequently to her own working-class background. (Significantly, Twiggy herself started the fashion for thin models; before she came on the scene, models were full-figured.) But your background has to be incorporated into the larger ideal of an infinitely malleable woman who is nevertheless always unique. We should be able to identify your signature walk even in silhouette, says Tyra, but you also need to speak without an accent.

Imagine, for a moment, being one of the millions of teenage girls who watch this show. What message is she supposed to derive from this? *Be yourself—but not too much yourself. Be proud of who you are—but cover it up the moment someone else says it's offensive. Be unique—but unique in the right way, not in the wrong way. And if you want to know how to follow these contradictory instructions, well, we can't tell you exactly how, but don't worry, we'll know it when we see it. So just keep trying and trying and trying. If you're lucky, you'll figure it out. If not, well, you're off the program!*

On another episode, Tyra confronts a voluptuous young woman whose body doesn't fit the model stereotype. "Being a big girl is almost harder than being a black girl," Tyra says, pointing out that, like any minority, the "big girl" will have to work harder and present herself more cheerfully than her mainstream counterparts. The judges see no problem with giving the girl contradictory advice: she is encouraged both to glory in her unusual body (unusual by models' standards) and to compensate for it.

Clearly, looks aren't all that matter: ambition counts, too. Girls don't see their families or their boyfriends for several weeks as they remain shut up in the "model house" or travel to some exotic location, all the while working around the clock on each week's task. Any girl who loses focus is reprimanded, by the judges and by her fellow models; everyone agrees that boyfriends must come second if you expect to win. The show's theme song drives the point home: "Wanna be on top?" it asks, again and again and again.

Accordingly, Danielle, the model with the gap-toothed smile and "country" accent, drags herself out of a hospital bed, fighting the after-effects of dehydration, exhaustion, and food poisoning to pose for a photo shoot on top of an elephant. She seems haggard and frail as she climbs on the beast's back, but the moment the cameras start to click, she looks dreamy and beautiful. She overcomes her physical weakness like a man but offers herself up to the camera like a woman, all in the service of a unique identity that is nevertheless ultrafeminized and overly sexualized.

To her credit, Banks wants to send a positive message about body image and race: the show always includes several African American and Latina models, as well as one or two girls who don't fit the mold. One season, that girl is Kim, a self-avowed lesbian who openly agonizes over her gender presentation: does she want to come across as a boy or a girl? The judges praise her androgyny and are obviously reluctant to cut her from the show. Clearly, Kim's no traditional girl; she even has a mini-affair with one of the other contestants. (Significantly, the other models object not to the homosexual activity but to the way the affair seems to distract both girls from the contest.) 25

Still, like all the women on the show, Kim is *also* ultrafeminine and overly sexualized: made up, dressed up, obediently allowing herself to be styled and posed however the client wants. Sometimes the judges want her to keep her boyish air; at other times, she's expected to look girlishly cute and sexy. Her unconventional qualities—androgyny, sexual difference—don't free her from traditional femininity so much as give her a unique spin on it. Even a gender-bending lesbian doesn't get a free pass: she has to retain her own style *and* be a "girly girl," sometimes switching back and forth, sometimes doing both at once.

CHAPTER 5   FOCUS

Learning to be America's Next Top Model is clearly a balancing act even more demanding than staying on the back of an elephant. In true girl style, the models seek to please, to obey, to look good. In true boy style, they seek to prove their physical prowess and to reach the top. ("Suck it up," say the judges when the models complain about working in the cold or dangling upside down in the heat. "I'm here to win, not to make friends," say the models when asked about their competitors.) And any alternative identity or personal style they might develop, no matter how unique or apparently transgressive, is always cycled back into the demand to be ultrafeminized and overly sexualized, to make money for whatever corporate client has sponsored the photo shoot, to do whatever it takes to reach the top. Being a proud black woman, Danielle nonetheless accepts a long, silky hairstyle; being a boyish lesbian doesn't keep Kim from wanting to sell makeup. They don't see any contradictions, and perhaps girls watch the show so eagerly because they, too, need to reconcile so many conflicting demands.

"I like the show while I watch it, but it makes me feel bad afterwards," says fifteen-year-old Madeleine, a junior at a public high school in a small midwestern college town. When I ask her why, she explains, "Well, it's intriguing, but it's sort of sad. I feel bad about myself, because I don't look that way. And I feel bad for them, because they want to reach the top but you know most of them aren't going to. They're never going to get what they dream about—but they just don't realize it."

Yet Madeleine watches the show every week, riveted by the balancing act that is her own struggle writ large. Like the contestants she watches, she needs to be herself—and to please others; to radiate confidence—but not to be arrogant; to look sexy—but not slutty; to be ambitious—but not mean. And if she stumbles on her own private runway or falters at her personal judge's latest demand, she at least has the comfort of knowing that thinner, prettier, more famous girls are also struggling with the impossible contradictions posed by the Triple Bind.

## Responding to Reading

1. What is the "triple bind"? According to Hinshaw, in what sense is the triple bind "the greatest current threat to our daughters' health and well-being" (3)?

2. Hinshaw points out that at one time girls used to be able to escape from the narrow demands of femininity. How, according to Hinshaw, has this situation changed? How does he account for this change?

3. What does Hinshaw mean when he says, "Despite the apparent wealth of choices, our girls are ultimately presented with a very narrow, unrealistic set of standards that allow for no alternative" (13)? According to Hinshaw, how does the show America's Next Top Model illustrate this contradiction? What do teenage female viewers take away from this show?

## Responding in Writing

Do you think men suffer from a version of the triple bind? Write a few paragraphs in which you discuss this possibility.

# THE WAR AGAINST BOYS

## Christina Hoff Sommers

### 1950–

*In the following, the opening section of a long essay that appeared in the* Atlantic Monthly, *Sommers examines what she calls "the myth of girls in crisis" and demonstrates that, contrary to popular opinion, boys, not girls, are short-changed by today's educational establishment. (See page 105 for Sommers's biography.)*

It's a bad time to be a boy in America. The triumphant victory of the U.S. women's soccer team at the World Cup last summer has come to symbolize the spirit of American girls. The shooting at Columbine High last spring might be said to symbolize the spirit of American boys.

That boys are in disrepute is not accidental. For many years women's groups have complained that boys benefit from a school system that favors them and is biased against girls. "Schools short-change girls," declares the American Association of University Women. Girls are "undergoing a kind of psychological foot-binding," two prominent educational psychologists say. A stream of books and pamphlets cite research showing not only that boys are classroom favorites but also that they are given to schoolyard violence and sexual harassment.

In the view that has prevailed in American education over the past decade, boys are resented, both as the unfairly privileged sex and as obstacles on the path to gender justice for girls. This perspective is promoted in schools of education, and many a teacher now feels that girls need and deserve special indemnifying consideration. "It is really clear that boys are Number One in this society and in most of the world," says Patricia O'Reilly, a professor of education and the director of the Gender Equity Center, at the University of Cincinnati.

The idea that schools and society grind girls down has given rise to an array of laws and policies intended to curtail the advantage boys have and to redress the harm done to girls. That girls are treated as the second sex in school and consequently suffer, that boys are accorded privileges and consequently benefit—these are things everyone is presumed to know. But they are not true.

5    The research commonly cited to support claims of male privilege and male sinfulness is riddled with errors. Almost none of it has been published in peer-reviewed professional journals. Some of the data turn out to be mysteriously missing. A review of the facts shows boys, not girls, on the weak side of an education gender gap. The typical boy is a year and a half behind the typical girl in reading and writing; he is less committed to school and less likely to go to college. In 1997 college fulltime enrollments were 45 percent male and 55 percent female. The Department of Education predicts that the proportion of boys in college classes will continue to shrink.

Data from the U.S. Department of Education and from several recent university studies show that far from being shy and demoralized, today's girls outshine boys. They get better grades. They have higher educational aspirations. They follow more rigorous academic programs and participate in advanced-placement classes at higher rates. According to the National Center for Education Statistics, slightly more girls than boys enroll in high-level math and science courses. Girls, allegedly timorous and lacking in confidence, now outnumber boys in student government, in honor societies, on school newspapers, and in debating clubs. Only in sports are boys ahead, and women's groups are targeting the sports gap with a vengeance. Girls read more books. They outperform boys on tests for artistic and musical ability. More girls than boys study abroad. More join the Peace Corps. At the same time, more boys than girls are suspended from school. More are held back and more drop out. Boys are three times as likely to receive a diagnosis of attention-deficit hyperactivity disorder. More boys than girls are involved in crime, alcohol, and drugs. Girls attempt suicide more often than boys, but it is boys who more often succeed. In 1997, a typical year, 4,483 young people aged five to twenty-four committed suicide: 701 females and 3,782 males.

In the technical language of education experts, girls are academically more "engaged." Last year an article in *The CQ Researcher* about male and female academic achievement described a common parental observation: "Daughters want to please their teachers by spending extra time on projects, doing extra credit, making homework as neat as possible. Sons rush through homework assignments and run outside to play, unconcerned about how the teacher will regard the sloppy work."

School engagement is a critical measure of student success. The U.S. Department of Education gauges student commitment by the following criteria: "How much time do students devote to homework each night?" and "Do students come to class prepared and ready to learn? (Do they bring books and pencils? Have they completed their homework?)" According to surveys of fourth, eighth, and twelfth graders, girls consistently do more homework than boys. By the twelfth grade boys are four times as likely as girls not to do homework. Similarly, more boys than girls report that they "usually" or "often" come to school without supplies or without having done their homework.

The performance gap between boys and girls in high school leads directly to the growing gap between male and female admissions to college. The Department of Education reports that in 1996 there were 8.4 million women but only 6.7 million men enrolled in college. It predicts that women will hold on to and increase their lead well into the next decade, and that by 2007 the numbers will be 9.2 million women and 6.9 million men.

## Deconstructing the Test-Score Gap

Feminists cannot deny that girls get better grades, are more engaged    10 academically, and are now the majority sex in higher education. They argue, however, that these advantages are hardly decisive. Boys, they point out, get higher scores than girls on almost every significant standardized test—especially the Scholastic Assessment Test and law school, medical school, and graduate school admissions tests.

In 1996 I wrote an article for *Education Week* about the many ways in which girl students were moving ahead of boys. Seizing on the test-score data that suggest boys are doing better than girls, David Sadker, a professor of education at American University and a co-author with his wife, Myra, of *Failing at Fairness: How America's Schools Cheat Girls* (1994), wrote, "If females are soaring in school, as Christina Hoff Sommers writes, then these tests are blind to their flight." On the 1998 SAT boys were thirty-five points (out of 800) ahead of girls in math and seven points ahead in English. These results seem to run counter to all other measurements of achievement in school. In almost all other areas boys lag behind girls. Why do they test better? Is Sadker right in suggesting that this is a manifestation of boys' privileged status?

The answer is no. A careful look at the pool of students who take the SAT and similar tests shows that the girls' lower scores have little or nothing to do with bias or unfairness. Indeed, the scores do not even signify lower achievement by girls. First of all, according to *College Bound Seniors,* an annual report on standardized-test takers published by the College Board, many more "at risk" girls than "at risk" boys take the SAT—girls from lower-income homes or with parents who never graduated from high school or never attended college. "These characteristics," the report says, "are associated with lower than average SAT scores." Instead of wrongly using SAT scores as evidence of bias against girls, scholars should be concerned about the boys who never show up for the tests they need if they are to move on to higher education.

Another factor skews test results so that they appear to favor boys. Nancy Cole, the president of the Educational Testing Service, calls it the

CHAPTER 5 FOCUS

"spread" phenomenon. Scores on almost any intelligence or achievement test are more spread out for boys than for girls—boys include more prodigies and more students of marginal ability. Or, as the political scientist James Q. Wilson once put it, "There are more male geniuses and more male idiots."

Boys also dominate dropout lists, failure lists, and learning-disability lists. Students in these groups rarely take college-admissions tests. On the other hand, exceptional boys who take school seriously show up in disproportionately high numbers for standardized tests. Gender-equity activists like Sadker ought to apply their logic consistently: if the shortage of girls at the high end of the ability distribution is evidence of unfairness to girls, then the excess of boys at the low end should be deemed evidence of unfairness to boys.

15      Suppose we were to turn our attention away from the highly motivated, self-selected two fifths of high school students who take the SAT and consider instead a truly representative sample of American schoolchildren. How would girls and boys then compare? Well, we have the answer. The National Assessment of Educational Progress, started in 1969 and mandated by Congress, offers the best and most comprehensive measure of achievement among students at all levels of ability. Under the NAEP program 70,000 to 100,000 students, drawn from forty-four states, are tested in reading, writing, math, and science at ages nine, thirteen, and seventeen. In 1996, seventeen-year-old boys outperformed seventeen-year-old girls by five points in math and eight points in science, whereas the girls outperformed the boys by fourteen points in reading and seventeen points in writing. In the past few years girls have been catching up in math and science while boys have continued to lag far behind in reading and writing.

In the July, 1995, issue of *Science*, Larry V. Hedges and Amy Nowell, researchers at the University of Chicago, observed that girls' deficits in math were small but not insignificant. These deficits, they noted, could adversely affect the number of women who "excel in scientific and technical occupations." Of the deficits in boys' writing skills they wrote, "The large sex differences in writing . . . are alarming. . . . The data imply that males are, on average, at a rather profound disadvantage in the performance of this basic skill." They went on to warn,

> The generally larger numbers of males who perform near the bottom of the distribution on reading comprehension and writing also have policy implications. It seems likely that individuals with such poor literacy skills will have difficulty finding employment in an increasingly information-driven economy. Thus, some intervention may be required to enable them to participate constructively.

Hedges and Nowell were describing a serious problem of national scope, but because the focus elsewhere has been on girls' deficits, few

CHAPTER 5  FOCUS

Americans know much about the problem or even suspect that it exists.

Indeed, so accepted has the myth of girls in crisis become that even teachers who work daily with male and female students tend to reflexively dismiss any challenge to the myth, or any evidence pointing to the very real crisis among boys. Three years ago Scarsdale High School, in New York, held a gender-equity workshop for faculty members. It was the standard girls-are-being-shortchanged fare, with one notable difference. A male student gave a presentation in which he pointed to evidence suggesting that girls at Scarsdale High were well ahead of boys. David Greene, a social-studies teacher, thought the student must be mistaken, but when he and some colleagues analyzed department grading patterns, they discovered that the student was right. They found little or no difference in the grades of boys and girls in advanced-placement social-studies classes. But in standard classes the girls were doing a lot better.

And Greene discovered one other thing: few wanted to hear about his startling findings. Like schools everywhere, Scarsdale High has been strongly influenced by the belief that girls are systematically deprived. That belief prevails among the school's gender-equity committee and has led the school to offer a special senior elective on gender equity. Greene has tried to broach the subject of male underperformance with his colleagues. Many of them concede that in the classes they teach, the girls seem to be doing better than the boys, but they do not see this as part of a larger pattern. After so many years of hearing about silenced, diminished girls, teachers do not take seriously the suggestion that boys are not doing as well as girls even if they see it with their own eyes in their own classrooms.

## Responding to Reading

1. In paragraph 4, Sommers states her essay's thesis: "That girls are treated as the second sex in school and consequently suffer, that boys are accorded privileges and consequently benefit—these are things everyone is presumed to know. But they are not true." Do you agree that the supposed privileged position of boys is something "everyone is presumed to know"?

2. Paragraph 6 of this essay presents a long list of areas in which "girls outshine boys." Do you find this list convincing? What other information could Sommers have provided to support her case?

3. Sommers believes that "the myth of girls in crisis" is so entrenched that "even teachers who work daily with male and female students tend to reflexively dismiss any challenge to the myth" (17). If what she says is true, would you expect this belief among teachers to benefit boys or girls in the long run? Why?

## Responding in Writing

Based on your experience, who is more successful in school—girls or boys?

# MEN ARE FROM EARTH, AND SO ARE WOMEN: IT'S FAULTY RESEARCH THAT SETS THEM APART

## Rosalind C. Barnett

### 1937–

## Caryl Rivers

### 1937–

*Executive director at Brandeis University's Women's Studies Research Center's Community, Families, and Work Program, Rosalind C. Barnett is a widely published author on gender-related issues. Caryl Rivers, professor of journalism at Boston University, has written numerous books and articles exploring the nature of gender, family, work, and religion. Like Barnett and Rivers's most recent book,* The Truth about Boys and Girls: Challenging Toxic Stereotypes about Our Children *(2011), the following essay reexamines popular (and damaging) beliefs about gender difference.*

Are American college professors unwittingly misleading their students by teaching widely accepted ideas about men and women that are scientifically unsubstantiated?

Why is the dominant narrative about the sexes one of difference, even though it receives little support from carefully designed peer-reviewed studies?

One reason is that findings from a handful of small studies with nonrepresentative samples have often reported wildly overgeneralized but headline-grabbing findings about gender differences. Those findings have then been picked up by the news media—and found their way back into the academy, where they are taught as fact. At the same time, research that tends to debunk popular ideas is often ignored by the news media.

Even worse, many researchers have taken untested hypotheses at face value and used them to plan their studies. Many have also relied exclusively on statistical tests that are designed to find difference, without using tests that would show the degree of overlap between men and women. As a result, findings often suggest—erroneously—that the sexes are categorically different with respect to some specific variable or other.

5      Yet in the latest edition of its publications manual, the American Psychological Association explicitly asks researchers to consider and report the degree of overlap in statistical studies. For good reason: Even if the mean difference between groups being compared is statistically significant, it may be of trivial consequence if the distributions show a high degree of overlap. Indeed, most studies that do report the size of

effects indicate that the differences between the sexes are trivial or slight on a host of personality traits and cognitive and social behaviors.

Because of such serious and pervasive problems, we believe that college students get a distorted picture about the sexes, one that overstates differences while minimizing the more accurate picture—that of enormous overlap and similarity.

It is easy to understand why college professors might spread myths about gender differences. Many of the original studies on which such findings were based have been embraced by both the academy and the wider culture. As Martha T. Mednick, an emerita professor of psychology at Howard University, pointed out in an article some years ago, popular ideas that are intuitively appealing, even if inadequately documented, all too often take on lives of their own. They may have shaky research foundations; they may be largely disproved by later—and better—studies. But bandwagon concepts that have become unhitched from research moorings are rampant in academe, particularly in the classroom. For example:

## Women Are Inherently More Caring and More "Relational" than Men

The chief architect of this essentialist idea is Carol Gilligan, the longtime Harvard University psychologist who is now at New York University. In the early 1980s, she laid out a new narrative for women's lives that theorized that women have a unique, caring nature not shared by men. Her ideas have revolutionized the psychology of women and revamped curricula to an unprecedented degree, some observers say. Certainly, almost every student in women's studies and the psychology of women is familiar with Gilligan. But how many are aware of the critics of her theories about women's moral development and the relational self?

Many scholarly reviews of Gilligan's research contend that it does not back up her claims, that she simply created an intriguing hypothesis that needs testing. But the relational self has become near-sacred writ, cited in textbooks, classrooms, and the news media.

Anne Alonso, a Harvard psychology professor and director of the Center for Psychoanalytic Studies at Massachusetts General Hospital, told us recently that she is dismayed by the lightning speed at which Gilligan's ideas, based on slender evidence, have been absorbed into psychotherapy. Usually new theories go through a long and rigorous process of publication in peer-reviewed journals before they are accepted by the field. "None of this work has been published in such journals. It's hard to take seriously a whole corpus of work that hasn't been peer-reviewed," Alonso said. The idea of a relational self, she charged, is simply an "idea du jour," one that she called "penis scorn."

## Men Don't Value Personal Relations

According to essentialist theorists, men are uncomfortable with any kind of communication that has to do with personal conflicts. They avoid talking about their problems. They avoid responding too deeply to other people's problems, instead giving advice, changing the subject, making a joke, or giving no response. Unlike women, they don't react to troubles talk by empathizing with others and expressing sympathy. These ideas are often cited in textbooks and in popular manuals, like those written by John Gray, a therapist, and Deborah Tannen, a linguistics professor at Georgetown University. Men are from Mars, women are from Venus, we are told. They just don't understand each other. But systematic research does not support those ideas.

An important article, "The Myth of Gender Cultures: Similarities Outweigh Differences in Men's and Women's Provision of and Responses to Supportive Communication," was published this year in *Sex Roles: A Journal of Research.* Erina L. MacGeorge, of Purdue University, and her colleagues at the University of Pennsylvania find no support for the idea that women and men constitute different "communication cultures." Their article, based on three studies that used questionnaires and interviews, sampled 738 people—417 women and 321 men.

In fact, the authors find, the sexes are very much alike in the way they communicate: "Both men and women view the provision of support as a central element of close personal relationships; both value the supportive communication skills of their friends, lovers, and family members; both make similar judgments about what counts as sensitive, helpful support; and both respond quite similarly to various support efforts."

Yet, MacGeorge and her colleagues point out, we still read in textbooks that:

- "Men's and women's communication styles are startlingly dissimilar"—*The Interpersonal Communication Reader,* edited by Joseph A. DeVito (Allyn and Bacon, 2002).

- "American men and women come from different sociolinguistic subcultures, having learned to do different things with words in a conversation"—a chapter by Daniel N. Maltz and Ruth A. Borker in *Language and Social Identity* (Cambridge University Press, 1982), edited by John J. Gumperz.

- "Husbands and wives, especially in Western societies, come from two different cultures with different learned behaviors and communication styles"—a chapter by Carol J. S. Bruess and Judy C. Pearson in *Gendered Relationships* (Mayfield, 1996), edited by Julia T. Wood.

## Gender Differences in Mate Selection Are Pervasive and Well Established

Evolutionary psychologists like David M. Buss, a professor at the [15] University of Texas at Austin, tell us in such books as *The Evolution of Desire: Strategies of Human Mating* (Basic Books, 1994) that men and women differ widely with respect to the traits they look for in a potential mate. Men, such writers claim, lust after pretty, young, presumably fertile women. Pop culture revels in this notion: Men want young and beautiful mates. There is, it is presumed, a universal female type beloved by men—young, unlined, with features that are close to those of an infant—that signals fertility. If there were a universal male preference for beautiful young women, it would have to be based on a strong correlation between beauty and reproductive success. Sure, Richard Gere chose Julia Roberts in *Pretty Woman* because of her beauty and youth. But would those qualities have assured enhanced fertility?

The answer, according to empirical research, seems to be no. Having a pretty face as a young adult has no relationship to the number of children a woman produces or to her health across the life span. Among married women, physical attractiveness is unrelated to the number of children they produce. If beauty has little to do with reproductive success, why would nature insist that men select for it? It seems more likely that having a young beauty on his arm indicates, instead, that a man is living up to certain cultural and social norms.

According to some who take what we call an ultra-Darwinist stance, there is no mystery about whom women prefer as a mate: The man with resources to feed and protect her future children. The combination of wealth, status, and power (which usually implies an older man) makes "an attractive package in the eyes of the average woman," as Robert Wright, a journalist and author of *The Moral Animal: The New Science of Evolutionary Psychology* (Pantheon, 1994), sums up the argument.

But those who believe that gender roles are shaped at least as much by culture and environment as by biology point out that women's preference for older good providers fits perfectly with the rise of the industrial state. That system, which often called for a male breadwinner and a female working at home, arose in the United States in the 1830s, was dominant until the 1970s, and then declined.

If that is correct, then we should see a declining preference for older men who are good providers, particularly among women with resources. In fact, a study by Alice Eagley, a psychologist at Northwestern University, and Wendy Wood, of Duke University, suggests that as gender equality in society has increased, women have expressed less of a preference for older men with greater earning potential. The researchers have found that when women have access to their own resources, they do not look for age in mates, but prefer qualities like empathy, understanding, and the ability to bond with children. The desire for an older "provider" is evidently not in women's genes. Terri D. Fisher, a psychologist at Ohio State University, told a reporter last year that whenever she teaches her college students the ultra-Darwinian take on the power of youth and beauty, the young men smile and nod and the young women look appalled.

## For Girls, Self-Esteem Plummets at Early Adolescence

20  Girls face an inevitable crisis of self-esteem as they approach adolescence. They are in danger of losing their voices, drowning, and facing a devastating dip in self-regard that boys don't experience. This is the picture that Carol Gilligan presented on the basis of her research at the Emma Willard School, a private girls' school in Troy, N.Y. While Gilligan did not refer to genes in her analysis of girls' vulnerability, she did cite both the "wall of Western culture" and deep early childhood socialization as reasons.

Her theme was echoed in 1994 by the clinical psychologist Mary Pipher's surprise best seller, *Reviving Ophelia* (Putnam, 1994), which spent three years on the *New York Times* best-seller list. Drawing on case studies rather than systematic research, Pipher observed how naturally outgoing, confident girls get worn down by sexist cultural expectations. Gilligan's and Pipher's ideas have also been supported by a widely cited study in 1990 by the American Association of University Women. That report, published in 1991, claimed that teenage girls experience a "free-fall in self-esteem from which some will never recover."

The idea that girls have low self-esteem has by now become part of the academic canon as well as fodder for the popular media. But is it true? No.

Critics have found many faults with the influential AAUW study. When children were asked about their self-confidence and academic plans, the report said 60 percent of girls and 67 percent of boys in elementary school responded, "I am happy the way I am." But by high school, the percentage of girls happy with themselves fell to 29 percent. Could it be that 71 percent of the country's teenage girls were low in self-esteem? Not necessarily. The AAUW counted as happy only those girls who checked "always true" to the question about happiness. Girls who said they were "sometimes" happy with themselves or "sort of" happy with themselves were counted as unhappy.

A sophisticated look at the self-esteem data is far more reassuring than the headlines. A new analysis of all of the AAUW data, and a meta-analysis of hundreds of studies, done by Janet Hyde, a psychologist at the University of Wisconsin at Madison, showed no huge gap between boys and girls. Indeed, Hyde found that the self-esteem scores of boys and girls were virtually identical. In particular there was no plunge in scores for girls during the early teen years—the supposed basis for the idea that girls "lost their voices" in that period. Parents, understandably concerned about noxious, hypersexual media images, may gaze in horror at those images while underestimating the resilience of their daughters, who are able to thrive in spite of them.

## Boys Have a Mathematics Gene, or at Least a Biological Tendency to Excel in Math, That Girls Do Not Possess

Do boys have a mathematics gene—or at least a biological tendency to excel 25 in math—that girls lack, as a popular stereotype has it? Suffice it to say that, despite being discouraged from pursing math at almost every level of school, girls and women today are managing to perform in math at high levels.

Do data support arguments for hard-wired gender differences? No. In 2001 Erin Leahey and Guang Guo, then a graduate student and an assistant professor of sociology, respectively, at the University of North Carolina at Chapel Hill, looked at some 20,000 math scores of children ages 4 to 18 and found no differences of any magnitude, even in areas that are supposedly male domains, such as reasoning skills and geometry.

The bandwagon concepts that we have discussed here are strongly held and dangerous. Even though they have been seriously challenged, they continue to be taught by authority figures in the classroom. These ideas are embedded in the curricula of courses in child and adolescent development, moral development, education, moral philosophy, feminist pedagogy, evolutionary psychology, gender studies, and the psychology of women.

Few students have the ability to investigate the accuracy of the claims on their own. And since these ideas resonate with the cultural zeitgeist, students would have little reason to do so in any case. The essentialist perspective has so colored the dialogue about the sexes that there is scant room for any narrative other than difference.

Obviously the difference rhetoric can create harm for both men and women. Men are taught to believe that they are deficient in caring and empathy, while women are led to believe that they are inherently unsuited for competition, leadership, and technological professions. Given how little empirical support exists for essentialist ideas, it's crucial that professors broaden the dialogue, challenging the conventional wisdom and encouraging their students to do so as well.

### Responding to Reading

1. According to Barnett and Rivers, what problems cause college students to "get a distorted picture about the sexes . . ." (6)? In what sense is the view distorted?
2. What specific misleading ideas do Barnett and Rivers identify? How do they challenge these ideas? How effective are their responses to these ideas?
3. Why do Barnett and Rivers see the "bandwagon concepts" they discuss as dangerous (27)? Why do teachers continue to spread these ideas? What do Barnett and Rivers think should be done about this situation?

### Responding in Writing

Barnett and Rivers do not specifically address the issue of academic performance in their essay. Do you think they should have? How do you think they would respond to the discussion of academic performance in Christina Hoff Sommers's essay "The War against Boys" (p. 283)?

CHAPTER 5   FOCUS

# WIDENING THE FOCUS

### For Critical Reading and Writing

Referring specifically to the three readings in this chapter's Focus section, write an essay in which you answer the question, "Who Has It Harder, Girls or Boys?"

### For Further Reading

The following readings can suggest additional perspectives for thinking and writing about the roles of men and women:

- Alleen Pace Nilsen, "Sexism in English: Embodiment and Language" (p. 148)

- Judith Ortiz Cofer, "The Myth of the Latin Woman: I Just Met a Girl Named Maria" (p. 308)

- Arlie Hochschild, "The Second Shift" (p. 412)

### For Focused Research

Differences in the ways boys and girls are treated in school remain a contentious discussion topic. In preparation for writing an essay about the gender gap in education, open one of the popular Web search engines that compile news stories, such as <http://news.google.com> or <http://news.yahoo.com> and enter the search terms *gender gap and education*. From your search results, select readings about your topic, and use information from these sources to help you develop your essay. You can begin by visiting one or all of the following resources, which were found through the *Google* news site:

- Casserly, Meghan. "The Global Gender Gap Is Closing, but the U.S. Is Still Failing Its Women." *Forbes.* October 24, 2012. <http://www .forbes.com/sites/meghancasserly/2012/10/24/the-global-gender-gap-is-closing-but-the-u-s-is-still-failing-its-women>.

- "Narrowing the Gender Gap in Primary and Secondary Education [Video]." *Care2.* Nov. 21, 2011. <http://www.care2.com/causes/narrowing-the-gender-gap-in-primary-and-secondary-education-video.html>.

- Orwig, Jessica. "Engineering across the Gender Gap." *The Battalion.* Nov. 15, 2011. <http://www.thebatt.com/engineering-across-the-gender-gap-1.2699309>.

## Beyond the Classroom

Interview three female college students majoring in traditionally male fields (business, engineering, math, and so on) and three male students majoring in traditionally female fields (nursing, elementary education, social work, nutrition, and so on). In your interviews, ask the following questions:

- Were you encouraged or discouraged (by friends, parents, and teachers) to pursue this field of study?

- Have you experienced any gender discrimination in the classroom or in any related employment settings?

Based on the responses to these questions, write an essay in which you consider whether educational opportunities are broader or narrower (or the same) for men and for women.

——————————————— WRITING ———————————————

## GENDER AND IDENTITY

1. In her well-known work *A Room of One's Own,* novelist and critic Virginia Woolf observes that "any woman born with a great gift in the sixteenth century would certainly have gone crazed, shot herself, or ended her days in some lonely cottage outside the village, half witch, half wizard, feared and mocked at." Write an essay in which you discuss in what respects this statement may still apply to gifted women of your own generation or of your parents' generation. You may want to read Marge Piercy's poem "Barbie Doll" (p. 247) and Deborah Tannen's "Marked Women" (p. 268) before you plan your paper.

2. List all the stereotypes of women—and of men—identified in the selections you read in this chapter. Then, write an essay in which you discuss those that you think have had the most negative effects. Do you consider these stereotypes just annoying, or actually dangerous? Refer to one or two essays in this chapter to support your points.

3. Several of the selections in this chapter—for example, "Stay-at-Home Dads" (p. 265) and "Why I Want a Wife" (p. 263)—draw distinctions, implicitly or explicitly, between "men's work" and "women's work." Write an essay in which you consider the extent to which such distinctions exist today, and explain how they have affected your professional goals.

4. The title of a best-selling self-help book by John Gray, *Men Are from Mars, Women Are from Venus,* suggests that men and women are so completely different that they may as well be from different planets. Write an essay in which you support or contradict this title's claim. You may focus on men's and women's actions, tastes, values, preferences, or behavior.

5. Write a letter to Judy Brady in which you update (or challenge) her characterization of a wife in "Why I Want a Wife" (p. 263).

6. Could all-male (or all-female) schools solve the problems encountered by boys and girls in school? Write an essay in which you present your views on this issue.

7. In her essay "Marked Women" (p. 268), Deborah Tannen discusses the distinction between the terms *marked* and *unmarked.* Study the men and women around you, or those you see in films or on television, and determine whether or not your observations support Tannen's point that, unlike women, men have "the option of being unmarked" (12). Write an essay in which you agree or disagree with Tannen's conclusion, citing her essay as well as your own observations. (Be sure to define the terms *marked* and *unmarked* in your introduction.)

8. A number of the writers in this chapter examine current ideas about what it means to be male and what it means to be female. Write an essay in which you develop your own definitions of *male* and *female*. You may want to consider Jennifer Finney Boylan's "Is My Marriage Gay?" (p. 255), Kathleen Deveny's "Who You Callin' a Lady?" (p. 258), and E. J. Graff's "The M/F Boxes" (p. 249).

9. In "Who You Callin' a Lady?" (p. 258), Kathleen Deveny questions the public's reaction to a female soccer player's pulling an opponent to the ground by her ponytail. Deveny points out that although we expect bad behavior from male athletes, we don't tolerate it from female athletes. According to her, this "soft bigotry of high expectations" hurts women both in sports and in life. Choose two or three traditionally male sports that have female participants—basketball, boxing, and soccer, for example. Then, discuss how the female players challenge (or possibly reinforce) traditional gender stereotypes.

10. Several of the essays in this chapter deal with gender roles and how they influence relationships between men and women. Write an essay in which you discuss how gender roles have affected you. For example, do you think you have ever been held back or given an unfair advantage because of your gender? In addition to your own experience, you may include information from the experiences of friends or family members. In addition, use information in two of the essays in this chapter to support your points.

# 6

## CULTURE AND IDENTITY

The word *culture* generally refers to an identity shared by a particular racial, religious, or ethnic group or an identity that is characteristic of a specific geographic region. But in many cases, cultural identity is more complicated, a concept that includes but goes beyond a person's self-identification as an African American or a Muslim or a New Yorker.

For some, cultural identity is determined by shared language or national origin or family history; others may identify with a group on the basis of gender or sexual orientation; still others identify with a particular group because of a shared interest or professional affiliation. Thus, we can talk about computer culture, Wall Street culture, skateboard culture, or football culture as well as about Chinese culture, feminist culture, or gay culture.

Cultural identity can rest on a shared system of deeply held values and beliefs or simply a shared preference in personal style—for example, an affinity for body art or motorcycle gear. But regardless of how we define culture, cultural identity is not always something we actively choose. Sometimes cultural identity is conferred upon us at birth; sometimes we identify with a culture simply out of habit; sometimes a

48th annual Puerto Rican Day Parade, New York City, June 11, 2006

Atlanta, GA, Gay Pride Parade, October 9, 2011

cultural identity is imposed on us by others, determined by how others see us rather than by how we see ourselves.

When we examine the idea of cultural identity, we may consider whether it is possible to be loyal to two cultures or how it feels to abandon one culture and take on another. We may also consider how to maintain an individual identity while identifying with one or more groups. Finally, we may consider how loyalty to a particular culture defines an individual—and how the individual helps to define the culture.

In the Focus section of this chapter, "Are We Moving toward a Post-Racial Society?" (p. 324), three writers consider culture in the context of "black identity" in the United States, suggesting, as Brent Staples (p. 325) puts it, that "race isn't as 'black' and 'white' as we think."

## ——————— Preparing to Read and Write ———————

As you read and prepare to write about the essays in this chapter, you may consider the following questions:

- Does the essay focus on one particular culture or on culture in general?

- Is the culture the writer discusses defined by race, ethnicity, geography, vocation, or something else?

- Does the writer see his or her own culture in positive, neutral, or negative terms?

- Does the writer explore personal feelings and experiences?

- Would you describe the writer's voice as reflective, angry, resigned, or something else?

246th annual St. Patrick's Day Parade, New York City, March 17, 2007

73rd annual Pulaski Day Parade, New York City, October 3, 2010

- Does the writer identify with the culture he or she describes or feel like an outsider?

- Does the writer embrace his or her culture or try to distance himself or herself from it?

- Does the writer see culture as defining him or her or as only a small part of his or her identity?

- Has the writer chosen to identify with a particular culture, or has his or her cultural identity been determined by how others view him or her?

- Does the writer challenge the way a culture is commonly perceived?

- Does the writer consider the impact of a culture on other cultures or on society as a whole?

- Which of the various writers' ideas about culture and identity are most similar? Which are most like your own?

## PHOTO ESSAY

## TATTOOS AND CULTURAL IDENTITY

The eight photographs that appear on the following pages illustrate various ways in which tattoos express identity and help create a shared culture. Look closely at the images, and read the explanatory captions that accompany them. Then, answer the questions below.

### Responding to the Images

1. List some possible motives people might have for getting tattoos.
2. Do you see tattoos primarily as self-expression? Decoration? Mutilation? Explain.
3. Which of the tattoos shown in the photo essay do you think convey positive messages? Which do you think would have negative connotations for most people who see them? Why?
4. Which tattoo do you find the most visually appealing? Why?
5. Which tattoo has the most powerful impact on you? Why?
6. Would you get a tattoo? Why or why not? If you already have one or more tattoos, what do you think they tell other people about your cultural identity?

### Responding in Writing

Choose one of the images on the following pages, and write an analysis of its features. (Use the "Reacting to Visual Texts" discussion on page 8 of the Introduction as a guide.) What message do you think the tattoo art pictured is intended to convey about the wearer's identity? Do you think this message is communicated effectively? What story does the tattoo tell?

Member of New Zealand Maori Tribe with traditional tattoos

Survivor of the Auschwitz-Birkenau concentration camp Robert Cohen shows his concentration camp identification tattoo prior to the trial against Nazi war criminal John Demjanjuk at the District Court in Munich, Germany, November 30, 2009

U.S. Marine with tattoo reading "Death before Dishonor" and "Semper Fi," Fallujah, Iraq, 2004

Tattooed motorcyclist

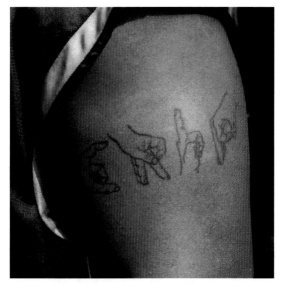

Tattoo on the arm of a member of the Eastside Crips spelling out the gang's name

Young woman with tattoos

Actress Angelina Jolie at the Cannes Film Festival, May 16, 2011

The new tokidoki Barbie doll, October 8, 2011

# BILINGUAL/BILINGUE

## Rhina Espaillat

### 1932–

*Born in the Dominican Republic and raised in New York City, Rhina Espaillat writes poetry in both English and Spanish. She is the author of eleven poetry collections, including, most recently,* Her Place in These Designs *(2008). The following poem considers how bilingualism shapes identity.*

My father liked them separate, one there,
one here (allá y aquí), as if aware

that words might cut in two his daughter's heart
(el corazón) and lock the alien part

to what he was—his memory, his name                                    5
(su nombre)—with a key he could not claim.

"English outside this door, Spanish inside,"
he said, "y basta." But who can divide

the world, the word (mundo y palabra) from
any child? I knew how to be dumb                                       10

and stubborn (testaruda); late, in bed,
I hoarded secret syllables I read

until my tongue (mi lengua) learned to run
where his stumbled. And still the heart was one.

I like to think he knew that, even when,                               15
proud (orgulloso) of his daughter's pen,

he stood outside mis versos, half in fear
of words he loved but wanted not to hear.

## Responding to Reading

1. Is this poem's central figure the speaker or her father? Explain.
2. Spanish words are defined throughout this poem, but no definitions are provided for *y basta* ("and enough"; line 8) or *mis versos* ("my poems"; line 17). Why do you suppose the poet chose not to define these two expressions?
3. What are the "secret syllables" (line 12) the speaker reads when she is in bed at night? Why does she keep them secret?

## Responding in Writing

The speaker's father has a rule: "English outside this door, Spanish inside" (line 7). Do you think the speaker's concept of *bilingual* is different from her father's? If so, how?

# The Struggle to Be an All-American Girl
## Elizabeth Wong
### 1958–

*A playwright and an adjunct assistant professor at the University of Southern California School of Theatre, Elizabeth Wong grew up in Los Angeles's Chinatown. The author of numerous award-winning plays and a former staff writer for the ABC sitcom* All-American Girl, *Wong explores Asian-American culture and identity in her work. In the following essay, she describes the difficult experience of being caught between two cultures.*

It's still there, the Chinese school on Yale Street where my brother and I used to go. Despite the new coat of paint and the high wire fence, the school I knew ten years ago remains remarkably, stoically the same.

Every day at 5 P.M., instead of playing with our fourth- and fifth-grade friends or sneaking out to the empty lot to hunt ghosts and animal bones, my brother and I had to go to Chinese school. No amount of kicking, screaming, or pleading could dissuade my mother, who was solidly determined to have us learn the language of our heritage.

Forcibly, she walked us the seven long, hilly blocks from our home to school, depositing our defiant tearful faces before the stern principal. My only memory of him is that he swayed on his heels like a palm tree, and he always clasped his impatient twitching hands behind his back. I recognized him as a repressed maniacal child killer, and knew that if we ever saw his hands we'd be in big trouble.

We all sat in little chairs in an empty auditorium. The room smelled like Chinese medicine, an imported faraway mustiness. Like ancient mothballs or dirty closets. I hated that smell. I favored crisp new scents. Like the soft French perfume that my American teacher wore in public school.

5      There was a stage far to the right, flanked by an American flag and the flag of the Nationalist Republic of China, which was also red, white and blue but not as pretty.

Although the emphasis at the school was mainly language—speaking, reading, writing—the lessons always began with an exercise in politeness. With the entrance of the teacher, the best student would tap a bell and everyone would get up, kowtow,[1] and chant, "Sing san ho," the phonetic for "How are you, teacher?"

Being 10 years old, I had better things to learn than ideographs copied painstakingly in lines that ran right to left from the tip of a *moc but*, a real ink pen that had to be held in an awkward way if blotches were to be avoided. After all, I could do the multiplication tables, name the satellites of Mars, and write reports on *Little Women* and *Black Beauty*. Nancy Drew, my favorite book heroine, never spoke Chinese.

The language was a source of embarrassment. More times than not, I had tried to disassociate myself from the nagging loud voice that followed me wherever I wandered in the nearby American supermarket outside Chinatown. The voice belonged to my grandmother, a fragile woman in her seventies who could outshout the best of the street vendors. Her humor was raunchy, her Chinese rhythmless, patternless. It was quick, it was loud, it was unbeautiful. It was not like the quiet, lilting romance of French or the gentle refinement of the American South. Chinese sounded pedestrian. Public.

In Chinatown, the comings and goings of hundreds of Chinese on their daily tasks sounded chaotic and frenzied. I did not want to be thought of as mad, as talking gibberish. When I spoke English, people nodded at me, smiled sweetly, said encouraging words. Even the people in my culture would cluck and say that I'd do well in life. "My, doesn't she move her lips fast," they would say, meaning that I'd be able to keep up with the world outside Chinatown.

My brother was even more fanatical than I about speaking English. 10 He was especially hard on my mother, criticizing her, often cruelly, for her pidgin speech—smatterings of Chinese scattered like chop suey in her conversation. "It's not 'What it is,' Mom," he'd say in exasperation. "It's 'What *is* it, what *is* it, what *is* it!'" Sometimes Mom might leave out an occasional "the" or "a," or perhaps a verb of being. He would stop her in mid-sentence: "Say it again, Mom. Say it right." When he tripped over his own tongue, he'd blame it on her: "See, Mom, it's all your fault. You set a bad example."

What infuriated my mother most was when my brother cornered her on her consonants, especially "r." My father had played a cruel joke on Mom by assigning her an American name that her tongue wouldn't allow her to say. No matter how hard she tried, "Ruth" always ended up "Luth" or "Roof."

After two years of writing with a *moc but* and reciting words with multiples of meanings, I finally was granted a cultural divorce. I was permitted to stop Chinese school.

I thought of myself as multicultural. I preferred tacos to egg rolls; I enjoyed Cinco de Mayo more than Chinese New Year.

---
[1]Kneel and bow in deference. [Eds.]

At last, I was one of you; I wasn't one of them.
15    Sadly, I still am.

## Responding to Reading

1.  In this essay, Wong looks back ten years to her childhood. Why is the Chinese school she remembers still such an important part of her identity? From the vantage point of adulthood, what does she feel she has lost?
2.  What differences does Wong identify between Chinese and American culture? Why, when she was a child, was American culture so much more appealing to her than Chinese culture?
3.  After leaving Chinese school, Wong says, "At last, I was one of you; I wasn't one of them" (14). Who are the *you* and *them* that Wong refers to? Was she really "one of you"? Is she now?

## Responding in Writing

How would you define an "all-American" boy or girl? Do you think it is possible to preserve one's cultural identity and still be "all-American"?

# What It Means to Be Latino

## Clara E. Rodríguez

### 1944–

*A sociology professor at Fordham University's College at Lincoln Center, Clara E. Rodríguez writes about issues pertaining to Latino culture and identity, media, and migration. Rodríguez has consulted for the children's television shows* Dora the Explorer *and* Sesame Street *and is the author of ten books, including* Heroes, Lovers and Others: The Story of Latinos in Hollywood *(2004). In the following essay, she describes the complexities of Latino culture.*

To be a Latino means that in the 2000 U.S. census, you were counted as one of 35.3 million people, of any race, classified as "Hispanic," and that you were part of a group that comprised 12.5% of the total U.S. population. It means you are part of a group that now equals, or has surpassed, African Americans in number. It also means that you are part of a group that is growing faster than all other groups (50% since 1990) and is expected to continue to grow rapidly because of high immigration, high fertility rates, and the youthfulness of the current population. Only Asian Americans, who represented 3.6% of the U.S. population in 2000, had greater rates of growth. Finally, it means that you are a member of a very diverse group, in terms of socioeconomic positions, religions, racial classifications and national origins.

If we look at the Hispanic/Latino population pie in 2000, we see that Mexicans comprised the majority of all Latinos (58.5% or 20.6 million).

Puerto Ricans were the second largest Latino group, constituting 9.6% of all Latinos or 3.4 million. However, if we include the 3.8 million Puerto Ricans who resided in Puerto Rico, then this figure more than doubles. Cubans were the next largest single national origin group and constitute 3.5% of the total Latino population, followed by Dominicans with 2.2%. Collectively, the Central American countries accounted for 4.8% of the total Latino pie, with Salvadorans (1.9%) and Guatemalans (1.1%) being the two largest groups among Central Americans. South Americans comprised another 3.8% of the total U.S. Latino population with Colombians (1.3%) the largest group here. All of the other countries in Central and South America constituted less than 1% each of the total Hispanic population. Interestingly, in view of the extensive diversity of national origins, there was a surprising 17.3% that reported they were Hispanic or Latino but did not indicate a national origin. Analyses have yet to be done on this group, but it may be that this fast-growing group represents either those who have parents from more than one country, or, those who consider themselves "Hispanic/Latino," but do not identify with a particular country.

Although historically there are important regional concentrations of each of these groups, e.g., Cubans in Florida, Puerto Ricans in the Northeast, and Mexicans in California and the Southwest, there is increasing Latino heterogeneity in all of these areas. All states now have Latino populations, many of which are increasing rapidly, and almost all cities are experiencing substantial changes in their Latino mix. For example, Miami now has an increasingly diverse Latin American population, with Colombians, Puerto Ricans, and diverse Central and South Americans increasing their presence. New York City now has substantial and growing Dominican, Colombian, Ecuadorian and Mexican populations. The same is true of Los Angeles and other large cities and many suburban areas.

Being Latino also means that you lay claim to one (or more) of the rich and unique histories that each of these groups brings to the United States. Likewise, each of these groups has had a unique narrative in the United States, involving different times of arrival, areas of settlement, and types of migration and reception experiences. Like so many other groups coming to the United States, some groups came mainly as political refugees, or, political exiles without the benefit of refugee status. Others came as free or contracted laborers, and still others simply as immigrants looking to improve the opportunities in their lives. Unlike most other groups, Latinos have come from this hemisphere. Therefore, they have been consistently impacted by U.S. hemispheric policy and they have had more "va y ven" (coming and going) between their countries and the United States. This has contributed to the sustenance of the Spanish language and multiculturalism within Latino communities while adding new infusions of Latinos to the United States.

5    Since Latinos have been part of the U.S. landscape for centuries, the nature of the migrations has also varied over time. For example, political immigrants or exiles were more characteristic of the migration from Puerto Rico in the late 19th century, while those who came in search of work characterized the exodus in the mid 20th century. There were also varying methods of migration, where some groups arrived mainly by boat, others by plane, and still others over land in cars, trains or buses. Some have arrived legally as immigrants, others were undocumented. Some became naturalized citizens, others became citizens because they were born in the United States and still others arrived as citizens or became citizens because their lands had become subject to United States rule. Different groups have also had different receptions in the U.S. at different times.

Being Latino means a connection to the Spanish language, although, in Latin America there are also a multiplicity of other languages spoken by various groups, e.g., the indigenous peoples. Each Latino group coming to the U.S. spoke Spanish, but each country has its particular way of speaking Spanish. Spanish speakers throughout Latin America and the Caribbean understand one another. However, the way the language is spoken varies according to class, regional, ethnic and racial differences within each country. If we think about how English is spoken in Australia, Britain, Brooklyn, New York, as well as the southern, eastern, and midwestern parts of the United States, we have some idea of how the same language can vary with regard to accent, intonation patterns, and vocabulary. Curiously, however, you can be called a Latino, or classified a Hispanic, and yet not speak Spanish very well or at all.

Finally, being Latino means you are a part of one or more groups that have their own unique cuisine, music, and cultural and artistic traditions. For example, spicy, hot food is common in some diets and relatively absent in others. But there are also some commonalties. For example, in the same way that meat and potatoes can be considered a staple of the U.S. American diet—though not everyone eats this—rice and beans are a staple throughout much of Latin America. Pink beans are preferred in some countries, black beans in others, and pinto beans in still yet others and so on. Most members of each group are proud of their own uniqueness and history—both in this country and in their country of origin. However, as Celia Cruz, the great Cuban Salsa singer, has said, "we are all brothers in a different country" and the level of bonding and common identification often goes beyond speaking Spanish.

## On Terminology: Hispanic or Latino?

The term "Hispanic" is often used interchangeably with the term "Latino." The term "Hispanic" was introduced into the English language and into the 1970 census by government officials who were searching for a generic term that would include all who came from, or who had parents who came from, Spanish-speaking countries. It is, therefore, an English-language term that is not generally used in Spanish-speaking countries. The term "Latino," on the other hand, is a Spanish-language term that has increased in usage since the introduction of the term Hispanic. Some Latinos/Hispanics feel strongly about which term they prefer. Some reject both terms, and insist they should be known by their national origin; still others use all terms and vary their usage depending on context.

Those who prefer "Latino" argue that the term preserves the flavor of national origin and the political relationship between the U.S. and Latin America. Also, they say that it is more culturally neutral and racially inclusive of all groups in Latin America. For example, those of indigenous, African, European and mixed origins are assumed to be Latinos, as are Brazilians, whose main language is Portuguese. In addition, they argue that it is less associated with Eurocentric Hispanistas, who were largely conservative wealthy landowning groups; and lastly, they maintain that it is the term most used in numerous editorials that are written in both Spanish and English.

Those who prefer the term "Hispanic" maintain that it should be 10 used because the data on this population is gathered using this term, and the data should not be re-labeled. It is seen to be preferable for scientific publications because it is seen to be more rigorous and consistent with the data. It is argued that Hispanic is a more universal term because this is the term used by most agencies and other data gatherers, while Latino is a regional term more often used in areas where there are large numbers of native Spanish-speakers. In essence, the argument is that this is the term that most people—particularly those living far from Spanish-speaking populations—will use. The term includes those from Spain, although it does not cover those from Brazil. It is also argued that the term "Latino" might be legally problematic, for others of "Latin" descent whose families have never lived in Latin America, e.g., the French, Italians, and others might conceivably argue that they are "Latinos" and therefore should be considered minorities.

## Responding to Reading

1. According to Rodríguez, what traits do Latinos share?
2. In paragraphs 8 through 10, Rodríguez explains why some groups prefer *Hispanic* while others prefer *Latino*. Summarize the two groups' positions. Do you think Rodríguez needs to explain why she uses the term *Latino* in this essay?
3. What differences among Latinos does Rodríguez identify? How does she explain why these differences exist?

## Responding in Writing

Given all the differences among Latinos that Rodríguez identifies, do you think there is really a distinctive "Latino culture"? Why or why not?

# THE MYTH OF THE LATIN WOMAN: I JUST MET A GIRL NAMED MARIA

## Judith Ortiz Cofer

### 1952–

*Born in Hormigueros, Puerto Rico, and raised in Paterson, New Jersey, Judith Ortiz Cofer teaches creative writing at the University of Georgia. She is an award-winning poet and novelist whose books include the novels* The Line of the Sun *(1989) and* Silent Dancing *(1990) as well as a collection of biographical essays. Her most recent books include* A Love Story Beginning in Spanish: Poems *(2005) and the young adult novels* Call Me Maria *(2005) and* If I Could Fly *(2011). In the following essay from her collection* The Latin Deli: Prose and Poetry *(1993), Cofer describes the stereotypes she has confronted as a Latina.*

On a bus trip to London from Oxford University where I was earning some graduate credits one summer, a young man, obviously fresh from a pub, spotted me and as if struck by inspiration went down on his knees in the aisle. With both hands over his heart he broke into an Irish tenor's rendition of "Maria" from *West Side Story*.[1] My politely amused fellow passengers gave his lovely voice the round of gentle applause it deserved. Though I was not quite as amused, I managed my version of an English smile: no show of teeth, no extreme contortions of the facial muscles—I was at this time of my life practicing reserve and cool. Oh, that British control, how I coveted it. But "Maria" had followed me to London, reminding me of a prime fact of my life: you can leave the island, master the English language, and travel as far as you can, but if you are a Latina, especially one like me who so obviously belongs to Rita Moreno's[2] gene pool, the island travels with you.

This is sometimes a very good thing—it may win you that extra minute of someone's attention. But with some people, the same things can make *you* an island—not a tropical paradise but an Alcatraz, a place nobody wants to visit. As a Puerto Rican girl living in the United States[3] and wanting like most children to "belong," I resented the stereotype that my Hispanic appearance called forth from many people I met.

Growing up in a large urban center in New Jersey during the 1960s, I suffered from what I think of as "cultural schizophrenia." Our life was

---

[1]A popular Broadway musical, loosely based on *Romeo and Juliet,* about two rival street gangs, one Anglo and one Puerto Rican, in New York City. [Eds.]

[2]Puerto Rico–born actress who won an Oscar for her role in the 1960 movie version of *West Side Story.* [Eds.]

[3]Although it is an island, Puerto Rico is part of the United States (it is a self-governing commonwealth). [Eds.]

designed by my parents as a microcosm of their *casas*[4] on the island. We spoke in Spanish, ate Puerto Rican food bought at the *bodega*,[5] and practiced strict Catholicism at a church that allotted us a one-hour slot each week for mass, performed in Spanish by a Chinese priest trained as a missionary for Latin America.

As a girl I was kept under strict surveillance by my parents, since my virtue and modesty were, by their cultural equation, the same as their honor. As a teenager I was lectured constantly on how to behave as a proper *señorita*. But it was a conflicting message I received, since the Puerto Rican mothers also encouraged their daughters to look and act like women and to dress in clothes our Anglo friends and their mothers found too "mature" and flashy. The difference was, and is, cultural; yet I often felt humiliated when I appeared at an American friend's party wearing a dress more suitable to a semi-formal than to a playroom birthday celebration. At Puerto Rican festivities, neither the music nor the colors we wore could be too loud.

I remember Career Day in our high school, when teachers told us   5
to come dressed as if for a job interview. It quickly became obvious that to the Puerto Rican girls "dressing up" meant wearing their mother's ornate jewelry and clothing, more appropriate (by mainstream standards) for the company Christmas party than as daily office attire. That morning I had agonized in front of my closet, trying to figure out what a "career girl" would wear. I knew how to dress for school (at the Catholic school I attended, we all wore uniforms), I knew how to dress for Sunday mass, and I knew what dresses to wear for parties at my relatives' homes. Though I do not recall the precise details of my Career Day outfit, it must have been a composite of these choices. But I remember a comment my friend (an Italian American) made in later years that coalesced my impressions of that day. She said that at the business school she was attending, the Puerto Rican girls always stood out for wearing "everything at once." She meant, of course, too much jewelry, too many accessories. On that day at school we were simply made the negative models by the nuns, who were themselves not credible fashion experts to any of us. But it was painfully obvious to me that to the others, in their tailored skirts and silk blouses, we must have seemed "hopeless" and "vulgar." Though I now know that most adolescents feel out of step much of the time, I also know that for the Puerto Rican girls of my generation that sense was intensified. The way our teachers and classmates looked at us that day in school was just a taste of the cultural clash that awaited us in the real world, where prospective employers and men on the street would often misinterpret our tight skirts and jingling bracelets as a "come-on."

---

[4]Homes. [Eds.]
[5]Small grocery store. [Eds.]

Mixed cultural signals have perpetuated certain stereotypes—for example, that of the Hispanic woman as the "hot tamale" or sexual firebrand. It is a one-dimensional view that the media have found easy to promote. In their special vocabulary, advertisers have designated "sizzling" and "smoldering" as the adjectives of choice for describing not only the foods but also the women of Latin America. From conversations in my house I recall hearing about the harassment that Puerto Rican women endured in factories where the "boss-men" talked to them as if sexual innuendo was all they understood, and worse, often gave them the choice of submitting to their advances or being fired.

It is custom, however, not chromosomes, that leads us to choose scarlet over pale pink. As young girls, it was our mothers who influenced our decisions about clothes and colors—mothers who had grown up on a tropical island where the natural environment was a riot of primary colors, where showing your skin was one way to keep cool as well as to look sexy. Most important of all, on the island, women perhaps felt freer to dress and move more provocatively since, in most cases, they were protected by the traditions, mores, and laws of a Spanish/Catholic system of morality and machismo whose main rule was: *You may look at my sister, but if you touch her I will kill you.* The extended family and church structure could provide a young woman with a circle of safety in her small pueblo on the island; if a man "wronged" a girl, everyone would close in to save her family honor.

My mother has told me about dressing in her best party clothes on Saturday nights and going to the town's plaza to promenade with her girlfriends in front of the boys they liked. The males were thus given an opportunity to admire the women and to express their admiration in the form of *piropos:* erotically charged street poems they composed on the spot. (I have myself been subjected to a few *piropos* while visiting the island, and they can be outrageous, although custom dictates that they must never cross into obscenity.) This ritual, as I understand it, also entails a show of studied indifference on the woman's part; if she is "decent," she must not acknowledge the man's impassioned words. So I do understand how things can be lost in translation. When a Puerto Rican girl dressed in her idea of what is attractive meets a man from the mainstream culture who has been trained to react to certain types of clothing as a sexual signal, a clash is likely to take place. I remember the boy who took me to my first formal dance leaning over to plant a sloppy, over-eager kiss painfully on my mouth; when I didn't respond with sufficient passion, he remarked resentfully: "I thought you Latin girls were supposed to mature early," as if I were expected to *ripen* like a fruit or vegetable, not just grow into womanhood like other girls.

It is surprising to my professional friends that even today some people, including those who should know better, still put others "in their place." It happened to me most recently during a stay at a classy metropolitan hotel favored by young professional couples for weddings. Late one evening after the theater, as I walked toward my room with a colleague (a woman with whom I was coordinating an arts program), a middle-aged man in a tuxedo, with a young girl in satin and lace on his arm, stepped directly into our path. With his champagne glass extended toward me, he exclaimed "Evita!"[6]

Our way blocked, my companion and I listened as the man half-recited, half-bellowed "Don't Cry for Me, Argentina." When he finished, the young girl said: "How about a round of applause for my daddy?" We complied, hoping this would bring the silly spectacle to a close. I was becoming aware that our little group was attracting the attention of the other guests. "Daddy" must have perceived this too, and he once more barred the way as we tried to walk past him. He began to shout-sing a ditty to the tune of "La Bamba"—except the lyrics were about a girl named Maria whose exploits rhymed with her name and gonorrhea. The girl kept saying "Oh, Daddy" and looking at me with pleading eyes. She wanted me to laugh along with the others. My companion and I stood silently waiting for the man to end his offensive song. When he finished, I looked not at him but at his daughter. I advised her calmly never to ask her father what he had done in the army. Then I walked between them and to my room. My friend complimented me on my cool handling of the situation, but I confessed that I had really wanted to push the jerk into the swimming pool. This same man—probably a corporate executive, well-educated, even worldly by most standards—would not have been likely to regale an Anglo woman with a dirty song in public. He might have checked his impulse by assuming that she could be somebody's wife or mother, or at least *somebody* who might take offense. But, to him, I was just an Evita or a Maria: merely a character in his cartoon-populated universe.

Another facet of the myth of the Latin woman in the United States is the menial, the domestic—Maria the housemaid or countergirl. It's true that work as domestics, as waitresses, and in factories is all that's available to women with little English and few skills. But the myth of the Hispanic menial—the funny maid, mispronouncing words and cooking up a spicy storm in a shiny California kitchen—has been perpetuated by the media in the same way that "Mammy" from *Gone with the Wind* became America's idea of the black woman for generations. Since I do not wear my diplomas around my neck for all to see, I have on occasion been sent to that "kitchen" where some think I obviously belong.

One incident has stayed with me, though I recognize it as a minor offense. My first public poetry reading took place in Miami, at a restaurant where a luncheon was being held before the event. I was nervous and excited as I walked in with notebook in hand. An older woman

---

[6]A Broadway musical, later made into a movie, about Eva Duarte de Perón, the former first lady of Argentina. [Eds.]

motioned me to her table, and thinking (foolish me) that she wanted me to autograph a copy of my newly published slender volume of verse, I went over. She ordered a cup of coffee from me, assuming that I was the waitress. (Easy enough to mistake my poems for menus, I suppose.) I know it wasn't an intentional act of cruelty. Yet of all the good things that happened later, I remember that scene most clearly, because it reminded me of what I had to overcome before anyone would take me seriously. In retrospect I understand that my anger gave my reading fire. In fact, I have almost always taken any doubt in my abilities as a challenge, the result most often being the satisfaction of winning a convert, of seeing the cold, appraising eyes warm to my words, the body language change, the smile that indicates I have opened some avenue for communication. So that day as I read, I looked directly at that woman. Her lowered eyes told me she was embarrassed at her faux pas, and when I willed her to look up at me, she graciously allowed me to punish her with my full attention. We shook hands at the end of the reading and I never saw her again. She has probably forgotten the entire incident, but maybe not.

Yet I am one of the lucky ones. There are thousands of Latinas without the privilege of an education or the entrees into society that I have. For them life is a constant struggle against the misconceptions perpetuated by the myth of the Latina. My goal is to try to replace the old stereotypes with a much more interesting set of realities. Every time I give a reading, I hope the stories I tell, the dreams and fears I examine in my work, can achieve some universal truth that will get my audience past the particulars of my skin color, my accent, or my clothes.

I once wrote a poem in which I called all Latinas "God's brown daughters." This poem is really a prayer of sorts, offered upward, but also, through the human-to-human channel of art, outward. It is a prayer for communication and for respect. In it, Latin women pray "in Spanish to an Anglo God/with a Jewish heritage," and they are "fervently hoping/that if not omnipotent,/at least He be bilingual."

## Responding to Reading

1. What exactly is the "myth of the Latin woman"? According to Cofer, what has perpetuated this stereotype? Do you see this "myth" as simply demeaning or as potentially dangerous? Why?
2. In paragraph 1, Cofer says, "you can leave [Puerto Rico], master the English language, and travel as far as you can, but if you are a Latina, . . . the island travels with you." What does she mean? Do you think this is also true of people from other ethnic groups (and other nations)? Can you think of any groups whose culture and ethnicity is *not* likely to travel with them?
3. Throughout this essay, Cofer speaks of the "cultural schizophrenia" (3) she felt, describing the "conflicting message" (4), the "cultural clash" (5), and the "mixed cultural signals" (6) she received from the two worlds she inhabited. Do you see this kind of "schizophrenia" as inevitable, or do you think it can be overcome? Do you think it *should* be overcome? Explain.

## Responding in Writing

What stereotypes are associated with your own ethnic group? Do you see these stereotypes as benign or harmful?

# Muslim in America
## Jeffery Sheler
## Michael Betzold

*Author of three books on religious issues, Jeffery Sheler is a religion writer at* U.S. News & World Report *and a correspondent for PBS's* Religion & Ethics NewsWeekly *television news program. Freelance writer Michael Betzold has written several articles and nonfiction books as well as a novel. In the following essay, Sheler and Betzold explore what it means to be a Muslim in America.*

Inside a storefront on West Warren Avenue, a gritty Dearborn, Mich., neighborhood of modest shops with hand-painted Arabic signs, a handful of men respond to the high-pitched chant of the muezzin[1] and form a line facing Mecca. They bow, sit, and prostrate on colorful rugs in a mostly silent rendition of the salat, the daily prayers Muslims have recited for nearly 1,400 years. In a smaller room, a cluster of women with head coverings also recite the prayers in response to the voice of the imam, which they can hear from across the hall. Most of the worshipers are recent refugees from Iraq who want a link to the country they still consider home. "They thank God they are here" in America, says Imam Hushan Al-Husainy, the mosque leader. "But their heart is back home with their loved ones who are suffering."

Meanwhile, 68 miles away, beneath a gleaming white dome and twin minarets that tower over the Ohio cornfields southwest of Toledo, hundreds of families assemble for worship—a largely upper-middle-class flock that represents some 22 nationalities, most U.S. citizens and some second- or third-generation Americans. Few of the women wear head coverings outside of the prayer hall, where only a 3-foot-high partition separates men and women, side by side. After prayers, they all gather for a potluck. The Toledo center, says its president, Cherrefe Kadri, represents a "progressive and middle-of-the-road" brand of Islam that, she says, is "very much at home in Middle America."

This, then, is American Islam: The modern Islamic Center of Greater Toledo and the traditionalist Karbala Islamic Education Center are but two examples of its wide-ranging diversity. And even though it is the nation's fastest-growing faith, with an estimated 7 million adherents

---

[1]At a mosque, the person who leads the call to prayer. [Eds.]

here—nearly double from a decade ago—Islam remains widely misunderstood in this country. The religion of more than a fifth of the world's population is viewed by many Americans as foreign, mysterious, even threatening to the nation's "Judeo-Christian heritage"—certainly no less so since the events of September 11—despite the fact that it shares common roots with Christianity and Judaism and has been present in North America for centuries.

**The rules.** Indeed, Islam embraces the monotheism of Christianity and Judaism, accepts the Hebrew Bible, and venerates Jesus as a prophet. It is centered on the Koran—the Islamic scriptures, which Muslims believe were revealed to the prophet Mohammed—which commands five basic devotional duties, called the "Five Pillars": a declaration of belief that "there is no God but Allah [Arabic for "the God"] and Mohammed is his prophet"; prayers offered five times a day; daytime fasting during the month of Ramadan; charitable giving; and at least one pilgrimage to Mecca. Muslims are forbidden to consume alcohol, illicit drugs, pork, or any meat that is not halal—the Islamic equivalent of kosher. Premarital sex and extramarital sex are sternly prohibited, as are most forms of unchaperoned dating. Emphasis on public modesty prompts many Muslims to cover themselves from the wrists to the ankles. Muslims also may not gamble or pay or accept interest on loans or savings accounts. It is a regimen that often runs in conflict with the dominant culture. Most American Muslims have no choice but to break the prohibition on usury to buy homes and automobiles, for example.

5        But if the intense scrutiny focused on world Islam since September 11 has revealed anything, it is that the faith is no monolith. While there is much that binds the world's 1.2 billion Muslims together, there is no authoritative hierarchy—no pope, no central group of elders—that speaks to them or for them. And American Islam, it emerges, is its own special brand. A recent study sponsored by the Council on American-Islamic Relations [CAIR] in cooperation with the Hartford Institute for Religion Research found that American Muslims generally are more accepting of differences, less inclined to fundamentalism, and more at home in a secular society than most Muslims elsewhere. They are also ethnically diverse: Most are immigrants or their descendants from Islamic countries in Asia, Africa, and the Middle East. About a third are African-Americans, and a small number are whites of European descent.

**Connections?** But while diversity may naturally include the extremes, the question on many people's minds has been what exactly the relationship is between American Islam and the kind of terror and anti-Americanism that came so horribly into focus last month under the guise of religious zealotry. One moderate American Islamic leader,

Sheik Muhammad Hisham Kabbani, told a State Department forum in 1999 that 80 percent of the nation's mosques are headed by clerics who espouse "extremist ideology"—which Kabbani associates with Wahhabism, an Islamic fundamentalist movement that began in Saudi Arabia in the 18th century. But Kabbani, head of the Islamic Supreme Council of America, a Washington, D.C.–based advocacy group, added that "a majority of American Muslims do not agree" with the extremist ideology.

Other American Muslim leaders say Kabbani's estimate of Wahhabi influence in U.S. mosques is exaggerated. "I don't know where he came up with that," says Ingrid Mattson, a Hartford Seminary professor and vice president of the Islamic Society of North America [ISNA]. African-Americans alone account for a third of the mosques, she notes, "and they clearly are not Wahhabis." The CAIR-Hartford study found that about 20 percent of mosques say they interpret the Koran literally, but 7 in 10 follow a more nuanced, nonfundamentalist approach.

Scholars say the democratic structure and autonomy of many American mosques protect them from extremist takeovers. Modern Islamic centers, like the one in Toledo, are "less likely to be dominated by a single teacher or viewpoint," says Frederick Denny, a scholar of Islam at the University of Colorado. That describes at least 60 percent of American mosques, according to the CAIR-Hartford study. Those that are more fundamentalist, he says, often are smaller, with transient members, such as those that "cater to foreign students who want something that feels like home." Even where fundamentalism exists, says Mattson, "there is a huge distinction between fundamentalist ideology and support of terrorism."

What divides American Muslims most often, says Denny, "is not liberal-versus-conservative ideology but how best to domesticate Islam in a Western society without doing violence to either." What, for example, are American Muslims to do with sharia, the Islamic legal and ethical codes that tradition says should undergird Islamic society? Radical clerics say it is a Muslim's duty to impose sharia throughout the world, by force if necessary. But moderates argue that Islamic law must be internalized. "It shouldn't be taken literally," says Imam Farooq Aboelzahab of the Toledo mosque. "The way sharia was applied 1,400 years ago may not always fit. It must be applied to the place and time where you live."

One indication that many Muslims are feeling more at home in 10 America is their growing involvement in the nation's public life. During the past five years, Islamic leaders and groups have become increasingly outspoken on social- and foreign-policy issues. Groups like CAIR, ISNA, the American Muslim Council, and the Islamic Institute maintain a high-visibility Washington presence, working to rally Muslim political activism and acting as media watchdogs. While American Islamic groups were virtually unanimous in condemning the terrorist attacks on New York and Washington, they remain vociferous critics of U.S. policy in the Middle East.

Stronger rhetoric, of course, has its price in this country. In late September, a prominent imam at a Cleveland mosque nearly lost his job over anti-Jewish remarks he had made in a speech 10 years ago. The board at the Islamic Center of Cleveland voted to keep Fawaz Damra after he apologized for the remarks, which appeared on a tape that surfaced recently, but local Jewish leaders are still upset.

**Incendiary rhetoric.** Meanwhile, a leading Muslim teacher in Northern California has apologized for his own rhetorical excesses. Hamza Yusuf, who was invited to the White House to pray with President Bush after the attacks, later came under criticism for saying in a speech two days before the attacks that the United States "stands condemned" and faced "a terrible fate" because of rampant immorality and injustice in its treatment of minorities. While their causes may be just, says Yusuf, "the rhetoric of some Muslim leaders has been too incendiary—I myself have been guilty of it." September 11, he says, "was a wake-up call to me. I don't want to contribute to the hate in any shape or form."

A decade ago, Sulayman Nyang, professor of African studies at Howard University in Washington, D.C., warned in a speech that Islam will be accepted in America only when Muslims fully take their place alongside other citizens, participating in the nation's civic life, and when what the Islamic faith can offer Western culture is recognized widely as something of value. Neither, he says, will be easy to accomplish. But in times like these, such hard work is more important than ever.

## Responding to Reading

1. This essay appeared in a newsmagazine on October 29, 2001, just weeks after the 9/11 terrorist attacks. What do you suppose the writers' purpose was? How can you tell?
2. According to Sheler and Betzold, how is Islam like other widely followed U.S. religions? How is it different?
3. In paragraph 5, the writers assert that the Muslim faith is "no monolith." What do they mean? What evidence do they offer to support this claim?

## Responding in Writing

What do you think it would take for Muslims to truly feel "at home in America" (10)? What elements of their culture might they have to sacrifice? Is this sacrifice worth making?

# THE GAYEST ONE

## Brett Krutzsch

*A Ph.D. student in religion at Temple University, Brett Krutzsch explores the connections between religion and LGBT (lesbian, gay, bisexual, and transgender) issues. He was a 2011 summer institute fellow in the Scholarship and Mentorship Program at the Human Rights Campaign Foundation, which promotes LGBT studies from a religious and theological perspective. His work has appeared in the* New York Blade *and* New York Press. *In the following essay, Krutzsch considers the nuances of gay identity from a personal perspective.*

"Everyone agreed that you're the gayest person in the department," my best friend from work said to me as we strolled through SoHo. Sara was recapping a conversation from a happy hour I missed because I had been at a book reading by Paula Deen, the eccentric Southern woman on the Food Network.

"What does that mean?" I asked.

"Nobody gave any reasons. Someone asked who was the biggest homosexual, people looked around, and Matt said your name. Everybody agreed."

I was immediately irritated and annoyed. Out of the 50 individuals who work in my division at NYU, 11 of us are gay men. How could I so quickly and unanimously be considered the fruitiest of the bunch?

Sara changed the topic to her upcoming wedding. As she talked    5 about whether or not to keep her hair straight or curly, I recalled a friend's birthday party a year ago. We were at a straight bar near Union Square, and an attractive woman, probably in her late 20s, repeatedly glanced my way the entire night. Eventually, she approached me and asked, "Are you here for Craig's party?"

"Yes, I am," I said, as I watched her eyes get big and the color drain from her face.

"Oh, you're gay," she interjected.

I had said three words. Three very little words. Each with one syllable. That was all it took for her to know my sexual orientation.

"I am," I said with an awkward laugh, realizing that she had wanted to hit on me.

"Oh, I thought. I mean, I'm sorry," she mumbled, and then ran off,    10 looking embarrassed.

I turned around and told my friends what happened, and they burst out laughing. I wasn't amused. I left the party soon after that and walked home, feeling sorry for myself.

Still talking about her wedding. Sara decided she should keep her hair curly since she was having an outdoor ceremony in July. "After all," she said. "It could never be completely straight anyway."

Apparently, with a voice like mine, neither could I.

That week I couldn't stop fixating on the idea of me as the biggest queen at work. I tried thinking of stereotypes I fit, but things still didn't make sense. Of all the gay men in my department, I was the only one in a long-term relationship. My boyfriend and I lived together, had joint finances, and shared holidays with each other's families. We were boringly monogamous. Our nights usually concluded with *Seinfeld*, not sex. So it couldn't be that I embodied the stereotype of the promiscuous gay man with a wild night life. I hadn't set foot in a gay club in three years. Of all the queer men I worked with, my homelife seemed the most heterosexual.

15 OK, my interests and hobbies were never particularly manly. I'd much rather be at a Broadway show than at a Yankees game. Given a choice, I always picked a day at the spa over a day of camping. I've typically been more comfortable at brunches with women chatting about sample sales than out having beers with the guys talking about cars or the stock market.

Not long ago I was walking down Third Avenue with my friend Lauren. It was raining and we shared an umbrella. We passed a homeless man sprawled out on the sidewalk who yelled to Lauren, "Hey, gorgeous, want to get married?"

"Sorry, I'm taken," Lauren said, looking up at me.

The homeless man screamed back, "Yeah, to a homo."

I wasn't singing "It's Raining Men" under the umbrella. I was just walking. Even the homeless man had enough gay-dar to know I wasn't heterosexual.

20 I assumed that I was decreed the gayest at my job because I was the least likely to pass as straight. I wore form-fitting Burberry polos, openly raved about Kelly Clarkson, and bought expensive Kiehl's skin care products even though I was only 28. If I were put in a lineup, it probably wouldn't take someone with Nancy Drew's investigative skills to finger me as the boy who likes boys. Nevertheless, I was still perplexed by people's need to ask, "Who among us is the biggest fairy?" I doubt straight guys ever sat around saying: "Bob, you're definitely the straightest one here." "No way, Harry. You're totally straighter."

When I moved to Manhattan four years ago I thought I was relocating to the gay mecca, as if the mother ship were calling me home. On my first outing to the bars of Chelsea and subsequent walks along Eighth Avenue I quickly observed that I didn't look like other gay men in the area. Standing six feet tall and weighing 140 pounds, I was a skinny Jewish bookworm who had no interest in going to the gym to become one of the musclemen who ruled the New York City gayborhoods. They paid little attention to me, so at that point in my life I felt like I wasn't gay enough.

I never believed my sexuality was a choice, but how I presented myself to the world was. Until I came out of the closet my senior year at Emory University, I wore oversized T-shirts and pretended to have a crush on Jennifer Aniston, like many of the straight, beer-drinking guys my age, never letting on that my lust was actually for Brad Pitt. I've since learned that I wasn't fooling anyone—my family members and friends have said they always assumed I was gay.

Growing up in Indiana, the boys in my school constantly asked why I talked like a girl. I didn't understand what they meant until I was in third grade, when I heard myself on an answering machine. I sounded just like my friend Liz, so each night I prayed for my voice to deepen and be like my dad's. After puberty, when I thought my prayers had been answered, the same boys asked why I talked like Michael Jackson. I always felt my voice was a reminder that I was different, a freak, and less than a real man.

When I came out at 22, my shrink said it could take several years to fully accept my sexuality. Six years have passed, and I'm now sharing my life with an incredible partner, but I still struggle, because I think of myself as a liberal Jewish pseudo-intellectual, not an über-homosexual. I know it isn't a bad thing to be the gayest one. I'm just not sure how to accept the title or if I'm ready to wear the tiara and sash.

## Responding to Reading

1. Despite his apparent comfort with and acceptance of his gay identity, Krutzsch objects to being so easily recognized as gay—and to being characterized as the "gayest person in the department" (1). Why?
2. How, according to Krutzsch, is gay culture stereotyped? In what respects does he believe he does not fit that stereotype?
3. In paragraph 22, Krutzsch says, "I never believed my sexuality was a choice, but how I presented myself to the world was." How much choice do you think he actually has in determining how others perceive him?

## Responding in Writing

Do you think Krutzsch should take steps to present himself to the world differently? If so, what should he do? If not, why not?

# ON THE MEANING OF PLUMBING
# AND POVERTY

## Melanie Scheller

*Melanie Scheller is the author of the children's book* My Grandfather's Hat *(1992) and the writer and director of the short film* No Where, USA *(2009). In the following essay, Scheller explores the cultural identity of the rural poor.*

Several years ago I spent some time as a volunteer on the geriatric ward of a psychiatric hospital. I was fascinated by the behavior of one of the patients, an elderly woman who shuffled at regular intervals to the bathroom, where she methodically flushed the toilet. Again and again she carried out her sacred mission as if summoned by some supernatural force, until the flush of the toilet became a rhythmic counterpoint for the ward's activity. If someone blocked her path or if, God forbid, the bathroom was in use when she reached it, she became agitated and confused.

Obviously, that elderly patient was a sick woman. And yet I felt a certain kinship with her, for I too have suffered from an obsession with toilets. I spent much of my childhood living in houses without indoor plumbing, and while I don't feel compelled to flush a toilet at regular intervals, I sometimes feel that toilets, or the lack thereof, have shaped my identity in ways that are painful to admit.

I'm not a child of the Depression,[1] but I grew up in an area of the South that had changed little since the day of the New Deal.[2] My mother was a widow with six children to support, not an easy task under any circumstances, but especially difficult in rural North Carolina during the 1960s. To her credit, we were never seriously in danger of going hungry. Our vegetable garden kept us stocked with tomatoes and string beans. We kept a few chickens and sometimes a cow. Blackberries were free for the picking in the fields nearby. Neighbors did their good Christian duty by bringing us donations of fresh fruit and candy at Christmastime. But a roof over our heads—that wasn't so easily improvised.

Like rural Southern gypsies, we moved from one dilapidated Southern farmhouse to another in a constant search for a decent place to live. Sometimes we moved when the rent increased beyond the 30 or 40 dollars my mother could afford. Or the house burned down, not an unusual occurrence in substandard housing. One year when we were gathered together for Thanksgiving dinner, a stranger walked in without knocking and announced that we were being evicted. The house had been sold without our knowledge and the new owner wanted to start remodeling immediately. We tried to finish our meal with an attitude of thanksgiving while he worked around us with his tape measure.

5    Usually we rented from farm families who'd moved from the old home place to one of the brick boxes that are now the standard in rural Southern architecture. The old farmhouse wasn't worth fixing up with a septic tank and flush toilet, but it was good enough to rent for a few

---

[1]Great Depression (1929–1939). [Eds.]

[2]Economic relief and reform program implemented by the U.S. government between 1933–1939. [Eds.]

dollars a month to families like mine. The idea of tenants' rights hadn't trickled down yet from the far reaches of the liberal North. It never occurred to us to demand improvements in the facilities. The ethic of the land said we should take what we could get and be grateful for it.

Without indoor plumbing, getting clean is a tiring and time consuming ritual. At one point I lived in a five-room house with six or more people, all of whom congregated in the one heated room to eat, do homework, watch television, dress and undress, argue, wash dishes. During cold weather we dragged mattresses from the unheated rooms and slept huddled together on the floor by the woodstove. For my bathing routine, I first pinned a sheet to a piece of twine strung across the kitchen. That gave me some degree of privacy from the six other people in the room. At that time our house had an indoor cold-water faucet, from which I filled a pot of water to heat on the kitchen stove. It took several pots of hot water to fill the metal washtub we used.

Since I was a teenager and prone to sulkiness if I didn't get special treatment, I got to take the first bath while the water was still clean. The others used the water I left behind, freshened up with hot water from the pot on the stove. Then the tub had to be dragged to the door and the bath water dumped outside. I longed to be like the woman in the Calgon bath oil commercials, luxuriating in a marble tub full of scented water with bubbles piled high and stacks of thick, clean towels nearby.

People raised in the land of the bath-and-a-half may wonder why I make such a fuss about plumbing. Maybe they spent a year in the Peace Corps, or they back-packed across India, or they worked at a summer camp and, gosh, using a latrine isn't all that bad. And of course it's *not* that bad. Not when you can catch the next plane out of the country, or pick up your duffel bag and head for home, or call mom and dad to come and get you when things get too tedious. A sojourn in a Third World country, where everyone shares the same primitive facilities, may cause some temporary discomfort, but the experience is soon converted into amusing anecdotes for cocktail-party conversation. It doesn't corrode your self-esteem with a sense of shame the way a childhood spent in chronic, unrelenting poverty can.

In the South of my childhood, not having indoor plumbing was the indelible mark of poor white trash. The phrase "so poor they didn't have a pot to piss in" said it all. Poor white trash were viciously stereotyped, and never more viciously than on the playground. White-trash children had cooties—everybody knew that. They had ringworm and pinkeye—don't get near them or you might catch it. They picked their noses. They messed in their pants. If a white-trash child made the mistake of catching a softball during recess, the other children made an elaborate show of wiping it clean before they would touch it.

Once a story circulated at school about a family whose infant 10
daughter had fallen into the "slop jar" and drowned. When I saw the
smirks and heard the laughter with which the story was told, I felt sick
and afraid in the pit of my stomach. A little girl had died, but people
were laughing. What had she done to deserve that laughter? I could
only assume that using a chamber pot was something so disgusting, so
shameful, that it made a person less than human.

My family was visibly and undeniably poor. My clothes were obviously hand-me-downs. I got free lunches at school. I went to the health
department for immunizations. Surely it was equally obvious that we
didn't have a flush toilet. But like an alcoholic who believes no one will
know he has a problem as long as he doesn't drink in public, I convinced myself that no one knew my family's little secret. It was a form
of denial that would color my relationships with the outside world for
years to come.

Having a friend from school spend the night at my house was out
of the question. Better to be friendless than to have my classmates know
my shameful secret. Home visits from teachers or ministers left me in
a dither of anticipatory anxiety. As they chattered on and on with
Southern small talk about tomato plants and relish recipes, I sat on the
edge of my seat, tensed against the dreaded words, "May I use your
bathroom, please?" When I began dating in high school, I'd lie in wait
behind the front door, ready to dash out as soon as my date pulled in
the driveway, never giving him a chance to hear the call of nature while
on our property.

With the help of a scholarship I was able to go away to college,
where I could choose from dozens of dormitory toilets and take as
many hot showers as I wanted, but I could never openly express my
joy in using the facilities. My roommates, each a pampered only child
from a well-to-do family, whined and complained about having to
share a bathroom. I knew that if I expressed delight in simply having
a bathroom, I would immediately be labeled as a hick. The need to
conceal my real self by stifling my emotions created a barrier around
me and I spent my college years in a vacuum of isolation.

Almost 20 years have passed since I first tried to leave my family's
chamber pot behind. For many of those years it followed behind me—
the ghost of chamber pots past—clanging and banging and threatening
to spill its humiliating contents at any moment. I was convinced that
everyone could see it, could smell it even. No college degree or job title
seemed capable of banishing it.

15    If finances had permitted, I might have become an Elvis Presley
or a Tammy Faye Bakker, easing the pain of remembered poverty with
gold-plated bathtub fixtures and leopard-skinned toilet seats. I feel
blessed that gradually, ever so gradually, the shame of poverty has
begun to fade. The pleasures of the present now take priority over

where a long-ago bowel movement did or did not take place. But for many Southerners, chamber pots and outhouses are more than just memories.

In North Carolina alone, 200,000 people still live without indoor plumbing.[3] People who haul their drinking water home from a neighbor's house or catch rainwater in barrels. People who can't wash their hands before handling food, the way restaurant employees are required by state law to do. People who sneak into public restrooms every day to wash, shave, and brush their teeth before going to work or to school. People who sacrifice their dignity and self-respect when forced to choose between going homeless and going to an outhouse. People whose children think they deserve the conditions in which they live and hold their heads low to hide the shame. But they're not the ones who should feel ashamed. No, they're not the ones who should feel ashamed.

## Responding to Reading

1. In paragraph 2, Scheller says, "I sometimes feel that toilets, or the lack thereof, have shaped my identity in ways that are painful to admit." Exactly how has the issue of indoor plumbing shaped her identity?
2. How does Scheller see herself as different from those who were "raised in the land of the bath-and-a-half" (8)? What does she mean by "the land of the bath-and-a-half"?
3. What specific problems, apart from the lack of indoor plumbing, did Scheller and her family face because they were poor? Why do you think she focuses on toilets instead of on another problem?

## Responding in Writing

The culture of rural poverty Scheller describes in this essay is not a culture that is generally freely chosen. How might their shared experiences and memories nevertheless create a sense of cultural identity for the rural poor?

---

[3]According to the North Carolina Housing Coalition, more than 13,000 homes in the state are still without indoor plumbing. [Eds.]

——————————————— FOCUS ———————————————

## Are We Moving toward a Post-Racial Society?

→ **NOTE: Please answer BOTH Question 8 about Hispanic origin and Question 9 about race. For this census, Hispanic origins are not races.**

**8. Is Person 1 of Hispanic, Latino, or Spanish origin?**

☐ **No,** not of Hispanic, Latino, or Spanish origin
☐ Yes, Mexican, Mexican Am., Chicano
☐ Yes, Puerto Rican
☐ Yes, Cuban
☐ Yes, another Hispanic, Latino, or Spanish origin — *Print origin, for example, Argentinean, Colombian, Dominican, Nicaraguan, Salvadoran, Spaniard, and so on.* ↗

**9. What is Person 1's race?** *Mark* X *one or more boxes.*

☐ White
☐ Black, African Am., or Negro
☐ American Indian or Alaska Native — *Print name of enrolled or principal tribe.* ↗

☐ Asian Indian    ☐ Japanese    ☐ Native Hawaiian
☐ Chinese    ☐ Korean    ☐ Guamanian or Chamorro
☐ Filipino    ☐ Vietnamese    ☐ Samoan
☐ Other Asian — *Print race, for example, Hmong, Laotian, Thai, Pakistani, Cambodian, and so on.* ↗    ☐ Other Pacific Islander — *Print race, for example, Fijian, Tongan, and so on.* ↗

☐ Some other race — *Print race.* ↗

Two questions on 2010 census form

## Responding to the Image

1. Do you think questions 8 and 9 on the census form offer enough choices? Do you think these questions offer *too many* choices? Explain.
2. Which box (or boxes) would you check to describe your own racial and ethnic identity? Why?

# WHY RACE ISN'T AS "BLACK" AND "WHITE" AS WE THINK

## Brent Staples

### 1951–

*After earning a Ph.D. in psychology from the University of Chicago in 1977, Brent Staples turned to journalism, writing for the* Chicago Sun-Times *and the* New York Times. *In 1990, he joined the editorial board of the* New York Times, *where his columns now appear regularly. His memoir* Parallel Time *(1994), which was inspired by his brother's murder in a dispute over a cocaine deal, describes Staples's own internal struggles. In the following essay, he considers the ways in which we live in a post-racial society.*

People have occasionally asked me how a black person came by a "white" name like Brent Staples. One letter writer ridiculed it as "an anchorman's name" and accused me of making it up. For the record, it's a British name—and the one my parents gave me. "Staples" probably arrived in my family's ancestral home in Virginia four centuries ago with the British settlers.

The earliest person with that name we've found—Richard Staples—was hacked to death by Powhatan Indians not far from Jamestown in 1622. The name moved into the 18th century with Virginians like John Staples, a white surveyor who worked in Thomas Jefferson's home county, Albemarle, not far from the area where my family was enslaved.

The black John Staples who married my paternal great-great-grandmother just after Emancipation—and became the stepfather of her children—could easily have been a Staples family slave. The transplanted Britons who had owned both sides of my family had given us more than a preference for British names. They had also given us their DNA. In what was an almost everyday occurrence at the time, my great-great-grandmothers on both sides gave birth to children fathered by white slave masters.

I've known all this for a long time, and was not surprised by the results of a genetic screening performed by DNAPrint Genomics, a company that traces ancestral origins to far-flung parts of the globe. A little more than half of my genetic material came from sub-Saharan Africa—common for people who regard themselves as black—with slightly more than a quarter from Europe.

The result that knocked me off my chair showed that one-fifth of my ancestry is Asian. Poring over the charts and statistics, I said out loud, "This has got to be a mistake." 5

That's a common response among people who are tested. Ostensibly white people who always thought of themselves as 100 percent European find they have substantial African ancestry. People who regard themselves as black sometimes discover that the African ancestry is a minority portion of their DNA.

These results are forcing people to re-examine the arbitrary calculations our culture uses to decide who is "white" and who is "black."

As with many things racial, this story begins in the slave-era South, where sex among slaves, masters and mistresses got started as soon as the first slave ship sailed into Jamestown Harbor in 1619. By the time of the American Revolution, there was a visible class of light-skinned black people who no longer looked or sounded African. Free mulattos, emancipated by guilt-ridden fathers, may have accounted for up to three-quarters of the tiny free-black population before the Revolution.

By the eve of the Civil War, the swarming numbers of mixed-race slaves on Southern plantations had become a source of constant anguish to planters' wives, who knew quite well where those racially ambiguous children were coming from.

10      Faced with widespread fear that racial distinctions were losing significance, the South decided to define the problem away. People with any ascertainable black ancestry at all were defined as black under the law and stripped of basic rights. The "one drop" laws defined as black even people who were blond and blue-eyed and appeared white.

Black people snickered among themselves and worked to subvert segregation at every turn. Thanks to white ancestry spread throughout the black community, nearly every family knew of someone born black who successfully passed as white to get access to jobs, housing and public accommodations that were reserved for white people only. Black people who were not quite light enough to slip undetected into white society billed themselves as Greek, Spanish, Portuguese, Italian, South Asian, Native American—you name it. These defectors often married into ostensibly white families at a time when interracial marriage was either illegal or socially stigmatized.

Those of us who grew up in the 1950's and 60's read black-owned magazines and newspapers that praised the racial defectors as pioneers while mocking white society for failing to detect them. A comic newspaper column by the poet Langston Hughes—titled "Why Not Fool Our White Folks?"—typified the black community's sense of smugness about knowing the real racial score. In keeping with this history, many black people I know find it funny when supposedly white Americans profess shock at the emergence of blackness in the family tree. But genetic testing holds plenty of surprises for black folks, too.

Which brings me back to my Asian ancestry. It comes as a surprise, given that my family's oral histories contain not a single person who is described as Asian. More testing on other family members should clarify the issue, but for now, I can only guess. This ancestry could well have come through a 19th-century ancestor who was incorrectly described as Indian, often a catchall category at the time.

The test results underscore what anthropologists have said for eons: racial distinctions as applied in this country are social categories and not scientific concepts. In addition, those categories draw hard, sharp distinctions among groups of people who are more alike than they are different. The ultimate point is that none of us really know who we are, ancestrally speaking. All we ever really know is what our parents and grandparents have told us.

## Responding to Reading

1.  What do the following pieces of information lead you to conclude about Staples's racial heritage?

    -   Two of his great-great-grandmothers had children by white slave masters.

    -   About half of his genetic material is from sub-Saharan Africa.

    -   About a quarter of his genetic material is from Europe.

    -   Twenty percent of his ancestry is Asian.

2.  Given what we learn about Staples's roots, do you think *black* is the most appropriate term he could use to describe his racial identity? On what grounds would John H. McWhorter (p. 327) agree with this choice? What term might Elizabeth Chang (p. 330) recommend? Why?
3.  In his conclusion, Staples points out that "racial distinctions as applied in this country are social categories and not scientific concepts" (14). Do you think his conclusion suggests an optimistic or pessimistic view of future race relations? Explain.

## Responding in Writing

In paragraph 7, Staples says that results of DNA analysis are "forcing people to re-examine the arbitrary calculations our culture uses to decide who is 'white' and who is 'black.'" Do you agree that the re-examination he refers to is actually occurring, or do you believe the "arbitrary calculations" will continue to rule?

# WHY I'M BLACK, NOT AFRICAN AMERICAN

## John H. McWhorter

### 1965–

*A Manhattan Institute senior fellow in public policy and a contributing editor to the Institute's* City Journal, *John H. McWhorter teaches linguistics at the Center for American Studies at Columbia University. McWhorter is also a contributing editor at the* New Republic *and* TheRoot.com *and the author of numerous books on language, race, culture, and music, including, most recently,* What Language Is:

*And What It Isn't and What It Could Be (2011). His work has appeared in numerous publications, such as the* Chronicle of Higher Education, *the* Los Angeles Times, New York *magazine, the* New York Times, *the* Wall Street Journal, *and the* Washington Post. *In the following essay, McWhorter considers the cultural significance of the terms we use to define racial identity.*

It's time we descendants of slaves brought to the United States let go of the term "African American" and go back to calling ourselves Black— with a capital B.

Modern America is home now to millions of immigrants who were born in Africa. Their cultures and identities are split between Africa and the United States. They have last names like Onwughalu and Senkofa. They speak languages like Wolof, Twi, Yoruba and Hausa, and speak English with an accent. They were raised on African cuisine, music, dance and dress styles, customs and family dynamics. Their children often speak or at least understand their parents' native language.

Living descendants of slaves in America neither knew their African ancestors nor even have elder relatives who knew them. Most of us worship in Christian churches. Our cuisine is more southern U.S. than Senegalese. Starting with ragtime and jazz, we gave America intoxicating musical beats based on African conceptions of rhythm, but with melody and harmony based on Western traditions.

Also, we speak English. Black Americans' home speech is largely based on local dialects of England and Ireland. Africa echoes in the dialect only as a whisper, in certain aspects of sound and melody. A working-class black man in Cincinnati has more in common with a working-class white man in Providence than with a Ghanaian.

5　　With the number of African immigrants in the U.S. nearly tripling since 1990, the use of "African American" is becoming increasingly strained. For example, Alan Keyes, the Republican Senate candidate in Illinois, has claimed that as a descendant of slaves, he is the "real" African American, compared with his Democratic rival, Barack Obama, who has an African father and white mother. And the reason Keyes and others are making arguments such as this is rather small, the idea being that "African American" should refer only to people with a history of subordination in this country—as if African immigrants such as Amadou Diallo, who was killed by police while reaching for his wallet, or Caribbean ones such as torture victim Abner Louima have found the U.S. to be the Land of Oz.

We are not African to any meaningful extent, but we are not white either—and that is much of why Jesse Jackson's presentation of the term "African American" caught on so fast. It sets us apart from the mainstream. It carries an air of standing protest, a reminder that our ancestors were brought here against their will, that their descendants were treated like animals for centuries, and that we have come a long way since then.

But we need a way of sounding those notes with a term that, first, makes some sense and, second, does not insult the actual African

Americans taking their place in our country. And our name must also celebrate our history here, in the only place that will ever be our home. To term ourselves as part "African" reinforces a sad implication: that our history is basically slave ships, plantations, lynching, fire hoses in Birmingham, and then South Central,[1] and that we need to look back to Mother Africa to feel good about ourselves.

But what about the black business districts that thrived across the country after slavery was abolished? What about Frederick Douglass, Ida B. Wells, W.E.B. Du Bois, Gwendolyn Brooks, Richard Wright and Thurgood Marshall, none born in Africa and all deeply American people? And while we're on Marshall, what about the civil rights revolution, a moral awakening that we gave to ourselves and the nation. My roots trace back to working-class Black people—Americans, not foreigners—and I'm proud of it. I am John Hamilton McWhorter the Fifth. Four men with my name and appearance, doing their best in a segregated America, came before me. They and their dearest are the heritage that I can feel in my heart, and they knew the sidewalks of Philadelphia and Atlanta, not Sierra Leone.

So, we will have a name for ourselves—and it should be Black. "Colored" and "Negro" had their good points but carry a whiff of *Plessy v. Ferguson* and Bull Connor[2] about them, so we will let them lie. "Black" isn't perfect, but no term is.

Meanwhile, the special value of "Black" is that it carries the same   10 potent combination of pride, remembrance and regret that "African American" was designed for. Think of what James Brown meant with "Say it loud, I'm Black and I'm proud." And then imagine: "Say it loud, I'm African American and I'm proud."

Since the late 1980s, I have gone along with using "African American" for the same reason that we throw rice at a bride—because everybody else was doing it. But no more. From now on, in my writings on race I will be returning to the word I grew up with, which reminds me of my true self and my ancestors who worked here to help make my life possible: Black.

## Responding to Reading

1. Why does McWhorter believe that *African American* is an inappropriate term for black Americans?
2. According to McWhorter, what negative associations does the term *African American* have? What positive connotations does he associate with *black*? Does he make a convincing argument for his characterization of these two terms?
3. Throughout this essay, McWhorter capitalizes the word *black* but not the word *white*. Why? What is your reaction to this stylistic decision?

---

[1]The 1992 South Central Los Angeles race riots. [Eds.]

[2]The Birmingham, Alabama, Commissioner of Public Safety (1897–1973) who, in 1963, ordered police officers to use police dogs and fire hoses to break up civil rights demonstrations. [Eds.]

## Responding in Writing

What different terms are used to identify the ethnic or racial group from which you draw your primary cultural identity? Which term do you prefer, and why?

# Why Obama Should Not Have Checked "Black" on His Census Form

## Elizabeth Chang

*An editor of the* Washington Post's *Sunday magazine, Elizabeth Chang also contributes articles to the newspaper on such topics as books, style, and travel. In the following essay, she examines the implications of racial labels.*

I have always considered Barack Obama to be biracial, and I had hoped that his election would help our country move beyond the tired concept of race. Unfortunately, the president is not getting with my program.

Although I knew Obama self-identifies as African American, I was disappointed when I read that that's what he checked on his census form. The federal government, finally heeding the desires of multiracial people to be able to accurately define themselves, had changed the rules in 2000, so he could have also checked white. Or he could have checked "some other race." Instead, Obama went with black alone.

Despite being raised by a white mother and white grandparents, despite have spent most of his childhood in the rainbow state of Hawaii, despite clearly being comfortable in almost any type of crowd (though I suppose Tea Partyers might give him pause), the president apparently considers himself only black. "I self-identify as an African American. That's how I am treated and that's how I am viewed. And I'm proud of it," he has said. But he also argued in his famous speech about race that he could no more disown the Reverend Jeremiah Wright[1] "than I can my white grandmother." With his census choice, he has done precisely that.

I am the mother of biracial children (Asian/Caucasian) and believe that multiracial people need to be accepted and acknowledged—even celebrated. The president's choice disappoints me, and it seems somewhat disingenuous. Obama, who has also referred to himself as a "mutt," made a big deal during the 2008 campaign of being able to relate to Hawaiians and Midwesterners, Harvard grads and salespeople, blacks, whites, Latinos, whatever—precisely because of his "unconventional"

[1]African-American pastor and polarizing figure (1941– ) whose condemnation of the U. S. government after 9/11 invoked harsh criticism. [Eds.]

background and multicultural exposure. On the census, however, he has effectively said that when it counts, he is black.

Michelle Hughes, president of the Chicago Biracial Family Network, told a reporter that she, too, was disappointed. "I think his choice will have political, social and cultural ramifications," she added. 5

I agree. I also wonder: Aren't people supposed to fill out their census forms accurately? Why else are we doing it? If everyone put down on the form how they "identified," I don't know what kind of count we'd wind up with, but clearly it would not reflect the racial makeup of the United States. As many have argued, race is an almost useless construct, so that might not matter, except in one very important area: If every biracial person chose one race, as Obama did, or as people had to do before the forms were changed in 2000, the census would portray a society more divided than it actually is. I'm all for tossing the whole racial-classification bit now, but I also know that if we fill out our forms accurately, the numbers will someday do that for us by quantifying the ridiculousness of race. In the meantime, if we aren't going to get rid of the racial category, we need to do it right.

Some have said that by putting himself in one box instead of two, Obama is simply exhibiting pride in being African American. I can appreciate that. But there is an important consequence when our president does not acknowledge half of his heritage, or, more basically, the mother and grandparents who raised him, or even his commonality with his sister, who is also biracial, though with a different mix. If the most powerful person in this country says that because society thinks he looks black, he is black, it sends a message that biracial children have to identify with the side they most resemble. That might be a problem for my daughters, who consider themselves Jewish, Chinese and, because it's the Chang family's home state, Hawaiian, yet are most often mistaken for Latinas. They usually shrug off that misperception, and I am glad. After all, if we let society determine what we are, we will never change society.

## Responding to Reading

1. How does Barack Obama explain why he identified himself as black on the U.S. Census form? Why does Chang believe this designation is inappropriate as well as "somewhat disingenuous" (4)?
2. In paragraph 6, Chang says, "If everyone put down on the form how they 'identified,' I don't know what kind of count we'd wind up with, but clearly it would not reflect the racial makeup of the United States." Do you think a person's racial identity is more or less important than his or her actual racial heritage? Explain.
3. Do you agree with Chang's conclusion that "if we let society determine what we are, we will never change society" (7)? Why or why not?

## Responding in Writing

Who, if anyone, do you believe should check "black" on the U.S. Census form? Review Brent Staples's essay on page 325 before you respond.

# WIDENING THE FOCUS

## For Critical Reading and Writing

Referring specifically to the three readings in this chapter's Focus section, write an essay in which you answer the question, "Are We Moving toward a Post-Racial Society?"

## For Further Reading

The following readings can suggest additional perspectives for thinking and writing about the role of race and culture in American society.

- Oscar Hijuelos, "Lost in Time and Words, a Child Begins Anew" (p. 131)

- Brent Staples, "Just Walk On By" (p. 356)

- Jasmin Darznik, "Persian, English" (p. 140)

- Martin Luther King, Jr., "Letter from Birmingham Jail" (p. 464)

## For Focused Research

The diverse cultural makeup of the United States has defined the country since its inception. Today, population of some cultural groups, such as Asian Americans and Hispanics, is growing exponentially. To gain greater insight into the various cultural groups in the United States, consult the following Web sites:

- <http://education.byu.edu/diversity/culture.html>, a page that provides information on various cultural groups in the United States.

- <http://pewhispanic.org/reports/report.php?ReportID=140>, a 2011 report about the country's growing Hispanic population

Then, write an essay about the fastest-growing cultural groups in the United States. Who is in the majority now, and who will be in the majority in 25 or 50 years? How do you think the growing population of these groups will change the United States? Support your points with information from the online resources you use.

## Beyond the Classroom

Survey ten classmates representing several different races, and ask them the following questions:

- Would you date a person of another race? Why or why not?
- Would you marry a person of another race? Why or why not?
- How would your parents react in each case?

Compare the responses you get from people of different races. Based on this very limited sample, do the respondents from one background seem more open to interracial dating and marriage than the respondents from another background? If so, how do you account for these differences? Write an essay that summarizes your conclusions.

---
# WRITING
---

## CULTURE AND IDENTITY

1. Write an essay in which you define your cultural identity. With which group or groups do you identify most strongly, and why? Begin your essay by analyzing how one writer in this chapter views his or her personal cultural identity. Then, discuss how your own attitudes toward culture are like and unlike those held by the writer you chose.

2. Do you think there is a distinctly "American" culture? If so, what are its key characteristics? Do you think that this "American" culture will endure? Write an essay in which you answer these questions, using information from readings in this chapter to support your points.

3. Some writers represented in this chapter (for example, Judith Ortiz Cofer, p. 308) feel pulled in two directions, torn between their own culture and the "American" society in which they live. Do you believe this conflict can ever be resolved, or do you think first-generation Americans (and perhaps their children and even their children's children) will always feel torn?

4. Is it possible to identify equally with two cultures—for example, black and Latino, Christian and Asian, urban and Native American? Write an essay that answers this question, referring to one or more essays in this chapter as well as to your own experiences.

5. How do tattoos or other kinds of body art (or fashion choices) express a person's cultural identity and build a group culture? Review the photo essay on page 300, and then write an essay that answers this question. You may refer to the images in the photo essay as well as to examples drawn from your own life.

6. Write an extended definition of a culture that is not based on race, ethnicity, geography, or religion—for example, business culture or hockey culture.

7. Many people believe that a "culture of poverty" exists in our nation. Define this culture, enumerating its features, and explain how and why members of this culture are set apart from mainstream culture. Refer to Melanie Scheller's essay (p. 319) in your discussion.

8. In what sense does a person's religion constitute a cultural identity? Is this culture based on shared beliefs and values, or is it defined by history, geography, family, or tradition? Write an essay that answers these questions. Include a discussion of your own religious identity (or lack of one).

9. Write an essay that defines rural, suburban, or urban culture.
10. Some writers in this chapter choose to identify with one particular culture; others try to straddle two cultures; still others seem to have a cultural identity thrust upon them by others. Write an essay that considers the differences among these three kinds of cultural identity.

# 7

# THE AMERICAN DREAM

The American Dream—of political and religious freedom, equal access to education, equal opportunity in the workplace, upward mobility, and the possibility of success and wealth—is often elusive. In the process of working toward the dream, people struggle to overcome their status as newcomers or outsiders—to fit in, to belong, to be accepted. As they work toward their goals, however, some must make painful decisions, for full participation in American society may mean assimilating: giving up language, custom, and culture and becoming more like others. Thus, although the American Dream may ultimately mean winning something, it can often mean losing something—a vital part of oneself—as well.

African-American man at "colored" drinking fountain, Oklahoma City, OK, 1939

For many people, an important part of the American Dream is the chance to reinvent themselves—the opportunity to become someone different, someone better. From Benjamin Franklin to Malcolm X, Americans have a long tradition of reinvention, which can involve anything from undertaking a program of self-improvement to undergoing a complete change of social identity.

In a free and mobile society, people can (theoretically, at least) become whatever they want to be. In the United States, reinvention has often come about through education and hard work, but Americans have also been able to change who they are and how they are perceived by changing their professions, their associations, or their places of residence. Along with this process of reinvention comes a constant self-analysis, as we Americans continue to question who we are and what we can become.

Many of the essays in this chapter are written from the point of view of outsiders looking in. These writers want to be accepted, to belong. Still, while some of these outsiders eagerly anticipate full acceptance, with all the rights and responsibilities that this entails, others are more cautious, afraid of the personal or cultural price they will have to pay for full acceptance into the American mainstream.

In recent years, with the worsening of the U.S. economy, the American Dream has become more elusive—not just for recent

President-elect Barack Obama saluted by U.S. Capitol Police guards at his inauguration in January 2009

immigrants but also for those whose families have been in this country for many generations. With unemployment rising, college costs soaring, and many homeowners unable to keep up with their mortgage payments, the American Dream is increasingly becoming out of reach for many.

This chapter's Focus section, "Should Undocumented Immigrants Have a Path to Citizenship?" (p. 376), zeroes in on the implications of the American Dream for those young people whose parents came to this country illegally. (Note that the DREAM Act—federal legislation that would have provided a path to citizenship for those who were brought to the United States as minors—was defeated by Congress. In June 2012, President Obama issued an executive order offering those who entered the United States illegally when under the age of 16 an opportunity to apply for deferred action for a period of two years, with an option to renew. During this period, they can work legally and cannot be deported.)

## PREPARING TO READ AND WRITE

As you read and prepare to write about the essays in this chapter, you may consider the following questions:

- What does the American Dream mean to the writer? Is the American Dream defined in social, political, economic, or cultural terms?

- Is the essay a personal narrative? an analysis of a problem facing a group? both of these?

- Is the writer's purpose to explain his or her dream to others? to explore his or her place in American society? to persuade others to take action?

- Has the writer been able to achieve the American Dream? If so, by what means? If not, why not?

- What are the greatest obstacles that stand between the writer and the American Dream? Would you characterize these obstacles as primarily cultural, social, political, racial, economic, religious, or educational?

- Who do you think has the easiest access to the American Dream? For whom is access most difficult? Why?

- Is the writer looking at the United States from the point of view of an insider or an outsider?

- Does the writer want to change his or her status? to change the status of others? What steps, if any, does he or she take to do so? What additional steps could he or she take?

- With what ethnic, racial, geographic, or economic group does the writer most strongly identify? What is the writer's attitude toward this group? What is the writer's attitude toward what he or she identifies as mainstream American culture?

- Does the writer speak as an individual or as a representative of a particular group?

- Which writers' views of the American Dream are most similar? Most different? Most like your own?

# *FORBES* SPECIAL REPORT:
# THE AMERICAN DREAM
## David M. Ewalt
1976–

## Michael Noer
1969–

*A senior editor at* Forbes *magazine, David M. Ewalt writes about technology and video games. He runs the blog* Metagamer *and is currently writing his first book,* Of Dice and Men: The Story of Dungeons & Dragons and the People Who Play It, *which traces the history of the popular fantasy role-playing game. The executive news editor for* Forbes.com, *Michael Noer writes about business and work. Noer is also interested in the history of Santa Claus, a research pursuit that has led him around the world. In the following* Forbes *special report, Ewalt and Noer collect various well-known people's responses to the question, "What Is the American Dream?" (Before you read, do a* Google *search to identify any of the people whose names you do not recognize.)*

America is a land built by immigrants, a patchwork of different cultures and creeds. But despite many differences, Americans are held together by the promise of a better life. In celebration of the tenth anniversary of *Forbes.com*, this three-part series examines the idea of the American Dream. In part one, we ask more than 60 great achievers to answer the question, "What is the American Dream?"

### Maya Angelou on the American Dream

#### What is the American Dream?

The American Dream, whether attainable or not, is to have freedom, freedom in all things. To go as far as ambition impels us, in work, in play, and religion and even in love.

I think that is what sent the first pioneers away from Europe and caused them to struggle with the Native Americans here and caused them to bring people, unwillingly from Africa, to indulge in slavery, and it is what caused the slaves to struggle against slavery.

Everyone is looking for freedom, freedom to live their lives, to control their own destiny.

—Interviewed by Evelyn Rusli

## Ben Nighthorse Campbell on the American Dream

### What is the American Dream?

The American Dream is freedom of success. It's the freedom to be what you want and to strive for what you want. I think it differs from a lot of countries where they have no dreams or can't implement their dreams.

I was in trouble [when I was younger] and I was a high school dropout. My dad was an alcoholic. I was from what you might call a dysfunctional home. . . . Those experiences are not conducive to what you might call a normal life of opportunities.

I joined the Air Force at the beginning of the Korean War . . . After serving in Korea, I returned to the U.S. for college and began to participate in judo competitions. I eventually won three judo national championships and served as captain of the U.S. Olympic team's judo squad at the 1964 Tokyo games, where I carried the American flag from the closing ceremonies.

I think that the discipline and the structured lifestyle of both of those experiences are really what helped turn me around.

If it hadn't been for sports and the Air Force, I might have ended up in a different kind of institution than the U.S. Senate.

—Interviewed by Brian Wingfield

## Henry Cisneros on the American Dream

### What is the American Dream?

I know the American Dream when I see it. I see it in the joyful tears of the people who strive, those who work hard for something they care deeply about and who attain it. I have always been moved by the experience of people who work, who apply themselves, who sacrifice, who discipline themselves, who play by the rules—who strive.

Sometimes they strive because they want something for themselves, such as an economic advancement, a prize, an honor or an achievement. I am especially moved when people strive because they love others and want something better for those they love: a home, an education, a career success, an opportunity. I say I know the American Dream when I see it because I am moved to tears myself and feel it as deeply as I feel anything else in my experience when I see it.

What makes this striving in fact American is that it is so much at the core of our culture. It is not that people don't strive in other societies or that they don't achieve. Clearly many do. I think it is that we try to make it possible for every person. Many other cultures are more class-bound, fatalistic, rigid, prejudiced or unfair. The American Dream is the right to strive, with the best chance in the world of being rewarded for it. Our American Dream is not perfect, but in America, if you strive you have a good shot at the reward—if not for you, then for someone you love who comes behind you.

—Interviewed by Hannah Clark

## Mark Cuban on the American Dream

### What is the American Dream?

The American Dream is knowing that you can create the life you want on your own terms. The American Dream is not about how much money you acquire—it's about reaching the pinnacle of success, waking up every morning with a smile on your face and looking forward to the day. The American Dream is trying the wrong things any number of times knowing it doesn't matter, because finding the one thing you love to do makes it all worthwhile. It makes every day fun, so that you feel like you will never work a day in your life. The American Dream is choosing whether you have a family and being able to raise them exactly as you choose if you do.

The American Dream is knowing there is an American Dream.

—Interviewed by Dan Frommer

## Joe Frazier on the American Dream

### What is the American Dream?

I'm not sure that, in my case, I would call it a dream so much as a vision. Since I was a boy of 5 or 6, I had in my mind that I would be a world boxing champion. Much of that "vision" was influenced by my family and their friends who would sit in my parents' living room watching on TV (we had one of the few in our community) the Wednesday and Friday night fights sponsored by Pabst Blue Ribbon and Gillette. They would remark about me quite often, especially my Uncle Rock, "Look at that boy—he looks like a young Joe Louis. He'll be champ one day." My mother allowed me to take an old burlap bag and fill it with moss, corn stalks and rocks, then hang it from a tree and spend an hour a day punching my "heavy bag."

That family support and the negative environment of the day toward blacks in South Carolina became the forces that led me out of the south—first to New York, then to Philadelphia where I found opportunity in the form of a PAL gym and my trainer, Yank Durham. This led me to accomplish three parts of my dream: first, as the only American boxer in the 1964 Tokyo Olympics to come home with a gold medal; second, winning the world heavyweight boxing championship; and now, almost four decades later, leading a fulfilling life with the respect of tens of millions of fans around the world.

There are discussions in Hollywood about a film around my life, and documentaries are being developed on different aspects of my career. Fans stream out to meet me when I make public appearances or do corporate meet and greets. I've achieved the American Dream and I believe others can too. I feel it's my duty to help them in their efforts to achieve their vision, especially the youth. Giving back is very important to me, and a very important part of the American Dream.

—Interviewed by James M. Clash

## Ha Jin on the American Dream

### What is the American Dream?

People tend to associate the American Dream with professional and material success, but some immigrants have not come to the States just for better opportunities or more existential space. To them, America is somewhat like an idealized place where you are entitled to pursue your own vision and fulfillment. In this sense, the American Dream should be very personal—each individual should have their own version of the American Dream, which should not exclude the willingness to face failure if one has to run risk.

It's too simpleminded to claim to have achieved one's American Dream, because the real dream should not be something to be realized but should be something to be pursued only. In pursuit of such an ideal, we can grow wiser and better as a human being. In brief, the American Dream should be like a blazing star in the sky—a matter of spirit.

—Interviewed by Hannah Clark

## Azar Nafisi on the American Dream

### What is the American Dream?

Saul Bellow[1] wrote, "everything that can be imagined is bound to be realized at least once–everything that mankind is capable of conceiving it seems compelled to do." For me that is one of the most important aspects of the American dream: to be able to actualize, to make something great out of nothing. This country could not exist without the vision of some amazing people who thought they could create something out of nothing.

The best work of literature to represent the American Dream is *The Great Gatsby* by F. Scott Fitzgerald. It shows us how dreaming can be tainted by reality, and that if you don't compromise, you may suffer. Gatsby refused to compromise. But also in order to actualize his dream, he demeaned himself, and in the end he paid with his life. The negative side of the American Dream comes when people pursue success at any cost, which in turn destroys the vision and the dream.

The great side of the dream is personified in *The Adventures of Huckleberry Finn* by Mark Twain. Huck Finn is told that if he doesn't

---

[1]American novelist (1915–2005). [Eds.]

give up the runaway slave, his traveling companion Jim, he'll go to hell. First he prepares to turn Jim in, but in the end he decides, "all right, then, I'll go to Hell!"

Huck has courage. For me the question is, Do those of us who believe in the American dream have that kind of courage?

America was based on a poetic vision. What will happen when it loses its poetry? This is a serious question these days. In my field I see a system of education that more and more neglects humanities and the arts, where information has become more important than real knowledge. I see people who talk about America, and then undermine it by not paying attention to its soul, to its poetry. I see polarization, reductionism and superficiality. I see libraries becoming downgraded, a system of education that is not funded and sound bites taking the place of imagination and thought.

If you come to America in search of the dream that Gatsby had, and then you realize that many people over here don't read Gatsby anymore, don't even dream anymore—how do you suppose that feels?

—Interviewed by Elisabeth Eaves

## Colin Powell on the American Dream

### What Is the American Dream?

The American Dream is something that every immigrant brought to this country, as my parents did, and that is the ability to go as far as you can in life, limited only by your own dreams and willingness to work hard.

And above all, the American Dream for these folks meant that your children will have the opportunity to do better than you will.

I lived the dream that my parents brought to this country, as did my sister. My parents came here as poor laborers. They left the country they loved—Jamaica—to go to a place where there was opportunity, a place where they could dream, a place they came to love deeply. They worked hard and watched their children become successful, one as an educator and one as a soldier.

—Interviewed by Brian Wingfield

## Condoleezza Rice on the American Dream

### What is the American Dream?

The American Dream is being dealt with and considered on your own merits. In America it doesn't matter where you came from; it matters where you're going. If you get ahead on your own determination and your own drive and your own merits, there should be no obstacles—not race, not creed nor color. And it's so important that that be the case, that there be no obstacles in America.

One of the great things about being a Stanford professor was that, in the classroom, in one corner there would be a fourth-generation Stanford legatee, and in the other corner there would be the child of an itinerant farm worker. And in this country, to obtain the American Dream, we need good educational options for every American.

—Interviewed by Brian Wingfield

## Martha Stewart on the American Dream

### What is the American Dream?

A couple of hundred years ago, writer Samuel Johnson so wisely said: "To be happy at home is the ultimate result of all ambition." Though Johnson was himself an Englishman, the statement is, to my mind, at the heart of the American Dream. I have worked hard all my life and I take great pride and pleasure in the business I created and the success I have been so fortunate to enjoy. But there is nothing I treasure more than time spent at home with my friends, family members and pets.

I know I'm not alone in this sentiment. Our families and our homes are the center of American life. And everything we do is to make those homes—and the lives in them—more beautiful, more comfortable, more functional and more full of life and light and joy for those we love. At the end of the day, that is the American Dream. All the rest is window dressing.

—Interviewed by Hannah Clark

## Responding to Reading

1. Explain what you think the speaker meant by each of the following statements:

   - "I know the American Dream when I see it." (Henry Cisneros)

   - "The American Dream is knowing there is an American Dream." (Marc Cuban)

   - "[T]he real dream should not be something to be realized but should be something to be pursued only." (Ha Jin)

2. Many of the people interviewed here (for example, Colin Powell) see the American Dream in concrete terms; others, like Ha Jin, describe it in more abstract terms. Review the interviews, and identify the word or brief phrase in each—such as *opportunity* or *helping others*—that best characterizes each person's idea of the American Dream.

3. Read the last paragraph of the interview with Azar Nafisi. What do you think she is saying about the American Dream? Would you characterize her view of the American Dream as positive or negative? Is it different from the view she expresses in her essay on page 363? If so, how?

## Responding in Writing

Which of these interviews best expresses what the American Dream means to you? Why?

# THE LIBRARY CARD

## Richard Wright

### 1908–1960

*Born on a former plantation near Natchez, Mississippi, Richard Wright spent much of his childhood in an orphanage or with various relatives. He attended schools in Jackson and in 1934 moved to Chicago, where he worked at a number of unskilled jobs before joining the Federal Writers' Project. When his politics became radical, he wrote poetry for leftist publications. In 1938, he published his first book,* Uncle Tom's Children: Four Novellas; *two years later, his novel* Native Son *made him famous. After World War II, Wright lived as an expatriate in Paris, where he wrote* Black Boy *(1945), an autobiography that celebrates African-American resilience and courage much as nineteenth-century slave narratives do. In this excerpt from* Black Boy, *Wright tells how he took advantage of an opportunity to feed his hunger for an intellectual life.*

One morning I arrived early at work and went into the bank lobby where the Negro porter was mopping. I stood at a counter and picked up the Memphis *Commercial Appeal* and began my free reading of the press. I came finally to the editorial page and saw an article dealing with one H. L. Mencken.[1] I knew by hearsay that he was the editor of the *American Mercury*, but aside from that I knew nothing about him. The article was a furious denunciation of Mencken, concluding with one hot, short sentence: Mencken is a fool.

I wondered what on earth this Mencken had done to call down upon him the scorn of the South. The only people I had ever heard denounced in the South were Negroes, and this man was not a Negro. Then what ideas did Mencken hold that made a newspaper like the *Commercial Appeal* castigate him publicly? Undoubtedly he must be advocating ideas that the South did not like. Were there, then, people other than Negroes who criticized the South? I knew that during the Civil War the South had hated northern whites, but I had not encountered such hate during my life. Knowing no more of Mencken than I did at that moment, I felt a vague sympathy for him. Had not the

---

[1]Henry Louis Mencken (1880–1956), journalist, critic, and essayist, who was known for his pointed, outspoken, and satirical comments about the blunders and imperfections of democracy and the cultural awkwardness of Americans. [Eds.]

South, which had assigned me the role of a non-man, cast at him its hardest words?

Now, how could I find out about this Mencken? There was a huge library near the riverfront, but I knew that Negroes were not allowed to patronize its shelves any more than they were the parks and playgrounds of the city. I had gone into the library several times to get books for the white men on the job. Which of them would now help me to get books? And how could I read them without causing concern to the white men with whom I worked? I had so far been successful in hiding my thoughts and feelings from them, but I knew that I would create hostility if I went about this business of reading in a clumsy way.

I weighed the personalities of the men on the job. There was Don, a Jew; but I distrusted him. His position was not much better than mine and I knew that he was uneasy and insecure; he had always treated me in an offhand, bantering way that barely concealed his contempt. I was afraid to ask him to help me to get books; his frantic desire to demonstrate a racial solidarity with the whites against Negroes might make him betray me.

Then how about the boss? No, he was a Baptist and I had the sus-  5
picion that he would not be quite able to comprehend why a black boy would want to read Mencken. There were other white men on the job whose attitudes showed clearly that they were Kluxers or sympathizers, and they were out of the question.

There remained only one man whose attitude did not fit into an anti-Negro category, for I had heard the white men refer to him as a "Pope lover." He was an Irish Catholic and was hated by the white Southerners. I knew that he read books, because I had got him volumes from the library several times. Since he, too, was an object of hatred, I felt that he might refuse me but would hardly betray me. I hesitated, weighing and balancing the imponderable realities.

One morning I paused before the Catholic fellow's desk.

"I want to ask you a favor," I whispered to him.

"What is it?"

"I want to read. I can't get books from the library. I wonder if you'd  10
let me use your card?"

He looked at me suspiciously.

"My card is full most of the time," he said.

"I see," I said and waited, posing my question silently.

"You're not trying to get me into trouble, are you, boy?" he asked, staring at me.

"Oh, no, sir."                                                          15

"What book do you want?"

"A book by H. L. Mencken."

"Which one?"

"I don't know. Has he written more than one?"

20     "He has written several."

"I didn't know that."

"What makes you want to read Mencken?"

"Oh, I just saw his name in the newspaper," I said.

"It's good of you to want to read," he said. "But you ought to read the right things."

25     I said nothing. Would he want to supervise my reading?

"Let me think," he said. "I'll figure out something."

I turned from him and he called me back. He stared at me quizzically.

"Richard, don't mention this to the other white men," he said.

"I understand," I said. "I won't say a word."

30     A few days later he called me to him.

"I've got a card in my wife's name," he said. "Here's mine."

"Thank you, sir."

"Do you think you can manage it?"

"I'll manage fine," I said.

35     "If they suspect you, you'll get in trouble," he said.

"I'll write the same kind of notes to the library that you wrote when you sent me for books," I told him. "I'll sign your name."

He laughed.

"Go ahead. Let me see what you get," he said.

That afternoon I addressed myself to forging a note. Now, what were the names of books written by H. L. Mencken? I did not know any of them. I finally wrote what I thought would be a foolproof note: *Dear Madam: Will you please let this nigger boy*—I used the word "nigger" to make the librarian feel that I could not possibly be the author of the note—*have some books by H. L. Mencken?* I forged the white man's name.

40     I entered the library as I had always done when on errands for whites, but I felt that I would somehow slip up and betray myself. I doffed my hat, stood a respectful distance from the desk, looked as unbookish as possible, and waited for the white patrons to be taken care of. When the desk was clear of people, I still waited. The white librarian looked at me.

"What do you want, boy?"

As though I did not possess the power of speech, I stepped forward and simply handed her the forged note, not parting my lips.

"What books by Mencken does he want?" she asked.

"I don't know, ma'am," I said, avoiding her eyes.

45     "Who gave you this card?"

"Mr. Falk," I said.

"Where is he?"

"He's at work, at the M—— Optical Company," I said. "I've been in here for him before."

"I remember," the woman said. "But he never wrote notes like this."

Oh, God, she's suspicious. Perhaps she would not let me have the 50
books? If she had turned her back at that moment, I would have ducked
out the door and never gone back. Then I thought of a bold idea.

"You can call him up, ma'am," I said, my heart pounding.

"You're not using these books, are you?" she asked pointedly.

"Oh, no, ma'am. I can't read."

"I don't know what he wants by Mencken," she said under her
breath.

I knew now that I had won; she was thinking of other things and 55
the race question had gone out of her mind. She went to the shelves.
Once or twice she looked over her shoulder at me, as though she was
still doubtful. Finally she came forward with two books in her hand.

"I'm sending him two books," she said. "But tell Mr. Falk to come
in next time, or send me the names of the books he wants. I don't know
what he wants to read."

I said nothing. She stamped the card and handed me the books.
Not daring to glance at them, I went out of the library, fearing that
the woman would call me back for further questioning. A block away
from the library I opened one of the books and read a title: *A Book of
Prefaces.* I was nearing my nineteenth birthday and I did not know
how to pronounce the word "preface." I thumbed the pages and saw
strange words and strange names. I shook my head, disappointed. I
looked at the other book; it was called *Prejudices.* I knew what that
word meant; I had heard it all my life. And right off I was on guard
against Mencken's books. Why would a man want to call a book
*Prejudices*? The word was so stained with all my memories of racial
hate that I could not conceive of anybody using it for a title. Perhaps
I had made a mistake about Mencken? A man who had prejudices
must be wrong.

When I showed the books to Mr. Falk, he looked at me and frowned.

"That librarian might telephone you," I warned him.

"That's all right," he said. "But when you're through reading those 60
books, I want you to tell me what you get out of them."

That night in my rented room, while letting the hot water run over
my can of pork and beans in the sink, I opened *A Book of Prefaces* and
began to read. I was jarred and shocked by the style, the clear, clean,
sweeping sentences. Why did he write like that? And how did one
write like that? I pictured the man as a raging demon, slashing with his
pen, consumed with hate, denouncing everything American, extolling
everything European or German, laughing at the weaknesses of people,
mocking God, authority. What was this? I stood up, trying to realize
what reality lay behind the meaning of the words. . . . Yes, this man was
fighting, fighting with words. He was using words as a weapon, using
them as one would use a club. Could words be weapons? Well, yes, for
here they were. Then, maybe, perhaps, I could use them as a weapon?

No. It frightened me. I read on and what amazed me was not what he said, but how on earth anybody had the courage to say it.

Occasionally I glanced up to reassure myself that I was alone in the room. Who were these men about whom Mencken was talking so passionately? Who was Anatole France? Joseph Conrad? Sinclair Lewis, Sherwood Anderson, Dostoevski, George Moore, Gustave Flaubert, Maupassant, Tolstoy, Frank Harris, Mark Twain, Thomas Hardy, Arnold Bennett, Stephen Crane, Zola, Norris, Gorky, Bergson, Ibsen, Balzac, Bernard Shaw, Dumas, Poe, Thomas Mann, O. Henry, Dreiser, H. G. Wells, Gogol, T. S. Eliot, Gide, Baudelaire, Edgar Lee Masters, Stendhal, Turgenev, Huneker, Nietzsche, and scores of others? Were these men real? Did they exist or had they existed? And how did one pronounce their names?

I ran across many words whose meanings I did not know, and I either looked them up in a dictionary or, before I had a chance to do that, encountered the word in a context that made its meaning clear. But what strange world was this? I concluded the book with the conviction that I had somehow overlooked something terribly important in life. I had once tried to write, had once reveled in feeling, had let my crude imagination roam, but the impulse to dream had been slowly beaten out of me by experience. Now it surged up again and I hungered for books, new ways of looking and seeing. It was not a matter of believing or disbelieving what I read, but of feeling something new, of being affected by something that made the look of the world different.

As dawn broke I ate my pork and beans, feeling dopey, sleepy. I went to work, but the mood of the book would not die; it lingered, coloring everything I saw, heard, did. I now felt that I knew what the white men were feeling. Merely because I had read a book that had spoken of how they lived and thought, I identified myself with that book. I felt vaguely guilty. Would I, filled with bookish notions, act in a manner that would make the whites dislike me?

65   I forged more notes and my trips to the library became frequent. Reading grew into a passion. My first serious novel was Sinclair Lewis's *Main Street*.[2] It made me see my boss, Mr. Gerald, and identify him as an American type. I would smile when I saw him lugging his golf bags into the office. I had always felt a vast distance separating me from the boss, and now I felt closer to him, though still distant. I felt now that I knew him, that I could feel the very limits of his narrow life. And this had happened because I had read a novel about a mythical man called George F. Babbitt.[3]

---

[2]*Main Street*, published in 1920, examines the smugness, intolerance, and lack of imagination that characterize small-town American life. [Eds.]

[3]The central character in Sinclair Lewis's *Babbitt* (1922), who believed in the virtues of home, the Republican Party, and middle-class conventions. To Wright, Babbitt symbolizes the mindless complacency of white middle-class America. [Eds.]

The plots and stories in the novels did not interest me so much as the point of view revealed. I gave myself over to each novel without reserve, without trying to criticize it; it was enough for me to see and feel something different. And for me, everything was something different. Reading was like a drug, a dope. The novels created moods in which I lived for days. But I could not conquer my sense of guilt, my feeling that the white men around me knew that I was changing, that I had begun to regard them differently.

Whenever I brought a book to the job, I wrapped it in newspaper— a habit that was to persist for years in other cities and under other circumstances. But some of the white men pried into my packages when I was absent and they questioned me.

"Boy, what are you reading those books for?"

"Oh, I don't know, sir."

"That's deep stuff you're reading, boy." 70

"I'm just killing time, sir."

"You'll addle your brains if you don't watch out."

I read Dreiser's *Jennie Gerhardt* and *Sister Carrie*[4] and they revived in me a vivid sense of my mother's suffering; I was overwhelmed. I grew silent, wondering about the life around me. It would have been impossible for me to have told anyone what I derived from these novels, for it was nothing less than a sense of life itself. All my life had shaped me for the realism, the naturalism of the modern novel, and I could not read enough of them.

Steeped in new moods and ideas, I bought a ream of paper and tried to write; but nothing would come, or what did come was flat beyond telling. I discovered that more than desire and feeling were necessary to write and I dropped the idea. Yet I still wondered how it was possible to know people sufficiently to write about them. Could I ever learn about life and people? To me, with my vast ignorance, my Jim Crow station in life, it seemed a task impossible of achievement. I now knew what being a Negro meant. I could endure the hunger. I had learned to live with hate. But to feel that there were feelings denied me, that the very breath of life itself was beyond my reach, that more than anything else hurt, wounded me. I had a new hunger.

In buoying me up, reading also cast me down, made me see what 75 was possible, what I had missed. My tension returned, new, terrible, bitter, surging, almost too great to be contained. I no longer *felt* that the world about me was hostile, killing; I *knew* it. A million times I asked myself what I could do to save myself, and there were no answers. I seemed forever condemned, ringed by walls.

I did not discuss my reading with Mr. Falk, who had lent me his library card; it would have meant talking about myself and that would

---

[4]Both *Jennie Gerhardt* (1911) and *Sister Carrie* (1900), by Theodore Dreiser, tell the stories of working women who struggle against poverty and social injustice. [Eds.]

have been too painful. I smiled each day, fighting desperately to maintain my old behavior, to keep my disposition seemingly sunny. But some of the white men discerned that I had begun to brood.

"Wake up there, boy!" Mr. Olin said one day.

"Sir!" I answered for the lack of a better word.

"You act like you've stolen something," he said.

80      I laughed in the way I knew he expected me to laugh, but I resolved to be more conscious of myself, to watch my every act, to guard and hide the new knowledge that was dawning within me.

If I went north, would it be possible for me to build a new life then? But how could a man build a life upon vague, unformed yearnings? I wanted to write and I did not even know the English language. I bought English grammars and found them dull. I felt that I was getting a better sense of the language from novels than from grammars. I read hard, discarding a writer as soon as I felt that I had grasped his point of view. At night the printed page stood before my eyes in sleep.

Mrs. Moss, my landlady, asked me one Sunday morning: "Son, what is this you keep on reading?"

"Oh, nothing. Just novels."

"What you get out of 'em?"

85      "I'm just killing time," I said.

"I hope you know your own mind," she said in a tone which implied that she doubted if I had a mind.

I knew of no Negroes who read the books I liked and I wondered if any Negroes ever thought of them. I knew that there were Negro doctors, lawyers, newspapermen, but I never saw any of them. When I read a Negro newspaper I never caught the faintest echo of my preoccupation in its pages. I felt trapped and occasionally, for a few days, I would stop reading. But a vague hunger would come over me for books, books that opened up new avenues of feeling and seeing, and again I would forge another note to the white librarian. Again I would read and wonder as only the naïve and unlettered can read and wonder, feeling that I carried a secret, criminal burden about with me each day.

That winter my mother and brother came and we set up housekeeping, buying furniture on the installment plan, being cheated and yet knowing no way to avoid it. I began to eat warm food and to my surprise found that regular meals enabled me to read faster. I may have lived through many illnesses and survived them, never suspecting that I was ill. My brother obtained a job and we began to save toward the trip north, plotting our time, setting tentative dates for departure. I told none of the white men on the job that I was planning to go north; I knew that the moment they felt I was thinking of the North they would change toward me. It would have made them feel that I did not like the life I was living, and because my life was completely conditioned by what they said or did, it would have been tantamount to challenging them.

I could calculate my chances for life in the South as a Negro fairly clearly now.

I could fight the southern whites by organizing with other Negroes, 90 as my grandfather had done. But I knew that I could never win that way; there were many whites and there were but few blacks. They were strong and we were weak. Outright black rebellion could never win. If I fought openly I would die and I did not want to die. News of lynchings were frequent.

I could submit and live the life of a genial slave, but that was impossible. All of my life had shaped me to live by my own feelings and thoughts. I could make up to Bess and marry her and inherit the house. But that, too, would be the life of a slave; if I did that, I would crush to death something within me, and I would hate myself as much as I knew the whites already hated those who had submitted. Neither could I ever willingly present myself to be kicked, as Shorty had done. I would rather have died than do that.

I could drain off my restlessness by fighting with Shorty and Harrison. I had seen many Negroes solve the problem of being black by transferring their hatred of themselves to others with a black skin and fighting them. I would have to be cold to do that, and I was not cold and I could never be.

I could, of course, forget what I had read, thrust the whites out of my mind, forget them; and find release from anxiety and longing in sex and alcohol. But the memory of how my father had conducted himself made that course repugnant. If I did not want others to violate my life, how could I voluntarily violate it myself?

I had no hope whatever of being a professional man. Not only had I been so conditioned that I did not desire it, but the fulfillment of such an ambition was beyond my capabilities. Well-to-do Negroes lived in a world that was almost as alien to me as the world inhabited by whites.

What, then, was there? I held my life in my mind, in my conscious- 95 ness each day, feeling at times that I would stumble and drop it, spill it forever. My reading had created a vast sense of distance between me and the world in which I lived and tried to make a living, and that sense of distance was increasing each day. My days and nights were one long, quiet, continuously contained dream of terror, tension, and anxiety. I wondered how long I could bear it.

## Responding to Reading

1. In what sense did access to books bring Wright closer to achieving the American Dream? What new obstacles did books introduce?
2. In paragraph 74, Wright mentions his "Jim Crow station in life." The term *Jim Crow*, derived from a character in a minstrel show, refers to laws enacted in Southern states that legalized racial segregation. What is Wright's "station

in life"? In what ways does he adapt his behavior to accommodate this Jim Crow image? In what ways does he defy this stereotype?

3.  After World War II, Wright left the United States to live in Paris. Given what you have read in this essay, does his decision surprise you? Do you think he made the right choice? What other options did he have?

### Responding in Writing

If Wright were alive today, what books, magazines, newspapers, and Web sites would you recommend he look at? Why?

# COMING INTO THE COUNTRY
## Gish Jen
### 1956–

*Gish Jen is the author of a short-story collection and four novels, most recently* World and Town *(2010). Her work is frequently anthologized and published in the* New York Times Magazine, *the* New Yorker, *and the* New Republic. *Jen, born to Chinese immigrants, writes primarily about the challenges of cultural assimilation faced by American immigrants and descendants of recent immigrants. The following essay explores the immigrant's process of shaping a distinctly American identity.*

In the Old World, there was one way of life, or 2, maybe 10. Here there are dozens, hundreds, all jammed in together, cheek by jowl, especially in the dizzying cities. Everywhere has a somewhere else just around the corner. We newish Americans leap-frog from world to world, reinventing ourselves en route. We perform our college selves, our waitress selves, our dot-com selves, our parent selves, our downtown selves, our Muslim, Greek, Hindi, South African selves. Even into the second or third generation, we speak different languages—more languages, often, than we know we know. We sport different names. I am Gish, Geesh, Jen, Lillian, Lil, Bilien, Ms. Jen, Miss Ren, Mrs. O'Connor. Or maybe we insist on one name. The filmmaker Mira Nair, for example, will be called *NIGH-ear*, please; she is not a depilatory product.

Of course, there are places where she does not have to insist, and places that don't get the joke, that need—that get—other jokes. It's a kind of high, switching spiels, eating Ethiopian, French, Thai, getting around. And the inventing! The moments of grand inspiration: *I think I will call myself Houdini.* Who could give up even the quotidian luxury of choosing, that small swell of power: to walk or to drive? The soup or the salad? The green or the blue? We bubble with pleasure. *It's me. I'm taking the plane. I'll take the sofa, the chair, the whole shebang—why not?*

Why not, indeed? A most American question, a question that comes to dominate our most private self-talk. In therapy-speak, we Americans like *to give ourselves permission.* To do what? To take care of ourselves, to express ourselves, to listen to ourselves. We tune out the loudspeaker of duty, tune in to the whisper of desire. This is faint at first, but soon proves easily audible; indeed, irresistible. *Why not go to town? Why not move away? Why not marry out? Why not? Why not? Why not?*

To come to America is to be greatly disoriented for many a day. The smell of the air is wrong, the taste of the water, the strength of the sun, the rate the trees grow. The rituals are strange—the spring setting out of mulch, the summer setting out of barbecues. How willingly the men heat themselves with burgers! Nobody eats the wildlife, certainly not the bugs or leaves. And beware, beware the rules about smoking. Your skin feels tight, your body fat or thin, your children stranger than they were already. Your sensations are exhausting.

Yet one day a moment comes—often, strangely, abroad—when we 5 find ourselves missing things. Our choice of restaurants, perhaps, or our cheap gas and good roads; or, more tellingly, our rights. To be without freedom of movement, to be without freedom of speech—these things pain everyone. But to be without *our* freedom of movement, without *our* freedom of speech is an American affliction; and in this, as in many facets of American life, possession matters. The moment we feel certain rights to be inalienable, when we feel them to be ours as our lungs are ours, so that their loss is an excision and a death, we have become American.

It's not always a happy feeling. For the more at home we become with our freedom, the more we become aware of its limits. There's much true opportunity in the land of opportunity, but between freedom in theory and freedom in practice gapes a grand canyon. As often as not, what we feel is the burn of injustice. A rise of anger, perhaps followed by a quick check on our impulse to act rashly; perhaps followed by a decision to act courageously. *We gather here today to make known our grievance. For is this not America?*

We wonder who we are—what does it mean to be Irish-American, Cuban-American, Armenian-American?—and are amazed to discover that others wonder, too. Indeed, nothing seems more typically American than to obsess about identity. Can so many people truly be so greatly confused? We feel very much a part of the contemporary gestalt.

Yet two or three generations later, we still may not be insiders. Recently, I heard about a basketball game starring a boy from the Cochiti pueblo in Santa Fe. The kids on his team, a friend reported, had one water bottle, which they passed around, whereas the kids on the other team each had his own. This was a heartening story, signaling the survival of a communal culture against the pressures of individualism. But did the Cochiti boy notice the other team? I couldn't help wondering.

Did he feel the glass pane between himself and the mainstream, so familiar, so tangible, so bittersweet? *Nobody has been here longer than we; how come our ways need protecting?* Later a member of the pueblo told me that the Cochiti have started a language-immersion program for the younger generation, and that it has been a success. They are saving their language from extinction.

Hooray! The rest of us cheer. How awed we feel in the presence of tradition, of authenticity. How avidly we will surf to such sites, some of us, and what we will pay to do so! We will pay for bits of the Southwest the way we will pay handsomely, in this generation or the next, for a home. Whatever that looks like; we find ourselves longing for some combination of Martha Stewart and what we can imagine, say, of our family seat in Brazil. At any rate, we can say this much: the home of our dreams is a safe place, a still place. A communal place, to which we contribute; to which we have real ties; a place that feels more stable, perhaps, than ourselves. How American this is—to long, at day's end, for a place where we belong more, invent less; for a heartland with more heart.

## Responding to Reading

1. In paragraph 1, Jen says, "We newish Americans leap-frog from world to world, reinventing ourselves en route." Is the concept of reinvention as she describes it limited to "newish Americans," or could it also apply to more assimilated Americans? Explain.
2. Jen says, "the more at home we become with our freedom, the more we become aware of its limits" (6). What does she mean? Do you think she is correct?
3. In paragraph 7, Jen observes, "nothing seems more typically American than to obsess about identity." Why, according to Jen, is this obsession "typically American"?

## Responding in Writing

Do you consider yourself an American (in Jen's terms, an "insider"), a "hyphenated American" (for example, Irish-American or Cuban-American), or something else?

# Just Walk On By

## Brent Staples

### 1951–

*Originally published in Ms. in 1986, the following essay conveys Staples's reactions to white people's images of black men. (See page 325 for Staples's biography.)*

My first victim was a woman—white, well dressed, probably in her early twenties. I came upon her late one evening on a deserted street in Hyde Park, a relatively affluent neighborhood in an otherwise mean, impoverished section of Chicago. As I swung onto the avenue behind her, there seemed to be a discreet, uninflammatory distance between us. Not so. She cast back a worried glance. To her, the youngish black man—a broad six feet two inches with a beard and billowing hair, both hands shoved into the pockets of a bulky military jacket—seemed menacingly close. After a few more quick glimpses, she picked up her pace and was soon running in earnest. Within seconds she disappeared into a cross street.

That was more than a decade ago. I was 22 years old, a graduate student newly arrived at the University of Chicago. It was in the echo of that terrified woman's footfalls that I first began to know the unwieldy inheritance I'd come into—the ability to alter public space in ugly ways. It was clear that she thought herself the quarry of a mugger, a rapist, or worse. Suffering a bout of insomnia, however, I was stalking sleep, not defenseless wayfarers. As a softy who is scarcely able to take a knife to a raw chicken—let alone hold it to a person's throat—I was surprised, embarrassed, and dismayed all at once. Her flight made me feel like an accomplice in tyranny. It also made it clear that I was indistinguishable from the muggers who occasionally seeped into the area from the surrounding ghetto. That first encounter, and those that followed, signified that a vast, unnerving gulf lay between nighttime pedestrians—particularly women—and me. And I soon gathered that being perceived as dangerous is a hazard in itself. I only needed to turn a corner into a dicey situation, or crowd some frightened, armed person in a foyer somewhere, or make an errant move after being pulled over by a policeman. Where fear and weapons meet—and they often do in urban America—there is always the possibility of death.

In that first year, my first away from my hometown, I was to become thoroughly familiar with the language of fear. At dark, shadowy intersections in Chicago, I could cross in front of a car stopped at a traffic light and elicit the *thunk, thunk, thunk, thunk* of the driver—black, white, male, or female—hammering down the door locks. On less traveled streets after dark, I grew accustomed to but never comfortable with people who crossed to the other side of the street rather than pass me. Then there were the standard unpleasantries with police, doormen, bouncers, cab drivers, and others whose business it is to screen out troublesome individuals *before* there is any nastiness.

I moved to New York nearly two years ago and I have remained an avid night walker. In central Manhattan, the near-constant crowd cover minimizes tense one-on-one street encounters. Elsewhere—visiting friends in SoHo, where sidewalks are narrow and tightly spaced buildings shut out the sky—things can get very taut indeed.

5      Black men have a firm place in New York mugging literature. Norman Podhoretz in his famed (or infamous) 1963 essay, "My Negro Problem—And Ours," recalls growing up in terror of black males; they "were tougher than we were, more ruthless," he writes—and as an adult on the Upper West Side of Manhattan, he continues, he cannot constrain his nervousness when he meets black men on certain streets. Similarly, a decade later, the essayist and novelist Edward Hoagland extols a New York where once "Negro bitterness bore down mainly on other Negroes." Where some see mere panhandlers, Hoagland sees "a mugger who is clearly screwing up his nerve to do more than just *ask* for money." But Hoagland has "the New Yorker's quickhunch posture for broken-field maneuvering," and the bad guy swerves away.

I often witness that "hunch posture," from women after dark on the warrenlike streets of Brooklyn where I live. They seem to set their faces on neutral and, with their purse straps strung across their chests bandolier style, they forge ahead as though bracing themselves against being tackled. I understand, of course, that the danger they perceive is not a hallucination. Women are particularly vulnerable to street violence, and young black males are drastically overrepresented among the perpetrators of that violence. Yet these truths are no solace against the kind of alienation that comes of being ever the suspect, against being set apart, a fearsome entity with whom pedestrians avoid making eye contact.

It is not altogether clear to me how I reached the ripe old age of 22 without being conscious of the lethality nighttime pedestrians attributed to me. Perhaps it was because in Chester, Pennsylvania, the small, angry industrial town where I came of age in the 1960s, I was scarcely noticeable against a backdrop of gang warfare, street knifings, and murders. I grew up one of the good boys, had perhaps a half-dozen fist fights. In retrospect, my shyness of combat has clear sources.

Many things go into the making of a young thug. One of those things is the consummation of the male romance with the power to intimidate. An infant discovers that random flailings send the baby bottle flying out of the crib and crashing to the floor. Delighted, the joyful babe repeats those motions again and again, seeking to duplicate the feat. Just so, I recall the points at which some of my boyhood friends were finally seduced by the perception of themselves as tough guys. When a mark cowered and surrendered his money without resistance, myth and reality merged—and paid off. It is, after all, only manly to embrace the power to frighten and intimidate. We, as men, are not supposed to give an inch of our lane on the highway; we are to seize the fighter's edge in work and in play and even in love; we are to be valiant in the face of hostile forces.

Unfortunately, poor and powerless young men seem to take all this nonsense literally. As a boy, I saw countless tough guys locked away;

I have since buried several, too. They were babies, really—a teenage cousin, a brother of 22, a childhood friend in his mid-twenties—all gone down in episodes of bravado played out in the streets. I came to doubt the virtues of intimidation early on. I chose, perhaps even unconsciously, to remain a shadow—timid, but a survivor.

The fearsomeness mistakenly attributed to me in public places 10 often has a perilous flavor. The most frightening of these confusions occurred in the late 1970s and early 1980s when I worked as a journalist in Chicago. One day, rushing into the office of a magazine I was writing for with a deadline story in hand, I was mistaken for a burglar. The office manager called security and, with an ad hoc posse, pursued me through the labyrinthine halls, nearly to my editor's door. I had no way of proving who I was. I could only move briskly toward the company of someone who knew me.

Another time I was on assignment for a local paper and killing time before an interview. I entered a jewelry store on the city's affluent Near North Side. The proprietor excused herself and returned with an enormous red Doberman pinscher straining at the end of a leash. She stood, the dog extended toward me, silent to my questions, her eyes bulging nearly out of her head. I took a cursory look around, nodded, and bade her good night. Relatively speaking, however, I never fared as badly as another black male journalist. He went to nearby Waukegan, Illinois, a couple of summers ago to work on a story about a murderer who was born there. Mistaking the reporter for the killer, police hauled him from his car at gunpoint and but for his press credentials would probably have tried to book him. Such episodes are not uncommon. Black men trade tales like this all the time.

In "My Negro Problem—And Ours," Podhoretz writes that the hatred he feels for blacks makes itself known to him through a variety of avenues—one being his discomfort with that "special brand of paranoid touchiness" to which he says blacks are prone. No doubt he is speaking here of black men. In time, I learned to smother the rage I felt at so often being taken for a criminal. Not to do so would surely have led to madness—via that special "paranoid touchiness" that so annoyed Podhoretz at the time he wrote the essay.

I began to take precautions to make myself less threatening. I move about with care, particularly late in the evening. I give a wide berth to nervous people on subway platforms during the wee hours, particularly when I have exchanged business clothes for jeans. If I happen to be entering a building behind some people who appear skittish, I may walk by, letting them clear the lobby before I return, so as not to seem to be following them. I have been calm and extremely congenial on those rare occasions when I've been pulled over by the police.

And on late-evening constitutionals along streets less traveled by, I employ what has proved to be an excellent tension-reducing measure:

I whistle melodies from Beethoven and Vivaldi and the more popular classical composers. Even steely New Yorkers hunching toward night-time destinations seem to relax, and occasionally they even join in the tune. Virtually everybody seems to sense that a mugger wouldn't be warbling bright, sunny selections from Vivaldi's *Four Seasons*. It is my equivalent of the cowbell that hikers wear when they know they are in bear country.

## Responding to Reading

1. Staples speaks quite matter-of-factly about the fear he inspires. Does your experience support his assumption that black men have the "ability to alter public space" (2)? Why or why not? Do you believe white men also have this ability?
2. In paragraph 13, Staples suggests some strategies that he believes make him "less threatening." What else, if anything, do you think he could do? Do you believe he *should* adopt such strategies?
3. Although Staples says he arouses fear in others, he also admits that he himself feels fearful. Why? Do you think he has reason to be fearful? What does this sense of fear say about his access to the American Dream?

## Responding in Writing

Imagine you are the woman Staples describes in paragraph 1. Draft an email to Staples in which you explain why you reacted as you did.

# Fatherland

## Kiran Desai
### 1971–

*A novelist born in India and now living in the United States, Kiran Desai often writes about how she, an American immigrant, sees her Indian cultural heritage. Desai is the author of two acclaimed novels,* Hullabaloo in the Guava Orchard *(1998) and* The Inheritance of Loss *(2006). In the following essay, she describes her complex feelings about the two worlds in which she has lived.*

The evening after my green card was approved, my father climbed to our rooftop, in Delhi, which lay under the direct flight path to the airport, and beneath the bobbing plane lights he mourned: "We brought up our children to become perfect foreigners." In a second, the sadness veered into scorn: "Call yourselves global citizens. Global bastards, more like!"

Almost all the children of my parents' friends had been brought up to emigrate; across India, the parents were aging alone, summoning and soothing the melancholic tides with whiskey brought back by the global bastards, drifting to the familiar Indian feeling of being left behind. My father kept a certificate in his drawer that awarded him, for his loyalty to the smoky pleasures of Laphroaig,[1] a square inch of peat in Scotland. He joked, "I own land in Delhi and Islay!"

Our emotional rhythms had long followed common migration patterns: winter crowds of immigrants winging back to India bearing gifts of marshmallows, zip-lock bags, and makeup cases they'd received free; Indian relatives heading north, filling the summer skies with ginger pickles, paisley stoles, the last of the twisted family silver.

As the nights turned cold, when I was small, we awaited the Indian-Americans, some of whom had metamorphosed into hippies, some into Republicans. Instead of being considered lowly Indians, they reported that they were mistaken for Spanish people in the streets of America. They bought carpets and cashmere; sampled perfumed dishes that resurrected the forgotten recipes of nawabs;[2] went on luxury tours of Rajasthan,[3] which my father paid for, so that they might reimburse him in dollars on his rare summer visits. I knew that those dollars wouldn't allow him to travel or eat in America any way but meanly, cheaply.

Some years later in the States, I experienced the mounting dread of 5 the revenge visit. The Indians were coming to reclaim their pride! They'd dry their underpants on our subdivision's bushes and, when they were told they were breaking rules, they'd pooh-pooh American freedom. They'd say that the grandchildren were greater morons than the children of the Delhi maid, who travelled from the slums and left the soap black. They'd show what they thought of waste by packing empty jam jars to take back to India. They'd ask, "How many American friends do you have?" to point out that you still didn't belong. Korean-American, Jewish, or Hispanic friends did not count.

During my twenties and thirties, while slowly writing my first novels, I rented a series of minute rooms within dark jigsaws of shared apartments. I lived out of two suitcases, refused to get a job, and spent entire days reading atop a wooden platform bed I'd found abandoned on the street. I had squandered my pride. I was, my father observed, even frightened of waiters.

"Kiran Desai! What are you thanking and thanking the waiter for? Oh thank you, oh thank you—for chicken that has less flavor than a potato."

And: "Roast your spices! Brown your spices!" he urged. It was not worth it to eat out. It was also miserable work to enliven the washed-out supermarket produce of the First World.

---

[1]Brand of whiskey. [Eds.]
[2]Governors or distinguished people. [Eds.]
[3]Indian state. [Eds.]

"Papa, I've had enough. . . ."

10   "Fine. I'll take care of myself," he said.

When he died, I went about like a ragged crow telling even strangers, "My father died, my father died." My indiscretion embarrassed me, but I could not help it. Without my father on his Delhi rooftop, why was I here? Without him there, why should I go back? Without that ache between us, what was I made of?

He'd said, "Don't be sentimental when it comes to giving up your Indian passport." He'd said, "Why do you want to stay there and work like a dog?" He'd said, "There's nothing for you here, don't return." He'd said, "Return without shame if you don't get your visa, O.K.?"

A year after his death, I went to the courthouse in lower Manhattan.

"How many wives do you have, sir?" an official was asking a man inside, who looked uncertain. "Two? Three? Think it over and then come back and tell me."

15   "Take off your hat, your *hat*," another official instructed an anxious Chinese man who kept taking off his glasses. Someone else was being chastised for donning a furry yellow tracksuit instead of formal attire. The judge walked in. We stood up. Twenty-three years after I arrived, I became a citizen.

Out in the streets, surveying crowds of New Yorkers, my father used to be astonished by the low quality of immigrants on show. "With the whole world to choose from. . ." he would muse. Then, as if catching sight of the future, he expanded to direful warning: "And what's going to happen if this lot takes over?"

## Responding to Reading

1. What does Desai's father mean by the expressions "perfect foreigners," "global citizens," and "global bastards" (1)? What does his use of these expressions reveal about his view of the American Dream?
2. In paragraph 12, Desai enumerates things her father used to say to her. What do his comments suggest about his attitude toward her life in America?
3. Why did Indian visitors to the United States believe that when immigrants counted their "American friends," "Korean-American, Jewish, or Hispanic friends did not count" (5)? Do you think such friends would "count" for Desai? Why or why not?

## Responding in Writing

How do you interpret the title of this essay? Is the "fatherland" Desai refers to India? Or is it something else entirely? Explain.

# VAGABOND NATION

## Azar Nafisi

### 1947–

*Azar Nafisi is a visiting fellow and the executive director of cultural conversations at the Foreign Policy Institute at Johns Hopkins University's Paul H. Nitze School of Advanced International Studies. An Iranian writer now living in the United States, Nafisi is the author of* Anti-Terra: A Study of Vladimir Nabokov's Novels *(1994),* Reading Lolita in Tehran: A Memoir in Books *(2003),* La Voce Verde *(2006), and* Things I've Been Silent About: Memories *(2008). Nafisi specializes in Middle Eastern culture, women's issues, and human rights. In the following essay, she considers what it means to become an American citizen.*

On December 1, 2008, I became an American, eleven years and five months after I started living here. It was a bright, cold morning, and my son dropped me off at the Immigration and Naturalization office in Fairfax, Virginia, and wished me luck. The office was in a glass-and-metal building, in a parking lot close to the highway. In its total lack of character or beauty, it seemed invulnerable and imposing. Inside, I sat in a huge waiting room and frantically reviewed my citizenship questions, even though I knew them by heart.

The interview turned out to be much more pleasant than I had feared. I was asked only two civics questions, and was told to write a simple English sentence. My interviewer was a friendly young African-American woman who asked me about my job. When I told her I was a writer, she wanted to know what kind of books I wrote. I offered to send her one, and was reminded that as a government worker she could not accept gifts. She told me that, if I waited until two o'clock, I could take the oath and become naturalized the same day.

There was nowhere to wait but a small diner nearby. I bought a paper, ordered coffee and eggs, and sat at a table by the window. I opened my notebook to jot down my thoughts, but it all seemed too confusing. How did it start, this relationship with America? When I was a young girl, in Tehran, my English tutor told me the story of the Wizard of Oz. It was the first time I had heard of America, of Kansas, and of cyclones. Later, I came to hear of a river called Mississippi: *Adventures of Huckleberry Finn* was the book that I returned to most often, during the years I taught English in the Islamic Republic of Iran. Throughout the book, Huck and Jim turn the decent, civilized world on its head. They are subversives, but compassionate ones, trusting their own instincts and experiences. The more I read of American books, the more I encountered other characters who seemed to do something similar—Ralph Ellison's Invisible Man, F. Scott Fitzgerald's Gatsby, Zora Neale Hurston's Janie. It was this aspect of America—its vagrant nature—that I connected to. America somehow encourages this vagabond self, and that is surely why so many people who migrate feel at home here: they can be outsiders yet still belong. Years before I became an American, I had already made my home in the imaginary America.

After lunch, I joined a long queue of people waiting to get naturalization packages, which included a booklet containing the Declaration of Independence and the Constitution, and a small American flag on a gold-colored plastic flagpole. We filed into a room and sat down. The national anthem played in the background, and a television projected images of the flag and of American landscapes. My seat was No. 30; on my left was No. 29 and on my right No. 31. No. 31 interested me. Unlike me and the man to my left, he seemed to have taken some trouble with his appearance, and wore a pink shirt and a salmon-colored tie. He had deep-brown eyes and an engaging smile. At one point, I overheard him speaking in Arabic. He must have been in his mid-thirties. He fidgeted, looking in my direction, with the movements of a man who is dying to talk. I smiled at him encouragingly and he smiled back, pointing to the small flag in my hand. He waved his, and said, "For the past ten years, I have kept an American flag in my apartment. I take it out, dust it, and put it back again." He paused and then said, "And now this!" The next time he took his flag out, he would do so as an American citizen. He went on to describe what awaited us: first, there would be the President's message of welcome, some speeches about citizenship, then each of us would be called. "Remember to keep your flag in your hand," he told me. "And smile, because someone will take our pictures." But no one did.

5    He was like an ecstatic bridegroom just before his wedding, relating to a perfect stranger his good fortune, the years he had hidden the picture of his beloved, taking it out every once in a while to gaze—and now this! I listened to him but did not say much. Could I have said that I became a citizen because of Huck Finn and Jim, because of Dorothy and Oz? Nothing I could have said would have matched his joy, his complete immersion in the moment.

Afterward, we all stepped out into the cold, brilliant day. I called my husband to say that I was now the first American in the family. As I walked down the street, a car stopped, and my Arab friend rolled the window down to ask me if I wanted a ride. I thanked him and declined; a bit nostalgic, I watched the car move on and disappear. It occurred to me that I did not know his name, and that I had not asked him where he was from.

## Responding to Reading

1. Why do you think Nafisi spends so much time describing the Immigration and Naturalization office? Why does she describe the man she calls "No. 31" so fully?
2. How are Nafisi's emotions about becoming an American citizen different from those of No. 31, whom she describes as "like an ecstatic bridegroom just before his wedding" (5)?

3. What does Nafisi mean when she says she "became a citizen because of Huck Finn and Jim, because of Dorothy and Oz" (5)? What is the "imaginary America" (3) she felt a part of even before she came to the United States to live?

## Responding in Writing

What particularly "American" characteristics do you think Nafisi is referring to with words like "vagabond" (title) and "vagrant" (3)? What does she mean when she says that America "encourages this vagabond self" (3)? Do you think she is right?

# THE DECLARATION OF INDEPENDENCE

## Thomas Jefferson

### 1743–1826

*Thomas Jefferson—lawyer, statesman, diplomat, architect, scientist, politician, writer, education theorist, and musician—graduated from William and Mary College in 1762 and went on to lead an impressive political life. Jefferson served as a member of the Continental Congress, governor of Virginia, secretary of state to George Washington, and vice president to John Adams and also served two terms as the U.S. president (1801–1809), during which he oversaw the Louisiana Purchase. After retiring from public office, Jefferson founded the University of Virginia in 1819. He was an avid collector of books and owned nearly ten thousand, which later became the foundation of the Library of Congress. A firm believer in reason and the natural rights of individuals, Jefferson drafted the Declaration of Independence, which was later amended by the Continental Congress. In this document, he presents the colonists' grievances in order to justify their decision to declare their independence from England.*

## In Congress, July 4, 1776: The Unanimous Declaration of the Thirteen United States of America

When in the Course of human events it becomes necessary for one people to dissolve the political bands which have connected them with another, and to assume among the powers of the earth, the separate and equal station to which the Laws of Nature and of Nature's God entitle them, a decent respect to the opinions of mankind requires that they should declare the causes which impel them to the separation.

We hold these truths to be self-evident, that all men are created equal, that they are endowed by their Creator with certain unalienable Rights, that among these are Life, Liberty and the pursuit of Happiness. That to secure these rights, Governments are instituted among Men, deriving their just powers from the consent of the governed. That whenever any Form of Government becomes destructive of these ends, it is the Right of the People to alter or to abolish it, and to institute new Government, laying its foundation on such principles and organizing its powers in such form, as to them shall seem most likely to effect their Safety and Happiness. Prudence, indeed, will dictate that Governments long established should not be changed for light and transient causes; and accordingly all experience hath shewn, that mankind are more disposed to suffer, while evils are sufferable, than to right themselves by abolishing the forms to which they are accustomed. But when a long train of abuses and usurpations, pursuing invariably the same Object, evinces a design to reduce them under absolute Despotism, it is their right, it is their duty, to throw off such Government, and to provide new Guards for their future security. Such has been the patient sufferance of these Colonies; and such is now the necessity which constrains them to alter their former Systems of Governors. The history of the present King of Great Britain is a history of repeated injuries and usurpations, all having in direct object the establishment of an absolute Tyranny over these States. To prove this, let Facts be submitted to a candid world.

He has refused his Assent to Laws, the most wholesome and necessary for the public good.

He has forbidden his Governors to pass laws of immediate and pressing importance, unless suspended in their operation till his Assent should be obtained; and when so suspended, he has utterly neglected to attend to them.

5    He has refused to pass other Laws for the accommodation of large districts of people, unless those people would relinquish the right of Representation in the Legislature, a right inestimable to them and formidable to tyrants only.

He has called together legislative bodies at places unusual, uncomfortable, and distant from the depository of their Public Records, for the sole purpose of fatiguing them into compliance with his measures.

He has dissolved Representative Houses repeatedly, for opposing with manly firmness his invasions on the rights of the people.

He has refused for a long time, after such dissolutions, to cause others to be elected; whereby the Legislative Powers, incapable of Annihilation, have returned to the People at large for their exercise; the State remaining in the mean time exposed to all the dangers of invasion from without, and convulsions within.

He has endeavored to prevent the population of these States; for that purpose obstructing the Laws for Naturalization of Foreigners; refusing to pass others to encourage their migration hither, and raising the conditions of new Appropriations of Lands.

10    He has obstructed the Administration of Justice, by refusing his Assent to Laws for establishing Judiciary Powers.

He has made Judges dependent on his Will alone, for the tenure of their offices, and the amount and payment of their salaries.

He has erected a multitude of New Offices, and sent hither swarms of Officers to harass our people, and eat out their substance.

He has kept among us, in times of peace, Standing Armies without the Consent of our legislatures.

He has affected to render the Military independent of and superior to the Civil Power.

He has combined with others to subject us to a jurisdiction foreign 15 to our constitution, and unacknowledged by our laws; giving his Assent to their Acts of pretended Legislation: For quartering large bodies of armed troops among us: For protecting them, by a mock Trial, from punishment for any Murders which they should commit on the Inhabitants of these States: For cutting off our Trade with all parts of the world: For imposing Taxes on us without our Consent: For depriving us in many cases, of the benefits of Trial by Jury; For transporting us beyond Seas to be tried for pretended offenses: For abolishing the free System of English Laws in a neighboring Province, establishing therein an Arbitrary government, and enlarging its Boundaries so as to render it at once an example and fit instrument for introducing the same absolute rule into these Colonies: For taking away our Charters, abolishing our most valuable Laws and altering fundamentally the Forms of our Governments: For suspending our own Legislatures, and declaring themselves invested with power to legislate for us in all cases whatsoever.

He has abdicated Government here, by declaring us out of his Protection and waging War against us.

He has plundered our seas, ravaged our Coasts, burnt our towns, and destroyed the lives of our people.

He is at this time transporting large Armies of foreign Mercenaries to complete the works of death, desolation and tyranny, already begun with circumstances of Cruelty & Perfidy scarcely paralleled in the most barbarous ages, and totally unworthy the Head of a civilized nation.

He has constrained our fellow Citizens taken Captive on the high Seas to bear Arms against their Country, to become the executioners of their friends and Brethren, or to fall themselves by their Hands.

He has excited domestic insurrections amongst us, and has endeav- 20 ored to bring on the inhabitants of our frontiers, the merciless Indian Savages, whose known rule of warfare, is an undistinguished destruction of all ages, sexes, and conditions.

In every stage of these Oppressions We have Petitioned for Redress in the most humble terms: Our repeated Petitions have been answered only by repeated injury. A Prince, whose character is thus marked by every act which may define a Tyrant, is unfit to be the ruler of a free people.

Nor have We been wanting in attention to our British brethren. We have warned them from time to time of attempts by their legislature to extend an unwarrantable jurisdiction over us. We have reminded them of the circumstances of our emigration and settlement here. We have appealed to their native justice and magnanimity, and we have conjured them by the ties of our common kindred to disavow these usurpations, which would inevitably interrupt our connections and correspondence. They too have been deaf to the voice of justice and of consanguinity. We must, therefore, acquiesce in the necessity, which denounces our Separation, and hold them, as we hold the rest of mankind, Enemies in War, in Peace Friends.

We, therefore, the Representatives of the United States of America, in General Congress, Assembled, appealing to the Supreme Judge of the world for the rectitude of our intentions, do, in the Name, and by Authority of the good People of these Colonies, solemnly publish and declare, That these United Colonies are, and of Right ought to be free and independent states; that they are Absolved from all Allegiance to the British Crown, and that all political connection between them and the State of Great Britain, is and ought to be totally dissolved; and that as Free and Independent States, they have full Power to levy War, conclude Peace, contract Alliances, establish Commerce, and to do all other Acts and Things which Independent States may of right do. And for the support of this Declaration, with a firm reliance on the protection of Divine Providence, we mutually pledge to each other our Lives, our Fortunes, and our sacred Honor.

## Responding to Reading

1. The Declaration of Independence was written in the eighteenth century, a time when logic and reason were thought to be the supreme achievements of human beings. Do you think this document appeals just to reason, or does it also appeal to the emotions?
2. Paragraphs 3–20 consist of a litany of grievances, expressed in forceful parallel language. How is this use of parallelism similar to (or different from) the language used by John F. Kennedy (p. 510) and Martin Luther King, Jr. (p. 370)?
3. Do you think it is fair, as some have done, to accuse the framers of the Declaration of Independence of being racist? of being sexist?

## Responding in Writing

Rewrite five or six sentences from paragraphs 3–20 of the Declaration of Independence in modern English, substituting contemporary examples for the injustices Jefferson enumerates.

# THE GETTYSBURG ADDRESS

## Abraham Lincoln

### 1809–1865

*The sixteenth president of the United States, Abraham Lincoln led the Union to victory in the American Civil War. Known as the "Great Emancipator," Lincoln freed the slaves of the Confederacy with the Emancipation Proclamation, which was issued on January 1, 1863. On November 19, 1863, Lincoln delivered the Gettysburg Address during the dedication of the National Cemetery at Gettysburg, Pennsylvania, where the Battle of Gettysburg had claimed more than 40,000 Union and Confederate lives in July of that year.*

Four score and seven years ago our fathers brought forth on this continent, a new nation, conceived in Liberty, and dedicated to the proposition that all men are created equal.

Now we are engaged in a great civil war, testing whether that nation, or any nation so conceived and so dedicated, can long endure. We are met on a great battle-field of that war. We have come to dedicate a portion of that field, as a final resting place for those who here gave their lives that that nation might live. It is altogether fitting and proper that we should do this.

But, in a larger sense, we can not dedicate—we can not consecrate—we can not hallow—this ground. The brave men, living and dead, who struggled here, have consecrated it, far above our poor power to add or detract. The world will little note, nor long remember what we say here, but it can never forget what they did here. It is for us the living, rather, to be dedicated here to the unfinished work which they who fought here have thus far so nobly advanced. It is rather for us to be here dedicated to the great task remaining before us—that from these honored dead we take increased devotion to that cause for which they gave the last full measure of devotion—that we here highly resolve that these dead shall not have died in vain—that this nation, under God, shall have a new birth of freedom—and that government of the people, by the people, for the people, shall not perish from the earth.

## Responding to Reading

1. To Lincoln and his audience, what is the "great task remaining before us" (3)?
2. The first paragraph of this speech looks back, the second paragraph describes the present, and the third paragraph looks ahead. Using contemporary conversational style, write a one-sentence summary of each of these paragraphs.
3. In paragraph 3, Lincoln says, "The world will little note, nor long remember what we say here, but it can never forget what they [the brave soldiers] did here." Is he correct? Explain.

## Responding in Writing

What "great tasks" do you believe still face our nation's leaders? Which of these do you think will still be a challenge in fifty years? Why?

# I Have a Dream

## Martin Luther King, Jr.

### 1929–1968

*One of the greatest civil rights leaders and orators of the last century, Baptist minister Martin Luther King, Jr., earned a B.A. degree from Morehouse College (1948), a B.D. degree from Crozer Theological Seminary in Pennsylvania (1951), and a Ph.D. from Boston University (1955). Influenced by Thoreau and Gandhi, King altered the spirit of African-American protest in the United States by advocating nonviolent civil disobedience to achieve racial equality. King was arrested more than twenty times and assaulted at least four times for his activities, but he also was awarded five honorary degrees, was named Man of the Year by* Time *magazine in 1963, and the following year was awarded the Nobel Peace Prize. His books include* Letter from Birmingham Jail *(1963) and* Where Do We Go from Here: Chaos or Community? *(1967). King was assassinated on April 4, 1968, in Memphis, Tennessee. He delivered the following speech from the steps of the Lincoln Memorial on August 28, 1963, during the March on Washington in support of civil rights.*

I am happy to join with you today in what will go down in history as the greatest demonstration for freedom in the history of our nation.

Fivescore years ago, a great American, in whose symbolic shadow we stand today, signed the Emancipation Proclamation. This momentous decree came as a great beacon light of hope to millions of Negro slaves who had been seared in the flames of withering injustice. It came as a joyous daybreak to end the long night of their captivity.

But one hundred years later, the Negro still is not free; one hundred years later, the life of the Negro is still sadly crippled by the manacles of segregation and the chains of discrimination; one hundred years later, the Negro lives on a lonely island of poverty in the midst of a vast ocean of material prosperity; one hundred years later, the Negro is still languishing in the corners of American society and finds himself in exile in his own land.

So we've come here today to dramatize a shameful condition. In a sense we've come to our nation's capital to cash a check. When the architects of our republic wrote the magnificent words of the Constitution and the Declaration of Independence, they were signing a promissory note to which every American was to fall heir. This note was the promise that all men, yes, black men as well as white men, would be guaranteed the unalienable rights of life, liberty, and the pursuit of happiness.

It is obvious today that America has defaulted on this promissory 5 note in so far as her citizens of color are concerned. Instead of honoring this sacred obligation, America has given the Negro people a bad check; a check which has come back marked "insufficient funds." We refuse to believe that there are insufficient funds in the great vaults of opportunity of this nation. And so we've come to cash this check, a check that will give us upon demand the riches of freedom and the security of justice.

We have also come to this hallowed spot to remind America of the fierce urgency of now. This is no time to engage in the luxury of cooling off or to take the tranquilizing drug of gradualism. Now is the time to make real the promises of democracy; now is the time to rise from the dark and desolate valley of segregation to the sunlit path of racial justice; now is the time to lift our nation from the quicksands of racial injustice to the solid rock of brotherhood; now is the time to make justice a reality for all God's children. It would be fatal for the nation to overlook the urgency of the moment. This sweltering summer of the Negro's legitimate discontent will not pass until there is an invigorating autumn of freedom and equality.

Nineteen sixty-three is not an end, but a beginning. And those who hope that the Negro needed to blow off steam and will now be content, will have a rude awakening if the nation returns to business as usual.

There will be neither rest nor tranquility in America until the Negro is granted his citizenship rights. The whirlwinds of revolt will continue to shake the foundations of our nation until the bright day of justice emerges.

But there is something that I must say to my people who stand on the warm threshold which leads into the palace of justice. In the process of gaining our rightful place we must not be guilty of wrongful deeds.

Let us not seek to satisfy our thirst for freedom by drinking from 10 the cup of bitterness and hatred. We must forever conduct our struggle on the high plane of dignity and discipline. We must not allow our creative protest to degenerate into physical violence. Again and again we must rise to the majestic heights of meeting physical force with soul force.

The marvelous new militancy which has engulfed the Negro community must not lead us to a distrust of all white people, for many of our white brothers, as evidenced by their presence here today, have come to realize that their destiny is tied up with our destiny and they have come to realize that their freedom is inextricably bound to our freedom. This offense we share mounted to storm the battlements of injustice must be carried forth by a biracial army. We cannot walk alone.

And as we walk, we must make the pledge that we shall always march ahead. We cannot turn back. There are those who are asking the devotees of civil rights, "When will you be satisfied?" We can never be satisfied as long as the Negro is the victim of the unspeakable horrors of police brutality.

We can never be satisfied as long as our bodies, heavy with fatigue of travel, cannot gain lodging in the motels of the highways and the hotels of the cities. We cannot be satisfied as long as the Negro's basic mobility is from a smaller ghetto to a larger one.

We can never be satisfied as long as our children are stripped of their selfhood and robbed of their dignity by signs stating "for whites only." We cannot be satisfied as long as a Negro in Mississippi cannot vote and a Negro in New York believes he has nothing for which to vote. No, we are not satisfied, and we will not be satisfied until justice rolls down like waters and righteousness like a mighty stream.

15    I am not unmindful that some of you have come here out of excessive trials and tribulation. Some of you have come fresh from narrow jail cells. Some of you have come from areas where your quest for freedom left you battered by the storms of persecution and staggered by the winds of police brutality. You have been the veterans of creative suffering. Continue to work with the faith that unearned suffering is redemptive.

Go back to Mississippi; go back to Alabama; go back to South Carolina; go back to Georgia; go back to Louisiana; go back to the slums and ghettos of the northern cities, knowing that somehow this situation can, and will be changed. Let us not wallow in the valley of despair.

So I say to you, my friends, that even though we must face the difficulties of today and tomorrow, I still have a dream. It is a dream deeply rooted in the American dream that one day this nation will rise up and live out the true meaning of its creed—we hold these truths to be self-evident, that all men are created equal.

I have a dream that one day on the red hills of Georgia, sons of former slaves and sons of former slave-owners will be able to sit down together at the table of brotherhood.

I have a dream that one day, even the state of Mississippi, a state sweltering with the heat of injustice, sweltering with the heat of oppression, will be transformed into an oasis of freedom and justice.

20    I have a dream my four little children will one day live in a nation where they will not be judged by the color of their skin but by the content of their character. I have a dream today!

I have a dream that one day, down in Alabama, with its vicious racists, with its governor having his lips dripping with the words of interposition and nullification, that one day, right there in Alabama, little black boys and black girls will be able to join hands with little white boys and white girls as sisters and brothers. I have a dream today!

I have a dream that one day every valley shall be exalted, every hill and mountain shall be made low, the rough places shall be made plain, and the crooked places shall be made straight and the glory of the Lord will be revealed and all flesh shall see it together.

This is our hope. This is the faith that I go back to the South with.

With this faith we will be able to hew out of the mountain of despair a stone of hope. With this faith we will be able to transform the jangling discords of our nation into a beautiful symphony of brotherhood.

With this faith we will be able to work together, to pray together, 25 to struggle together, to go to jail together, to stand up for freedom together, knowing that we will be free one day. This will be the day when all of God's children will be able to sing with new meaning— "my country 'tis of thee; sweet land of liberty; of thee I sing; land where my fathers died, land of the pilgrim's pride; from every mountain side, let freedom ring"—and if America is to be a great nation, this must become true.

So let freedom ring from the prodigious hilltops of New Hampshire.

Let freedom ring from the mighty mountains of New York.

Let freedom ring from the heightening Alleghenies of Pennsylvania.

Let freedom ring from the snow-capped Rockies of Colorado.

Let freedom ring from the curvaceous slopes of California.    30

But not only that.

Let freedom ring from Stone Mountain of Georgia.

Let freedom ring from Lookout Mountain of Tennessee.

Let freedom ring from every hill and molehill of Mississippi, from every mountainside, let freedom ring.

And when we allow freedom to ring, when we let it ring from every 35 village and hamlet, from every state and city, we will be able to speed up that day when all of God's children—black men and white men, Jews and Gentiles, Catholics and Protestants—will be able to join hands and to sing in the words of the old Negro spiritual, "Free at last, free at last; thank God Almighty, we are free at last."

## Responding to Reading

1. What exactly is King's dream? Do you believe it has come true? If he were alive today, do you think he would believe his dream has been realized?

2. Speaking as a representative of his fellow African-American citizens, King tells his audience that African Americans find themselves "in exile in [their] own land" (3). Do you believe this is still true of African Americans? Of members of other minority groups? Which groups? Why?

3. Thomas Jefferson (p. 365) wrote the Declaration of Independence in the eighteenth century; King wrote his speech in the twentieth. Jefferson wrote as an insider, a man of privilege; King, as an outsider. What do their dreams have in common? How did each man intend to achieve his dream?

## Responding in Writing

What dreams do you have for yourself and for your family? What dreams do you have for your country? Do you expect these dreams to be realized?

# LA MIGRA¹

## Pat Mora

### 1942–

*Pat Mora's work focuses on Latino and Mexican-American culture, history, and identity. She is the author of numerous poetry collections and children's books, most recently* The Beautiful Lady: Our Lady of Guadalupe. *The following poem offers a particular view of U.S. immigration.*

I

Let's play *La Migra*
I'll be the Border Patrol.
You be the Mexican maid.
I get the badge and sunglasses.
5   You can hide and run,
but you can't get away
because I have a jeep.
I can take you wherever
I want, but don't ask
10   questions because
I don't speak Spanish.
I can touch you wherever
I want but don't complain
too much because I've got
15   boots and kick—if I have to,
and I have handcuffs.
Oh, and a gun.
Get ready, get set, run.

II

Let's play *La Migra*
20   You be the Border Patrol.

---

¹U.S. border patrol (Mexican slang). [Eds.]

I'll be the Mexican woman.
Your jeep has a flat,
and you have been spotted
by the sun.
All you have is heavy: hat                                    25
glasses, badge, shoes, gun.
I know this desert,
where to rest,
where to drink.
Oh, I am not alone.                                           30
You hear us singing
and laughing with the wind,
*Agua dulce brota aqui,*
*aqui, aqui,*[2] but since you
can't speak Spanish,                                          35
you do not understand.
Get ready.

## Responding to Reading

1. How would you characterize the tone of this poem? For example, does the speaker's "Let's play" (lines 1 and 19) really seem playful, or does it have a serious or ironic undertone?
2. What is the relationship between this poem's two stanzas? How are the stanzas alike in style, form, and content? How are they different?
3. What is the significance of the fact, mentioned in lines 11 and 35, that the Border Patrol agent cannot speak Spanish? (Consider this fact particularly in light of the Spanish expression that is not translated into English.)

## Responding in Writing

Who do you think has the upper hand here, the Border Patrol or the Mexican woman? Who does the speaker believe has the advantage? Why?

---

[2]"Sweet water springs here, here, here." [Eds.]

---

### FOCUS

---

## Should Undocumented Immigrants
## Have a Path to Citizenship?

Student demonstrating in support of the DREAM
Act, Detroit, 2010

### Responding to the Image

1. What argument does the graduate's T-shirt in the photo above make in favor of passage of the DREAM Act, which would offer a path to citizenship for some undocumented immigrants? Is this a convincing argument? What counterarguments can you suggest?
2. What do you see as the relationship between the DREAM Act and the American Dream?
3. If you were to design a T-shirt to express your position on this issue, what would it say?

# OUTLAW: MY LIFE IN AMERICA AS AN UNDOCUMENTED IMMIGRANT

## Jose Antonio Vargas

### 1981–

*Jose Antonio Vargas is a Filipino journalist and a former reporter for the* Washington Post. *Vargas was a member of the team of journalists who won the Pulitzer Prize in 2008 for breaking news reporting about the Virginia Tech campus shootings. He also started the online project* Define American *to promote "a new conversation about immigration." In the following essay, originally published in 2011 in the* New York Times Magazine, *Vargas reveals himself as an "undocumented immigrant" who has been living illegally in the United States since he was twelve years old. (Note that Vargas is too old to take advantage of President Obama's 2012 executive order.)*

One August morning nearly two decades ago, my mother woke me and put me in a cab. She handed me a jacket. *"Baka malamig doon"* were among the few words she said. ("It might be cold there.") When I arrived at the Philippines' Ninoy Aquino International Airport with her, my aunt and a family friend, I was introduced to a man I'd never seen. They told me he was my uncle. He held my hand as I boarded an airplane for the first time. It was 1993, and I was 12.

My mother wanted to give me a better life, so she sent me thousands of miles away to live with her parents in America—my grandfather (*Lolo* in Tagalog[1]) and grandmother (*Lola*). After I arrived in Mountain View, Calif., in the San Francisco Bay Area, I entered sixth grade and quickly grew to love my new home, family and culture. I discovered a passion for language, though it was hard to learn the difference between formal English and American slang. One of my early memories is of a freckled kid in middle school asking me, "What's up?" I replied, "The sky," and he and a couple of other kids laughed. I won the eighth-grade spelling bee by memorizing words I couldn't properly pronounce. (The winning word was "indefatigable.")

One day when I was 16, I rode my bike to the nearby D.M.V. office to get my driver's permit. Some of my friends already had their licenses, so I figured it was time. But when I handed the clerk my green card as proof of U.S. residency, she flipped it around, examining it. "This is fake," she whispered. "Don't come back here again."

Confused and scared, I pedaled home and confronted Lolo. I remember him sitting in the garage, cutting coupons. I dropped my

[1]Official language of the Philippines. [Eds.]

bike and ran over to him, showing him the green card. *"Peke ba ito?"* I asked in Tagalog. ("Is this fake?") My grandparents were naturalized American citizens—he worked as a security guard, she as a food server—and they had begun supporting my mother and me financially when I was 3, after my father's wandering eye and inability to properly provide for us led to my parents' separation. Lolo was a proud man, and I saw the shame on his face as he told me he purchased the card, along with other fake documents, for me. "Don't show it to other people," he warned.

5　　I decided then that I could never give anyone reason to doubt I was an American. I convinced myself that if I worked enough, if I achieved enough, I would be rewarded with citizenship. I felt I could earn it.

I've tried. Over the past 14 years, I've graduated from high school and college and built a career as a journalist, interviewing some of the most famous people in the country. On the surface, I've created a good life. I've lived the American dream.

But I am still an undocumented immigrant. And that means living a different kind of reality. It means going about my day in fear of being found out. It means rarely trusting people, even those closest to me, with who I really am. It means keeping my family photos in a shoebox rather than displaying them on shelves in my home, so friends don't ask about them. It means reluctantly, even painfully, doing things I know are wrong and unlawful. And it has meant relying on a sort of 21st-century underground railroad of supporters, people who took an interest in my future and took risks for me.

Last year I read about four students who walked from Miami to Washington to lobby for the Dream Act, a nearly decade-old immigration bill that would provide a path to legal permanent residency for young people who have been educated in this country. At the risk of deportation—the Obama administration has deported almost 800,000 people in the last two years—they are speaking out. Their courage has inspired me.[2]

There are believed to be 11 million undocumented immigrants in the United States. We're not always who you think we are. Some pick your strawberries or care for your children. Some are in high school or college. And some, it turns out, write news articles you might read. I grew up here. This is my home. Yet even though I think of myself as an American and consider America my country, my country doesn't think of me as one of its own.

10　　My first challenge was the language. Though I learned English in the Philippines, I wanted to lose my accent. During high school, I spent hours at a time watching television (especially *Frasier, Home Improvement* and reruns of *The Golden Girls*) and movies (from *Goodfellas* to *Anne of*

---

[2]In 2011, the Obama administration instituted a policy that would generally not deport undocumented immigrants unless they posed a threat of some kind. [Eds.]

*Green Gables*), pausing the VHS to try to copy how various characters enunciated their words. At the local library, I read magazines, books and newspapers—anything to learn how to write better. Kathy Dewar, my high-school English teacher, introduced me to journalism. From the moment I wrote my first article for the student paper, I convinced myself that having my name in print—writing in English, interviewing Americans—validated my presence here.

The debates over "illegal aliens" intensified my anxieties. In 1994, only a year after my flight from the Philippines, Gov. Pete Wilson was re-elected in part because of his support for Proposition 187, which prohibited undocumented immigrants from attending public school and accessing other services. (A federal court later found the law unconstitutional.) After my encounter at the D.M.V. in 1997, I grew more aware of anti-immigrant sentiments and stereotypes: *they don't want to assimilate, they are a drain on society*. They're not talking about me, I would tell myself. I have something to contribute.

To do that, I had to work—and for that, I needed a Social Security number. Fortunately, my grandfather had already managed to get one for me. Lolo had always taken care of everyone in the family. He and my grandmother emigrated legally in 1984 from Zambales, a province in the Philippines of rice fields and bamboo houses, following Lolo's sister, who married a Filipino-American serving in the American military. She petitioned for her brother and his wife to join her. When they got here, Lolo petitioned for his two children—my mother and her younger brother—to follow them. But instead of mentioning that my mother was a married woman, he listed her as single. Legal residents can't petition for their married children. Besides, Lolo didn't care for my father. He didn't want him coming here too.

But soon Lolo grew nervous that the immigration authorities reviewing the petition would discover my mother was married, thus derailing not only her chances of coming here but those of my uncle as well. So he withdrew her petition. After my uncle came to America legally in 1991, Lolo tried to get my mother here through a tourist visa, but she wasn't able to obtain one. That's when she decided to send me. My mother told me later that she figured she would follow me soon. She never did.

The "uncle" who brought me here turned out to be a coyote,[3] not a relative, my grandfather later explained. Lolo scraped together enough money—I eventually learned it was $4,500, a huge sum for him—to pay him to smuggle me here under a fake name and fake passport. (I never saw the passport again after the flight and have always assumed that the coyote kept it.) After I arrived in America, Lolo obtained a new fake Filipino passport, in my real name this time, adorned with a fake student visa, in addition to the fraudulent green card.

---

[3]Someone who smuggles undocumented immigrants into the United States. [Eds.]

15    Using the fake passport, we went to the local Social Security Administration office and applied for a Social Security number and card. It was, I remember, a quick visit. When the card came in the mail, it had my full, real name, but it also clearly stated: "Valid for work only with I.N.S. authorization."

When I began looking for work, a short time after the D.M.V. incident, my grandfather and I took the Social Security card to Kinko's, where he covered the "I.N.S. authorization" text with a sliver of white tape. We then made photocopies of the card. At a glance, at least, the copies would look like copies of a regular, unrestricted Social Security card.

Lolo always imagined I would work the kind of low-paying jobs that undocumented people often take. (Once I married an American, he said, I would get my real papers, and everything would be fine.) But even menial jobs require documents, so he and I hoped the doctored card would work for now. The more documents I had, he said, the better.

While in high school, I worked part time at Subway, then at the front desk of the local Y.M.C.A., then at a tennis club, until I landed an unpaid internship at the *Mountain View Voice*, my hometown newspaper. First I brought coffee and helped around the office; eventually I began covering city-hall meetings and other assignments for pay.

For more than a decade of getting part-time and full-time jobs, employers have rarely asked to check my original Social Security card. When they did, I showed the photocopied version, which they accepted. Over time, I also began checking the citizenship box on my federal I-9 employment eligibility forms. (Claiming full citizenship was actually easier than declaring permanent resident "green card" status, which would have required me to provide an alien registration number.)

20    This deceit never got easier. The more I did it, the more I felt like an impostor, the more guilt I carried—and the more I worried that I would get caught. But I kept doing it. I needed to live and survive on my own, and I decided this was the way.

Mountain View High School became my second home. I was elected to represent my school at school-board meetings, which gave me the chance to meet and befriend Rich Fischer, the superintendent for our school district. I joined the speech and debate team, acted in school plays and eventually became co-editor of the *Oracle*, the student newspaper. That drew the attention of my principal, Pat Hyland. "You're at school just as much as I am," she told me. Pat and Rich would soon become mentors, and over time, almost surrogate parents for me.

After a choir rehearsal during my junior year, Jill Denny, the choir director, told me she was considering a Japan trip for our singing group. I told her I couldn't afford it, but she said we'd figure out a way.

I hesitated, and then decided to tell her the truth. "It's not really the money," I remember saying. "I don't have the right passport." When she assured me we'd get the proper documents, I finally told her. "I can't get the right passport," I said. "I'm not supposed to be here."

She understood. So the choir toured Hawaii instead, with me in tow. (Mrs. Denny and I spoke a couple of months ago, and she told me she hadn't wanted to leave any student behind.)

Later that school year, my history class watched a documentary on Harvey Milk, the openly gay San Francisco city official who was assassinated. This was 1999, just six months after Matthew Shepard's body was found tied to a fence in Wyoming. During the discussion, I raised my hand and said something like: "I'm sorry Harvey Milk got killed for being gay. . . . I've been meaning to say this. . . . I'm gay."

I hadn't planned on coming out that morning, though I had known 25 that I was gay for several years. With that announcement, I became the only openly gay student at school, and it caused turmoil with my grandparents. Lolo kicked me out of the house for a few weeks. Though we eventually reconciled, I had disappointed him on two fronts. First, as a Catholic, he considered homosexuality a sin and was embarrassed about having *"ang apo na bakla"* ("a grandson who is gay"). Even worse, I was making matters more difficult for myself, he said. I needed to marry an American woman in order to gain a green card.

Tough as it was, coming out about being gay seemed less daunting than coming out about my legal status. I kept my other secret mostly hidden.

While my classmates awaited their college acceptance letters, I hoped to get a full-time job at the *Mountain View Voice* after graduation. It's not that I didn't want to go to college, but I couldn't apply for state and federal financial aid. Without that, my family couldn't afford to send me.

But when I finally told Pat and Rich about my immigration "problem"—as we called it from then on—they helped me look for a solution. At first, they even wondered if one of them could adopt me and fix the situation that way, but a lawyer Rich consulted told him it wouldn't change my legal status because I was too old. Eventually they connected me to a new scholarship fund for high-potential students who were usually the first in their families to attend college. Most important, the fund was not concerned with immigration status. I was among the first recipients, with the scholarship covering tuition, lodging, books and other expenses for my studies at San Francisco State University.

As a college freshman, I found a job working part time at the *San Francisco Chronicle*, where I sorted mail and wrote some freelance articles. My ambition was to get a reporting job, so I embarked on a series of internships. First I landed at the *Philadelphia Daily News*, in the summer of 2001, where I covered a drive-by shooting and the wedding of the 76ers star Allen Iverson. Using those articles, I applied to the *Seattle Times* and got an internship for the following summer.

30        But then my lack of proper documents became a problem again. The *Times*'s recruiter, Pat Foote, asked all incoming interns to bring certain paperwork on their first day: a birth certificate, or a passport, or a driver's license plus an original Social Security card. I panicked, thinking my documents wouldn't pass muster. So before starting the job, I called Pat and told her about my legal status. After consulting with management, she called me back with the answer I feared: I couldn't do the internship.

This was devastating. What good was college if I couldn't then pursue the career I wanted? I decided then that if I was to succeed in a profession that is all about truth-telling, I couldn't tell the truth about myself.

After this episode, Jim Strand, the venture capitalist who sponsored my scholarship, offered to pay for an immigration lawyer. Rich and I went to meet her in San Francisco's financial district.

I was hopeful. This was in early 2002, shortly after Senators Orrin Hatch, the Utah Republican, and Dick Durbin, the Illinois Democrat, introduced the Dream Act—Development, Relief and Education for Alien Minors. It seemed like the legislative version of what I'd told myself: If I work hard and contribute, things will work out.

But the meeting left me crushed. My only solution, the lawyer said, was to go back to the Philippines and accept a 10-year ban before I could apply to return legally.

35        If Rich was discouraged, he hid it well. "Put this problem on a shelf," he told me. "Compartmentalize it. Keep going."

And I did. For the summer of 2003, I applied for internships across the country. Several newspapers, including the *Wall Street Journal,* the *Boston Globe* and the *Chicago Tribune,* expressed interest. But when the *Washington Post* offered me a spot, I knew where I would go. And this time, I had no intention of acknowledging my "problem."

The Post internship posed a tricky obstacle: It required a driver's license. (After my close call at the California D.M.V., I'd never gotten one.) So I spent an afternoon at the Mountain View Public Library, studying various states' requirements. Oregon was among the most welcoming—and it was just a few hours' drive north.

Again, my support network came through. A friend's father lived in Portland, and he allowed me to use his address as proof of residency. Pat, Rich and Rich's longtime assistant, Mary Moore, sent letters to me at that address. Rich taught me how to do three-point turns in a parking lot, and a friend accompanied me to Portland.

The license meant everything to me—it would let me drive, fly and work. But my grandparents worried about the Portland trip and the Washington internship. While Lola offered daily prayers so that I would not get caught, Lolo told me that I was dreaming too big, risking too much.

I was determined to pursue my ambitions. I was 22, I told them, responsible for my own actions. But this was different from Lolo's driving a confused teenager to Kinko's. I knew what I was doing now, and I knew it wasn't right. But what was I supposed to do?

I was paying state and federal taxes, but I was using an invalid Social Security card and writing false information on my employment forms. But that seemed better than depending on my grandparents or on Pat, Rich and Jim—or returning to a country I barely remembered. I convinced myself all would be O.K. if I lived up to the qualities of a "citizen": hard work, self-reliance, love of my country.

At the D.M.V. in Portland, I arrived with my photocopied Social Security card, my college I.D., a pay stub from the *San Francisco Chronicle* and my proof of state residence—the letters to the Portland address that my support network had sent. It worked. My license, issued in 2003, was set to expire eight years later, on my 30th birthday, on Feb. 3, 2011. I had eight years to succeed professionally, and to hope that some sort of immigration reform would pass in the meantime and allow me to stay.

It seemed like all the time in the world.

My summer in Washington was exhilarating. I was intimidated to be in a major newsroom but was assigned a mentor—Peter Perl, a veteran magazine writer—to help me navigate it. A few weeks into the internship, he printed out one of my articles, about a guy who recovered a long-lost wallet, circled the first two paragraphs and left it on my desk. "Great eye for details—awesome!" he wrote. Though I didn't know it then, Peter would become one more member of my network.

At the end of the summer, I returned to the *San Francisco Chronicle*. My plan was to finish school—I was now a senior—while I worked for the *Chronicle* as a reporter for the city desk. But when the *Post* beckoned again, offering me a full-time, two-year paid internship that I could start when I graduated in June 2004, it was too tempting to pass up. I moved back to Washington.

About four months into my job as a reporter for the *Post*, I began feeling increasingly paranoid, as if I had "illegal immigrant" tattooed on my forehead—and in Washington, of all places, where the debates over immigration seemed never-ending. I was so eager to prove myself that I feared I was annoying some colleagues and editors—and worried that any one of these professional journalists could discover my secret. The anxiety was nearly paralyzing. I decided I had to tell one of the higher-ups about my situation. I turned to Peter.

By this time, Peter, who still works at the *Post*, had become part of management as the paper's director of newsroom training and professional development. One afternoon in late October, we walked a couple of blocks to Lafayette Square, across from the White House. Over some 20 minutes, sitting on a bench, I told him everything: the Social Security card, the driver's license, Pat and Rich, my family.

Peter was shocked. "I understand you 100 times better now," he said. He told me that I had done the right thing by telling him, and that it was now our shared problem. He said he didn't want to do anything about it just yet. I had just been hired, he said, and I needed to prove myself. "When you've done enough," he said, "we'll tell Don and Len together." (Don Graham is the chairman of the Washington Post Company; Leonard Downie Jr. was then the paper's executive editor.) A month later, I spent my first Thanksgiving in Washington with Peter and his family.

In the five years that followed, I did my best to "do enough." I was promoted to staff writer, reported on video-game culture, wrote a series on Washington's H.I.V./AIDS epidemic and covered the role of technology and social media in the 2008 presidential race. I visited the White House, where I interviewed senior aides and covered a state dinner—and gave the Secret Service the Social Security number I obtained with false documents.

50      I did my best to steer clear of reporting on immigration policy but couldn't always avoid it. On two occasions, I wrote about Hillary Clinton's position on driver's licenses for undocumented immigrants. I also wrote an article about Senator Mel Martinez of Florida, then the chairman of the Republican National Committee, who was defending his party's stance toward Latinos after only one Republican presidential candidate—John McCain, the co-author of a failed immigration bill—agreed to participate in a debate sponsored by Univision, the Spanish-language network.

It was an odd sort of dance: I was trying to stand out in a highly competitive newsroom, yet I was terrified that if I stood out too much, I'd invite unwanted scrutiny. I tried to compartmentalize my fears, distract myself by reporting on the lives of other people, but there was no escaping the central conflict in my life. Maintaining a deception for so long distorts your sense of self. You start wondering who you've become, and why.

In April 2008, I was part of a *Post* team that won a Pulitzer Prize for the paper's coverage of the Virginia Tech shootings a year earlier. Lolo died a year earlier, so it was Lola who called me the day of the announcement. The first thing she said was, "*Anong mangyayari kung malaman ng mga tao?*"

What will happen if people find out?

I couldn't say anything. After we got off the phone, I rushed to the bathroom on the fourth floor of the newsroom, sat down on the toilet and cried.

In the summer of 2009, without ever having had that follow-up talk 55 with top *Post* management, I left the paper and moved to New York to join the *Huffington Post*. I met Arianna Huffington at a Washington Press Club Foundation dinner I was covering for the *Post* two years earlier, and she later recruited me to join her news site. I wanted to learn more about Web publishing, and I thought the new job would provide a useful education.

Still, I was apprehensive about the move: many companies were already using E-Verify, a program set up by the Department of Homeland Security that checks if prospective employees are eligible to work, and I didn't know if my new employer was among them. But I'd been able to get jobs in other newsrooms, I figured, so I filled out the paperwork as usual and succeeded in landing on the payroll.

While I worked at the *Huffington Post*, other opportunities emerged. My H.I.V./AIDS series became a documentary film called *The Other City*, which opened at the Tribeca Film Festival last year and was broadcast on Showtime. I began writing for magazines and landed a dream assignment: profiling Facebook's Mark Zuckerberg for the *New Yorker*.

The more I achieved, the more scared and depressed I became. I was proud of my work, but there was always a cloud hanging over it, over me. My old eight-year deadline—the expiration of my Oregon driver's license—was approaching.

After slightly less than a year, I decided to leave the *Huffington Post*. In part, this was because I wanted to promote the documentary and write a book about online culture—or so I told my friends. But the real reason was, after so many years of trying to be a part of the system, of focusing all my energy on my professional life, I learned that no amount of professional success would solve my problem or ease the sense of loss and displacement I felt. I lied to a friend about why I couldn't take a weekend trip to Mexico. Another time I concocted an excuse for why I couldn't go on an all-expenses-paid trip to Switzerland. I have been unwilling, for years, to be in a long-term relationship because I never wanted anyone to get too close and ask too many questions. All the while, Lola's question was stuck in my head: What will happen if people find out?

Early this year, just two weeks before my 30th birthday, I won a 60 small reprieve: I obtained a driver's license in the state of Washington. The license is valid until 2016. This offered me five more years of acceptable identification—but also five more years of fear, of lying to people I respect and institutions that trusted me, of running away from who I am.

I'm done running. I'm exhausted. I don't want that life anymore.

So I've decided to come forward, own up to what I've done, and tell my story to the best of my recollection. I've reached out to former bosses and employers and apologized for misleading them—a mix of humiliation and liberation coming with each disclosure. All the people mentioned in this article gave me permission to use their names. I've also talked to family and friends about my situation and am working with legal counsel to review my options. I don't know what the consequences will be of telling my story.

I do know that I am grateful to my grandparents, my Lolo and Lola, for giving me the chance for a better life. I'm also grateful to my other family—the support network I found here in America—for encouraging me to pursue my dreams.

It's been almost 18 years since I've seen my mother. Early on, I was mad at her for putting me in this position, and then mad at myself for being angry and ungrateful. By the time I got to college, we rarely spoke by phone. It became too painful; after a while it was easier to just send money to help support her and my two half-siblings. My sister, almost 2 years old when I left, is almost 20 now. I've never met my 14-year-old brother. I would love to see them.

65   Not long ago, I called my mother. I wanted to fill the gaps in my memory about that August morning so many years ago. We had never discussed it. Part of me wanted to shove the memory aside, but to write this article and face the facts of my life, I needed more details. Did I cry? Did she? Did we kiss goodbye?

My mother told me I was excited about meeting a stewardess, about getting on a plane. She also reminded me of the one piece of advice she gave me for blending in: If anyone asked why I was coming to America, I should say I was going to Disneyland.

## Responding to Reading

1. List the specific illegal acts Vargas's grandfather (and Vargas himself) committed to hide the fact that Vargas was in the United States illegally. What motivated each of these acts? How does Vargas justify them? What finally motivated Vargas to (in his words) "come forward, own up to what I've done, and tell my story" (62)?
2. What obstacles did Vargas face because of his immigration status? How did he overcome them? How did his "support network" (38) help him? Do you think these people did the right thing by helping him?
3. How do you respond to each of these statements?

   • "I convinced myself that if I worked enough, if I achieved enough, I would be rewarded with citizenship." (5)

   • "Tough as it was, coming out about being gay seemed less daunting than coming out about my legal status." (26)

   • "I decided then that if I was to succeed in a profession that is all about truth-telling, I couldn't tell the truth about myself." (31)

Do you think Vargas is being completely honest with himself in each case? Do you see any irony in his words?

## Responding in Writing

What different connotations do the terms *undocumented immigrants* and *illegal aliens* have (11)? Which terms do you think should be used to refer to Vargas and others in his situation? Why?

# JOSE ANTONIO VARGAS IS AN AMERICAN HERO

## Rory O'Connor

### 1951–

*A managing editor and a columnist at* MediaChannel.org *and the founding editorial director of* Newstrust.net, *Rory O'Connor is a journalist, blogger, documentary filmmaker, and corporate executive. He is the coauthor of* Nukespeak: Nuclear Language, Visions, and Mindset *(1982) and author of* Shock Jocks: Hate Speech & Talk Radio *(2008). In the following essay, O'Connor calls Jose Antonio Vargas (p. 379) an "American hero."*

I first met Jose Antonio Vargas in the fall of 2008, in the midst of the historic Obama campaign for the presidency. At the time, I was a fellow at the Joan Shorenstein Center on the Press, Politics and Public Policy at Harvard's Kennedy School of Government, where I was researching the impact of the then-emerging social media on older legacy forms of journalism, such as newspapers.

A woman named Maralee Schwartz was also at the Kennedy School when I was there. Beginning in 1979, Maralee had spent her entire professional career at the *Washington Post*, largely as a political reporter and political editor. As national political editor, she led the *Post*'s award-winning teams of reporters in coverage including three presidential elections, the last term of the Clinton White House, and the first term of the Bush White House.

As a "lifer" at the *Post*, and like many of her peers at the time in the so-called "mainstream media," Maralee was, shall we say, extremely wary of the new media. When she heard upon our first meeting that I was researching how social networks were affecting journalism, for example, she promptly fired back, "Social networks? You mean those places online people go to get dates?"

Despite her pronounced skepticism, Maralee was still open enough to at least consider the possibility that there might be something to my seemingly wild contention that social media would have a major impact on the way journalism would be practiced in the near future. A few weeks after we met, she knocked loudly on my office door, and when I opened it, literally shoved a young man in. "This is Jose Antonio Vargas," she announced. "He gets what you're doing!" And then she marched off, leaving Vargas in her considerable wake.

CHAPTER 7 FOCUS

5    We spent the next hour talking, and I quickly ascertained that Maralee was right—this guy really did get it! Quick, articulate, savvy and full of energy, the twenty-seven-year-old immigrant from the Philippines had already been part of a Pulitzer Prize–winning team at the *Post*—and he certainly seemed poised to attain even greater honor and success in the near future, pursing a career that had already taken him at a still tender age (to me at least!) near the pinnacle of establishment journalism.

Vargas then surprised me by proceeding to castigate his employer as completely behind the curve and mired in a rapidly fading past glory. "These guys don't understand," Vargas complained. "They should fire most of the editors and hire a bunch of graphic designers and online journalists," he announced with the impatience and brashness of youth.

I realized immediately that Vargas, whose Pulitzer participation came about when he cleverly used social media like Facebook to break news about the Virginia Tech campus massacre, was exactly the sort of young, hip and connected reporter places like the *Post* desperately needed in order to make the transition to a new digital form of journalism. I also realized that Vargas probably was not long for that world.

In short order he did walk away—from what, in an earlier era, would have been seen as the opportunity of a lifetime—in order to join the online upstart *Huffington Post*. He was among the first, in what soon became a wave, and then a tsunami of journalists, who were abandoning major media platforms like the *Post*, the *New York Times* and national television networks to work in a new form of journalism online.

In the years that followed, Jose enjoyed great success at HuffPo, and also began freelancing for major national magazines, including writing a landmark piece for the *New Yorker* about Facebook founder Mark Zuckerberg. A series of articles he had written about H.I.V./AIDS became a documentary film called *The Other City*, which opened at the Tribeca Film Festival last year and was broadcast on Showtime—and along the way, Jose also came out as gay and wrote movingly about how he could and would no longer keep secrets about who he was and how he felt.

10    But despite his many amazing successes, Vargas still felt incomplete. Now we know why.

In an incredibly moving and important piece in the *New York Times* Sunday Magazine, "My Life as an Undocumented Immigrant," he has just "come out" again—this time bravely and dangerously revealing that he is an undocumented immigrant, who has lived in the shadows since arriving in the USA in 1993 as a 12-year-old. Yes, this young man, on the fast track to attaining the putative American Dream, has now exposed himself not as "American"—but as "other."

Jose Antonio Vargas is incredibly brave to risk everything he has accomplished in this country in order to tell the truth—and to shine yet another but still much-needed light on the pressing need for comprehensive immigration reform in this country. He, and millions like him, have much to contribute to America—and without people like them, our country will be far poorer.

If there isn't room in the United States for people like Jose Antonio—the precise type of people who made this country great—I despair for our collective future. I urge you to read his inspiring story, and then to take action to ensure that Jose Antonio—and the many others like him—aren't forced to choose between hiding in the shadows or risking it all by telling the truth.

## Responding to Reading

1. What specific professional strengths does O'Connor identify in Jose Antonio Vargas in his discussion of his "amazing successes" (10)? What personal strengths does he identify?
2. What is your reaction to O'Connor's account of his first meeting with Vargas? Do you see Vargas as simply "Quick, articulate, savvy and full of energy" (5), or do you think he is also arrogant and ungrateful?
3. Why does O'Connor see Vargas as a hero? Do you think he makes a convincing case? If not, what additional evidence do you think he needs to present?

## Responding in Writing

The portrait of Vargas presented by O'Connor is clearly sympathetic. What does O'Connor suggest about Vargas that Vargas himself does not convey in his own essay on page 377?

# JOSE ANTONIO VARGAS'S LIES DESERVE NO SYMPATHY

## Esther Cepeda

*A columnist for the* Chicago Sun-Times *and the* Washington Post, *Esther Cepeda writes about issues pertaining to Latino culture. She started working for the* Chicago Sun-Times *in 2006, when she became Chicago's first Latina metro columnist. In the following essay, Cepeda explains the dark side of Jose Antonio Vargas's immigration story.*

In retelling last week's revelation that Pulitzer Prize–winning journalist Jose Antonio Vargas is an illegal immigrant, civil rights metaphors have been trotted out to describe the plight of a talented young man who got caught up in an immigration mess but, through his shocking confession, has become to some people a new American hero.

But if a charismatic reporter with good intentions and the capacity to commit many different kinds of personal deceptions and federal offenses is the latest poster boy for the sad state of the melting pot, America's in big trouble.

Anyone with an ounce of compassion who read Vargas's essay "Outlaw: My Life in America as an Undocumented Immigrant" from last Sunday's *New York Times Magazine* couldn't have helped feeling the heart stir with sadness. A 12-year-old child was given up by a mother who only wished for her son to have a decent life. Until Vargas tried to get a driver's license, he believed that he was a legal U.S. resident.

The rest of Vargas's story makes the stomach ache.

5    His grandfather, a legal resident of the United States, smuggled Vargas into California under a false name with a fake passport and used it to obtain an authentic, but restricted, Social Security card that they later altered at a local Kinko's copy center to look as though Vargas was U.S.-born and thus a citizen.

Despite Vargas's anxieties about being an imposter, guilt over his web of lies, and his ever-present fear of getting caught, he excelled in high school as a choir member and journalist. The academic success led to his first flirtation with "coming out" of the illegal-immigrant closet: with the assistance of his scholastic "underground railroad" of school administrator friends who even considered adopting him, an immigration lawyer was consulted. He learned that the only way to get right with the law would have been to go back to the Philippines, accept a 10-year ban, and then apply to return legally.

He didn't consider returning to his family a viable option and instead went to the neighboring state of Oregon where, with the help of friends, he obtained the driver's license that would allow him to use a car, travel by airplane and take jobs in media, some of which included reporting on illegal-immigration issues. A journalistic rock star, his full complement of fake IDs even got him past the Secret Service and into the White House to report on a state dinner and interview senior aides.

What the general public was supposed to take from Vargas's "heroic" admission is that illegal immigrants generally are people who don't mean to break any laws, tell any lies or hurt anyone's feelings but are forced to do so because of the draconian and unjust immigration laws in this country. And they're not just janitors, nannies or grass-mowers, but also professionals who make many great contributions to society.

Here's what I, and many others, took from it.

Someone can lie to almost every person and institution he's come    10
in contact with while in the United States then cloak himself in the
American flag and, using the parlance of American civil rights history,
morph into a high-profile activist with little chance of being deported.

And never mind that respected colleagues were humiliated. A profession that is already suffering from perceptions of liberal political bias
was further tarred. And in newsrooms and offices around the country,
Hispanic and Asian professionals may be feeling now, more than ever,
that their honesty and residency status are also in doubt. That's supposed to be OK, because immigration reform is such an important
issue.

Even for those who have great empathy for the struggles of people
who come to this country to work hard, even for low wages, for a shot
at the mythical "better life," it's almost impossible to not be deeply
disturbed by the self-promotion disguised as sacrifice, the blatant criminal activity and distasteful comparisons to the experiences of African-
Americans in their struggle for equality.

This latest attempt at putting a human and familiar face on
immigration-policy concerns will go largely ignored or, at worse, backfire because though Vargas is a powerful storyteller, his chronicle isn't
really all that easy to commiserate with.

If he meant to inspire compassion for any of the other 11 million
illegal immigrants who wouldn't expect to be spared the full weight
of legal repercussions if they ran to the media, he has left many
unmoved.

## Responding to Reading

1. In the first paragraph of her essay, Cepeda identifies Vargas as both a "Pulitzer Prize–winning journalist" and an "illegal immigrant." What other terms does she use to characterize him? Having read Vargas's essay (p. 377), do you think Cepeda's characterizations are fair?

2. In paragraph 8, Cepeda says that what Vargas was trying to tell readers was that "illegal immigrants generally are people who don't mean to break any laws, tell any lies or hurt anyone's feelings but are forced to do so because of the draconian and unjust immigration laws in this country." Do you think this characterization is accurate? Why or why not?

3. Whom does Cepeda believe Vargas's deception has hurt? Do you think the long-term impact of his article will be largely positive, neutral, or negative? Explain.

## Responding in Writing

Do you agree with Cepeda that Vargas is a liar, a criminal, and a self-promoter whose "coming out" as an undocumented immigrant will hurt others in his situation? Do you see him as O'Connor (p. 387) does, as an "American hero"? Or do you have a different opinion of Vargas?

# WIDENING THE FOCUS

## For Critical Reading and Writing

Referring specifically to the three readings in this chapter's Focus section, write an essay in which you answer the question, "Should Undocumented Immigrants Have a Path to Citizenship?"

## For Further Reading

The following readings can suggest additional perspectives for thinking and writing about immigrants and the path to citizenship:

- Gary Shteyngart, "Sixty-Nine Cents" (p. 41)

- Bich Minh Nguyen, "The Good Immigrant Student" (p. 87)

- Clara E. Rodríguez, "What It Means to Be Latino" (p. 304)

- Gary Soto, "One Last Time" (p. 404)

## For Focused Research

As the immigrant population in the United States grows, the debate surrounding undocumented immigration in the United States continues. For current information about immigration in the United States, visit the following Web sites:

- <http://www.brookings.edu/topics/immigration.aspx>, the immigration page at the Brookings Institution

- <http://www.ccis-ucsd.org>, the Web site for the Center for Comparative Immigration Studies

- <http://www.cis.org>, the Web site for the Center for Immigration Studies

- <http://www.dhs.gov/files/statistics/immigration.shtm>, the Web site for the Office of Immigration Statistics at the U.S. Department of Homeland Security

- <http://www.immigrationforum.org>, the Web site for the National Immigration Forum

- <http://www.urban.org/toolkit/issues/immigration.cfm>, the Web site for the Urban Institute

After consulting these Web sites, write an essay in which you propose possible solutions to the problem of undocumented immigrants in the United States How should we deal with those who are already here illegally? What options have already been proposed, and which do you think will work best (and why)? Does it make sense to have a different solution for those brought here as children?

## Beyond the Classroom

Interview a first-generation American, a second-generation American, and a third-generation American. How are their views of the American Dream different? How are they like and unlike the dreams of various writers represented in this chapter? Write an essay summarizing your findings and examining the connection between immigration and the American Dream.

─────────────── WRITING ───────────────

### The American Dream

1. In an excerpt from his book *The Audacity of Hope,* President Barack Obama writes, "I believe that part of America's genius has always been its ability to absorb newcomers, to forge a national identity out of the disparate lot that arrived on our shores." Write an essay in which you support the idea that the strength of the United States comes from its ability to assimilate many different groups. In your essay, discuss specific contributions your own ethnic group and others have made to American society.

2. Both "The Library Card" (p. 346) and "Outlaw: My Life in America as an Undocumented Immigrant" (p. 377) deal with the uniquely American concept of reinventing oneself, taking on a new identity. Write an essay in which you outline the options available to newcomers to the United States who wish to achieve this kind of transformation. Whenever possible, give examples from the readings in this chapter.

3. In his keynote speech at the 2012 Democratic National Convention, Júlian Castro, the mayor of San Antonio, observed, "the American Dream is not a sprint, or even a marathon, but a relay." What do you think he meant? Do you think he is right? How do you think some of the other writers in this chapter would react to this statement?

4. In "Coming into the Country" (p. 354), Gish Jen identifies the ability to make choices—what she calls the "luxury of choosing"—as a distinctly American advantage (2). Do you think the United States is really a place in which all residents are free to plot out the course of their lives as they choose? Support your position on this issue with references to readings in this book.

5. Using the readings in this chapter as source material, write a manifesto that sets forth the rights and responsibilities of all Americans. (Begin by reading President John F. Kennedy's inaugural address, p. 510).

6. Discouraged by the racism he experienced in the United States, Richard Wright (p. 346) left his country in 1947 and lived the rest of his life as an expatriate in Paris. Under what circumstances could you imagine leaving the United States and becoming a citizen of another country?

7. Reread the interviews collected in "*Forbes* Special Report: The American Dream" (p. 340). Choose a statement from one of the interviews that you believe defines the American Dream, and use it as the thesis statement of an essay. Support this thesis statement with information from your own experiences and observations as well as from two or three of the other readings in this chapter.

8. How does the American Dream differ for those in the United States illegally and those who are legal residents? Do they have the same dreams? Do they have the same expectations of achieving those dreams? Write an essay that answers these questions. In your discussion, compare Jose Antonio Vargas's dreams with those expressed by Azar Nafisi, Kiran Desai, and Gish Jen.

9. In paragraph 3 of "Vagabond Nation" (p. 363), Azar Nafisi says that immigrants feel at home in America because "they can be outsiders and yet still belong." Do your own experiences and observations (and the experiences and observations of the writers represented in this chapter) support or challenge this statement? Be sure you define *outsider* somewhere in your essay.

10. In "Jose Antonio Vargas's Lies Deserve No Sympathy" (p. 389), Esther Cepeda criticizes Jose Antonio Vargas for "using the parlance of American civil rights history" (10) and making "distasteful comparisons to the experiences of African-Americans in their struggle for equality" (12). In what respects do you see Vargas's life as an undocumented immigrant to be like and unlike the life of an African American in the pre–civil rights era? As you plan your essay, consider the experiences described by Richard Wright and Martin Luther King, Jr., in this chapter.

# 8

## WHY WE WORK

Although work has always been a part of the human experience, the nature of work has evolved considerably—especially over the last two hundred years. During the Middle Ages and the Renaissance, work was often done by family units. Whether it involved planting and harvesting crops, tending livestock, or engaging in the manufacture of goods, parents, grandparents, and children (and possibly an apprentice or two) worked together, at home. With the Industrial Revolution, however, the nature of work changed. Manufacturing became centralized in factories, and tasks that were formerly divided among various members of a family were now carried out more efficiently by machines. People worked long hours—in many cases twelve to fifteen hours a day, six and sometimes seven days a week—and could be fired for any reason. By the middle of the nineteenth century, most of the great manufacturing cities of Europe were overcrowded and polluted, teeming with unskilled factory workers. It is no wonder that labor unions became increasingly

Auto workers making car radiators on assembly line, circa 1915

popular as they organized workers to fight for job security, shorter workdays, and minimum safety standards

Thanks to the labor struggles of the past, many workers today have pension plans, health insurance, sick leave, paid vacations, life insurance, and other benefits. In spite of these advances, however, there is a dark side to this situation. American workers—like all workers—are subject to unpredictable changes in both the national and the global economies. As a result, during good times workers experience low unemployment and receive high wages, and during economic downturns—such as the one that began in 2008—workers experience higher unemployment and receive lower wages. Add to this situation the tendency of American companies to move manufacturing and high-tech jobs overseas and to see employees as entities whose jobs can be phased out as the need arises, and it is no surprise that workers are often stressed, insecure, and unhappy. The result is that many of today's workers question the role that work plays in their lives and wonder if it is in their best interest to invest so much time and energy in their jobs.

The essays in the Focus section of this chapter (p. 436) address the question, "Are Internships Work Experience or Exploitation?" These essays ask important questions about the nature of internships. Are unpaid internships fair? Do internships benefit students, or do they really benefit the businesses that employ them? Do interns undercut and possibly displace workers whose jobs they perform? Finally, and perhaps most disturbing, do internships discriminate against students who cannot afford to forgo paid employment to gain experience in a particular field—and, as a result, do they actually perpetuate a system

Welding robots on a Volkswagen assembly line in Germany, 2004

in which wealthier students continue to have an advantage over those who are less well off?

## PREPARING TO READ AND WRITE

As you read and prepare to write about the essays in this chapter, you may consider the following questions:

• What do you know about the writer? In what way does the writer's economic and social position affect his or her definition of work?

• Is the writer male or female? Does the writer's gender affect his or her attitude toward work?

• When was the essay written? Does the date of publication affect its content?

• Does the essay seem fair? Balanced? Does the writer have any pre-conceived ideas about work and its importance?

• Is the writer generally sympathetic or unsympathetic toward workers?

• Does the writer have a realistic or unrealistic view of work?

• On what specific problems does the writer focus?

• What specific solutions does the writer suggest? Are these solutions practical?

• Is your interpretation of the problem the same as or different from the interpretation presented in the essay?

• Are there any aspects of the problem that the writer ignores?

• Does the essay challenge any of your ideas about work?

• In what ways is the essay like other essays in this chapter?

# WHY WE WORK
## Andrew Curry
### 1976–

*Currently a freelance writer and editor, Andrew Curry was an associate editor for* U.S. News and World Report. *"Why We Work" was the cover story of the February 24, 2003, issue. In this essay, Curry examines the nature of work and explains why many workers today feel unfulfilled.*

In 1930, W. K. Kellogg made what he thought was a sensible decision, grounded in the best economic, social, and management theories of the time. Workers at his cereal plant in Battle Creek, Mich., were told to go home two hours early. Every day. For good.

The Depression-era move was hailed in *Factory and Industrial Management* magazine as the "biggest piece of industrial news since [Henry] Ford announced his five-dollar-a-day policy." President Herbert Hoover summoned the eccentric cereal magnate to the White House and said the plan was "very worthwhile." The belief: Industry and machines would lead to a workers' paradise where all would have less work, more free time, and yet still produce enough to meet their needs.

So what happened? Today, work dominates Americans' lives as never before, as workers pile on hours at a rate not seen since the Industrial Revolution. Technology has offered increasing productivity and a higher standard of living while bank tellers and typists are replaced by machines. The mismatch between available work and those available to do it continues, as jobs go begging while people beg for jobs. Though Kellogg's six-hour day lasted until 1985, Battle Creek's grand industrial experiment has been nearly forgotten. Instead of working less, our hours have stayed steady or risen—and today many more women work so that families can afford the trappings of suburbia. In effect, workers chose the path of consumption over leisure.

But as today's job market shows so starkly, that road is full of potholes. With unemployment at a nine-year high and many workers worried about losing their jobs—or forced to accept cutbacks in pay and benefits—work is hardly the paradise economists once envisioned.

Instead, the job market is as precarious today as it was in the early 5 1980s, when business began a wave of restructurings and layoffs to maintain its competitiveness. Many workers are left feeling insecure, unfulfilled, and underappreciated. It's no wonder surveys of today's workers show a steady decline in job satisfaction. "People are very emotional about work, and they're very negative about it," says David Rhodes, a principal at human resource consultants Towers Perrin. "The biggest issue is clearly workload. People are feeling crushed."

The backlash comes after years of people boasting about how hard they work and tying their identities to how indispensable they are. Ringing cellphones, whirring faxes, and ever present E-mail have blurred the lines between work and home. The job penetrates every aspect of life. Americans don't exercise, they work out. We manage our time and work on our relationships. "In reaching the affluent society, we're working longer and harder than anyone could have imagined," says Rutgers University historian John Gillis. "The work ethic and identifying ourselves with work and through work is not only alive and well but more present now than at any time in history."

## Stressed Out

It's all beginning to take a toll. Fully one third of American workers—who work longer hours than their counterparts in any industrialized country—felt overwhelmed by the amount of work they had to do, according to a 2001 Families and Work Institute survey. "Both men and women wish they were working about 11 hours [a week] less," says Ellen Galinsky, the institute's president. "A lot of people believe if they do work less they'll be seen as less committed, and in a shaky economy no one wants that."

The modern environment would seem alien to pre-industrial laborers. For centuries, the household—from farms to "cottage" craftsmen—was the unit of production. The whole family was part of the enterprise, be it farming, blacksmithing, or baking. "In pre-industrial society, work and family were practically the same thing," says Gillis.

The Industrial Revolution changed all that. Mills and massive iron smelters required ample labor and constant attendance. "The factory took men, women and children out of the workshops and homes and put them under one roof and timed their movements to machines," writes Sebastian de Grazia in *Of Time, Work and Leisure.* For the first time, work and family were split. Instead of selling what they produced, workers sold their time. With more people leaving farms to move to cities and factories, labor became a commodity, placed on the market like any other.

10    Innovation gave rise to an industrial process based on machinery and mass production. This new age called for a new worker. "The only safeguard of order and discipline in the modern world is a standardized worker with interchangeable parts," mused one turn-of-the-century writer.

Business couldn't have that, so instead it came up with the science of management. The theories of Frederick Taylor, a Philadelphia factory foreman with deep Puritan roots, led to work being broken down into component parts, with each step timed to coldly quantify jobs that skilled craftsmen had worked a lifetime to learn. Workers resented

Taylor and his stopwatch, complaining that his focus on process stripped their jobs of creativity and pride, making them irritable. Long before anyone knew what "stress" was, Taylor brought it to the workplace—and without sympathy. "I have you for your strength and mechanical ability, and we have other men paid for thinking," he told workers.

## Long Hours

The division of work into components that could be measured and easily taught reached its apex in Ford's River Rouge plant in Dearborn, Mich., where the assembly line came of age. "It was this combination of a simplification of tasks . . . with moving assembly that created a manufacturing revolution while at the same time laying waste human potential on a massive scale," author Richard Donkin writes in *Blood, Sweat and Tears*.

To maximize the production lines, businesses needed long hours from their workers. But it was no easy sell. "Convincing people to work 9 to 5 took a tremendous amount of propaganda and discipline," says the University of Richmond's Joanne Ciulla, author of *The Working Life: The Promise and Betrayal of Modern Work*. Entrepreneurs, religious leaders, and writers like Horatio Alger created whole bodies of literature to glorify the work ethic.

Labor leaders fought back with their own propaganda. For more than a century, a key struggle for the labor movement was reducing the amount of time workers had to spend on the job. "They were pursuing shorter hours and increased leisure. In effect, they were buying their time," says University of Iowa Prof. Benjamin Hunnicutt, author of *Work Without End: Abandoning Shorter Hours for the Right to Work*.

The first labor unions were organized in response to the threat of 15 technology, as skilled workers sought to protect their jobs from mechanization. Later, semi- and unskilled workers began to organize as well, agitating successfully for reduced hours, higher wages, and better work conditions. Unions enjoyed great influence in the early 20th century, and at their height in the 1950s, 35 percent of U.S. workers belonged to one.

Union persistence and the mechanization of factories gradually made shorter hours more realistic. Between 1830 and 1930, work hours were cut nearly in half, with economist John Maynard Keynes famously predicting in 1930 that by 2030 a 15-hour workweek would be standard. The Great Depression pressed the issue, with job sharing proposed as a serious solution to widespread unemployment. Despite business and religious opposition over worries of an idle populace, the Senate passed a bill that would have mandated a 30-hour week in 1933; it was narrowly defeated in the House.

Franklin Delano Roosevelt struck back with a new gospel that lives to this very day: consumption. "The aim . . . is to restore our rich domestic market by raising its vast consuming capacity," he said. "Our first purpose is to create employment as fast as we can." And so began the modern work world. "Instead of accepting work's continuing decline and imminent fall from its dominant social position, businessmen, economists, advertisers, and politicians preached that there would never be 'enough,'" Hunnicutt writes in *Kellogg's Six-Hour Day*. "The entrepreneur and industry could invent new things for advertising to sell and for people to want and work for indefinitely."

The New Deal dumped government money into job creation, in turn encouraging consumption. World War II fueled the fire, and American workers soon found themselves in a "golden age"—40-hour workweeks, plenty of jobs, and plenty to buy. Leisure was the road not taken, a path quickly forgotten in the postwar boom of the 1950s and 1960s.

## Discontent

Decades of abundance, however, did not bring satisfaction. "A significant number of Americans are dissatisfied with the quality of their working lives," said the 1973 report "Work in America" from the Department of Health, Education and Welfare. "Dull, repetitive, seemingly meaningless tasks, offering little challenge or autonomy, are causing discontent among workers at all occupational levels." Underlying the dissatisfaction was a very gradual change in what the "Protestant work ethic" meant. Always a source of pride, the idea that hard work was a calling from God dated to the Reformation and the teachings of Martin Luther. While work had once been a means to serve God, two centuries of choices and industrialization had turned work into an end in itself, stripped of the spiritual meaning that sustained the Puritans who came ready to tame the wilderness.

20    By the end of the '70s, companies were reaching out to spiritually drained workers by offering more engagement while withdrawing the promise of a job for life, as the American economy faced a stiff challenge from cheaper workers abroad. "Corporations introduced feel-good programs to stimulate jaded employees with one hand while taking away the elements of a 'just' workplace with the other," says Andrew Ross, author of *No Collar: The Humane Workplace and Its Hidden Costs*. Employees were given more control over their work and schedules, and "human relations" consultants and motivational speakers did a booming business. By the 1990s, technology made working from home possible for a growing number of people. Seen as a boon at first, telecommuting and the rapidly proliferating "electronic leash" of cellphones made work inescapable, as employees found themselves on call 24/7. Today, almost half of American workers use computers,

cellphones, E-mail, and faxes for work during what is supposed to be nonwork time, according to the Families and Work Institute. Home is no longer a refuge but a cozier extension of the office.

The shift coincided with a shortage of highly skilled and educated workers, some of whom were induced with such benefits as stock options in exchange for their putting the company first all the time. But some see a different explanation for the rise in the amount of time devoted to work. "Hours have crept up partly as a consequence of the declining power of the trade-union movement," says Cornell University labor historian Clete Daniel. "Many employers find it more economical to require mandatory overtime than hire new workers and pay their benefits." Indeed, the trend has coincided with the steady decline in the percentage of workers represented by unions, as the labor movement failed to keep pace with the increasing rise of white-collar jobs in the economy. Today fewer than 15 percent of American workers belong to unions.

## Nirvana?

The Internet economy of the '90s gave rise to an entirely new corporate climate. The "knowledge worker" was wooed with games, gourmet chefs, and unprecedented freedom over his schedule and environment. Employees at Intuit didn't have to leave their desks for massages; Sun Microsystems offered in-house laundry, and Netscape workers were offered an on-site dentist. At first glance, this new corporate world seemed like nirvana. But "for every attractive feature, workers found there was a cost," says Ross. "It was both a worker's paradise and a con game."

When the stock market bubble burst and the economy fell into its recent recession, workers were forced to re-evaluate their priorities. "There used to be fat bonuses and back rubs, free bagels and foosball tables—it didn't really feel like work," says Allison Hemming, who organizes "pink-slip parties" for laid-off workers around the country and has written *Work It! How to Get Ahead, Save Your Ass, and Land a Job in Any Economy.* "I think people are a lot wiser about their choices now. They want a better quality of life; they're asking for more flextime to spend with their families."

In a study of Silicon Valley culture over the past decade, San Jose State University anthropologist Jan English-Lueck found that skills learned on the job were often brought home. Researchers talked to families with mission statements, mothers used conflict-resolution buzzwords with their squabbling kids, and engineers used flowcharts to organize Thanksgiving dinner. Said one participant: "I don't live life; I manage it."

In some ways, we have come full circle. "Now we're seeing the return of work to the home in terms of telecommuting," says Gillis. 25

"We may be seeing the return of households where work is the central element again."

But there's still the question of fulfillment. In a recent study, human resources consultants Towers Perrin tried to measure workers' emotions about their jobs. More than half of the emotion was negative, with the biggest single factor being workload but also a sense that work doesn't satisfy their deeper needs. "We expect more and more out of our jobs," says Hunnicutt. "We expect to find wonderful people and experiences all around us. What we find is Dilbert."

### Responding to Reading

1.  Why does "work dominate Americans' lives as never before" (3)? According to Curry, what toll does this situation take on American workers?
2.  How did the Industrial Revolution change the nature of work? What effect did Frederick Taylor have on work? According to Curry, why were the first labor unions formed? Why was the New Deal the "golden age" for workers (18)?
3.  Why does Curry think that workers today are unfulfilled? What evidence does he offer to support this contention? What view of work do you think he has? Do you agree or disagree with his assessment?

### Responding in Writing

Why do the people you know work? Do their motives support or challenge Curry's conclusion?

# ONE LAST TIME

## Gary Soto

### 1952–

*Gary Soto grew up working along with his family as a migrant laborer in California's San Joaquin Valley. Soto often writes of the struggles of Mexican Americans, as he does in the following autobiographical essay, in which he describes his experiences picking grapes and cotton. This essay is taken from* Living Up the Street: Narrative Recollections, *for which he won the American Book Award in 1985. The author of numerous poetry collections, Soto has also published short story collections, novels, and picture books for children. He is also involved with two organizations that work for justice for migrant workers: California Rural Legal Assistance (CRLA) and the United Farm Workers of America (UFWA).*

Yesterday I saw the movie *Gandhi*[1] and recognized a few of the people— not in the theater but in the film. I saw my relatives, dusty and thin as

---

[1]The 1982 film biography of the nonviolent revolutionary Mohandas Gandhi (known as Mahatma), which was set in part among the peasants of India. [Eds.]

sparrows, returning from the fields with hoes balanced on their shoulders. The workers were squinting, eyes small and veined, and were using their hands to say what there was to say to those in the audience with popcorn and Cokes. I didn't have anything, though. I sat thinking of my family and their years in the fields, beginning with Grandmother who came to the United States after the Mexican revolution to settle in Fresno where she met her husband and bore children, many of them. She worked in the fields around Fresno, picking grapes, oranges, plums, peaches, and cotton, dragging a large white sack like a sled. She worked in the packing houses, Bonner and Sun-Maid Raisin, where she stood at a conveyor belt passing her hand over streams of raisins to pluck out leaves and pebbles. For over twenty years she worked at a machine that boxed raisins until she retired at sixty-five.

Grandfather worked in the fields, as did his children. Mother also found herself out there when she separated from Father for three weeks. I remember her coming home, dusty and so tired that she had to rest on the porch before she trudged inside to wash and start dinner. I didn't understand the complaints about her ankles or the small of her back, even though I had been in the grape fields watching her work. With my brother and sister I ran in and out of the rows; we enjoyed ourselves and pretended not to hear Mother scolding us to sit down and behave ourselves. A few years later, however, I caught on when I went to pick grapes rather than play in the rows.

Mother and I got up before dawn and ate quick bowls of cereal. She drove in silence while I rambled on how everything was now solved, how I was going to make enough money to end our misery and even buy her a beautiful copper tea pot, the one I had shown her in Long's Drugs. When we arrived I was frisky and ready to go, self-consciously aware of my grape knife dangling at my wrist. I almost ran to the row the foreman had pointed out, but I returned to help Mother with the grape pans and jug of water. She told me to settle down and reminded me not to lose my knife. I walked at her side and listened to her explain how to cut grapes; bent down, hands on knees, I watched her demonstrate by cutting a few bunches into my pan. She stood over me as I tried it myself, tugging at a bunch of grapes that pulled loose like beads from a necklace. "Cut the stem all the way," she told me as last advice before she walked away, her shoes sinking in the loose dirt, to begin work on her own row.

I cut another bunch, then another, fighting the snap and whip of vines. After ten minutes of groping for grapes, my first pan brimmed with bunches. I poured them on the paper tray, which was bordered by a wooden frame that kept the grapes from rolling off, and they spilled like jewels from a pirate's chest. The tray was only half filled, so I hurried to jump under the vines and begin groping, cutting, and tugging at the grapes again. I emptied the pan, raked the grapes with my hands to make them look like they filled the tray, and jumped back under the vine on my knees. I tried to cut faster because Mother, in the next row, was slowly moving ahead. I peeked into her row and saw five trays gleaming in the early morning. I cut, pulled hard, and stopped to gather the grapes that missed the pan; already bored, I spat on a few to wash them before tossing them like popcorn into my mouth.

5 So it went. Two pans equaled one tray—or six cents. By lunchtime I had a trail of thirty-seven trays behind me while mother had sixty or more. We met about halfway from our last trays, and I sat down with a grunt, knees wet from kneeling on dropped grapes. I washed my hands with the water from the jug, drying them on the inside of my shirt sleeve before I opened the paper bag for the first sandwich, which I gave to Mother. I dipped my hand in again to unwrap a sandwich without looking at it. I took a first bite and chewed it slowly for the tang of mustard. Eating in silence I looked straight ahead at the vines, and only when we were finished with cookies did we talk.

"Are you tired?" she asked.

"No, but I got a sliver from the frame," I told her. I showed her the web of skin between my thumb and index finger. She wrinkled her forehead but said it was nothing.

"How many trays did you do?"

I looked straight ahead, not answering at first. I recounted in my mind the whole morning of bend, cut, pour again and again, before answering a feeble "thirty-seven." No elaboration, no detail. Without looking at me she told me how she had done field work in Texas and Michigan as a child. But I had a difficult time listening to her stories. I played with my grape knife, stabbing it into the ground, but stopped when Mother reminded me that I had better not lose it. I left the knife sticking up like a small, leafless plant. She then talked about school, the junior high I would be going to that fall, and then about Rick and Debra, how sorry they would be that they hadn't come out to pick grapes because they'd have no new clothes for the school year. She stopped talking when she peeked at her watch, a bandless one she kept in her pocket. She got up with an *"Ay, Dios,"* and told me that we'd work until three, leaving me cutting figures in the sand with my knife and dreading the return to work.

10 Finally I rose and walked slowly back to where I had left off, again kneeling under the vine and fixing the pan under bunches of grapes. By that time, 11:30, the sun was over my shoulder and made me squint and think of the pool at the Y.M.C.A. where I was a summer member. I saw myself diving face first into the water and loving it. I saw myself gleaming like something new, at the edge of the pool. I had to day-dream and keep my mind busy because boredom was a terror almost as awful as the work itself. My mind went dumb with stupid things, and I had to keep it moving with dreams of baseball and would-be

girlfriends. I even sang, however softly, to keep my mind moving, my hands moving.

I worked less hurriedly and with less vision. I no longer saw that copper pot sitting squat on our stove or Mother waiting for it to whistle. The wardrobe that I imagined, crisp and bright in the closet, numbered only one pair of jeans and two shirts because, in half a day, six cents times thirty-seven trays was two dollars and twenty-two cents. It became clear to me. If I worked eight hours, I might make four dollars. I'd take this, even gladly, and walk downtown to look into store windows on the mall and long for the bright madras shirts from Walter Smith or Coffee's, but settling for two imitation ones from Penney's.

That first day I laid down seventy-three trays while Mother had a hundred and twenty behind her. On the back of an old envelope, she wrote out our numbers and hours. We washed at the pump behind the farm house and walked slowly to our car for the drive back to town in the afternoon heat. That evening after dinner I sat in a lawn chair listening to music from a transistor radio while Rick and David King played catch. I joined them in a game of pickle, but there was little joy in trying to avoid their tags because I couldn't get the fields out of my mind: I saw myself dropping on my knees under a vine to tug at a branch that wouldn't come off. In bed, when I closed my eyes, I saw the fields, yellow with kicked up dust, and a crooked trail of trays rotting behind me.

The next day I woke tired and started picking tired. The grapes rained into the pan, slowly filling like a belly, until I had my first tray and started my second. So it went all day, and the next, and all through the following week, so that by the end of thirteen days the foreman counted out, in tens mostly, my pay of fifty-three dollars. Mother earned one hundred and forty-eight dollars. She wrote this on her envelope, with a message I didn't bother to ask her about.

The next day I walked with my friend Scott to the downtown mall where we drooled over the clothes behind fancy windows, bought popcorn, and sat at a tier of outdoor fountains to talk about girls. Finally we went into Penney's for more popcorn, which we ate walking around, before we returned home without buying anything. It wasn't until a few days before school that I let my fifty-three dollars slip quietly from my hands, buying a pair of pants, two shirts, and a maroon T-shirt, the kind that was in style. At home I tried them on while Rick looked on enviously; later, the day before school started, I tried them on again wondering not so much if they were worth it as who would see me first in those clothes.

Along with my brother and sister I picked grapes until I was fif- 15 teen, before giving up and saying that I'd rather wear old clothes than stoop like a Mexican. Mother thought I was being stuck-up, even stupid, because there would be no clothes for me in the fall. I told her I didn't care, but when Rick and Debra rose at five in the morning, I lay awake in bed feeling that perhaps I had made a mistake but unwilling to change my mind. That fall Mother bought me two pairs of socks, a packet of colored T-shirts, and underwear. The T-shirts would help, I thought, but who would see that I had new underwear and socks? I wore a new T-shirt on the first day of school, then an old shirt on Tuesday, then another T-shirt on Wednesday, and on Thursday an old Nehru shirt that was embarrassingly out of style. On Friday I changed into the corduroy pants my brother had handed down to me and slipped into my last new T-shirt. I worked like a magician, blinding my classmates, who were all clothes conscious and small-time social climbers, by arranging my wardrobe to make it seem larger than it really was. But by spring I had to do something—my blue jeans were almost silver and my shoes had lost their form, puddling like black ice around my feet. That spring of my sixteenth year, Rick and I decided to take a labor bus to chop cotton. In his old Volkswagen, which was more noise than power, we drove on a Saturday morning to West Fresno—or Chinatown as some call it—parked, walked slowly toward a bus, and stood gawking at the winos, toothy blacks, Okies, *Tejanos*[2] with gold teeth, whores, Mexican families, and labor contractors shouting "Cotton" or "Beets," the work of spring.

We boarded the "Cotton" bus without looking at the contractor who stood almost blocking the entrance because he didn't want winos. We boarded scared and then were more scared because two blacks in the rear were drunk and arguing loudly about what was better, a two-barrel or four-barrel Ford carburetor. We sat far from them, looking straight ahead, and only glanced briefly at the others who boarded, almost all of them broken and poorly dressed in loudly mismatched clothes. Finally when the contractor banged his palm against the side of the bus, the young man at the wheel, smiling and talking in Spanish, started the engine, idled it for a moment while he adjusted the mirrors, and started off in slow chugs. Except for the windshield there was no glass in the windows, so as soon as we were on the rural roads outside Fresno, the dust and sand began to be sucked into the bus, whipping about like irate wasps as the gravel ticked about us. We closed our eyes, clotted up our mouths that wanted to open with embarrassed laughter because we couldn't believe we were on that bus with those people and the dust attacking us for no reason.

When we arrived at a field we followed the others to a pickup where we each took a hoe and marched to stand before a row. Rick and I, self-conscious and unsure, looked around at the others who leaned on their hoes or squatted in front of the rows, almost all talking in Spanish, joking, lighting cigarettes—all waiting for the foreman's whistle to begin work. Mother had explained how to chop cotton by showing us with a broom in the backyard.

---

[2]Descendants of early Mexican settlers in Texas. [Eds.]

"Like this," she said, her broom swishing down weeds. "Leave one plant and cut four—and cut them! Don't leave them standing or the foreman will get mad."

The foreman whistled and we started up the row stealing glances at other workers to see if we were doing it right. But after awhile we worked like we knew what we were doing, neither of us hurrying or falling behind. But slowly the clot of men, women, and kids began to spread and loosen. Even Rick pulled away. I didn't hurry, though. I cut smoothly and cleanly as I walked at a slow pace, in a sort of funeral march. My eyes measured each space of cotton plants before I cut. If I missed the plants, I swished again. I worked intently, seldom looking up, so when I did I was amazed to see the sun, like a broken orange coin, in the east. It looked blurry, unbelievable, like something not of this world. I looked around in amazement, scanning the eastern horizon that was a taut line jutted with an occasional mountain. The horizon was beautiful, like a snapshot of the moon, in the early light of morning, in the quiet of no cars and few people.

The foreman trudged in boots in my direction, stepping awkwardly 20 over the plants, to inspect the work. No one around me looked up. We all worked steadily while we waited for him to leave. When he did leave, with a feeble complaint addressed to no one in particular, we looked up smiling under straw hats and bandanas.

By 11:00, our lunch time, my ankles were hurting from walking on clods the size of hardballs. My arms ached and my face was dusted by a wind that was perpetual, always busy whipping about. But the work was not bad, I thought. It was better, so much better, than picking grapes, especially with the hourly wage of a dollar twenty-five instead of piece work. Rick and I walked sorely toward the bus where we washed and drank water. Instead of eating in the bus or in the shade of the bus, we kept to ourselves by walking down to the irrigation canal that ran the length of the field, to open our lunch of sandwiches and crackers. We laughed at the crackers, which seemed like a cruel joke from our Mother, because we were working under the sun and the last thing we wanted was a salty dessert. We ate them anyway and drank more water before we returned to the field, both of us limping in exaggeration. Working side by side, we talked and laughed at our predicament because our Mother had warned us year after year that if we didn't get on track in school we'd have to work in the fields and then we would see. We mimicked Mother's whining voice and smirked at her smoky view of the future in which we'd be trapped by marriage and screaming kids. We'd eat beans and then we'd see.

Rick pulled slowly away to the rhythm of his hoe falling faster and smoother. It was better that way, to work alone. I could hum made-up songs or songs from the radio and think to myself about school and friends. At the time I was doing badly in my classes, mainly because of a difficult stepfather, but also because I didn't care anymore. All through junior high and into my first year of high school there were those who said I would never do anything, be anyone. They said I'd work like a donkey and marry the first Mexican girl that came along. I was reminded so often, verbally and in the way I was treated at home, that I began to believe that chopping cotton might be a lifetime job for me. If not chopping cotton, then I might get lucky and find myself in a car wash or restaurant or junkyard. But it was clear; I'd work, and work hard.

I cleared my mind by humming and looking about. The sun was directly above with a few soft blades of clouds against a sky that seemed bluer and more beautiful than our sky in the city. Occasionally the breeze flurried and picked up dust so that I had to cover my eyes and screw up my face. The workers were hunched, brown as the clods under our feet, and spread across the field that ran without end—fields that were owned by corporations, not families.

I hoed, trying to keep my mind busy with scenes from school and pretend girlfriends until finally my brain turned off and my thinking went fuzzy with boredom. I looked about, no longer mesmerized by the beauty of the landscape, no longer wondering if the winos in the fields could hold out for eight hours, no longer dreaming of the clothes I'd buy with my pay. My eyes followed my chopping as the plants, thin as their shadows, fell with each strike. I worked slowly with ankles and arms hurting, neck stiff, and eyes stinging from the dust and the sun that glanced off the field like a mirror.

25     By quitting time, 3:00, there was such an excruciating pain in my ankles that I walked as if I were wearing snowshoes. Rick laughed at me and I laughed too, embarrassed that most of the men were walking normally and I was among the first timers who had to get used to this work. "And what about you, wino," I came back at Rick. His eyes were meshed red and his long hippie hair was flecked with dust and gnats and bits of leaves. We placed our hoes in the back of a pickup and stood in line for our pay, which was twelve fifty. I was amazed at the pay, which was the most I had ever earned in one day, and thought that I'd come back the next day, Sunday. This was too good.

Instead of joining the others in the labor bus, we jumped in the back of a pickup when the driver said we'd get to town sooner and were welcome to join him. We scrambled into the truck bed to be joined by a heavy-set and laughing *Tejano* whose head was shaped like an egg, particularly so because the bandana he wore ended in a point on the top of his head. He laughed almost demonically as the pickup roared up the dirt path, a gray cape of dust rising behind us. On the highway, with the wind in our faces, we squinted at the fields as if we were look-ing for someone. The *Tejano* had quit laughing but was smiling broadly, occasionally chortling tunes he never finished. I was scared of him, though Rick, two years older and five inches taller, wasn't. If the *Tejano* looked at him, Rick stared back for a second or two before he looked away to the fields.

I felt like a soldier coming home from war when we rattled into Chinatown. People leaning against car hoods stared, their necks following us, owl-like; prostitutes chewed gum more ferociously and showed us their teeth; Chinese grocers stopped brooming their storefronts to raise their cadaverous faces at us. We stopped in front of the Chi Chi Club where Mexican music blared from the juke box and cue balls cracked like dull ice. The *Tejano,* who was dirty as we were, stepped awkwardly over the side rail, dusted himself off with his bandana, and sauntered into the club.

Rick and I jumped from the back, thanked the driver who said *de nada* and popped his clutch, so that the pickup jerked and coughed blue smoke. We returned smiling to our car, happy with the money we had made and pleased that we had, in a small way, proved ourselves to be tough; that we worked as well as other men and earned the same pay.

We returned the next day and the next week until the season was over and there was nothing to do. I told myself that I wouldn't pick grapes that summer, saying all through June and July that it was for Mexicans, not me. When August came around and I still had not found a summer job, I ate my words, sharpened my knife, and joined Mother, Rick, and Debra for one last time.

## Responding to Reading

1. What types of work did Soto's relatives do? What does he mean when he says that they reminded him of some of the characters in the film *Gandhi*?
2. What is Soto's attitude toward picking grapes? How is his attitude different from his mother's? What does he mean when he says, "I'd rather wear old clothes than stoop like a Mexican" (15)?
3. What do you think Soto learned about work by picking grapes and cotton? What did he learn about his mother? about himself? about Mexicans?

## Responding in Writing

Write about a difficult, unpleasant, or even dangerous job that you had. What did you learn from doing this job?

# THE SECOND SHIFT

## Arlie Hochschild

### 1940–

*Arlie Hochschild was co-director of the Center for Working Families and has done extensive research into the role of work in personal and family life. Hochschild has published* The Second Shift: Working Parents and the Revolution at Home *(1989),* The Time Bind: When Work Becomes Home and Home Becomes Work *(1997), and, most recently,* The Outsourced Self: Intimate Life in Market Times *(2012). The following essay, taken from* The Second Shift, *makes the point that most working women have two jobs: one that lasts from nine to five and another that begins the moment they return home.*

Every American household bears the footprints of economic and cultural trends that originate far outside its walls. A rise in inflation eroding the earning power of the male wage, an expanding service sector opening for women, and the inroads made by women into many professions—all these changes do not simply go on around the American family. They occur *within* a marriage or living-together arrangement and transform it. Problems between couples, problems that seem "unique" or "marital," are often the individual ripples of powerful economic and cultural shock waves. Quarrels between husbands and wives in households across the nation result mainly from a friction between faster-changing women and slower-changing men.

The exodus of women from the home to the workplace has not been accompanied by a new view of marriage and work that would make this transition smooth. Most workplaces have remained inflexible in the face of the changing needs of workers with families, and most men have yet to really adapt to the changes in women. I call the strain caused by the disparity between the change in women and the absence of change elsewhere the "stalled revolution."

If women begin to do less at home because they have less time, if men do little more, and if the work of raising children and tending a home requires roughly the same effort, then the questions of who does what at home and of what "needs doing" become a source of deep tension in a marriage.

Over the past 30 years in the United States, more and more women have begun to work outside the home, and more have divorced. While some commentators conclude that women's work *causes* divorce, my research into changes in the American family suggests something else. Since all the wives in the families I studied (over an eight-year period) worked outside the home, the fact that they worked did not account for why some marriages were happy and others were not. What *did* contribute to happiness was the husband's willingness to do the work at home. Whether they were traditional or more egalitarian in their relationship, couples were happier when the men did a sizable share of housework and child care.

In one study of 600 couples filing for divorce, researcher George Levinger found that the second most common reason women cited for wanting to divorce—after "mental cruelty"—was their husbands' "neglect of home or children." Women mentioned this reason more often than financial problems, physical abuse, drinking, or infidelity.

A happy marriage is supported by a couple's being economically secure, by their enjoying a supportive community, and by their having compatible needs and values. But these days it may also depend on a shared appreciation of the work it takes to nurture others. As the role of the homemaker is being abandoned by many women, the homemaker's work has been continually devalued and passed on to low-paid house-keepers, baby-sitters, or day-care workers. Long devalued by men, the contribution of cooking, cleaning, and care-giving is now being devalued as mere drudgery by many women, too.

In the era of the stalled revolution, one way to make housework and child care more valued is for men to share in that work. Many working mothers are already doing all they can at home. Now it's time for men to make the move.

If more mothers of young children are working at full-time jobs outside the home, and if most couples can't afford household help, who's doing the work at home? Adding together the time it takes to do a paid job and to do housework and child care and using estimates from major studies on time use done in the 1960s and 1970s, I found that women worked roughly 15 more hours each week than men. Over a year, they worked an extra month of 24-hour days. Over a dozen years, it was an extra year of 24-hour days. Most women without children spend much more time than men on housework. Women with children devote more time to both housework and child care. Just as there is a wage gap between men and women in the workplace, there is a "leisure gap" between them at home. Most women work one shift at the office or factory and a "second shift" at home.

In my research, I interviewed and observed 52 couples over an eight-year period as they cooked dinner, shopped, bathed their children, and in general struggled to find enough time to make their complex lives work. The women I interviewed seemed to be far more deeply torn between the demands of work and family than were their husbands. They talked more about the abiding conflict between work and family. They felt the second shift was *their* issue, and most of their husbands agreed. When I telephoned one husband to arrange an interview with him, explaining that I wanted to ask him how he managed work and family life, he replied genially, "Oh, this will *really* interest my *wife*."

10    Men who shared the load at home seemed just as pressed for time as their wives, and as torn between the demands of career and small children. But of the men I surveyed, the majority did not share the load at home. Some refused outright. Others refused more passively, often offering a loving shoulder to lean on, or an understanding ear, as their working wife faced the conflict they both saw as hers. At first it seemed to me that the problem of the second shift *was* hers. But I came to realize that those husbands who helped very little at home were often just as deeply affected as their wives—through the resentment their wives felt toward them and through their own need to steel themselves against that resentment.

A clear example of this phenomenon is Evan Holt, a warehouse furniture salesman who did very little housework and played with his four-year-old son, Joey, only at his convenience. His wife, Nancy, did the second shift, but she resented it keenly and half-consciously expressed her frustration and rage by losing interest in sex and becoming overly absorbed in Joey.

Even when husbands happily shared the work, their wives *felt* more responsible for home and children. More women than men kept track of doctor's appointments and arranged for kids' playmates to come over. More mothers than fathers worried about a child's Halloween costume or a birthday present for a school friend. They were more likely to think about their children while at work and to check in by phone with the baby-sitter.

Partly because of this, more women felt torn between two kinds of urgency, between the need to soothe a child's fear of being left at day-care and the need to show the boss she's "serious" at work. Twenty percent of the men in my study shared housework equally. Seventy percent did a substantial amount (less than half of it, but more than a third), and 10 percent did less than a third. But even when couples more equitably share the work at home, women do two thirds of the daily jobs at home, such as cooking and cleaning up—jobs that fix them into a rigid routine. Most women cook dinner, for instance, while men change the oil in the family car. But, as one mother pointed out, dinner needs to be prepared every evening around six o'clock, whereas the car oil needs to be changed every six months, with no particular deadline. Women do more child care than men, and men repair more household appliances. A child needs to be tended to daily, whereas the repair of household appliances can often wait, said the men, "until I have time." Men thus have more control over when they make their contributions than women do. They may be very busy with family chores, but, like the executive who tells his secretary to "hold my calls," the man has more control over his time.

Another reason why women may feel under more strain than men is that women more often do two things at once—for example, write checks and return phone calls, vacuum and keep an eye on a three-year-old, fold laundry and think out the shopping list. Men more often will either cook dinner *or* watch the kids. Women more often do both at the same time.

Beyond doing more at home, women also devote proportionately, more of their time at home to housework than men and proportionately less of it to child care. Of all the time men spend working at home, a growing amount of it goes to child care. Since most parents prefer to tend to their children than to clean house, men do more of what they'd rather do. More men than women take their children on "fun" outings to the park, the zoo, the movies. Women spend more time on maintenance, such as feeding and bathing children—enjoyable activities, to be sure, but often less leisurely or "special" than going to the zoo. Men also do fewer of the most undesirable household chores, such as scrubbing the toilet.

As a result, women tend to talk more intensely about being over-tired, sick, and emotionally drained. Many women interviewed were fixated on the topic of sleep. They talked about how much they could "get by on"—six and a half, seven, seven and a half, less, more. They talked about who they knew who needed more or less. Some apologized for how much sleep they needed—"I'm afraid I need eight hours of sleep"—as if eight was "too much." They talked about how to avoid fully waking up when a child called them at night, and how to get back to sleep. These women talked about sleep the way a hungry person talks about food.

If, all in all, the two-job family is suffering from a speedup of work and family life, working mothers are its primary victims. It is ironic, then, that often it falls to women to be the time-and-motion experts of family life. As I observed families inside their homes, I noticed it was often the mother who rushed children, saying, "Hurry up! It's time to go," "Finish your cereal now," "You can do that later," or "Let's go!" When a bath needed to be crammed into a slot between 7:45 and 8:00, it was often the mother who called out "Let's see who can take their bath the quickest." Often a younger child would rush out, scurrying to be first in bed, while the older and wiser one stalled, resistant, sometimes resentful: "Mother is always rushing us." Sadly, women are more often the lightning rods for family tensions aroused by this speedup of work and family life. They are the villains in a process in which they are also the primary victims. More than the longer hours and the lack of sleep, this is the saddest cost to women of their extra month of work each year.

Raising children in a nuclear family is still the overwhelming preference of most people. Yet in the face of new problems for this family mode we have not created an adequate support system so that the nuclear family can do its job well in the era of the two-career couple.

Corporations have done little to accommodate the needs of working parents, and the government has done little to prod them.

We really need, as sociologist Frank Furstenberg has suggested, a Marshall Plan for the family. After World War II we saw that it was in our best interests to aid the war-torn nations of Europe. Now—it seems obvious in an era of growing concern over drugs, crime, and family instability—it is in our best interests to aid the overworked two-job families right here at home. We should look to other nations for a model of what could be done. In Sweden, for example, upon the birth of a child every working couple is entitled to 12 months of paid parental leave—nine months at 90 percent of the worker's salary, plus an additional three months at about three hundred dollars a month. The mother and father are free to divide this year off between them as they wish. Working parents of a child under eight have the opportunity to work no more than six hours a day, at six hours' pay. Parental insurance offers parents money for work time lost while visiting a child's school or caring for a sick child. That's a true pro-family policy.

20    A pro-family policy in the United States could give tax breaks to companies that encourage job sharing, part-time work, flex time, and family leave for new parents. By implementing comparable worth policies we could increase pay scales for "women's" jobs. Another key element of a pro-family policy would be instituting fewer-hour, more flexible options—called "family phases"—for all regular jobs filled by parents of young children.

Day-care centers could be made more warm and creative through generous public and private funding. If the best form of day-care comes from the attention of elderly neighbors, students, or grandparents, these people could be paid to care for children through social programs.

In these ways, the American government would create a safer environment for the two-job family. If the government encouraged corporations to consider the long-range interests of workers and their families, they would save on long-range costs caused by absenteeism, turnover, juvenile delinquency, mental illness, and welfare support for single mothers.

These are real pro-family reforms. If they seem utopian today, we should remember that in the past the eight-hour day, the abolition of child labor, and the vote for women seemed utopian, too. Among top rated employers listed in *The 100 Best Companies to Work for in America* are many offering country-club memberships, first-class air travel, and million-dollar fitness centers. But only a handful offer job sharing, flex time, or part-time work. Not one provides on-site day-care, and only three offer child-care deductions: Control Data, Polaroid, and Honeywell. In his book *Megatrends*, John Naisbitt reports that 83 percent of corporate executives believed that more men feel the need to share the responsibilities of parenting; yet only 9 percent of corporations offer paternity leave.

Public strategies are linked to private ones. Economic and cultural trends bear on family relations in ways it would be useful for all of us to understand. The happiest two-job marriages I saw during my research were ones in which men and women shared the housework and parenting. What couples called good communication often meant that they were good at saying thanks to one another for small aspects of taking care of the family. Making it to the school play, helping a child read, cooking dinner in good spirit, remembering the grocery list, taking responsibility for cleaning up the bedrooms—these were the silver and gold of the marital exchange. Until now, couples committed to an equal sharing of housework and child care have been rare. But, if we as a culture come to see the urgent need of meeting the new problems posed by the second shift, and if society and government begin to shape new policies that allow working parents more flexibility then we will be making some progress toward happier times at home and work. And as the young learn by example, many more women and men will be able to enjoy the pleasure that arises when family life is family life, and not a second shift.

## Responding to Reading

1. Hochschild coined the terms *second shift* and *stalled revolution*. Define each of these terms. Are they appropriate for what they denote? Would other terms—for example, *late shift* or *swing shift* and *postponed revolution* or *failed revolution*—be more appropriate? Explain.
2. According to Hochschild, women *think* that they are "under more strain than men" (14), even when their husbands do their share of housework and child-care. How does Hochschild account for this impression?
3. Beginning with paragraph 18, Hochschild recommends changes that she believes will ease the strain on working families—because, as she says in paragraph 24, "public strategies are linked to private ones." Given what Hochschild has said about the basic differences in men's and women's approaches to family roles, do you believe that government and corporations can solve the problem she identifies?

## Responding in Writing

Would you say that your parents are committed to equal sharing of housework and childcare? What changes, if any, would you suggest?

# IT'S NOT ABOUT YOU

## David Brooks

### 1961–

*The following essay describes the particular challenges facing today's college graduates as they look for work. (See page 57 for Brooks's biography.)*

Over the past few weeks, America's colleges have sent another class of graduates off into the world. These graduates possess something of inestimable value. Nearly every sensible middle-aged person would give away all their money to be able to go back to age 22 and begin adulthood anew.

But, especially this year, one is conscious of the many ways in which this year's graduating class has been ill served by their elders. They enter a bad job market, the hangover from decades of excessive borrowing. They inherit a ruinous federal debt.

More important, their lives have been perversely structured. This year's graduates are members of the most supervised generation in American history. Through their childhoods and teenage years, they have been monitored, tutored, coached and honed to an unprecedented degree.

Yet upon graduation they will enter a world that is unprecedentedly wide open and unstructured. Most of them will not quickly get married, buy a home and have kids, as previous generations did. Instead, they will confront amazingly diverse job markets, social landscapes and lifestyle niches. Most will spend a decade wandering from job to job and clique to clique, searching for a role.

5    No one would design a system of extreme supervision to prepare people for a decade of extreme openness. But this is exactly what has emerged in modern America. College students are raised in an environment that demands one set of navigational skills, and they are then cast out into a different environment requiring a different set of skills, which they have to figure out on their own.

Worst of all, they are sent off into this world with the whole baby-boomer theology ringing in their ears. If you sample some of the commencement addresses being broadcast on C-Span these days, you see that many graduates are told to: Follow *your* passion, chart *your* own course, march to the beat of *your* own drummer, follow *your* dreams and find *your*self. This is the litany of expressive individualism, which is still the dominant note in American culture.

But, of course, this mantra misleads on nearly every front.

College grads are often sent out into the world amid rapturous talk of limitless possibilities. But this talk is of no help to the central business

of adulthood, finding serious things to tie yourself down to. The successful young adult is beginning to make sacred commitments—to a spouse, a community and calling—yet mostly hears about freedom and autonomy.

Today's graduates are also told to find their passion and then pursue their dreams. The implication is that they should find themselves first and then go off and live their quest. But, of course, very few people at age 22 or 24 can take an inward journey and come out having discovered a developed self.

Most successful young people don't look inside and then plan a 10 life. They look outside and find a problem, which summons their life. A relative suffers from Alzheimer's and a young woman feels called to help cure that disease. A young man works under a miserable boss and must develop management skills so his department can function. Another young woman finds herself confronted by an opportunity she never thought of in a job category she never imagined. This wasn't in her plans, but this is where she can make her contribution.

Most people don't form a self and then lead a life. They are called by a problem, and the self is constructed gradually by their calling.

The graduates are also told to pursue happiness and joy. But, of course, when you read a biography of someone you admire, it's rarely the things that made them happy that compel your admiration. It's the things they did to court unhappiness—the things they did that were arduous and miserable, which sometimes cost them friends and aroused hatred. It's excellence, not happiness, that we admire most.

Finally, graduates are told to be independent-minded and to express their inner spirit. But, of course, doing your job well often means suppressing yourself. As Atul Gawande mentioned during his countercultural address last week at Harvard Medical School, being a good doctor often means being part of a team, following the rules of an institution, going down a regimented checklist.

Today's grads enter a cultural climate that preaches the self as the center of a life. But, of course, as they age, they'll discover that the tasks of a life are at the center. Fulfillment is a byproduct of how people engage their tasks, and can't be pursued directly. Most of us are egotistical and most are self-concerned most of the time, but it's nonetheless true that life comes to a point only in those moments when the self dissolves into some task. The purpose in life is not to find yourself. It's to lose yourself.

## Responding to Reading

1.  What does Brooks mean when he says that today's young people are victims of "extreme supervision" (5)?
2.  What is the "baby-boomer theology" to which Brooks refers in paragraph 6? In what sense does he think this philosophy reverses life's priorities? Why does it create problems for new college graduates?

3. According to Brooks, "The purpose in life is not to find yourself. It's to lose yourself" (14). What does he mean? Do you agree?

## Responding in Writing

Do you think Brooks is correct when he characterizes you and your peers as members "of the most supervised generation in American history" (3)?

# DO SECRETARIES HAVE A FUTURE?

## Lynn Peril

*An op-ed contributor to the* New York Times, *Lynn Peril is a secretary who is also the author of the books* Pink Think: Becoming a Woman in Many Uneasy Lessons *(2002),* College Girls: Bluestockings, Sex Kittens, and Coeds, Then and Now *(2006), and* Swimming in the Steno Pool: A Retro Guide to Making It in the Office *(2011). In the following essay, Peril considers the viability of her profession.*

The 1950s and '60s brought many new things to American offices, including the Xerox machine, word processing and—perhaps less famously—the first National Secretaries Day, in 1952. Secretaries of that era envisioned a rosy future, and many saw their jobs as a ticket to a better life.

In 1961, the trade magazine *Today's Secretary* predicted that, 50 years hence, the "secretary of the future" would start her workday at noon and take monthlong vacations thanks to the "electronic computer." According to another optimistic assessment, secretaries (transported through office hallways "via trackless plastic bubble") would be in ever-higher demand because of what was vaguely referred to as "business expansion."

But nearly 60 years later, on the date now promoted as Administrative Professionals Day, we're living through the end of a recession in which around two million administrative and clerical workers lost their jobs after bosses discovered they could handle their calendars and travel arrangements online and rendered their assistants expendable. Clearly, while the secretary hasn't joined the office boy and the iceman in the elephant's graveyard of outmoded occupations, technological advancements haven't panned out quite the way those midcentury futurists imagined. There are satisfactions to the job, to be sure, but for many secretaries, it remains often taxing, sometimes humiliating and increasingly precarious.

New technologies did make the lives of 20th-century secretaries easier. By the 1920s the typewriter had cemented women's place in the outer office, and later versions made for faster, less strenuous typing ("Alive After Five!" was the way a 1957 ad put it). The introduction of the Xerox 914 photocopier in 1959 did away with the laborious routine of carbon copies.

But even from the start, the relationship between secretaries and technology was fraught. One turn-of-the-last-century secretarial guidebook offered the cautionary tale of a secretary who refused to learn how to use an early transcribing recorder called a "business phonograph," and was promptly replaced by a younger stenographer, at $3 more a week.

As early as 1966, with the introduction of the first computerized word-processing system (I.B.M.'s Magnetic Tape Selectric Typewriter), secretaries were worrying that machines could replace them. They no longer had to retype a page because of a dropped letter—but would they be relegated to a "space-age typing pool" that offered little opportunity for advancement?

Indeed, that has come to pass, in good ways and bad, as some secretaries have moved from physical offices to virtual ones. Commenting on this newspaper's Web site[1] in 2008, one virtual assistant named Barbara Saunders claimed that the cyberoffice, where "symbols of social rank" like corner offices have no meaning, might upend the hierarchy of boss and staff once and for all. "For those of us who have always found the rank-based social system distasteful, the loss of 'the office' is liberating," she wrote.

It's interesting, then, to note that reinforcing these "symbols of social rank" has often been one way secretaries tried to keep their jobs from becoming obsolete. Back in 1961, a past president of the National Secretaries Association told the *Los Angeles Times* that secretaries should cheerfully perform menial tasks like emptying ashtrays because that was their "security against being replaced by a computer." That same year, *Life* magazine joked that the voice-activated typewriter "wasn't likely to automate any secretaries out of their jobs very soon," as—here it mimicked the machine's inability to translate spoken language into properly spelled English—the "klumsi masheen kan nivver make kawfi."

Coffee has long been a flashpoint for strong emotions about the differences between service and servility in offices; in the 1970s, when the second wave of feminism began to undo the traditional dyad of male boss and female secretary, more than one secretary was fired for refusing to make, fetch or serve coffee. In Los Angeles in 1973, one Leonor Pendleton was fired for "incompetence, insubordination and failure to comply with job instructions" after refusing to make coffee. Two years later, a Manhattan secretary was fired 20 minutes after she

---

[1] <www.nytimes.com>. [Eds.]

refused to get "four regulars" from a nearby coffee shop for a man who stopped her in the hallway—and turned out to be a vice president of the company.

10    This sort of thing still happens today. In 20-some years as an office worker, I've made coffee when the pot has run dry, asked clients if they'd like a cup, and picked up an extra for my boss when getting myself one. But others have it harder. "I don't have a problem getting coffee and/or water for our guests," wrote Tamara Klopfenstein, a clerk and receptionist, in an e-mail to her two male bosses in 2007. But she wasn't willing to "serve and wait on you by making and serving you coffee." She would be "happy to sit down and talk" about the matter, but she never got the chance. Nine minutes after hitting send, she was fired.

Secretaries of today and 60 years ago would probably agree on something: the one technological advancement they wish existed never will. After all these years, a human being still needs to plug in Mr. Coffee and deliver his output. But that won't save an administrative assistant's job from the maw of computerization. Secretaries can only hope that bosses won't take the human in question for granted, a sign that not everyone will be celebrating this Administrative Professionals Day.

## Responding to Reading

1. What future was predicted for secretaries in the 1950s and '60s? How does this vision of the future clash with the situation today?
2. How has technology affected the working lives of secretaries? Has it been a positive or negative influence?
3. What are the "symbols of social rank" (7) that Peril discusses? How do these symbols keep secretaries from becoming obsolete? Overall, do you think Peril is optimistic or pessimistic about the future of secretaries?

## Responding in Writing

The annual observance of Secretaries Day was instituted in 1952. Today, that same day is called Administrative Professionals Day. What is the significance of this name change? What, if anything, does it reveal about how secretaries (and their employers) have changed?

# DON'T BLAME WAL-MART

## Robert B. Reich

### 1946–

*A professor of public policy at the University of California at Berkeley, Robert B. Reich was the United States secretary of labor from 1993 to 1997. He is the author of numerous books, including, most recently,* Beyond Outrage: What Has Gone Wrong with Our Economy and Our Democracy, and How to

Fix It *(2012). He has published articles in the* New York Times, *the* New Yorker, *the* Atlantic Monthly, *the* Washington Post, *and the* Wall Street Journal. *In the following essay, Reich considers the economic and cultural influence of the mega-store Wal-Mart.*

Bowing to intense pressure from neighborhood and labor groups, a real estate developer has just given up plans to include a Wal-Mart store in a mall in Queens, thereby blocking Wal-Mart's plan to open its first store in New York City. In the eyes of Wal-Mart's detractors, the Arkansas-based chain embodies the worst kind of economic exploitation: it pays its 1.2 million American workers an average of only $9.68 an hour, doesn't provide most of them with health insurance, keeps out unions, has a checkered history on labor law and turns main streets into ghost towns by sucking business away from small retailers.

But isn't Wal-Mart really being punished for our sins? After all, it's not as if Wal-Mart's founder, Sam Walton, and his successors created the world's largest retailer by putting a gun to our heads and forcing us to shop there.

Instead, Wal-Mart has lured customers with low prices. "We expect our suppliers to drive the costs out of the supply chain," a spokeswoman for Wal-Mart said. "It's good for us and good for them."

Wal-Mart may have perfected this technique, but you can find it almost everywhere these days. Corporations are in fierce competition to get and keep customers, so they pass the bulk of their cost cuts through to consumers as lower prices. Products are manufactured in China at a fraction of the cost of making them here, and American consumers get great deals. Back-office work, along with computer programming and data crunching, is "offshored" to India, so our dollars go even further.

Meanwhile, many of us pressure companies to give us even better    5
bargains. I look on the Internet to find the lowest price I can and buy airline tickets, books, merchandise from just about anywhere with a click of a mouse. Don't you?

The fact is, today's economy offers us a Faustian bargain:[1] it can give consumers deals largely because it hammers workers and communities.

We can blame big corporations, but we're mostly making this bargain with ourselves. The easier it is for us to get great deals, the stronger the downward pressure on wages and benefits. Last year, the real wages of hourly workers, who make up about 80 percent of the work force, actually dropped for the first time in more than a decade; hourly

[1]Reference to a legendary German magician who makes a deal with the devil. [Eds.]

workers' health and pension benefits are in free fall. The easier it is for us to find better professional services, the harder professionals have to hustle to attract and keep clients. The more efficiently we can summon products from anywhere on the globe, the more stress we put on our own communities.

But you and I aren't just consumers. We're also workers and citizens. How do we strike the right balance? To claim that people shouldn't have access to Wal-Mart or to cut-rate airfares or services from India or to Internet shopping, because these somehow reduce their quality of life, is paternalistic tripe. No one is a better judge of what people want than they themselves.

The problem is, the choices we make in the market don't fully reflect our values as workers or as citizens. I didn't want our community bookstore in Cambridge, Mass., to close (as it did last fall) yet I still bought lots of books from Amazon.com. In addition, we may not see the larger bargain when our own job or community isn't directly at stake. I don't like what's happening to airline workers, but I still try for the cheapest fare I can get.

10    The only way for the workers or citizens in us to trump the consumers in us is through laws and regulations that make our purchases a social choice as well as a personal one. A requirement that companies with more than 50 employees offer their workers affordable health insurance, for example, might increase slightly the price of their goods and services. My inner consumer won't like that very much, but the worker in me thinks it a fair price to pay. Same with an increase in the minimum wage or a change in labor laws making it easier for employees to organize and negotiate better terms.

I wouldn't go so far as to re-regulate the airline industry or hobble free trade with China and India—that would cost me as a consumer far too much—but I'd like the government to offer wage insurance to ease the pain of sudden losses of pay. And I'd support labor standards that make trade agreements a bit more fair.

These provisions might end up costing me some money, but the citizen in me thinks they are worth the price. You might think differently, but as a nation we aren't even having this sort of discussion. Instead, our debates about economic change take place between two warring camps: those who want the best consumer deals, and those who want to preserve jobs and communities much as they are. Instead of finding ways to soften the blows, compensate the losers or slow the pace of change—so the consumers in us can enjoy lower prices and better products without wreaking too much damage on us in our role as workers and citizens—we go to battle.

I don't know if Wal-Mart will ever make it into New York City. I do know that New Yorkers, like most other Americans, want the great deals that can be had in a rapidly globalizing high-tech economy. Yet the prices on sales tags don't reflect the full prices we have to pay as workers and citizens. A sensible public debate would focus on how to make that total price as low as possible.

## Responding to Reading

1. According to Reich, why do some people oppose Wal-Mart? What does he mean when he says that Wal-Mart is "really being punished for our sins" (2)?
2. What does Reich mean when he says that today's economy "offers us a Faustian bargain" (6)? Do you think this Faustian bargain is fair? Do you think it is inevitable?
3. What does Reich think should be done to address the problem he identifies? Why does he think his "inner consumer" (10) will not like the suggestions he proposes?

## Responding in Writing

How do the interests of "workers," "citizens," and "consumers" differ? Which interests do you see as most important? Why?

# DELUSIONS OF GRANDEUR
## Henry Louis Gates, Jr.
### 1950–

*Henry Louis Gates, Jr., earned a Ph.D. (1979) in English literature from Clare College at the University of Cambridge, where he was the first African American to do so. At age thirty, he received a MacArthur Foundation Genius Grant (1980). He has taught at Yale, Cornell, Duke, and Harvard. One of Gates's best-known works is* Loose Canons: Notes on the Culture Wars *(1992), in which he discusses gender, literature, and multiculturalism in American arts and letters. His latest book is* Black in Latin America *(2011). He is general editor of the first (1996) and second (2003) editions of* The Norton Anthology of African American Literature; *a staff writer for the* New Yorker; *and the author of essays, reviews, and profiles in many other publications. In the following essay, Gates points out how few African Americans actually succeed as professional athletes and argues that the schools should do more to encourage young black men to pursue more realistic goals.*

Standing at the bar of an all-black VFW post in my hometown of Piedmont, W.Va., I offered five dollars to anyone who could tell me how many African-American professional athletes were at work today. There are 35 million African-Americans, I said.

"Ten million!" yelled one intrepid soul, too far into his cups.

"No way . . . more like 500,000," said another.

"You mean *all* professional sports," someone interjected, "including golf and tennis, but not counting the brothers from Puerto Rico?" Everyone laughed.

5    "Fifty thousand, minimum," was another guess.
Here are the facts:

There are 1,200 black professional athletes in the U.S.
There are 12 times more black lawyers than black athletes.
There are $2^1/_2$ times more black dentists than black athletes.
There are 15 times more black doctors than black athletes.

Nobody in my local VFW believed these statistics; in fact, few people would believe them if they weren't reading them in the pages of *Sports Illustrated*. In spite of these statistics, too many African-American youngsters still believe that they have a much better chance of becoming another Magic Johnson or Michael Jordan than they do of matching the achievements of Baltimore Mayor Kurt Schmoke or neurosurgeon Dr. Benjamin Carson, both of whom, like Johnson and Jordan, are black.

In reality, an African-American youngster has about as much chance of becoming a professional athlete as he or she does of winning the lottery. The tragedy for our people, however, is that few of us accept that truth.

Let me confess that I love sports. Like most black people of my generation—I'm 40—I was raised to revere the great black athletic heroes, and I never tired of listening to the stories of triumph and defeat that, for blacks, amount to a collective epic much like those of the ancient Greeks: Joe Louis's demolition of Max Schmeling; Satchel Paige's dazzling repertoire of pitches; Jesse Owens's in-your-face performance in Hitler's 1936 Olympics; Willie Mays's over-the-shoulder basket catch; Jackie Robinson's quiet strength when assaulted by racist taunts; and a thousand other grand tales.

10    Nevertheless, the blind pursuit of attainment in sports is having a devastating effect on our people. Imbued with a belief that our principal avenue to fame and profit is through sport, and seduced by a win-at-any-cost system that corrupts even elementary school students, far too many black kids treat basketball courts and football fields as if they were classrooms in an alternative school system. "O.K., I flunked English," a young athlete will say. "But I got an A plus in slamdunking."

The failure of our public schools to educate athletes is part and parcel of the schools' failure to educate almost everyone. A recent survey of the Philadelphia school system, for example, stated that "more than half of all students in the third, fifth and eighth grades cannot perform minimum math and language tasks." One in four middle school students in that city fails to pass to the next grade each year. It is a sad truth that such statistics are repeated in cities throughout the nation. Young athletes—particularly young black athletes—are especially ill-served. Many of them are functionally illiterate, yet they are passed along from year to year for the greater glory of good old Hometown High. We should not be surprised to learn, then, that only 26.6%

of black athletes at the collegiate level earn their degrees. For every successful educated black professional athlete, there are thousands of dead and wounded. Yet young blacks continue to aspire to careers as athletes, and it's no wonder why; when the University of North Carolina recently commissioned a sculptor to create archetypes of its student body, guess which ethnic group was selected to represent athletes?

Those relatively few black athletes who do make it in the professional ranks must be prevailed upon to play a significant role in the education of all of our young people, athlete and nonathlete alike. While some have done so, many others have shirked their social obligations: to earmark small percentages of their incomes for the United Negro College Fund; to appear on television for educational purposes rather than merely to sell sneakers; to let children know the message that becoming a lawyer, a teacher or a doctor does more good for our people than winning the Super Bowl; and to form productive liaisons with educators to help forge solutions to the many ills that beset the black community. These are merely a few modest proposals.

A similar burden falls upon successful blacks in all walks of life. Each of us must strive to make our young people understand the realities. Tell them to cheer Bo Jackson but to emulate novelist Toni Morrison or businessman Reginald Lewis or historian John Hope Franklin or Spelman College president Johnetta Cole—the list is long.

Of course, society as a whole bears responsibility as well. Until colleges stop using young blacks as cannon fodder in the big-business wars of so-called nonprofessional sports, until training a young black's mind becomes as important as training his or her body, we will continue to perpetuate a system akin to that of the Roman gladiators, sacrificing a class of people for the entertainment of the mob.

## Responding to Reading

1. Why does Gates begin his essay with an anecdote? What does this story reveal about African Americans' assumptions about sports? According to Gates, what harm do these assumptions do?

2. What does Gates mean when he says, "The failure of our public schools to educate athletes is part and parcel of the schools' failure to educate almost everyone" (11)? Do you agree? In addition to the public schools, who or what else could be responsible for the situation Gates describes?

3. What does Gates mean when he says that colleges are using young blacks as "cannon fodder" (14)? According to Gates, how are young black athletes like Roman gladiators? Do you think that this comparison is accurate? fair?

## Responding in Writing

What were your reactions to the statistics presented in paragraph 6? Write the text of a children's picture book designed to convey this information accurately to preschoolers.

# EXPLOITING THE GENDER GAP

## Warren Farrell

### 1943–

*Described as "the Gloria Steinem of Men's Liberation," Warren Farrell*
*teaches and writes about men's and women's issues. He is the chair of the*
*Commission to Create a White House Council on Boys to Men and has taught*
*at the School of Medicine at the University of California, San Diego, as well*
*as at Georgetown University, Rutgers University, and American University.*
*The author of numerous books, Farrell is currently coauthoring* Boys to Men
*with John Gray. In the following essay, Farrell examines the wage disparity*
*between men and women.*

Nothing disturbs working women more than the statistics often mentioned on Labor Day showing that they are paid only 76 cents to men's
dollar for the same work. If that were the whole story, it should disturb all
of us; like many men, I have two daughters and a wife in the work force.

When I was on the board of the National Organization for Women
in New York City, I blamed discrimination for that gap. Then I asked
myself, "If an employer has to pay a man one dollar for the same work
a woman would do for 76 cents, why would anyone hire a man?"

Perhaps, I thought, male bosses undervalue women. But I discovered that in 2000, women without bosses—who own their own businesses—earned only 49 percent of male business owners. Why? When
the Rochester Institute of Technology surveyed business owners with
M.B.A.'s from one top business school, they found that money was the
primary motivator for only 29 percent of the women, versus 76 percent
of the men. Women put a premium on autonomy, flexibility (25- to
35-hour weeks and proximity to home), fulfillment and safety.

After years of research, I discovered 25 differences in the work-life
choices of men and women. All 25 lead to men earning more money,
but to women having better lives.

5      High pay, as it turns out, is about tradeoffs. Men's tradeoffs include
working more hours (women work more around the home); taking
more dangerous, dirtier and outdoor jobs (garbage collecting, construction, trucking); relocating and traveling; and training for technical jobs
with less people contact (like engineering).

Is the pay gap, then, about the different choices of men and women?
Not quite. It's about parents' choices. Women who have never been
married and are childless earn 117 percent of their childless male counterparts. (This comparison controls for education, hours worked and

age.) T~~~~~~~~~~~~~~~~~~~~~~~~~~~never-married
men's decisions a.~~~~~~~~~~~~~~~~~~eers in arts, no
weekend work, etc.).

Does this imply that mothers sacrifice caree~~. ~ : really. Surveys of men and women in their 20's find that both sexes (70 percent of men, and 63 percent of women) would sacrifice pay for more family time. The next generation's discussion will be about who gets to be the primary parent.

Don't women, though, earn less than men in the same job? Yes and no. For example, the Bureau of Labor Statistics lumps together all medical doctors. Men are more likely to be surgeons (versus general practitioners) and work in private practice for hours that are longer and less predictable, and for more years. In brief, the same job is not the same. Are these women's choices? When I taught at a medical school, I saw that even my first-year female students eyed specialties with fewer and more predictable hours.

But don't female executives also make less than male executives? Yes. Discrimination? Let's look. The men are more frequently executives of national and international firms with more personnel and revenues, and responsible for bottom-line sales, marketing and finances, not human resources or public relations. They have more experience, relocate and travel overseas more, and so on.

Comparing men and women with the "same jobs," then, is to compare apples and oranges. However, when all 25 choices are the same, the great news for women is that then the women make more than the men. Is there discrimination against women? Yes, like the old boys' network. And sometimes discrimination against women becomes discrimination against men: in hazardous fields, women suffer fewer hazards. For example, more than 500 marines have died in the war in Iraq. All but two were men. In other fields, men are virtually excluded—try getting hired as a male dental hygienist, nursery school teacher, cocktail waiter.

There are 80 jobs in which women earn more than men—positions like financial analyst, speech-language pathologist, radiation therapist, library worker, biological technician, motion picture projectionist. Female sales engineers make 143 percent of their male counterparts; female statisticians earn 135 percent.

I want my daughters to know that people who work 44 hours a week make, on average, more than twice the pay of someone working 34 hours a week. And that pharmacists now earn almost as much as doctors. But only by abandoning our focus on discrimination against women can we discover these opportunities for women.

## Responding to Reading

1.  In paragraph 1, Farrell mentions that he has "two daughters and a wife in the work force." In paragraph 2, he points out that he was on the board of the New

York chapter of the National Organization for Women. Why do you think he includes these facts? What assumptions is he making about his readers?

2.  How does Farrell explain the wage disparity that exists between men and women? Do you think his explanation makes sense?

3.  What does Farrell mean when he concludes, "Comparing men and women with the 'same jobs,' then, is to compare apples and oranges" (10)? Do you think this analogy is accurate? Is it fair?

### Responding in Writing

Do you think Farrell is oversimplifying the issue of wage discrimination when he says, "But only by abandoning our focus on discrimination against women can we discover these opportunities for women" (12)? Explain.

# A&P

## John Updike
### 1932–2009

*One of the most influential and prolific American authors of the twentieth century, John Updike was a fiction writer, poet, playwright, and essayist. He published numerous novels, poetry collections, and essay collections, and his work frequently appeared in the* New Yorker *and the* New York Review of Books, *among other publications. His last books, both published posthumously in 2009, are* Endpoint and Other Poems *and* My Father's Tears and Other Stories. *In the following 1961 short story, Updike captures the experience of a young man working in a New England supermarket.*

In walks these three girls in nothing but bathing suits. I'm in the third check-out slot, with my back to the door, so I don't see them until they're over by the bread. The one that caught my eye first was the one in the plaid green two-piece. She was a chunky kid, with a good tan and a sweet broad soft-looking can with those two crescents of white just under it, where the sun never seems to hit, at the top of the backs of her legs. I stood there with my hand on a box of HiHo crackers trying to remember if I rang it up or not. I ring it up again and the customer starts giving me hell. She's one of these cash-register-watchers, a witch about fifty with rouge on her cheekbones and no eyebrows, and I know it made her day to trip me up. She'd been watching cash registers forty years and probably never seen a mistake before.

By the time I got her feathers smoothed and her goodies into a bag—she gives me a little snort in passing, if she'd been born at the right time they would have burned her over in Salem—by the time I get her on her way the girls had circled around the bread and were coming back, without a pushcart, back my way along the counters, in the aisle between the check-outs and the Special bins. They didn't even have shoes on. There was this chunky one, with the two-piece—it was bright green and the seams on the bra were still sharp and her belly was still pretty pale so I guessed she just got it (the suit)—there was this one, with one of those chubby berry-faces, the lips all bunched together under her nose, this one, and a tall one, with black hair that hadn't quite frizzed right, and one of these sunburns right across under the eyes, and a chin that was too long—you know, the kind of girl other girls think is very "striking" and "attractive" but never quite makes it, as they very well know, which is why they like her so much—and then the third one, that wasn't quite so tall. She was the queen. She kind of led them, the other two peeking around and making their shoulders round. She didn't look around, not this queen, she just walked straight on slowly, on these long white prima donna legs. She came down a little hard on her heels, as if she didn't walk in her bare feet that much, putting down her heels and then letting the weight move along to her toes as if she was testing the floor with every step, putting a little deliberate extra action into it. You never know for sure how girls' minds work (do you really think it's a mind in there or just a little buzz like a bee in a glass jar?) but you got the idea she had talked the other two into coming in here with her, and now she was showing them how to do it, walk slow and hold yourself straight.

She had on a kind of dirty-pink—beige maybe, I don't know— bathing suit with a little nubble all over it and, what got me, the straps were down. They were off her shoulders looped loose around the cool tops of her arms, and I guess as a result the suit had slipped a little on her, so all around the top of the cloth there was this shining rim. If it hadn't been there you wouldn't have known there could have been anything whiter than those shoulders. With the straps pushed off, there was nothing between the top of the suit and the top of her head except just her, this clean bare plane of the top of her chest down from the shoulder bones like a dented sheet of metal tilted in the light. I mean, it was more than pretty.

She had sort of oaky hair that the sun and salt had bleached, done up in a bun that was unravelling, and a kind of prim face. Walking into the A&P with your straps down, I suppose it's the only kind of face you *can* have. She held her head so high her neck, coming up out of those white shoulders, looked kind of stretched, but I didn't mind. The longer her neck was, the more of her there was.

She must have felt in the corner of her eye me and over my shoul- 5 der Stokesie in the second slot watching, but she didn't tip. Not this queen. She kept her eyes moving across the racks, and stopped, and turned so slow it made my stomach rub the inside of my apron, and buzzed to the other two, who kind of huddled against her for relief, and they all three of them went up the cat-and-dog-food-breakfast-cereal-macaroni-rice-raisins-seasonings-spreads-spaghetti-soft drinks-crackers-and-cookies aisle. From the third slot I look straight up this aisle to the meat counter, and I watched them all the way. The fat one with the tan sort of fumbled with the cookies, but on second thought she put the packages back. The sheep pushing their carts down the aisle—the girls were walking against the usual traffic (not that we have one-way signs or anything)—were pretty hilarious. You could see them, when Queenie's white shoulders dawned on them, kind of jerk, or hop, or hiccup, but their eyes snapped back to their own baskets and on they pushed. I bet you could set off dynamite in an A&P and the people would by and large keep reaching and checking oatmeal off their lists and muttering "Let me see, there was a third thing, began with A, asparagus, no, ah, yes, applesauce!" or whatever it is they do mutter. But there was no doubt, this jiggled them. A few house-slaves in pin curlers even looked around after pushing their carts past to make sure what they had seen was correct.

You know, it's one thing to have a girl in a bathing suit down on the beach, where what with the glare nobody can look at each other much anyway, and another thing in the cool of the A&P, under the fluorescent lights, against all those stacked packages, with her feet paddling along naked over our checkerboard green-and-cream rubber-tile floor.

"Oh Daddy," Stokesie said beside me. "I feel so faint."

"Darling," I said. "Hold me tight." Stokesie's married, with two babies chalked up on his fuselage already, but as far as I can tell that's the only difference. He's twenty-two, and I was nineteen this April.

"Is it done?" he asks, the responsible married man finding his voice. I forgot to say he thinks he's going to be manager some sunny day, maybe in 1990 when it's called the Great Alexandrov and Petrooshki Tea Company or something.

10    What he meant was, our town is five miles from a beach, with a big summer colony out on the Point, but we're right in the middle of town, and the women generally put on a shirt or shorts or something before they get out of the car into the street. And anyway these are usually women with six children and varicose veins mapping their legs and nobody, including them, could care less. As I say, we're right in the middle of town, and if you stand at our front doors you can see two banks and the Congregational church and the newspaper store and three real-estate offices and about twenty-seven old free-loaders tearing up Central Street because the sewer broke again. It's not as if we're on the Cape; we're north of Boston and there's people in this town haven't seen the ocean for twenty years.

The girls had reached the meat counter and were asking McMahon something. He pointed, they pointed, and they shuffled out of sight behind a pyramid of Diet Delight peaches. All that was left for us to see was old McMahon patting his mouth and looking after them sizing up their joints. Poor kids, I began to feel sorry for them, they couldn't help it.

Now here comes the sad part of the story, at least my family says it's sad but I don't think it's sad myself. The store's pretty empty, it being Thursday afternoon, so there was nothing much to do except lean on the register and wait for the girls to show up again. The whole store was like a pinball machine and I didn't know which tunnel they'd come out of. After a while they come around out of the far aisle, around the light bulbs, records at discount of the Caribbean Six or Tony Martin Sings or some such gunk you wonder they waste the wax on, sixpacks of candy bars, and plastic toys done up in cellophane that fall apart when a kid looks at them anyway. Around they come, Queenie still leading the way, and holding a little gray jar in her hand. Slots Three through Seven are unmanned and I could see her wondering between Stokes and me, but Stokesie with his usual luck draws an old party in baggy gray pants who stumbles up with four giant cans of pineapple juice (what do these bums *do* with all that pineapple juice? I've often asked myself) so the girls come to me. Queenie puts down the jar and I take it into my fingers icy cold. Kingfish Fancy Herring Snacks in Pure Sour Cream: 49¢. Now her hands are empty, not a ring or a bracelet, bare as God made them, and I wonder where the money's coming from. Still with that prim look she lifts a folded dollar bill out of the hollow at the center of her nubbled pink top. The jar went heavy in my hand. Really, I thought that was so cute.

Then everybody's luck begins to run out. Lengel comes in from haggling with a truck full of cabbages on the lot and is about to scuttle into that door marked MANAGER behind which he hides all day when the girls touch his eye. Lengel's pretty dreary, teaches Sunday school and the rest, but he doesn't miss that much. He comes over and says, "Girls, this isn't the beach."

Queenie blushes, though maybe it's just a brush of sunburn I was noticing for the first time, now that she was so close. "My mother asked me to pick up a jar of herring snacks." Her voice kind of startled me, the way voices do when you see the people first, coming out so flat and dumb yet kind of tony, too, the way it ticked over "pick up" and "snacks." All of a sudden I slid right down her voice into her living room. Her father and the other men were standing around in ice-cream coats and bow ties and the women were in sandals picking up herring snacks on toothpicks off a big plate and they were all holding drinks the color of water with olives and sprigs of mint in them. When my parents have somebody over they get lemonade and if it's a real racy affair Schlitz in tall glasses with "They'll Do It Every Time" cartoons stencilled on.

"That's all right," Lengel said. "But this isn't the beach." His repeat-ing this struck me as funny, as if it had just occurred to him, and he had 15 been thinking all these years the A&P was a great big dune and he was the head lifeguard. He didn't like my smiling—as I say he doesn't miss much—but he concentrates on giving the girls that sad Sunday-school-superintendent stare.

Queenie's blush is no sunburn now, and the plump one in plaid, that I liked better from the back—a really sweet can—pipes up, "We weren't doing any shopping. We just came in for the one thing."

"That makes no difference," Lengel tells her, and I could see from the way his eyes went that he hadn't noticed she was wearing a two-piece before. "We want you decently dressed when you come in here."

"We are decent," Queenie says suddenly, her lower lip pushing, getting sore now that she remembers her place, a place from which the crowd that runs the A&P must look pretty crummy. Fancy Herring Snacks flashed in her very blue eyes.

"Girls, I don't want to argue with you. After this come in here with your shoulders covered. It's our policy." He turns his back. That's policy for you. Policy is what the kingpins want. What the others want is juvenile delinquency.

20    All this while, the customers had been showing up with their carts but, you know, sheep, seeing a scene, they had all bunched up on Stokesie, who shook open a paper bag as gently as peeling a peach, not wanting to miss a word. I could feel in the silence everybody getting nervous, most of all Lengel, who asks me, "Sammy, have you rung up this purchase?"

I thought and said "No" but it wasn't about that I was thinking. I go through the punches, 4, 9, GROC, TOT—it's more complicated than you think, and after you do it often enough, it begins to make a little song, that you hear words to, in my case "Hello *(bing)* there, you *(gung)* hap-py pee-pul *(splat)*"—the splat being the drawer flying out. I uncrease the bill, tenderly as you may imagine, it just having come from between the two smoothest scoops of vanilla I had ever known were there, and pass a half and a penny into her narrow pink palm, and nestle the herrings in a bag and twist its neck and hand it over, all the time thinking.

The girls, and who'd blame them, are in a hurry to get out, so I say "I quit" to Lengel quick enough for them to hear, hoping they'll stop and watch me, their unsuspected hero. They keep right on going, into the electric eye; the door flies open and they flicker across the lot to their car, Queenie and Plaid and Big Tall Goony-Goony (not that as raw material she was so bad), leaving me with Lengel and a kink in his eyebrow.

"Did you say something, Sammy?"

"I said I quit."

25    "I thought you did."

"You didn't have to embarrass them."

"It was they who were embarrassing us."

I started to say something that came out "Fiddle-de-doo." It's a saying of my grandmother's, and I know she would have been pleased.

"I don't think you know what you're saying," Lengel said.

"I know you don't," I said. "But I do." I pull the bow at the back of my apron and start shrugging it off my shoulders. A couple customers that had been heading for my slot begin to knock against each other, like scared pigs in a chute.

Lengel sighs and begins to look very patient and old and gray. He's been a friend of my parents for years. "Sammy, you don't want to do this to your Mom and Dad," he tells me. It's true, I don't. But it seems to me that once you begin a gesture it's fatal not to go through with it. I fold the apron, "Sammy" stitched in red on the pocket, and put it on the counter, and drop the bow tie on top of it. The bow tie is theirs, if you've ever wondered. "You'll feel this for the rest of your life," Lengel says, and I know that's true, too, but remembering how he made that pretty girl blush makes me so scrunchy inside I punch the No Sale tab and the machine whirs "pee-pul" and the drawer splats out. One advantage to this scene taking place in summer, I can follow this up with a clean exit, there's no fumbling around getting your coat and galoshes, I just saunter into the electric eye in my white shirt that my mother ironed the night before, and the door heaves itself open, and outside the sunshine is skating around on the asphalt.

I look around for my girls, but they're gone, of course. There wasn't anybody but some young married screaming with her children about some candy they didn't get by the door of a powder-blue Falcon station wagon. Looking back in the big windows, over the bags of peat moss and aluminum lawn furniture stacked on the pavement, I could see Lengel in my place in the slot, checking the sheep through. His face was dark gray and his back stiff, as if he'd just had an injection of iron, and my stomach kind of fell as I felt how hard the world was going to be to me hereafter.

## Responding to Reading

1. What is Sammy's attitude toward his job? toward Lengel, the store manager? toward the customers of the A&P? What words and phrases in the story lead you to your conclusions?
2. How accurate are Sammy's judgments about Queenie and her friends? How would these characters be described if Lengel were telling the story?
3. Why does Sammy quit his job? Is his quitting some form of rebellion, or does he do it for some other reason? What do you think Sammy is trying to accomplish with this action? (Consider all possible motives.)

## Responding in Writing

If you were in Sammy's place, would you have made the same choice he did? Why or why not?

—————————————— FOCUS ——————————————

## Are Internships Work Experience or Exploitation?

Bulletin board advertising internships

### Responding to the Image

1. The photo above shows an advertisement for internships posted on a bulletin board at a college. What positive things about the positions does the ad emphasize? What things does it downplay or fail to mention?
2. In your opinion, what does the ad highlight as the internships' main selling point? Is this tactic in any way deceptive?
3. How does the ad attempt to establish credibility? Is this effort successful?

## INTERNING OR INDENTURED?

## Elizabeth Cronin

*A student in the M.A. arts journalism program at the School of the Art Institute of Chicago, Elizabeth Cronin is the grants and program coordinator for the SALRC blog and a writer for F Newsmagazine. In the following essay, Cronin considers the real costs involved in unpaid student internships.*

While the reality of interning next year may interfere with plans for finally obtaining a Ramen-free diet and an actual lease (not with your parents), it isn't like we weren't warned. Internships have become synonymous with the word unpaid. Discussed last April in both the *Washington Times* article, "Is Use of Interns Abuse of Labor?" and Ross Perlin's *New York Times* op-ed, "Unpaid Interns, Complicit Colleges," it's clear that the practice of employers hiring unpaid student interns while schools charge tuition for the privilege is garnering critical attention. Though many students may be complacent about the practice, are schools to blame for this potentially exploitative relationship?

"[The schools] should stop charging students to work without pay—and ensure that the currency of academic credit, already cheapened by internships, doesn't lose all its value," argues Ross Perlin. This may not be an issue for students with unlimited parental support. But for students like Abraham Ritchie, whose internship comes with a heavy course load and a part-time job at the Art Institute, it's grounds for a serious reappraisal of a system seemingly oblivious to the needs of students.

Ritchie, a New Arts Journalism student at SAIC[1] graduating this May, is an intern at *Bad at Sports* (a blog and weekly podcast series about contemporary art). "In art school, the internship is seen as 'good experience,' and payment is optional," Ritchie said. "This is silly. Students have to live in the real world just like everyone else. We have rents to pay, we need to eat and we need jobs."

Sarah Taylor, a first-year New Arts Journalism student, agrees—and as a nearly five-year internship veteran, she admits she's torn. "On one hand, I agree with the internship requirement. It truly teaches you outside of the program and I think it should be mandatory. That being said, requiring us to pay tuition money to essentially work for free seems a little suspect."

To successfully meet the requirements of their programs, New Arts 5 Journalism (MANAJ) students must complete six internship credits over two semesters, and Arts Administration (MAAAP) students must complete three. Those three credits equal 210 hours of work per semester, which breaks down to two eight-hour shifts a week—but it's not the requirement most students are questioning. It's the price tag.

"For the money we spend [$7,548 over two semesters], there should be a significant return," adds Ritchie. "If the internships that the school generates aren't creating valuable and marketable work experience, or leading directly to a job after graduation, then the students will start to question the return on their mandatory investment [tuition]. I think that they are widely starting to do so, which isn't to say that's good or bad, it just seems to be the case."

Kelly Reaves, a 2010 MANAJ graduate who interned at *Gapers Block* (a web-based guide to art events in Chicago) explained, "I'm irritated with the school system, not the employers. I arranged my own internship.

---

[1]School of the Art Institute of Chicago. [Eds.]

I didn't need to do it through the school. But then again, a lot of places won't hire interns who aren't students because they're skeptical about your motivation or dedication if you're not paying for it, and you have nothing tangible to lose from not showing up."

Vicki Engonopoulos is the Director of the Cooperative Education Internship Program (Co-op) at SAIC, which counsels students through the internship process and works with employers to post up to 700 internships per semester (including BFA, MA & MFA opportunities). According to Engonopoulos, the internship should be looked at "like a course, a learning experience, like you're going to a different kind of classroom."

Students can begin their internship search by either calling the office to schedule an appointment with one of the eight full-time faculty advisers, or they can search for opportunities online using SAIC Launch. Once the employer has been vetted and the student has been placed, the student's faculty adviser continues to monitor his or her progress with regular site visits, as well as more informal meetings with the student off-site. Engonopoulos states the program's goal is to make sure that "employers meet their criteria so students have a good experience."

10    Reaves acknowledges her internship has been instrumental to her professional development and advises students to "do the work well. Be enthusiastic. The only thing worse than having to pay to do an internship through the Co-op program is paying to do an internship through the Co-op program, and then doing a half-assed job and not learning anything. Then you're really throwing your money away."

SAIC's Jim Yood, Professor of Art History and Director of the New Arts Journalism Program, explained that arts journalism is a profession as well as an intellectual discipline. The hours spent outside the classroom are meant to provide students with the professional training necessary to be competitive. When asked about the concern some MANAJ students had expressed about the Co-op program's tuition policy, Yood replied, "We expect people who employ our students as interns to provide them with intriguing work to do. The aim is not simply to provide non-profits and corporations with unpaid labor, but to provide our students with professional experience."

Editor and publisher Andrew Huff of *Gapers Block* has employed two MANAJ interns over the years, and says that he's been "very happy with their abilities and enthusiasm for the work." The staff at *Gapers Block* consists solely of volunteers, so it would be a "little odd to pay interns in our case," says Huff. Although he wasn't aware that tuition dollars were being applied to help fund the program, and concludes it does seem a "little unfair," he imagines that it must be tied in with the administrative time spent overseeing the program.

Reaves described her internship at *Gapers Block* as a "great experience" with a full-time editorial position waiting for her at the end of her run (although pay still remains an issue). However, she also shared that her continued education has translated into paying thousands of dollars for a master's degree which has left her with "less skills and experience than my boyfriend, who is also in the arts field, and who didn't graduate from college. Now I'm finding myself having to choose between continuing to work there during the day for pennies, going to work in a bar at night for money, or taking a boring clerical job instead of having my nights free. SAIC's a great school—it teaches you to think. But it doesn't teach you how to make money."

Should it? Art schools like SAIC aren't exactly in the business of grooming graduate students to secure high-paying jobs after graduation— its focus is art, not business. And the internship experience is meant to reflect that philosophy. But how do you translate "experience" into "practical" and turn it into "profitable"? Furthermore, how do you manage to stay financially afloat while making it happen? Should SAIC charge students for experience gained outside the classroom?

A good internship may turn out to be a great experience, but unfortunately, I don't think my landlord will care. 15

## Responding to Reading

1. According to Cronin, what is wrong with most internship programs? Do you agree with her?
2. In paragraph 1, Cronin refers to Ross Perlin's article, "Unpaid Interns, Complicit Colleges" (p. 439). Why? Does she agree or disagree with Perlin?
3. Beginning in paragraph 7, Cronin discusses the experiences of Kelly Reaves, a student who majored in New Arts Journalism. Do you think this extended example is effective? Would another example (or a series of short examples) have been a better choice? Explain.

## Responding in Writing

Do you think the primary purpose of an internship should be to help a student get a job? Or should an internship accomplish something else?

# UNPAID INTERNS, COMPLICIT COLLEGES

## Ross Perlin

### 1983–

*A researcher at the Himalayan Languages Project, Ross Perlin is currently completing his doctoral dissertation on Trung, a rare language spoken in southwestern China. He is the author of* Intern Nation: How to Earn Nothing and Learn Little in the Brave New Economy *(2011). In the following essay, Perlin takes a critical look at the "unpaid internship boom."*

On college campuses, the annual race for summer internships, many of them unpaid, is well under way. But instead of steering students toward the best opportunities and encouraging them to value their work, many institutions of higher learning are complicit in helping companies skirt a nebulous area of labor law.

Colleges and universities have become cheerleaders and enablers of the unpaid internship boom, failing to inform young people of their rights or protect them from the miserly calculus of employers. In hundreds of interviews with interns over the past three years, I found dejected students resigned to working unpaid for summers, semesters and even entire academic years—and, increasingly, to paying for the privilege.

For the students, the problems are less philosophical and legal than practical. In 2007, for instance, Will Batson, a Colgate University student from Augusta, Ga., and a son of two public-interest lawyers, worked as an unpaid, full-time summer intern for WNBC and had to scramble for shelter in New York City.

"It definitely hurt my confidence," Mr. Batson told me. He recalled crashing on more than 20 floors and couches, being constantly short on cash and fearing he would have to quit and go home. His father, he said, felt like a failure for not being able to help him rent an apartment.

5      What makes WNBC—whose parent company, General Electric, is valued at more than $200 billion—think it can get away with this? In Mr. Batson's case, a letter from Colgate, certifying that he was receiving credit for doing the internship. (Now 24, he gave up on journalism and is at a technology start-up. NBC calls its internship program "an important recruiting tool.")

The uncritical internship fever on college campuses—not to mention the exploitation of graduate student instructors, adjunct faculty members and support staff—is symptomatic of a broader malaise. Far from being the liberal, pro-labor bastions of popular image, universities are often blind to the realities of work in contemporary America.

In politics, film, fashion, journalism and book publishing, unpaid internships are seen as a way to break in. (The *New York Times* has paid and unpaid interns.) But the phenomenon goes beyond fields seen as glamorous.

Three-quarters of the 10 million students enrolled in America's four-year colleges and universities will work as interns at least once before graduating, according to the College Employment Research Institute. Between one-third and half will get no compensation for their efforts, a study by the research firm Intern Bridge found. Unpaid interns also lack protection from laws prohibiting racial discrimination and sexual harassment.

The United States Department of Labor says an intern at a for-profit company may work without pay only when the program is similar to that offered in a vocational school, benefits the student, does not displace a regular employee and does not entitle the student to a job; in addition, the employer must derive "no immediate advantage" from the student's work and both sides must agree that the student is not entitled to wages.

Employers and their lawyers appear to believe that unpaid interns  10 who get academic credit meet those criteria, but the law seems murky; the Labor Department has said that "academic credit alone does not guarantee that the employer is in compliance."

Fearing a crackdown by regulators, some colleges are asking the government, in essence, to look the other way. In a letter last year, 13 university presidents told the Labor Department, "While we share your concerns about the potential for exploitation, our institutions take great pains to ensure students are placed in secure and productive environments that further their education."

Far from resisting the exploitation of their students, colleges have made academic credit a commodity. Just look at Menlo College, a business-focused college in northern California, which sold credits to a business called Dream Careers. Menlo grossed $50,000 from the arrangement in 2008, while Dream Careers sold Menlo-accredited internships for as much as $9,500.

To meet the credit requirement of their employers, some interns have essentially had to pay to work for free: shelling out $2,700 to the University of Pennsylvania in the case of an intern at NBC Universal and $1,600 to New York University by an intern at *The Daily Show*, to cite two examples from news reports.

Charging students tuition to work in unpaid positions might be justifiable in some cases—if the college plays a central role in securing the internship and making it a substantive academic experience. But more often, internships are a cheap way for universities to provide credit—cheaper than paying for faculty members, classrooms and equipment.

A survey of more than 700 colleges by the National Association of  15 Colleges and Employers found that 95 percent allowed the posting of unpaid internships in campus career centers and on college Web sites. And of those colleges, only 30 percent required that their students obtain academic credit for those unpaid internships; the rest, evidently, were willing to overlook potential violations of labor law.

Campus career centers report being swamped; advisers I spoke to flatly denied being able to "monitor and reassess" all placements or even postings, as the 13 university presidents claim to do—their ability to visit students' workplaces, for instance, is almost nil. They described feeling caught between the demands of employers and interns, and scrambling to make accommodations: issuing vague letters of support for interns to show employers; offering sketchy "internship transcript notations" or "internship certificates"; and even handing out "0.0 credit"—a mysterious work-around by which credit both is and isn't issued.

CHAPTER 8  FOCUS

Is there a better way? Cooperative education, in which students alternate between tightly integrated classroom time and paid work experience, represents a humane and pragmatic model.

Colleges shouldn't publicize unpaid internships at for-profit companies. They should discourage internship requirements for graduation—common practice in communications, psychology, social work and criminology. They should stop charging students to work without pay—and ensure that the currency of academic credit, already cheapened by internships, doesn't lose all its value.

To be sure, the unpaid internship is only part of a phenomenon that includes the growing numbers of temps, freelancers, adjuncts, self-employed "entrepreneurs" and other low-wage or precariously employed workers who live gig by gig. The academy should critique, not amplify, those trends.

20      While higher education has tried to stand for fairness in the past few decades through affirmative action and financial aid, the internship boom gives the well-to-do a foot in the door while consigning the less well-off to dead-end temporary jobs. Colleges have turned internships into a prerequisite for the professional world but have neither ensured equal access to these opportunities, nor insisted on fair wages for honest work.

## Responding to Reading

1. What are Perlin's general objections to unpaid internships? Are these objections reasonable? Why or why not?
2. What specific legal objections to internships does Perlin have? Do these objections make sense? Are they convincing?
3. What solution does Perlin suggest for the problems he discusses? Is this solution practical?

## Responding in Writing

Do you think an internship is necessary for your future success, or do you think you could do just as well in your career without one?

# UNPAID INTERNS: REWARDED OR EXPLOITED?

*The following four letters to the editor of the* New York Times *were written in response to Ross Perlin's essay "Unpaid Interns, Complicit Colleges"* (p. 439).

## To the Editor:

Ross Perlin unfairly views colleges as complicit in labor law abuses ("Unpaid Interns, Complicit Colleges," Op-Ed, April 3). Most interns do benefit—not monetarily, but by gaining experience. This bridges education and the workplace and helps students get jobs.

Unfortunately, most interns have to pay for college credits, do unpaid work and forsake paying jobs that won't further a career. But many are later hired in their chosen profession. For example, the advertising company Young & Rubicam has hired more than 12 City College of New York interns.

Well-run internships benefit everyone. The college supervisor identifies qualified students and suitable environments, doing quality control for sponsors—and for interns. If there are abuses, the supervisor intervenes and advocates on students' behalf.

If all internships had to be paid, opportunities would decline, hurting the professional path for many, especially minorities.

LYNN APPELBAUM
Closter, N.J., April 3, 2011

*The writer is a professor of media and communications arts at City College.*

## To the Editor:

Beyond the potential exploitation of interns' labor and the devaluing of academic achievement, reliance on unpaid internships can actually harm the businesses that are the recipients of the interns' largess.

In my own field of documentary television production, the endless supply of willing unpaid interns, with or without college credit, has altered our creative work force, limiting it to those who have had the financial ability to work without pay at the start of their careers.

We will never know what talented filmmakers we've lost because they couldn't afford to make that economic sacrifice.

DAVID AXELROD
Los Angeles, April 3, 2011

## To the Editor:

Internships, whether paid or not, can be quite valuable to a college student. Having worked at a college in Manhattan, and having benefited from a very low-paying internship, I have seen firsthand how internships can open doors for college students to industries that otherwise might be tough to break into without connections.

Given that there are people with years of work experience who are currently unemployed and taking volunteer positions in the hopes of securing a paid job, college students can hardly expect their internship to be more than the apprenticeship and foot-in-the-door opportunity that it is.

The competitive nature of today's job market is what enables companies to make use of unpaid internships. Rather than being "blind to the realities of work in contemporary America," universities are aware of the growing shortcomings of having only a college degree, and therefore encourage the job experience and networks that will bolster students after graduation.

MARIA CAMPO
New York, April 6, 2011

## To the Editor:

Ross Perlin cites the communications profession as one of many industries that routinely hire unpaid interns. His assessment that colleges and firms are perpetuating a degradation of the value of professional experience for college students is admirable in its effort to raise exposure for this important issue. Recently, the Public Relations Society of America issued new guidance to public relations professionals concerning the ethical use of interns. We made clear our belief that it is unethical not to provide some type of compensation to interns, whether monetary or college credit.

It seems a stretch, however, for Mr. Perlin to argue that all forms of for-credit unpaid internships should be terminated. Instead, we should focus on the quality of professional experience and acumen these arrangements provide and the direct role that plays in an intern's ability to obtain fulfilling postgraduate work.

We have a responsibility to prepare the next generation of professionals for more prosperous career prospects than ours.

FRANCIS C. McDONALD
New York, April 6, 2011

*The writer is on the Board of Ethics and Professional Standards of the Public Relations Society of America.*

## Responding to Reading

1. Which of the letter writers agree with Ross Perlin (p. 439)? Which ones disagree with him? What are their specific objections?
2. What is the most convincing point in each letter? Why?
3. What parts of Perlin's essay does each letter writer seem to ignore? On which points does each focus?

## Responding in Writing

Which letter do you think is the strongest response to Perlin's essay? Why?

# WIDENING THE FOCUS

## For Critical Reading and Writing

Referring specifically to the three readings in this chapter's Focus section, write an essay in which you answer the question, "Are Internships Work Experience or Exploitation?"

## For Further Reading

The following readings can suggest additional perspectives for thinking and writing about college internship programs.

- Scott Adams, "How to Get a Real Education" (p. 98)

- Stephen G. Emerson, "Is College Worth the Money?" (p. 119)

- Hilda Solis, Commencement Speech, Los Angeles City College, 2010 (p. 548)

## For Focused Research

Child labor is a topic that has sparked debate around the globe. In the United States, for example, students at several colleges and universities have protested their bookstores' sale of merchandise made in foreign sweatshops by child laborers. To gain greater insight into worldwide child labor, visit the Web site for the International Programme on the Elimination of Child Labour (IPEC), <http://www.ilo.org/ipec/lang--en/index.htm>. Then, write an essay that examines child labor in various countries, considering such factors as the pay and working conditions of child laborers as well as the kinds of industries that use child labor. What alternatives are available to the children in these countries? What happens to the children who do not get these jobs? Could an argument be made in defense of child labor?

## Beyond the Classroom

Assemble a group of friends and classmates, and lead a discussion about internships, gathering opinions on whether they see internships as education, exploitation, or something else. (You will want to record this group session so you can listen to the responses later.) Then, write an essay summarizing the group's opinions, quoting individual group members to illustrate various points of view. Then develop your own conclusions about how valuable internships—particularly unpaid internships—are to students.

─────────────── **WRITING** ───────────────

## Why We Work

1. In "Exploiting the Gender Gap" (p. 428), Warren Farrell asserts that the gap between men's and women's pay has more to do with quality-of-life choices than with discrimination; in "The Second Shift" (p. 412), Arlie Hochschild makes the point that most working women have two jobs: the one they do at work and the one that begins when they get home. Write an essay in which you consider to what extent the gender gap affects the way women work. Make sure you refer to both Farrell and Hochschild in your essay.
2. What do young people learn by having a job—even a bad job? Read "One Last Time" by Gary Soto (p. 404) and "A&P" by John Updike (p. 430). Then, discuss what the young Soto and Updike's character Sammy learned about work.
3. Write an essay in which you describe in detail the worst job you ever had.
4. Considering the essays in this chapter—especially "Why We Work" (p. 399), "One Last Time" (p. 404), and "The Second Shift" (p. 412)—write an essay in which you discuss what you believe the purpose of work should be. For example, should it be to earn money, or should it be to gain personal satisfaction and fulfillment? Are these two goals mutually exclusive? Does the way we work in this country help people achieve these goals?
5. In "The Second Shift" (p. 412), Arlie Hochschild says that both society and the government should institute new policies that would allow workers to have more time at home. Write an essay in which you briefly summarize Hochschild's ideas and then go on to explain in detail why people need more time with their families.
6. In "It's Not about You" (p. 418), David Brooks sees working in positive terms—as the way a person achieves his or her full potential as a human being. In "Why We Work" (p. 399), however, Andrew Curry makes the point that most workers dislike their jobs. Which of these two views of work do you hold? Write an essay in which you give the reasons for your belief. Illustrate your points with your own experiences as well as with references to the essays by Brooks and Curry.
7. Imagine that you have been asked by your former high school to address students in this year's graduating class about how to get part-time and summer jobs to offset the high cost of college. Write a speech that is inspirational but also offers specific advice.

8. In his essay "Delusions of Grandeur, "Henry Lewis Gates, Jr. points out that "only 26% of African-American athletes at the collegiate level earn their degrees" (11). According to Gates, colleges should stop using African-American athletes "as cannon fodder in the big-business wars" of non-professional sports (14). Do you agree with Gates that colleges are exploiting African-American athletes? Do you think these student-athletes would be better off preparing themselves for careers in the workplace?

9. In "Do Secretaries Have a Future?" (p. 420), Lynn Peril writes about the indignities that modern secretaries face, and in "One Last Time" (p. 404), Gary Soto examines the working conditions of Mexican farm workers. After reading these essays, write a Bill of Rights for workers. What basic working conditions should they be guaranteed? What rights should they have? What protections should be afforded them? In your Bill of Rights, be sure to address the issues that Peril and Soto bring up in their essays.

10. In "Don't Blame Wal-Mart" (p. 422), Robert B. Reich discusses the harm that he thinks people do by shopping at Wal-Mart. Write an essay in which you present your own view of Wal-Mart. Make sure you refer to Reich's essay. Document all ideas that are not your own, and include a works-cited page.

# 9

# MAKING ETHICAL CHOICES

As Robert Frost suggests in his poem "The Road Not Taken" (p. 451), making choices is fundamental to our lives. The ability—and, in fact, the need—to make complex decisions is part of what makes us human. On a practical level, we choose friends, mates, careers, and places to live. On a more abstract level, we struggle to make the moral and ethical choices that people have struggled with over the years.

Many times, complex questions have no easy answers; occasionally, they have no answers at all. For example, should we obey a law that we

Peace Corps volunteer checking literacy workbook in Djiliki, Niger

believe to be morally wrong? Should we stand up to authority even if our stand puts us at risk? Should we help less fortunate individuals if such help threatens our own social or economic status? Should we strive to do well or to do good? Should we tell the truth even if the truth may hurt us—or hurt someone else? Which road should we take, the easy one or the more difficult one?

Most of the time, the choice we (and the writers whose essays appear in this chapter) face is the same: to act or not to act. To make a decision, we must understand both the long- and short-term consequences of acting in a particular way or of choosing not to act. We must struggle with the possibility of compromise—and with the possibility of making a morally or ethically objectionable decision. And, perhaps most important, we must learn to take responsibility for our decisions.

In the context of the pressure on today's college students to make the right ethical choices, the Focus section of this chapter, "What Has Happened to Academic Integrity?" (p. 493), considers the erosion of academic integrity and the persistence of plagiarism.

Young businesspeople in office complex

─────── **Preparing to Read and Write** ───────

As you read and prepare to write about the selections in this chapter, you may consider the following questions:

- On what specific choice or choices does the essay focus? Is the decision to be made moral? ethical? political? practical?

- Does the writer introduce a **dilemma,** a choice between equally problematic alternatives?

- Does the choice the writer presents apply only to one specific situation or case, or does it also have a wider application?

- Is the writer emotionally involved with the issue he or she is discussing? Does this involvement (or lack of involvement) affect the effectiveness of the writer's argument?

- What social, political, or religious ideas influence the writer? How can you tell? Are these ideas similar to or different from your own views?

- Does the choice being considered lead the writer to examine his or her own values? The values of others? The values of the society at large? Does the writer lead you to examine your own values?

- Does the writer offer a solution to a problem? If so, do you find this solution reasonable?

- Does the choice the writer advocates require sacrifice? If so, does the sacrifice seem worth it?

- Which writers' views seem most alike? Which seem most different?

# THE ROAD NOT TAKEN
## Robert Frost
### 1874–1963

*Robert Frost, four-time Pulitzer Prize–winning poet of rural New England,
lived most of his life in New Hampshire and taught at Amherst College, Harvard
University, and Dartmouth College. His subjects at first seem familiar and
comfortable, as does his language, but the symbols, allusions, and underlying
meanings in many of his poems are quite complex. Some of Frost's most famous
poems are "Birches," "Mending Wall," and "Stopping by Woods on a Snowy
Evening." In the poem that follows, the speaker hesitates before making a choice.*

Two roads diverged in a yellow wood,
And sorry I could not travel both
And be one traveller, long I stood
And looked down one as far as I could
To where it bent in the undergrowth;                        5

Then took the other, as just as fair,
And having perhaps the better claim,
Because it was grassy and wanted wear;
Though as for that the passing there
Had worn them really about the same,                        10

And both that morning equally lay
In leaves no step had trodden black.
Oh, I kept the first for another day!
Yet knowing how way leads on to way,
I doubted if I should ever come back.                        15

I shall be telling this with a sigh
Somewhere ages and ages hence:
Two roads diverged in a wood, and I—
I took the one less travelled by,
And that has made all the difference.                        20

## Responding to Reading

1. What is the difference between the two paths Frost's speaker considers? Why
   does he make the choice he does?

2. Is "The Road Not Taken" simply about two paths in the wood, or does it suggest more? What makes you think so? To what larger choices might the speaker be alluding?
3. What does the speaker mean by "that has made all the difference" (line 20)?

## Responding in Writing

In your own words, write a short prose summary of this poem. Use first person and past tense (as Frost does).

## ETHICS

## Linda Pastan

### 1932–

*The winner of numerous prizes for her poetry, Linda Pastan often focuses on the complexity of domestic life, using intense imagery to bring a sense of mystery to everyday matters. She has been a lecturer at the Breadloaf Writers Conference in Vermont and an instructor at American University, and she has published numerous collections of poetry, including* Waiting for My Life *(1981),* PM/ AM: New and Selected Poems *(1983),* Carnival Evening: New and Selected Poems 1968–1998 *(1998),* The Last Uncle: Poems (2002), Queen of a Rainy Country *(2006), and* Traveling Light: Poems *(2011). In "Ethics," from* Waiting for My Life, *the speaker introduces an ethical dilemma.*

In ethics class so many years ago
our teacher asked this question every fall:
if there were a fire in a museum
which would you save, a Rembrandt painting
5   or an old woman who hadn't many
years left anyhow? Restless on hard chairs
caring little for pictures or old age
we'd opt one year for life, the next for art
and always half-heartedly. Sometimes
10   the woman borrowed my grandmother's face
leaving her usual kitchen to wander
some drafty, half imagined museum.
One year, feeling clever, I replied
why not let the woman decide herself?
15   Linda, the teacher would report, eschews
the burdens of responsibility.
This fall in a real museum I stand
before a real Rembrandt, old woman,
or nearly so, myself. The colors

within this frame are darker than autumn,                                    20
darker even than winter—the browns of earth,
though earth's most radiant elements burn
through the canvas. I know now that woman
and painting and season are almost one
and all beyond saving by children.                                           25

## Responding to Reading

1. What choice actually confronts Pastan's speaker? What answer do you think
   the teacher expects the students to give?
2. Do you agree with the teacher that refusing to choose means avoiding
   responsibility? Does Frost's speaker (p. 453) have the option not to choose?
3. When the speaker says that "woman / and painting and season are almost
   one" (lines 23–24), what does she mean? Does she imply that the teacher's
   question really has no answer? that the children who would "opt one year
   for life, the next for art" (line 8) are right?

## Responding in Writing

Confronted with the choice facing the speaker, would you save the Rembrandt
painting or the elderly woman? Why? Would you find this a difficult choice to
make?

# THE UNACKNOWLEDGED ETHICISTS ON CAMPUSES

## David A. Hoekema

*The chair of the philosophy department and a philosophy professor at Calvin
College, David A. Hoekema specializes in political philosophy, African philoso-
phy, and aesthetics. He is the author of four published books and two forthcoming
books,* Finding the Hidden Path: Contexts of Conflict and Possibilities for
Peace *and* Growing Up in College: A User's Guide. *In the following essay,
Hoekema examines possible sources of ethical guidance for college students.*

Catalogs and presidential speeches assure us repeatedly that the study
of the liberal arts strengthens morality and instills virtue, but they do
not tell us how. If virtue can indeed be taught, where can we find its
teachers? College study is widely assumed to foster a deeper sense of
moral conviction, but scarcely a trace of moral instruction remains anywhere in the curriculum.

   One of the distinctive features of the university environment is the
openness of students to new ideas and challenges. What, then, are the
dominant influences on students' thinking concerning moral choices?
Who, and where, are the ethics experts on campuses? And is it possible

for them to instill a more rigorous and more demanding vision of the moral life than that of the surrounding culture?

We can find the answers to such questions primarily by understanding the influence of three distinct groups. None of the groups bear a close resemblance to a 19th-century college president holding forth on moral philosophy to assembled seniors. But each plays a vital role in shaping students' sense of what is expected of them as responsible adults.

The first and most prominent group consists of the professors standing in front of their classrooms. Whether consciously or unconsciously, whether systematically or haphazardly, they serve as moral guides to students. Many professors would deny if asked that this has anything to do with their responsibilities or their function as members of the faculty. But it is a role that all faculty members do in fact occupy, and which contributes one of the most important elements of the moral atmosphere on any campus. It is not just professors in humanities disciplines like religion, philosophy, and history who play this role but also those in social sciences and sciences. Even if only a few courses explicitly deal with ethical questions, every class is to some degree a class in ethics.

5      For it is not so much the content as the conduct of classroom discourse that shapes students' conceptions of how to lead their lives. Students learn what it means to disagree forcefully but respectfully, and they observe how much or how little concern their instructors show when a student is unable to grasp critical concepts. Professors teach students about morality by the ways in which they grade tests, structure assignments, and respond to student complaints.

Further, only a minority of students envision their future selves following the same vocation as their professors, but they all are influenced by what they see in their instructors' understanding of their own vocation. They can see the difference between a dedicated teacher and one who is merely earning a paycheck, between an insincere and a genuine commitment to students' intellectual and personal welfare. They can distinguish between a scholar engaged in passionate pursuit of deeper understanding and a status seeker always trying to climb the ladder to a more prestigious institution. Those differences inform students' reflections on their vocational plans and shape students' sense of what it means to do one's life work with integrity and commitment.

A smaller but equally influential army of ethics teachers can be found in the student-life staff. It is not just when students do something foolish and shortsighted, and then face disciplinary sanctions, that such administrators become involved in students' personal and moral lives. From the first days of orientation through senior-week activities, they help students learn who they are and decide what they value.

And what sort of guidance do they offer? At best, student-life administrators challenge students to advance to a deeper level of critical awareness of their own choices through conversations, programmed activities, and interactions related to campus discipline. They emphasize that compliance with campus rules is only a small part of the important task of developing a strong sense of moral direction and personal integrity. Discipline for misbehavior becomes the occasion for serious reflection on why a student has fallen short, not just of college expectations, but also of the expectations other students have of her—and indeed that she has of herself.

Whether student-life administrators see themselves as having the authority to offer any specific moral guidance to students varies widely from campus to campus and person to person, and their influence is often implicit and indirect. Yet on every campus, we will find some student-life administrators who are deeply engaged in the most serious and searching moral inquiry with the students. No other group exercises so profound an influence over students' moral growth.

A subset of the student-life community includes those who coordinate religious life. The relationship between a campus pastor and a student involved in worship leadership may be as close as any relationship between adults and students on a campus. But at most institutions, the scope of such relationships is limited to a relatively small group of the student population. 10

The third major group of ethics experts are the student leaders of major campus organizations. Adolescents, we know, are profoundly influenced by the examples and opinions of their peers and are particularly likely to admire and emulate those who have risen to high levels of visibility and responsibility. Which students play the most important role depends on the specifics of each campus's history and culture, but captains and star players on sports teams, student-government leaders, and student journalists are usually among them. The relationship of student leaders to the members of their organizations is likely to involve little explicit discussion of matters of morality and personal responsibility, but beneath the surface a great deal of ethical instruction takes place. Indeed, some of the most influential teachers of ethics on our campuses, in the long run, are probably other students—people whom we as faculty and staff members tend to see as recipients rather than sources of instruction.

It is clear that serious and sustained problems of student conduct, particularly in upholding academic integrity and taking responsibility for destructive and self-destructive behaviors, are present at every college. For example, the prevalence of cheating on assignments and tests is notoriously difficult to measure accurately, but anyone who asserts that it is absent from his campus is kidding himself. Still, there are teachers of ethics on our campuses: the professoriate, the student-life staff, and the leadership of student organizations and activities.

But do the members of any of these groups really believe that they have something of substance to teach? Many do not. Professors believe they have the duty and authority to convey to students a deeper understanding of history or biology or accounting, but not of morality. They hold themselves responsible for preparing engaging lectures, setting challenging assignments, and keeping their own intellects continually sharpened by research and scholarship. How students conduct their lives outside class, however, is considered to lie wholly outside the faculty's concerns.

Meanwhile, members of the second group, student-life administrators, see their role as settling conflicts, enforcing serious campus rules, and helping everyone get along better. But, not wanting to appear judgmental, they usually scrupulously avoid applying moral categories to students. And those who make up the third group, student leaders, are themselves often in need of moral guidance as they learn to shoulder adult responsibilities.

15      If few of those potential teachers of virtue have anything that they believe they can teach, from whom will students learn? In the end, students will learn from one another, without any systematic assistance in learning what it means to grow morally—to critique, challenge, and refine a vision of what makes a life worthwhile. Offered no coherent or articulate ethical framework beyond the encouragement to fit in and enjoy their lives, students will model themselves on peers and adults whom they admire. In good times they will make themselves comfortable and get along. But in times of crisis and conflict, when hard choices arise and it takes a keen eye for moral nuance and a courageous heart to move forward, they will be woefully unprepared.

And what will be the outcome? That is a question that should trouble the sleep of anyone involved in higher education today. The absence of any effective ethical content in the curriculum may produce a future generation of parents and corporate leaders who are no better prepared to solve the urgent problems of the day than physicians would be to perform surgery if they had learned medicine from their friends and conferred their own diplomas.

We need to adjust our expectations of both students and faculty members in ways that will enhance, not impede, more-effective relationships of moral guidance and effective ethical modeling. For the resources needed for a renewed sense of the ethical core of liberal education are already in place on every campus. Neglect of moral issues has arisen not from ignorance of what morality is, but rather from the conviction that morality is no longer the business of the university. Yet there remain some faculty members, and many campus-life staff members and campus chaplains, who hold to a more integrated vision of students' lives. They are ready to engage more thoughtfully and intensively in the moral formation of their students.

When we make room in our academic institutions for all to relate to one another as thoughtful and responsible moral agents, we will find that we can actually teach each other a great deal. There are lots of ethicists in the house. We need only to build institutional structures and expectations that will encourage them to get to work.

## Responding to Reading

1. What three groups of "unacknowledged ethicists" does Hoekema discuss in this essay? What does each group contribute? Why does Hoekema believe that ethical guidance is so important?
2. According to Hoekema, if the three groups he identifies are unwilling or unable to teach ethics and morals to students, students will have to "learn from one another" (15). Why does Hoekema believe this kind of learning is not ideal? Do you think students can learn ethics and morals from one another?
3. In paragraph 4, Hoekema says, "Even if only a few courses explicitly deal with ethical questions, every class is to some degree a class in ethics." Do you agree with him? Do you think that formal, systematic "moral instruction" and "ethical content" (16) should be required in the college curriculum? If so, what form should this instruction take, and where (and by whom) should it be taught? If not, why not?

## Responding in Writing

Who are the ethicists on your campus? at your workplace? in your family? in your community? What moral and ethical guidance does each group provide? Which do you rely on most, and why?

# Shooting an Elephant

## George Orwell

### 1903–1950

*George Orwell was born Eric Arthur Blair in Bengal, India, the son of a British colonial civil servant. He joined the Indian Imperial Police in Burma, where he came to question the British methods of colonialism. This detailed account of an incident with an elephant in Burma is Orwell's most powerful criticism of imperialism and the impossible position of British police officers— himself among them—in the colonies. Orwell says about the incident, "It was perfectly clear to me what I ought to do," but then he thinks of "the watchful yellow faces from behind" and realizes that his choice is not so simple. An enemy of totalitarianism and a spokesperson for the oppressed, Orwell criticized totalitarian regimes in his bitterly satirical novels* Animal Farm *(1945) and* 1984 *(1949). He wrote many literary essays and is much admired for his lucid prose style.*

In Moulmein, in lower Burma, I was hated by large numbers of people— the only time in my life that I have been important enough for this to happen to me. I was sub-divisional police officer of the town, and in an aimless, petty kind of way anti-European feeling was very bitter. No one had the guts to raise a riot, but if a European woman went through the bazaars alone somebody would probably spit betel juice over her dress. As a police officer I was an obvious target and was baited whenever it seemed safe to do so. When a nimble Burman tripped me up on the football field and the referee (another Burman) looked the other way, the crowd yelled with hideous laughter. This happened more than once. In the end the sneering yellow faces of young men that met me everywhere, the insults hooted after me when I was at a safe distance, got badly on my nerves. The young Buddhist priests were the worst of all. There were several thousands of them in the town and none of them seemed to have anything to do except stand on street corners and jeer at Europeans.

All this was perplexing and upsetting. For at that time I had already made up my mind that imperialism was an evil thing and the sooner I chucked up my job and got out of it the better. Theoretically—and secretly, of course—I was all for the Burmese and all against their oppressors, the British. As for the job I was doing, I hated it more bitterly than I can perhaps make clear. In a job like that you see the dirty work of Empire at close quarters. The wretched prisoners huddling in the stinking cages of the lock-ups, the grey, cowed faces of the long-term convicts, the scarred buttocks of the men who had been flogged with bamboos—all these oppressed me with an intolerable sense of guilt. But I could get nothing into perspective. I was young and ill-educated and I had to think out my problems in the utter silence that is imposed on every Englishman in the East. I did not even know that the British Empire is dying, still less did I know that it is a great deal better than the younger empires that are going to supplant it.[1] All I knew was that I was stuck between my hatred of the empire I served and my rage against the evil-spirited little beasts who tried to make my job impossible. With one part of my mind I thought of the British Raj[2] as an unbreakable tyranny, as something clamped down, in *saecula saeculorum*,[3] upon the will of prostrate peoples; with another part I thought that the greatest joy in the world would be to drive a bayonet into a Buddhist priest's guts. Feelings like these are the normal by-products of imperialism; ask any Anglo-Indian official, if you can catch him off duty.

One day something happened which in a roundabout way was enlightening. It was a tiny incident in itself, but it gave me a better glimpse than I had before of the real nature of imperialism—the real motives for which despotic governments act. Early one morning the sub-inspector at a police station the other end of the town rang me up on the phone and said that an elephant was ravaging the bazaar. Would I please come and do something about it? I did not know what I could do, but I wanted to see what was happening and I got on to a pony and

---

[1]This essay was written in 1936, three years before the start of World War II; Stalin and Hitler were in power. [Eds.]
[2]Sovereignty. [Eds.]
[3]From time immemorial. [Eds.]

started out. I took my rifle, an old .44 Winchester and much too small to kill an elephant, but I thought the noise might be useful in *terrorem*. Various Burmans stopped me on the way and told me about the elephant's doings. It was not, of course, a wild elephant, but a tame one which had gone "must." It had been chained up, as tame elephants always are when their attack of "must"[4] is due, but on the previous night it had broken its chain and escaped. Its mahout,[5] the only person who could manage it when it was in that state, had set out in pursuit, but had taken the wrong direction and was now twelve hours' journey away, and in the morning the elephant had suddenly reappeared in the town. The Burmese population had no weapons and were quite helpless against it. It had already destroyed somebody's bamboo hut, killed a cow, and raided some fruit-stalls and devoured the stock; also it had met the municipal rubbish van and, when the driver jumped out and took to his heels, had turned the van over and inflicted violences upon it.

The Burmese sub-inspector and some Indian constables were waiting for me in the quarter where the elephant had been seen. It was a very poor quarter, a labyrinth of squalid bamboo huts, thatched with palm-leaf, winding all over a steep hillside. I remember that it was a cloudy, stuffy morning at the beginning of the rains. We began questioning the people as to where the elephant had gone and, as usual, failed to get any definite information. That is invariably the case in the East; a story always sounds clear enough at a distance, but the nearer you get to the scene of events the vaguer it becomes. Some of the people said that the elephant had gone in one direction, some said that he had gone in another, some professed not even to have heard of any elephant. I had almost made up my mind that the whole story was a pack of lies, when we heard yells a little distance away. There was a loud, scandalized cry of "Go away, child! Go away this instant!" and an old woman with a switch in her hand came round the corner of a hut, violently shooing away a crowd of naked children. Some more women followed, clicking their tongues and exclaiming; evidently there was something that the children ought not to have seen. I rounded the hut and saw a man's dead body sprawling in the mud. He was an Indian, a black Dravidian coolie,[6] almost naked, and he could not have been dead many minutes. The people said that the elephant had come suddenly upon him round the corner of the hut, caught him with its trunk, put its foot on his back, and ground him into the earth. This was the rainy season and the ground was soft, and his face had scored a trench a foot deep and a couple of yards long. He was lying on his belly with arms crucified and head sharply twisted to one side. His face was coated with mud, the eyes wide open, the teeth bared and grinning with an expression of unendurable agony. (Never tell me, by

---

[4]Frenzy. [Eds.]
[5]Keeper. [Eds.]
[6]An unskilled laborer. [Eds.]

the way, that the dead look peaceful. Most of the corpses I have seen looked devilish.) The friction of the great beast's foot had stripped the skin from his back as neatly as one skins a rabbit. As soon as I saw the dead man I sent an orderly to a friend's house nearby to borrow an elephant rifle. I had already sent back the pony, not wanting it to go mad with fright and throw me if it smelt the elephant.

5      The orderly came back in a few minutes with a rifle and five cartridges, and meanwhile some Burmans had arrived and told us that the elephant was in the paddy fields below, only a few hundred yards away. As I started forward practically the whole population of the quarter flocked out of the houses and followed me. They had seen the rifle and were all shouting excitedly that I was going to shoot the elephant. They had not shown much interest in the elephant when he was merely ravaging their homes, but it was different now that he was going to be shot. It was a bit of fun to them, as it would be to an English crowd; besides they wanted the meat. It made me vaguely uneasy. I had no intention of shooting the elephant—I had merely sent for the rifle to defend myself if necessary—and it is always unnerving to have a crowd following you. I marched down the hill, looking and feeling a fool, with the rifle over my shoulder and an ever-growing army of people jostling at my heels. At the bottom, when you got away from the huts, there was a metalled road and beyond that a miry waste of paddy fields a thousand yards across, not yet ploughed but soggy from the first rains and dotted with coarse grass. The elephant was standing eight yards from the road, his left side towards us. He took not the slightest notice of the crowd's approach. He was tearing up bunches of grass, beating them against his knees to clean them and stuffing them into his mouth.

I had halted on the road. As soon as I saw the elephant I knew with perfect certainty that I ought not to shoot him. It is a serious matter to shoot a working elephant—it is comparable to destroying a huge and costly piece of machinery—and obviously one ought not to do it if it can possibly be avoided. And at that distance, peacefully eating, the elephant looked no more dangerous than a cow. I thought then and I think now that his attack of "must" was already passing off; in which case he would merely wander harmlessly about until the mahout came back and caught him. Moreover, I did not in the least want to shoot him. I decided that I would watch him for a little while to make sure that he did not turn savage again, and then go home.

But at that moment I glanced round at the crowd that had followed me. It was an immense crowd, two thousand at the least and growing every minute. It blocked the road for a long distance on either side. I looked at the sea of yellow faces above the garish clothes—faces all happy and excited over this bit of fun, all certain that the elephant was going to be shot. They were watching me as they would watch a conjurer about to perform a trick. They did not like me, but with the magical rifle in my hands I was momentarily worth watching. And suddenly I realized that I should have to shoot the elephant after all. The people expected it of me and I had got to do it; I could feel their two thousand wills pressing me forward, irresistibly. And it was at this moment, as I stood there with the rifle in my hands, that I first grasped the hollowness, the futility of the white man's dominion in the East. Here was I, the white man with his gun, standing in front of the unarmed native crowd—seemingly the leading actor of the piece; but in reality I was only an absurd puppet pushed to and fro by the will of those yellow faces behind. I perceived in this moment that when the white man turns tyrant it is his own freedom that he destroys. He becomes a sort of hollow, posing dummy, the conventionalized figure of a sahib.[7] For it is the condition of his rule that he shall spend his life in trying to impress the "natives," and so in every crisis he has got to do what the "natives" expect of him. He wears a mask, and his face grows to fit it. I had got to shoot the elephant. I had committed myself to doing it when I sent for the rifle. A sahib has got to act like a sahib; he has got to appear resolute, to know his own mind and do definite things. To come all that way, rifle in hand, with two thousand people marching at my heels, and then to trail feebly away, having done nothing—no, that was impossible. The crowd would laugh at me. And my whole life, every white man's life in the East, was one long struggle not to be laughed at.

But I did not want to shoot the elephant. I watched him beating his bunch of grass against his knees, with that preoccupied grandmotherly air that elephants have. It seemed to me that it would be murder to shoot him. At that age I was not squeamish about killing animals, but I had never shot an elephant and never wanted to. (Somehow it always seems worse to kill a *large* animal.) Besides, there was the beast's owner to be considered. Alive, the elephant was worth at least a hundred pounds; dead, he would only be worth the value of his tusks, five pounds, possibly. But I had got to act quickly. I turned to some experienced looking Burmans who had been there when we arrived, and asked them how the elephant had been behaving. They all said the same thing: he took no notice of you if you left him alone, but he might charge if you went too close to him.

It was perfectly clear to me what I ought to do. I ought to walk up to within, say, twenty-five yards of the elephant and test his behavior. If he charged, I could shoot; if he took no notice of me, it would be safe to leave him until the mahout came back. But also I knew that I was going to do no such thing. I was a poor shot with a rifle and the ground was soft mud into which one would sink at every step. If the elephant charged and I missed him, I should have about as much chance as a toad under a steam-roller. But even then I was not thinking particularly of

---

[7]Term used by natives of colonial India when referring to a European of rank. [Eds.]

my own skin, only of the watchful yellow faces behind. For at that moment, with the crowd watching me, I was not afraid in the ordinary sense, as I would have been if I had been alone. A white man mustn't be frightened in front of "natives"; and so, in general, he isn't frightened. The sole thought in my mind was that if anything went wrong those two thousand Burmans would see me pursued, caught, trampled on, and reduced to a grinning corpse like that Indian up the hill. And if that happened it was quite probable that some of them would laugh. That would never do. There was only one alternative. I shoved the cartridges into the magazine and lay down on the road to get a better aim.

10     The crowd grew very still, and a deep, low, happy sigh, as of people who see the theatre curtain go up at last, breathed from innumerable throats. They were going to have their bit of fun after all. The rifle was a beautiful German thing with cross-hair sights. I did not then know that in shooting an elephant one would shoot to cut an imaginary bar running from ear-hole to ear-hole. I ought, therefore, as the elephant was sideways on, to have aimed straight at his ear-hole; actually I aimed several inches in front of this, thinking the brain would be further forward.

When I pulled the trigger I did not hear the bang or feel the kick— one never does when a shot goes home—but I heard the devilish roar of glee that went up from the crowd. In that instant, in too short a time, one would have thought, even for the bullet to get there, a mysterious, terrible change had come over the elephant. He neither stirred nor fell, but every line of his body had altered. He looked suddenly stricken, shrunken, immensely old, as though the frightful impact of the bullet had paralysed him without knocking him down. At last, after what seemed a long time—it might have been five seconds, I dare say— he sagged flabbily to his knees. His mouth slobbered. An enormous senility seemed to have settled upon him. One could have imagined him thousands of years old. I fired again into the same spot. At the second shot he did not collapse but climbed with desperate slowness to his feet and stood weakly upright, with legs sagging and head dropping. I fired a third time. That was the shot that did for him. You could see the agony of it jolt his whole body and knock the last remnant of strength from his legs. But in falling he seemed for a moment to rise, for as his hind legs collapsed beneath him he seemed to tower upward like a huge rock toppling, his trunk reaching skywards like a tree. He trumpeted, for the first and only time. And then down he came, his belly towards me, with a crash that seemed to shake the ground even where I lay.

I got up. The Burmans were already racing past me across the mud. It was obvious that the elephant would never rise again, but he was not dead. He was breathing very rhythmically with long rattling gasps, his great mound of a side painfully rising and falling. His mouth was wide open—I could see far down into caverns of pale pink throat. I waited a long time for him to die, but his breathing did not weaken. Finally I fired my two remaining shots into the spot where I thought his heart must be. The thick blood welled out of him like red velvet, but still he did not die. His body did not even jerk when the shots hit him, the tortured breathing continued without a pause. He was dying, very slowly and in great agony, but in some world remote from me where not even a bullet could damage him further. I felt that I had got to put an end to that dreadful noise. It seemed dreadful to see the great beast lying there, powerless to move and yet powerless to die, and not even to be able to finish him. I sent back for my small rifle and poured shot after shot into his heart and down his throat. They seemed to make no impression. The tortured gasps continued as steadily as the ticking of a clock.

In the end I could not stand it any longer and went away. I heard later that it took him half an hour to die. Burmans were bringing dahs[8] and baskets even before I left, and I was told they had stripped his body almost to the bones by the afternoon.

Afterwards, of course, there were endless discussions about the shooting of the elephant. The owner was furious, but he was only an Indian and could do nothing. Besides, legally I had done the right thing, for a mad elephant has to be killed, like a mad dog, if its owner fails to control it. Among the Europeans opinion was divided. The older men said I was right, the younger men said it was a damn shame to shoot an elephant for killing a coolie, because an elephant was worth more than any damn Coringhee coolie. And afterwards I was very glad that the coolie had been killed; it put me legally in the right and it gave me a sufficient pretext for shooting the elephant. I often wondered whether any of the others grasped that I had done it solely to avoid looking a fool.

## Responding to Reading

1. The central focus of this essay is Orwell's struggle to decide how to control the elephant. Do you think he really has a choice?
2. Orwell says that his encounter with the elephant, although "a tiny incident in itself," gave him an understanding of "the real nature of imperialism—the real motives for which despotic governments act" (3). In light of this statement, do you think his purpose in this essay is to explore something about himself or something about the nature of British colonialism—or both?
3. In paragraphs 5–6, Orwell introduces the elephant as peaceful and innocent; in paragraphs 11–12, he describes the animal's misery. What do these paragraphs contribute to the essay?

## Responding in Writing

Compare paragraphs 11–12 of Orwell's essay with paragraphs 27–33 of Claire McCarthy's essay (p. 479). How are the descriptions alike? How are they different?

---

[8]Large knives. [Eds.]

# LETTER FROM BIRMINGHAM JAIL

## Martin Luther King, Jr.

### 1929–1968

*The following letter, written by Martin Luther King, Jr., in 1963, is his eloquent and impassioned response to a public statement by eight fellow clergymen in Birmingham, Alabama, who appealed to the citizenry of that city to "observe the principles of law and order and common sense" rather than join in the principled protests that King was leading. (See page 372 for King's biography.)*

MY DEAR FELLOW CLERGYMEN:[1]

While confined here in the Birmingham city jail, I came across your recent statement calling my present activities "unwise and untimely." Seldom do I pause to answer criticism of my work and ideas. If I sought to answer all the criticisms that cross my desk, my secretaries would have little time for anything other than such correspondence in the course of the day, and I would have no time for constructive work. But since I feel that you are men of genuine good will and that your criticisms are sincerely set forth, I want to try to answer your statement in what I hope will be patient and reasonable terms.

I think I should indicate that I am here in Birmingham, since you have been influenced by the view which argues against "outsiders coming in." I have the honor of serving as president of the Southern Christian Leadership Conference, an organization operating in every southern state, with headquarters in Atlanta, Georgia. We have some eighty-five affiliated organizations across the South, and one of them is the Alabama Christian Movement for Human Rights. Frequently we share staff, educational, and financial resources with our affiliates. Several months ago the affiliate here in Birmingham asked us to be on call to engage in a non-violent direct-action program if such were deemed necessary. We readily consented, and when the hour came we lived up to our promise. So I, along with several members of my staff, am here because I was invited here. I am here because I have organizational ties here.

But more basically, I am in Birmingham because injustice is here. Just as the prophets of the eighth century B.C. left their villages and

---

[1]This response to a published statement by eight fellow clergymen from Alabama (Bishop C. C. J. Carpenter, Bishop Joseph A. Durick, Rabbi Milton L. Grafman, Bishop Paul Hardin, Bishop Holan B. Harmon, the Reverend George M. Murray, the Reverend Edward V. Ramage and the Reverend Earl Stallings) was composed under somewhat constricting circumstances. Begun on the margins of the newspaper in which the statement appeared while I was in jail, the letter was continued on scraps of writing paper supplied by a friendly Negro trusty, and concluded on a pad my attorneys were eventually permitted to leave me. Although the text remains in substance unaltered, I have indulged in the author's prerogative of polishing it for publication.

carried their "thus saith the Lord" far beyond the boundaries of their home towns, and just as the Apostle Paul left his village of Tarsus and carried the gospel of Jesus Christ to the far corners of the Greco-Roman world, so am I compelled to carry the gospel of freedom beyond my own home town. Like Paul, I must constantly respond to the Macedonian call for aid.

Moreover, I am cognizant of the interrelatedness of all communities and states. I cannot sit idly by in Atlanta and not be concerned about what happens in Birmingham. Injustice anywhere is a threat to justice everywhere. We are caught in an inescapable network of mutuality, tied in a single garment of destiny. Whatever affects one directly, affects all indirectly. Never again can we afford to live with the narrow, provincial "outside agitator" idea. Anyone who lives inside the United States can never be considered an outsider anywhere within its bounds.

You deplore the demonstrations taking place in Birmingham. But 5 your statement, I am sorry to say, fails to express a similar concern for the conditions that brought about the demonstrations. I am sure that none of you would want to rest content with the superficial kind of social analysis that deals merely with effects and does not grapple with underlying causes. It is unfortunate that demonstrations are taking place in Birmingham, but it is even more unfortunate that the city's white power structure left the Negro community with no alternative.

In any nonviolent campaign there are four basic steps: collection of the facts to determine whether injustices exist; negotiation; self-purification; and direct action. We have gone through all these steps in Birmingham. There can be no gainsaying the fact that racial injustice engulfs this community. Birmingham is probably the most thoroughly segregated city in the United States. Its ugly record of brutality is widely known. Negroes have experienced grossly unjust treatment in the courts. There have been more unsolved bombings of Negro homes and churches in Birmingham than in any other city in the nation. These are the hard, brutal facts of the case. On the basis of these conditions, Negro leaders sought to negotiate with the city fathers. But the latter consistently refused to engage in good-faith negotiation.

Then, last September, came the opportunity to talk with leaders of Birmingham's economic community. In the course of the negotiations, certain promises were made by the merchants—for example, to remove the stores' humiliating racial signs. On the basis of these promises, the Reverend Fred Shuttlesworth and the leaders of the Alabama Christian Movement for Human Rights agreed to a moratorium on all demonstrations. As the weeks and months went by, we realized that we were the victims of a broken promise. A few signs, briefly removed, returned; the others remained.

As in so many past experiences, our hopes had been blasted, and the shadow of deep disappointment settled upon us. We had no alternative except to prepare for direct action, whereby we would present our very bodies as a means of laying our case before the conscience of the local and the national community. Mindful of the difficulties involved, we decided to undertake a process of self-purification. We began a series of workshops on nonviolence, and we repeatedly asked ourselves: "Are you able to accept blows without retaliating?" "Are you able to endure the ordeal of jail?" We decided to schedule our direct-action program for the Easter season, realizing that except for Christmas, this is the main shopping period of the year. Knowing that a strong economic-withdrawal program would be the by-product of direct action, we felt that this would be the best time to bring pressure to bear on the merchants for the needed change.

Then it occurred to us that Birmingham's mayoral election was coming up in March, and we speedily decided to postpone action until after election day. When we discovered that the Commissioner of Public Safety, Eugene "Bull" Connor,[2] had piled up enough votes to be in the run-off, we decided again to postpone action until the day after the run-off so that the demonstrations could not be used to cloud the issues. Like many others, we wanted to see Mr. Connor defeated, and to this end we endured postponement after postponement. Having aided in this community need, we felt that our direct-action program could be delayed no longer.

10    You may well ask, "Why direct action? Why sit-ins, marches, and so forth? Isn't negotiation a better path?" You are quite right in calling for negotiation. Indeed, this is the very purpose of direct action. Nonviolent direct action seeks to create such a crisis and foster such a tension that a community which has constantly refused to negotiate is forced to confront the issue. It seeks so to dramatize the issue that it can no longer be ignored. My citing the creation of tension as part of the work of the nonviolent-resister may sound rather shocking. But I must confess that I am not afraid of the word "tension." I have earnestly opposed violent tension, but there is a type of constructive, nonviolent tension which is necessary for growth. Just as Socrates felt that it was necessary to create a tension in the mind so that individuals could rise from the bondage of myths and half-truths to the unfettered realm of creative analysis and objective appraisal, so must we see the need for nonviolent gadflies to create the kind of tension in society that will help men rise from the dark depths of prejudice and racism to the majestic heights of understanding and brotherhood.

The purpose of our direct-action program is to create a situation so crisis-packed that it will inevitably open the door to negotiation. I therefore concur with you in your call for negotiation. Too long has our

---

[2]An ardent segregationist, Connor ordered police officers to use police dogs and fire hoses to break up civil rights demonstrations. (Conner lost his bid for mayor.) [Eds.]

beloved Southland been bogged down in a tragic effort to live in monologue rather than dialogue.

One of the basic points in your statement is that the action that I and my associates have taken in Birmingham is untimely. Some have asked: "Why didn't you give the new city administration time to act?" The only answer that I can give to this query is that the new Birmingham administration must be prodded about as much as the outgoing one, before it will act. We are sadly mistaken if we feel that the election of Albert Boutwell as mayor will bring the millennium to Birmingham. While Mr. Boutwell is a much more gentle person than Mr. Connor, they are both segregationists, dedicated to maintenance of the status quo. I have hoped that Mr. Boutwell will be reasonable enough to see the futility of massive resistance to desegregation. But he will not see this without pressure from devotees of civil rights. My friends, I must say to you that we have not made a single gain in civil rights without determined legal and nonviolent pressure. Lamentably, it is an historical fact that privileged groups seldom give up their privileges voluntarily. Individuals may see the moral light and voluntarily give up their unjust posture; but, as Reinhold Niebuhr[3] has reminded us, groups tend to be more immoral than individuals.

We know through painful experience that freedom is never voluntarily given by the oppressor; it must be demanded by the oppressed. Frankly, I have yet to engage in a direct-action campaign that was "well timed" in the view of those who have not suffered unduly from the disease of segregation. For years now I have heard the word "Wait!" It rings in the ear of every Negro with piercing familiarity. This "Wait!" has almost always meant "Never." We must come to see, with one of our distinguished jurists, that "justice too long delayed is justice denied."[4]

We have waited for more than 340 years for our constitutional and God-given rights. The nations of Asia and Africa are moving with jet-like speed toward gaining political independence, but we still creep at horse-and-buggy pace toward gaining a cup of coffee at a lunch counter. Perhaps it is easy for those who have never felt the stinging darts of segregation to say, "Wait." But when you have seen vicious mobs lynch your mothers and fathers at will and drown your sisters and brothers at whim; when you have seen hate-filled policemen curse, kick, and even kill your black brothers and sisters; when you see the vast majority of your twenty million Negro brothers smothering in an airtight cage of poverty in the midst of an affluent society; when you suddenly find your tongue twisted and your speech stammering as you seek to explain to your six-year-old daughter why she can't go to the

---

[3]American religious and social thinker (1892–1971). [Eds.]

[4]Attributed to British statesman William Ewart Gladstone (1809–1898), a stalwart of the Liberal Party who also said, "You cannot fight the future. Time is on our side." [Eds.]

public amusement park that has just been advertised on television, and see tears welling up in her eyes when she is told that Funtown is closed to colored children, and see ominous clouds of inferiority beginning to form in her little mental sky, and see her beginning to distort her personality by developing an unconscious bitterness toward white people; when you have to concoct an answer for a five-year-old son who is asking, "Daddy, why do white people treat colored people so mean?"; when you take a cross-country drive and find it necessary to sleep night after night in the uncomfortable corners of your automobile because no motel will accept you; when you are humiliated day in and day out by nagging signs reading "white" and "colored"; when your first name becomes "nigger," your middle name becomes "boy" (however old you are) and your last name becomes "John," and your wife and mother are never given the respected title "Mrs."; when you are harried by day and haunted by night by the fact that you are a Negro, living constantly at tiptoe stance, never quite knowing what to expect next, and are plagued with inner fears and outer resentments; when you are forever fighting a degenerating sense of "nobodiness"—then you will understand why we find it difficult to wait. There comes a time when the cup of endurance runs over, and men are no longer willing to be plunged into the abyss of despair. I hope, sirs, you can understand our legitimate and unavoidable impatience.

15    You express a great deal of anxiety over our willingness to break laws. This is certainly a legitimate concern. Since we so diligently urge people to obey the Supreme Court's decision of 1954 outlawing segregation in the public schools, at first glance it may seem rather paradoxical for us consciously to break laws. One may well ask: "How can you advocate breaking some laws and obeying others?" The answer lies in the fact that there are two types of laws: just and unjust. I would be the first to advocate obeying just laws. One has not only a legal but a moral responsibility to obey just laws. Conversely, one has a moral responsibility to disobey unjust laws. I would agree with St. Augustine[5] that "an unjust law is no law at all."

Now, what is the difference between the two? How does one determine whether a law is just or unjust? A just law is a man-made code that squares with the moral law or the law of God. An unjust law is a code that is out of harmony with the moral law. To put it in the terms of St. Thomas Aquinas:[6] An unjust law is a human law that is not rooted in eternal law and natural law. Any law that uplifts human personality is just. Any law that degrades human personality is unjust. All segregation statutes are unjust because segregation distorts the soul and damages the personality. It gives the segregator a false sense of superiority and the

---

[5]Italian-born missionary and theologian (?–c. 604). [Eds.]
[6]Italian philosopher and theologian (1225–1274). [Eds.]

segregated a false sense of inferiority. Segregation, to use the terminology of the Jewish philosopher Martin Buber,[7] substitutes an "I-it"
relationship for an "I-thou" relationship and ends up relegating persons
to the status of things. Hence segregation is not only politically, economically, and sociologically unsound, it is morally wrong and sinful.
Paul Tillich[8] has said that sin is separation. Is not segregation an existential expression of man's tragic separation, his awful estrangement,
his terrible sinfulness? Thus it is that I can urge men to obey the 1954
decision of the Supreme Court, for it is morally right; and I can urge
them to disobey segregation ordinances, for they are morally wrong.

Let us consider a more concrete example of just and unjust laws.
An unjust law is a code that a numerical or power majority group compels a minority group to obey but does not make binding on itself. This
is *difference* made legal. By the same token, a just law is a code that a
majority compels a minority to follow and that it is willing to follow
itself. This is *sameness* made legal.

Let me give another explanation. A law is unjust if it is inflicted on
a minority that, as a result of being denied the right to vote, had no part
in enacting or devising the law. Who can say that the legislature of
Alabama which set up that state's segregation laws was democratically
elected? Throughout Alabama all sorts of devious methods are used to
prevent Negroes from becoming registered voters, and there are some
counties in which, even though Negroes constitute a majority of the
population, not a single Negro is registered. Can any law enacted under
such circumstances be considered democratically structured?

Sometimes a law is just on its face and unjust in its application. For
instance, I have been arrested on a charge of parading without a permit.
Now, there is nothing wrong in having an ordinance which requires a
permit for a parade. But such an ordinance becomes unjust when it is
used to maintain segregation and to deny citizens the First-Amendment
privilege of peaceful assembly and protest.

I hope you are able to see the distinction I am trying to point out. 20
In no sense do I advocate evading or defying the law, as would the
rabid segregationist. That would lead to anarchy. One who breaks an
unjust law must do so openly, lovingly, and with a willingness to
accept the penalty. I submit that an individual who breaks a law that
conscience tells him is unjust, and who willingly accepts the penalty of
imprisonment in order to arouse the conscience of the community over
its injustice, is in reality expressing the highest respect for law.

Of course, there is nothing new about this kind of civil disobedience. It was evidenced sublimely in the refusal of Shadrach, Meshach,
and Abednego to obey the laws of Nebuchadnezzar, on the ground that

---

[7]Austrian existentialist philosopher and Judaic scholar (1878–1965). [Eds.]

[8]American philosopher and theologian (1886–1965). [Eds.]

a higher moral law was at stake.[9] It was practiced superbly by the early Christians, who were willing to face hungry lions and the excruciating pain of chopping blocks rather than submit to certain unjust laws of the Roman Empire. To a degree, academic freedom is a reality today because Socrates practiced civil disobedience.[10] In our own nation, the Boston Tea Party represented a massive act of civil disobedience.

We should never forget that everything Adolf Hitler did in Germany was "legal" and everything the Hungarian freedom fighters[11] did in Hungary was "illegal." It was "illegal" to aid and comfort a Jew in Hitler's Germany. Even so, I am sure that, had I lived in Germany at the time, I would have aided and comforted my Jewish brothers. If today I lived in a Communist country where certain principles dear to the Christian faith are suppressed, I would openly advocate disobeying that country's anti-religious laws.

I must make two honest confessions to you, my Christian and Jewish brothers. First, I must confess that over the past few years I have been gravely disappointed with the white moderate. I have almost reached the regrettable conclusion that the Negro's great stumbling block in his stride toward freedom is not the White Citizen's Counciler or the Ku Klux Klanner, but the white moderate, who is more devoted to "order" than to justice; who prefers a negative peace which is the absence of tension to a positive peace which is the presence of justice; who constantly says, "I agree with you in the goal you seek, but I cannot agree with your methods of direct action"; who paternalistically believes he can set the timetable for another man's freedom; who lives by a mythical concept of time and who constantly advises the Negro to wait for a "more convenient season." Shallow understanding from people of good will is more frustrating than absolute misunderstanding from people of ill will. Lukewarm acceptance is much more bewildering than outright rejection.

I had hoped that the white moderate would understand that law and order exist for the purpose of establishing justice and that when they fail in this purpose they become the dangerously structured dams that block the flow of social progress. I had hoped that the white moderate would understand that the present tension in the South is a necessary phase of the transition from an obnoxious negative peace, in which the Negro passively accepted his unjust plight, to a substantive and

---

[9]In the book of Daniel, Nebuchadnezzar commanded the people to worship a golden statue or be thrown into a furnace of blazing fire. When Shadrach, Meshach, and Abednego refused to worship any god but their own, they were bound and thrown into a blazing furnace, but the fire had no effect on them. Their escape led Nebuchadnezzar to make a decree forbidding blasphemy against their god. [Eds.]

[10]The ancient Greek philosopher Socrates was tried by the Athenians for corrupting their youth through his use of questions to teach. When he refused to change his methods of teaching, he was condemned to death. [Eds.]

[11]The Hungarian anti-Communist uprising of 1956 was quickly crushed by the army of the USSR. [Eds.]

positive peace, in which all men will respect the dignity and worth of human personality. Actually, we who engage in nonviolent direct action are not the creators of tension. We merely bring to the surface the hidden tension that is already alive. We bring it out in the open, where it can be seen and dealt with. Like a boil that can never be cured so long as it is covered up but must be opened with all its ugliness to the natural medicines of air and light, injustice must be exposed, with all the tension its exposure creates, to the light of human conscience and the air of national opinion, before it can be cured.

In your statement you assert that our actions, even though peace- 25 ful, must be condemned because they precipitate violence. But is this a logical assertion? Isn't this like condemning a robbed man because his possession of money precipitated the evil act of robbery? Isn't this like condemning Socrates because his unswerving commitment to truth and his philosophical inquiries precipitated the act by the misguided populace in which they made him drink hemlock? Isn't this like condemning Jesus because his unique God-consciousness and never-ceasing devotion to God's will precipitated the evil act of crucifixion? We must come to see that, as the federal courts have consistently affirmed, it is wrong to urge an individual to cease his efforts to gain his basic constitutional rights because the quest may precipitate violence. Society must protect the robbed and punish the robber.

I had also hoped that the white moderate would reject the myth concerning time in relation to the struggle for freedom. I have just received a letter from a white brother in Texas. He writes: "All Christians know that the colored people will receive equal rights eventually, but it is possible that you are in too great a religious hurry. It has taken Christianity almost two thousand years to accomplish what it has. The teachings of Christ take time to come to earth." Such an attitude stems from a tragic misconception of time, from the strangely irrational notion that there is something in the very flow of time that will inevitably cure all ills. Actually, time itself is neutral; it can be used either destructively or constructively. More and more I feel that the people of ill will have used time much more effectively than have the people of good will. We will have to repent in this generation not merely for the hateful words and actions of the bad people, but for the appalling silence of the good people. Human progress never rolls in on wheels of inevitability; it comes through the tireless efforts of men willing to be co-workers with God, and without this hard work, time itself becomes an ally of the forces of social stagnation. We must use time creatively, in the knowledge that the time is always ripe to do right. Now is the time to make real the promise of democracy and transform our pending national elegy into a creative psalm of brotherhood. Now is the time to lift our national policy from the quicksand of racial injustice to the solid rock of human dignity.

You speak of our activity in Birmingham as extreme. At first I was rather disappointed that fellow clergymen would see my nonviolent efforts as those of an extremist. I began thinking about the fact that I stand in the middle of two opposing forces in the Negro community. One is a force of complacency, made up in part of Negroes who, as a result of long years of oppression, are so drained of self-respect and a sense of "somebodiness" that they have adjusted to segregation; and in part of a few middle-class Negroes who, because of a degree of academic and economic security and because in some ways they profit by segregation, have become insensitive to the problems of the masses. The other force is one of bitterness and hatred, and it comes perilously close to advocating violence. It is expressed in the various black nationalist groups that are springing up across the nation, the largest and best-known being Elijah Muhammad's Muslim movement. Nourished by the Negro's frustration over the continued existence of racial discrimination, this movement is made up of people who have lost faith in America, who have absolutely repudiated Christianity, and who have concluded that the white man is an incorrigible "devil."

I have tried to stand between these two forces, saying that we need emulate neither the "do-nothingism" of the complacent nor the hatred and despair of the black nationalist. For there is the more excellent way of love and nonviolent protest. I am grateful to God that, through the influence of the Negro church, the way of nonviolence became an integral part of our struggle.

If this philosophy had not emerged, by now many streets of the South would, I am convinced, be flowing with blood. And I am further convinced that if our white brothers dismiss as "rabblerousers" and "outside agitators" those of us who employ nonviolent direct action, and if they refuse to support our nonviolent efforts, millions of Negroes will, out of frustration and despair, seek solace and security in black-nationalist ideologies—a development that would inevitably lead to a frightening racial nightmare.

30    Oppressed people cannot remain oppressed forever. The yearning for freedom eventually manifests itself, and that is what has happened to the American Negro. Something within has reminded him of his birthright of freedom, and something without has reminded him that it can be gained. Consciously or unconsciously, he has been caught up by the *Zeitgeist*,[12] and with his black brothers of Africa and his brown and yellow brothers of Asia, South America, and the Caribbean, the United States Negro is moving with a sense of great urgency toward the promised land of racial justice. If one recognizes this vital urge that has engulfed the Negro community, one should readily understand why public demonstrations are taking place. The Negro has many pent-up

---

[12]The spirit of the times. [Eds.]

resentments and latent frustrations, and he must release them. So let him march; let him make prayer pilgrimages to the city hall; let him go on freedom rides—and try to understand why he must do so. If his repressed emotions are not released in nonviolent ways, they will seek expression through violence; this is not a threat but a fact of history. So I have not said to my people, "Get rid of your discontent." Rather, I have tried to say that this normal and healthy discontent can be channeled into the creative outlet of nonviolent direct action. And now this approach is being termed extremist.

But though I was initially disappointed at being categorized as an extremist, as I continued to think about the matter I gradually gained a measure of satisfaction from the label. Was not Jesus an extremist for love: "Love your enemies, bless them that curse you, do good to them that hate you, and pray for them which despitefully use you, and persecute you." Was not Amos an extremist for justice: "Let justice roll down like waters and righteousness like an ever-flowing stream." Was not Paul an extremist for the Christian gospel: "I bear in my body the marks of the Lord Jesus." Was not Martin Luther an extremist: "Here I stand; I cannot do otherwise, so help me God." And John Bunyan: "I will stay in jail to the end of my days before I make a butchery of my conscience." And Abraham Lincoln: "This nation cannot survive half slave and half free." And Thomas Jefferson: "We hold these truths to be self-evident, that all men are created equal. . . . " So the question is not whether we will be extremists, but what kind of extremists we will be. Will we be extremists for hate or for love? Will we be extremists for the preservation of injustice or for the extension of justice? In that dramatic scene on Calvary's hill three men were crucified. We must never forget that all three were crucified for the same thing—the crime of extremism. Two were extremists for immorality, and thus fell below their environment. The other, Jesus Christ, was an extremist for love, truth, and goodness, and thereby rose above his environment. Perhaps the South, the nation, and the world are in dire need of creative extremists.

I had hoped that the white moderate would see this need. Perhaps I was too optimistic; perhaps I expected too much. I suppose I should have realized that few members of the oppressor race can understand the deep groans and passionate yearnings of the oppressed race, and still fewer have the vision to see that injustice must be rooted out by strong, persistent, and determined action. I am thankful, however, that some of our white brothers in the South have grasped the meaning of this social revolution and committed themselves to it. They are still all too few in quantity, but they are big in quality. Some—such as Ralph McGill, Lillian Smith, Harry Golden, James McBride Dabbs, Ann Braden, and Sarah Patton Boyle—have written about our struggle in eloquent and prophetic terms. Others have marched with us down nameless streets of the South. They have languished in filthy, roach-infested jails, suffering the abuse and brutality of policemen who view them as "dirty nigger-lovers." Unlike so many of their moderate brothers and sisters, they have recognized the urgency of the moment and sensed the need for powerful "action" antidotes to combat the disease of segregation.

Let me take note of my other major disappointment. I have been so greatly disappointed with the white church and its leadership. Of course, there are some notable exceptions. I am not unmindful of the fact that each of you has taken some significant stands on this issue. I commend you, Reverend Stallings, for your Christian stand on this past Sunday, in welcoming Negroes to your worship service on a nonsegregated basis. I commend the Catholic leaders of this state for integrating Spring Hill College several years ago.

But despite these notable exceptions, I must honestly reiterate that I have been disappointed with the church. I do not say this as one of those negative critics who can always find something wrong with the church. I say this as a minister of the gospel, who loves the church; who was nurtured in its bosom; who has been sustained by its spiritual blessings and who will remain true to it as long as the cord of life shall lengthen.

35     When I was suddenly catapulted into the leadership of the bus protest in Montgomery, Alabama, a few years ago, I felt we would be supported by the white church. I felt that the white ministers, priests, and rabbis of the South would be among our strongest allies. Instead, some have been outright opponents, refusing to understand the freedom movement and misrepresenting its leaders; all too many others have been more cautious than courageous and have remained silent behind the anesthetizing security of stained glass windows.

In spite of my shattered dreams, I came to Birmingham with the hope that the white religious leadership of this community would see the justice of our cause and, with deep moral concern, would serve as the channel through which our just grievances could reach the power structure. I had hoped that each of you would understand. But again I have been disappointed.

I have heard numerous southern religious leaders admonish their worshipers to comply with a desegregation decision because it is the law, but I have longed to hear white ministers declare: "Follow this decree because integration is morally right and because the Negro is your brother." In the midst of blatant injustices inflicted upon the Negro, I have watched white churchmen stand on the sideline and mouth pious irrelevancies and sanctimonious trivialities. In the midst of a mighty struggle to rid our nation of racial and economic injustice, I have heard many ministers say: "Those are social issues, with which the gospel has no real concern." And I have watched many churches commit themselves to a completely otherworldly religion which makes a strange, un-Biblical distinction between body and soul, between the sacred and the secular.

I have traveled the length and breadth of Alabama, Mississippi, and all the other southern states. On sweltering summer days and crisp autumn mornings I have looked at the South's beautiful churches with their lofty spires pointing heavenward. I have beheld the impressive outlines of her massive religious-education buildings. Over and over I have found myself asking: "What kind of people worship here? Who is their God? Where were their voices when the lips of Governor Barnett[13] dripped with words of interposition and nullification? Where were they when Governor Wallace[14] gave a clarion call for defiance and hatred? Where were their voices of support when bruised and weary Negro men and women decided to rise from the dark dungeons of complacency to the bright hills of creative protest?"

Yes, these questions are still in my mind. In deep disappointment I have wept over the laxity of the church. But be assured that my tears have been tears of love. There can be no deep disappointment where there is not deep love. Yes, I love the church. How could I do otherwise? I am in the rather unique position of being the son, the grandson, and the great-grandson of preachers. Yes, I see the church as the body of Christ. But, oh! How we have blemished and scarred that body through social neglect and through fear of being nonconformists.

There was a time when the church was very powerful—in the time    40
when the early Christians rejoiced at being deemed worthy to suffer for what they believed. In those days the church was not merely a thermometer that recorded the ideas and principles of popular opinion; it was a thermostat that transformed the mores of society. Whenever the early Christians entered a town, the people in power became disturbed and immediately sought to convict the Christians for being "disturbers of the peace" and "outside agitators." But the Christians pressed on, in the conviction that they were "a colony of heaven," called to obey God rather than man. Small in number, they were big in commitment. They were too God-intoxicated to be "astronomically intimidated." By their effort and example they brought an end to such ancient evils as infanticide and gladiatorial contests.

Things are different now. So often the contemporary church is a weak, ineffectual voice with an uncertain sound. So often it is an archdefender to the status quo. Far from being disturbed by the presence of the church, the power structure of the average community is consoled by the church's silent—and often even vocal—sanction of things as they are.

---

[13]Ross Barnett, segregationist governor of Mississippi, who strongly resisted the integration of the University of Mississippi in 1962. [Eds.]

[14]George Wallace, segregationist governor of Alabama, best known for standing in the doorway of a University of Alabama building to block the entrance of two black students who were trying to register. [Eds.]

But the judgment of God is upon the church as never before. If today's church does not recapture the sacrificial spirit of the early church, it will lose its authenticity, forfeit the loyalty of millions, and be dismissed as an irrelevant social club with no meaning for the twentieth century. Every day I meet young people whose disappointment with the church has turned into outright disgust.

Perhaps I have once again been too optimistic. Is organized religion too inextricably bound to the status quo to save our nation and the world? Perhaps I must turn my faith to the inner spiritual church, the church within the church, as the true *ekklesia*[15] and the hope of the world. But again I am thankful to God that some noble souls from the ranks of organized religion have broken loose from the paralyzing chains of conformity and joined us as active partners in the struggle for freedom. They have left their secure congregations and walked the streets of Albany, Georgia, with us. They have gone down the highways of the South on tortuous rides for freedom. Yes, they have gone to jail with us. Some have been dismissed from their churches, have lost the support of their bishops and fellow ministers. But they have acted in the faith that right defeated is stronger than evil triumphant. Their witness has been the spiritual salt that has preserved the true meaning of the gospel in these troubled times. They have carved a tunnel of hope through the dark mountain of disappointment.

I hope the church as a whole will meet the challenge of this decisive hour. But even if the church does not come to the aid of justice, I have no despair about the future. I have no fear about the outcome of our struggle in Birmingham, even if our motives are at present misunderstood. We will reach the goal of freedom in Birmingham and all over the nation, because the goal of America is freedom. Abused and scorned though we may be, our destiny is tied up with America's destiny. Before the pilgrims landed at Plymouth, we were here. Before the pen of Jefferson etched the majestic words of the Declaration of Independence across the pages of history, we were here. For more than two centuries our forebears labored in this country without wages; they made cotton king; they built the homes of their masters while suffering gross injustice and shameful humiliation—and yet out of a bottomless vitality they continued to thrive and develop. If the inexpressible cruelties of slavery could not stop us, the opposition we now face will surely fail. We will win our freedom because the sacred heritage of our nation and the eternal will of God are embodied in our echoing demands.

45    Before closing I feel impelled to mention one other point in your statement that has troubled me profoundly. You warmly commended the Birmingham police force for keeping "order" and "preventing

---

[15]The Greek word for the early Christian church. [Eds.]

violence." I doubt that you would have so warmly commended the police force if you had seen its dogs sinking their teeth into unarmed, nonviolent Negroes. I doubt that you would so quickly commend the policemen if you were to observe their ugly and inhumane treatment of Negroes here in the city jail; if you were to watch them push and curse old Negro women and young Negro girls; if you were to see them slap and kick old Negro men and young boys; if you were to observe them, as they did on two occasions, refuse to give us food because we wanted to sing our grace together. I cannot join you in your praise of the Birmingham police department.

It is true that the police have exercised a degree of discipline in handling the demonstrators. In this sense they have conducted themselves rather "nonviolently" in public. But for what purpose? To preserve the evil system of segregation. Over the past few years I have consistently preached that nonviolence demands that the means we use must be as pure as the ends we seek. I have tried to make clear that it is wrong to use immoral means to attain moral ends. But now I must affirm that it is just as wrong, or perhaps even more so, to use moral means to preserve immoral ends. Perhaps Mr. Connor and his policemen have been rather nonviolent in public, as was Chief Pritchett in Albany, Georgia, but they have used the moral means of nonviolence to maintain the immoral end of racial injustice. As T. S. Eliot[16] has said, "The last temptation is the greatest treason: To do the right deed for the wrong reason."

I wish you had commended the Negro sit-inners and demonstrators of Birmingham for their sublime courage, their willingness to suffer, and their amazing discipline in the midst of great provocation. One day the South will recognize its real heroes. They will be the James Merediths,[17] with the noble sense of purpose that enables them to face jeering and hostile mobs, and with the agonizing loneliness that characterizes the life of the pioneer. They will be old, oppressed, battered Negro women, symbolized in a seventy-two-year-old woman in Montgomery, Alabama, who rose up with a sense of dignity and with her people decided not to ride segregated buses, and who responded with ungrammatical profundity to one who inquired about her weariness: "My feets is tired, but my soul is at rest." They will be the young high school and college students, the young ministers of the gospel and a host of their elders, courageously and nonviolently sitting in at lunch counters and willingly going to jail for conscience' sake. One day the South will know that when these disinherited children of God sat down at lunch counters, they were in reality standing up for what is

---

[16]American-born British poet (1888–1965), winner of the 1948 Nobel Prize in Literature. [Eds.]

[17]First African American to enroll at the University of Mississippi, after federal troops were brought in to control demonstrators protesting his enrollment. [Eds.]

best in the American dream and for the most sacred values in our Judaeo-Christian heritage, thereby bringing our nation back to those great wells of democracy which were dug deep by the founding fathers in their formulation of the Constitution and the Declaration of Independence.

Never before have I written so long a letter. I'm afraid it is much too long to take your precious time. I can assure you that it would have been much shorter if I had been writing from a comfortable desk, but what else can one do when he is alone in a narrow jail cell, other than write long letters, think long thoughts, and pray long prayers?

If I have said anything in this letter that overstates the truth and indicates an unreasonable impatience, I beg you to forgive me. If I have said anything that understates the truth and indicates my having a patience that allows me to settle for anything less than brotherhood, I beg God to forgive me.

I hope this letter finds you strong in the faith. I also hope that circumstances will soon make it possible for me to meet each of you, not as an integrationist or a civil-rights leader but as a fellow clergyman and a Christian brother. Let us all hope that the dark clouds of racial prejudice will soon pass away and the deep fog of misunderstanding will be lifted from our fear-drenched communities, and in some not too distant tomorrow the radiant stars of love and brotherhood will shine over our great nation with all their scintillating beauty.

Yours for the cause of Peace and Brotherhood,

MARTIN LUTHER KING, JR.

## Responding to Reading

1. Do you believe King would have been justified in arguing that he had no alternative other than protest? Would you accept this argument?
2. In paragraph 30, King says, "Oppressed people cannot remain oppressed forever." Do you think world events of the last few years confirm or contradict this statement?
3. Throughout this letter, King uses elaborate diction and complex rhetorical strategies. He addresses his audience directly; makes frequent use of balance and parallelism, understatement, and metaphor; and makes many historical and religious allusions. What effect do you think King intended these rhetorical strategies to have on the letter's original audience of clergymen? Does King's elaborate style enhance his argument, or does it just get in the way?

## Responding in Writing

Write a short manifesto advocating civil disobedience for a cause you strongly believe in. To inspire others to follow the course of action you propose, explain the goal you are seeking, and identify the opposing forces that you believe make civil disobedience necessary. Then, outline the form you expect your peaceful protest to take.

# DOG LAB
## Claire McCarthy
### 1963–

*A graduate of Harvard Medical School, Claire McCarthy is now a primary care physician and the medical communications editor at Children's Hospital Boston. During her medical training, she kept detailed journals, which provided the basis for her books* Learning How the Heart Beats: The Making of a Pediatrician *(1995) and* Everyone's Children: A Pediatrician's Story of an Inner-City Practice *(1998). In the following essay, a chapter from* Learning How the Heart Beats, *McCarthy recalls her reluctance to attend an optional lab lesson in which students studied the cardiovascular system of a sedated living dog, which was then euthanized.*

When I finished college and started medical school, the learning changed fundamentally. Whereas in college I had been learning mostly for learning's sake, learning in order to know something, in medical school I was learning in order to *do* something, do the thing I wanted to do with my life. It was exhilarating and at the same time a little scary. My study now carried responsibility.

The most important course in the first year besides Anatomy was Physiology, the study of the functions and processes of the human body. It was the most fascinating subject I had ever studied. I found the intricacies of the way the body works endlessly intriguing and ingenious: the way the nervous system is designed to differentiate a sharp touch from a soft one; the way muscles move and work together to throw a ball; the wisdom of the kidneys, which filter the blood and let pass out only waste products and extra fluid, keeping everything else carefully within. It was magical to me that each organ and system worked so beautifully and in perfect concert with the rest of the body.

The importance of Physiology didn't lie just in the fact that it was fascinating, however. The other courses I was taking that semester, like Histology and Biochemistry, were fascinating, too. But because Physiology was the study of how the body actually works, it seemed the most pertinent to becoming a physician. The other courses were more abstract. Physiology was practical, and I felt that my ability to master Physiology would be a measure of my ability to be a doctor.

When the second-year students talked about Physiology, they always mentioned "dog lab." They mentioned it briefly but significantly, sharing knowing looks. I gathered that it involved cutting dogs open and that it was controversial, but that was all I knew. I didn't pursue it, I didn't ask questions. That fall I was living day to day, lecture to lecture, test to test. My life was organized around putting as much information into my brain as possible, and I didn't pay much attention to anything else.

5    I would get up around six, make coffee, and eat my bowl of cereal while I sat at my desk. There was nowhere else to sit in my dormitory room, and if I was going to sit at my desk, I figured I might as well study, so I always studied as I ate. I had a small refrigerator and a hot plate so that I could fix myself meals. After breakfast it was off to a morning of lectures, back to the room at lunchtime for a yogurt or soup and more studying, then afternoon lectures and labs. Before dinner I usually went for a run or a swim; although it was necessary for my sanity and my health, I always felt guilty that I wasn't studying instead. I ate dinner at my desk or with other medical students at the cafeteria in Beth Israel Hospital. We sat among the doctors, staff, and patients, eating our food quickly. Although we would try to talk about movies, current affairs, or other "nonmedical" topics, sooner or later we usually ended up talking about medicine; it was fast becoming our whole life. After dinner it was off to the eerie quiet of the library, where I sat surrounded by my textbooks and notes until I got tired or frustrated, which was usually around ten-thirty. Then I'd go back to the dorm, maybe chat with the other students on my floor, maybe watch television, probably study some more, and then fall asleep so that I could start the routine all over again the next morning.

My life had never been so consuming. Sometimes I felt like a true student in the best sense of the word, wonderfully absorbed in learning; other times I felt like an automaton. I was probably a combination of the two. It bothered me sometimes that this process of teaching me to take care of people was making me live a very study-centered, self-centered life. However, it didn't seem as though I had a choice.

One day at the beginning of a physiology lecture the instructor announced that we would be having a laboratory exercise to study the cardiovascular system, and that dogs would be used. The room was quickly quiet; this was the infamous "dog lab." The point of the exercise, he explained, was to study the heart and blood vessels in vivo[1] to learn the effects of different conditions and chemicals by seeing them rather than just by reading about them. The dogs would be sedated and the changes in their heart rates, respiratory rates, and blood pressure would be monitored with each experiment. As the last part of the exercise the sleeping dogs' chests would be cut open so we could actually watch the hearts and lungs in action, and then the dogs would be killed, humanely. We would be divided up into teams of four, and each team would work with a teaching assistant. Because so many teaching assistants were required, the class would be divided in half, and the lab would be held on two days.

The amphitheater buzzed.

---

[1]Latin phrase for "in the living being." [Eds.]

The lab was optional, the instructor told us. We would not be marked off in any way if we chose not to attend. He leaned against the side of the podium and said that the way he saw it there was a spectrum of morality when it came to animal experimentation. The spectrum, he said, went from mice or rats to species like horses or apes, and we had to decide at which species we would draw our lines. He hoped, though, that we would choose to attend. It was an excellent learning opportunity, and he thought we ought to take advantage of it. Then he walked behind the podium and started the day's lecture.

It was all anyone could talk about: should we do dog lab or 10 shouldn't we? We discussed it endlessly.

There were two main camps. One was the "excellent learning opportunity" camp, which insisted that dog lab was the kind of science we came to medical school to do and that learning about the cardiovascular system on a living animal would make it more understandable and would therefore make us better doctors.

Countering them was the "importance of a life" camp. The extreme members of this camp insisted that it was always wrong to murder an animal for experimentation. The more moderate members argued that perhaps animal experimentation was useful in certain kinds of medical research, but that dog lab was purely an exercise for our education and didn't warrant the killing of a dog. We could learn the material in other ways, they said.

On and on the arguments went, with people saying the same things over and over again in every conceivable way. There was something very important about this decision. Maybe it was because we were just beginning to figure out how to define ourselves as physicians—were we scientists, eager for knowledge, or were we defenders of life? The dog lab seemed to pit one against the other. Maybe it was because we thought that our lives as physicians were going to be filled with ethical decisions, and this was our first since entering medical school. It was very important that we do the right thing, but the right thing seemed variable and unclear.

I was quiet during these discussions. I didn't want to kill a dog, but I certainly wanted to take advantage of every learning opportunity offered me. And despite the fact that the course instructor had said our grades wouldn't be affected if we didn't attend the lab, I wasn't sure I believed him, and I didn't want to take any chances. Even if he didn't incorporate the lab report into our grades, I was worried that there would be some reference to it in the final exam, some sneaky way that he would bring it up. Doing well had become so important that I was afraid to trust anyone; doing well had become more important than anything.

I found myself waiting to see what other people would decide. I 15 was ashamed not to be taking a stand, but I was stuck in a way I'd never been before. I didn't like the idea of doing the lab; it felt wrong. Yet for some reason I was embarrassed that I felt that way, and the lab seemed so important. The more I thought about it, the more confused I became.

Although initially the students had appeared divided more or less evenly between the camps, as the lab day drew nearer the majority chose to participate. The discussions didn't stop, but they were fewer and quieter. The issue seemed to become more private.

I was assigned to the second lab day. My indecision was becoming a decision since I hadn't crossed my name off the list. I can still change my mind, I told myself. I'm not on a team yet, nobody's counting on me to show up. One of my classmates asked me to join his group. I hedged.

The day before group lists had to be handed in, the course instructor made an announcement. It was brief and almost offhand: he said that if any of us wished to help anesthetize the dogs for the lab, we were welcome to do so. He told us where to go and when to be there for each lab day. I wrote the information down.

Somehow, this was what I needed. I made my decision. I would do the lab, but I would go help anesthetize the dogs first.

20    Helping with the anesthesia, I thought, would be taking full responsibility for what I was doing, something that was very important to me. I was going to *face* what I was doing, see the dogs awake with their tails wagging instead of meeting them asleep and sort of pretending they weren't real. I also thought it might make me feel better to know that the dogs were treated well as they were anesthetized and to be there, helping to do it gently. Maybe in part I thought of it as my penance.

The day of the first lab came. Around five o'clock I went down to the Friday afternoon "happy hour" in the dormitory living room to talk to the students as they came back. They came back singly or in pairs, quiet, looking dazed. They threw down their coats and backpacks and made their way to the beer and soda without talking to anyone. Some, once they had a cup in their hands, seemed to relax and join in conversations; others took their cups and sat alone on the couches. They all looked tired, worn out.

"Well?" I asked several of them. "What was it like?"

Most shrugged and said little. A few said that it was interesting and that they'd learned a lot, but they said it without any enthusiasm. Every one of them said it was hard. I thought I heard someone say that their dog had turned out to be pregnant. Nobody seemed happy.

The morning of my lab was gray and dreary. I overslept, which I hardly ever do. I got dressed quickly and went across the street to the back entrance of the lab building. It was quiet and still and a little dark. The streets were empty except for an occasional cab. I found the open door and went in.

There was only one other student waiting there, a blond-haired 25 woman named Elise. I didn't know her well. We had friends in common, but we'd never really talked. She was sweet and soft-spoken; she wore old jeans and plaid flannel shirts and hung out with the activist crowd. She had always intimidated me. I felt as though I weren't political enough when I was around her. I was actually a little surprised that she was doing the lab at all, as many of her friends had chosen not to.

We greeted each other awkwardly, nodding hello and taking our places leaning against the wall. Within a few minutes one of the teaching assistants came in, said good morning, pulled out some keys, and let us into a room down the hall. Two more teaching assistants followed shortly.

The teaching assistants let the dogs out of cages, and they ran around the room. They were small dogs; I think they were beagles. They seemed happy to be out of their cages, and one of them, white with brown spots, came over to me with his tail wagging. I leaned over to pet him, and he licked my hand, looking up at me eagerly. I stood up again quickly.

The teaching assistant who had let us in, a short man with tousled brown hair and thick glasses, explained that the dogs were to be given intramuscular injections of a sedative that would put them to sleep. During the lab they would be given additional doses intravenously as well as other medications to stop them from feeling pain. We could help, he said, by holding the dogs while they got their injections. Elise and I nodded.

So we held the dogs, and they got their injections. After a few minutes they started to stumble, and we helped them to the floor. I remember that Elise petted one of the dogs as he fell asleep and that she cried. I didn't cry, but I wanted to.

When we were finished, I went back to my room. I sat at my desk, 30 drank my coffee, and read over the lab instructions again. I kept thinking about the dogs running around, about the little white one with the brown spots, and I felt sick. I stared at the instructions without really reading them, looking at my watch every couple of minutes. At five minutes before eight I picked up the papers, put them in my backpack with my books, and left.

The lab was held in a big open room with white walls and lots of windows. The dogs were laid out on separate tables lined up across the room; they were on their backs, tied down. They were all asleep, but some of them moved slightly, and it chilled me.

We walked in slowly and solemnly, putting our coats and backpacks on the rack along the wall and going over to our assigned tables. I started to look for the dog who had licked my hand, but I stopped myself. I didn't want to know where he was.

Our dog was brown and black, with soft floppy ears. His eyes were shut. He looked familiar. We took our places, two on each side of the table, laid out our lab manuals, and began.

The lab took all day. We cut through the dog's skin to find an artery and vein, into which we placed catheters. We injected different drugs and chemicals and watched what happened to the dog's heart rate and blood pressure, carefully recording the results. At the end of the day, when we were done with the experiments, we cut open the dog's chest. We cut through his sternum and pulled open his rib cage. His heart and lungs lay in front of us. The heart was a fist-size muscle that squeezed itself as it beat, pushing blood out. The lungs were white and solid and glistening under the pleura that covered them. The instructor pointed out different blood vessels, like the aorta and the superior vena cava. He showed us the stellate ganglion, which really did look like a star. I think we used the electrical paddles of a defibrillator and shocked the dog's heart into ventricular fibrillation, watching it shiver like Jell-O in front of us. I think that's how we killed them—or maybe it was with a lethal dose of one of the drugs. I'm not sure. It's something I guess I don't want to remember.

35    Dan was the anesthesiologist, the person assigned to making sure that the dog stayed asleep throughout the entire procedure. Every once in a while Dan would get caught up in the experiment and the dog would start to stir. I would nudge Dan, and he would quickly give more medication. The dog never actually woke up, but every time he moved even the slightest bit, every time I had to think about him being a real dog who was never going to wag his tail or lick any-one's hand again because of us, I got so upset that I couldn't concen-trate. In fact, I had trouble concentrating on the lab in general. I kept staring at the dog.

As soon as we were finished, or maybe a couple of minutes before, I left. I grabbed my coat and backpack and ran down the stairs out into the dusk of the late afternoon. It was drizzling, and the medical school looked brown and gray. I walked quickly toward the street.

I was disappointed in the lab and disappointed in myself for doing it. I knew now that doing the lab was wrong. Maybe not wrong for everyone—it was clearly a complicated and individual choice—but wrong for me. The knowledge I had gained wasn't worth the life of a dog to me. I felt very sad.

The drizzle was becoming rain. I slowed down; even though it was cold, the rain felt good. A couple of people walking past me put up their umbrellas. I let the rain fall on me. I wanted to get wet.

From the moment you enter the field of medicine as a medical stu-dent, you have an awareness that you have entered something bigger and more important than you are. Doctors are different from other people, we are told implicitly, if not explicitly. Medicine is a way of life, with its own values and guidelines for daily living. They aren't bad values; they include things like the importance of hard work, the pursuit of knowledge, and the preservation of life—at least human life. There's room for individuality and variation, but that's something I realized later, much later. When I started medical school I felt that not only did I have to learn information and skills, I had to become a certain kind of person, too. It was very important to me to learn to do the thing that a doctor would do in a given situation. Since the course instructor, who represented Harvard Medical School to me, had recommended that we do the lab, I figured that a doctor would do it. That wasn't the only reason I went ahead with the lab, but it was a big reason.

The rain started to come down harder and felt less pleasant. I 40 walked more quickly, across Longwood Avenue into Vanderbilt Hall. I could hear familiar voices coming from the living room, but I didn't feel like talking to anyone. I ducked into the stairwell.

I got to my room, locked the door behind me, took off my coat, and lay down on my bed. The rain beat against my window. It was the time I usually went running, but the thought of going back out in the rain didn't appeal to me at all. I was suddenly very tired.

As I lay there I thought about the course instructor's discussion of the spectrum of morality and drawing lines. Maybe it's not a matter of deciding which animals I feel comfortable killing, I thought. Maybe it's about drawing different kinds of lines: drawing the lines to define how much of myself I will allow to change. I was proud of being a true student, even if it did mean becoming a little like an automaton. But I still needed to be the person I was before; I needed to be able to make some decisions without worrying about what a doctor would do.

I got up off the bed, opened a can of soup, and put it in a pan on the hot plate to warm. I got some bread and cheese out of the refrigerator, sat down at my desk, and opened my Biochemistry text.

Suddenly I stopped. I closed the text, reached over, and turned on the television, which sat on a little plastic table near the desk. There would be time to study later. I was going to watch television, read a newspaper, and call some friends I hadn't called since starting medical school. It was time to make some changes, some changes back.

## Responding to Reading

1. Summarize the two main schools of thought about whether or not to participate in "dog lab." Do the students really have a choice? Explain.
2. Why did McCarthy decide to help anesthetize the dogs? Does her decision make sense to you?
3. Does McCarthy believe that the knowledge she gained was worth the sacrifice of the dog? Do you agree with her? Do you think her experience in "dog lab" changed her? Do you think it made her a better doctor?

## Responding in Writing

Do you see a difference in the relative value of the lives of a laboratory animal, an animal in the wild, and a pet? Or, do you think the lives of all three kinds of animals have equal value? Explain your beliefs.

# A Modest Proposal

## Jonathan Swift

### 1667–1745

*Jonathan Swift was an Irish essayist, satirist, and poet. He wrote numerous works, many of which dealt with Irish/British political tensions and religious issues. His best-known works include* A Tale of a Tub *(1704),* Gulliver's Travels *(1726), and "A Modest Proposal" (1729), which follows. In this essay, Swift proposes a satirical solution to a social and ethical problem.*

It is a melancholy object to those, who walk through this great town, or travel in the country, when they see the streets, the roads and cabbin-doors crowded with beggars of the female sex, followed by three, four, or six children, all in rags, and importuning every passenger for an alms. These mothers instead of being able to work for their honest livelihood, are forced to employ all their time in stroling to beg sustenance for their helpless infants who, as they grow up, either turn thieves for want of work, or leave their dear native country, to fight for the Pretender in Spain,[1] or sell themselves to the Barbadoes.

I think it is agreed by all parties, that this prodigious number of children in the arms, or on the backs, or at the heels of their mothers, and frequently of their fathers, is in the present deplorable state of the kingdom, a very great additional grievance; and therefore whoever could find out a fair, cheap and easy method of making these children sound and useful members of the common-wealth, would deserve so well of the publick, as to have his statue set up for a preserver of the nation.

But my intention is very far from being confined to provide only for the children of professed beggars: it is of a much greater extent, and shall take in the whole number of infants at a certain age, who are born of parents in effect as little able to support them, as those who demand our charity in the streets.

As to my own part, having turned my thoughts for many years, upon this important subject, and maturely weighed the several schemes of our projectors, I have always found them grossly mistaken in their computation. It is true, a child just dropt from its dam, may be supported by her milk, for a solar year, with little other nourishment:

---

[1]The descendant of King James II (1644–85), who, as a Catholic, was an exile in Spain. [Eds.]

at most not above the value of two shillings, which the mother may certainly get, or the value in scraps, by her lawful occupation of begging; and it is exactly at one year old that I propose to provide for them in such a manner, as, instead of being a charge upon their parents, or the parish, or wanting food and raiment for the rest of their lives, they shall, on the contrary, contribute to the feeding, and partly to the cloathing of many thousands.

There is likewise another great advantage in my scheme, that it will prevent those voluntary abortions, and that horrid practice of women murdering their bastard children, alas! too frequent among us, sacrificing the poor innocent babes, I doubt, more to avoid the expence than the shame, which would move tears and pity in the most savage and inhuman breast.

The number of souls in this kingdom being usually reckoned one million and a half, of these I calculate there may be about two hundred thousand couple whose wives are breeders; from which number I subtract thirty thousand couple, who are able to maintain their own children, (although I apprehend there cannot be so many, under the present distresses of the kingdom) but this being granted, there will remain an hundred and seventy thousand breeders. I again subtract fifty thousand, for those women who miscarry, or whose children die by accident or disease within the year. There only remain an hundred and twenty thousand children of poor parents annually born. The question therefore is, How this number shall be reared, and provided for? which, as I have already said, under the present situation of affairs, is utterly impossible by all the methods hitherto proposed. For we can neither employ them in handicraft or agriculture; we neither build houses, (I mean in the country) nor cultivate land: they can very seldom pick up a livelihood by stealing till they arrive at six years old; except where they are of towardly parts, although I confess they learn the rudiments much earlier; during which time they can however be properly looked upon only as probationers: As I have been informed by a principal gentleman in the county of Cavan, who protested to me, that he never knew above one or two instances under the age of six, even in a part of the kingdom so renowned for the quickest proficiency in that art.

I am assured by our merchants, that a boy or a girl before twelve years old, is no saleable commodity, and even when they come to this age, they will not yield above three pounds, or three pounds and half a crown at most, on the exchange; which cannot turn to account either to the parents or kingdom, the charge of nutriments and rags having been at least four times that value.

I shall now therefore humbly propose my own thoughts, which I hope will not be liable to the least objection.

I have been assured by a very knowing American of my acquaintance in London, that a young healthy child well nursed, is, at a year old, a most delicious nourishing and wholesome food, whether stewed, roasted, baked, or boiled; and I make no doubt that it will equally serve in a fricasie, or a ragoust.

10     I do therefore humbly offer it to publick consideration, that of the hundred and twenty thousand children, already computed, twenty thousand may be reserved for breed, whereof only one fourth part to be males; which is more than we allow to sheep, black cattle, or swine, and my reason is, that these children are seldom the fruits of marriage, a circumstance not much regarded by our savages, therefore, one male will be sufficient to serve four females. That the remaining hundred thousand may, at a year old, be offered in sale to the persons of quality and fortune, through the kingdom, always advising the mother to let them suck plentifully in the last month, so as to render them plump, and fat for a good table. A child will make two dishes at an entertainment for friends, and when the family dines alone, the fore or hind quarter will make a reasonable dish, and seasoned with a little pepper or salt, will be very good boiled on the fourth day, especially in winter.

I have reckoned upon a medium, that a child just born will weigh 12 pounds, and in a solar year, if tolerably nursed, encreaseth to 28 pounds.

I grant this food will be somewhat dear, and therefore very proper for landlords, who, as they have already devoured most of the parents, seem to have the best title to the children.

Infant's flesh will be in season throughout the year, but more plentiful in March, and a little before and after; for we are told by a grave author,[2] an eminent French physician, that fish being a prolifick dyet, there are more children born in Roman Catholick countries about nine months after Lent, the markets will be more glutted than usual, because the number of Popish infants, is at least three to one in this kingdom, and therefore it will have one other collateral advantage, by lessening the number of Papists among us.

I have already computed the charge of nursing a beggar's child (in which list I reckon all cottagers, labourers, and four-fifths of the farmers) to be about two shillings per annum, rags included; and I believe no gentleman would repine to give ten shillings for the carcass of a good fat child, which, as I have said, will make four dishes of excellent nutritive meat, when he hath only some particular friend, or his own family to dine with him. Thus the squire will learn to be a good landlord, and grow popular among his tenants, the mother will have eight shillings neat profit, and be fit for work till she produces another child.

15     Those who are more thrifty (as I must confess the times require) may flea the carcass; the skin of which, artificially dressed, will make admirable gloves for ladies, and summer boots for fine gentlemen.

As to our City of Dublin, shambles may be appointed for this purpose, in the most convenient parts of it, and butchers we may be assured

---

[2]François Rabelais (1494–1553?). [Eds.]

will not be wanting; although I rather recommend buying the children alive, and dressing them hot from the knife, as we do roasting pigs.

A very worthy person, a true lover of his country, and whose virtues I highly esteem, was lately pleased, in discoursing on this matter, to offer a refinement upon my scheme. He said, that many gentlemen of this kingdom, having of late destroyed their deer, he conceived that the want of venison might be well supply'd by the bodies of young lads and maidens, not exceeding fourteen years of age, nor under twelve; so great a number of both sexes in every country being now ready to starve for want of work and service: And these to be disposed of by their parents if alive, or otherwise by their nearest relations. But with due deference to so excellent a friend, and so deserving a patriot, I cannot be altogether in his sentiments; for as to the males, my American acquaintance assured me from frequent experience, that their flesh was generally tough and lean, like that of our school-boys, by continual exercise, and their taste disagreeable, and to fatten them would not answer the charge. Then as to the females, it would, I think, with humble submission, be a loss to the publick, because they soon would become breeders themselves: And besides, it is not improbable that some scrupulous people might be apt to censure such a practice, (although indeed very unjustly) as a little bordering upon cruelty, which, I confess, hath always been with me the strongest objection against any project, how well soever intended.

But in order to justify my friend, he confessed, that this expedient was put into his head by the famous Salmanaazor,[3] a native of the island Formosa, who came from thence to London, above twenty years ago, and in conversation told my friend, that in his country, when any young person happened to be put to death, the executioner sold the carcass to persons of quality, as a prime dainty; and that, in his time, the body of a plump girl of fifteen, who was crucified for an attempt to poison the Emperor, was sold to his imperial majesty's prime minister of state, and other great mandarins of the court in joints from the gibbet, at four hundred crowns. Neither indeed can I deny, that if the same use were made of several plump young girls in this town, who without one single groat to their fortunes, cannot stir abroad without a chair, and appear at a play-house and assemblies in foreign fineries which they never will pay for; the kingdom would not be the worse.

Some persons of a desponding spirit are in great concern about that vast number of poor people, who are aged, diseased, or maimed; and I have been desired to employ my thoughts what course may be taken, to ease the nation of so grievous an incumbrance. But I am not in the least pain upon that matter, because it is very well known, that they are every day dying, and rotting, by cold and famine, and filth, and vermin, as fast as can be reasonably expected. And as to the young labourers, they are now in almost as hopeful a condition. They cannot get work,

---

[3]George Psalmanazar (1679?–1763), a Frenchman who fraudulently claimed to come from Formosa (now Taiwan), which he wrote about in a book. [Eds.]

and consequently pine away from want of nourishment, to a degree, that if at any time they are accidentally hired to common labour, they have not strength to perform it, and thus the country and themselves are happily delivered from the evils to come.

20    I have too long digressed, and therefore shall return to my subject. I think the advantages by the proposal which I have made are obvious and many, as well as of the highest importance.

For first, as I have already observed, it would greatly lessen the number of Papists, with whom we are yearly over-run, being the principal breeders of the nation, as well as our most dangerous enemies, and who stay at home on purpose with a design to deliver the kingdom to the Pretender, hoping to take their advantage by the absence of so many good Protestants, who have chosen rather to leave their country, than stay at home and pay tithes against their conscience to an episcopal curate.

Secondly, The poorer tenants will have something valuable of their own, which by law may be made liable to a distress, and help to pay their landlord's rent, their corn and cattle being already seized, and money a thing unknown.

Thirdly, Whereas the maintainance of an hundred thousand children, from two years old, and upwards, cannot be computed at less than ten shillings a piece per annum, the nation's stock will be thereby encreased fifty thousand pounds per annum, besides the profit of a new dish, introduced to the tables of all gentlemen of fortune in the kingdom, who have any refinement in taste. And the money will circulate among our selves, the goods being entirely of our own growth and manufacture.

Fourthly, The constant breeders, besides the gain of eight shillings sterling per annum by the sale of their children, will be rid of the charge of maintaining them after the first year.

25    Fifthly, This food would likewise bring great custom to taverns, where the vintners will certainly be so prudent as to procure the best receipts for dressing it to perfection; and consequently have their houses frequented by all the fine gentlemen, who justly value themselves upon their knowledge in good eating; and a skilful cook, who understands how to oblige his guests, will contrive to make it as expensive as they please.

Sixthly, This would be a great inducement to marriage, which all wise nations have either encouraged by rewards, or enforced by laws and penalties. It would encrease the care and tenderness of mothers towards their children, when they were sure of a settlement for life to the poor babes, provided in some sort by the publick, to their annual profit instead of expence. We should soon see an honest emulation among the married women, which of them could bring the fattest child to the market. Men would become as fond of their wives, during the time of their pregnancy, as they are now of their mares in foal, their cows in calf, or sow when they are ready to farrow; nor offer to beat or kick them (as is too frequent a practice) for fear of a miscarriage.

Many other advantages might be enumerated. For instance, the addition of some thousand carcasses in our exportation of barrel'd beef: the propagation of swine's flesh, and improvement in the art of making good bacon, so much wanted among us by the great destruction of pigs, too frequent at our tables; which are no way comparable in taste or magnificence to a well grown, fat yearly child, which roasted whole will make a considerable figure at a Lord Mayor's feast, or any other publick entertainment. But this, and many others, I omit, being studious of brevity.

Supposing that one thousand families in this city, would be constant customers for infants flesh, besides others who might have it at merry meetings, particularly at weddings and christenings, I compute that Dublin would take off annually about twenty thousand carcasses; and the rest of the kingdom (where probably they will be sold somewhat cheaper) the remaining eighty thousand.

I can think of no one objection, that will possibly be raised against this proposal, unless it should be urged, that the number of people will be thereby much lessened in the kingdom. This I freely own, and 'twas indeed one principal design in offering it to the world. I desire the reader will observe, that I calculate my remedy for this one individual Kingdom of Ireland, and for no other that ever was, is, or, I think, ever can be upon Earth. Therefore let no man talk to me of other expedients: Of taxing our absentees at five shillings a pound: Of using neither cloaths, nor houshold furniture, except what is of our own growth and manufacture: Of utterly rejecting the materials and instruments that promote foreign luxury: Of curing the expensiveness of pride, vanity, idleness, and gaming in our women: Of introducing a vein of parsimony, prudence and temperance: Of learning to love our country, wherein we differ even from Laplanders, and the inhabitants of Topinamboo: Of quitting our animosities and factions, nor acting any longer like the Jews, who were murdering one another at the very moment their city was taken: Of being a little cautious not to sell our country and consciences for nothing: Of teaching landlords to have at least one degree of mercy towards their tenants. Lastly, of putting a spirit of honesty, industry, and skill into our shop-keepers, who, if a resolution could now be taken to buy only our native goods, would immediately unite to cheat and exact upon us in the price, the measure, and the goodness, nor could ever yet be brought to make one fair proposal of just dealing, though often and earnestly invited to it.

Therefore I repeat, let no man talk to me of these and the like expedients, 'till he hath at least some glympse of hope, that there will ever be some hearty and sincere attempt to put them into practice. 30

But, as to my self, having been wearied out for many years with offering vain, idle, visionary thoughts, and at length utterly despairing of success, I fortunately fell upon this proposal, which, as it is wholly new, so it hath something solid and real, of no expence and little trouble, full in our own power, and whereby we can incur no danger in disobliging England.

For this kind of commodity will not bear exportation, and flesh being of too tender a consistence, to admit a long continuance in salt, although perhaps I could name a country, which would be glad to eat up our whole nation without it.

After all, I am not so violently bent upon my own opinion, as to reject any offer, proposed by wise men, which shall be found equally innocent, cheap, easy, and effectual. But before something of that kind shall be advanced in contradiction to my scheme, and offering a better, I desire the author or authors will be pleased maturely to consider two points. First, As things now stand, how they will be able to find food and raiment for a hundred thousand useless mouths and backs. And secondly, There being a round million of creatures in humane figure throughout this kingdom, whose whole subsistence put into a common stock, would leave them in debt two million of pounds sterling, adding those who are beggars by profession, to the bulk of farmers, cottagers and labourers, with their wives and children, who are beggars in effect; I desire those politicians who dislike my overture, and may perhaps be so bold to attempt an answer, that they will first ask the parents of these mortals, whether they would not at this day think it a great happiness to have been sold for food at a year old, in the manner I prescribe, and thereby have avoided such a perpetual scene of misfortunes, as they have since gone through, by the oppression of landlords, the impossibility of paying rent without money or trade, the want of common sustenance, with neither house nor cloaths to cover them from the inclemencies of the weather, and the most inevitable prospect of intailing the like, or greater miseries, upon their breed for ever.

I profess, in the sincerity of my heart, that I have not the least personal interest in endeavouring to promote this necessary work, having no other motive than the publick good of my country, by advancing our trade, providing for infants, relieving the poor, and giving some pleasure to the rich. I have no children, by which I can propose to get a single penny; the youngest being nine years old, and my wife past child-bearing.

## Responding to Reading

1. In this essay, Swift identifies a serious problem. What is this problem? How would his "modest proposal" solve it?
2. In what respects does Swift believe that the British government's treatment of the Irish is unethical? Do you think his purpose in this essay is just to get readers to think more deeply about this problem, or do you think he expects them to take some kind of action?
3. Find a definition of *satire*. How does "A Modest Proposal" fit this definition?

## Responding in Writing

Write your own satirical "modest proposal" for solving a problem on your college campus—for example, academic cheating, student debt, or binge drinking.

— FOCUS —

## What Has Happened to Academic Integrity?

*Google* search results for "student papers for sale"

## Responding to the Image

1. What, if anything, does the list pictured above tell you about the state of academic integrity in the 21st century? Could you argue that the availability of papers for sale is irrelevant to the way students view plagiarism?
2. Do your own search for "student papers for sale," click on one of the links listed, and evaluate the site it leads you to. Do you think this site makes an effective appeal to its intended audience? Why or why not? (Remember to evaluate the site's language as well as its content and appearance.)
3. Some term paper sites include a disclaimer stating that they assume users will not hand in the papers they purchase but will rather use them as research sources. What is your response to such disclaimers?

# PLAGIARISM LINES BLUR FOR STUDENTS IN DIGITAL AGE

## Trip Gabriel

### 1955–

*A reporter for the* New York Times, *Trip Gabriel writes on issues related to education and politics. In the following essay, Gabriel considers the changing nature of academic integrity in the Internet Age.*

At Rhode Island College, a freshman copied and pasted from a Web site's frequently asked questions page about homelessness—and did not think he needed to credit a source in his assignment because the page did not include author information.

At DePaul University, the tip-off to one student's copying was the purple shade of several paragraphs he had lifted from the Web; when confronted by a writing tutor his professor had sent him to, he was not defensive—he just wanted to know how to change purple text to black.

And at the University of Maryland, a student reprimanded for copying from *Wikipedia* in a paper on the Great Depression said he thought its entries—unsigned and collectively written—did not need to be credited since they counted, essentially, as common knowledge.

Professors used to deal with plagiarism by admonishing students to give credit to others and to follow the style guide for citations, and pretty much left it at that.

5      But these cases—typical ones, according to writing tutors and officials responsible for discipline at the three schools who described the plagiarism—suggest that many students simply do not grasp that using words they did not write is a serious misdeed.

It is a disconnect that is growing in the Internet age as concepts of intellectual property, copyright and originality are under assault in the unbridled exchange of online information, say educators who study plagiarism.

Digital technology makes copying and pasting easy, of course. But that is the least of it. The Internet may also be redefining how students—who came of age with music file-sharing, *Wikipedia* and Web-linking—understand the concept of authorship and the singularity of any text or image.

"Now we have a whole generation of students who've grown up with information that just seems to be hanging out there in cyberspace and doesn't seem to have an author," said Teresa Fishman, director of the Center for Academic Integrity at Clemson University. "It's possible to believe this information is just out there for anyone to take."

Professors who have studied plagiarism do not try to excuse it—many are champions of academic honesty on their campuses—but rather try to understand why it is so widespread.

In surveys from 2006 to 2010 by Donald L. McCabe, a co-founder of the Center for Academic Integrity and a business professor at Rutgers University, about 40 percent of 14,000 undergraduates admitted to copying a few sentences in written assignments.

Perhaps more significant, the number who believed that copying from the Web constitutes "serious cheating" is declining—to 29 percent on average in recent surveys from 34 percent earlier in the decade.

Sarah Brookover, a senior at the Rutgers campus in Camden, N.J., said many of her classmates blithely cut and paste without attribution.

"This generation has always existed in a world where media and intellectual property don't have the same gravity," said Ms. Brookover, who at 31 is older than most undergraduates. "When you're sitting at your computer, it's the same machine you've downloaded music with, possibly illegally, the same machine you streamed videos for free that showed on HBO last night."

Ms. Brookover, who works at the campus library, has pondered the differences between researching in the stacks and online. "Because you're not walking into a library you're not physically holding the article, which takes you closer to 'this doesn't belong to me,'" she said. Online, "everything can belong to you really easily."

A University of Notre Dame anthropologist, Susan D. Blum, disturbed by the high rates of reported plagiarism, set out to understand how students view authorship and the written word, or "texts" in Ms. Blum's academic language.

She conducted her ethnographic research among 234 Notre Dame undergraduates. "Today's students stand at the crossroads of a new way of conceiving texts and the people who create them and who quote them," she wrote last year in the book *My Word!: Plagiarism and College Culture*, published by Cornell University Press.

Ms. Blum argued that student writing exhibits some of the same qualities of pastiche that drive other creative endeavors today—TV shows that constantly reference other shows or rap music that samples from earlier songs.

In an interview, she said the idea of an author whose singular effort creates an original work is rooted in Enlightenment ideas of the individual. It is buttressed by the Western concept of intellectual property rights as secured by copyright law. But both traditions are being challenged.

"Our notion of authorship and originality was born, it flourished, and it may be waning," Ms. Blum said.

She contends that undergraduates are less interested in cultivating a unique and authentic identity—as their 1960s counterparts were—than in trying on many different personas, which the Web enables with social networking.

"If you are not so worried about presenting yourself as absolutely unique, then it's O.K. if you say other people's words, it's O.K. if you say things you don't believe, it's O.K. if you write papers you couldn't care less about because they accomplish the task, which is turning something in and getting a grade," Ms. Blum said, voicing student attitudes. "And it's O.K. if you put words out there without getting any credit."

The notion that there might be a new model young person, who freely borrows from the vortex of information to mash up a new creative work, fueled a brief brouhaha earlier this year with Helene Hegemann, a German teenager whose best-selling novel about Berlin club life turned out to include passages lifted from others.

Instead of offering an abject apology, Ms. Hegemann insisted, "There's no such thing as originality anyway, just authenticity." A few critics rose to her defense, and the book remained a finalist for a fiction prize (but did not win).

That theory does not wash with Sarah Wilensky, a senior at Indiana University, who said that relaxing plagiarism standards "does not foster creativity, it fosters laziness."

25     "You're not coming up with new ideas if you're grabbing and mixing and matching," said Ms. Wilensky, who took aim at Ms. Hegemann in a column in her student newspaper headlined "Generation Plagiarism."

"It may be increasingly accepted, but there are still plenty of creative people—authors and artists and scholars—who are doing original work," Ms. Wilensky said in an interview. "It's kind of an insult that that ideal is gone, and now we're left only to make collages of the work of previous generations."

In the view of Ms. Wilensky, whose writing skills earned her the role of informal editor of other students' papers in her freshman dorm, plagiarism has nothing to do with trendy academic theories.

The main reason it occurs, she said, is because students leave high school unprepared for the intellectual rigors of college writing.

"If you're taught how to closely read sources and synthesize them into your own original argument in middle and high school, you're not going to be tempted to plagiarize in college, and you certainly won't do so unknowingly," she said.

30     At the University of California, Davis, of the 196 plagiarism cases referred to the disciplinary office last year, a majority did not involve students ignorant of the need to credit the writing of others.

Many times, said Donald J. Dudley, who oversees the discipline office on the campus of 32,000, it was students who intentionally copied—knowing it was wrong—who were "unwilling to engage the writing process."

"Writing is difficult, and doing it well takes time and practice," he said.

And then there was a case that had nothing to do with a younger generation's evolving view of authorship. A student accused of plagiarism came to Mr. Dudley's office with her parents, and the father admitted that he was the one responsible for the plagiarism. The wife assured Mr. Dudley that it would not happen again.

## Responding to Reading

1. What is Gabriel's purpose in writing this article? Does he simply want to present information, or does he want to make a point about the issue he discusses?
2. According to Gabriel, how—and why—have the "concepts of intellectual property, copyright and originality" (6) changed in the Internet Age?
3. Gabriel quotes a number of experts (and nonexperts). Do these quotations present a balanced view of the issue, or should he have included comments from other sources as well? Explain.

## Responding in Writing

Do you think Gabriel is excusing students who plagiarize unintentionally? Do you think such unintentional plagiarism should be punished? If so, how?

# THE TRUTH ABOUT PLAGIARISM

## Richard A. Posner

### 1939–

*A judge of the U.S. Court of Appeals for the Seventh Circuit and a senior lecturer at the University of Chicago Law School, Richard A. Posner is a legal expert whose work focuses on the economics of intellectual property and health policy. A contributor to the* Becker-Posner Blog, *he has written numerous academic articles, book reviews, and books, including the recent book* The Crisis of Capitalist Democracy *(2010). In the following essay, Posner considers the difference between plagiarism and theft.*

Plagiarism is considered by most writers, teachers, journalists, scholars and even members of the general public to be the capital intellectual crime. Being caught out in plagiarism can blast a politician's career, earn a college student expulsion and destroy a writer's, scholar's or journalist's reputation. In recent days, for example, the *New York Times* has referred to "widespread fabrication and plagiarism" by reporter Jayson Blair as "a low point in the 152-year history of the newspaper."

In James Hynes' splendid satiric novella of plagiarism, *Casting the Runes,* the plagiarist, having by black magic murdered one of the historians whom he plagiarized and tried to murder a second, is himself killed by the very same black magic, deployed by the widow of his murder victim.

There is a danger of overkill. Plagiarism can be a form of fraud, but it is no accident that, unlike real theft, it is not a crime. If a thief steals your car, you are out the market value of the car, but if a writer copies material from a book you wrote, you don't have to replace the book. At worst, the undetected plagiarist obtains a reputation that he does not deserve (that is the element of fraud in plagiarism). The real victim of his fraud is not the person whose work he copies, but those of his competitors who scruple to enhance their own reputations by such means.

The most serious plagiarisms are by students and professors, whose undetected plagiarisms disrupt the system of student and scholarly evaluation. The least serious are those that earned the late Stephen Ambrose and Doris Kearns Goodwin such obloquy last year. Popular historians, they jazzed up their books with vivid passages copied from previous historians without quotation marks, though with footnote attributions that made their "crime" easy to detect.

5   (One reason that plagiarism, like littering, is punished heavily, even though an individual act of plagiarism usually does little or no harm, is that it is normally very difficult to detect—but not in the case of Ambrose and Goodwin.) Competing popular historians might have been injured, but I'm not aware of anyone actually claiming this.

Confusion of plagiarism with theft is one reason plagiarism engenders indignation; another is a confusion of it with copyright infringement. Wholesale copying of copyrighted material is an infringement of a property right, and legal remedies are available to the copyright holder. But the copying of brief passages, even from copyrighted materials, is permissible under the doctrine of "fair use," while wholesale copying from material that is in the public domain—material that never was copyrighted, or on which the copyright has expired—presents no copyright issue at all.

Plagiarism of work in the public domain is more common than otherwise. Consider a few examples: *West Side Story* is a thinly veiled copy (with music added) of *Romeo and Juliet*, which in turn plagiarized Arthur Brooke's *The Tragicall Historye of Romeo and Juliet*, published in 1562, which in turn copied from several earlier Romeo and Juliets, all of which were copies of Ovid's story of Pyramus and Thisbe.

*Paradise Lost* plagiarizes the book of Genesis in the Old Testament. Classical musicians plagiarize folk melodies (think only of Dvorak, Bartok, and Copland) and often "quote" (as musicians say) from earlier classical works. Edouard Manet's most famous painting, *Dejeuner sur l'herbe,* copies earlier paintings by Raphael, Titian, and Courbet, and *My Fair Lady* plagiarized Shaw's play *Pygmalion,* while Woody Allen's movie *Play It Again, Sam* "quotes" a famous scene from *Casablanca.* Countless movies are based on books, such as *The Thirty-Nine Steps* on John Buchan's novel of that name or *For Whom the Bell Tolls* on Hemingway's novel.

Many of these "plagiarisms" were authorized, and perhaps none was deceptive; they are what Christopher Ricks in his excellent book *Allusions to the Poets* helpfully terms *allusion* rather than *plagiarism.* But what they show is that copying with variations is an important form of creativity, and this should make us prudent and measured in our condemnations of plagiarism.

10   Especially when the term is extended from literal copying to the copying of ideas. Another phrase for copying an idea, as distinct from the form in which it is expressed, is dissemination of ideas. If one needs

a license to repeat another person's idea, or if one risks ostracism by one's professional community for failing to credit an idea to its originator, who may be forgotten or unknown, the dissemination of ideas is impeded.

I have heard authors of history textbooks criticized for failing to document their borrowing of ideas from previous historians. This is an absurd criticism. The author of a textbook makes no claim to originality; rather the contrary—the most reliable, if not necessarily the most exciting, textbook is one that confines itself to ideas already well accepted, not at all novel.

It would be better if the term *plagiarism* were confined to literal copying, and moreover literal copying that is not merely unacknowledged but deceptive. Failing to give credit where credit is due should be regarded as a lesser, indeed usually merely venial, offense.

The concept of plagiarism has expanded, and the sanctions for it, though they remain informal rather than legal, have become more severe, in tandem with the rise of individualism. Journal articles are no longer published anonymously, and ghostwriters demand that their contributions be acknowledged.

Individualism and a cult of originality go hand in hand. Each of us supposes that our contribution to society is unique rather than fungible and so deserves public recognition, which plagiarism clouds.

This is a modern view. We should be aware that the high value 15 placed on originality is a specific cultural, and even field-specific, phenomenon, rather than an aspect of the universal moral law.

Judges, who try to conceal rather than to flaunt their originality, far from crediting their predecessors with original thinking like to pretend that there is no original thinking in law, that judges are just a transmission belt for rules and principles laid down by the framers of statutes or the Constitution.

Resorting to plagiarism to obtain a good grade or a promotion is fraud and should be punished, though it should not be confused with "theft." But I think the zeal to punish plagiarism reflects less a concern with the real injuries that it occasionally inflicts than with a desire on the part of leaders of professional communities, such as journalists and historians, to enhance their profession's reputation.

Journalists (like politicians) have a bad reputation for truthfulness, and historians, in this "postmodernist" era, are suspected of having embraced an extreme form of relativism and of having lost their regard for facts. Both groups hope by taking a very hard line against plagiarism and fabrication to reassure the public that they are serious diggers after truth whose efforts, a form of "sweat equity," deserve protection against copycats.

Their anxieties are understandable; but the rest of us will do well to keep the matter in perspective, realizing that the term *plagiarism* is used loosely and often too broadly; that much plagiarism is harmless and (when the term is defined broadly) that some has social value.

### Responding to Reading

1. In paragraph 3, Posner says, "There is a danger of overkill. Plagiarism can be a form of fraud, but it is no accident that, unlike real theft, it is not a crime." How do you think David Callahan (p. 500) would react to this statement?
2. According to Posner, what is the difference between plagiarism and theft? Between plagiarism and copyright infringement? Between plagiarism and allusion? Do you see these distinctions as valid in cases of academic plagiarism? Why or why not?
3. Read Posner's concluding paragraph. Does his statement that "much plagiarism is harmless" adequately sum up his essay's position? What else, if anything, do you think he should address in this paragraph?

### Responding in Writing

Do you agree with Posner that "much plagiarism is harmless" (19)? Under what circumstances, if any, do you think academic cheating is "harmless"?

# A BETTER WAY TO PREVENT CHEATING: APPEAL TO FAIRNESS

## David Callahan

### 1965–

*A senior fellow at the think tank Demos, the editor of the blog* PolicyShop. net, *and a radio and television commentator, David Callahan explores issues related to finances and ethics. He is the author of eight books, including, most recently,* Fortunes of Change: The Rise of the Liberal Rich and the Remaking of America *(2010). His articles have appeared in such publications as the* Nation, *the* New York Times, *and the* Washington Post. *In the following essay, Callahan offers suggestions to help prevent cheating in college.*

As professors sit down to grade mid-term exams, it's time for some to play their least favorite role: cop. With surveys finding that up to three-quarters of college students cheat, faculty and administrators are making a bigger push for integrity. What most still lack, however, is a compelling moral argument against cheating.

A growing number of universities have enacted honor codes, but many of these codes—along with campus efforts to publicize them—fail to make a strong case for why cheating is wrong. Often they invoke fuzzy ideals of honor or, conversely, dwell on the negative consequences for cheaters who are caught. Neither approach gets very far, not these days.

Honor, with its emphasis on doing the right thing for its own sake, is no match for the anxious cynicism of many college students. This point was driven home to me by a junior I met in North Carolina. Why not cheat, he argued, given how many of America's most successful people cut corners to get where they are? Cheating is how the real world works, he said. Look at the politicians who lie or the sluggers who take steroids, or the CEOs who cook the books. The student also pointed to the hurdles he faced as he tried to get ahead: high tuition costs, heavy student loans, low-paying jobs without benefits. America wasn't a fair place for kids like him, so it made sense to try to level the playing field by bending a few rules.

Many young people take this bleak view. A 2008 poll of high school students found that 59 percent agreed that "successful people do what they have to do to win, even if others consider it cheating." Young people believe in honor and value integrity; they also worry that living by these beliefs could mean ending up as a loser. In justifying her cheating, one student told a researcher: "Good grades can make the difference between going to medical school and being a janitor." Few professors have a ready retort to this logic.

Appeals to self-interest only worsen the problem. If you tell a student that she shouldn't cheat because she might get caught, or that she's "just cheating herself" by not learning the material, or that integrity is an asset in life to be cultivated, she might respond—as the student I met in North Carolina did—by spelling out the ways that successful cheating could advance one's self-interest, especially if "everybody else" is doing it. 5

Students with a strong sense of right and wrong, learned early in life, may be more willing to sacrifice personal advancement for the sake of their values. Some research has shown, for instance, that students with a theistic outlook are less likely to cheat. But most colleges aren't in the position to reshape students' character at this level. Likewise, our universities have limited influence over the broader socioeconomic trends that help fuel cheating, such as rising economic inequality and increasing middle-class insecurity.

What can faculty and administrators do to stem epidemic cheating? Their best hope is to cast cheating as an issue of justice.

Students may be cynical about what it takes to succeed these days, but they do care about fairness. And cheating is nothing if not unfair. Cheaters get rewards they don't deserve, like scholarships, admission to college or grad school, internships, and jobs. Cheating is the antithesis of equal opportunity: the notion that we all should have a fair shot at success and that the people who get rewarded are the people who deserve those rewards because they worked the hardest.

Many students understand that the ideal of equal opportunity is threatened in an era of rising inequality. Quite a few say they want to do something about this. Anticheating efforts offer a way to build, on campus, a microcosm of the kind of society they want to live in—one with a level playing field for all. I've met many students who see this and many who are organizing to fight cheating.

CHAPTER 9 FOCUS

10      Maybe academic integrity will never become a great campus cause. But if faculty can cast this issue as a matter of justice, and empower students to take action, perhaps some day they won't have to spend so much time playing cop.

## Responding to Reading

1. What practical objections does Callahan have to the kind of appeals to students that stress the idea of "doing the right thing for its own sake" (3)? To what he calls "appeals to self-interest" (5)? Do his objections make sense to you?
2. Reread Callahan's criticisms of college honor codes in paragraph 2. What do you suppose Richard Posner (p. 497) would think of honor codes?
3. How do you react to the following two statements (the first by a student, the second by Callahan)?

   • "Cheating is how the real world works. . . . " (3)

   • "Students may be cynical about what it takes to succeed these days, but they do care about fairness." (8)

Given your reactions to these two statements, do you think Callahan's recommendations for how to prevent cheating are unrealistically optimistic?

## Responding in Writing

Do you think professors should take on the role of "cops" when it comes to uncovering cheating and other forms of academic dishonesty? Why or why not?

# WIDENING THE FOCUS

## For Critical Reading and Writing

Referring specifically to the three readings in this chapter's Focus section, write an essay in which you answer the question, "What Has Happened to Academic Integrity?"

## For Further Reading

The following readings can suggest additional perspectives for thinking and writing about the issue of academic integrity:

- Amy Chua, "Why Chinese Mothers Are Superior" (p. 52)
- John Holt, "School Is Bad for Children" (p. 72)
- Christina Hoff Sommers, "The War against Boys" (p. 283)
- David A. Hoekema, "The Unacknowledged Ethicists on Campuses" (p. 453)

## For Focused Research

Honor codes are an integral part of the academic policies at many colleges and universities across the United States. However, not all honor codes are alike: they vary considerably from school to school. In preparation for writing an essay about higher-education honor codes, do a *Google* search using the search terms *honor codes and US colleges,* and read information about the honor codes at various schools. In your essay, explain the range of honor codes at US colleges and universities and what these schools hope to accomplish by enforcing them. Are honor codes a good solution to the problems created by the decline of academic integrity? Support your points with examples and evidence from the school Web sites you use.

## Beyond the Classroom

Interview the following people: several professors (in different fields), one student from every year at your school, and two college librarians. Ask each of them if they think plagiarism and other forms of academic dishonesty are on the rise—and, if so, why. Then, ask them what solutions they propose to address the problems they identify. Write an essay in the form of a proposal that summarizes the recommendations you have gathered.

---
# WRITING
---

## Making Ethical Choices

1. The question of whether or not to act to end another's suffering—possibly at one's own expense—is explored in "Shooting an Elephant" by George Orwell (p. 457). Do you think we as a society should act to end suffering even if it causes us some hardship?

2. Martin Luther King, Jr. (p. 464) considers the difficulties of resisting majority rule, standing up to authority, and protesting against established rules and laws. Choose a law or practice that you consider unjust, and write an essay in which you explain why you believe it should be challenged (or even disobeyed).

3. What do you believe we gain and lose by using animals in scientific research? Do you believe this practice should be continued? If so, with which animals? Under what circumstances? If not, why not? What alternative do you propose? Read Claire McCarthy's "Dog Lab" (p. 479) before you begin to plan your essay.

4. Which of the two roads identified in Robert Frost's "The Road Not Taken" (p. 451) have you chosen? In what sense has that choice "made all the difference" (line 20)?

5. Do you believe it is possible both to do good (that is, to help others) and to do well (that is, to be financially successful), or do you believe these two goals are mutually exclusive? Write an essay in which you answer this question, citing examples of people you know as well as public figures who have (or have not) managed both to do good and to do well.

6. Are you essentially optimistic or pessimistic about your own life and about the world we live in? Choose several readings from this chapter that you believe express either an optimistic or a pessimistic worldview, and use the writers' ideas to support your position.

7. Do you believe that people can be guided by a moral and ethical code that is strictly secular, or do you believe it is only possible to live a moral, ethical life if one believes in a higher power and follows the guidelines set by a particular religion? Write an essay that explains your position.

8. Do you believe that decisions about what steps to take to preserve the environment are essentially ethical choices? Or, do you think a person's behavior in situations like this has nothing to do with ethics or morals?

9. Imagine that you are in charge of an almost-full lifeboat and can take on only one additional passenger. Which of the following people would you choose, and why?

- A healthy three-year-old
- An elderly Nobel Prize winner
- A single father of two young children
- A thirty-year-old decorated combat veteran
- A middle-aged doctor who has performed life-saving surgery

Write an essay in which you consider which of the candidates most deserves to be saved (not which one can be of most practical help to the others in the lifeboat). Before you focus on the person you would save, evaluate the pros and cons of saving each of the others.

# 10

## FACING THE FUTURE

In the early part of the twentieth century, people envisioned the future as a place of infinite possibilities, where human intellect would create a society in which technology and industry could solve all the world's problems. War would be a thing of the past, and so would famine and disease. Soon, however, two World Wars (and many small ones) revealed the folly of these forecasts. Instead of creating a utopia, technology enabled human beings to create destruction on a scale never witnessed before in human history.

Of course, the new developments were not all bad. In the early part of the twentieth century, people traveled mainly on foot, by horse, or by train. By the middle of the century, the automobile and the jet plane enabled them to travel great distances in hours instead of weeks. In 1969, the same rocket technology that had enabled Nazi Germany to launch

View of a future city from the 1927 science fiction movie *Metropolis*

V2 rockets against England in 1944 also enabled the United States to send astronauts to the moon. Throughout the twentieth century, medicine made advances that enabled doctors to cure diseases—such as polio, typhus, and cholera—that had decimated human populations for centuries. With the inventions of the telephone, radio, and television, people were able to transmit and receive information instantly, regardless of distance. And the computer gave people access to information on a scale that earlier generations could never have imagined.

Now, at the beginning of the twenty-first century, people understandably wonder what is in store for them.

- Will the family look much as it does today, or will *family* be defined differently?

- Will education as we know it endure, or will online education replace face-to-face classroom instruction?

- How will social media affect our language?

- Will cultural identity become more or less important?

- Will technology bring people closer together or push them further apart?

- How will gender roles change? Will these changes be for the better?

- How will the nature of work and workers' roles change? What new jobs will emerge?

Contemporary view of the Brooklyn Bridge and the Manhattan skyline at night

- Will more people realize the American Dream, or will it remain out of reach for many?

- What new ethical dilemmas will the future bring?

- Finally, will the future be benign or harmful? Will human beings achieve the society that they have always wished for, or will this century be as destructive as the last one?

The three college commencement speeches in the Focus section of this chapter (p. 547) address the question "What Comes Next?" and reflect the hopes, fears, and mood of the speakers, the nation, and the graduates. The speeches deal with traditional themes, such as success, happiness, personal fulfillment, and service, as well as more contemporary issues, such as saving the environment, continuing the work of fighting racism, and dealing with the state of the economy.

## ——————— PREPARING TO READ AND WRITE ———————

As you read and prepare to write about the selections in this chapter, you may consider the following questions:

- On what specific issue does the writer focus?

- Is the writer optimistic, pessimistic, or ambivalent about the future?

- Does the writer believe that the future he or she envisions is inevitable, or does he or she believe that people can influence future events?

- Does the writer identify a specific problem? Does he or she think the problem can be solved?

- Is the writer emotionally involved with the issue he or she is discussing? Does this involvement (or lack of involvement) affect the writer's credibility?

- What social, political, or religious ideas influence the writer's view of the future? How can you tell? Are these ideas similar to or different from your own ideas?

- Does the predicted future cause the writer to examine his or her own values? The values of society? Does the writer lead you to examine your own values?

- Which writers' views of the future seem most similar? Which seem most different?

- Which writer's view of the future seems the most plausible? Which seems the least plausible?

POETRY

## Dover Beach

## Matthew Arnold

### 1822–1888

*Matthew Arnold was an English Victorian poet, literary and social critic, essayist, and lecturer. In addition to his poetry, Arnold is known for such works as* Essays in Criticism *(1865) and* Culture and Anarchy *(1869). Considered one of the most influential Victorian poets, Arnold explained that his poems portray "the main movement of mind over the last quarter of a century." The following famous poem conveys a vision of the future.*

The sea is calm to-night.
The tide is full, the moon lies fair
Upon the straits; on the French coast the light
Gleams and is gone; the cliffs of England stand;
Glimmering and vast, out in the tranquil bay.                    5
Come to the window, sweet is the night-air!
Only, from the long line of spray
Where the sea meets the moon-blanched land,
Listen! you hear the grating roar
Of pebbles which the waves draw back, and fling,                10
At their return, up the high strand,
Begin, and cease, and then again begin,
With tremulous cadence slow, and bring
The eternal note of sadness in.

Sophocles[1] long ago                                           15
Heard it on the Aegean,[2] and it brought
Into his mind the turbid ebb and flow
Of human misery; we
Find also in the sound a thought,
Hearing it by this distant northern sea.                        20

The Sea of Faith
Was once, too, at the full, and round earth's shore
Lay like the folds of a bright girdle furled.
But now I only hear
Its melancholy, long, withdrawing roar,                         25
Retreating, to the breath

---

[1] Ancient Greek dramatist (c. 496 BC–406 BC). [Eds.]
[2] Aegean Sea. [Eds.]

Of the night-wind, down the vast edges drear
And naked shingles of the world.
Ah, love, let us be true
30    To one another! for the world, which seems
To lie before us like a land of dreams,
So various, so beautiful, so new,
Hath really neither joy, nor love, nor light,
Nor certitude, nor peace, nor help for pain;
35    And we are here as on a darkling plain
Swept with confused alarms of struggle and flight,
Where ignorant armies clash by night.

## Responding to Reading

1. How would you describe the mood of the poem? How does the poem's mood reflect its subject?
2. The poem's first stanza opens with a description of the calm night sea. In the second stanza, the sea is said to remind Sophocles of "the turbid ebb and flow of human misery." In the third stanza, the sea is called the "sea of faith," but the speaker hears its "melancholy, long, withdrawing roar." What is the significance of these changing characterizations of the sea?
3. Who are the "ignorant armies" (line 37)? Why do they "clash by night"?

## Responding in Writing

What vision of the future is presented in the poem's last stanza?

# INAUGURAL ADDRESS

## John F. Kennedy

### 1917–1963

*Born in Brookline, Massachusetts, John Fitzgerald Kennedy received a bachelor's degree from Harvard University and served in the navy during World War II as a PT boat commander in the South Pacific. A charismatic politician, he was elected to the United States House of Representatives in 1947 and to the Senate in 1953. In 1960, defeating Republican candidate (and later president) Richard Nixon, Kennedy became the youngest man and the first Catholic to be elected president. During his tenure, he supported policies promoting racial equality, aid to the poor and to education, and increased availability of medical care; he also conceived of the idea of the Peace Corps. However, Kennedy was also responsible for involving the country further in the doomed Vietnam conflict. He was assassinated in November of 1963, a year before the end of his first term.*

Vice President Johnson, Mr. Speaker, Mr. Chief Justice, President Eisenhower, Vice President Nixon, President Truman, Reverend Clergy, fellow citizens:

We observe today not a victory of party but a celebration of freedom— symbolizing an end as well as a beginning—signifying renewal as well as change. For I have sworn before you and Almighty God the same solemn oath our forebears prescribed nearly a century and three-quarters ago.

The world is very different now. For man holds in his mortal hands the power to abolish all forms of human poverty and all forms of human life. And yet the same revolutionary beliefs for which our forebears fought are still at issue around the globe—the belief that the rights of man come not from the generosity of the state but from the hand of God.

We dare not forget today that we are the heirs of that first revolution. Let the word go forth from this time and place, to friend and foe alike, that the torch has been passed to a new generation of Americans— born in this century, tempered by war, disciplined by a hard and bitter peace, proud of our ancient heritage—and unwilling to witness or permit the slow undoing of those human rights to which this nation has always been committed, and to which we are committed today at home and around the world.

Let every nation know, whether it wishes us well or ill, that we shall pay any price, bear any burden, meet any hardship, support any friend, oppose any foe to assure the survival and the success of liberty.

This much we pledge—and more.

To those old allies whose cultural and spiritual origins we share, we pledge the loyalty of faithful friends. United there is little we cannot do in a host of cooperative ventures. Divided there is little we can do— for we dare not meet a powerful challenge at odds and split asunder.

To those new states whom we welcome to the ranks of the free, we pledge our word that one form of colonial control shall not have passed away merely to be replaced by a far more iron tyranny. We shall not always expect to find them supporting our view. But we shall always hope to find them strongly supporting their own freedom—and to remember that, in the past, those who foolishly sought power by riding the back of the tiger ended up inside. To those people in the huts and villages of half the globe struggling to break the bonds of mass misery, we pledge our best efforts to help them help themselves, for whatever period is required—not because the communists may be doing it, not because we seek their votes, but because it is right. If a free society cannot help the many who are poor, it cannot save the few who are rich.

To our sister republics south of our border, we offer a special pledge—to convert our good words into good deeds—in a new alliance for progress—to assist free men and free governments in casting off the chains of poverty. But this peaceful revolution of hope cannot become the prey of hostile powers. Let all our neighbors know that we shall join with them to oppose aggression or subversion anywhere in the Americas. And let every other power know that this Hemisphere intends to remain the master of its own house.

10　　To that world assembly of sovereign states, the United Nations, our last best hope in an age where the instruments of war have far outpaced the instruments of peace, we renew our pledge of support— to prevent it from becoming merely a forum for invective—to strengthen its shield of the new and the weak—and to enlarge the area in which its writ may run.

Finally, to those nations who would make themselves our adversary, we offer not a pledge but a request: that both sides begin anew the quest for peace, before the dark powers of destruction unleashed by science engulf all humanity in planned or accidental self-destruction.

We dare not tempt them with weakness. For only when our arms are sufficient beyond doubt can we be certain beyond doubt that they will never be employed.

But neither can two great and powerful groups of nations take comfort from our present course—both sides overburdened by the cost of modern weapons, both rightly alarmed by the steady spread of the deadly atom, yet both racing to alter that uncertain balance of terror that stays the hand of mankind's final war.

So let us begin anew—remembering on both sides that civility is not a sign of weakness, and sincerity is always subject to proof. Let us never negotiate out of fear. But let us never fear to negotiate.

15　　Let both sides explore what problems unite us instead of belaboring those problems which divide us.

Let both sides, for the first time, formulate serious and precise proposals for the inspection and control of arms and bring the absolute power to destroy other nations under the absolute control of all nations.

Let both sides seek to invoke the wonders of science instead of its terrors. Together let us explore the stars, conquer the deserts, eradicate disease, tap the ocean depths and encourage the arts and commerce.

Let both sides unite to heed in all corners of the earth the command of Isaiah—to "undo the heavy burdens . . . (and) let the oppressed go free."

And if a beachhead of cooperation may push back the jungle of suspicion, let both sides join in creating a new endeavor, not a new balance of power, but a new world of law, where the strong are just and the weak secure and the peace preserved.

20　　All this will not be finished in the first one hundred days. Nor will it be finished in the first one thousand days, nor in the life of this Administration, nor even perhaps in our lifetime on this planet. But let us begin.

In your hands, my fellow citizens, more than mine, will rest the final success or failure of our course. Since this country was founded, each generation of Americans has been summoned to give testimony to its national loyalty. The graves of young Americans who answered the call to service surround the globe.

Now the trumpet summons us—again not as a call to bear arms, though arms we need—not as a call to battle, though embattled we are—but a call to bear the burden of a long twilight struggle, year in and year out, "rejoicing in hope, patient in tribulation"—a struggle against the common enemies of man: tyranny, poverty, disease and war itself. Can we forge against these enemies a grand and global alliance, North and South, East and West, that can assure a more fruitful life for all mankind? Will you join in that historic effort?

In the long history of the world, only a few generations have been granted the role of defending freedom in its hour of maximum danger. I do not shrink from this responsibility—I welcome it. I do not believe that any of us would exchange places with any other people or any other generation. The energy, the faith, the devotion which we bring to this endeavor will light our country and all who serve it—and the glow from that fire can truly light the world. And so, my fellow Americans: ask not what your country can do for you—ask what you can do for your country. My fellow citizens of the world: ask not what America will do for you, but what together we can do for the freedom of man.

Finally, whether you are citizens of America or citizens of the world, ask of us here the same high standards of strength and sacrifice which we ask of you. With a good conscience our only sure reward, with history the final judge of our deeds, let us go forth to lead the land we love, asking His blessing and His help, but knowing that here on earth God's work must truly be our own.

## Responding to Reading

1. At the beginning of his speech, Kennedy alludes to the "revolutionary beliefs" of Thomas Jefferson and asserts, "We are the heirs of that first revolution" (3-4). What does he mean? Do you think his speech offers adequate support for this statement?

2. What are Kennedy's hopes for the future? What problems does he think the United States must solve? Has the United States solved the problems that Kennedy mentions in his speech, or have they yet to be fully addressed?

3. Near the end of his speech, Kennedy says, "And so, my fellow Americans: ask not what your country can do for you—ask what you can do for your country" (23). What does this famous, often-quoted passage actually mean in practical terms? Do you think this call to action is realistic? Do you think it is fair? Explain.

## Responding in Writing

Exactly what do you expect America to do for you, and what do you expect to do for your country?

# The Obligation to Endure

## Rachel Carson

### 1907–1964

*Naturalist and environmentalist Rachel Carson was a specialist in marine biology. She won the National Book Award for* The Sea Around Us *(1951), which, like her other books, appeals to scientists and nonscientists alike. While working as an aquatic biologist for the U.S. Fish and Wildlife Service, Carson became concerned about ecological hazards and wrote* Silent Spring *(1962), in which she warned readers about the indiscriminate use of pesticides. This book influenced President John F. Kennedy to begin investigations into this and other environmental problems. Recently, however, critics have challenged the accuracy of Carson's science and questioned the validity of her conclusions concerning the dangers of DDT. In the excerpt from* Silent Spring *that follows, Carson urges readers to question the use of chemical pesticides.*

The history of life on earth has been a history of interaction between living things and their surroundings. To a large extent, the physical form and the habits of the earth's vegetation and its animal life have been molded by the environment. Considering the whole span of earthly time, the opposite effect, in which life actually modifies its surroundings, has been relatively slight. Only within the moment of time represented by the present century has one species—man—acquired significant power to alter the nature of his world.

During the past quarter century this power has not only increased to one of disturbing magnitude but it has changed in character. The most alarming of all man's assaults upon the environment is the contamination of air, earth, rivers, and sea with dangerous and even lethal materials. This pollution is for the most part irrecoverable; the chain of evil it initiates not only in the world that must support life but in living tissues is for the most part irreversible. In this now universal contamination of the environment, chemicals are the sinister and little-recognized partners of radiation in changing the very nature of the world—the very nature of its life. Strontium 90, released through nuclear explosions into the air, comes to earth in rain or drifts down in fallout, lodges in soil, enters into the grass or corn or wheat grown there, and in time takes up its abode in the bones of a human being, there to remain until his death. Similarly, chemicals sprayed on croplands or forests or gardens lie long in soil, entering into living organisms, passing from one to another in a chain of poisoning and death. Or they pass mysteriously by underground streams until they emerge and, through the alchemy of air and sunlight, combine into new forms that kill vegetation, sicken cattle, and work unknown harm on those who drink from once pure wells. As Albert Schweitzer[1] has said, "Man can hardly even recognize the devils of his own creation."

It took hundreds of millions of years to produce the life that now inhabits the earth—eons of time in which that developing and evolving and diversifying life reached a state of adjustment and balance with its surroundings. The environment, rigorously shaping and directing the life it supported, contained elements that were hostile as well as supporting. Certain rocks gave out dangerous radiation; even within the light of the sun, from which all life draws its energy, there were short-wave radiations with power to injure. Given time—time not in years but in millennia—life adjusts, and a balance has been reached. For time is the essential ingredient; but in the modern world there is no time.

The rapidity of change and the speed with which new situations are created follow the impetuous and heedless pace of man rather than the deliberate pace of nature. Radiation is no longer merely the background radiation of rocks, the bombardment of cosmic rays, the ultra-violet of the sun that have existed before there was any life on earth; radiation is now the unnatural creation of man's tampering with the atom. The chemicals to which life is asked to make its adjustment are no longer merely the calcium and silica and copper and all the rest of the minerals washed out of the rocks and carried in rivers to the sea; they are the synthetic creations of man's inventive mind, brewed in his laboratories, and having no counterparts in nature.

To adjust to these chemicals would require time on the scale that is   5 nature's; it would require not merely the years of a man's life but the life of generations. And even this, were it by some miracle possible, would be futile, for the new chemicals come from our laboratories in an endless stream; almost five hundred annually find their way into actual use in the United States alone. The figure is staggering and its implications are not easily grasped—500 new chemicals to which the bodies of men and animals are required somehow to adapt each year, chemicals totally outside the limits of biologic experience.

Among them are many that are used in man's war against nature. Since the mid-1940s over 200 basic chemicals have been created for use in killing insects, weeds, rodents, and other organisms described in the modern vernacular as "pests"; and they are sold under several thousand different brand names.

These sprays, dusts, and aerosols are now applied almost universally to farms, gardens, forests, and homes—nonselective chemicals that have the power to kill every insect, the "good" and the "bad," to still the songs of birds and the leaping of fish in the streams, to coat the leaves with a deadly film, and to linger on in soil—all this though the

---

[1]French theologian (1875-1965) honored for his work as a scientist, humanitarian, musician, and religious thinker. In 1952, he was awarded the Nobel Peace Prize. [Eds.]

intended target may be only a few weeds or insects. Can anyone believe it is possible to lay down such a barrage of poisons on the surface of the earth without making it unfit for all life? They should not be called "insecticides," but "biocides."

The whole process of spraying seems caught up in an endless spiral. Since DDT was released for civilian use, a process of escalation has been going on in which ever more toxic materials must be found. This has happened because insects, in a triumphant vindication of Darwin's principle of the survival of the fittest, have evolved super races immune to the particular insecticide used, hence a deadlier one has always to be developed—and then a deadlier one than that. It has happened also because, for reasons to be described later, destructive insects often undergo a "flare-back" or resurgence, after spraying in numbers greater than before. Thus the chemical war is never won, and all life is caught in its violent crossfire.

Along with the possibility of the extinction of mankind by nuclear war, the central problem of our age has therefore become the contamination of man's total environment with such substances of incredible potential for harm—substances that accumulate in the tissues of plants and animals and even penetrate the germ cells to shatter or alter the very material of heredity upon which the shape of the future depends.

10    Some would-be architects of our future look toward a time when it will be possible to alter the human germ plasm by design. But we may easily be doing so now by inadvertence, for many chemicals, like radiation, bring about gene mutations. It is ironic to think that man might determine his own future by something so seemingly trivial as the choice of an insect spray.

All this has been risked—for what? Future historians may well be amazed by our distorted sense of proportion. How could intelligent beings seek to control a few unwanted species by a method that contaminated the entire environment and brought the threat of disease and death even to their own kind? Yet this is precisely what we have done. We have done it, moreover, for reasons that collapse the moment we examine them. We are told that the enormous and expanding use of pesticides is necessary to maintain farm production. Yet is our real problem not one of *overproduction?* Our farms, despite measures to remove acreages from production and to pay farmers *not* to produce, have yielded such a staggering excess of crops that the American taxpayer in 1962 is paying out more than one billion dollars a year as the total carrying cost of the surplus-food storage program. And is the situation helped when one branch of the Agriculture Department tries to reduce production while another states, as it did in 1958, "It is believed generally that reduction of crop acreages under provisions of the Soil Bank will stimulate interest in use of chemicals to obtain maximum production on the land retained in crops."

All this is not to say there is no insect problem and no need of control. I am saying, rather, that control must be geared to realities, not to mythical situations, and that the methods employed must be such that they do not destroy us along with the insects.

The problem whose attempted solution has brought such a train of disaster in its wake is an accomplishment of our modern way of life. Long before the age of man, insects inhabited the earth—a group of extraordinarily varied and adaptable beings. Over the course of time since man's advent, a small percentage of the more than half a million species of insects have come into conflict with human welfare in two principal ways: as competitors for the food supply and as carriers of human disease.

Disease-carrying insects become important where human beings are crowded together, especially under conditions where sanitation is poor, as in time of natural disaster or war or in situations of extreme poverty and deprivation. Then control of some sort becomes necessary. It is a sobering fact, however, as we shall presently see, that the method of massive chemical control has had only limited success, and also threatens to worsen the very conditions it is intended to curb.

Under primitive agricultural conditions the farmer had few insect problems. These arose with the intensification of agriculture—the devotion of immense acreages to a single crop. Such a system set the stage for explosive increases in specific insect populations. Single-crop farming does not take advantage of the principles by which nature works; it is agriculture as an engineer might conceive it to be. Nature has introduced great variety into the landscape, but man has displayed a passion for simplifying it. Thus he undoes the built-in checks and balances by which nature holds the species within bounds. One important natural check is a limit on the amount of suitable habitat for each species. Obviously then, an insect that lives on wheat can build up its population to much higher levels on a farm devoted to wheat than on one in which wheat is intermingled with other crops to which the insect is not adapted.

The same thing happens in other situations. A generation or more ago, the towns of large areas of the United States lined their streets with the noble elm tree. Now the beauty they hopefully created is threatened with complete destruction as disease sweeps through the elms, carried by a beetle that would have only limited chance to build up large populations and to spread from tree to tree if the elms were only occasional trees in a richly diversified planting.

Another factor in the modern insect problem is one that must be viewed against a background of geologic and human history: the spreading of thousands of different kinds of organisms from their native homes to invade new territories. This worldwide migration has been studied and graphically described by the British ecologist Charles

15

Elton in his recent book *The Ecology of Invasions.* During the Cretaceous Period, some hundred million years ago, flooding seas cut many land bridges between continents and living things found themselves confined in what Elton calls "colossal separate nature reserves." There, isolated from others of their kind, they developed many new species. When some of the land masses were joined again, about 15 million years ago, these species began to move out into new territories—a movement that is not only still in progress but is now receiving considerable assistance from man.

The importation of plants is the primary agent in the modern spread of species, for animals have almost invariably gone along with the plants, quarantine being a comparatively recent and not completely effective innovation. The United States Office of Plant Introduction alone has introduced almost 200,000 species and varieties of plants from all over the world. Nearly half of the 180 or so major insect enemies of plants in the United States are accidental imports from abroad, and most of them have come as hitchhikers on plants.

In new territory, out of reach of the restraining hand of the natural enemies that kept down its numbers in its native land, an invading plant or animal is able to become enormously abundant. Thus it is no accident that our most troublesome insects are introduced species.

20    These invasions, both the naturally occurring and those dependent on human assistance, are likely to continue indefinitely. Quarantine and massive chemical campaigns are only extremely expensive ways of buying time. We are faced, according to Dr. Elton, "with a life-and-death need not just to find new technological means of suppressing this plant or that animal"; instead we need the basic knowledge of animal populations and their relations to their surroundings that will "promote an even balance and damp down the explosive power of outbreaks and new invasions."

Much of the necessary knowledge is now available but we do not use it. We train ecologists in our universities and even employ them in our governmental agencies but we seldom take their advice. We allow the chemical death rain to fall as though there were no alternative, whereas in fact there are many, and our ingenuity could soon discover many more if given opportunity.

Have we fallen into a mesmerized state that makes us accept as inevitable that which is inferior or detrimental, as though having lost the will or the vision to demand that which is good? Such thinking, in the words of the ecologist Paul Shepard, "idealizes life with only its head out of water, inches above the limits of toleration of the corruption of its own environment. . . . Why should we tolerate a diet of weak poisons, a home in insipid surroundings, a circle of acquaintances who are not quite our enemies, the noise of motors with just enough relief to prevent insanity? Who would want to live in a world which is just not quite fatal?"

Yet such a world is pressed upon us. The crusade to create a chemically sterile, insect-free world seems to have engendered a fanatic zeal on the part of many specialists and most of the so-called control agencies. On every hand there is evidence that those engaged in spraying operations exercise a ruthless power. "The regulatory entomologists . . . function as prosecutor, judge and jury, tax assessor and collector and sheriff to enforce their own orders," said Connecticut entomologist Neely Turner. The most flagrant abuses go unchecked in both state and federal agencies.

It is not my contention that chemical insecticides must never be used. I do contend that we have put poisonous and biologically potent chemicals indiscriminately into the hands of persons largely or wholly ignorant of their potentials for harm. We have subjected enormous numbers of people to contact with these poisons, without their consent and often without their knowledge. If the Bill of Rights contains no guarantee that a citizen shall be secure against lethal poisons distributed either by private individuals or by public officials, it is surely only because our forefathers, despite their considerable wisdom and foresight, could conceive of no such problem.

I contend, furthermore, that we have allowed these chemicals to be 25 used with little or no advance investigation of their effect on soil, water, wildlife, and man himself. Future generations are unlikely to condone our lack of prudent concern for the integrity of the natural world that supports all life.

There is still very limited awareness of the nature of the threat. This is an era of specialists, each of whom sees his own problem and is unaware of or intolerant of the larger frame into which it fits. It is also an era dominated by industry, in which the right to make a dollar at whatever cost is seldom challenged. When the public protests, confronted with some obvious evidence of damaging results of pesticide applications, it is fed little tranquilizing pills of half truth. We urgently need an end to these false assurances, to the sugar coating of unpalatable facts. It is the public that is being asked to assume the risks that the insect controllers calculate. The public must decide whether it wishes to continue on the present road, and it can do so only when in full possession of the facts. In the words of Jean Rostand, "The obligation to endure gives us the right to know."

## Responding to Reading

1. In paragraph 9, Carson says, "Along with the possibility of the extinction of mankind by nuclear war, the central problem of our age has . . . become the contamination of man's total environment with such substances of incredible potential for harm. . . . " Do you think she makes a good point, or do you think she overstates her case?

2. What future scenario does Carson predict if the use of pesticides is not curtailed? Does she provide enough evidence to support her prediction? Explain.

3. In paragraph 24, Carson attempts to address critics' objections by saying that she does not believe insecticides "must never be used." Is she successful? Do you think she should have discussed the problems that could result if the use of insecticides such as DDT were reduced or eliminated?

## Responding in Writing

Since Carson wrote her book, DDT has been banned. Recently, however, some scientists have said that it should be reintroduced on a limited basis because some insects have developed resistance to safer insecticides. Do you think this information strengthens or weakens Carson's position?

# THE CHANGING DEMOGRAPHICS OF AMERICA

## Joel Kotkin

*A presidential fellow in urban futures at Chapman University, Joel Kotkin is an executive editor of* www.newgeography.com *and a columnist for* Forbes.com *and* Politico.com. *His work has appeared in such publications as* Newsweek, *the* New York Times, *the* Wall Street Journal, *and the* Washington Post. *He is the author of several books, including, most recently,* The Next Hundred Million: America in 2050 *(2010), from which the following essay was adapted. Kotkin is currently writing a book on the future of the United States.*

Estimates of the U.S. population at the middle of the 21st century vary, from the U.N.'s 404 million to the U.S. Census Bureau's 422 to 458 million. To develop a snapshot of the nation at 2050, particularly its astonishing diversity and youthfulness, I use the nice round number of 400 million people, or roughly 100 million more than we have today.

The United States is also expected to grow somewhat older. The portion of the population that is currently at least 65—13 percent—is expected to reach about 20 percent by 2050. This "graying of America" has helped convince some commentators of the nation's declining eminence. For example, international relations expert Parag Khanna envisions a "shrunken America" lucky to eke out a meager existence between a "triumphant China" and a "retooled Europe." Morris Berman, a cultural historian, says America "is running on empty."

But even as the baby boomers age, the population of working and young people is also expected to keep rising, in contrast to most other advanced nations. America's relatively high fertility rate—the number of children a woman is expected to have in her lifetime—hit 2.1 in 2006, with 4.3 million total births, the highest levels in 45 years. That's thanks largely to recent immigrants, who tend to have more children than residents whose families have been in the United States for several generations. Moreover, the nation is on the verge of a baby boomlet, when the children of the original boomers have children of their own.

Between 2000 and 2050, census data suggest, the U.S. 15-to-64 age group is expected to grow 42 percent. In contrast, because of falling fertility rates, the number of young and working-age people is expected to decline elsewhere: by 10 percent in China, 25 percent in Europe, 30 percent in South Korea and more than 40 percent in Japan.

Within the next four decades, most of the developed countries in 5 Europe and East Asia will become veritable old-age homes: A third or more of their populations will be over 65. By then, the United States is likely to have more than 350 million people under 65.

The prospect of an additional 100 million Americans by 2050 worries some environmentalists. A few have joined traditionally conservative xenophobes and anti-immigration activists in calling for a national policy to slow population growth by severely limiting immigration. The U.S. fertility rate—50 percent higher than that of Russia, Germany and Japan and well above that of China, Italy, Singapore, South Korea and virtually all the rest of Europe—has also prompted criticism.

Colleen Heenan, a feminist author and environmental activist, says Americans who favor larger families are not taking responsibility for "their detrimental contribution" to population growth and "resource shortages." Similarly, Peter Kareiva, the chief scientist at the Nature Conservancy, compared different conservation measures and concluded that not having a child is the most effective way of reducing carbon emissions and becoming an "eco hero."

Such critiques don't seem to take into account that a falling population and a dearth of young people may pose a greater threat to the nation's well-being than population growth. A rapidly declining population could create a society that doesn't have the work force to support the elderly and, overall, is less concerned with the nation's long-term future.

The next surge in growth may be delayed if tough economic times continue, but over time the rise in births, producing a generation slightly larger than the boomers, will add to the work force, boost consumer spending and generate new entrepreneurial businesses. And even with 100 million more people, the United States will be only one-sixth as crowded as Germany is today.

Immigration will continue to be a major force in U.S. life. The 10 United Nations estimates that 2 million people a year will move from poorer to developed nations over the next 40 years, and more than half of those will come to the United States, the world's preferred destination for educated, skilled migrants. In 2000, according to the Organization for Economic Co-operation and Development, an association of 30 democratic, free-market countries, the United States was home to 12.5 million skilled immigrants, equaling the combined total for Germany, France, the United Kingdom, Australia, Canada and Japan.

If recent trends continue, immigrants will play a leading role in our future economy. Between 1990 and 2005, immigrants started one out of four venture-backed public companies. Large American firms are also increasingly led by people with roots in foreign countries, including 15 of the Fortune 100 CEOs in 2007.

For all these reasons, the United States of 2050 will look different from that of today: Whites will no longer be in the majority. The U.S. minority population, currently 30 percent, is expected to exceed 50 percent before 2050. No other advanced, populous country will see such diversity.

In fact, most of America's net population growth will be among its minorities, as well as in a growing mixed-race population. Latino and Asian populations are expected to nearly triple, and the children of immigrants will become more prominent. Today in the United States, 25 percent of children under age 5 are Hispanic; by 2050, that percentage will be almost 40 percent.

Growth places the United States in a radically different position from that of Russia, Japan and Europe. Russia's low birth and high mortality rates suggest its overall population will drop 30 percent by 2050, to less than a third of the United States'. While China's population will continue to grow for a while, it may begin to experience decline as early as 2035, first in work force and then in actual population, mostly because of the government's one-child mandate, instituted in 1979 and still in effect. By 2050, 31 percent of China's population will be older than 60. More than 41 percent of Japanese will be that old.

15    Political prognosticators say China and India pose the greatest challenges to American predominance. But China, like Russia, lacks the basic environmental protections, reliable legal structures, favorable demographics and social resilience of the United States. India still has an overwhelmingly impoverished population and suffers from ethnic, religious and regional divisions. The vast majority of the Indian population remains semiliterate and lives in poor rural villages.

Suburbia will continue to be a mainstay of American life. Despite criticisms that suburbs are culturally barren and energy-inefficient, most U.S. metropolitan population growth has taken place in suburbia, confounding oft-repeated predictions of its decline.

Some aspects of suburban life—notably long-distance commuting and heavy reliance on fossil fuels—will have to change. The new suburbia will be far more environmentally friendly—what I call "green-urbia." The Internet, wireless phones, video conferencing and other communication technologies will allow more people to work from home: At least one in four or five will do so full time or part time, up from roughly one in six or seven today.

A new landscape may emerge, one that resembles the network of smaller towns characteristic of 19th-century America. The nation's landmass is large enough—about 3 percent is currently urbanized—to accommodate this growth, while still husbanding critical farmland and open space.

In other advanced nations where housing has become both expensive and dense—Japan, Germany, South Korea and Singapore—birthrates have fallen, partly because of the high cost of living, particularly for homes large enough to comfortably raise children. Preserving suburbs may therefore be critical for U.S. demographic vitality.

A 2009 study by the Brookings Institution found that between 1998 20 and 2006, jobs shifted away from the center and to the periphery in 95 out of 98 leading metropolitan regions—from Dallas and Los Angeles to Chicago and Seattle. Walter Siembab, a planning consultant, calls the process of creating sustainable work environments on the urban periphery "smart sprawl."

Super-fuel-efficient cars of the future are likely to spur smart sprawl. They may be a more reasonable way to meet environmental needs than shifting back to the mass-transit-based models of the industrial age; just 5 percent of the U.S. population uses mass transit on a daily basis.

Suburbs epitomize much of what constitutes the American dream for many people. Minorities, once largely associated with cities, tend to live in the suburbs; in 2008 they were a majority of residents in Texas, New Mexico, California and Hawaii. Nationwide, about 25 percent of suburbanites are minorities; by 2050 immigrants, their children and native-born minorities will become an even more dominant force in shaping suburbia.

The baby boom generation is poised for a large-scale "back to the city" movement, according to many news reports. But Sandra Rosenbloom, a University of Arizona gerontology professor, says roughly three-quarters of retirees in the first bloc of boomers appear to be sticking close to the suburbs, where the vast majority reside.

"Everybody in this business wants to talk about the odd person who moves downtown," Rosenbloom observes. "[But] most people retire in place. When they move, they don't move downtown, they move to the fringes."

To be sure, there will be 15 million to 20 million new urban dwell- 25 ers by 2050. Many will live in what Wharton business professor Joseph Gyourko calls "superstar cities," such as San Francisco, Boston, Manhattan and western Los Angeles—places adapted to business and recreation for the elite and those who work for them. By 2050, Seattle, Portland and Austin could join their ranks.

But because these elite cities are becoming too expensive for the middle class, the focus of urban life will shift to cities that are more spread out and, by some standards, less attractive. They're what I call "cities of aspiration," such as Phoenix, Houston, Dallas, Atlanta and

Charlotte. They'll facilitate upward mobility, as New York and other great industrial cities once did, and begin to compete with the superstar cities for finance, culture and media industries, and the amenities that typically go along with them.

What the United States does with its demographic dividend—its relatively young working-age population—is critical. Simply to keep pace with the growing U.S. population, the nation needs to add 125,000 jobs a month, the New America Foundation estimates. Without robust economic growth but with an expanding population, the country will face a massive decline in living standards.

Entrepreneurs, small businesses and self-employed workers will become more common. Between 1980 and 2000 the number of self-employed individuals expanded, to about 15 percent of the work force. More workers will live in an economic environment like that of Hollywood or Silicon Valley, with constant job hopping and changes in alliances among companies.

For much of American history, race has been the greatest barrier to a common vision of community. Race still remains all too synonymous with poverty: Considerably higher poverty rates for blacks and Hispanics persist. But the future will most likely see a dimming of economic distinctions based on ethnic origins.

30   The most pressing social problem facing mid-21st-century America will be fulfilling the historic promise of upward mobility. In recent decades, certain high-end-occupation incomes grew rapidly, while wages for lower-income and middle-class workers stagnated. Even after the 2008 economic downturn, largely brought on by Wall Street, it was primarily middle-class homeowners and jobholders who bore the brunt, sometimes losing their residences.

Most disturbingly, the rate of upward mobility has stagnated overall, as wages have largely failed to keep up with the cost of living. It is no easier for poor and working-class people to move up the socioeconomic ladder today than it was in the 1970s; in some ways, it's more difficult. The income of college-educated younger people, adjusted for inflation, has been in decline since 2000.

To reverse these trends, I think Americans will need to attend to the nation's basic investments and industries, including manufacturing, energy and agriculture. This runs counter to the fashionable assertion that the American future can be built around a handful of high-end creative jobs and will not require reviving the old industrial economy.

A more competitive and environmentally sustainable America will rely on technology. Fortunately, no nation has been more prodigious in its ability to apply new methods and techniques to solve fundamental problems; the term "technology" was invented in America in 1829. New energy finds, unconventional fuel sources and advanced technology are likely to ameliorate the long-prophesied energy catastrophe.

And technology can ease or even reverse the environmental costs of growth. With a population of 300 million, the United States has cleaner air and water now than 40 years ago, when the population was 200 million.

The America of 2050 will most likely remain the one truly transcend-   35 ent superpower in terms of society, technology and culture. It will rely on what has been called America's "civil religion"—its ability to forge a unique common national culture amid great diversity of people and place. We have no reason to lose faith in the possibilities of the future.

## Responding to Reading

1. How does Kotkin respond to those who say that the United States is in decline? How does he respond to those who encourage American families to have fewer children? Do you find his arguments convincing?
2. According to Kotkin, what role will immigrants play in the future of the United States? Does Kotkin think that their influence will be positive or negative? What evidence does he present to support his conclusion?
3. What effect will the demographic trends Kotkin describes have on cities? on suburbs? on workers? What does Kotkin think will be the most pressing social problem facing mid-twenty-first-century America?

## Responding in Writing

Overall, do you think Kotkin's view of the Unites States is optimistic or pessimistic?

# EARTHLY EMPIRES
## William C. Symonds
### 1951–

## Brian Grow
### 1969–

## John Cady
### 1932–

*William C. Symonds,* Businessweek *magazine's former Boston bureau chief, is currently the director of the Pathways to Prosperity Project at Harvard Graduate School of Education. Brian Grow is a senior writer at* Business-week, *based in Atlanta. John Cady, a former* Businessweek *researcher and technology manager, is now a librarian. The following essay discusses the business aspects of the "megachurch" phenomenon.*

There's no shortage of churches in Houston, deep in the heart of the Bible Belt. So it's surprising that the largest one in the city—and in the entire country—is tucked away in a depressed corner most Houstonians would never dream of visiting. Yet 30,000 people endure punishing traffic on the narrow roads leading to Lakewood Church every weekend to hear Pastor Joel Osteen deliver upbeat messages of hope. A youthful-looking 42-year-old with a ready smile, he reassures the thousands who show up at each of his five weekend services that "God has a great future in store for you." His services are rousing affairs that often include his wife, Victoria, leading prayers and his mother, Dodie, discussing passages from the Bible.

Osteen is so popular that he has nearly quadrupled attendance since taking over the pulpit from his late father in 1999, winning over believers from other churches as well as throngs of the "unsaved." Many are drawn first by his ubiquitous presence on television. Each week 7 million people catch the slickly produced broadcast of his Sunday sermons on national cable and network channels, for which Lakewood shells out $15 million a year. Adherents often come clutching a copy of Osteen's best-seller, *Your Best Life Now*, which has sold 2.5 million copies since its publication last fall.

To keep them coming back, Lakewood offers free financial counseling, low-cost bulk food, even a "fidelity group" for men with "sexual addictions." Demand is brisk for the self-help sessions. Angie Mosqueda, 34, who was brought up a Catholic, says she and her husband, Mark, first went to Lakewood in 2000 when they were on the brink of a divorce. Mark even threw her out of the house after she confessed to infidelity. But over time, Lakewood counselors "really helped us to forgive one another and start all over again," she says.

## Disney Look

Osteen's flourishing Lakewood enterprise brought in $55 million in contributions last year, four times the 1999 amount, church officials say. Flush with success, Osteen is laying out $90 million to transform the massive Compaq Center in downtown Houston—former home of the NBA's Houston Rockets—into a church that will seat 16,000, complete with a high-tech stage for his TV shows and Sunday School for 5,000 children. After it opens in July, he predicts weekend attendance will rocket to 100,000. Says Osteen: "Other churches have not kept up, and they lose people by not changing with the times."

5      Pastor Joel is one of a new generation of evangelical entrepreneurs transforming their branch of Protestantism into one of the fastest-growing and most influential religious groups in America. Their runaway success is modeled unabashedly on business. They borrow tools ranging from niche marketing to MBA hiring to lift their share of U.S. churchgoers.

Like Osteen, many evangelical pastors focus intently on a huge potential market—the millions of Americans who have drifted away from
mainline Protestant denominations or simply never joined a church in
the first place.

To reach these untapped masses, savvy leaders are creating Sunday
Schools that look like Disney World and church cafes with the appeal
of Starbucks. Although most hold strict religious views, they scrap
staid hymns in favor of multimedia worship and tailor a panoply of
services to meet all kinds of consumer needs, from divorce counseling
to help for parents of autistic kids. Like Osteen, many offer an upbeat
message intertwined with a religious one. To make newcomers feel at
home, some do away with standard religious symbolism—even basics
like crosses and pews—and design churches to look more like modern
entertainment halls than traditional places of worship.

## Branding Whiz

So successful are some evangelicals that they're opening up branches
like so many new Home Depots or Subways. This year, the 16.4 million-
member Southern Baptist Convention plans to "plant" 1,800 new
churches using by-the-book niche-marketing tactics. "We have cowboy
churches for people working on ranches, country music churches, even
several motorcycle churches aimed at bikers," says Martin King, a
spokesman for the Southern Baptists' North American Mission Board.

Branding whizzes that they are, the new church leaders are spreading their ideas through every available outlet. A line of "Biblezines"
packages the New Testament in glossy magazines aimed at different
market segments—there's a hip-hop version and one aimed at teen
girls. Christian music appeals to millions of youths, some of whom
otherwise might never give church a second thought, serving up everything from alternative rock to punk and even "screamo" (they scream
religious lyrics). California megachurch pastor Rick Warren's 2002
book, *The Purpose-Driven Life,* has become the fastest-selling nonfiction
book of all time, with more than 23 million copies sold, in part through
a novel "pyro marketing" strategy. Then there's the Left Behind phenomenon, a series of action-packed, apocalyptic page-turners about
those left on earth after Christ's second coming, selling more than 60
million copies since 1995.

Evangelicals' eager embrace of corporate-style growth strategies is
giving them a tremendous advantage in the battle for religious market
share, says Roger Finke, a Pennsylvania State University sociology professor and co-author of a new book, *The Churching of America, 1776–2005:
Winners and Losers in Our Religious Economy.* A new Pope has given
Catholicism a burst of global publicity, but its nominal membership
growth in the U.S. stems largely from the influx of Mexican immigrants.

Overall, the Catholic Church's long-term decline in U.S. attendance accelerated after the recent sex-abuse scandals, there's a severe priest shortage, and parish churches and schools are closing in the wake of a financial crisis.

10      Similarly, the so-called mainline Protestants who dominated 20th century America have become the religious equivalent of General Motors Corp. The large denominations—including the United Methodist Church and the Episcopal Church—have been shrinking for decades and have lost more than 1 million members in the past 10 years alone. Today, mainline Protestants account for just 16% of the U.S. population, says University of Akron political scientist John C. Green.

In contrast, evangelicalism's theological flexibility gives it the freedom to adapt to contemporary culture. With no overarching authority like the Vatican, leaders don't need to wrestle with a bureaucratic hierarchy that dictates acceptable behavior. "If you have a vision for ministry, you just do it, which makes it far easier to respond to market demand," says University of North Carolina at Chapel Hill sociology professor Christian Smith.

With such low barriers to entry, the number of evangelical megachurches—defined as those that attract at least 2,000 weekly worshippers—has shot up to 880 from 50 in 1980, figures John N. Vaughan, founder of research outfit Church Growth Today in Bolivar, Mo. He calculates that a new megachurch emerges in the U.S. an average of every two days. Overall, white evangelicals make up more than a quarter of Americans today, experts estimate. The figures are fuzzy because there's no common definition of evangelical, which typically refers to Christians who believe the Bible is the literal word of God. They may include many Southern Baptists, nondenominational churches, and some Lutherans and Methodists. There are also nearly 25 million black Protestants who consider themselves evangelicals but largely don't share the conservative politics of most white ones. Says pollster George Gallup, who has studied religious trends for decades: "The evangelicals are the most vibrant branch of Christianity."

The triumph of evangelical Christianity is profoundly reshaping many aspects of American politics and society. Historically, much of the U.S. political and business elite has been mainline Protestant. Today, President George W. Bush and more than a dozen members of Congress, including House Speaker Dennis Hastert, are evangelicals. More important, the Republican Right has been fueled by the swelling ranks of evangelicals, whose leaders tend to be conservative politically despite their progressive marketing methods. In the 1960s and '70s, prominent evangelicals like Billy Graham kept a careful separation of pulpit and politics—even though he served as a spiritual adviser to President Richard M. Nixon. That began to change in the early 1980s, when Jerry Falwell formed the Moral Majority to express evangelicals' political views. Many of today's evangelicals hope to expand their clout even further. They're also gaining by taking their views into Corporate America. Exhibit A: the recent clash at software giant Microsoft.

As they thrive, though, there are growing tensions, with some mainline Protestants offended by their conservative politics and brazen marketing. "Jesus was not a capitalist; check out what [He] says about how hard it is to get into heaven if you're a rich man," says the Reverend Robert W. Edgar, general secretary of the liberal National Council of Churches.

Especially controversial are leaders like Osteen and the flamboyant    15
Creflo A. Dollar, pastor of World Changers Church International in College Park, Ga., who preach "the prosperity gospel." They endorse material wealth and tell followers that God wants them to be prosperous. In his book, Osteen talks about how his wife, Victoria, a striking blonde who dresses fashionably, wanted to buy a fancy house some years ago, before the money rolled in. He thought it wasn't possible. "But Victoria had more faith," he wrote. "She convinced me we could live in an elegant home . . . and several years later, it did come to pass." Dollar, too, defends materialistic success. Dubbed "Pass-the-Dollar" by critics, he owns two Rolls Royces and travels in a Gulfstream 3 jet. "I practice what I preach, and the Bible says . . . that God takes pleasure in the prosperity of his servants," says Dollar, 43, nattily attired in French cuffs and a pinstriped suit.

## Hucksters?

Some evangelical leaders acknowledge that flagrant materialism can raise the specter of religious hucksterism à la Sinclair Lewis' fictional Elmer Gantry[1] or Jim and Tammy Faye Bakker.[2] "Our goal is not to turn the church into a business," insists Warren, the founder of Saddleback megachurch in Lake Forest, Calif. After *The Purpose-Driven Life* made him millions, he repaid Saddleback all the salary he had taken over the years and still lives modestly. Cautions Kurt Frederickson, a director of the Fuller Theological Seminary in Pasadena, Calif.: "We have to be careful when a pastor moves into the CEO mode and becomes too market-oriented, or there might be a reaction against megachurches just as there is against Wal-Mart."

Many evangelicals say they're just trying to satisfy demands not met by traditional churches. Craig Groeschel, who launched Life

---

[1]Evangelical preacher and con man. [Eds.]

[2]Jim Bakker, Assemblies of God minister and former host (with his wife Tammy Faye Bakker) of the evangelical Christian TV program *The PTL Club*. Indicted on federal charges of fraud and tax evasion. [Eds.]

Church in Edmond, Okla., in 1996, started out doing market research with non-churchgoers in the area—and got an earful. "They said churches were full of hypocrites and were boring," he recalls. So he designed Life Church to counter those preconceptions, with lively, multimedia-filled services in a setting that's something between a rock concert and a coffee shop.

Once established, some ambitious churches are making a big business out of spreading their expertise. Willow Creek Community Church in South Barrington, Ill., formed a consulting arm called Willow Creek Assn. It earned $17 million last year, partly by selling marketing and management advice to 10,500 member churches from 90 denominations. Jim Mellado, the hard-charging Harvard MBA who runs it, last year brought an astonishing 110,000 church and lay leaders to conferences on topics such as effective leadership. "Our entrepreneurial impulse comes from the Biblical mandate to get the message out," says Willow Creek founder Bill Hybels, who hired Stanford MBA Greg Hawkins, a former McKinsey & Co. consultant, to handle the church's day-to-day management. Willow Creek's methods have even been lauded in a Harvard Business School case study.

Hybels's consumer-driven approach is evident at Willow Creek, where he shunned stained glass, Bibles, or even a cross for the 7,200-seat, $72 million sanctuary he recently built. The reason? Market research suggested that such traditional symbols would scare away non-churchgoers. He also gives practical advice. On a recent Wednesday evening, one of his four "teaching" pastors gave a service that started with 20 minutes of music, followed by a lengthy sermon about the Christian approach to personal finances. He told the 5,000 listeners about resisting advertising aimed at getting people to buy things they don't need and suggested they follow up at home by e-mailing questions. Like Osteen, Hybels packages self-help programs with a positive message intended to make people feel good about themselves. "When I walk out of a service, I feel completely relieved of any stress I walked in with," says Phil Earnest, 38, a sales manager who in 2003 switched to Willow Creek from the Methodist Church he found too stodgy.

20   So adept at the sell are some evangelicals that it can be difficult to distinguish between their religious aims and the secular style they mimic. Last December, Prestonwood Baptist Church in Plano, Tex., staged a spectacular Christmas festival, including a 500-person choir, that attracted 70,000 people even though the cheapest ticket was $20. Throughout the year, some 16,000 people take part in its sports program, which uses eight playing fields and six gyms on its $100 million, 140-acre campus. The teams, coached by church members, bring in converts, many of them children, says Executive Pastor Mike Buster.

## Gushers of Cash

Kids are often a prime target audience for megachurches. The main campus of Groeschel's Life Church in Edmond, Okla., includes a "Toon Town" of 3D buildings, a 16-foot high slide, and an animatronic police chief who recites rules. All the razzmatazz has helped Life Church quadruple its Sunday school attendance to more than 2,500 a week. "The kids are bringing their parents to church," says children's pastor Scott Werner.

Such marketing and services help to create brand loyalty any CEO would envy. Willow Creek ranks in the top 5% of 250 major brands, right up with Nike and John Deere, says Eric Arnson. He helped develop a consumer-brand practice that McKinsey then bought and recently did a pro bono study for Willow Creek using that methodology.

Other megachurches are franchising their good name. Life Church now has five campuses in Oklahoma and will expand into Phoenix this fall. Pastor Groeschel jumped the 1,000 miles to Arizona after market research pinpointed Phoenix as an area with a large population but few effective churches. Atlanta's Dollar, who is African American, has pushed into five countries, including Nigeria and South Africa.

All this growth, plus the tithing many evangelicals encourage, is generating gushers of cash. A traditional U.S. church typically has fewer than 200 members and an annual budget of around $100,000. The average megachurch pulls in $4.8 million, according to a 1999 study by the Hartford Seminary, one of the few surveys on the topic. The money is also fueling a megachurch building boom. First Baptist Church of Woodstock, near Atlanta, for example, has just finished a $62 million, 7,000-seat sanctuary.

Megachurch business ventures sometimes grow beyond the bounds of the church itself. In the mid-1990s, Kirbyjon Caldwell, a Wharton MBA who sold bonds for First Boston before he enrolled in seminary, formed an economic development corporation that revived a depressed neighborhood near Houston's 14,000-member Windsor Village United Methodist Church, which he heads. A former Kmart now houses a mix of church and private businesses employing 270 people, including a Christian school and a bank. New plans call for a massive center with senior housing, retailing, and a public school.

For all their seemingly unstoppable success, evangelicals must contend with powerful forces in U.S. society. The ranks of Americans who express no religious preference have quadrupled since 1991, to 14%, according to a recent poll. Despite the megachurch surge, overall church attendance has remained fairly flat. And if anything, popular culture has become more vulgar in recent years. Still, experts like pollster Gallup see clear signs of a rising fascination with spirituality in the U.S. The September 11 attacks are one reason. So is the aging of the culturally influential Baby Boom, since spirituality tends to increase with age, he says. If so, no one is better poised than evangelicals to capitalize on the trend.

## Responding to Reading

1. Can you tell whether the writers have a positive, negative, or neutral view of the evangelical churches they describe? Of those who worship there? Of Pastor Osteen? Do the writers think that institutions like Lakewood Church represent the future of religion in the United States? Do you?
2. What does Lakewood Church offer its parishioners? What do you think attracts worshippers to this church and to its pastor?
3. This essay appeared in *Businessweek,* and the writers use business terms to describe the rise of evangelical churches like Lakewood. Identify some examples of such language. Do you think this kind of language is effective? Do you think it is appropriate?

## Responding in Writing

What do you see as the advantages of a "megachurch" like Lakewood? What do you see as the disadvantages?

# THE ELUSIVE BIG IDEA

## Neal Gabler

*A senior fellow at the University of Southern California's Annenberg Norman Lear Center, Neal Gabler is a journalist, cultural historian, political commentator, and film critic. He has authored and coauthored several books, including, most recently,* Walt Disney: The Triumph of the American Imagination *(2006). His work has appeared in such publications as* Esquire, *the* Los Angeles Times, New York *magazine, the* New York Times, Salon, Us, *and* Vogue. *Gabler is currently writing a biography of the late senator Edward M. Kennedy. In the following essay, Gabler considers the future of ideas.*

The July/August issue of the *Atlantic* trumpets the "14 Biggest Ideas of the Year." Take a deep breath. The ideas include "The Players Own the Game" (No. 12), "Wall Street: Same as it Ever Was" (No. 6), "Nothing Stays Secret" (No. 2), and the very biggest idea of the year, "The Rise of the Middle Class—Just Not Ours," which refers to growing economies in Brazil, Russia, India and China.

Now exhale. It may strike you that none of these ideas seem particularly breathtaking. In fact, none of them are ideas. They are more on the order of observations. But one can't really fault the *Atlantic* for mistaking commonplaces for intellectual vision. Ideas just aren't what they used to be. Once upon a time, they could ignite fires of debate, stimulate other thoughts, incite revolutions and fundamentally change the ways we look at and think about the world.

They could penetrate the general culture and make celebrities out of thinkers—notably Albert Einstein, but also Reinhold Niebuhr, Daniel Bell, Betty Friedan, Carl Sagan and Stephen Jay Gould, to name a few. The ideas themselves could even be made famous: for instance, for "the end of ideology," "the medium is the message," "the feminine mystique," "the Big Bang theory," "the end of history." A big idea could capture the cover of *Time*—"Is God Dead?"—and intellectuals like Norman Mailer, William F. Buckley Jr. and Gore Vidal would even occasionally be invited to the couches of late-night talk shows. How long ago that was.

If our ideas seem smaller nowadays, it's not because we are dumber than our forebears but because we just don't care as much about ideas as they did. In effect, we are living in an increasingly post-idea world—a world in which big, thought-provoking ideas that can't instantly be monetized are of so little intrinsic value that fewer people are generating them and fewer outlets are disseminating them, the Internet notwithstanding. Bold ideas are almost passé.

It is no secret, especially here in America, that we live in a post- 5 Enlightenment age in which rationality, science, evidence, logical argument and debate have lost the battle in many sectors, and perhaps even in society generally, to superstition, faith, opinion and orthodoxy. While we continue to make giant technological advances, we may be the first generation to have turned back the epochal clock—to have gone backward intellectually from advanced modes of thinking into old modes of belief. But post-Enlightenment and post-idea, while related, are not exactly the same.

Post-Enlightenment refers to a style of thinking that no longer deploys the techniques of rational thought. Post-idea refers to thinking that is no longer done, regardless of the style.

The post-idea world has been a long time coming, and many factors have contributed to it. There is the retreat in universities from the real world, and an encouragement of and reward for the narrowest specialization rather than for daring—for tending potted plants rather than planting forests.

There is the eclipse of the public intellectual in the general media by the pundit who substitutes outrageousness for thoughtfulness, and the concomitant decline of the essay in general-interest magazines. And there is the rise of an increasingly visual culture, especially among the young—a form in which ideas are more difficult to express.

But these factors, which began decades ago, were more likely harbingers of an approaching post-idea world than the chief causes of it.

The real cause may be information itself. It may seem counterintuitive that at a time when we know more than we have ever known, we think about it less.

10      We live in the much vaunted Age of Information. Courtesy of the Internet, we seem to have immediate access to anything that anyone could ever want to know. We are certainly the most informed generation in history, at least quantitatively. There are trillions upon trillions of bytes out there in the ether—so much to gather and to think about.

And that's just the point. In the past, we collected information not simply to know things. That was only the beginning. We also collected information to convert it into something larger than facts and ultimately more useful—into ideas that made sense of the information. We sought not just to apprehend the world but to truly comprehend it, which is the primary function of ideas. Great ideas explain the world and one another to us.

Marx pointed out the relationship between the means of production and our social and political systems. Freud taught us to explore our minds as a way of understanding our emotions and behaviors. Einstein rewrote physics. More recently, McLuhan theorized about the nature of modern communication and its effect on modern life. These ideas enabled us to get our minds around our existence and attempt to answer the big, daunting questions of our lives.

But if information was once grist for ideas, over the last decade it has become competition for them. We are like the farmer who has too much wheat to make flour. We are inundated with so much information that we wouldn't have time to process it even if we wanted to, and most of us don't want to.

The collection itself is exhausting: what each of our friends is doing at that particular moment and then the next moment and the next one; who Jennifer Aniston is dating right now; which video is going viral on YouTube this hour; what Princess Letizia or Kate Middleton is wearing that day. In effect, we are living within the nimbus of an informational Gresham's law[1] in which trivial information pushes out significant information, but it is also an ideational Gresham's law in which information, trivial or not, pushes out ideas.

15      We prefer knowing to thinking because knowing has more immediate value. It keeps us in the loop, keeps us connected to our friends and our cohort. Ideas are too airy, too impractical, too much work for too little reward. Few talk ideas. Everyone talks information, usually personal information. Where are you going? What are you doing? Whom are you seeing? These are today's big questions.

It is certainly no accident that the post-idea world has sprung up alongside the social networking world. Even though there are sites and

---

[1]Economics law that states devalued money makes more valuable forms of money obsolete over time. [Eds.]

blogs dedicated to ideas, Twitter, Facebook, Myspace, Flickr, etc., the most popular sites on the Web, are basically information exchanges, designed to feed the insatiable information hunger, though this is hardly the kind of information that generates ideas. It is largely useless except insofar as it makes the possessor of the information feel, well, informed. Of course, one could argue that these sites are no different than conversation was for previous generations, and that conversation seldom generated big ideas either, and one would be right.

But the analogy isn't perfect. For one thing, social networking sites are the primary form of communication among young people, and they are supplanting print, which is where ideas have typically gestated. For another, social networking sites engender habits of mind that are inimical to the kind of deliberate discourse that gives rise to ideas. Instead of theories, hypotheses and grand arguments, we get instant 140-character tweets about eating a sandwich or watching a TV show. While social networking may enlarge one's circle and even introduce one to strangers, this is not the same thing as enlarging one's intellectual universe. Indeed, the gab of social networking tends to shrink one's universe to oneself and one's friends, while thoughts organized in words, whether online or on the page, enlarge one's focus.

To paraphrase the famous dictum, often attributed to Yogi Berra, that you can't think and hit at the same time, you can't think and tweet at the same time either, not because it is impossible to multitask but because tweeting, which is largely a burst of either brief, unsupported opinions or brief descriptions of your own prosaic activities, is a form of distraction or anti-thinking.

The implications of a society that no longer thinks big are enormous. Ideas aren't just intellectual playthings. They have practical effects.

An artist friend of mine recently lamented that he felt the art world [20] was adrift because there were no longer great critics like Harold Rosenberg and Clement Greenberg to provide theories of art that could fructify the art and energize it. Another friend made a similar argument about politics. While the parties debate how much to cut the budget, he wondered where were the John Rawlses and Robert Nozicks who could elevate our politics.

One could certainly make the same argument about economics, where John Maynard Keynes remains the center of debate nearly 80 years after propounding his theory of government pump priming. This isn't to say that the successors of Rosenberg, Rawls and Keynes don't exist, only that if they do, they are not likely to get traction in a culture that has so little use for ideas, especially big, exciting, dangerous ones, and that's true whether the ideas come from academics or others who are not part of elite organizations and who challenge the conventional wisdom. All thinkers are victims of information glut, and the ideas of today's thinkers are also victims of that glut.

But it is especially true of big thinkers in the social sciences like the cognitive psychologist Steven Pinker, who has theorized on everything from the source of language to the role of genetics in human nature, or the biologist Richard Dawkins, who has had big and controversial ideas on everything from selfishness to God, or the psychologist Jonathan Haidt, who has been analyzing different moral systems and drawing fascinating conclusions about the relationship of morality to political beliefs. But because they are scientists and empiricists rather than generalists in the humanities, the place from which ideas were customarily popularized, they suffer a double whammy: not only the whammy against ideas generally but the whammy against science, which is typically regarded in the media as mystifying at best, incomprehensible at worst. A generation ago, these men would have made their way into popular magazines and onto television screens. Now they are crowded out by informational effluvium.

No doubt there will be those who say that the big ideas have migrated to the marketplace, but there is a vast difference between profit-making inventions and intellectually challenging thoughts. Entrepreneurs have plenty of ideas, and some, like Steven P. Jobs of Apple, have come up with some brilliant ideas in the "inventional" sense of the word.

Still, while these ideas may change the way we live, they rarely transform the way we think. They are material, not ideational. It is thinkers who are in short supply, and the situation probably isn't going to change anytime soon.

25    We have become information narcissists, so uninterested in anything outside ourselves and our friendship circles or in any tidbit we cannot share with those friends that if a Marx or a Nietzsche were suddenly to appear, blasting his ideas, no one would pay the slightest attention, certainly not the general media, which have learned to service our narcissism.

What the future portends is more and more information—Everests of it. There won't be anything we won't know. But there will be no one thinking about it.

Think about that.

## Responding to Reading

1. According to Gabler, what is the difference between an idea and an observation? Why is this distinction important to him?

2. Gabler says that we live in "an increasingly post-idea world" (4), noting that the most popular social networking sites on the Web are "information exchanges" that do little to "generate ideas" (16). What does he mean? Do you agree?

3. What does Gabler mean when he says that entrepreneurs like Steve Jobs have ideas in the "inventional sense of the word" (23)? Why do their ideas "rarely transform the way we think" (24)? What are the implications of this situation for the future?

## Responding in Writing

Do you agree with Gabler's assertion that we live in a culture that has "little use for ideas, especially big, exciting, dangerous ones . . . " (21)?

# THE NEXT AMERICAN FRONTIER
## Michael S. Malone
### 1954–

*Michael S. Malone writes about a range of topics related to business and technology. He is the author of several books, including, most recently,* No Size Fits All: From Mass Marketing to Mass Handselling *(2009), coauthored with Tom Hayes. His work has appeared in such publications as the* Economist, *the* New York Times, *and the* Wall Street Journal. *In the following essay, Malone considers "new American frontiers."*

The entire world seems to be heading toward points of inflection. The developing world is embarking on the digital age. The developed world is entering the Internet era. And the United States, once again at the vanguard, is on the verge of becoming the world's first Entrepreneurial Nation.

At the Chicago World's Fair in 1893, Frederick Jackson Turner delivered a paper to the American Historical Association—the most famous ever by an American historian. In "The Significance of the Frontier in American History," he noted that, according to the most recent U.S. census, so much of the nation had been settled that there was no longer an identifiable western migration. The very notion of a "frontier" was obsolete.

For three centuries the frontier had defined us, tantalized us with the perpetual chance to "light out for the territories" and start our lives over. It was the foundation of those very American notions of "federalism" and "rugged individualism." But Americans had crossed an invisible line in history, entering a new world with a new set of rules.

What Turner couldn't guess was that the unexplored prairie would become the uninvented new product, the unexploited new market and the untried new business plan.

The great new American frontiers proved to be those of business, 5 science and technology. In the course of the 20th century, Americans invented more milestone technologies and inventions, created more wealth and leisure time, and reorganized their institutions more times than any country had ever done before—despite a massive economic depression and two world wars. It all reached a crescendo in the magical year of 1969, with the creation of the Internet, the invention of the microprocessor and, most of all, a man walking on the moon.

Along with genetic engineering, we are still busily spinning out the implications of these marvels. Yet it is becoming increasingly apparent that the cultural underpinnings of these activities have changed in some fundamental way.

We still have schools, but a growing number of our children are studying at home or attending private schools—and those in public schools are doing ever more amounts of their class work on the Internet.

We still have companies and corporations, but now they are virtualized, with online work teams handing off assignments to each other 24/7 around the world. Men and women go to work, but the office is increasingly likely to be in the den. In 2005, an Intel survey of its employees found that nearly 20% of its professionals had never met their boss face-to-face. Half of them never expected to. Last summer, when the Media X institute at Stanford extended that survey to IBM, Sun, HP, Microsoft and Cisco, the percentages turned out to be even greater.

Newspapers are dying, networks are dying, and if teenage boys playing GTA 4 and World of Warcraft have any say about it, so is television. More than 200 million people now belong to just two social networks: MySpace and Facebook. And there are more than 80 million videos on YouTube, all put there by the same individual initiative.

10    The most compelling statistic of all? Half of all new college graduates now believe that self-employment is more secure than a full-time job. Today, 80% of the colleges and universities in the U.S. now offer courses on entrepreneurship; 60% of Gen Y business owners consider themselves to be serial entrepreneurs, according to *Inc.* magazine. Tellingly, 18 to 24-year-olds are starting companies at a faster rate than 35 to 44-year-olds. And 70% of today's high schoolers intend to start their own companies, according to a Gallup poll.

An upcoming wave of new workers in our society will never work for an established company if they can help it. To them, having a traditional job is one of the biggest career failures they can imagine.

Much of childhood today is spent, not in organized sports or organizations, but in ad hoc teams playing online games such as Half Life, or competing in robotics tournaments, or in constructing and decorating MySpace pages. Without knowing it, we have been training a whole generation of young entrepreneurs.

And who is going to dissuade them? Mom, who is a self-employed consultant working out of the spare bedroom? Or Dad, who is at Starbucks working on the spreadsheet of his new business plan?

In the past there have been trading states like Venice, commercial regions like the Hanseatic League, and even so-called nations of shopkeepers. But there has never been a nation in which the dominant paradigm is entrepreneurship. Not just self-employment or sole proprietorship, but serial company-building, entire careers built on perpetual change, independence and the endless pursuit of the next opportunity.

Without noticing it, we have once again discovered, and then raced 15 off to settle, a new frontier. Not land, not innovation, but ourselves and a growing control over our own lives and careers.

And why not? Each step in the development of American society has been towards an ever-greater level of independence, freedom and personal liberty. And as the rest of the world catches up to where we were, we've already moved on to the next epoch in the national story.

But liberty exacts its own demands. Entrepreneurial America is likely to become even more innovative than it is today. And that innovation is likely to spread across society, not just as products and inventions, but new ways of living and new types of organizations.

The economy will be much more volatile and much more competitive. In the continuous fervor to create new institutions, it will become increasingly difficult to sustain old ones. New political parties, new social groupings, thousands of new manias and movements and millions of new companies will pop up over the next few decades. Large corporations that don't figure out how to combine permanence with perpetual change will be swept away.

This higher level of anarchy will be exciting, but it will also sometimes be very painful. Entire industries will die almost overnight, laying off thousands, while others will just as suddenly appear, hungry for employees. Continuity and predictability will become the rarest of commodities. And if the entrepreneurial personality honors smart failures, by the same token it has little pity for weakness. That fraction of Americans—10%, 20%—who still dream of the gold watch or the 30-year pin will suffer the most . . . and unless their needs are somehow met as well, they will remain a perpetually open wound in our society.

Scary, exciting, liberating, frustrating, infinitely ambitious and 20 thoroughly amnesic. If you live in a high-tech community like Silicon Valley or Redmond or Austin, you already live in this world. It's hard to imagine more exciting places to be.

For all of our fears about privacy and security, for all the added pressures that will be created by heightened competition and clashing ambitions, America as an entrepreneurial nation will reward each of us with greater independence—and perhaps even greater happiness—than ever before. It waits out there for each of us. Being good entrepreneurs, it's time to look ahead, develop a good plan, and then bet everything on ourselves.

## Responding to Reading

1. Why does Malone begin his essay by talking about Frederick Jackson Turner? How do Turner's ideas set the stage for the rest of the essay?
2. According to Malone, what are "the great new American frontiers" (5)? Why was 1969 a "magical year" (5)?

3.  In paragraph 15, Malone says that the new frontier we are settling is "Not land, not innovation, but ourselves and a growing control of our own lives and careers." What does he mean? What are the implications for the future of Malone's new frontier? Do you agree?

## Responding in Writing

In paragraph 11, Malone says that "new workers in our society" consider getting "a traditional job" with an "established company" to be "one of the biggest career failures" they can imagine. Why? Do you think these workers have a point?

# INNOVATION STARVATION

## Neal Stephenson

### 1959–

*Neal Stephenson writes science fiction and essays with an emphasis on technology and the future. He is the author of several novels, including, most recently,* Reamde *(2011). His work has also appeared in* Wired *magazine,* World Policy Journal, *and other publications. In the following essay, Stephenson considers the future of creativity.*

My lifespan encompasses the era when the United States of America was capable of launching human beings into space. Some of my earliest memories are of sitting on a braided rug before a hulking black-and-white television, watching the early Gemini missions. This summer, at the age of 51—not even old—I watched on a flatscreen as the last Space Shuttle lifted off the pad. I have followed the dwindling of the space program with sadness, even bitterness. Where's my donut-shaped space station? Where's my ticket to Mars? Until recently, though, I have kept my feelings to myself. Space exploration has always had its detractors. To complain about its demise is to expose oneself to attack from those who have no sympathy that an affluent, middle-aged white American has not lived to see his boyhood fantasies fulfilled.

Still, I worry that our inability to match the achievements of the 1960s space program might be symptomatic of a general failure of our society to get big things done. My parents and grandparents witnessed the creation of the airplane, the automobile, nuclear energy, and the computer to name only a few. Scientists and engineers who came of age during the first half of the 20th century could look forward to building things that would solve age-old problems, transform the landscape, build the economy, and provide jobs for the burgeoning middle class that was the basis for our stable democracy.

The Deepwater Horizon oil spill of 2010 crystallized my feeling that we have lost our ability to get important things done. The OPEC oil shock was in 1973—almost 40 years ago. It was obvious then that it was crazy for the United States to let itself be held economic hostage to the kinds of countries where oil was being produced. It led to Jimmy Carter's proposal for the development of an enormous synthetic fuels industry on American soil. Whatever one might think of the merits of the Carter presidency or of this particular proposal, it was, at least, a serious effort to come to grips with the problem.

Little has been heard in that vein since. We've been talking about wind farms, tidal power, and solar power for decades. Some progress has been made in those areas, but energy is still all about oil. In my city, Seattle, a 35-year-old plan to run a light rail line across Lake Washington is now being blocked by a citizen initiative. Thwarted or endlessly delayed in its efforts to build things, the city plods ahead with a project to paint bicycle lanes on the pavement of thoroughfares.

In early 2011, I participated in a conference called Future Tense, 5 where I lamented the decline of the manned space program, then pivoted to energy, indicating that the real issue isn't about rockets. It's our far broader inability as a society to execute on the big stuff. I had, through some kind of blind luck, struck a nerve. The audience at Future Tense was more confident than I that science fiction [SF] had relevance—even utility—in addressing the problem. I heard two theories as to why:

1. The Inspiration Theory. SF inspires people to choose science and engineering as careers. This much is undoubtedly true, and somewhat obvious.
2. The Hieroglyph Theory. Good SF supplies a plausible, fully thought-out picture of an alternate reality in which some sort of compelling innovation has taken place. A good SF universe has a coherence and internal logic that makes sense to scientists and engineers. Examples include Isaac Asimov's robots, Robert Heinlein's rocket ships, and William Gibson's cyberspace. As Jim Karkanias of Microsoft Research puts it, such icons serve as hieroglyphs—simple, recognizable symbols on whose significance everyone agrees.

Researchers and engineers have found themselves concentrating on more and more narrowly focused topics as science and technology have become more complex. A large technology company or lab might employ hundreds or thousands of persons, each of whom can address only a thin slice of the overall problem. Communication among them can become a mare's nest of email threads and Powerpoints. The fondness that many such people have for SF reflects, in part, the usefulness of an over-arching narrative that supplies them and their colleagues with a shared vision. Coordinating their efforts through a command-and-control management system is a little like trying to run a modern economy out of a Politburo.[1] Letting them work toward an agreed-on goal is something more like a free and largely self-coordinated market of ideas.

## Spanning the Ages

SF has changed over the span of time I am talking about—from the 1950s (the era of the development of nuclear power, jet airplanes, the space race, and the computer) to now. Speaking broadly, the techno-optimism of the Golden Age of SF has given way to fiction written in a generally darker, more skeptical and ambiguous tone. I myself have tended to write a lot about hackers—trickster archetypes who exploit the arcane capabilities of complex systems devised by faceless others.

10       Believing we have all the technology we'll ever need, we seek to draw attention to its destructive side effects. This seems foolish now that we find ourselves saddled with technologies like Japan's ramshackle 1960's-vintage reactors at Fukushima when we have the possibility of clean nuclear fusion on the horizon. The imperative to develop new technologies and implement them on a heroic scale no longer seems like the childish preoccupation of a few nerds with slide rules. It's the only way for the human race to escape from its current predicaments. Too bad we've forgotten how to do it.

"You're the ones who've been slacking off!" proclaims Michael Crow, president of Arizona State University (and one of the other speakers at Future Tense). He refers, of course, to SF writers. The scientists and engineers, he seems to be saying, are ready and looking for things to do. Time for the SF writers to start pulling their weight and supplying big visions that make sense. Hence the Hieroglyph project, an effort to produce an anthology of new SF that will be in some ways a conscious throwback to the practical techno-optimism of the Golden Age.

## Spaceborne Civilizations

China is frequently cited as a country now executing on Big Stuff, and there's no doubt they are constructing dams, high-speed rail systems, and rockets at an extraordinary clip. But those are not fundamentally innovative. Their space program, like all other countries' (including our own), is just parroting work that was done 50 years ago by the Soviets and the Americans. A truly innovative program would involve taking

---

[1]Communist political committee. [Eds.]

risks (and accepting failures) to pioneer some of the alternative space launch technologies that have been advanced by researchers all over the world during the decades dominated by rockets.

Imagine a factory mass-producing small vehicles, about as big and complicated as refrigerators, which roll off the end of an assembly line, are loaded with space-bound cargo, and topped off with non-polluting liquid hydrogen fuel, then exposed to intense concentrated heat from an array of ground-based lasers or microwave antennas. Heated to temperatures beyond what can be achieved through a chemical reaction, the hydrogen erupts from a nozzle on the base of the device and sends it rocketing into the air. Tracked through its flight by the lasers or microwaves, the vehicle soars into orbit, carrying a larger payload for its size than a chemical rocket could ever manage, but the complexity, expense, and jobs remain grounded. For decades, this has been the vision of such researchers as physicists Jordin Kare and Kevin Parkin. A similar idea, using a pulsed ground-based laser to blast propellant from the backside of a space vehicle, was being talked about by Arthur Kantrowitz, Freeman Dyson, and other eminent physicists in the early 1960s.

If that sounds too complicated, then consider the 2003 proposal of Geoff Landis and Vincent Denis to construct a 20-kilometer-high tower using simple steel trusses. Conventional rockets launched from its top would be able to carry twice as much payload as comparable ones launched from ground level. There is even abundant research, dating all the way back to Konstantin Tsiolkovsky, the father of astronautics beginning in the late 19th century, to show that a simple tether—a long rope, tumbling end-over-end while orbiting the earth—could be used to scoop payloads out of the upper atmosphere and haul them up into orbit without the need for engines of any kind. Energy would be pumped into the system using an electrodynamic process with no moving parts.

All are promising ideas—just the sort that used to get an earlier 15 generation of scientists and engineers fired up about actually building something.

But to grasp just how far our current mindset is from being able to attempt innovation on such a scale, consider the fate of the space shuttle's external tanks [ETs]. Dwarfing the vehicle itself, the ET was the largest and most prominent feature of the space shuttle as it stood on the pad. It remained attached to the shuttle—or perhaps it makes as much sense to say that the shuttle remained attached to it—long after the two strap-on boosters had fallen away. The ET and the shuttle remained connected all the way out of the atmosphere and into space. Only after the system had attained orbital velocity was the tank jettisoned and allowed to fall into the atmosphere, where it was destroyed on re-entry.

At a modest marginal cost, the ETs could have been kept in orbit indefinitely. The mass of the ET at separation, including residual propellants, was about twice that of the largest possible Shuttle payload. Not destroying them would have roughly tripled the total mass launched into orbit by the Shuttle. ETs could have been connected to build units that would have humbled today's International Space Station. The residual oxygen and hydrogen sloshing around in them could have been combined to generate electricity and produce tons of water, a commodity that is vastly expensive and desirable in space. But in spite of hard work and passionate advocacy by space experts who wished to see the tanks put to use, NASA—for reasons both technical and political—sent each of them to fiery destruction in the atmosphere. Viewed as a parable, it has much to tell us about the difficulties of innovating in other spheres.

## Executing the Big Stuff

Innovation can't happen without accepting the risk that it might fail. The vast and radical innovations of the mid-20th century took place in a world that, in retrospect, looks insanely dangerous and unstable. Possible outcomes that the modern mind identifies as serious risks might not have been taken seriously—supposing they were noticed at all—by people habituated to the Depression, the World Wars, and the Cold War, in times when seat belts, antibiotics, and many vaccines did not exist. Competition between the Western democracies and the communist powers obliged the former to push their scientists and engineers to the limits of what they could imagine and supplied a sort of safety net in the event that their initial efforts did not pay off. A grizzled NASA veteran once told me that the Apollo moon landings were communism's greatest achievement.

In his recent book *Adapt: Why Success Always Starts with Failure*, Tim Harford outlines Charles Darwin's discovery of a vast array of distinct species in the Galapagos Islands—a state of affairs that contrasts with the picture seen on large continents, where evolutionary experiments tend to get pulled back toward a sort of ecological consensus by interbreeding. "Galapagan isolation" vs. the "nervous corporate hierarchy" is the contrast staked out by Harford in assessing the ability of an organization to innovate.

20    Most people who work in corporations or academia have witnessed something like the following: A number of engineers are sitting together in a room, bouncing ideas off each other. Out of the discussion emerges a new concept that seems promising. Then some laptop-wielding person in the corner, having performed a quick Google search, announces that this "new" idea is, in fact, an old one—or at least vaguely similar—and has already been tried. Either it failed, or it succeeded. If it failed,

then no manager who wants to keep his or her job will approve spending money trying to revive it. If it succeeded, then it's patented and entry to the market is presumed to be unattainable, since the first people who thought of it will have "first-mover advantage" and will have created "barriers to entry." The number of seemingly promising ideas that have been crushed in this way must number in the millions.

What if that person in the corner hadn't been able to do a Google search? It might have required weeks of library research to uncover evidence that the idea wasn't entirely new—and after a long and toilsome slog through many books, tracking down many references, some relevant, some not. When the precedent was finally unearthed, it might not have seemed like such a direct precedent after all. There might be reasons why it would be worth taking a second crack at the idea, perhaps hybridizing it with innovations from other fields. Hence the virtues of Galapagan isolation.

The counterpart to Galapagan isolation is the struggle for survival on a large continent, where firmly established ecosystems tend to blur and swamp new adaptations. Jaron Lanier, a computer scientist, composer, visual artist, and author of the recent book *You Are Not a Gadget: A Manifesto,* has some insights about the unintended consequences of the Internet—the informational equivalent of a large continent—on our ability to take risks. In the pre-net era, managers were forced to make decisions based on what they knew to be limited information. Today, by contrast, data flows to managers in real time from countless sources that could not even be imagined a couple of generations ago, and powerful computers process, organize, and display the data in ways that are as far beyond the hand-drawn graph-paper plots of my youth as modern video games are to tic-tac-toe. In a world where decision-makers are so close to being omniscient, it's easy to see risk as a quaint artifact of a primitive and dangerous past.

The illusion of eliminating uncertainly from corporate decision-making is not merely a question of management style or personal preference. In the legal environment that has developed around publicly traded corporations, managers are strongly discouraged from shouldering any risks that they know about—or, in the opinion of some future jury, should have known about—even if they have a hunch that the gamble might pay off in the long run. There is no such thing as "long run" in industries driven by the next quarterly report. The possibility of some innovation making money is just that—a mere possibility that will not have time to materialize before the subpoenas from minority shareholder lawsuits begin to roll in.

Today's belief in ineluctable certainty is the true innovation-killer of our age. In this environment, the best an audacious manager can do is to develop small improvements to existing systems—climbing the hill, as it were, toward a local maximum, trimming fat, eking out the occasional tiny innovation—like city planners painting bicycle lanes on the streets as a gesture toward solving our energy problems. Any strategy that involves crossing a valley—accepting short-term losses to reach a higher hill in the distance—will soon be brought to a halt by the demands of a system that celebrates short-term gains and tolerates stagnation, but condemns anything else as failure. In short, a world where big stuff can never get done.

## Responding to Reading

1.  Do you think Stephenson's career as a science fiction writer gives him special insight into his subject? What references to science fiction does he make in his essay? How do these references help to reinforce his essay's central point?
2.  Stephenson says that he wonders if our failure "to match the achievements of the 1960s space program" is symptomatic of our general inability "to get big things done" (2). What does he mean? What evidence does he present to support this concern? Does he make a convincing case?
3.  What is the difference between "Galapagan isolation" and the "nervous corporate hierarchy" (19)? According to Stephenson, how do these two concepts help explain the ability (or inability) of an organization to innovate?

## Responding in Writing

Do you, like Stephenson, worry that we will not be able to match the scientific and technical achievements of the past? Or, do you believe our greatest achievements in these areas are yet to come?

─────────── **FOCUS** ───────────

## What Comes Next?

Hillary Rodham at her Wellesley College graduation, 1969

## Responding to the Image

1. The photo above shows Hillary Rodham Clinton (then Hillary D. Rodham) at her 1969 graduation, where she delivered a commencement speech to her class. In her speech, she mentions that her fellow students have always questioned the basic assumptions underlying their education and that this questioning forced Wellesley to make certain changes. How much influence do you think students should have concerning academic policy decisions?

2. Later in her speech, Clinton says, "We're searching for [a] more immediate, ecstatic and penetrating mode of living. And so our questions, our questions about our institutions, about our colleges, about our churches, about our government continue." When you think about the future—after you graduate—what specific questions do you have? Which questions do you think you will be able to answer? Which do you think will remain unanswered?

3. Toward the end of her speech, Clinton says, "I was talking to [a] woman who said that she wouldn't want to be me for anything in the world. She wouldn't want to live today and look ahead to what it is she sees because she's afraid. Fear is always with us but we just don't have time for it. Not now." If Clinton were graduating this year (instead of 1969), do you think that she would express the same optimism about the future? Explain.

# Commencement Speech, Los Angeles City College, 2010

## Hilda L. Solis

### 1957–

*Hilda L. Solis, the United States Secretary of Labor in the Obama administra-*
*tion, coauthored the 2010 book* Reinvesting in America's Youth: Lessons
from the 2009 Recovery Act Summer Youth Employment Initiative. *
*Solis delivered the following commencement address at Los Angeles City Col-*
*lege in 2010.*

Good morning Los Angeles City College 2010 graduates! Thank you
Dr. (Jamillah) Moore for your warm introduction. It's great to see you
again. Dr. Moore and I have known each other from our days in the
California State Assembly. Dr. Moore's passion for community colleges is evident as her leadership extends to issues at both the state
and federal levels. And I think that we can all agree that she always
puts her students and those in most need at the forefront of everything she does.

I want to acknowledge and thank the faculty and staff that are
present. I also want to welcome your City Controller Wendy Gruel and
Assemblyman Warren Furatani for joining us as well.

It's an honor to speak at the 2010 Los Angeles City College graduation ceremony! I think that now is the appropriate time to say . . .
congratulations class of 2010! You deserve a big round of applause.

I know many family members are here. . . . I want to congratulate
all the parents, grandparents, wives, husbands and children. Today, we
also celebrate all of the support you gave these graduates during their
time here at Los Angeles City College. Even if it was just that delicious
breakfast your mom made you or that $50.00 your grandfather gave
you for your textbook. Or that tender hug you received from your
spouse after your exam! Your family played an important role in your
education!

5      And at this time, I want to extend a special welcome and congratulate the nineteen U.S. veterans who are graduating today. I
thank each and every one of you for your sacrifice and service to our
country!

I must say, from where I'm standing the class of 2010 looks like
they are going to conquer the world!

Standing here in front of you reminds me of the moment I was in
your place . . . boy was it challenging . . . especially to have been the first
in the family to go to college. I understand that 50% of today's graduates
are the first in their family to graduate from college. Graduates, this is

a remarkable accomplishment and you are setting a wonderful example for your families and community.

Who would have thought that one day this farm land—once the original campus for UCLA—would become an institution that would prepare generations of professionals? In September of 1929 Los Angeles City College opened its doors to 1,300 students, with close to 60 teachers on staff. Fast-track to 2010 and you have more than 17,000 students enrolled here! Today 1,600 degrees and certificates will be awarded, which is the most since 1985. This is a remarkable milestone and Dr. Moore, I congratulate you and your staff!

Great minds and great students do come out of community colleges. That is why I began my career in public service as a Board Member of the Rio Hondo Community College Board of Trustees. And, as I look around, I am filled with a sense of pride and excitement for this graduating class. We are here to celebrate your achievements and your hard work. You've put in your time and it has paid off. Yes, some days I'm sure were more difficult than others, but you always found a solution. You've learned from one another; you've helped each other . . . regardless of where you come from, your paths have crossed here at this campus and today we celebrate the finish line for this part of your life.

One day, many of you will be behind this podium telling your story. With all honesty, I never imagined a moment like this would come in my life. You want to know why? Because in high school a counselor told me I was not the type of person that could go to college. He told me I should settle for a secretarial job. Apparently, he thought I had a bright future as an office assistant. I guess he could predict the future because I did become a secretary, the Secretary of Labor. 10

Students, I tell you, it's easy to give up, especially when we come from a family with financial difficulties and when our parents don't fully understand the educational system in this country. In my case, my mother migrated from Nicaragua and my father came from Mexico . . . both worked hard and barely earned the minimum wage. They worked to provide for us, sacrificing their health along the way to make sure we had a roof over our heads and food on our table. But that did not matter because we had things more valuable than money; we had love, dignity and respect in our home.

And one thing I will never forget: my father taught me to not be afraid to ask questions. So I started to ask a lot of questions. I wanted to know how people obtained Pell Grants, Cal Grants, Financial Aid, work-study . . . all of those things . . . I asked and I found out.

Soon, I was working at the bookstore and then at the public library; I was earning money while going to school . . . just like many of you did. My siblings realized the opportunities too . . . and today, my twin sisters are engineers and another sister has a PhD in public health.

You still have a road to travel . . . and it won't be easy, but you are determined to make your dreams a reality. Just remember that the steps you take after today will be extremely important for your future. Don't wait around too long to think about what you're going to do next because the clock is ticking. Go out and take risks . . . find mentors, network, set goals for yourself, learn about other cultures and issues. Little did I know that the people I was meeting in high school and college were shaping the person I am today!

15     My education and involvement with the community made me aware of the social and civic turmoil taking place in my own neighborhood. I grew up in La Puente, about 30 minutes from here. You want to know who and what inspired me to pursue the field that I am in today? It was the people around me . . . my community!

The more I learned about the issues affecting my immediate environment, the more reasons I had to stand up on behalf of a united voice. It broke my heart to learn that people were being mistreated at the workplace. Some were facing discrimination, some were not getting paid for their work, and many were exposed to toxic chemicals and landfills. I wanted to do something about it. That was my calling . . . a calling for me to take action and help to be a voice and champion for my community's most vulnerable citizens!

My first task as a public servant would be to help community colleges increase the diversity among minorities and women. Following that, I worked to improve community colleges' vocational job training programs. When I became a legislator, I tackled other important issues like health care, domestic violence . . . and veterans needed a voice too . . . I saw the need for representation in different places. Also, during the late 90's, I noticed that polluting projects were operating here in Los Angeles . . . and primarily in minority and low-income neighborhoods!

The 90210 zip code was not touched or polluted that's for sure, but the poor were breathing harmful air. I went against the businesses that were profiting from this tragedy and other politicians refused to stand with me. I always think that "fighting for what is just is not always popular but it is necessary." And that's exactly what I did. As a result, in 1999 Governor Gray Davis signed into law Senate Bill 115, the first of its kind. This law was defined as "the fair treatment of all races, cultures, and incomes with respect to the development, adoption, implementation, and enforcement of environmental laws."

I would soon be surprised with a prestigious award for my environmental work. I was the first woman to receive the John F. Kennedy Profile in Courage Award—for my courage to stand and fight on behalf of disadvantaged communities. But my work did not stop in the California State Senate and Legislature! During my eight years in Congress I worked to help ease the burden of working families:

- I fought to allow immigrant students to attend state colleges at in-state tuition rates;

- I have proudly supported the Dream Act;

- I pressed for legislation to help reduce teen pregnancy within Latinas and African Americans; and

- I helped pass legislation to fund domestic violence programs.

Now, as your Secretary of Labor, it is my obligation to help American workers and all of you prepare for jobs in the 21st century economy. An education can fortify you against the uncertainties of a 21st century economy. And your education is even more important now that you're entering a tough job market. You're accepting your degrees as international competition increases, and with an economy that's still rebounding. In the words of President Obama—"let there be no doubt—the future belongs to the nation that best educates its citizens." 20

With your degree and certificates in hand, you're in a stronger position to outcompete workers around the globe. Workers with more technical expertise and critical thinking capacity will be best positioned to secure the higher wage jobs of the future. Today, the reality is that African-Americans and Latinos are not entering fields related to science, technology, engineering, and math! STEM jobs as they call it. Even fewer women are bound to go into those careers.

And along that field of work will be "green jobs." Green jobs are more than a job; they are the future careers of the 21st century economy. The President and I strongly believe that green jobs will be a key driver behind America's economic recovery. These clean energy jobs are available to anyone willing to upgrade their skills. However, the bigger question is . . . who will lead the world in making the fuel-efficient vehicles, wind turbines, solar panels and other technologies of tomorrow? Let me tell you who will . . . American workers will and many of you here today.

This Administration's number one priority in confronting the economic crisis is to put Americans back to work. Therefore, the Labor Department is making the necessary investments for workers and as of now . . . we are:

- investing $720 million in job training programs that focus on careers in allied health, clean and renewable energy and information technology.

- enforcing our labor laws, so that you are paid fairly and have a safe workplace.

- protecting vulnerable workers, because no one should be subject to workplace discrimination.

In essence, we are preparing the next generation of the U.S. labor force and I want to make sure you're part of it.

Class of 2010, the opportunities for a better life and a better tomorrow are all in your hands. Let this be "only" the beginning of the great things you have yet to accomplish. Ask yourself . . . what will I do after today? Will you take the easy path from here? Or, will you be ready for the next challenge? "Let us think of education as the means of developing our greatest abilities, because in each of us there is a private hope and dream which, fulfilled, can be translated into benefit for everyone and greater strength for our Nation." Those were the words of President John F. Kennedy.

25    Starting today, your dreams and aspirations will continue to fuel the next generation of scholars. Your education will benefit your families, communities and ultimately our country because you are the future of our nation.

So, class of 2010, many great opportunities await you . . . it's up to you to go after them!

It was an honor to be here with you on this very important day.

Congratulations . . . you deserve to celebrate!

Felicidades y si se puede![1]

## Responding to Reading

1. Solis's speech has two parts. In the first part, she tells listeners about herself. In the second part, she discusses her role as Secretary of Labor. How do these two parts complement each other? Are both topics relevant to her audience? Explain.

2. In her speech, Solis tells about a high school counselor who advised her to become a secretary. What lesson does this story teach about success? About failure?

3. Solis delivered her speech to graduates who were about to enter a very difficult job market. What advice does she give them? In light of the economic situation, do you think her advice is useful? Explain.

## Responding in Writing

If you were giving a speech to the graduates of Los Angeles City College, what advice would you give them?

---

[1]Spanish for *Congratulations and yes you can!* [Eds.]

# Commencement Speech, University of Portland, 2009
## Paul Hawken
### 1946–

*An environmentalist and entrepreneur, Paul Hawken is the CEO of OneSun Solar and the cofounder of Highwater Global Fund. Hawken is the author of numerous books, including, most recently,* Blessed Unrest: How the Largest Movement in the World Came into Being, and Why No One Saw It Coming *(2007). He has published articles in* BioScience, *the* Boston Globe, Esquire, Harvard Business Review, Inc., Mother Jones, Nation's Business, Orion, *the* San Francisco Chronicle, Sierra, *and* Utne Reader. *Hawken delivered the following commencement address at the University of Portland in 2009.*

When I was invited to give this speech, I was asked if I could give a simple short talk that was "direct, naked, taut, honest, passionate, lean, shivering, startling, and graceful." No pressure there.

Let's begin with the startling part. Class of 2009: you are going to have to figure out what it means to be a human being on earth at a time when every living system is declining, and the rate of decline is accelerating. Kind of a mind-boggling situation . . . but not one peer-reviewed paper published in the last thirty years can refute that statement. Basically, civilization needs a new operating system, you are the programmers, and we need it within a few decades.

This planet came with a set of instructions, but we seem to have misplaced them. Important rules like don't poison the water, soil, or air, don't let the earth get overcrowded, and don't touch the thermostat have been broken. Buckminster Fuller[1] said that spaceship earth was so ingeniously designed that no one has a clue that we are on one, flying through the universe at a million miles per hour, with no need for seatbelts, lots of room in coach, and really good food—but all that is changing.

There is invisible writing on the back of the diploma you will receive, and in case you didn't bring lemon juice to decode it, I can tell you what it says: You are Brilliant, and the Earth is Hiring. The earth couldn't afford to send recruiters or limos to your school. It sent you rain, sunsets, ripe cherries, night blooming jasmine, and that unbelievably cute person you are dating. Take the hint. And here's the deal: Forget that this task of planet-saving is not possible in the time required. Don't be put off by people who know what is not possible. Do what

---

[1]American engineer and architect (1895–1983). [Eds.]

needs to be done, and check to see if it was impossible only after you are done.

5    When asked if I am pessimistic or optimistic about the future, my answer is always the same: If you look at the science about what is happening on earth and aren't pessimistic, you don't understand the data. But if you meet the people who are working to restore this earth and the lives of the poor, and you aren't optimistic, you haven't got a pulse. What I see everywhere in the world are ordinary people willing to confront despair, power, and incalculable odds in order to restore some semblance of grace, justice, and beauty to this world. The poet Adrienne Rich wrote, "So much has been destroyed I have cast my lot with those who, age after age, perversely, with no extraordinary power, reconstitute the world." There could be no better description. Humanity is coalescing. It is reconstituting the world, and the action is taking place in schoolrooms, farms, jungles, villages, campuses, companies, refugee camps, deserts, fisheries, and slums.

You join a multitude of caring people. No one knows how many groups and organizations are working on the most salient issues of our day: climate change, poverty, deforestation, peace, water, hunger, conservation, human rights, and more. This is the largest movement the world has ever seen. Rather than control, it seeks connection. Rather than dominance, it strives to disperse concentrations of power. Like Mercy Corps,[2] it works behind the scenes and gets the job done. Large as it is, no one knows the true size of this movement. It provides hope, support, and meaning to billions of people in the world. Its clout resides in idea, not in force. It is made up of teachers, children, peasants, businesspeople, rappers, organic farmers, nuns, artists, government workers, fisherfolk, engineers, students, incorrigible writers, weeping Muslims, concerned mothers, poets, doctors without borders, grieving Christians, street musicians, the President of the United States of America, and as the writer David James Duncan would say, the Creator, the One who loves us all in such a huge way.

There is a rabbinical teaching that says if the world is ending and the Messiah arrives, first plant a tree, and then see if the story is true. Inspiration is not garnered from the litanies of what may befall us; it resides in humanity's willingness to restore, redress, reform, rebuild, recover, reimagine, and reconsider. "One day you finally knew what you had to do, and began, though the voices around you kept shouting their bad advice," is Mary Oliver's[3] description of moving away from the profane toward a deep sense of connectedness to the living world.

---

[2]Global aid organization. [Eds.]
[3]American poet (1935– ). [Eds.]

Millions of people are working on behalf of strangers, even if the evening news is usually about the death of strangers. This kindness of strangers has religious, even mythic origins, and very specific eighteenth-century roots. Abolitionists were the first people to create a national and global movement to defend the rights of those they did not know. Until that time, no group had filed a grievance except on behalf of itself. The founders of this movement were largely unknown— Granville Sharp, Thomas Clarkson, Josiah Wedgwood—and their goal was ridiculous on the face of it: at that time three out of four people in the world were enslaved. Enslaving each other was what human beings had done for ages. And the abolitionist movement was greeted with incredulity. Conservative spokesmen ridiculed the abolitionists as liberals, progressives, do-gooders, meddlers, and activists. They were told they would ruin the economy and drive England into poverty. But for the first time in history a group of people organized themselves to help people they would never know, from whom they would never receive direct or indirect benefit. And today tens of millions of people do this every day. It is called the world of non-profits, civil society, schools, social entrepreneurship, non-governmental organizations, and companies who place social and environmental justice at the top of their strategic goals. The scope and scale of this effort is unparalleled in history.

The living world is not "out there" somewhere, but in your heart. What do we know about life? In the words of biologist Janine Benyus, life creates the conditions that are conducive to life. I can think of no better motto for a future economy. We have tens of thousands of abandoned homes without people and tens of thousands of abandoned people without homes. We have failed bankers advising failed regulators on how to save failed assets. We are the only species on the planet without full employment. Brilliant. We have an economy that tells us that it is cheaper to destroy earth in real time rather than renew, restore, and sustain it. You can print money to bail out a bank but you can't print life to bail out a planet. At present we are stealing the future, selling it in the present, and calling it gross domestic product. We can just as easily have an economy that is based on healing the future instead of stealing it. We can either create assets for the future or take the assets of the future. One is called restoration and the other exploitation. And whenever we exploit the earth we exploit people and cause untold suffering. Working for the earth is not a way to get rich, it is a way to be rich.

The first living cell came into being nearly 40 million centuries ago, and its direct descendants are in all of our bloodstreams. Literally you are breathing molecules this very second that were inhaled by Moses, Mother Teresa, and Bono. We are vastly interconnected. Our fates are inseparable. We are here because the dream of every cell is to become two cells. And dreams come true. In each of you are one quadrillion cells, 90 percent of which are not human cells. Your body is a community, and without those other microorganisms you would perish in hours. Each human cell has 400 billion molecules conducting millions of processes between trillions of atoms. The total cellular activity in one human body is staggering: one septillion actions at any one moment, a one with twenty-four zeros after it. In a millisecond, our body has undergone ten times more processes than there are stars in the universe, which is exactly what Charles Darwin foretold when he said science would discover that each living creature was a "little universe, formed of a host of self-propagating organisms, inconceivably minute and as numerous as the stars of heaven."

So I have two questions for you all: First, can you feel your body? Stop for a moment. Feel your body. One septillion activities going on simultaneously, and your body does this so well you are free to ignore it, and wonder instead when this speech will end. You can feel it. It is called life. This is who you are. Second question: Who is in charge of your body? Who is managing those molecules? Hopefully not a political party. Life is creating the conditions that are conducive to life inside you, just as in all of nature. Our innate nature is to create the conditions that are conducive to life. What I want you to imagine is that collectively humanity is evincing a deep innate wisdom in coming together to heal the wounds and insults of the past.

Ralph Waldo Emerson once asked what we would do if the stars only came out once every thousand years. No one would sleep that night, of course. The world would create new religions overnight. We would be ecstatic, delirious, made rapturous by the glory of God. Instead, the stars come out every night and we watch television.

This extraordinary time when we are globally aware of each other and the multiple dangers that threaten civilization has never happened, not in a thousand years, not in ten thousand years. **Each of us is as complex and beautiful as all the stars in the universe. We have done great things and we have gone way off course in terms of honoring creation.** You are graduating to the most amazing, stupefying challenge ever bequeathed to any generation. The generations before you failed. They didn't stay up all night. They got distracted and lost sight of the fact that life is a miracle every moment of your existence. Nature beckons you to be on her side. You couldn't ask for a better boss. The most unrealistic person in the world is the cynic, not the dreamer. Hope only makes sense when it doesn't make sense to be hopeful. This is your century. Take it and run as if your life depends on it.

## Responding to Reading

1. Hawken begins his speech by stating that "every living system is declining, and the rate of decline is accelerating" (2). What evidence does he offer to support this claim? How convincing is this supporting evidence?

2. In paragraph 6, Hawken tells graduating students, "You join a multitude of caring people." Do you think the optimism about the future that this statement reveals is justified? Explain.
3. What is Hawken's actual message to the graduating class of University of Portland? Do you think his message is both realistic and appropriate? Does this 2009 message seem dated in any way?

## Responding in Writing

In paragraph 9, Hawken says, "Working for the earth is not a way to get rich, it is a way to be rich." What does he mean? Do you agree with this sentiment?

# COMMENCEMENT SPEECH, HOWARD UNIVERSITY, 1994
## Colin Powell
### 1937–

*Colin Powell was the first African-American chairman of the United States Joint Chiefs of Staff, serving from 1989 to 1993, and United States Secretary of State, serving from 2001 to 2005. He is the author of numerous books, including, most recently,* It Worked for Me: In Life and Leadership *(2012). Powell delivered the following commencement address at Howard University in 1994.*

The real challenge in being a commencement speaker is figuring out how long to speak. The graduating students want a short speech, five to six minutes and let's get it over. They are not going to remember who their commencement speaker was anyway. P O W E L L.

Parents are another matter. Arrayed in all their finery they have waited a long time for this day, some not sure it would ever come, and they want it to last. So go on and talk for two or three hours. We brought our lunch and want our money's worth.

The faculty member who suggested the speaker hopes the speech will be long enough to be respectable, but not so long that he has to take leave for a few weeks beginning Monday.

So the poor speaker is left figuring out what to do. My simple rule is to respond to audience reaction. If you are appreciative and applaud a lot early on, you get a nice, short speech. If you make me work for it, we're liable to be here a long time.

You know, the controversy over Howard's speaking policy has its positive side. It has caused the university to go through a process of self-examination, which is always a healthy thing to do. Since many people have been giving advice about how to handle this matter, I thought I might as well too.

First, I believe with all my heart that Howard must continue to serve as an institute of learning excellence where freedom of speech is strongly encouraged and rigorously protected. That is at the very essence of a great university and Howard is a great university.

And freedom of speech means permitting the widest range of views to be present for debate, however controversial those views may be. The First Amendment right of free speech is intended to protect the controversial and even outrageous word, and not just comforting platitudes, too mundane to need protection.

Some say that by hosting controversial speakers who shock our sensibilities, Howard is in some way promoting or endorsing their message. Not at all. Howard has helped put their message in perspective while protecting their right to be heard. So that the message can be exposed to the full light of day.

I have every confidence in the ability of the administration, the faculty and the students of Howard to determine who should speak on this campus. No outside help needed, thank you.

10    I also have complete confidence in the students of Howard to make informed, educated judgments about what they hear.

But for this freedom to hear all views, you bear a burden to sort out wisdom from foolishness. There is great wisdom in the message of self reliance, of education, of hard work, and of the need to raise strong families. There is utter foolishness, evil, and danger in the message of hatred, or of condoning violence, however cleverly the message is packaged or entertainingly it is presented. We must find nothing to stand up and cheer about or applaud in a message of racial or ethnic hatred.

I was at the inauguration of President Mandela in South Africa earlier this week. You were there too by television and watched that remarkable event. Together, we saw what can happen when people stop hating and begin reconciling. DeKlerk the jailer became DeKlerk the liberator, and Mandela the prisoner became Mandela the president. Twenty seven years of imprisonment did not embitter Nelson Mandela. He invited his three jail keepers to the ceremony. He used his liberation to work his former tormentors to create a new South Africa and to eliminate the curse of apartheid from the face of the earth. What a glorious example! What a glorious day it was!

Last week you also saw Prime Minister Rabin and PLO Chairman Arafat sign another agreement on their still difficult, long road to peace, trying to end hundreds of years of hatred and two generations of violence. Palestinian authorities have now begun entering Gaza and Jericho.

In these two historic events, intractable enemies of the past have shown how you can join hands to create a force of moral authority more powerful than any army and which can change the world.

Although there are still places of darkness in the world where the  15
light of reconciliation has not penetrated, these two beacons of hope
show what can be done when men and women of goodwill work
together for peace and for progress.

There is a message in these two historic events for us assembled
here today. As the world goes forward, we cannot start going backward. African Americans have come too far and we have too far yet to
go to take a detour into the swamp of hatred. We, as a people who have
suffered so much from the hatred of others must not now show toler-
ance for any movement or philosophy that has at its core the hatred of
Jews or anyone else. Our future lies in the philosophy of love and
understanding and caring and building. Not of hatred and tearing
down.

We know that. We must stand up for it and speak up for it! We
must not be silent if we would live up to the legacy of those who have
gone before us from this campus.

I have no doubt that this controversy will pass and Howard University will emerge even stronger, even more than ever a symbol of
hope, of promise, and of excellence. That is Howard's destiny!

Ambassador Annenberg, one of your honorees today, is a dear
friend of mine and is one of America's leading businessmen and greatest philanthropists. You have heard of his recent contribution to American education and his generous gift to Howard. A few years ago I told
Mr. Annenberg about a project I was involved in to build a memorial
to the Buffalo Soldiers, those brave black cavalrymen of the West whose
valor had long gone unrecognized. Ambassador Annenberg responded
immediately, and with his help the memorial now stands proudly at
Fort Leavenworth, Kansas.

The Buffalo Soldiers were formed in 1867, at the same time as How-  20
ard University. It is even said that your mascot, the bison, came from
the bison, or buffalo, soldiers. Both Howard and the Buffalo Soldiers
owe their early success to the dedication and faith of white military
officers who served in the Civil War. In Howard's case, of course, it was
your namesake, Major General Oliver Howard.

For the 10th Cavalry Buffalo Soldiers, it was Colonel Benjamin
Grierson who formed and commanded that regiment for almost
twenty five years. And he fought that entire time to achieve equal
status for his black comrades.

Together, Howard University and the Buffalo Soldiers showed
what black Americans were capable of when given the education and
opportunity; and when shown respect and when accorded dignity.

I am a direct descendant of those Buffalo Soldiers, of the Tuskegee
Airmen, and of the Navy's Golden Thirteen, and Montfort Point
Marines, and all the black men and women who served this nation in
uniform for over three hundred years. All of whom served in their time
and in their way and with whatever opportunity existed then to break

CHAPTER 10  FOCUS

down the walls of discrimination and racism to make the path easier for those of us who came after them.

I climbed on their backs and stood on their shoulders to reach the top of my chosen profession to become chairman of the American Joint Chiefs of Staff. I will never forget my debt to them and to the many white "Colonel Griersons" and "General Howards" who helped me over the thirty five years of my life as a soldier. They would say to me now, "Well done. And now let others climb up on your shoulders."

25    Howard's Buffalo Soldiers did the same thing, and on their shoulders now stand governors and mayors and congressmen and generals and doctors and artists and writers and teachers and leaders in every segment of American society. And they did it for the class of 1994. So that you can now continue climbing to reach the top of the mountain, while reaching down and back to help those less fortunate.

You face "Great Expectations." Much has been given to you and much is expected from you. You have been given a quality education, presented by a distinguished faculty who sit here today in pride of you. You have inquiring minds and strong bodies given to you by God and by your parents, who sit behind you and pass on to you today their still unrealized dreams and ambitions. You have been given citizenship in a country like none other on earth, with opportunities available to you like nowhere else on earth, beyond anything available to me when I sat in a place similar to this thirty six years ago.

What will be asked of you is hard work. Nothing will be handed to you. You are entering a life of continuous study and struggle to achieve your goals. A life of searching to find that which you do well and love doing. Never stop seeking.

I want you to have faith in yourselves. I want you to believe to the depth of your soul that you can accomplish any task that you set your mind and energy to. I want you to be proud of your heritage. Study your origins. Teach your children racial pride and draw strength and inspiration from the cultures of our forebears.

Not as a way of drawing back from American society and its European roots. But as a way of showing that there are other roots as well. African and Caribbean roots that are also a source of nourishment for the American family tree. To show that African Americans are more than a product of our slave experience. To show that our varied backgrounds are as rich as that of any other American—not better or greater, but every bit as equal.

30    Our black heritage must be a foundation stone we can build on, not a place to withdraw into. I want you to fight racism. But remember, as Dr. King and Dr. Mandela have taught us, racism is a disease of the racist. Never let it become yours. White South Africans were cured of the outward symptoms of the disease by President Mandela's inauguration, just as surely as black South Africans were liberated from apartheid.

Racism is a disease you can help cure by standing up for your rights and by your commitment to excellence and to performance. By being ready to take advantage of your rights and the opportunities that will come from those rights.

Never let the dying hand of racism rest on your shoulder, weighing you down. Let racism always be someone else's burden to carry. As you seek your way in the world, never fail to find a way to serve your community. Use your education and your success in life to help those still trapped in cycles of poverty and violence. Above all, never lose faith in America. Its faults are yours to fix, not to curse.

America is a family. There may be differences and disputes in the family, but we must not allow the family to be broken into warring factions. From the diversity of our people, let us draw strength and not cause weakness. Believe in America with all your heart and soul and mind. It remains the "last best hope of Earth." You are its inheritors and its future is today placed in your hands.

Go forth from this place today inspired by those who went before you. Go forth with the love of your families and the blessings of your teachers.

Go forth to make this a better country and society. Prosper, raise strong families, remembering that all you will leave behind is your good works and your children.

Go forth with my humble congratulations.                                         35

And let your dreams be your only limitations. Now and forever.

Thank you and God bless you.

Have a great life!

## Responding to Reading

1.  Powell delivered his speech at Howard University, a school that has allowed some highly controversial individuals to speak on campus. Why do you think Powell begins his speech by addressing this situation? Is this an effective strategy?
2.  In his speech, Powell refers to the inauguration of Nelson Mandela as President of South Africa as well as to the signing of peace accords by Yitzhak Rabin, former Prime Minister of Israel, and Yasser Arafat, former Chairman of the PLO. What do these two events show? What message does Powell think they send to his listeners?
3.  What does Powell mean in paragraph 30 when he says, "Our black heritage must be a foundation stone we can build on, not a place to withdraw into"?

## Responding in Writing

Speaking nearly twenty years ago, Powell says, "America is a family. There may be differences and disputes in the family, but we must not allow the family to be broken into warring factions" (32). How do you think he would characterize America today?

# WIDENING THE FOCUS

### For Critical Reading and Writing

Referring specifically to the three speeches in this chapter's Focus section, write an essay in which you answer the question, "What Comes Next?"

### For Further Reading

The following readings can suggest additional perspectives for thinking and writing about the issues that society will face in the future:

- Charles Murray, "Should the Obama Generation Drop Out?" (p. 95)
- Louis Menand, "Thumbspeak: Is Texting Here to Stay?" (p. 185)
- David Carr, "Why Twitter Will Endure" (p. 231)
- Jennifer Finney Boylan, "Is My Marriage Gay?" (p. 255)
- Brent Staples, "Why Race Isn't as 'Black' and 'White' as We Think" (p. 325)
- Lynn Peril, "Do Secretaries Have a Future?" (p. 420)

### For Focused Research

This Focus section offers three examples of recent commencement addresses. Consider the similarities and differences among these addresses. Then, do a *Google* search for additional examples of commencement addresses from the past thirty years, and write an essay that considers the following questions: What dominant themes are present in the addresses over the years? What changes do you see in the subject matter of commencement addresses over time, and how do these changes reflect changes in society? Quote from key commencement addresses to support your points.

### Beyond the Classroom

Choose two or three classic science fiction movies that are set in a future that is close to our own time—for example, *2001: A Space Odyssey* (made in 1968 and set in 2001), *Blade Runner* (made in 1982 and set in 2019), and *Back to the Future Part II* (made in 1989 and set in 2015). After viewing the movies, write an essay in which you report how accurate their predictions are. What did the movies get right? What did they get wrong? What conclusions can you draw about Hollywood's ability to predict the future?

--- **WRITING** ---

## Facing the Future

1. Will the structure of the American family stay the same, or will it change in the future? Write an essay in which you answer this question, using material from Jennifer Finney Boylan's "Is My Marriage Gay?"(p. 255), Glenn Sacks's "Stay-at-Home Dads" (p. 265), and Arlie Hochschild's "The Second Shift" (p. 412).

2. How do you think higher education will change in the future? Will it be widely available or limited to a privileged few? Will traditional instruction be replaced by technology? Will students be offered more practical options than they currently have? Read Charles Murray's "Should the Obama Generation Drop Out?" (p. 95), Scott Adams's "How to Get a Real Education" (p. 98), and Michael S. Malone's "The Next American Frontier" (p. 537). Then, incorporating the information in these essays, write an essay in which you present your ideas on this issue.

3. Read Nicholas Carr's "Does the Internet Make You Dumber?" (p. 216) and Alice Mathias's "The Fakebook Generation" (p. 229). Then, citing material from these essays, discuss the ways in which you believe changes in information technology (the Internet, smartphones, tablets, and so on) will affect your life in the future.

4. Over the past fifty years, gender roles have changed considerably. Read Alleen Pace Nilsen's "Sexism in English: Embodiment and Language" (p. 148), Kathleen Deveny's "Who You Callin' a Lady?" (p. 258), and Glenn Sacks's "Stay-at-Home Dads" (p. 265). Then, write an essay in which you discuss how equal (or unequal) male/female roles will be twenty years from now. Be specific, and refer to the essays you read for this assignment.

5. In his poem "Dover Beach" (p. 509), Matthew Arnold paints a dark picture of a world without religious faith. In "Earthly Empires" (p. 525), William C. Symonds and his coauthors discuss the increasing popularity of the megachurch among evangelical Christians. What do you see as the future of religion in the United States? Do you think that the United States is a country in which religious faith is declining or is increasing? In addition to considering the ideas developed in Arnold's poem and Symonds' essay, use material from Colin Powell's Commencement Speech, Howard University, 1994 (p. 557) in your essay.

6. For some, the American Dream is an elusive, if not impossible, goal. Write an essay in which you define the American Dream and discuss what could be done to make it more achievable. In your essay, refer

to Melanie Scheller's "On the Meaning of Plumbing and Poverty" (p. 319), Jose Antonio Vargas's "Outlaw: My Life in America as an Undocumented Immigrant" (p. 377), and Hilda Solis's Commencement Speech, Los Angeles City College, 2010 (p. 548).

7. Write an essay in which you examine where you expect to be ten years after you graduate. Before you write, read "Why We Work" by Andrew Curry (p. 399), "The Next American Frontier" by Michael Malone (p. 537), and Commencement Speech, Los Angeles City College, 2010, by Hilda Solis (p. 548).

8. What do you think will be the most pressing ethical choice facing people in 2020? Will it concern poverty? unemployment? the environment? energy? terrorism? something else? Write an essay in which you answer this question. Make sure you define the problem, the possible solutions to the problem, and the choice that you think should be made. In your essay refer to David A. Hoekema's "The Unacknowledged Ethicists on Campuses" (p. 453), Neal Gabler's "The Elusive Big Idea" (p. 532), and Michael S. Malone's "The Next American Frontier" (p. 537).

9. Currently, the United States as well as the rest of the world is in an economic downturn. Whatever the causes of this situation, the results are clear—high unemployment and an increasing sense of insecurity. Given this situation, how useful is the advice given to graduating students by the three graduation speakers in the Focus section of this chapter? Write an essay in which you answer this question in light of recent economic developments.

10. Overall, are you optimistic or pessimistic about the future? Do you think human beings will achieve the society that they have always wished for, or do you think this century will be as destructive as the last one? Write an essay in which you answer these questions. To support your position, refer to two or three readings in this chapter.

# CREDITS

Hochschild, Arlie, and Ann Machung, "UTNE Reader Selection," from *The Second Shift*. Copyright © 1989, 2003 by Arlie Hochschild. Used by permission of Viking Penguin, a division of Penguin Group (USA) Inc.

Hoekema, David A., "The Unacknowledged Ethicist on Campus," from *The Chronicle of Higher Education*, January 24, 2010. Copyright © 2010 by David A. Hoekema. Reprinted with permission of the author.

Hogan, Linda, "Heritage," from *Red Clay*. Copyright © 1994 by Linda Hogan. (Greenfield Center, NY: Greenfield Review Press, 1994). Reprinted with permission of The Permissions Company, Inc. on behalf of the author, www.permissionscompany.com.

Holt, John, "Schools Are Bad Places for Kids," from *The Underachieving School*, as appeared in *Saturday Evening Post*, 1989. Copyright © 2005 by John Holt. Published by Sentient Publications, Boulder, CO. Reprinted with permission.

Humphrys, John, "I h8 text msgs: How Texting is Wrecking Our Language," from *Daily Mail*, September 24, 2007. Copyright © 2007 by Solo Syndication. Reprinted with permission.

Jacobson, David, "Reflections: Growing Up Grown," from *Daily Grito* website, July 15, 2011. Copyright © 2011 by David Jacobson. Reprinted with permission by the author.

Jin, Ha, and Hannah Clark, "The American Dream: Ha Jin on the American Dream," from the *Forbes* website, March 2007. Copyright © 2007 by Ha Jin and Hannah Clark, Reprinted with permission of Forbes Media LLC.

Jones, Edward P., "First Day," from *Lost In The City*. Copyright © 1992 by Edward P. Jones. Reprinted with permission of HarperCollins Publishers.

King, Jr., Martin Luther, "I Have a Dream" by Martin Luther King, Jr. Copyright © 1963 by Dr. Martin Luther King, Jr.; Copyright © renewed 1991 by Coretta Scott King. Reprinted by arrangement with The Heirs to the Estate of Martin Luther King, Jr., c/o Writers House as agent for the proprietor, New York, NY.

King, Jr., Martin Luther, "Letter from Birmingham Jail.". Copyright © 1963 by Dr. Martin Luther King, Jr.; Copyright © renewed 1991 by Coretta Scott King. Reprinted by arrangement with The Heirs to the Estate of Martin Luther King, Jr., c/o Writers House as agent for the proprietor, New York, NY.

Kingston, Maxine Hong "No Name Woman" from *The Woman Warrior*. Copyright © 1975, 1976 by Maxine Hong Kingston. Used by permission of Alfred A. Knopf, a division of Random House, Inc. For on-line information about other Random House, Inc. books and authors, see the Internet web site at http://www.randomhouse.com

Kotkin, Joel, "The Changing Demographics of Americans," from *Smithsonian Magazine*, August 2010. Copyright © 2010 by Joel Kotkin. Reprinted with permission of the author.

Kozol, Jonathan, "The Human Cost of an Illiterate Society," from *Illiterate America*. Copyright © 1985 by Jonathan Kozol. Used by permission of Doubleday, a division of Random House, Inc. and International Creative Management, Inc.

Krutzsch, Brett, "The Gayest One," from *The Advocate*, November 6, 2007. Copyright © 2007 by Here Media, Inc. Reprinted with permission. All rights reserved.

Last, Jonathan V., "TV for Tots: Not What You Remember," from *Wall Street Journal*, April 22, 2010. Copyright © 2010 Dow Jones & Company, Inc. Reproduced with permission of Dow Jones & Company, Inc. via Copyright Clearance Center.

Malone, Michael S., "The Next American Frontier," from *Wall Street Journal*, May 19, 2008. Copyright © 2008 Dow Jones & Company, Inc. Reproduced with permission of Dow Jones & Company, Inc. via Copyright Clearance Center.

McCarthy, Claire, "Dog Lab," from *Learning How the Heart Beats*. Copyright © 1995 by Claire McCarthy, M.D. Published by Viking Penguin, a division of Penguin Group (USA) Inc. Reprinted with permission.

McGonigal, Jane, "Introduction: Reality Is Broken," from *Reality Is Broken*. Copyright © 2011 by Jane McGonigal. Used by permission of The Penguin Press, a division of Penguin Group (USA) Inc.

McWhorter, John, "Why I'm Black, Not African American," from *Los Angeles Times*, September 8, 2004. Copyright © 2004 by John McWhorter. Reprinted with permission of the author.

Menand, Louis, "Thumbspeak: Is Texting Here to Stay?," from *The New Yorker*, October 20, 2008. Copyright © 2008 by Louis Menand. Reprinted with permission of The Wylie Agency LLC.

Mora, Pat, "La Migra," from *Agua Santa: Holy Water*. Copyright © 1995 by Pat Mora. Reprinted with permission of Curtis Brown, Ltd.

Nafisi, Azar, "Vagabond Nation," from *The New Yorker*, April 18, 2011. Copyright © 2011 by Azar Nafisi. Used with permission of The Wylie Agency LLC.

Sheler, Jeffery, and Michael Betzhold, "Muslim in America," from *U.S. News & World Report*, October 29, 2001. Copyright © 2001 by U.S. News & World Report. Reprinted with permission of Wright's Media on behalf of the publisher.

Shteyngart, Gary, "Sixty-Nine Cents" from *The New Yorker*, September 3, 2007. Copyright © 2007 by Gary Shteyngart. Reprinted with permission of the Denise Shannon Literary Agency, Inc. All rights reserved.

Solis, Hilda L., from Remarks by Secretary of Labor, Hilda L. Solis at Los Angeles City College Graduation, June 8, 2010, from the United States Department of Labor

Sommers, Christina Hoff, "For More Balance on Campus," from *The Young America's Foundation Speakers Program*, May 6, 2002. Copyright © 2002 by Christine Hoff Sommers. Reprinted with permission of the author.

Sommers, Christine Hoff, "The War Against Boys," from *The Atlantic Monthly*, May 2000. Copyright © 2000 by Christine Hoff Sommers. Reprinted with permission of the author.

Soto, Gary, "One Last Time," from *Living Up the Street*. Copyright © 1985 by Gary Soto. Published by Dell. Reprinted with permission of the author.

Staples, Brent, "Just Walk On By," from *Harper's*, December 1986. Copyright © 1986 by Brent Staples. Reprinted with permission of the author.

Stephenson, Neal, "Innovation Starvation," originally published in *World Policy Journal*, XXVIII, No. 3, fall 2011, doi: 10.1177/0740277511425349. Copyright © 2011 by Neal Stephenson. Reprinted with permission.

Stewart, Martha, and Hannah Clark, "The American Dream: Martha Stewart on the American Dream," from the *Forbes* website, March 2007. Copyright © 2007 by Martha Steward and Hannah Clark, Reprinted with permission of Forbes Media LLC.

Symonds, William C., Brian Grow, and John Cady, "Earthly Empires," from *Business Weekly*, May 23, 2005. Copyright © 2005 by William C. Symonds, Brian Grow, and John Cady. Reprinted with permission.

Tan, Amy, "Mother Tongue," from *The Threepenny Review*. Copyright © 1990 by Amy Tan. Reprinted with permission of the author and the Sandra Dijkstra Literary Agency.

Tannen, Deborah, "Wears Jump Suit. Sensible Shoes. Uses Husband's Last Name," from *The New York Times Magazine*, June 20, 1993, adapted from *Talking From 9 ot 5: Women and Men at Work*, HaperCollins Publishers. Copyright © 1993 by Deborah Tannen. Reprinted with permission of the author.

Turkle, Sherry, "Connectivity and Its Discontents," from *Alone Together: Why We Expect More Technology and Less from Each Other*. Copyright © 2011 by Sherry Turkle. Reprinted with permission of Basic Books, a member of the Perseus Books Group.

Updike, John, "A&P," from *Pigeon Feather and Other Stories*. Copyright © 1962, copyright renewed 1990 by John Updike. Used by permission of Alfred A. Knopf, a division of Random House, Inc. For on-line information about other Random House, Inc. books and authors, see the Internet web site at http://www.randomhouse.com

Walker, Alice, "Beauty: When the Other Dancer is the Self," from *In Search of Our Mothers' Gardens: Womanist Prose*, published by Harcourt. Copyright © 1983 by Alice Walker. Reprinted with permission of The Wendy Weil Agency, Inc. and Houghton Mifflin Harcourt Publishing Company. All rights reserved.

White, E. B., "Once More to the Lake" from *One Man's Meat*. Copyright © 1941 by E. B. White. Reprinted with permission of International Creative Management and Tilbury House Publishers.

Wong, Elizabeth, "The Struggle to Be the All-American Girl." Copyright © 1980 by Elizabeth Wong. Reprinted with permission of the author. www.elizabethwong.net

Wright, Richard, "Library Card," from *Black Boy*. Copyright © 1937, 1942, 1945 by Richard Wright; renewed © 1973 by Ellen Wright. Reprinted by permission of HarperCollins Publishers.

## Photo Credits

**Page 10:** Adbusters Media Foundation; **page 12:** Robert W. Woodruff Library, Emory University; **page 13:** David Jacobsen; **page 52:** Erin Patrice O'Brien for The Wall Street Journal; **page 66:** ChipPix/Shutterstock.com; **page 67:** lightpoet/Shutterstock.com; **page 113:** © John McPherson/Distributed by Universal Uclick via Cartoonstock.com; **page 128:** Eve Arnold/Magnum Photos; **page 129:** Heinz-Jürgen Göttert/picture-alliance/

# INDEX OF AUTHORS AND TITLES